BabyLM Challenge 2023

Held at the 27th Conference on Computational Natural Language Learning

Singpore
6 – 7 December 2023

ISBN: 978-1-7138-8586-3

Printed from e-media with permission by:

Curran Associates, Inc.
57 Morehouse Lane
Red Hook, NY 12571

Association for Computational Linguistics
209 N. Eighth Street
Stroudsburg, Pennsylvania 18360

Phone: 1-570-476-8006
Fax: 1-570-476-0860

acl@aclweb.org

Additional copies of this publication are available from:

Curran Associates, Inc.
57 Morehouse Lane
Red Hook, NY 12571 USA
Phone: 845-758-0400
Fax: 845-758-2633
Email: curran@proceedings.com
Web: www.proceedings.com

CoNLL 2023

The BabyLM Challenge at the 27th Conference on Computational Natural Language Learning

Proceedings of the BabyLM Challenge

December 6-7, 2023

Introduction

Greetings "babies"! and welcome to the proceedings and session of the 2023 BabyLM Challenge, held on December 6, 2023 as part of CoNLL (co-hosted with EMNLP) in Singapore. This challenge aims to bring together researchers interested in developmentally plausible pre-training, sample efficiency, and human language acquisition. Our challenge encourages researchers to "think small" by using training corpora containing 100 million words—approximately the amount of data available to human language learners, but far less data than is typically used for pre-training language models.

We received 31 papers, all of which were accepted on the basis of scientific and technical validity, rather than model performance. We received 162 individual model submissions, the scores of which are hosted online, at `www.https://dynabench.org/babylm`.

We are grateful to the participants for advancing our understanding of how best to train language models on scaled-down and more developmentally plausible corpora.. Their contributions have provided insight into important questions related to cognitive modeling, computational psycholinguistics, and sample-efficient language modeling. We are also grateful to the program committee for their thoughtful reviews of the submissions we received this year. Likewise, we are thankful to the CoNLL organizers for their work in integrating the BabyLM challenge into their program.

– The BabyLM Organization Committee: Alex Warstadt, Aaron Mueller, Leshem Choshen, Ethan Wilcox, Chengxu Zhuang, Adina Williams, Tal Linzen, Ryan Cotterell.

Organizing Committee

Organizers

Alex Warstadt, ETH Zürich, Switzerland
Aaron Mueller, Northeastern University
Leshem Choshen, MIT, IBM
Ethan Wilcox, ETH Zürich, Switzerland
Chengxu Zhuang, Massachusetts Institute of Technology
Juan Ciro, MLCommons
Rafael Mosquera, MLCommons
Bhargavi Paranjabe, University of Washington
Adina Williams, Meta AI (FAIR)
Tal Linzen, New York University
Ryan Cotterell, ETH Zürich, Switzerland

Table of Contents

Findings of the BabyLM Challenge: Sample-Efficient Pretraining on Developmentally Plausible Corpora

Alex Warstadt[1*] Aaron Mueller[2,3*] Leshem Choshen[4,5] Ethan Wilcox[1] Chengxu Zhuang[4]
Juan Ciro[6] Rafael Mosquera[6] Bhargavi Paranjape[8]
Adina Williams[6,7] Tal Linzen[9] Ryan Cotterell[1]
[1]ETH Zürich [2]Northeastern University [3]Technion [4]MIT
[5]IBM Research [6]MLCommons [7]Meta AI (FAIR)
[8]University of Washington [9]New York University
warstadt@inf.ethz.ch aa.mueller@northeastern.edu

Abstract

Children can acquire language from less than 100 million words of input. Large language models are far less data-efficient: they typically require 3 or 4 orders of magnitude more data and still do not perform as well as humans on many evaluations. These intensive resource demands limit the ability of researchers to train new models and use existing models as developmentally plausible cognitive models. The BabyLM Challenge is a communal effort in which participants compete to optimize language model training on a fixed data budget. Submissions are compared on various evaluation tasks targeting grammatical ability, downstream task performance, and generalization. Participants can submit to up to three tracks with progressively looser data restrictions. From over 30 submissions, we extract concrete recommendations on how best to train data-efficient language models, and on where future efforts should (and perhaps should not) focus. The winning submissions using the LTG-BERT architecture (Samuel et al., 2023) outperformed models trained on trillions of words. Other submissions achieved strong results through training on shorter input sequences or training a student model on a pretrained teacher. Curriculum learning attempts, which accounted for a large number of submissions, were largely unsuccessful, though some showed modest improvements.

1 Introduction

Although there have massive improvements in the effectiveness of neural language models in the last decade, humans are still the state of the art in language learning. To achieve impressive results, language models need to be trained on hundreds of times more language input than a typical human will be exposed to in an entire lifetime. The BabyLM Challenge is a shared task that invites

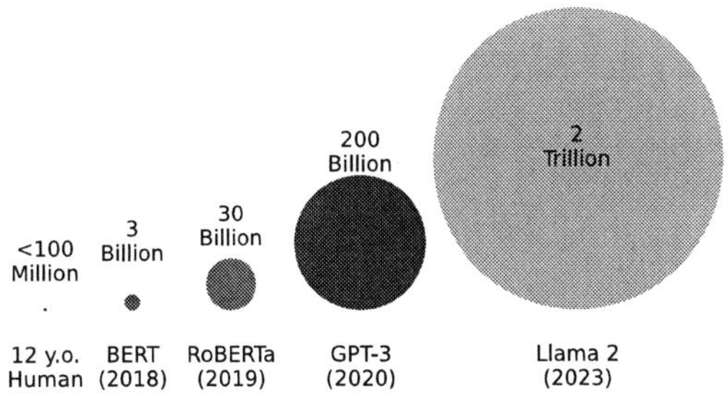

Figure 1: **Data Scale:** Modern Language Models are trained multiple orders of magnitude more word tokens than the amount available to a typical child. This image is based on Fig. 1 from Warstadt and Bowman (2022).

members of the natural language processing, linguistics, and cognitive science communities to train language models in low-resource data settings, where the amount of linguistic input resembles the amount received by human language learners. In doing so, our motivations (Section 2) are to improve the relevance of language models as cognitive models of human language acquisition, find more effective and data-efficient training algorithms for language models, and democratize research on language model training by emphasizing research questions that can be addressed on a smaller training budget.

Participants in the shared task could submit to the *Strict*, *Strict-Small*, or *Loose* track, which, respectively, required models to be trained on corpora that constituted either 10 million words, 100 million words, or 100 million words plus an unlimited amount of additional non-linguistic data (Section 3). These corpora were constructed from a mixture of sources including developmentally plausible domains such as child-directed speech, transcribed dialogue, and children's literature (Section 4). To enable standardized evaluation and easy comparison of the resulting models, we create a leaderboard and release an evaluation pipeline (Section 5) targeting zero-shot grammatical performance, finetunability on language understanding

*Equal contribution.

Proceedings of the 27th Conference on Computational Natural Language Learning: Volume 2: The BabyLM Challenge, pages 1–34

tasks, and model inductive bias. We also contribute a novel set of zero-shot evaluation tasks targeting semantic and discourse-level phenomena.

We received 31 papers making a variety of contributions, ranging from designing novel architectures and tuning hyperparameters to employing curriculum learning and training teacher–student model pairs (Section 6). We conduct a meta-analysis of the results, yielding several concrete recommendations and scientific conclusions (Section 7). The winners of the challenge's various tracks made contributions that led to impressive improvements in our evaluation over not just the BabyLM baselines, but also the massively pretrained Llama 2 model (Touvron et al., 2023). The best-performing models overall (Charpentier and Samuel, 2023) use the LTG-BERT architecture (Samuel et al., 2023), which synthesizes a number of recent optimizations of the Transformer architecture. The winner of the *Loose* track (Xiao et al., 2023) trains the models continuously on the training samples belonging to the same source dataset while randomizing the dataset orders in each training epoch. Other submissions did not achieve strong downstream results, but still provided valuable scientific contributions. We received many curriculum learning submissions, including one that systematically tested a variety of strategies (Martinez et al., 2023) and reported few improvements over non-curriculum baselines. Steuer et al. (2023) found that benchmark performance is not correlated with a greater ability to predict human psycholinguistic data.

We plan to organize future BabyLM Challenges that will build on the success of this first iteration (Section 8). The winning submission from this year sets a high baseline for next year. Future iterations will need harder and more varied evaluations, including those that emphasize human-like processing and learning; they should emphasize new approaches that were not thoroughly explored this year, such as multimodality; and, they should incentivize compute-efficiency. Altogether, the first BabyLM Challenge has been a successful initiative, and we hope that this will continue to advance research on small-scale language models.

2 Motivation

The observation at the center of the BabyLM Challenge is this: Children are incredibly data-efficient language learners, and language models are not. Children are exposed to less than 100 million word tokens by age 13 (Gilkerson et al., 2017), while modern language models are typically trained on 3 or 4 orders-of-magnitude more data (Figure 1). This discrepancy raises two important questions: First, how is it that humans are able to learn language so efficiently? Second, what insights from human language learning can be used to improve language models?

A great deal of recent work in language model training seeks improvements by scaling up pretraining data and parameters (Raffel et al., 2020; Brown et al., 2020; Hoffmann et al., 2022; Touvron et al., 2023). Scaling is undoubtedly central to building deployable models (though see McKenzie et al. 2023 for counterexamples) and raises its own set of scientific questions, such as quantitative scaling laws (Kaplan et al., 2020) and the emergence of new abilities (Wei et al., 2022). However, increased emphasis on scaling is unlikely to lead to answers to the two questions we raised, and it excludes researchers without access to massive computational resources.

Thus, there are three principal benefits to data-limited language model training which the BabyLM Challenge aims to highlight:

1. Building more cognitively and developmentally plausible models of human language acquisition and processing,
2. Optimizing training pipelines prior to scaling by allowing for faster iteration on architectures and hyperparameters, and
3. Enabling research on language model training beyond highly funded industry groups.

Cognitive Modeling. Language models have been used to model aspects of human language learning and processing for decades (Elman, 1990; Hale, 2001; Reali and Christiansen, 2005, o.a.). While many researchers continue to advocate for language models as cognitive models (Keller, 2010; Dupoux, 2018; Linzen, 2019; Baroni, 2022; Warstadt and Bowman, 2022; Piantadosi, 2023; Wilcox et al., 2023), most agree that it is critical to make LMs learn in more human-like ways. Warstadt and Bowman (2022) and Linzen (2020) point to data quantity as the most egregious advantage that modern language models have over humans. When restricted to developmentally plausible data volumes, language models no longer perform well on benchmarks for human-like syntactic and semantic behavior (van Schijndel et al., 2019; Zhang et al., 2021).

Working to close the data-efficiency gap between language models and humans will have two principal advantages for cognitive modeling. First, by reverse-engineering known and hypothetical aspects of the human learning scenario—from multimodal inputs and multi-agent interaction to innate linguistic structural biases—we can determine which factors are critical to our unique ability to learn language efficiently (Dupoux, 2018). Second, by minimizing differences between humans and models, we make results from controlled experiments carried out on models more likely to be applicable to humans (Warstadt and Bowman, 2022).

Faster iteration on architectures and hyperparameters for language modeling. Reducing the scale of training provides researchers with a sandbox in which to more fully explore this design space and better optimize training pipelines. The search space for design choices when training language models is enormous. Thus, it can be impractical, especially at large scales, to experiment with new model architectures, training objectives, or data preprocessing steps, in addition to necessary hyperparameter tuning. Models such as RoBERTa (Liu et al., 2019) have succeeded in making some optimizations to the BERT training pipeline, but more optimizations remain. Indeed, there are anecdotes of basic design choices for popular pipelines, such as the masking rate for BERT training (Wettig et al., 2023), being poorly tuned for years, despite hundreds or even thousands of papers using this training pipeline.

There are numerous dimensions along which to scale down training. Some works seek to optimize pipelines for a limited amount of compute, time, or money. Notable examples of such pipelines for bidirectional encoder-only include ELECTRA (Clark et al., 2020), 24-hour BERT (Izsak et al., 2021), and MosaicBERT (Portes et al., 2023). These pipelines typically combine multiple approaches, such as modifying training objectives to increase the number of supervised predictions per forward pass, using low-precision floating-point computations for certain components, reducing sequence length or padding, and altering the attention or feed-forward layers of the transformer block.

However, the objective of optimizing pipelines for a fixed data budget is relatively underexplored. This is changing in the last year with new models optimized for small datasets such as LTG-BERT (Samuel et al., 2023) and community-oriented events centered around data-limited training such as the Learning from Small Data workshop (Breitholtz et al., 2023) and the MiniPile Challenge (Kaddour, 2023).

Democratizing language model training research. The third goal of the BabyLM Challenge is to democratize research on pretraining—typically thought to be practical only for large industry groups—by drawing attention to challenging and important open problems that can be explored on a university budget. In recent years, efforts aimed at widening participation in LM research often take different avenues from the one proposed here, including aggregation of distributed computation power (Diskin et al., 2021), reliance on public computing infrastructure (Scao et al., 2022), aggregation of expertise, data and stepwise contributions (Don-Yehiya et al., 2023; Raffel, 2023) and modularity (Pfeiffer et al., 2023). Such a line of pretraining research proposes to keep costs large but to distribute them across funding sources through many contributing factors.

Other works on decentralizing computation (Diskin et al., 2021; Li et al., 2022; Lialin et al., 2023) or model recycling works generally take existing models and build upon them, proposing a single adaptation finetuning (Choshen et al., 2022), a single knowledge edit (De Cao et al., 2021), combining several models (Yadav et al., 2023), or iterative approaches showing that stacking such improvements can continually improve models (Don-Yehiya et al., 2023). Recently, a framework for doing so was also released (Kandpal et al., 2023). One can see the BabyLM challenge in this context as a suggestion to persist in using a centralized approach to pretraining, but making it tractable, by reducing the cost through increased focus on tractable research questions.

3 Guidelines and Timeline

Tracks. Submissions to BabyLM had to conform to one of three sets of guidelines, which we term **tracks**. In this section, we describe each competition track; for specific details about wording, see the original Call for Papers (Warstadt et al., 2023). The three tracks for the BabyLM challenges were ***Strict***, ***Strict-Small***, and ***Loose***. Participants in all tracks were allowed a constant number of English-language training tokens (100 million in *Strict* and

Loose and 10 million in *Strict-Small*) to be used in total for all software used in the pipeline. This data was released by the organizing committee and is described, in detail, in Section 4. *Loose* track submissions were encouraged to train on data beyond just the linguistic text data provided through the shared task (e.g., speech audio signal, code, music, or visual input). The *Loose* track also permitted the use of expert-annotated data, but any language data used to train the LM or auxiliary models counted towards the 100M word budget. Thus, for example, a *Loose* track submission could train a parser on the Penn Treebank (Marcus et al., 1993) and self-train to parse the pretraining corpus, as long as the number of words in the Penn Treebank plus the pretraining corpus total less than 100M.[1]

In general, seeing the same data twice (e.g., across different epochs) did not count as seeing more text. While it is unlikely that humans process data iteratively in a manner similar to epoch-based training, there is evidence that humans do repeat some of the information they process (e.g., in memory replay, Carr et al., 2011). Furthermore, epochs are very useful for gradient-based methods.

Finally, participants across all tracks were encouraged to submit models and papers even if their work did not fit into any of the three tracks. As the goal of the shared task is to advance efficient and cognitively plausible LM training, we did not want to curtail participant creativity. While submissions using external linguistic data did not qualify to win any of the tracks, they still qualified to be presented in the competition and to be published in the proceedings.

Community building. Given that the BabyLM Challenge aims to encourage research in efficient and cognitively plausible model pretraining, one of our goals was to encourage the formation of a research community with shared interests. Towards that end, we hosted a public messaging forum on Slack and enabled participants to interact with each other and with the task organizers. At the time of paper writing, this forum had over 250 members, including many interested researchers who did not ultimately submit to the challenge. An interactive forum was useful for both establishing a community and building interest; it allowed the community to clarify the track rules, debug the evaluation pipeline, and receive announcements from the organizers.

Timeline. Below, we replicate the timeline from the website.

- December 2022: The BabyLM Challenge is announced at CoNLL 2022, as well as on Twitter and in several mailing lists.
- January 2023: The pretraining datasets for the *Strict* and *Strict-Small* tracks were released.
- March 2023: The initial evaluation pipeline was made public.
- 1 June 2023: Hidden (surprise) evaluations were released and the Dynabench submission portal was opened.
- 22 June 2023: Deadline for model submissions (extended from 15 June 2023).
- 1 August 2023: Deadline for paper submissions.
- 6-7 December 2023: Presentation of the shared task at CoNLL.

4 Pretraining Corpus

We compiled and distributed a pretraining corpus inspired by the input received by children.[2] Submissions to the *Strict* track are required to train exclusively on this corpus. Submissions to the *Strict-Small* track are required to use only a scaled-down version of the dataset, approximately 10% the size of the *Strict*-track corpus. Two key properties of the dataset—its size and its domain—are controlled in order to make the data more developmentally plausible than typical LM pretraining data.

Size: 100M words or less. The pretraining corpus for the *Strict* track consists of under 100M words, and the corpus for the *Strict-Small* track is under 10M words. Children are exposed to 2M-7M words per year (Gilkerson et al., 2017). Choosing the beginning of adolescence (age 12) as a cutoff, the dataset should be between 24M-84M words, which we round up to 100M words. The 10M word

[1]In our initial announcement, external software trained on linguistic input or expert annotations not included in our corpus—including taggers, parsers, tokenizers, or models were *not* allowed. However, numerous questions from participants prompted an announcement in April 2023 that we were modifying the rules of the *Loose* track to allow such methods. We made this decision because we determined that the interests of the community were better served by emphasizing creativity and discovery in the *Loose* track. Text generated by a language model that was trained only on a BabyLM corpus was not counted towards the 100M word budget, nor was data bootstrapped by such models.

[2]Clicking on the following link will download the dataset (240MB zipped, 700MB unzipped): `https://github.com/babylm/babylm.github.io/raw/main/babylm_data.zip`

Dataset	Domain	# Words Strict-Small	# Words Strict	Proportion
CHILDES (MacWhinney, 2000)	Child-directed speech	0.44M	4.21M	5%
British National Corpus (BNC),[1] dialogue portion	Dialogue	0.86M	8.16M	8%
Children's Book Test (Hill et al., 2016)	Children's books	0.57M	5.55M	6%
Children's Stories Text Corpus[2]	Children's books	0.34M	3.22M	3%
Standardized Project Gutenberg Corpus (Gerlach and Font-Clos, 2020)	Written English	0.99M	9.46M	10%
OpenSubtitles (Lison and Tiedemann, 2016)	Movie subtitles	3.09M	31.28M	31%
QCRI Educational Domain Corpus (QED; Abdelali et al., 2014)	Educational video subtitles	1.04M	10.24M	11%
Wikipedia[3]	Wikipedia (English)	0.99M	10.08M	10%
Simple Wikipedia[4]	Wikipedia (Simple English)	1.52M	14.66M	15%
Switchboard Dialog Act Corpus (Stolcke et al., 2000)	Dialogue	0.12M	1.18M	1%
Total	–	9.96M	98.04M	100%

Table 1: The datasets we release for the *Strict* and *Strict-Small* tracks of the BabyLM Challenge. We present the number of words in the training set of each corpus that we include. [1]`http://www.natcorp.ox.ac.uk` [2]`https://www.kaggle.com/datasets/edenbd/children-stories-text-corpus` [3]`https://dumps.wikimedia.org/enwiki/20221220/` [4]`https://dumps.wikimedia.org/simplewiki/20221201/`

Strict-Small dataset corresponds to the amount of input in the first two to five years of development. By contrast, contemporary widely used LMs such as Llama 2 (Touvron et al., 2023) are trained on trillions of words (Figure 1). Even BERT (Devlin et al., 2019), which is comparatively small by today's standards, was trained on over 3B words, well over the amount of input to a human in an entire lifetime. This discrepancy in input volume between LMs and humans is an oft-cited criticism of using these artifacts out-of-the-box as cognitive models (Warstadt and Bowman, 2022; Frank, 2023, a.o.).

Domain: Mostly transcribed speech. We source the majority ($\approx 56\%$) of the pretraining corpus from transcribed or scripted speech. We made this choice because the majority of the input to a hearing child comes from speech (though this proportion decreases with age as consumption of written media increases). This contrasts with standard LM training corpora, which consist mostly of text that was intended to be read and potentially edited. This is particularly significant for studying grammar learning, as some grammatical constructions (such as nominalizations and passives) are far more frequent in writing, while others (such as first- and second-person pronouns) are more frequent in speech (Biber, 1991).

Domain: Child-directed language. About 40% of the data in the pretraining corpus comes from sources either intended for children or appropriate for children, including child-directed speech, children's books, educational videos, and simplified English. Child-directed speech has been used as the sole or primary data source in some previous work aiming to model child language acquisition with LMs (Reali and Christiansen, 2005; Perfors et al., 2011; Pannitto and Herbelot, 2020; Huebner et al., 2021; Yedetore et al., 2023). We chose to include data from other domains (both child-directed and not) for several reasons. First, fewer than 10M words of transcribed child-directed speech are available, far below our 100M word budget. Second, child-directed speech makes up only part of the input to children. This amount can vary by a factor of 10 or more across cultures and socio-economic groups (Cristia et al., 2019). The estimate on which we base the 100M word budget (Gilkerson et al., 2017) counts *all* speech in the child's environment including overheard speech.

4.1 Contents

The contents of the BabyLM pretraining dataset are summarized in Table 1. Descriptions of each data source are provided in Appendix A.

4.2 Preprocessing

We release *Strict* and *Strict-Small* train, development, and test splits of each of the ten data sources, split approximately 83.3%/8.3%/8.3%. The 10M word *Strict-Small* training set is sampled randomly from the *Strict* training set. After any preprocessing, we downsample and split each source by randomly sampling chunks of 2000 lines or longer. The code and instructions for downloading and preprocessing the raw data are publicly available.[3]

We perform minimal preprocessing in terms of filtering and reformatting text. Notably, we gener-

[3]`https://github.com/babylm/babylm_data_preprocessing`.

ally preserve newlines in the original texts, meaning newlines do not consistently delimit documents, paragraphs, or sentences, as in some pretraining datasets. We use WikiExtractor (Attardi, 2015) to extract text from the `xml` Simple English Wikipedia dump dated 2022-12-01. We perform additional preprocessing on Simple English Wikipedia to remove `<doc>` tags. We select the spoken subset of the BNC by selecting only lines from the `xml` containing the `<stext>` tag and extracting only the text from the `xml`. We use code by Gerlach and Font-Clos (2020) to download and preprocess data from Project Gutenberg, which we additionally filter to contain only English texts by authors born after 1850. The OpenSubtitles and Wikipedia portions of the pretraining corpus were shared with us in preprocessed form, having had duplicate documents removed from OpenSubtitles and preprocessing steps performed to Wikipedia similar to our Simple English Wikipedia procedure.[4] We use regular expressions to remove speaker and dialog act annotations from the Switchboard Dialog Act Corpus. We perform no preprocessing on the remaining datasets.

5 Evaluation

To evaluate submissions, participants were asked to upload their model predictions to Dynabench, which is an online platform for dynamic data collection and model benchmarking.[5] Multiple submissions to the Dynabench platform were allowed, but at most one candidate was allowed to be chosen as a competitor from each team.

5.1 Evaluation Tasks

The goal of the evaluation pipeline is to assess the extent to which submitted models have learned the latent syntactic and semantic structure of their pretraining language. To evaluate the grammatical abilities of LMs, we use BLiMP (Warstadt et al., 2020a). BLiMP consists of tasks that evaluate the ability of language models to behave in a manner consistent with the structure of English. Each example consists of a minimal pair of sentences, where one sentence is acceptable and the other is unacceptable (differing as minimally as possible from the acceptable sentence otherwise); a model is correct on a given example if it assigns higher probability to the correct sentence in the minimal pair. We also release a supplement to the BLiMP tasks, which tests for phenomena not captured by BLiMP (see §5.1.1).

To assess the abilities of LMs on more typical downstream NLP tasks, we evaluate on a mixture of tasks from a subsample of (Super)GLUE, which consists of text classification tasks. We include a variety of task types, including paraphrase detection (MRPC, QQP), sentiment classification (SST-2), natural language inference (MNLI, QNLI, RTE), question answering (BoolQ, MultiRC), acceptability judgments (CoLA), and commonsense reasoning (WSC).

5.1.1 Hidden Tasks

Two weeks before the results deadline, we released three hidden evaluation tasks: the Mixed Signals Generalization Set (MSGS), a supplement to BLiMP, and an age-of-acquisition (AoA) prediction task. MSGS and the BLiMP supplement were mandatory; AoA prediction was provided as an additional analysis point for participants in writing their papers. The motivation for using these hidden tasks was to prevent our evaluations from rewarding submissions that overfit to the BLiMP and (Super)GLUE tasks.

The BLiMP supplement includes five test suites consisting of BLiMP-style minimal pairs that cover areas of linguistic knowledge not tested by BLiMP—namely, dialogue and questions. The test suites are semi-automatically generated using manually filled templates. As with BLiMP, models are evaluated on the supplement in a zero-shot manner, by comparing the probabilities of the sequences in a minimal pair, under the assumption that the acceptable sequence will be more probable than its unacceptable counterpart.

HYPERNYMS. We evaluate LMs' knowledge of lexical entailment, i.e., hypernym–hyponym relationships. This task bears similarity to natural language inference (Dagan et al., 2006; Bowman et al., 2015; Williams et al., 2018), but we instead measure whether models assign a higher likelihood to valid statements of entailment compared to minimally differing invalid statements. The evaluation data is designed around manually written triples consisting of ⟨`hypernym`, `base`, `hyponym`⟩—for example, ⟨*plant*, *herb*, *basil*⟩. We also specify an `other` noun (for example, *flower*) which shares the `hypernym` but not the `hyponym` with the `base` noun. From these nouns, plus a set of manually written

[4] We thank Haau-Sing Li for allowing us to use this preprocessed data.

[5] `https://dynabench.org/`

contexts, we generate six types of minimal pairs, shown in Table 5 in Appendix C. Additionally, we randomly vary the text used to convey entailment, e.g., *If p then q*, *If p that means q*, *p therefore q*, etc.

SUBJECT–AUXILIARY INVERSION. The subject–auxiliary inversion rule applies in question formation in English (e.g., relating *Logan will go.* to *Will Logan go?*). This task has been used to evaluate language models' syntactic abilities and preferences (e.g., McCoy et al., 2020; Mueller et al., 2022; Yedetore et al., 2023; Mueller and Linzen, 2023). Our test data was created by Warstadt (2022, Ch. 6), where it is described in more detail.

TURN-TAKING. Comprehending dialogue requires tracking the grammatical properties of utterances from multiple speakers. Pronouns such as *I*, *you*, and *she* are indexicals, meaning their interpretation depends on the speaker's context and identity. This test suite evaluates whether LMs can predict which pronoun is appropriate to use when there is a change in speaker. For example, if person A asks person B a question of the form *Can I ...*, person B's response should begin with *You*, not *I*. Our tests include (i) cases where the pronoun is expected to change, and (ii) cases where it is not. We also vary the context length (and therefore the distance between the context pronoun and the target), and whether the context contains a distractor pronoun in an embedded position. Finally, for each example, we randomly select one from a set of formats for indicating the speaker, e.g., *A: ..., B: ...*, or *"...," he asked. "...," she said.*, etc. Examples of each format can be found in Table 6 in Appendix C.

QUESTION–ANSWER CONGRUENCE. The syntax of a question constrains the acceptable responses. For example, a congruent answer to a *who*-question must be an animate noun (or contain one in a suitable context). This test suite evaluates whether LMs assign a higher likelihood to congruent answers compared to incongruent ones, and therefore learn the cross-sentential dependency between a *wh*-word and an answer. In addition to a set of EASY test cases, we construct a set of adversarial TRICKY test cases where there is a highly salient distractor answer that is not congruent with the *wh*-word. We randomly vary whether the answer appears as a fragment or in a complete sentence as well as the format for indicating the speaker. See Table 7 in Appendix C for examples.

Mixed Signals Generalization Set. The Mixed Signals Generalization Set (MSGS; Warstadt et al., 2020b) is a text classification task that evaluates the inductive biases of language models. For a MSGS subtask, models are finetuned on an ambiguous training set where the labels are consistent with both a syntactic generalization and a surface generalization, and then evaluated on examples that disambiguate which generalization the model converged on (if any).[6]

Ideally, models would be more sensitive to linguistic features than surface features, as a systematic preference for abstract linguistic properties allows models to generalize more robustly to unseen structures. The metric for MSGS is the Matthews correlation coefficient between the model's predictions and the labels according to the linguistic generalization on the test set. A coefficient of 1 corresponds to a systematic linguistic generalization, and -1 to a systematic surface generalization. Indeed, Warstadt et al. (2020c) find that linguistic bias increases with the volume of pretraining data, and that models with RoBERTa-like architectures require more than a billion words of pretraining data to achieve an overall linguistic bias (i.e., a score greater than 0).

Age-of-acquisition Prediction. Optionally, participants could evaluate on the age of acquisition (AoA) prediction task of Portelance et al. (2023). When humans are learning language, they tend to acquire certain words at specific ages; the age of acquisition of a word refers to the age at which humans acquire that word. The AoA prediction task compares LMs' word surprisals with children's AoA of the same words. A language model's average surprisals are converted into AoA predictions, and these are then compared to the actual average AoA (in months) of those words. Models achieving lower mean absolute deviation between the actual

[6]For example, one of the subtasks tests which of the following two generalizations the model's inductive bias favors: whether the word "the" is present (the surface generalization), or whether the sentence contains an adjective (the syntactic generalization). Thus, training examples will include only ambiguous labeled pairs where these two properties are both perfectly correlated with each other and with the binary labels, such as `(The big dog barked, 1)` and `(A dog barked, 0)`. At test time, the model must classify held-out sentences where the features are anti-correlated, such as `A big dog barked` and `The dog barked`. If the model predicts labels `1` and `0` respectively for these and other analogous examples, we infer that it classifies examples based on the linguistic feature, while if it predicts `0` and `1` respectively, it adopted the surface generalization.

age and predicted age are said to perform better on the task.[7] While we did not require participants to submit these scores as part of their predictions, we provided code to make evaluation on this task simple, such that they could include this score as an additional analysis point in their paper submissions. 7 teams (22.6%) evaluated on the AoA prediction task; see Appendix E for results and discussion.

5.2 Evaluation Pipeline

The organizers provided code to unify the evaluation setup across submissions. This was released as a public repository on GitHub.[8] The evaluation pipeline supports models implemented in HuggingFace, though we did not restrict the model submissions to HuggingFace-based models.[9] For model and result submissions, users were required to (i) upload a link to their model (on any file-hosting service), and (ii) provide model predictions for each example of each task (via Dynabench); we provided a template specifying the format of the predictions file.

Data preprocessing. NLP tasks in our evaluation pipeline often contained vocabulary that is not contained in the BabyLM pretraining corpora. To address this mismatch, we filtered each task according to its lexical content: if an example contained any words that appear less than twice in the *Strict-Small* training corpus, we filtered the example out. Otherwise, each dataset is presented in its original format. See Table 4 in Appendix B for details on the size of the filtered datasets.

5.2.1 Evaluation Paradigms

Zero-shot evaluation. For zero-shot tasks—BLiMP and the BLiMP supplement—we modify the BigScience fork of the `lm-eval-harness` repository, originally by EleutherAI (Gao et al., 2021). This provides functionality for scoring autoregressive decoder-only LMs and encoder-decoder LMs. For encoder-only LMs, we modify the repository to support masked language model scoring as described in Salazar et al. (2020).[10]

Finetuning. We first attempted zero-shot learning and few-shot in-context learning for (Super)GLUE and MSGS tasks. However, this often resulted in random-chance accuracies from each of our baselines; we, therefore employ finetuning.[11] For tasks requiring finetuning—(Super)GLUE (Wang et al., 2018, 2019) and MSGS (Warstadt et al., 2020b)—we base our scripts on HuggingFace's example finetuning scripts for text classification.[12] We modified the script to support encoder-decoder models, and to work for a wider variety of tasks. We provide a default set of hyperparameters that we found to work well across our baseline models, though participants were allowed to freely modify hyperparameters.

5.3 Dynabench Leaderboard

Dynabench is an open-source platform for dynamic dataset creation, model evaluation, and leaderboard hosting (Kiela et al., 2021). In addition to open-sourcing datasets—including adversarial and human-in-the-loop datasets (Nie et al., 2020; Bartolo et al., 2021; Potts et al., 2021; Sheng et al., 2021; Vidgen et al., 2021; Kirk et al., 2022)—Dynabench has offered leaderboard support for several community challenges in the past (Wenzek et al., 2021; Bartolo et al., 2022; Mazumder et al., 2022). Given that we desire a dynamic leaderboard that allows for submissions even after the end of the challenge, this platform was well-suited to the BabyLM Challenge. All model submissions to the challenge were submitted via the Dynabench platform, to the respective leaderboards for the *Strict*,[13] *Strict-Small*,[14] and *Loose*[15] tracks.

Each leaderboard presents aggregate scores across all tasks, which can be interactively bro-

[7]It is not clear whether optimizing LM performance on this task necessarily leads to better language models. It is possible instead that LMs could have a different pattern of surprisals than humans while learning particular linguistic concepts more or less efficiently than humans. Thus, this task should be used more as a measure of how well LMs align with humans—and thus, as a measure of their usefulness as cognitive models of language acquisition and processing—rather than as a measure of quality or performance.

[8]`https://github.com/babylm/evaluation-pipeline`

[9]Upon release of the evaluation pipeline, we announced that we would provide support as needed to teams training LMs not based in HuggingFace.

[10]We use the implementation of Misra (2022) in the `minicons` library.

[11]finetuning technically adds to the training set size. We consider this acceptable, as finetuning on a single GLUE or MSGS task does not meaningfully add to the domain-general linguistic abilities of language models. The LM is finetuned separately for each task, so we still see this as an evaluation of the LM's abilities in itself (albeit more confounded than the zero-shot evaluations).

[12]`https://github.com/huggingface/transformers/blob/211f93aab95d1c683494e61c3cf8ff10e1f5d6b7/examples/pytorch/text-classification/run_glue.py`

[13]`https://dynabench.org/tasks/baby_strict`

[14]`https://dynabench.org/tasks/baby_strict_small`

[15]`https://dynabench.org/tasks/baby_loose`

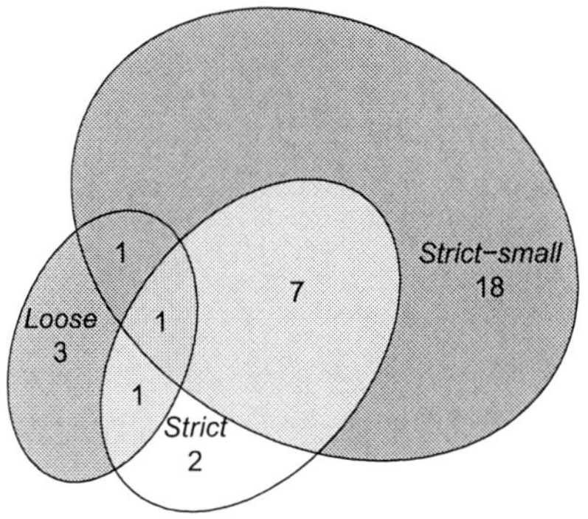

Figure 2: Number of participants who submitted to each track, with multiple submissions counted once.

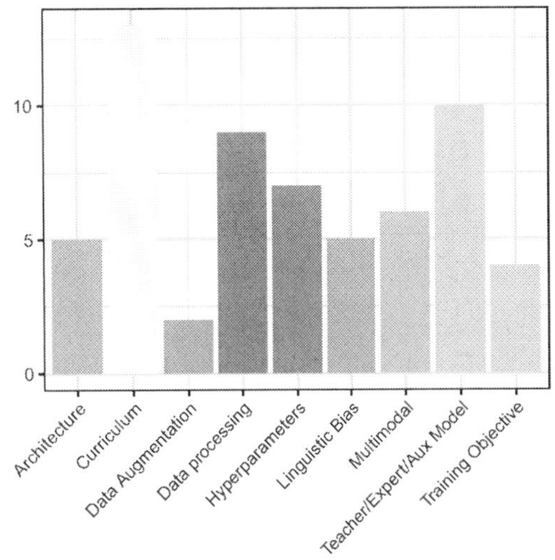

Figure 3: Total number of submitted models that used each of the nine approaches in our typology. We count at most one submitted model per participant per track.

ken down into more fine-grained scores per task and per subtask. To compute the aggregate score, we weigh BLiMP and the BLiMP-supplement together at 50% (all subtasks weighted equally), (Super)GLUE at 30%, and MSGS at 20%. This weighting scheme was arrived at heuristically, though we did observe that the winners for each track were stable across a wide range of reasonable weightings. Dynabench allows users to specify a custom task weighting to compute an alternative aggregate score. The leaderboard for the BabyLM challenge will continue to accept submissions indefinitely.

5.4 Baselines and Skylines

Baselines. To provide simple baselines for our evaluation tasks, we train multiple models on the data released for *Strict-Small* and *Strict* tracks and evaluate them on the evaluation tasks. Three baseline models are provided: OPT-125M, RoBERTa-base, and T5-base. These models use the same objective function and network architecture corresponding to their original papers (OPT; Zhang et al., 2022, RoBERTa; Liu et al., 2019, T5; Raffel et al., 2020). The network architecture of these models covers both encoder-decoder (T5-base and RoBERTa-base) and decoder-only (OPT-125M) architectures. Their objective functions include next-token prediction (OPT-125M), masked-token prediction (RoBERTa-base), and sequence-to-sequence (T5-base) matching losses. The baseline models are trained using a fixed context length of 128, a constant learning rate of 1e-4, a linear learning-rate warmup from 0 in the first 5000 steps, a batch size of 128, and AdamW (Loshchilov and Hutter, 2019) as the optimizer. They are trained for 20 epochs on the data, where each epoch randomly and independently shuffles the whole dataset. Although most of these hyperparameters are loosely inspired by Huebner et al., we expect that the specific choices on them can be further improved and leave these potential improvements as possible topics for submissions. We find that our baseline models achieve reasonable performance on the evaluation tasks, with clear improvement from more data from *Strict-Small* to *Strict* track and notable gap towards their counterparts pretrained on much larger datasets.

Skylines. To get an approximation of how well larger models could, in principle, perform in our task and setting, we ran Llama 2 70B (Touvron et al., 2023) and the fully trained RoBERTa-base model through our evaluation pipeline. This is meant to provide a comparison point to the state of the art in 2023, as the Llama 2 model is pretrained on much more data (2T tokens) than the challenge allows, and it has far more parameters than we expect to find in submissions. We evaluate Llama 2 on (Super)GLUE using in-context learning, but it is fully finetuned on MSGS. BabyLM submissions that approach these scores can be considered to have greater sample efficiency than the skyline models, and may therefore provide stronger starting points for future research in sample-efficient NLP.

6 Submissions Summary

We received 31 papers and 162 models in total. Table 3 shows the submission counts for each track.

	Model	BLiMP	GLUE	MSGS	BLiMP-Supp.	*Aggregated*
	Llama 2	0.84	0.84	0.26	0.75	0.71
	RoBERTa-Base	0.87	0.79	0.24	0.76	0.70
Strict	ELC-BERT (Charpentier and Samuel, 2023)	0.85	0.78	**0.47**	**0.77**	**0.74**
	BootBERT (Samuel, 2023)	**0.86**	**0.79**	0.28	0.72	0.70
	McGill-BERT (Cheng et al., 2023)	0.84	0.72	0.25	0.71	0.67
	Best Baseline (OPT-125M)	0.75	0.70	0.13	0.68	0.60
Strict-Small	ELC-BERT (Charpentier and Samuel, 2023)	**0.80**	**0.74**	**0.29**	0.67	**0.66**
	MLSM (Berend, 2023b)	0.79	0.71	0.17	0.57	0.61
	McGill-BERT (Cheng et al., 2023)	0.75	0.70	0.13	**0.68**	0.60
	Best Baseline (OPT-125M)	0.63	0.62	0.10	0.53	0.50
Loose	Contextualizer (Xiao et al., 2023)	**0.86**	**0.73**	**0.58**	0.63	**0.73**
	McGill-BERT (Cheng et al., 2023)	0.80	0.68	-0.02	0.57	0.57
	BabyStories (Zhao et al., 2023)	0.78	0.61	0.03	**0.65**	0.56

Table 2: Top 3 systems for each track, as well as the baseline model with the highest aggregate score. We also show "skyline" models: RoBERTa-base and Llama 2 trained on their full pre-training corpora. Each task score is simply the mean score across each of its subtasks. The aggregate score is a weighted average of each task. We **bold** the highest-scoring system for each task within each track.

	# Models	# Participants
Loose	20	8
Strict-Small	118	29
Strict	24	11
total	*162*	*31*

Table 3: Total number of models and participants per track. Participants who submitted to multiple tracks are counted once in the total.

Some participants submitted to multiple tracks; we show data for unique participants in Figure 2.

We found that many submissions focused their efforts on similar techniques. To better quantify this, we devised a typology of the nine most common approaches and assigned each submitted model one or more labels. Figure 3 shows the number of submissions employing each approach. §7.3 provides more detailed descriptions of each approach, as well as results indicating which ones were most effective.

All participants are affiliated with universities or independent research institutions. Participants' home institutions are located in 16 different countries. The number of participants by country is as follows (multinational participants are counted more than once): US (9), Germany (5), Netherlands (3), UK (4), Canada (2), Norway (2), Austria (1), Denmark (1), France (1), Hungary (1), Israel (1), Japan (1), Norway (1), Switzerland (1), Turkey (1).

The official leaderboard is available on Dynabench.[16] With the consent of participants, we release links to submitted models, their complete predictions for the evaluation tasks, their scores for each task and subtask, and metadata about each submission at the BabyLM's GitHub at `https://github.com/babylm/submissions2023`. We provide a summary of each submission in Appendix F.

7 Results & Analysis

7.1 Overall Results & Track Winners

The results from all submissions are shown in Figure 4, with the scores of the top-performing models in each track detailed in Table 2. In the figure, dashed green lines show the performance of the Llama 2 skyline. Solid green lines show human performance on GLUE reported in Nangia and Bowman (2019), and human performance on BLiMP as reported by Warstadt et al. (2020a).

Before discussing the winning systems in each track, we note a few high-level takeaways from these results. The strongest results were achieved by models in the *Strict* track. Given the *Strict* track's larger training corpus relative to the *Strict-Small* corpus, it is not surprising that these models could outperform those in the *Strict-Small* track. However, there are two interesting trends: First, *Strict* models did not outperform those in *Strict-Small* by a large amount, even though the size of training data was an order-of-magnitude larger. For example, there are only

[16] `https://dynabench.org/babylm`

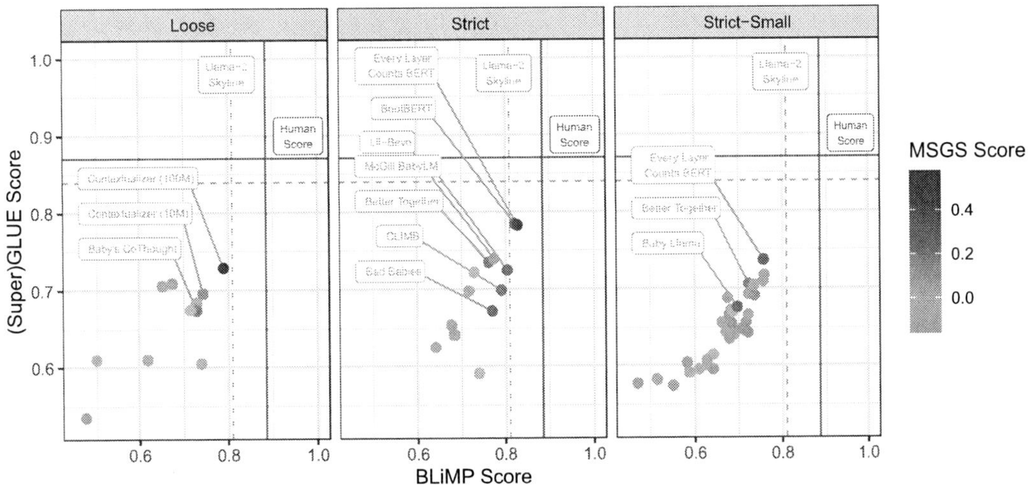

Figure 4: **Summary of BabyLM Submission Results:** Each point represents an official model submission. Scores are broken down into performance on BLiMP (x-axis), GLUE (y-axis) and MSGS (color). Submissions that achieve an aggregate score above 0.6 are labeled in gray. Green dashed lines show Llama 2 skyline performance, and green solid lines show the human performance ceiling.

two models in the *Strict* track that achieve higher GLUE scores than the best-performing *Strict-Small* model. Second, models in the *Loose* track tended to perform worse in the aggregate than those in the *Strict-Small* track, even though they potentially had access to additional (non-linguistic) data. One conclusion we can draw from this is that learning from multiple modalities of data presents a challenge in its own right, and that current model architectures are not optimized to efficiently utilize multiple types of inputs during training.

The other important high-level takeaway is that many BabyLM models are very close to the Llama 2 skyline, and to achieving human-level performance on BLiMP and GLUE (i.e., they are near the green lines in Figure 4). Strong performance could be expected in the case of (Super)GLUE, where models were finetuned with additional data, but we note that even for BLiMP, the top-performing model is only about 3% shy of human performance. Note that prior to the start of the challenge, we explored the possibility of measuring zero-shot performance on (Super)GLUE test sets, and found zero-shot performance to be at or below chance for our baselines. This fact, as well as the consideration that GLUE has been traditionally evaluated using finetuning, leads us to select finetuning evaluations for the (Super)GLUE benchmark(s).

Given that successful training on developmentally plausible corpora could have ramifications for cognitive and linguistic theories of learnability (Wilcox et al., 2023; Warstadt and Bowman, 2022), these results point to two important takeaways: (1) Human-level results have not been achieved *yet*. However, (2) given the strong performance of the top-scoring models, human-level results appear likely to be achieved very soon, possibly within the next few years. Of course, one possible concern is the following: current models may not be close to human-level performance; rather, current performance metrics, like BLiMP, might not accurately measure human-level linguistic competence. We are sympathetic to such concerns, but we also note that BLiMP, and other related syntactic benchmarks such as those presented in Marvin and Linzen (2018) and Gauthier et al. (2020), were specifically designed to mimic the types of tests invented by linguists and cognitive scientists to reveal syntactic competence—i.e., they are all based on minimal pair sentences. Thus, while it is imperative to continue building more comprehensive and larger datasets, we believe it is fair to say that the close-to-human scores observed in the BabyLM challenge on BLiMP reflect genuine grammatical generalizations learned by the models.

7.2 Winning Submissions

Below, we discuss the winning submissions from each track in greater detail. We also mention the winners of our "Most Interesting Paper" awards and provide a brief justification for each.

***Strict* track.** The winner of the *Strict* track is ELC-BERT submitted by Charpentier and Samuel (2023). This model, as well as the runner-up submission Boot-BERT (Samuel, 2023), used as their starting point the LTG-BERT architecture from Samuel et al. (2023). Although these submissions make additional incremental improvements to the LTG-BERT training regime, their own baselines suggest that the backbone architecture plays a large role in the submissions' successes. LTG-BERT's main contribution is a synthesis of several optimizations to the Transformer architecture, namely: (1) additional layer normalization, following (Shleifer et al., 2021); (2) GEGLU feed-forward modules (Shazeer, 2020); (3) disentangled attention following DeBERTa (He et al., 2021); and (4) scaled weight initialization following (Nguyen and Salazar, 2019). ELC-BERT modifies this backbone such that the input to each layer is a weighted sum of the outputs of all previous layers. Another notable property of LTG-BERT is that all models with this architecture so far have been trained for a large number of epochs. Charpentier and Samuel (2023) train models for over 450 epochs for their *Strict* submission, and over 2000 epochs for their *Strict-Small* submission. LTG-BERT models performed exceptionally well on our set of evaluations, outperforming not only every other submission to the shared task but also the Llama 2 and RoBERTa-Base skylines on overall score and on all test suites except for (Super)GLUE (Table 2). The second runner-up for this track was McGill-BERT (Cheng et al., 2023).

***Strict-Small* track.** The winner of the *Strict-Small* track is, again, ELC-BERT (Charpentier and Samuel, 2023). This double-win demonstrates that the model's architectural choices work well with multiple scales of pretraining data. The runners-up were MLSM (Berend, 2023b) and McGill-BERT (Cheng et al., 2023).

***Loose* track.** The winner of the *Loose* track is the Contextualizer model of Xiao et al. (2023), which used a data processing scheme in which extra training samples are created by combining chunks of texts from different contexts. Repeating this process 40 times for each chunk gives a dataset that has as many training samples as 4B word dataset, but based on a dataset of only 100M words. This augmentation technique outperforms training for 40 epochs using the same training samples. Runners-up for this track were McGill-BERT (Cheng et al., 2023) and the BabyStories model of Zhao et al. (2023).

Most interesting paper awards. These awards are given to papers that go beyond achieving high scores on a leaderboard, and instead demonstrate contributions to the shared task based on interesting analyses, useful negative results, creative modeling choices, or a combination thereof. We awarded two most interesting paper awards in two different categories.

Outstanding evaluation. The most interesting paper award for outstanding evaluation was given to "Large GPT-like Models are Bad Babies: A Closer Look at the Relationship between Linguistic Competence and Psycholinguistic Measures" (Steuer et al., 2023). This work goes beyond the BabyLM evaluation tasks: the authors use measures of human cognitive processing effort and linguistic competence and additionally correlate these with BabyLM task performance. Their work assesses BabyLM submissions as models of human language processing, thus contributing to our understanding of how to better train cognitive models.

Compelling negative results. The most interesting paper award for compelling negative results was given to "CLIMB—Curriculum Learning for Infant-inspired Model Building" (Martinez et al., 2023). This work proposes a typology of common curriculum learning approaches and performs a thorough and principled evaluation exploring this design space. Although they find that none of the tested approaches leads to widespread improvements across the evaluation tasks, the exhaustiveness of this search and the careful controls and baselines in the study make this negative result a valuable contribution.

7.3 Common Methods

One of the main objectives of the BabyLM Challenge is to compare and contrast methodological choices for sample-efficient pretraining. To do so, we hand-coded each submission based on the method(s) it employs. Figure 3 shows the number of submissions using each approach, and we visualize the performance of different methods in Figure 5. We also present a similar figure separated by the underlying architecture (Figure 6). Each of these approaches is discussed

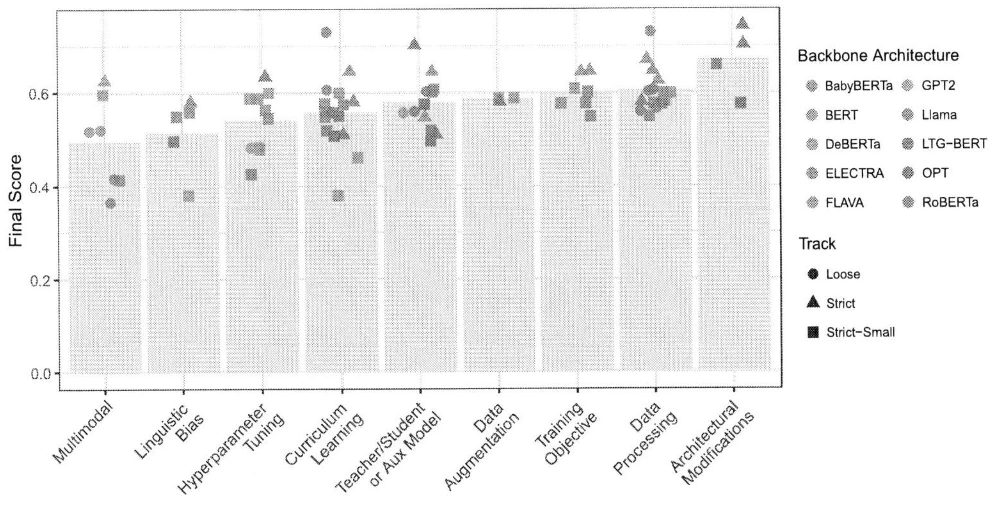

Figure 5: **Effect of Training Strategy and Backbone Architecture:** Each point represents a submission. Some submissions may appear more than once if they use multiple strategies. Shapes show the challenge track to which the model was submitted. Colors show the backbone architecture on which the model is based. Gray bars show within-category aggregates.

in further detail below. We highlight two high-level takeaways to start: First, curriculum learning, which was the most popular approach, did not tend to produce high scores (although one curriculum learning model did perform well). Second, the highest-performing models were ones that made architectural modifications—namely, those based on the LTG-BERT architecture.

Curriculum learning. This approach entails sorting training steps with respect to some complexity metric(s). This was the most popular approach, with 13 teams (41.9%) attempting some variant of curriculum learning. The majority of these attempts did not produce consistent improvements across the BabyLM evaluation tasks. However, they did explore a large space of possible curricula, for example: ranking sentences by surprisal (Chobey et al., 2023; Hong et al., 2023), lexical frequency (Borazjanizadeh, 2023; Martinez et al., 2023), length (DeBenedetto, 2023; Edman and Bylinina, 2023), and syntactic complexity (Mi, 2023; Oba et al., 2023; Bunzeck and Zarrieß, 2023); sorting entire datasets by difficulty (Opper et al., 2023; Martinez et al., 2023; Xiao et al., 2023); gradually increasing vocabulary size (Thoma et al., 2023; Edman and Bylinina, 2023); and gradually increasing the difficulty of the training objective (Martinez et al., 2023).

Teacher–student or auxiliary model. Many papers trained their submitted models with the aid of additional models. According to our rules, this was permissible as long as any auxiliary models were trained on the BabyLM corpus. Knowledge distillation using auxiliary models was often a successful approach: Samuel (2023) considered an exponential moving average teacher model (Tarvainen and Valpola, 2017), while Berend (2023b) modeled a latent semantic feature distribution from a teacher model. Timiryasov and Tastet (2023) performed distillation on an ensemble of features. Others used auxiliary models to select appropriate training examples for a curriculum (Chobey et al., 2023; Hong et al., 2023), or trained a reward model for use in reinforcement learning (Zhao et al., 2023).

Data preprocessing. Many submissions modified the format of the pretraining corpus. When controlled comparisons were performed, these preprocessing steps often led to improvements. In §7.2 we discuss the successful Contextualizer method for constructing new training samples. Other successful approaches used short sequences or individual sentences as training samples, rather than long portions of documents (Govindarajan et al., 2023; Cheng et al., 2023; Edman and Bylinina, 2023). Among the more unique approaches in this space was Baby's CoThought (Zhang et al., 2023), which used an LLM to reformat unrelated sentences from the corpus into coherent paragraphs.

Hyperparameter tuning and model scaling. This was a relatively common approach. Many

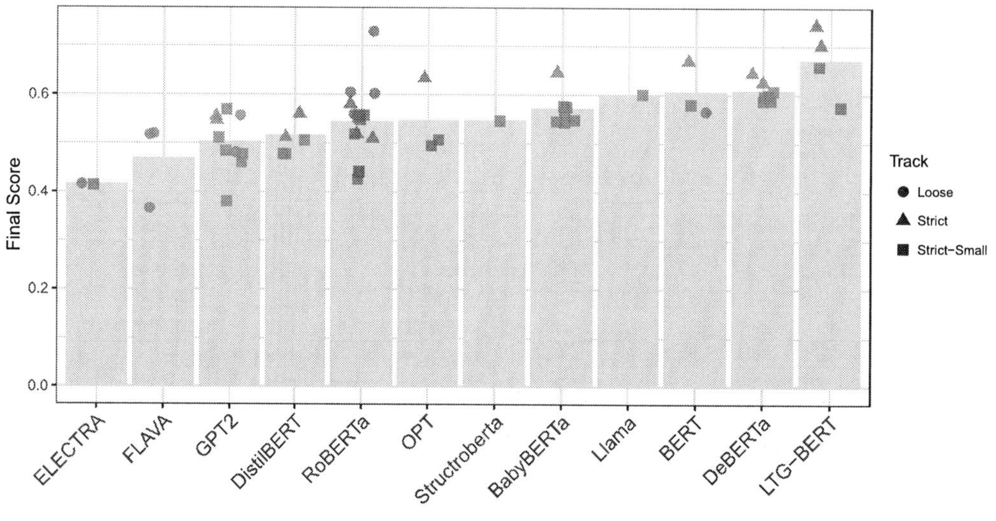

Figure 6: **Effect of Backbone Architecture:** Each point represents a submission. Shape indicates the challenge track. Gray bars show within-category aggregates.

submissions performed extensive hyperparameter searches, producing hard-won hyperparameters that work well on smaller datasets while preserving features of the dataset. While extensive hyperparameter searching can be expensive and challenging when scaling up to full-sized pretraining, in our limited data regime, consistently successful modifications include reducing context length (see "Data preprocessing", above), and training for more epochs or long epochs with data augmentation (Jumelet et al., 2023; Bhardwaj et al., 2023; Yang et al., 2023; Xiao et al., 2023; Samuel, 2023; Charpentier and Samuel, 2023).

However, results are mixed when modifying model size: some participants achieved better results when scaling model sizes up (Çağatan, 2023), while others were able to perform well when using very small models (Proskurina et al., 2023). More controlled studies using a variety of architectures and datasets are needed to determine whether scaling up or down is a better solution.

Multimodal learning. Multimodal learning was one of the directions where we expected the most interest and the most submissions; however, we received few submissions based on multimodal inputs, and the multimodal submissions did not reliably contribute to higher overall accuracy. One submission used music (Govindarajan et al., 2023), another used vision and language data (Amariucai and Warstadt, 2023), a third explored text-and-audio (Wolf et al., 2023), and a fourth incorporated text-and-image data and lexical sensorimotor data as part of the embedding process using multiplex networks (Stella et al., 2017; Ciaglia et al., 2023). Music training produced minor improvements on some subtasks, while the vision-and-language system marginally improved over the baselines in the *Strict-Small* track. The multiplex network did not produce performance gains, though it did allow the participants to reduce the number of parameters while preserving performance relative to the baselines. WhisBERT was reported to be undertrained, making its results difficult to interpret.

Architecture modifications. The winning submission made architectural modifications: Charpentier and Samuel (2023) made slight improvements to LTG-BERT (see §7.2 for more on this architecture) by taking a weighted sum over the outputs of all previous layers. Momen et al. (2023) used the relatively novel StructFormer architecture (Shen et al., 2021), which encourages tree-structured representations of inputs.

Training objectives. Some submissions trained language models using a mixture of both a language modeling objective and some other objective. Knowledge distillation from teacher models (see paragraphed titled "Teacher–student or auxiliary model" above) was the most common modification. Martinez et al. (2023) simplified the masked language modeling objective by coarse-graining the output classes, with little effect. Govindarajan et al. (2023) achieved improvements on specific BLiMP subtasks by modifying the masking procedure to preferentially mask specific words thought to be relevant to a particular phenomenon tested by BLiMP.

Linguistic bias. Some submissions tried to impart human linguistic biases to models. Such approaches discussed above include curriculum learning based on linguistically motivated data sorting methods and architectures like StructFormer that encourage hierarchical analyses of inputs. Chen and Portelance (2023) also pretrained with token embeddings obtained via grammar induction, and Thoma et al. (2023) iteratively updated the vocabulary of the LM based on word simplicity measures (motivated by human age-of-acquisition analyses).

Data augmentation. Arguably, the effective Contextualizer approach (Xiao et al., 2023) is a form of data augmentation (see §7.2). Jumelet et al. (2023) used regular expressions to generate question-answer pairs given the BabyLM training data. Zhao et al. (2023) used an LLM to generate text merging disparate sentences into cohesive paragraphs.

8 Future BabyLM Challenges

The first iteration of the BabyLM Challenge yielded many successes, but also some organizational and scientific challenges. The lessons learned from our findings can improve future iterations of this challenge.

We were surprised that there were significantly more submissions to the *Strict-Small* track than the other two tracks combined, considering that the *Loose* track allows for a much wider variety of methods. However, this is understandable from the perspective of compute: training on *Strict-Small* is the least computationally expensive of each of the tracks, and it constrains the model search space enough that ideas are perhaps easier to define and execute. In future iterations of the BabyLM challenge, it could be interesting to provide more specific and constrained *Loose* tracks, which focus on particular research directions—for example, LLM-assisted low-resource pretraining, allowing expert annotations during pretraining, or joint text and audio modeling.

We can also draw insights from the data preprocessing and hyperparameter tuning submissions in particular, and standardize them into the dataset/evaluation pipeline. For example, we could preprocess the data in ways the present challenge has shown to be effective. This could include sorting the data according to the curriculum learning method that yielded performance gains, providing better-starting hyperparameters, and training a baseline with the best architecture.

Although data quantity was the main focus of this iteration, we may also consider rewarding compute efficiency in the future. Many of the most successful submissions consumed a lot of compute by training for many epochs. Indeed, the winning submission trained on about as many samples as BERT, despite having a training set only about 3% as large. While this finding is interesting, it does little to help achieve our goals in §2. Training for hundreds of epochs is not cognitively plausible, and it is does not make it easier and more accessible to test novel training approaches or train models on a university budget.

The evaluation pipeline was built on the existing `lm-evaluation-harness` repository,[17] but maintaining and updating it for this challenge was no small feat for a single organizer. In future iterations of the challenge, it would be beneficial to have a larger dedicated support team for the evaluations. A dedicated team could also allow us to handle a greater variety of submissions, including those not supported by HuggingFace.

9 Conclusions

The BabyLM Challenge encouraged participants to *think small*. We asked: can we improve language modeling on smaller and more cognitively plausible datasets? The submitted systems employed diverse methods, but the most consistent gains came from modified model architectures, new training objectives, principled preprocessing of the pretraining corpora, and hyperparameter searches. In one case, a curriculum learning method resulted in significant improvements. Future work can build on these findings to further improve language modeling for low-resource settings and for cognitive modeling research.

Acknowledgments

We would like to thank the participants of the BabyLM Challenge for their valuable contributions—not just their models and papers, but also their contributions to the evaluation pipeline and the reviewing process.

[17]Originally released at `https://github.com/EleutherAI/lm-evaluation-harness`. Note that we based our implementation on the BigScience fork at `https://github.com/bigscience-workshop/lm-evaluation-harness`.

We would also like to thank the Dynabench team at MLCommons for hosting our leaderboards and integrating our challenge's unique requirements into their implementation. Thanks especially to Max Bartolo, Douwe Kiela, and Hannah Rose Kirk for feedback on earlier iterations of the BabyLM evaluation setup.

Author Contributions

- **Original concept:** Alex Warstadt, Leshem Choshen
- **Primary organizers:** Alex Warstadt, Ethan Wilcox, Leshem Choshen, Aaron Mueller, Chengxu Zhuang
- **Pipeline implementation and maintenance:** Aaron Mueller
- **Baseline model training**: Chengxu Zhuang
- **Publicity and communications with participants:** Leshem Choshen, Ethan Wilcox
- **Training dataset compilation:** Alex Warstadt
- **BLiMP Supplement evaluation data creation:** Alex Warstadt
- **Dynabench integration:** Juan Ciro, Rafael Mosquera, Adina Williams
- **Llama 2 evaluation:** Bhargavi Paranjape
- **Guidance on concept and workshop organization:** Ryan Cotterell, Tal Linzen, Adina Williams
- **Reviewing submissions:** Alex Warstadt, Ethan Wilcox, Leshem Choshen, Aaron Mueller, Chengxu Zhuang, Adina Williams
- **Initial draft of findings paper:** Alex Warstadt, Ethan Wilcox, Leshem Choshen, Aaron Mueller, Chengxu Zhuang
- **Editing:** All authors

References

Ahmed Abdelali, Francisco Guzman, Hassan Sajjad, and Stephan Vogel. 2014. The AMARA corpus: Building parallel language resources for the educational domain. In *Proceedings of the Ninth International Conference on Language Resources and Evaluation*, pages 1856–1862, Reykjavik, Iceland. European Language Resources Association (ELRA).

Theodor Amariucai and Alexander Scott Warstadt. 2023. Acquiring linguistic knowledge from multimodal input. In *Proceedings of the BabyLM Challenge*. Association for Computational Linguistics (ACL).

Giuseppe Attardi. 2015. Wikiextractor. `https://github.com/attardi/wikiextractor`.

Marco Baroni. 2022. On the proper role of linguistically-oriented deep net analysis in linguistic theorizing. *Algebraic Structures in Natural Language*, pages 1–16.

Max Bartolo, Hannah Kirk, Pedro Rodriguez, Katerina Margatina, Tristan Thrush, Robin Jia, Pontus Stenetorp, Adina Williams, and Douwe Kiela, editors. 2022. *Proceedings of the First Workshop on Dynamic Adversarial Data Collection*. Association for Computational Linguistics, Seattle, WA.

Max Bartolo, Tristan Thrush, Robin Jia, Sebastian Riedel, Pontus Stenetorp, and Douwe Kiela. 2021. Improving question answering model robustness with synthetic adversarial data generation. In *Proceedings of the 2021 Conference on Empirical Methods in Natural Language Processing*, pages 8830–8848, Online and Punta Cana, Dominican Republic. Association for Computational Linguistics.

Eden Bensaid, Mauro Martino, Benjamin Hoover, Jacob Andreas, and Hendrik Strobelt. 2021. Fairytailor: A multimodal generative framework for storytelling. *CoRR*, abs/2108.04324.

Gábor Berend. 2023a. Masked latent semantic modeling: an efficient pre-training alternative to masked language modeling. In *Findings of the Association for Computational Linguistics: ACL 2023*, pages 13949–13962, Toronto, Canada. Association for Computational Linguistics.

Gábor Berend. 2023b. Better together: Jointly using masked latent semantic modeling and masked language modeling for sample efficient pre-training. In *Proceedings of the BabyLM Challenge*. Association for Computational Linguistics (ACL).

Khushi Bhardwaj, Raj Sanjay Shah, and Sashank Varma. 2023. Pre-training LLMs using human-like development data corpus. In *Proceedings of the BabyLM Challenge*. Association for Computational Linguistics (ACL).

Douglas Biber. 1991. *Variation across Speech and Writing*. Cambridge University Press.

Nasim Borazjanizadeh. 2023. Optimizing GPT-2 pretraining on BabyLM corpus with difficulty-based sentence reordering. In *Proceedings of the BabyLM Challenge*. Association for Computational Linguistics (ACL).

Samuel R. Bowman, Gabor Angeli, Christopher Potts, and Christopher D. Manning. 2015. A large annotated corpus for learning natural language inference. In *Proceedings of the 2015 Conference on Empirical Methods in Natural Language Processing*, pages 632–642, Lisbon, Portugal. Association for Computational Linguistics.

Ellen Breitholtz, Shalom Lappin, Sharid Loaiciga, Nikolai Ilinykh, and Simon Dobnik, editors. 2023. *Proceedings of the 2023 CLASP Conference on Learning with Small Data*. Association for Computational Linguistics, Gothenburg, Sweden.

Tom Brown, Benjamin Mann, Nick Ryder, Melanie Subbiah, Jared D. Kaplan, Prafulla Dhariwal, Arvind Neelakantan, Pranav Shyam, Girish Sastry, Amanda Askell, Sandhini Agarwal, Ariel Herbert-Voss, Gretchen Krueger, Tom Henighan, Rewon Child, Aditya Ramesh, Daniel Ziegler, Jeffrey Wu, Clemens Winter, Chris Hesse, Mark Chen, Eric Sigler, Mateusz Litwin, Scott Gray, Benjamin Chess, Jack Clark, Christopher Berner, Sam McCandlish, Alec Radford, Ilya Sutskever, and Dario Amodei. 2020. Language models are few-shot learners. In *Advances in Neural Information Processing Systems*, volume 33, pages 1877–1901.

Bastian Bunzeck and Sina Zarrieß. 2023. GPT-wee: Effective pre-training for downsized language models. In *Proceedings of the BabyLM Challenge*. Association for Computational Linguistics (ACL).

Margaret F. Carr, Shantanu P. Jadhav, and Loren M. Frank. 2011. Hippocampal replay in the awake state: a potential substrate for memory consolidation and retrieval. *Nature Neuroscience*, 14(2):147–153.

Lucas Georges Gabriel Charpentier and David Samuel. 2023. Not all layers are equally as important: Every layer counts BERT. In *Proceedings of the BabyLM Challenge*. Association for Computational Linguistics (ACL).

Xuanda Chen and Eva Portelance. 2023. Grammar induction pretraining for language modeling in low resource contexts. In *Proceedings of the BabyLM Challenge*. Association for Computational Linguistics (ACL).

Ziling Cheng, Rahul Aralikatte, Ian Porada, Cesare Spinoso-Di Piano, and Jackie C. K. Cheung. 2023. McGill BabyLM shared task submission: The effects of data formatting and structure biases. In *Proceedings of the BabyLM Challenge*. Association for Computational Linguistics (ACL).

Aryaman Chobey, Oliver Smith, Anzi Wang, and Grusha Prasad. 2023. Can training neural language models on a curriculum with developmentally plausible data improve alignment with human reading behavior? In *Proceedings of the BabyLM Challenge*. Association for Computational Linguistics (ACL).

Leshem Choshen, Elad Venezian, Shachar Don-Yehiya, Noam Slonim, and Yoav Katz. 2022. Where to start? analyzing the potential value of intermediate models. *CoRR*, abs/2211.00107.

Floriana Ciaglia, Massimo Stella, and Casey Kennington. 2023. Investigating preferential acquisition and attachment in early word learning through cognitive, visual and latent multiplex lexical networks. *Physica A: Statistical Mechanics and its Applications*, 612:128468.

Kevin Clark, Minh-Thang Luong, Quoc V. Le, and Christopher D. Manning. 2020. ELECTRA: pretraining text encoders as discriminators rather than generators. In *Proceedings of the 8th International Conference on Learning Representations*. OpenReview.net.

BNC Consortium. 2007. *The British National Corpus, XML Edition*. Oxford Text Archive.

Alejandrina Cristia, Emmanuel Dupoux, Michael Gurven, and Jonathan Stieglitz. 2019. Child-directed speech is infrequent in a forager-farmer population: A time allocation study. *Child Development*, 90(3):759–773.

Ido Dagan, Oren Glickman, and Bernardo Magnini. 2006. The PASCAL recognising textual entailment challenge. In *Machine Learning Challenges. Evaluating Predictive Uncertainty, Visual Object Classification, and Recognising Textual Entailment*. Springer.

Nicola De Cao, Wilker Aziz, and Ivan Titov. 2021. Editing factual knowledge in language models. In *Proceedings of the 2021 Conference on Empirical Methods in Natural Language Processing*, pages 6491–6506, Online and Punta Cana, Dominican Republic. Association for Computational Linguistics.

Justin DeBenedetto. 2023. Byte-ranked curriculum learning for BabyLM strict-small shared task 2023. In *Proceedings of the BabyLM Challenge*. Association for Computational Linguistics (ACL).

Jacob Devlin, Ming-Wei Chang, Kenton Lee, and Kristina Toutanova. 2019. BERT: Pre-training of deep bidirectional transformers for language understanding. In *Proceedings of the 2019 Conference of the North American Chapter of the Association for Computational Linguistics: Human Language Technologies, Volume 1 (Long and Short Papers)*, pages 4171–4186, Minneapolis, Minnesota. Association for Computational Linguistics.

Michael Diskin, Alexey Bukhtiyarov, Max Ryabinin, Lucile Saulnier, Quentin Lhoest, Anton Sinitsin, Dmitry Popov, Dmitriy Pyrkin, Maxim Kashirin, Alexander Borzunov, Albert Villanova del Moral, Denis Mazur, Ilia Kobelev, Yacine Jernite, Thomas

Wolf, and Gennady Pekhimenko. 2021. Distributed deep learning in open collaborations. In *Advances in Neural Information Processing Systems*.

Shachar Don-Yehiya, Elad Venezian, Colin Raffel, Noam Slonim, and Leshem Choshen. 2023. ColD fusion: Collaborative descent for distributed multitask finetuning. In *Proceedings of the 61st Annual Meeting of the Association for Computational Linguistics (Volume 1: Long Papers)*, pages 788–806, Toronto, Canada. Association for Computational Linguistics.

Emmanuel Dupoux. 2018. Cognitive science in the era of artificial intelligence: A roadmap for reverse-engineering the infant language-learner. *Cognition*, 173:43–59.

Lukas Edman and Lisa Bylinina. 2023. Too much information: Keeping training simple for BabyLMs. In *Proceedings of the BabyLM Challenge*. Association for Computational Linguistics (ACL).

Jeffrey L. Elman. 1990. Finding structure in time. *Cognitive Science*, 14(2):179–211. Wiley Online Library.

Clayton Fields, Osama Natouf, Andrew McMains, Catherine Henry, and Casey Kennington. 2023. Tiny language models enriched with multimodal knowledge from multiplex networks. In *Proceedings of the BabyLM Challenge*. Association for Computational Linguistics (ACL).

Michael C. Frank. 2023. Bridging the data gap between children and large language models. *Trends in Cognitive Sciences*.

Leo Gao, Jonathan Tow, Stella Biderman, Sid Black, Anthony DiPofi, Charles Foster, Laurence Golding, Jeffrey Hsu, Kyle McDonell, Niklas Muennighoff, Jason Phang, Laria Reynolds, Eric Tang, Anish Thite, Ben Wang, Kevin Wang, and Andy Zou. 2021. A framework for few-shot language model evaluation.

Jon Gauthier, Jennifer Hu, Ethan Wilcox, Peng Qian, and Roger Levy. 2020. SyntaxGym: An online platform for targeted evaluation of language models. In *Proceedings of the 58th Annual Meeting of the Association for Computational Linguistics: System Demonstrations*, pages 70–76, Online. Association for Computational Linguistics.

Martin Gerlach and Francesc Font-Clos. 2020. A standardized project gutenberg corpus for statistical analysis of natural language and quantitative linguistics. *Entropy. An International and Interdisciplinary Journal of Entropy and Information Studies*, 22(1). Number: 126 tex.pubmedid: 33285901.

Jill Gilkerson, Jeffrey A. Richards, Steven F. Warren, Judith K. Montgomery, Charles R. Greenwood, D. Kimbrough Oller, John HL Hansen, and Terrance D. Paul. 2017. Mapping the early language environment using all-day recordings and automated analysis. *American Journal of Speech-Language Pathology*, 26(2):248–265.

J.J. Godfrey, E.C. Holliman, and J. McDaniel. 1992. SWITCHBOARD: Telephone speech corpus for research and development. In *IEEE International Conference on Acoustics, Speech, and Signal Processing*, volume 1, pages 517–520 vol.1.

Venkata Subrahmanyan Govindarajan, Juan Diego Rodriguez, Kaj Bostrom, and Kyle Mahowald. 2023. Lil-bevo: Explorations of strategies for training language models in more humanlike ways. In *Proceedings of the BabyLM Challenge*. Association for Computational Linguistics (ACL).

John Hale. 2001. A probabilistic Earley parser as a psycholinguistic model. In *Second Meeting of the North American Chapter of the Association for Computational Linguistics*.

Pengcheng He, Xiaodong Liu, Jianfeng Gao, and Weizhu Chen. 2021. DeBERTa: Decoding-enhanced BERT with disentangled attention. In *International Conference on Learning Representations*.

Felix Hill, Antoine Bordes, Sumit Chopra, and Jason Weston. 2016. The Goldilocks principle: Reading children's books with explicit memory representations. In *4th International Conference on Learning Representations*.

Jordan Hoffmann, Sebastian Borgeaud, Arthur Mensch, Elena Buchatskaya, Trevor Cai, Eliza Rutherford, Diego de las Casas, Lisa Anne Hendricks, Johannes Welbl, Aidan Clark, Tom Hennigan, Eric Noland, Katherine Millican, George van den Driessche, Bogdan Damoc, Aurelia Guy, Simon Osindero, Karen Simonyan, Erich Elsen, Oriol Vinyals, Jack William Rae, and Laurent Sifre. 2022. An empirical analysis of compute-optimal large language model training. In *Advances in Neural Information Processing Systems*.

Xudong Hong, Sharid Loáiciga, and Asad B. Sayeed. 2023. A surprisal oracle for active curriculum language modeling. In *Proceedings of the BabyLM Challenge*. Association for Computational Linguistics (ACL).

Philip A. Huebner, Elior Sulem, Fisher Cynthia, and Dan Roth. 2021. BabyBERTa: Learning more grammar with small-scale child-directed language. In *Proceedings of the 25th conference on computational natural language learning*, pages 624–646, Online. Association for Computational Linguistics.

Philip A. Huebner and Jon A. Willits. 2021. Using lexical context to discover the noun category: Younger children have it easier. In Kara D. Federmeier and Lili Sahakyan, editors, *The Context of Cognition: Emerging Perspectives*, volume 75 of *Psychology of learning and motivation*, pages 279–331. Academic Press. ISSN: 0079-7421.

Peter Izsak, Moshe Berchansky, and Omer Levy. 2021. How to train BERT with an academic budget. In *Proceedings of the 2021 conference on empirical meth-*

ods in natural language processing, pages 10644–10652, Online and Punta Cana, Dominican Republic. Association for Computational Linguistics.

Jaap Jumelet, Michael Hanna, Marianne De Heer Kloots, Anna Langedijk, Charlotte Pouw, and Oskar van der Wal. 2023. ChapGTP, ILLC's attempt at raising a BabyLM: Improving data efficiency by automatic task formation. In *Proceedings of the BabyLM Challenge*. Association for Computational Linguistics (ACL).

Jean Kaddour. 2023. The minipile challenge for data-efficient language models. *CoRR*, abs/2304.08442.

Nikhil Kandpal, Brian Lester, Mohammed Muqeeth, Anisha Mascarenhas, Monty Evans, Vishal Baskaran, Tenghao Huang, Haokun Liu, and Colin Raffel. 2023. Git-theta: A git extension for collaborative development of machine learning models. 202:15708–15719.

Jared Kaplan, Sam McCandlish, Tom Henighan, Tom B. Brown, Benjamin Chess, Rewon Child, Scott Gray, Alec Radford, Jeffrey Wu, and Dario Amodei. 2020. Scaling laws for neural language models. *CoRR*, abs/2001.08361.

Frank Keller. 2010. Cognitively plausible models of human language processing. In *Proceedings of the ACL 2010 Conference Short Papers*, pages 60–67, Uppsala, Sweden. Association for Computational Linguistics.

Douwe Kiela, Max Bartolo, Yixin Nie, Divyansh Kaushik, Atticus Geiger, Zhengxuan Wu, Bertie Vidgen, Grusha Prasad, Amanpreet Singh, Pratik Ringshia, Zhiyi Ma, Tristan Thrush, Sebastian Riedel, Zeerak Waseem, Pontus Stenetorp, Robin Jia, Mohit Bansal, Christopher Potts, and Adina Williams. 2021. Dynabench: Rethinking benchmarking in NLP. In *Proceedings of the 2021 Conference of the North American Chapter of the Association for Computational Linguistics: Human Language Technologies*, pages 4110–4124, Online. Association for Computational Linguistics.

Hannah Kirk, Bertie Vidgen, Paul Rottger, Tristan Thrush, and Scott Hale. 2022. Hatemoji: A test suite and adversarially-generated dataset for benchmarking and detecting emoji-based hate. In *Proceedings of the 2022 Conference of the North American Chapter of the Association for Computational Linguistics: Human Language Technologies*, pages 1352–1368, Seattle, United States. Association for Computational Linguistics.

Margaret Li, Suchin Gururangan, Tim Dettmers, Mike Lewis, Tim Althoff, Noah A. Smith, and Luke Zettlemoyer. 2022. Branch-train-merge: Embarrassingly parallel training of expert language models. In *First Workshop on Interpolation Regularizers and Beyond at NeurIPS 2022*.

Vladislav Lialin, Namrata Shivagunde, Sherin Muckatira, and Anna Rumshisky. 2023. Stack more layers differently: High-rank training through low-rank updates. *CoRR*, abs/2307.05695.

Tal Linzen. 2019. What can linguistics and deep learning contribute to each other? Response to Pater. *Language*, 95(1):e99–e108.

Tal Linzen. 2020. How can we accelerate progress towards human-like linguistic generalization? In *Proceedings of the 58th Annual Meeting of the Association for Computational Linguistics*, pages 5210–5217, Online. Association for Computational Linguistics.

Pierre Lison and Jörg Tiedemann. 2016. OpenSubtitles2016: Extracting large parallel corpora from movie and TV subtitles. In *Proceedings of the Tenth International Conference on Language Resources and Evaluation*, pages 923–929, Portorož, Slovenia. European Language Resources Association (ELRA).

Yinhan Liu, Myle Ott, Naman Goyal, Jingfei Du, Mandar Joshi, Danqi Chen, Omer Levy, Mike Lewis, Luke Zettlemoyer, and Veselin Stoyanov. 2019. Roberta: A robustly optimized BERT pretraining approach. *CoRR*, abs/1907.11692.

Ilya Loshchilov and Frank Hutter. 2019. Decoupled weight decay regularization. In *International Conference on Learning Representations*.

Brian MacWhinney. 2000. *The CHILDES project: The database*, volume 2. Psychology Press.

Mitchell P. Marcus, Beatrice Santorini, and Mary Ann Marcinkiewicz. 1993. Building a large annotated corpus of English: The Penn Treebank. *Computational Linguistics*, 19(2):313–330.

Richard Diehl Martinez, Hope McGovern, Zebulon Goriely, Christopher Davis, Andrew Caines, Paula Buttery, and Lisa Beinborn. 2023. Climb – curriculum learning for infant-inspired model building. In *Proceedings of the BabyLM Challenge*. Association for Computational Linguistics (ACL).

Rebecca Marvin and Tal Linzen. 2018. Targeted syntactic evaluation of language models. In *Proceedings of the 2018 Conference on Empirical Methods in Natural Language Processing*, pages 1192–1202, Brussels, Belgium. Association for Computational Linguistics.

Mark Mazumder, Colby R. Banbury, Xiaozhe Yao, Bojan Karlas, William Gaviria Rojas, Sudnya Frederick Diamos, Greg Diamos, Lynn He, Douwe Kiela, David Jurado, David Kanter, Rafael Mosquera, Juan Ciro, Lora Aroyo, Bilge Acun, Sabri Eyuboglu, Amirata Ghorbani, Emmett D. Goodman, Tariq Kane, Christine R. Kirkpatrick, Tzu-Sheng Kuo, Jonas Mueller, Tristan Thrush, Joaquin Vanschoren, Margaret Warren, Adina Williams, Serena Yeung, Newsha Ardalani, Praveen K. Paritosh, Ce Zhang, James Zou, Carole-Jean Wu, Cody Coleman, Andrew Y. Ng,

Peter Mattson, and Vijay Janapa Reddi. 2022. Dataperf: Benchmarks for data-centric AI development. *CoRR*, abs/2207.10062.

R. Thomas McCoy, Robert Frank, and Tal Linzen. 2020. Does syntax need to grow on trees? sources of hierarchical inductive bias in sequence-to-sequence networks. *Transactions of the Association for Computational Linguistics*, 8:125–140.

Ian R. McKenzie, Alexander Lyzhov, Michael Martin Pieler, Alicia Parrish, Aaron Mueller, Ameya Prabhu, Euan McLean, Xudong Shen, Joe Cavanagh, Andrew George Gritsevskiy, Derik Kauffman, Aaron T. Kirtland, Zhengping Zhou, Yuhui Zhang, Sicong Huang, Daniel Wurgaft, Max Weiss, Alexis Ross, Gabriel Recchia, Alisa Liu, Jiacheng Liu, Tom Tseng, Tomasz Korbak, Najoung Kim, Samuel R. Bowman, and Ethan Perez. 2023. Inverse scaling: When bigger isn't better. *Transactions on Machine Learning Research*.

Maggie Mi. 2023. Mmi01 at the BabyLM challenge: Linguistically motivated curriculum learning for pretraining in low-resource settings. In *Proceedings of the BabyLM Challenge*. Association for Computational Linguistics (ACL).

Kanishka Misra. 2022. minicons: Enabling flexible behavioral and representational analyses of transformer language models. *CoRR*, abs/2203.13112.

Omar Momen, David Arps, and Laura Kallmeyer. 2023. Increasing the performance of cognitively inspired data-efficient language models via implicit structure building. In *Proceedings of the BabyLM Challenge*. Association for Computational Linguistics (ACL).

Aaron Mueller, Robert Frank, Tal Linzen, Luheng Wang, and Sebastian Schuster. 2022. Coloring the blank slate: Pre-training imparts a hierarchical inductive bias to sequence-to-sequence models. In *Findings of the Association for Computational Linguistics: ACL 2022*, pages 1352–1368, Dublin, Ireland. Association for Computational Linguistics.

Aaron Mueller and Tal Linzen. 2023. How to plant trees in language models: Data and architectural effects on the emergence of syntactic inductive biases. In *Proceedings of the 61st Annual Meeting of the Association for Computational Linguistics (Volume 1: Long Papers)*, pages 11237–11252, Toronto, Canada. Association for Computational Linguistics.

Nikita Nangia and Samuel R. Bowman. 2019. Human vs. muppet: A conservative estimate of human performance on the GLUE benchmark. In *Proceedings of the 57th Annual Meeting of the Association for Computational Linguistics*, pages 4566–4575, Florence, Italy. Association for Computational Linguistics.

Toan Q. Nguyen and Julian Salazar. 2019. Transformers without tears: Improving the normalization of self-attention. In *Proceedings of the 16th International Conference on Spoken Language Translation*, Hong Kong. Association for Computational Linguistics.

Yixin Nie, Adina Williams, Emily Dinan, Mohit Bansal, Jason Weston, and Douwe Kiela. 2020. Adversarial NLI: A new benchmark for natural language understanding. In *Proceedings of the 58th Annual Meeting of the Association for Computational Linguistics*, pages 4885–4901, Online. Association for Computational Linguistics.

Miyu Oba, Akari Haga, Akiyo Fukatsu, and Yohei Oseki. 2023. CoNLL shared task BabyLM challenge: Curriculum learning based on sentence complexity approximating language acquisition. In *Proceedings of the BabyLM Challenge*. Association for Computational Linguistics (ACL).

Mattia Opper, J. Morrison, and N. Siddharth. 2023. On the effect of curriculum learning with developmental data for grammar acquisition. In *Proceedings of the BabyLM Challenge*. Association for Computational Linguistics (ACL).

Ludovica Pannitto and Aurélie Herbelot. 2020. Recurrent babbling: evaluating the acquisition of grammar from limited input data. In *Proceedings of the 24th Conference on Computational Natural Language Learning*, pages 165–176, Online. Association for Computational Linguistics.

Isabel Papadimitriou and Dan Jurafsky. 2020. Learning Music Helps You Read: Using transfer to study linguistic structure in language models. In *Proceedings of the 2020 Conference on Empirical Methods in Natural Language Processing (EMNLP)*, pages 6829–6839, Online. Association for Computational Linguistics.

Andy Perfors, Joshua B. Tenenbaum, and Terry Regier. 2011. The learnability of abstract syntactic principles. *Cognition*, 118(3):306–338.

Jonas Pfeiffer, Sebastian Ruder, Ivan Vulic, and Edoardo Maria Ponti. 2023. Modular deep learning. *CoRR*, abs/2302.11529.

Steven Piantadosi. 2023. Modern language models refute chomsky's approach to language. *Lingbuzz*. Preprint.

Eva Portelance, Yuguang Duan, Michael C. Frank, and Gary Lupyan. 2023. Predicting age of acquisition for children's early vocabulary in five languages using language model surprisal. *Cognitive Science*.

Jacob Portes, Alexander R. Trott, Sam Havens, Daniel King, Abhinav Venigalla, Moin Nadeem, Nikhil Sardana, Daya Khudia, and Jonathan Frankle. 2023. MosaicBERT: How to train BERT with a lunch money budget. In *Workshop on Efficient Systems for Foundation Models at ICML2023*.

Christopher Potts, Zhengxuan Wu, Atticus Geiger, and Douwe Kiela. 2021. DynaSent: A dynamic benchmark for sentiment analysis. In *Proceedings of the 59th Annual Meeting of the Association for Computational Linguistics and the 11th International Joint*

Conference on Natural Language Processing (Volume 1: Long Papers), pages 2388–2404, Online. Association for Computational Linguistics.

Ofir Press, Noah A. Smith, and Mike Lewis. 2021. Shortformer: Better language modeling using shorter inputs. In *Proceedings of the 59th Annual Meeting of the Association for Computational Linguistics and the 11th International Joint Conference on Natural Language Processing (Volume 1: Long Papers)*, pages 5493–5505, Online. Association for Computational Linguistics.

Irina Proskurina, Guillaume Metzler, and Julien Velcin. 2023. Mini minds: Exploring Bebeshka and Zlata baby models. In *Proceedings of the BabyLM Challenge*. Association for Computational Linguistics (ACL).

Colin Raffel. 2023. Building machine learning models like open source software. *Communications of the ACM*, 66(2):38–40.

Colin Raffel, Noam Shazeer, Adam Roberts, Katherine Lee, Sharan Narang, Michael Matena, Yanqi Zhou, Wei Li, and Peter J. Liu. 2020. Exploring the limits of transfer learning with a unified text-to-text transformer. *Journal of Machine Learning Research*, 21(140):1–67.

Florencia Reali and Morten H. Christiansen. 2005. Uncovering the richness of the stimulus: Structure dependence and indirect statistical evidence. *Cognitive Science*, 29(6):1007–1028.

Julian Salazar, Davis Liang, Toan Q. Nguyen, and Katrin Kirchhoff. 2020. Masked language model scoring. In *Proceedings of the 58th Annual Meeting of the Association for Computational Linguistics*, pages 2699–2712, Online. Association for Computational Linguistics.

David Samuel. 2023. Mean BERTs make erratic language teachers: the effectiveness of latent bootstrapping in low-resource settings. In *Proceedings of the BabyLM Challenge*. Association for Computational Linguistics (ACL).

David Samuel, Andrey Kutuzov, Lilja Øvrelid, and Erik Velldal. 2023. Trained on 100 million words and still in shape: BERT meets British National Corpus. In *Findings of the Association for Computational Linguistics: EACL 2023*, pages 1954–1974, Dubrovnik, Croatia. Association for Computational Linguistics.

Teven Le Scao, Angela Fan, Christopher Akiki, Ellie Pavlick, Suzana Ilic, Daniel Hesslow, Roman Castagné, Alexandra Sasha Luccioni, François Yvon, Matthias Gallé, Jonathan Tow, Alexander M. Rush, Stella Biderman, Albert Webson, Pawan Sasanka Ammanamanchi, Thomas Wang, Benoît Sagot, Niklas Muennighoff, Albert Villanova del Moral, Olatunji Ruwase, Rachel Bawden, Stas Bekman, Angelina McMillan-Major, Iz Beltagy, Huu Nguyen, Lucile Saulnier, Samson Tan, Pedro Ortiz Suarez, Victor Sanh, Hugo Laurençon, Yacine Jernite, Julien Launay, Margaret Mitchell, Colin Raffel, and et al. 2022. BLOOM: A 176b-parameter open-access multilingual language model. *CoRR*, abs/2211.05100.

Noam Shazeer. 2020. GLU variants improve transformer. *CoRR*, abs/2002.05202.

Yikang Shen, Yi Tay, Che Zheng, Dara Bahri, Donald Metzler, and Aaron Courville. 2021. StructFormer: Joint unsupervised induction of dependency and constituency structure from masked language modeling. In *Proceedings of the 59th Annual Meeting of the Association for Computational Linguistics and the 11th International Joint Conference on Natural Language Processing (Volume 1: Long Papers)*, pages 7196–7209, Online. Association for Computational Linguistics.

Sasha Sheng, Amanpreet Singh, Vedanuj Goswami, Jose Magana, Tristan Thrush, Wojciech Galuba, Devi Parikh, and Douwe Kiela. 2021. Human-adversarial visual question answering. In *Advances in Neural Information Processing Systems*, volume 34, pages 20346–20359.

Sam Shleifer, Jason Weston, and Myle Ott. 2021. Normformer: Improved transformer pretraining with extra normalization. *CoRR*, abs/2110.09456.

Massimo Stella, Nicole M. Beckage, and Markus Brede. 2017. Multiplex lexical networks reveal patterns in early word acquisition in children. *Scientific Reports*, 7(1):46730.

Julius Steuer, Marius Mosbach, and Dietrich Klakow. 2023. GPT-like models are bad babies: A closer look into the relationship of linguistic competence and psycholinguistic measures. In *Proceedings of the BabyLM Challenge*. Association for Computational Linguistics (ACL).

Andreas Stolcke, Klaus Ries, Noah Coccaro, Elizabeth Shriberg, Rebecca Bates, Daniel Jurafsky, Paul Taylor, Rachel Martin, Carol Van Ess-Dykema, and Marie Meteer. 2000. Dialogue act modeling for automatic tagging and recognition of conversational speech. *Computational Linguistics*, 26(3):339–374.

Antti Tarvainen and Harri Valpola. 2017. Mean teachers are better role models: Weight-averaged consistency targets improve semi-supervised deep learning results. In *Advances in Neural Information Processing Systems*, volume 30.

Lukas Thoma, Ivonne Weyers, Erion Çano, Stefan Schweter, Jutta L. Mueller, and Benjamin Roth. 2023. Cogmemlm: Human-like memory mechanisms improve performance and cognitive plausibility of LLMs. In *Proceedings of the BabyLM Challenge*. Association for Computational Linguistics (ACL).

Inar Timiryasov and Jean-Loup Tastet. 2023. Baby Llama: knowledge distillation from an ensemble of teachers trained on a small dataset with no performance penalty. In *Proceedings of the BabyLM Challenge*. Association for Computational Linguistics (ACL).

Hugo Touvron, Louis Martin, Kevin Stone, Peter Albert, Amjad Almahairi, Yasmine Babaei, Nikolay Bashlykov, Soumya Batra, Prajjwal Bhargava, Shruti Bhosale, Dan Bikel, Lukas Blecher, Cristian Canton-Ferrer, Moya Chen, Guillem Cucurull, David Esiobu, Jude Fernandes, Jeremy Fu, Wenyin Fu, Brian Fuller, Cynthia Gao, Vedanuj Goswami, Naman Goyal, Anthony Hartshorn, Saghar Hosseini, Rui Hou, Hakan Inan, Marcin Kardas, Viktor Kerkez, Madian Khabsa, Isabel Kloumann, Artem Korenev, Punit Singh Koura, Marie-Anne Lachaux, Thibaut Lavril, Jenya Lee, Diana Liskovich, Yinghai Lu, Yuning Mao, Xavier Martinet, Todor Mihaylov, Pushkar Mishra, Igor Molybog, Yixin Nie, Andrew Poulton, Jeremy Reizenstein, Rashi Rungta, Kalyan Saladi, Alan Schelten, Ruan Silva, Eric Michael Smith, Ranjan Subramanian, Xiaoqing Ellen Tan, Binh Tang, Ross Taylor, Adina Williams, Jian Xiang Kuan, Puxin Xu, Zheng Yan, Iliyan Zarov, Yuchen Zhang, Angela Fan, Melanie Kambadur, Sharan Narang, Aurélien Rodriguez, Robert Stojnic, Sergey Edunov, and Thomas Scialom. 2023. Llama 2: Open foundation and fine-tuned chat models. *CoRR*, abs/2307.09288.

Marten van Schijndel, Aaron Mueller, and Tal Linzen. 2019. Quantity doesn't buy quality syntax with neural language models. In *Proceedings of the 2019 Conference on Empirical Methods in Natural Language Processing and the 9th International Joint Conference on Natural Language Processing (EMNLP-IJCNLP)*, pages 5831–5837, Hong Kong, China. Association for Computational Linguistics.

Bertie Vidgen, Tristan Thrush, Zeerak Waseem, and Douwe Kiela. 2021. Learning from the worst: Dynamically generated datasets to improve online hate detection. In *Proceedings of the 59th Annual Meeting of the Association for Computational Linguistics and the 11th International Joint Conference on Natural Language Processing (Volume 1: Long Papers)*, pages 1667–1682, Online. Association for Computational Linguistics.

Alex Wang, Yada Pruksachatkun, Nikita Nangia, Amanpreet Singh, Julian Michael, Felix Hill, Omer Levy, and Samuel Bowman. 2019. SuperGLUE: A stickier benchmark for general-purpose language understanding systems. In *Advances in Neural Information Processing Systems*, volume 32.

Alex Wang, Amanpreet Singh, Julian Michael, Felix Hill, Omer Levy, and Samuel Bowman. 2018. GLUE: A multi-task benchmark and analysis platform for natural language understanding. In *Proceedings of the 2018 EMNLP Workshop BlackboxNLP: Analyzing and Interpreting Neural Networks for NLP*, pages 353–355, Brussels, Belgium. Association for Computational Linguistics.

Alex Warstadt. 2022. *Artificial Neural Networks as Models of Human Language Acquisition*. PhD Thesis, New York University.

Alex Warstadt and Samuel R. Bowman. 2022. What artificial neural networks can tell us about human language acquisition. In *Algebraic Structures in Natural Language*, pages 17–60. CRC Press.

Alex Warstadt, Leshem Choshen, Aaron Mueller, Adina Williams, Ethan Wilcox, and Chengxu Zhuang. 2023. Call for papers - the babylm challenge: Sample-efficient pretraining on a developmentally plausible corpus. *CoRR*, abs/2301.11796.

Alex Warstadt, Alicia Parrish, Haokun Liu, Anhad Mohananey, Wei Peng, Sheng-Fu Wang, and Samuel R. Bowman. 2020a. BLiMP: The benchmark of linguistic minimal pairs for English. *Transactions of the Association for Computational Linguistics*, 8:377–392.

Alex Warstadt, Yian Zhang, Xiaocheng Li, Haokun Liu, and Samuel R. Bowman. 2020b. Learning which features matter: RoBERTa acquires a preference for linguistic generalizations (eventually). In *Proceedings of the 2020 Conference on Empirical Methods in Natural Language Processing (EMNLP)*, pages 217–235, Online. Association for Computational Linguistics.

Alex Warstadt, Yian Zhang, Xiaocheng Li, Haokun Liu, and Samuel R. Bowman. 2020c. Learning which features matter: RoBERTa acquires a preference for linguistic generalizations (eventually). In *Proceedings of the 2020 Conference on Empirical Methods in Natural Language Processing (EMNLP)*, pages 217–235, Online. Association for Computational Linguistics.

Jason Wei, Yi Tay, Rishi Bommasani, Colin Raffel, Barret Zoph, Sebastian Borgeaud, Dani Yogatama, Maarten Bosma, Denny Zhou, Donald Metzler, Ed H. Chi, Tatsunori Hashimoto, Oriol Vinyals, Percy Liang, Jeff Dean, and William Fedus. 2022. Emergent abilities of large language models. *Transactions on Machine Learning Research*.

Guillaume Wenzek, Vishrav Chaudhary, Angela Fan, Sahir Gomez, Naman Goyal, Somya Jain, Douwe Kiela, Tristan Thrush, and Francisco Guzmán. 2021. Findings of the WMT 2021 shared task on large-scale multilingual machine translation. In *Proceedings of the Sixth Conference on Machine Translation*, pages 89–99, Online. Association for Computational Linguistics.

Alexander Wettig, Tianyu Gao, Zexuan Zhong, and Danqi Chen. 2023. Should you mask 15% in masked language modeling? In *Proceedings of the 17th Conference of the European Chapter of the Association for Computational Linguistics*, pages 2985–3000, Dubrovnik, Croatia. Association for Computational Linguistics.

Ethan Gotlieb Wilcox, Richard Futrell, and Roger Levy. 2023. Using computational models to test syntactic learnability. *Linguistic Inquiry*, pages 1–44.

Adina Williams, Nikita Nangia, and Samuel Bowman. 2018. A broad-coverage challenge corpus for sentence understanding through inference. In *Proceedings of the 2018 Conference of the North American Chapter of the Association for Computational Linguistics: Human Language Technologies, Volume 1 (Long Papers)*, pages 1112–1122, New Orleans, Louisiana. Association for Computational Linguistics.

Lukas Wolf, Eghbal A. Hosseini, Greta Tuckute, Klemen Kotar, Alex Warstadt, Ethan Wilcox, and Tamar I Regev. 2023. WhisBERT: Multimodal text-audio language modeling on 100m words. In *Proceedings of the BabyLM Challenge*. Association for Computational Linguistics (ACL).

Chenghao Xiao, G. Thomas Hudson, and Noura Al Moubayed. 2023. Towards more human-like language models based on contextualizer pretraining strategy. In *Proceedings of the BabyLM Challenge*. Association for Computational Linguistics (ACL).

Prateek Yadav, Derek Tam, Leshem Choshen, Colin Raffel, and Mohit Bansal. 2023. Resolving interference when merging models. *CoRR*, abs/2306.01708.

Yahan Yang, Elior Sulem, Insup Lee, and Dan Roth. 2023. Penn & BGU BabyBERTa+ for strict-small BabyLM challenge. In *Proceedings of the BabyLM Challenge*. Association for Computational Linguistics (ACL).

Aditya Yedetore, Tal Linzen, Robert Frank, and R. Thomas McCoy. 2023. How poor is the stimulus? evaluating hierarchical generalization in neural networks trained on child-directed speech. In *Proceedings of the 61st Annual Meeting of the Association for Computational Linguistics (Volume 1: Long Papers)*, pages 9370–9393, Toronto, Canada. Association for Computational Linguistics.

Susan Zhang, Stephen Roller, Naman Goyal, Mikel Artetxe, Moya Chen, Shuohui Chen, Christopher Dewan, Mona T. Diab, Xian Li, Xi Victoria Lin, Todor Mihaylov, Myle Ott, Sam Shleifer, Kurt Shuster, Daniel Simig, Punit Singh Koura, Anjali Sridhar, Tianlu Wang, and Luke Zettlemoyer. 2022. OPT: Open pre-trained transformer language models. *CoRR*, abs/2205.01068.

Yian Zhang, Alex Warstadt, Xiaocheng Li, and Samuel R. Bowman. 2021. When do you need billions of words of pretraining data? In *Proceedings of the 59th Annual Meeting of the Association for Computational Linguistics and the 11th International Joint Conference on Natural Language Processing (Volume 1: Long Papers)*, pages 1112–1125, Online. Association for Computational Linguistics.

Zheyu Zhang, Han Yang, Bolei Ma, David Rügamer, and Ercong Nie. 2023. Baby's CoThought: Leveraging large language models for enhanced reasoning in compact models. In *Proceedings of the BabyLM Challenge*. Association for Computational Linguistics (ACL).

Xingmeng Zhao, Tongnian Wang, Sheri Osborn, and Anthony Rios. 2023. BabyStories: Can reinforcement learning teach baby language models to write better stories? In *Proceedings of the BabyLM Challenge*. Association for Computational Linguistics (ACL).

Ömer Veysel Çağatan. 2023. ToddlerBERTa: Exploiting BabyBERTa for grammar learning and language understanding. In *Proceedings of the BabyLM Challenge*. Association for Computational Linguistics (ACL).

A Data Source Descriptions

CHILDES. The Child Language Data Exchange System (CHILDES; MacWhinney, 2000) is a multilingual database compiling transcriptions from numerous researchers of adult–child interactions in a range of environments, from structured laboratory activities to the home. Huebner and Willits (2021) further process CHILDES, selecting only interactions with American English-speaking children ages 0–6, removing all child utterances, and tokenizing the data. The resulting dataset[18] contains about 5M words.

British National Corpus. The BNC (Consortium, 2007) is a 100M word multi-domain corpus of British English from the second half of the 20th century. We select only the dialogue portion of the corpus, totaling about 10M words.

Children's Book Test. CBT is a compilation of over a hundred children's books from Project Gutenberg by Hill et al. (2016). The dataset was originally released with a set of questions for testing named entity prediction, which we do not include in the pretraining data.

Children's Stories Text Corpus. This dataset consists of manually selected children's stories from Project Gutenberg. It was compiled by Bensaid et al. (2021) for the development of a story generation system.

Project Gutenberg. The Standardized Project Gutenberg Corpus (Gerlach and Font-Clos, 2020) is a curated and preprocessed selection of over 50k literary books in the public domain from Project Gutenberg totaling over 3B tokens.[19] This distribution comes with extensive metadata that allows us to filter texts by language and date.

OpenSubtitles. This dataset (Lison and Tiedemann, 2016) is a compilation of publicly available subtitles from TV and movies on a third-party website.[20] We use only the English portion.

QED. The QCRI Educational Domain Corpus (formerly QCRI AMARA Corpus; Abdelali et al., 2014) consists of volunteer-written subtitles for educational videos. We use only the English portion.

Wikipedia. Wikipedia is a volunteer-authored encyclopedia hosted by the Wikimedia Foundation. We use only the English portion.

Simple English Wikipedia. Simple English is classified as a separate language in Wikipedia, thus the texts here are disjoint from those in English Wikipedia. The texts use shorter sentences and high-frequency vocabulary and avoid idioms.

Switchboard Corpus. The Switchboard Corpus (Godfrey et al., 1992) is a collection of transcribed telephone conversations between pairs of strangers. We accessed the text through the Switchboard Dialog Act Corpus (Stolcke et al., 2000).

[18] `https://github.com/phueb/BabyBERTa/blob/master/data/corpora/aochildes.txt`
[19] `https://gutenberg.org/`
[20] `http://opensubtitles.org/`

B Evaluation Data Details

As described in Section 5.2, we filter out evaluation examples that do not have lexical overlap with the *Strict-Small* pretraining corpus. Here, we present the number of training and test examples for each evaluation task after filtering. This allows us to partially control for the confound of the language style of most NLP tasks not aligning well with the pretraining corpus that we constructed. However, we only control for lexical content: other factors, such as sentence length, syntactic complexity, and overall linguistic style, remain distinct between our corpus and these tasks. In the future, it would be helpful for researchers to focus on designing tasks on which both children *and* language models can be reasonably evaluated.

Note, too, that our filtering procedure means that we cannot directly compare results obtained from the BabyLM Challenge to prior evaluations using the full datasets. We use a subset of the training and evaluation examples, and therefore can only compare between models evaluated on our version of these tasks.

	Task	**|Train|**	**|Test|**
BLiMP	Anaphor Agreement	–	1956
	Argument Structure	–	8248
	Binding	–	6738
	Control Raising	–	4526
	Determiner-Noun Agreement	–	7542
	Ellipsis	–	1732
	Filler-Gap	–	6426
	Irregular Forms	–	1965
	Island Effects	–	2676
	NPI Licensing	–	6586
	Quantifiers	–	3882
	Subject-Verb Agreement	–	5535
BLiMP Supplement	Hypernym	–	860
	Question-Answer Congruence (easy)	–	64
	Question-Answer Congruence (tricky)	–	165
	Subject-Auxiliary Inversion	–	4099
	Turn-taking	–	280
(Super)GLUE	CoLA	8164	1019
	SST-2	50528	508
	MRPC	1579	177
	QQP	243498	26889
	MNLI	259780	6562
	MNLI-mismatched	259780	6284
	QNLI	43917	2286
	RTE	858	99
	BoolQ	2072	723
	MultiRC	4637	913
	WSC	487	83
MSGS	Control Raising (Control)	6570	6731
	Lexical Content (Control)	9086	9100
	Main Verb (Control)	8166	8249
	Relative Position (Control)	9068	9046
	Syntactic Category (Control)	8930	8824
	Control Raising–Lexical Content	6816	6910
	Control Raising–Relative Token Position	8166	8167
	Main Verb–Lexical Content	7306	7378
	Main Verb–Relative Token Position	8177	8059
	Syntactic Category–Lexical Content	8181	7597
	Syntactic Category–Relative Position	9159	8298

Table 4: Number of training and test examples for each BabyLM evaluation task. We show the number of examples *after* filtering based on the pre-training corpus vocabulary (Section 5.2).

C Examples from the BLiMP Supplement

Contrast name	Acceptable sentence	Unacceptable sentence
BASE_AND_HYPONYM/ HYPERNYM	If he is growing herbs, then he is growing plants.	If he is growing herbs, then he is growing basil.
BASE_NEG_AND_HYPERNYM_NEG/ CONVERSE	If he isn't growing herbs, that means he isn't growing basil.	If he isn't growing basil, that means he isn't growing herbs.
BASE_NEG_AND_HYPERNYM_NEG/ HYPONYM_NEG	If he isn't growing herbs, that means he isn't growing basil.	If he isn't growing herbs, that means he isn't growing plants.
HYPERNYM_AND_BASE/ CONVERSE	If he is growing basil, that means he is growing herbs.	If he is growing herbs, that means he is growing basil.
HYPERNYM_AND_BASE/ OTHER	If he is growing basil, then he is growing herbs	If he is growing basil, then he is growing flowers.
HYPERNYM_AND_OTHER_NEG/ BASE_NEG	He is growing basil, therefore he isn't growing flowers.	He is growing basil, therefore he isn't growing herbs.

Table 5: Representative examples from the HYPERNYMS test suite of the BLiMP supplement.

Type	Length	Acceptable dialogue	Unacceptable dialogue
single	short	David: Should you quit?\n Sarah: No, I shouldn't.	David: Should she quit?\n Sarah: No, I shouldn't.
single	long	Did they try to finish it on time or not?\n No, they didn't.	Did we try to finish it on time or not?\n No, they didn't.
double	short	A: Did we say that you finished?\n B: Yes, you did.	A: Did you say that you finished?\n B: Yes, you did.
double	long	"Did you say that you will go somewhere after the movie is over?" he asked.\n "No, I didn't," she said.	"Did you say that you will go somewhere after the movie is over?" he asked.\n "No, you didn't," she said.

Table 6: Representative examples from the TURN-TAKING test suite of the BLiMP supplement.

Contrast name	Dif.	Acceptable dialogue	Unacceptable dialogue
ANIMATE VS. INANIMATE	easy	A: What did you purchase?\n B: Bread.	A: What did you purchase?\n B: David.
INANIMATE VS. ANIMATE	easy	"Who played the piano?" he asked. "A teacher played the piano," she said.	"Who played the piano?" he asked. "A car played the piano," she said.
LOC VS. NP	easy	David: Where did you put it?\n Sarah: Behind the sofa.	David: Where did you put it?\n Sarah: Eggs.
ANIMATE VS. INANIMATE	tricky	David: Who mopped?\n Sarah: A doctor.	David: Who mopped?\n Sarah: The tiles.
LOC VS. NP	tricky	A: Where were you reading?\n B: By the lake.	A: Where were you reading?\n B: An essay.
TEMP VS. NP	tricky	When did you eat?\n Several minutes ago.	When did you eat?\n Dinner.
EXPL VS. NP	tricky	"Why were you reading?" he asked. "For fun," she said.	"Why were you reading?" he asked. "A book," she said.
NUM VS. NP	tricky	A: How many do you teach?\n B: A few.	A: How many do you teach?\n B: History.
MANNER VS. NP	tricky	David: How did you vacuum?\n Sarah: I vacuumed quickly.	David: How did you vacuum?\n Sarah: I vacuumed the patio.

Table 7: Representative examples from the QUESTION-ANSWER CONGRUENCE test suite of the BLiMP supplement.

D Subtask Results

Here, we present a more detailed breakdown of results by subtask. Each task has a subsection containing a table where results are described, as well as a textual description containing and overview of the main takeaways for each task.

D.1 MSGS

Matthews correlation coefficients on MSGS (Table 8) were largely negative, indicating that language models trained at this scale tend to prefer surface features over linguistic features in ambiguous contexts. However, certain models demonstrated a much stronger preference for linguistic features in specific contexts: ELC-BERT showed high positive scores on average (sometimes significantly higher than Llama 2), as did Contextualizer. This shows us that architectural modifications can significantly improve scores, as can princpled approaches to curriculum learning.

In general, comparable models trained on the *Strict* corpus have higher MCCs than those trained on the *Strict-Small* corpus, but not always. This suggests that, while more pretraining data generally lead to stronger syntactic inductive biases, these preferences may depend on the features being compared, and that this will not always be the case depending on the architecture used.

	Model	**Macro average**	**Ctl–Raising / Lexical content**	**Ctl–Raising / Relative position**	**Main verb / Lexical content**	**Main verb / Relative position**	**Syntactic cat. / Lexical content**	**Syntactic cat. / Relative position**
	Llama 2 (Touvron et al., 2023)	-0.24	**0.93**	0.23	-0.77	-0.96	-0.19	-0.74
	RoBERTa-base (Liu et al., 2019)	-0.37	0.46	-0.58	-0.95	-0.94	0.36	-0.57
Strict	ELC-BERT (Charpentier and Samuel, 2023)	0.10	-0.51	-0.46	0.71	**0.97**	**0.46**	-0.53
Strict	Boot-BERT (Samuel, 2023)	-0.22	0.37	-0.77	-0.99	0.96	-0.34	-0.58
Strict	McGill (Cheng et al., 2023)	-0.35	0.65	-0.70	-0.99	-0.73	0.17	-0.49
Strict	*Best Baseline (OPT-125M)*	-0.39	0.35	-0.70	-0.76	-0.99	0.34	-0.60
Strict-small	ELC-BERT (Charpentier and Samuel, 2023)	-0.01	0.02	-0.71	**0.95**	0.50	-0.26	-0.59
Strict-small	MLSM (Thoma et al., 2023)	-0.37	0.31	-0.56	-0.99	-0.49	-0.03	-0.44
Strict-small	McGill (Cheng et al., 2023)	-0.60	-0.68	-0.37	-1.00	-0.79	-0.35	-0.42
Strict-small	*Best Baseline (OPT-125M)*	-0.45	0.00	-0.70	-0.72	-0.77	0.13	-0.68
Loose	Contextualizer (Xiao et al., 2023)	**0.24**	**0.88**	**0.71**	-0.32	0.30	0.21	**-0.35**
Loose	McGill (Cheng et al., 2023)	-0.75	-0.56	-0.97	-0.99	-0.86	-0.66	-0.46
Loose	BabyStories (Zhao et al., 2023)	-0.71	-0.24	-0.99	-0.99	-0.99	-0.23	-0.78

Table 8: MSGS results for each ambiguous subtask for the top performing models (by overall score) from each track, as well as baselines and skylines. MCC (i.e., linguistic bias score) results presented, truncated to two decimal places.

D.2 BLiMP

Accuracies on BLiMP (Table **??**) show that bigger models do not, as a rule, perform better on targeted grammatical evaluation. RoBERTa is the best-performing skyline model, despite that Llama 2 has orders-of-magnitude more parameters and was trained on significantly more data. Among the BabyLM submissions, Boot-BERT generally performs best, with ELC-BERT and McGill's submission also performing well in general on the *Strict* and *Strict-Small* tracks. ELC-BERT and Boot-BERT are both based on LTG-BERT (Samuel et al., 2023), suggesting that this architecture is a good starting point for pretraining on developmentally plausible amounts of linguistic input.

Analyzing specific test suites, we see that unsurprisingly that models in all tracks typically perform best on agreement phenomena, though we find surprisingly high variability on ANAPHOR AGREEMENT. **?**

reported that ISLAND EFFECTS and QUANTIFIERS were the two most difficult test cases. We find that the best BabyLM submissions actually outperform Llama by a wide margin on ISLAND EFFECTS. However, QUANTIFIERS, on which most models achieve very consistent and mediocre results, is the one test suite on which the Llama 2 skyline is stronger.

D.3 BLiMP Supplement

Accuracies on the BLiMP supplement tasks (Table 9) demonstrate similar trends as those in the BLiMP tasks. As these individual test suites are new to this task, these fine-grained results are of particular interest. We find that the HYPERNYM test suite is clearly beyond the ability of language models. All models including the skylines perform very close to chance, suggesting either that their preferences are virtually random guessing, or they show systematic biases that essentially cancel out due to counterbalancing in the test data. However, we hesitate to conclude that these models have no knowledge of lexical entailment relations for two reasons: First, these test sentences are somewhat unnatural logical statements which are out-of-domain for the models, and second, there is less reason *a priori* to think that logically invalid statements have lower probability than valid statements.

Among the QUESTION–ANSWER CONGRUENCE test suites, we do indeed find that the "tricky" examples are far more difficult than the "easy" ones. The "tricky" set is highly discriminative, due probably to its adversarial nature, telling us that most models are easily fooled by locally coherent distractor answers and pay too little attention to cross-sentential long-distance dependency between a *wh*-word and a congruent answer. Only the top-performing models in the *Strict* track score better than chance, and the RoBERTa skyline outperforms all models by a wide margin.

The tests for SUBJECT–AUXILIARY INVERSION are relatively easy, with the best models reaching near-perfect accuracy. TURN TAKING is highly discriminative, with some models performing at or near chance, while the best model achieves accuracy over 90%. Again, ELC-BERT outperforms the skylines. This may be due in part to the fact that transcribed dialogue is a relatively large proportion of the BabyLM training data, compared to the training data for typical pretrained language models.

	Model	Macro average	Hypernym	Q–A congruence (easy)	Q–A congruence (tricky)	Subject–aux inversion	Turn taking
	Llama 2	0.74	**0.50**	0.85	0.63	0.91	0.83
	RoBERTa	0.75	0.48	**0.87**	**0.72**	**0.98**	0.73
Strict	ELC-BERT	**0.76**	0.47	**0.85**	**0.63**	0.94	**0.92**
Strict	Boot-BERT	0.72	0.45	0.75	0.58	**0.96**	0.86
Strict	McGill	0.71	0.46	0.84	0.58	0.82	0.83
Strict	OPT	0.67	0.46	0.76	0.47	0.85	0.82
Strict-small	ELC-BERT	0.67	0.48	0.68	0.44	0.88	0.83
Strict-small	MLSM	0.57	0.47	0.70	0.33	0.82	0.52
Strict-small	McGill	0.58	0.49	0.73	0.35	0.77	0.57
Strict-small	OPT	0.52	**0.50**	0.54	0.31	0.70	0.57
Loose	Contextualizer	0.63	0.47	0.73	0.42	0.91	0.62
Loose	McGill	0.56	0.49	0.64	0.29	0.80	0.61
Loose	BabyStories	0.64	0.49	0.71	0.50	0.79	0.73

Table 9: BLiMP Supplement accuracies for each subtask for the top performing systems (by overall score), best baseline, and skylines. For each subtask, we mark the best performing system for each track, and the **best** non-skyline and **best** performing system overall.

D.4 GLUE/SuperGLUE

Scores on (Super)GLUE tasks (Table 10) show that ELC-BERT is generally the best-performing system in both the *Strict* and *Strict-Small* tracks, and that Boot-BERT is also highly effective in the *Strict* track. Contextualizer also performs well. This largely confirms findings from the BLiMP and BLiMP Supplement tasks: LTG-BERT is an effective architecture for pretraining on smaller corpora, and curriculum learning can improve performance over a naïve corpus ordering.

	Model	Macro average	CoLA	SST-2	MRPC	QQP	MNLI	MNLI-mm	QNLI	RTE	BoolQ	MultiRC	WSC
	Llama 2	**0.83**	**0.63**	**0.95**	0.87	0.81	0.85	**0.87**	0.89	**0.81**	**0.85**	**0.86**	**0.75**
	RoBERTa	0.78	0.62	0.93	0.88	0.87	**0.86**	0.85	**0.92**	0.61	0.76	0.68	0.61
Strict	ELC-BERT	**0.78**	**0.59**	**0.92**	**0.90**	**0.88**	0.84	0.83	0.89	0.64	**0.73**	0.72	**0.62**
Strict	Boot-BERT	**0.78**	0.57	**0.92**	0.89	**0.88**	**0.85**	**0.84**	**0.91**	**0.65**	0.72	**0.73**	0.61
Strict	McGill	0.72	0.49	0.89	0.83	0.86	0.79	0.79	0.84	0.53	0.66	0.65	0.61
Strict	OPT	0.70	0.36	0.88	0.82	0.83	0.76	0.77	0.83	0.63	0.66	0.60	0.54
Strict-small	ELC-BERT	0.73	0.47	0.86	0.87	0.86	0.78	0.79	0.84	0.60	0.69	0.68	**0.62**
Strict-small	MLSM	0.70	0.41	0.90	0.78	0.85	0.75	0.76	0.82	0.59	0.66	0.58	0.61
Strict-small	McGill	0.69	0.41	0.87	0.79	0.81	0.73	0.74	0.79	0.54	0.66	0.62	0.61
Strict-small	OPT	0.62	0.15	0.84	0.74	0.78	0.67	0.69	0.65	0.55	0.65	0.51	0.59
Loose	Contextualizer	0.72	0.56	0.90	0.83	0.85	0.77	0.78	0.83	0.53	0.68	0.64	0.59
Loose	McGill	0.68	0.37	0.88	0.77	0.83	0.73	0.75	0.78	0.49	0.67	0.60	0.61
Loose	BabyStories	0.60	0.00	0.84	0.82	0.66	0.59	0.64	0.79	0.53	0.67	0.46	0.61

Table 10: (Super)GLUE results for each subtask for the top performing systems (by overall score), best baseline, and skylines. For each subtask, we mark the best performing system for each track, and the **best** non-skyline and **best** performing system overall.

E Age of Acquisition Prediction Results

Here, we present scores, separated by track, for each model that evaluated on the age of acquisition (AoA) prediction task (Table 11). We also compare to the best-performing baseline within each track, as in Table 2.

Almost all submissions which evaluated on the AoA prediction task were in the *Strict-Small* track. Here, no model achieved closer predictions than the OPT-125M baseline, though many got very close. In the *Strict* track, BabyStories achieved very close scores to the OPT-125M baseline.

	Model	Mean average deviation ↓ Overall	Nouns	Predicates	Function Words
Strict	BabyStories (GPT2-Large-PPO) (Zhao et al., 2023)	2.05	1.98	**1.82**	2.63
Strict	*Best Baseline (OPT-125M)*	**2.04**	**1.97**	1.83	**2.61**
Strict-Small	GPT-Wee (16k (cu.)) (Bunzeck and Zarrieß, 2023)	2.06	2.00	1.83	2.58
Strict-Small	Bebeshka (Proskurina et al., 2023)	2.06	1.98	1.84	2.66
Strict-Small	Zlata (Proskurina et al., 2023)	2.07	1.99	1.83	2.67
Strict-Small	Too Much Information (Edman and Bylinina, 2023)	2.05	1.99	1.85	2.58
Strict-Small	Mmi01 (RARITY) (Mi, 2023)	2.05	1.97	1.85	2.64
Strict-Small	Baby Llama (Timiryasov and Tastet, 2023)	2.06	1.99	1.84	2.63
Strict-Small	Lil-Bevo-X (Govindarajan et al., 2023)	2.05	1.99	1.85	2.59
Strict-Small	*Best Baseline (OPT-125M)*	**2.03**	1.98	**1.81**	**2.57**

Table 11: Mean average deviation (MAD) in months across cross-validation folds when predicting the age of acquisition of words. Lower MAD scores are better. We present all systems that evaluated on AoA prediction, as well as the baseline model with the best scores per track. We **bold** the highest-scoring system for each task within each track.

F Summary of Each Submission

GPT-wee (Bunzeck and Zarrieß, 2023). This paper tests various approaches to reordering the examples based on word and sentence statistics. The motivation comes from usage-based linguistics and the idea that frequent lexical items, such as phrases or common groups of words, are learned early (rather than words, for instance). They also find that training more—up to 10 epochs—helps, and that a medium-sized model might be as good as larger models.

Tiny Language Models with Multiplex Networks (Fields et al., 2023). This approach leverages multimodal data (including text/visual data and sensorimotor data) as part of the embeddings to an ELECTRA language model. The proposed models are very small (as few as 7M parameters) and perform well on BLiMP. For reference, the baseline models contain 125M to 220M parameters.

Mini Minds (Proskurina et al., 2023). This submission explores how scaling down models (in terms of number of parameters) can help in low-data settings. The authors conduct a parameter search for scaled-down versions of GPT-2 and RoBERTa, and find that optimal models have around a 2-to-1 ratio of attention heads to layers. They train two models and find that they perform about as well as larger parameter count models on GLUE. Furthermore, the authors test their models on an ethical reasoning benchmark and find that the small models perform about as well as models which have about ten times the parameters.

Grammar induction pretraining (Chen and Portelance, 2023). This submission introduces syntactic bias into the static token embeddings of an LM. An unsupervised grammar induction system is trained on a 1-million word subset of the *Strict-Small* corpus, and the resulting static token embeddings are used to initialize the LM token embeddings. Although the results improve over the BabyLM *Strict-Small* baseline, similar improvements are observed with a custom baseline model using randomly initialized token embeddings. Thus, there is no evidence that the grammar induction step had a positive impact on LM results.

ChapGTP (Jumelet et al., 2023). This work explores how targeted data augmentation can improve the performance of masked language models in the *Strict-Small* track. The authors used regex patterns to extract common phrases from the GLUE tasks and then used these patterns to generate follow-up questions that served as additional training data. They also found that increasing the training epochs up to 200 epochs continues to help performance.

BabyBerta+ (Yang et al., 2023). The submission replicates the BabyBERTa training setup (Huebner et al., 2021) and tests its ability after pretraining on the *Strict-Small* corpus. They find that a small model trained on many epochs keeps improving and becomes better than baseline models in grammatical aspects, but not downstream tasks.

Keeping Training Simple for BabyLMs (Edman and Bylinina, 2023). This paper proposes a variety of complexity metrics for reordering the BabyLM *Strict-Small* data from simple to complex. Compared to no curricula and reversed curricula, the proposed curricula do not result in consistent performance improvements on the BabyLM evaluation tasks. However, reducing the context length to 32 (from the baselines' 128) results in significant and consistent performance improvements.

Can Training Neural Language Models on a Curriculum with Developmentally Plausible Data Improve Alignment with Human Reading Behavior? (Chobey et al., 2023). This paper explores surprisal-based curricula for pretraining on the *Strict-Small* dataset of the BabyLM challenge. The authors use an ensemble of LSTM "teacher" models to rank sentences by average surprisal, on which a final OPT model is trained. Results are mixed. The authors find that their model does not outperform a random baseline. However, when this model is further trained on the randomly-ordered training dataset after training on the curriculum-ordered data, it does beat the baseline. As an additional analysis, the authors investigate the ability of their model to predict human reading times for syntactically complex sentences, finding that the model is not particularly good at the task, but that it is about equivalent to baselines which are trained on much larger datasets.

CLIMB (Martinez et al., 2023). This submission presents a thorough comparison of different approaches to curriculum learning in the *Strict-Small* setting. They consider three main criteria for curriculum design: the size of the input vocabulary, the difficulty of the training sample, and the size of the output space for MLM prediction. They conduct experiments exploring eight different curricula sorted into these three main approaches. While there are many small differences in performance among these settings, curricula provide no consistent improvements over more naive training algorithms.

Acquiring Linguistic Knowledge from Multimodal Input (Amariucai and Warstadt, 2023). The authors explored whether vision-language co-training helps the learning of linguistic knowledge. They trained models on Wiki texts with images using the state-of-the-art multi-modality model (FLAVA). After varying the amount of training data and how many images are used, the authors found that visual input only provides a slight improvement on grammar benchmarks for 10M-word training, but not for 100M-word training.

GPT-like Models are Bad Babies (Steuer et al., 2023). This paper trains a decoder-only model, trying different hyperparameters, including reordering the training data by different orders (based on cues which did not improve over regular shuffling), different sizes, layer widths, among other features. The main focus of the paper is to test if models that perform better on BabyLM evaluation tasks are also better at modeling reading difficulty in humans. Surprisingly, models performing better on BabyLM tasks performed *less* well in modeling reading difficulty.

Baby's CoThought (Zhang et al., 2023). This system leverages a large language model, GPT-3.5-Turbo, to reformat semantically unrelated sentences into cohesive paragraphs. In low-data settings, this approach can form better training examples for language models; the proposed approach results in improvements across BLiMP tasks, though performance is not significantly different on (Super)GLUE or MSGS. Note that the LLM is trained on far more than 100M words, so this submission technically does not qualify under any track. However, this method does improve the sample efficiency of the student model, and it aids our understanding of what types of data are best for supervising smaller language models.

ToddlerBERTa (Çağatan, 2023). This paper conducts a thorough hyperparameter investigation of the BabyBERTa model, exploring different options for model sizes and training algorithms. The author finds that larger models tend to perform better.

CogMemLM (Thoma et al., 2023). This work explores an approach to word segmentation and tokenization that is intended to model vocabulary growth during learning. A vocabulary is cumulatively built using a cognitively-inspired model of word segmentation, in which strings are split into chunks based on an activation weight which changes throughout training depending on how often the chunk is observed together. While the approach achieves consistent improvements over the BabyLM *Strict* baseline results, it is not clear whether these improvements are due to the segmentation scheme or other hyperparameter modifications.

BabyStories (Zhao et al., 2023). This paper investigates how reinforcement learning from human feedback (RLHF) improves the performance of causal language models pretrained on small scales of datasets. The authors report that models finetuned by RLHF on short stories yield better performance on language understanding benchmarks, though this improvement is only observed on larger models. Their findings suggest that benefiting from RLHF requires a large number of trainable parameters.

Byte-ranked Curriculum Learning (DeBenedetto, 2023). This paper proposes a curriculum learning approach for reordering data based on non-linguistic metrics. Specifically, they choose the order in which datasets are shown to the model starting from the minimal amount of bytes per sentence and going up. This happens to also start from spoken data and follow with text data later. The paper also shows that a larger model as well as more epochs improves the results.

McGill BabyLM Submission (Cheng et al., 2023). This paper finds that changes to the data format have large positive impacts. Specifically, not using sequence packing, using sentences and not documents as examples, not truncating, and reducing maximum sequence length are each highly effective. By contrast, adding supervision from POS tags and using unsupervised syntactic induction have negligible impact.

Mean BERTS make erratic language teachers (Samuel, 2023). This submission presents Boot-BERT, a latent bootstrapping approach to language modeling in low resource settings. In the latent bootstrapping set-up, a student model is trained to produce predictions over words as well as to match contextualized embeddings from a teacher model. In turn, the teacher's embeddings are obtained via a moving average of the student's. The authors use LTG-BERT (Samuel et al., 2023) as an encoder backbone, as well as for a baseline.[21] They find that their Boot-BERT outperforms LTG-BERT for some of the BabyLM tasks, including GLUE for both the *Strict* and *Strict-Small* tracks.

Every Layer Counts BERT (ELC-BERT) (Charpentier and Samuel, 2023). This submission takes as its starting point the very effective LTG-BERT architecture from Samuel et al. (2023) and modifies it such that the input to each layer is a weighted sum of the outputs of all previous layers, where the weights can be learned but also biased by initialization. Several variations are explored, including equal initial weights, and initial weights biased towards the previous layer. Results on BabyLM evaluations do not strongly suggest that any one variant is clearly better than the LTG-BERT baseline, though all models perform significantly better than the BabyLM RoBERTa baseline. Additionally, inspection of the learned weights for combining previous layer outputs suggests that the most important outputs are from the previous few layers and the static embedding layer.

WhisBERT (Wolf et al., 2023). In this submission, the authors explore whether text-and-audio co-training helps model performance on BLiMP tasks. After pretraining a multi-modal model (FLAVA) on 100M words with or without their corresponding word-aligned speech, they find that the speech-augmented model outperforms the text-only model on 11 out of 17 grammatical tasks.

Surprisal-based active curriculum learning (Hong et al., 2023). This submission combines curriculum and active learning to schedule training order for models. The authors use n-gram surprisals to determine the sentences with the highest surprisal and then train their models on structurally similar examples to these high-surprisal sentences. Models with active curriculum learning show noticeable performance gains in (Super)GLUE but underperform the models without such learning on MSGS.

Linguistically Motivated Curriculum Learning (Mi, 2023). This submission tests 6 linguistic metrics of complexity as curriculum learning approaches. On the *Strict-Small* track, this approach succeeds in finding improvements over training on the whole corpus in a random order.

Baby Llama (Timiryasov and Tastet, 2023). This submission proposes a knowledge distillation approach with two teacher models (a 300M-parameter Llama model and 700M-parameter GPT-2 model) trained on the *Strict-Small* corpus. These are distilled into a 58M-parameter Llama model called Baby Llama. The proposed model outperforms the BabyLM baselines, the teacher LMs, and a 58M-parameter Llama model trained from scratch on the *Strict-Small* data without distillation.

Curriculum learning based on sentence complexity approximating language acquisition (Oba et al., 2023). This submission assesses the impact of curriculum learning based on sentence complexity within the context of the *Strict-Small* task. The authors order training data based on three sentence-level complexity metrics: number of tokens, number of constituents, and max depth of the sentences'

[21]As described in §7.2, LTG-BERT makes multiple modifications to the standard Transformer encoder architecture: additional layer normalization (Shleifer et al., 2021), GEGLU feed-forward modules (Shazeer, 2020), disentangled attention following DeBERTa (He et al., 2021), and scaled weight initialization following (Nguyen and Salazar, 2019).

dependency parse. They find that the dependency-based ranking leads to better models, however, all curriculum-based models underperform a random baseline.

Masked Latent Semantic Modeling (Berend, 2023b). This paper adopts a method from Berend (2023a) called Masked Latent Semantic Modeling (MLSM) in which the target output distribution can be transformed from a one-hot distribution over the vocabulary into a sparse distribution over latent "semantic property" vectors. Then, the same kind of student-teacher optimization as in knowledge distillation is applied using this modified output distribution instead of the full vocabulary. MLSM on its own is found to lead to degradation in BLiMP performance, although combining MLSM with typical MLM training in a multitask setting leads to similar performance as MLM training alone.

Lil-Bevo (Govindarajan et al., 2023). This paper offered submissions to both *Strict-Small* and *Strict* tracks and used three design choices for LM training: (i) initially pretraining on music data, following work on transfer learning (Papadimitriou and Jurafsky, 2020), which suggested that musical structure may form a reasonable basis upon which to learn language structure; (ii) subsequently using a training curriculum starting from shorter sequences (128) before moving to longer ones (512), following insights from Press et al. (2021), and (iii) masking critical tokens necessary to perform some of the BLiMP subtasks (e.g., masking "not" for NPI-licensing). Taking final results into consideration alongside ablations, this team found that sequence length matters, music pretraining may help a little, and targeted MLM training seems to help (but only for some BLiMP subtasks, including NPI licensing and Argument Structure).

Contextualizer (Xiao et al., 2023). This paper sorts the corpora in the training dataset loosely based on their age of acquisition and reading difficulty. The authors then introduce techniques to begin and end the training with padding-separated datasets sorted from easy to hard, while the middle of the training employs a noisier padding and sorting strategy to improve the model's robustness. The final model performs similarly to its counterpart pretrained with thousands of times more data.

Implicit Structure Building (Momen et al., 2023). This submission introduces an unsupervised hierarchical bias into the transformer. The approach shows that such structural bias with StructFormer improves over the classic MLM Transformer approach. Improvements are not consistent across scenarios: the model excels in single-sentence or syntactic evaluation tasks, but less so in semantic tasks with multi-sentence inputs.

Pretraining LLMs using human-like development data (Bhardwaj et al., 2023). This submission trains RoBERTa, DistilBERT, and GPT-2 models on the *Strict* and *Strict-Small* data. They find that training DistilBERT for 60 epochs is better than 20 epochs. They also claim that the performance of the baseline RoBERTa model may not be replicable across random initializations and that hyperparameter searches should be more thorough to hedge against such outlier models.

On the Effect of Curriculum Learning with Developmental Data for Grammar Acquisition (Opper et al., 2023). This submission explores the effect of curriculum learning, using BabyBERTa models, on the *Strict-Small* data track. The authors contrast three types of curriculum learning: one that orders input by word frequency; one by sequence entropy; and one by increasing context length. They find that neither of these methods produces results above a baseline random presentation. In a series of follow-up experiments, the authors verify that model performance is linked to the amount of exposure to transcribed speech data and suggest that speech data is a good foundation for curriculum learning.

Difficulty-based Sentence Reordering (Borazjanizadeh, 2023). This study explores two broad approaches to dataset preprocessing to improve LM training in the 10M-word setting: data reordering (curriculum learning) and data cleaning. Results show that reordering a subset of the data by sentence difficulty may lead to marginal improvements, as long the local coherence of the samples is not damaged too greatly. However, the clearest improvements come from cleaning the data of incoherent, ungrammatical, or non-linguistic strings.

G Results Broken Down by GLUE / BLiMP Subtask

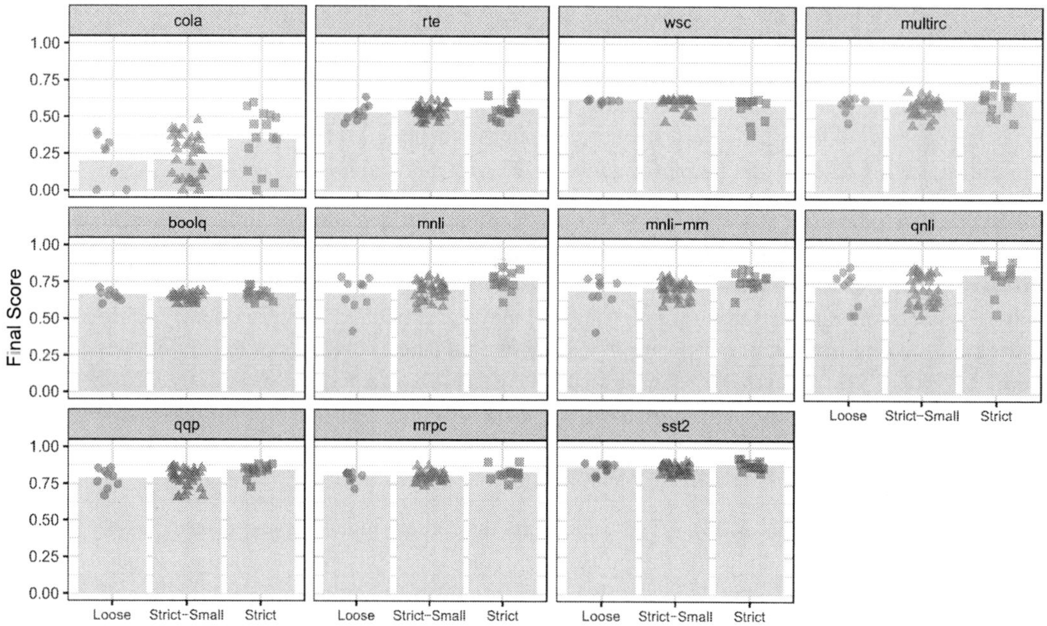

Figure 7: **Submission Results by GLUE subtask:** Points show the performance of each submission. Gray bars show the across-submission average in each category.

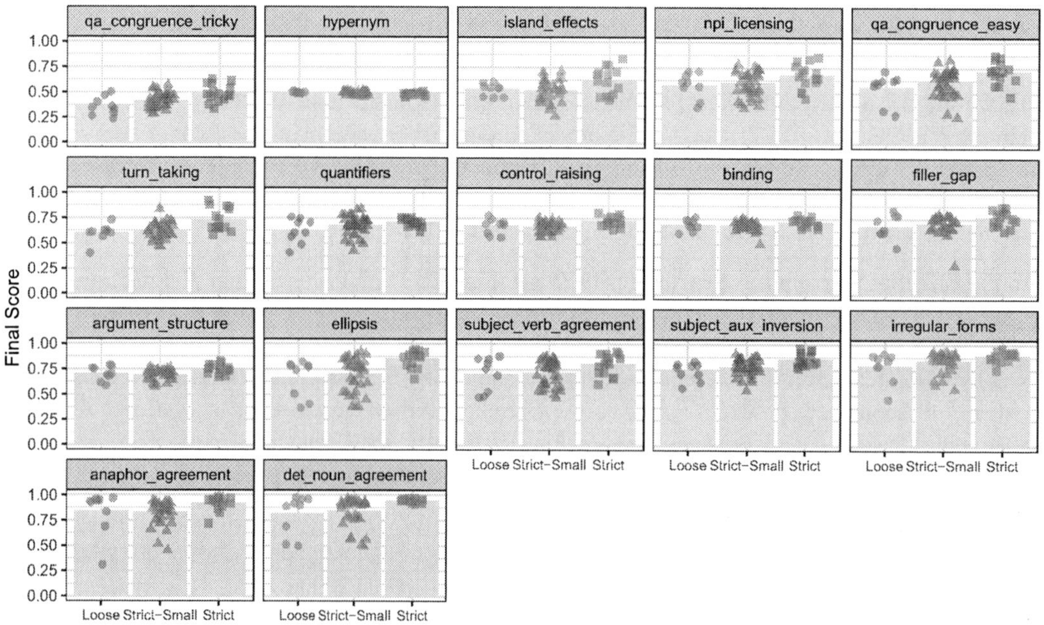

Figure 8: **Submission Results by BLiMP subtask:** Points show the performance of each submission. Gray bars show the across-submission average in each category.

GPT-wee: How Small Can a Small Language Model Really Get?

Bastian Bunzeck and **Sina Zarrieß**
Computational Linguistics, Department of Linguistics
Bielefeld University, Germany
{bastian.bunzeck, sina.zarriess}@uni-bielefeld.de

Abstract

In this model report, we present an alternative approach to improving language models through scaling up their architectures and training data. In contrast, we train significantly smaller GPT-wee language models for the CMCL and CoNLL shared task: the BabyLM challenge. Drawing inspiration from usage-based linguistics, specifically focusing on language acquisition factors such as frequency, word length, and lexical frames, we also conduct tests employing curriculum learning techniques. Our findings demonstrate that even very small models can achieve considerable proficiency in standard evaluation tasks, performing as good as or even better than much larger baseline models, both on zero-shot evaluation and tasks that require further fine-tuning. Our naïve curriculum approach, however, does not show any straightforward improvements, except for certain, very specific tasks. Overall, the results remain inconclusive and suggest interaction effects between model architecture, data make-up and learning processes that warrant further inspection.

1 Introduction

In recent years, language model-based NLP has witnessed remarkable advancements, surpassing numerous benchmarks and continuously achieving new breakthroughs through increasingly larger models. However, such large language models come with certain difficulties. As their size expands, they demand substantial amounts of computing power and training data, while also retaining a certain degree of opaqueness and consuming immense amounts of energy (Bender et al., 2021). Besides, their overblown and complex architectures hinder interpretability, while commonly used training data mostly comes from non-naturalistic sources such as book corpora, Wikipedia crawls, and web pages. Addressing these concerns, the BabyLM challenge (Warstadt et al., 2023b) emerges as an experimental test bed for "smaller" or more optimized (and possibly more cognitively plausible) models. By drastically reducing the allowed amount of training data compared to state-of-the-art models, and by sourcing it from more varied domains, it forces language model engineers to come up with new solutions that are not (only) grounded in increasing parameters, training data, and computing power. We respond to this challenge by exploring language models with drastically reduced GPT-2 architectures (Radford et al., 2019) and the value of curriculum learning (Bengio et al., 2009; Hacohen and Weinshall, 2019) in training them, inspired by findings from usage-based linguistics on the nature of child-directed and child speech. Among the submissions to the BabyLM challenge, our GPT-Wee models stand out in the sense that we did not implement intricate and highly complex learning strategies, but rather examined how much simple architectures can be reduced in size while still providing considerable performance. Our models feature some of the lowest, if not *the lowest* number of parameters among the submissions.

Elman (1993) discusses how learning processes (e.g. language acquisition) are tied to cognitive maturation, and how during these processes, increasingly complex human neural networks are confronted with increasingly complex input. With respect to the concrete nature of this linguistic input, usage-based research has shown that its vocabulary is compact and mainly concerned with children's immediate surroundings (Saxton, 2017). It features a high amount of fragmentary utterances and frequent, utterance-initial lexical frames (Cameron-Faulkner et al., 2003). In turn, children's earliest utterances also revolve around lexically highly specific pivot schemas and item-based constructions (Braine and Bowerman, 1976; Tomasello, 2000; Diessel, 2013a), which only gradually expand to more complex utterances. Due to the linguistically

Proceedings of the 27th Conference on Computational Natural Language Learning: Volume 2: The BabyLM Challenge, pages 35–46
December 6-7, 2023 ©2023 Association for Computational Linguistics

more diverse nature of training data in machine learning – in the case of the present challenge it is, for example, composed of realistic input from CHILDES (MacWhinney, 2000) and other sources like Wikipedia dumps or Open Subtitles – the common approach of providing it to the training algorithm in random order does not mirror a developmentally plausible input trajectory. To better understand the value of these two factors, the growing intricacy of natural neural networks and the growing diversity of input, we (1) explore artificial neural networks of increasing/decreasing complexity, and (2) experiment with ordering the training data according to its complexity and (with regard to child-directed speech) prototypicality.

In sum, we find that a reduction of key parameters, e.g. the number of hidden layers and attention heads or the vocabulary size, does not immediately materialize in detrimental effects. Only when they are *drastically* reduced, the performance is affected more strongly. Moreover, we find that the curriculum approach does not always increase performance, but indeed shows effects on the training and evaluation losses that warrant further inspection. To the shared task, we submit our medium-sized model, as we observe the best size–performance trade-offs for these variants. We submit the curriculum variant (with a vocabulary size of 8k) of this member of our model family, which we call GPT-wee[1] in honor of their *wee* architectures.

2 Language models and developmental plausibility

Cognitive maturation in the form of an increasing number of neurons (*nodes*) and synapses (*connections)* in human neural networks accompanies developmental processes, and thus also language acquisition (Elman, 1993). The learning mechanisms of current language models do not mirror this development. Their architecture is defined before the training process, and then the nodes' and connections' weights and biases are randomly initialized and finally optimized, often based on randomly ordered input examples and influenced by the choice of specific loss functions. Interestingly, alternative approaches to ANNs, like dynamically growing networks or weights with gradient values, which were proposed during the 1980s and 1990s (for example in Elman et al., 1996, 73), never achieved widespread adoption in NLP (although they exist, with examples like NEAT (Stanley and Miikkulainen, 2002) having been shown to be useful for a variety of tasks). The best proxy for investigating the effects of neuronal growth are smaller models like BabyBERTa (Huebner et al., 2021) or TinyStories (Eldan and Li, 2023). They show that for small data settings (in these cases further restrained by linguistic simplicity through child-directed speech or Simple English), much smaller architectures trained for shorter periods of time can still exhibit similar or even improved performance compared to larger models.

Apart from model architecture, also the concrete *learning* process (viz. the training goal) in current language models requires theoretical scrutiny. Whether it uses prediction in context, next word prediction or next sentence prediction, learning always involve a form of *prediction*. While prediction effects in language are well documented (for an overview, see Ryskin et al., 2020), it remains an open question whether the current flavor of prediction in language model training aligns with its cognitive counterpart. While the unidirectional prediction goal in autoregressive models (like those from the GPT-family) appears cognitively more plausible than bidirectional prediction, as employed in e.g. BERT-like models – after all, humans can only predict from what they have already processed, and not from the following (not yet perceived) contexts – other modalities of language acquisition like reading often involve explicit instruction with bi-directional prediction (e.g. fill-in-the-blank exercises).

3 Child-directed speech is tailored to children's needs

Child-directed speech differs from regular adult-adult conversation in several crucial aspects. It should be noted that its specific features[2] are not *exclusive* to child-directed speech, but rather *preferred* in this specific register. As such, child-directed speech is a gradient concept, where certain utterances stick out as more prototypical instances. We use the following four features of child-directed speech to define a prototypicality ranking that we employ in our curriculum approach.

[1]Our code can be found at `https://github.com/clause-bielefeld/gpt-wee`

[2]The following section only reiterates the features directly relevant to the current modelling task. For a more comprehensive overview across all layers of linguistic analysis, Saxton (2017) and Clark (2009, 32–41) should be consulted.

The first feature is word length. Saxton (2017) describes how the child-directed vocabulary is mostly restricted to short words grounded in the direct spatial and temporal proximity of the child. Concrete objects are favoured over abstract concepts. As Zipf (1935) already noted, word length is inversely proportional to word frequency. Furthermore, longer words have a higher informational content (Piantadosi et al., 2011) and are thus not ideal for the – still developing – linguistic and cognitive capabilities of children.

Secondly, word frequency itself, although it is a contested notion (Saxton, 2009), plays an important role in language acquisition. Apart from its role in the input, it is also reflected in children's earliest utterances, which are highly item-based and revolve around so-called pivot schemas (Braine and Bowerman, 1976; Tomasello, 2000; Diessel, 2013a), for example *more [NP]*, where *more* as the static lexical element is combined with a slot for a noun phrase. Ambridge et al. (2015) show evidence for a direct relationship between the age of acquisition of linguistic forms and their frequency in the input. Importantly, the Zipfian distribution of lexical elements in child-directed speech is stable across the development span of children as well as across typologically diverse languages (Lavi-Rotbain and Arnon, 2023). From these empirical findings, we deduce that child-directed utterances with more frequent lexical items (across the entirety of the input) can also be seen as more prototypical.

Thirdly, moving from the lexical to the syntactic level, Cameron-Faulkner et al. (2003) show that the majority of child-directed speech does not consist of canonical subject-predicate sentences, but rather of questions, imperatives and an enormous amount of fragments without a regular predicate. For different input types, these distributions vary considerably. Children's books, for example, feature a much higher amount of subject-predicate and complex sentences (with two or more lexical verbs) than ordinary speech (Cameron-Faulkner and Noble, 2013). Because the everyday child-directed input (e.g. in toyplay or meal sessions) contains more fragments compared to these specialised kinds of input, we conclude that shorter utterances are also more prototypical for child-directed speech.

Finally, Cameron Faulkner et al. (2003) also show that the majority of child-directed utterances begin with what they call "lexical frames" – highly frequent utterance-initial, mostly two- or three-word, lexical sequences which are stable across development and different caregivers. These specific frames are thought to facilitate the acquisition of item-based constructions, which then later gradually emerge into a complete mental grammar. From this, we conclude that child-directed utterances beginning with highly frequent frames, here measured in trigrams, are also more prototypical.

As Geeraerts (1989) notes, prototype theory is prototypical in itself and not a monolithic framework. For the sake of the present analysis, we define the overall prototypicality of an utterance as the shared centrality along all axes of the mentioned prototype criteria – in concrete terms this means that we combine the utterance ranks to determine a final rank for each utterance.

4 Curriculum learning

Curriculum learning is an approach to machine learning where "the examples are not randomly presented but organized in a meaningful order which illustrates gradually more concepts, and gradually more complex ones" (Bengio et al., 2009, 41). They propose two advantages: less training time (as the learner does not waste time on predicting noisy or hard examples too early), and an orientation into "better areas of the training space" – local minima during optimization.

This approach has been proven effective across a variety of tasks, for example in vision and language (Zhang et al., 2021) or reinforcement learning (Narvekar et al., 2020), but it remains questionable under which circumstances considerable advantages emerge. Wu et al. (2021) show that for established benchmarks, the advantages are marginal to non-existent. In contrast, the benefits are the most pronounced for problems with noisy training data. Child-directed speech, with its high amount of fragmentary utterances, can also be considered somewhat *noisy* input which, in conclusion, might benefit from a curriculum approach.

Importantly, our flavor of curriculum learning implements usage-based and cognitive principles as the source of the concrete curriculum ordering, and no engineering-based metrics, pacing functions or other kinds of transfer learning, e.g. those with teacher networks that determine the examples' difficulty (as in Hacohen and Weinshall, 2019). Due to the *a priori* nature of these aspects, we employ a vanilla approach to curriculum learning (Soviany et al., 2022), meaning that we only order the exam-

	Small	Medium	Large
Vocabulary size	4k	8k	16k
Hidden layers	2	2	4
Attention heads	2	2	4
Embedding size	64	128	256
Context size	64	128	128
Parameters	0.42M	1.55M	7.52M

Table 1: Model parameters

ples once and then provide them to the training algorithm in this static order, to maintain comparability with equivalent no-curriculum models. Interestingly, the BabyBERTa experiments implemented a somewhat comparable functionality. They showed that, in their own grammatical test suite, models benefit from this *scaffolding*, i.e. first training on child-directed speech and only later on more complex registers and non-dialogue input data.

5 Implementation

5.1 Training

As training data, we used the `babylm_10M` data set from the `strict-small` submission track for the BabyLM challenge. It consists of a mixture of child-directed and adult-directed speech, e.g. from CHILDES (MacWhinney, 2000), as well as written language, e.g. from Wikipedia. The exact composition of the corpus is described in Warstadt et al. (2023a). For evaluation during the training process, we used the `babylm_test`[3] data set.

We trained models of three different sizes, each once with and once without curriculum learning. Table 1 shows the different parameter configurations[4]. The training process was implemented in the huggingface transformers library (Wolf et al., 2020). As already mentioned, we decided on a GPT2 architecture (Radford et al., 2019) to account for the sequential nature of language. A BPE tokenizer was trained with a vocabulary size of 4k/8k/16k subword tokens. Before tokenization, all textual input was normalized in terms of capitalization and eventual diacritics. For the curriculum models, the pre-ordered examples were dynamically loaded in unshuffled batches during training time, which preserved the calculated order based on the prototypicality measures. We supplied the models with training batches of size 32. Regarding training hyperparameters, we used the cosine learning rate scheduler with a learning rate if 5e-4, weight decay of 0.1, 1k warm-up steps and 8 gradient accumulation steps. All models were trained for exactly 10 epochs in the non-curriculum setting and roughly 10 epochs in the curriculum setting, where we could not set the exact number of epochs due to the dynamic data loading. The models were evaluated after each training epoch. After those 10 epochs, the losses mostly stabilized. We did not conduct any kind of extensive hyperparameter search. Instead, we only used the default configurations for GPT-2 training, including dropout probabilities of 0.1 and layer normalization. By doing so, we tried to stay as close as possible to the vanilla configuration, which allows us to better assess the effects of smaller architectures in isolation.

The models were trained on a GPU workstation equipped with an Intel Core i7-4770 CPU (3.40GHz), 32GB of RAM and an NVIDIA GeForce GTX 1080 Ti GPU. Due to the small number of parameters, training times varied between 3–4 hours for the smallest models to 20h for the largest models.

5.2 Sentence scoring

To order the curriculum input sentences, we determined four different scores based on the aforementioned prototypicality criteria of child-directed speech. For each utterance/sentence in the training data (delimited by sentence-final punctuation or line breaks, dependening on the corpus file), we calculated the following:

- the **average word length** of a sequence, measured by the mean number of characters for all tokens in a sequence
- the **average word frequency** of a sequence, measured by taking the mean of the individual token frequencies across the whole training data
- the **utterance length**, measured as the number of lexical tokens in the sequence
- the **frame frequency**, calculated as the amount of times that the three utterance-initial tokens occur in that configuration through the training data

[3] A dev data set was also provided, but due to their equivalent size it the choice between did not affect the outcome of the training process.

[4] From this point onwards, we will denote the models by the vocabulary size of their tokenizer.

	Mean (SD)
Frame frequency	188.76 (917.04)
Utterance length	8.01 (9.21)
Mean word length	4.28 (1.37)
Mean word frequency	55153.93 (42877.18)

Table 2: Distribution of scoring variables

We operationalized the frame frequency as exactly three utterance-initial tokens because this number provides a good trade-off between the open-ended nature of sentences (and their long-tail distribution of final lexical items) and the number of fixed lexical items that certain syntactical constructions are associated with.

For each value, we calculated the respective rank of the utterance across all utterances. The final "prototypicality rank" for each utterance was calculated by taking the sum of these four ranks and then ranking by this sum.

Mean values and standard deviations for the four criteria are reported in table 2. Especially for the frame frequency and the utterance length, the distributions are heavily skewed and indicate long-tail distributions. The mean word length of approximately 4 with a standard deviation of 1.34 is to be expected, whereas the distribution of the sentences' mean word frequency also appears to be heavily skewed. As Lavi-Rotbain and Arnon (2023) show how pervasive Zipfian distributions are on a lexical level, it is not surprising that other properties of language, e.g. lexical frames, follow similar laws.

6 Results

6.1 Training

We evaluated the models after every 5k training steps during the approximately 40k training steps, returning 8 data points for training and evaluation loss. Their development is reported in appendix A (figures 1, 2 and 3). Across all models, the evaluation loss for the curriculum learning is initially much higher than the other losses, whereas the evaluation loss for the normal, randomized learning is the lowest. This is not surprising, however, as the evaluation data was not re-ordered and thus many linguistic features present in it were not yet processed by the curriculum models during earlier training steps. The regular training losses share a very similar development across all model sizes. Between the model sizes, differences are more pronounced in the later stages of training. Noticeably, the smallest model seems to converge the earliest, while the largest model might have benefited from even further training. Furthermore, the curriculum evaluation loss stays much higher for the larger model, whereas it converges in similar dimensions of the training losses for the smaller models. As such, both an effect of the curriculum learning (albeit not strictly positive) and an interaction between model size and (non-)curriculum learning can be reported.

6.2 Zero-shot evaluation with BLiMP

We tested our models with the evaluation suite supplied by the BabyLM challenge (Gao et al., 2022; Warstadt et al., 2023a), which included zero-shot evaluation tasks as well as tasks requiring additional fine-tuning. The zero-shot tasks are taken from the BLiMP evaluation suite (Warstadt et al., 2020a), which consists of minimal acceptable/unacceptable pairs of sentences across a wide variety of linguistic phenomena. To evaluate models, these sentences are scored by the models for their likelihood. A model is said to have acquired grammatical knowledge of a specific phenomenon if it consistently scores the acceptable sentences higher.

The results for the BLiMP tasks are shown in Tables 3 and 4. When comparing our own GPT-Wee models, we find that there is no straightforward effect of model size on task performance. For the majority of tasks, the performance increases with model size, whereas some tasks (e.g. hypernym, island effects) show light inverse scaling behavior. On most tasks, the effect of curriculum learning is small and rather mixed (positive or negative), when compared to the respective baseline (same model size, without curriculum). Overall, model size has a larger effect than curriculum learning. In a few task-model combinations, though, curriculum learning has a very strong positive effect (16k model/anaphor agreement, 8k model/irregular forms, 16kmodel /quantifiers) and in one case a strong negative effect(8k/NPI). Thus, if at all, it is rather the medium-sized or larger models than the small models which seem to benefit from the curriculum. For the quantifiers task, for example, the curriculum model with a 16k vocabulary outperforms all other models by approx. 18%.

Compared to the baseline results[5], we find that

[5]Taken from https://github.com/babylm/

	anaphor agreement:	argument structure:	binding:	control raising:	determiner noun agreement:	ellipsis:	filler gap:	irregular forms:	island effects:
4k	63.50	60.11	61.26	60.78	65.34	32.56	64.11	68.65	47.80
4k (cu.)	57.98	57.86	63.97	60.78	64.58	35.45	66.06	70.03	43.05
8k	71.06	64.69	65.75	62.64	78.69	44.11	62.68	82.29	42.49
8k (cu.)	64.37	63.86	65.94	62.88	75.96	44.86	65.70	90.13	37.07
16k	73.82	71.91	68.97	66.26	88.36	54.56	68.67	86.06	41.03
16k (cu.)	82.87	69.51	65.24	63.21	85.52	55.43	66.65	77.56	40.88
OPT	63.8	70.6	67.1	66.5	78.5	62	63.8	67.5	48.6
RoBERTa	81.5	67.1	67.3	67.9	90.8	76.4	63.5	87.4	39.9
T5	68.9	63.8	60.4	60.9	72.2	34.4	48.2	77.6	45.6

Table 3: Results (accuracies) of zeroshot BLiMP and BLiMP Supplement evaluation measures for our GPT-Wee models and baseline models (OPT, RoBERTa and T5)

	npi licensing:	quantifiers:	subject verb agreement:	hypernym:	qa congruence easy:	qa congruence tricky:	subject aux inversion:	turn taking:
4k	49.95	54.87	50.62	52.21	48.44	39.39	81.53	45.71
4k (cu.)	49.47	55.41	52.09	50.00	43.75	44.85	80.09	43.57
8k	52.10	60.90	56.24	49.77	51.56	32.12	82.58	50.36
8k (cu.)	37.97	60.38	57.81	49.88	50.00	40.00	85.44	46.43
16k	51.97	59.61	66.49	49.42	57.81	28.48	80.09	54.29
16k (cu.)	46.60	78.54	65.82	50.93	53.12	33.33	83.46	56.79
OPT	46.7	59.6	56.9	50.0	54.7	31.5	80.3	57.1
RoBERTa	55.9	70.5	65.4	49.4	31.3	32.1	71.7	53.2
T5	47.8	61.2	65.0	48.0	40.6	21.2	64.9	45.0

Table 4: Results (accuracies) of zeroshot BLiMP and BLiMP Supplement evaluation measures for our GPT-Wee models and baseline models (OPT, RoBERTa and T5), contd.

our smaller models do not perform considerably worse on average, and outperform the baseline models for selected tasks. For example, a few of our small models are surprisingly good at island effects, hypernyms, qa congruence, or subject-auxiliary inversion. As the baseline results are derived from BERT/OPT/T5 models with much larger architectures and higher parameter numbers (e.g. 125M parameters for the OPT model, with 12 hidden layers, 12 attention heads, a 50k token vocabulary and intermediate embeddings of size 768), we are pleasantly surprised by the comparatively good results which our models achieve.

6.3 (Super)GLUE and MSGS evaluation

For the evaluation tasks requiring additional fine-tuning, we only collected results for our submitted, medium-sized curriculum model due to constraints in computing power and time.

The GLUE (Wang et al., 2018) and SuperGLUE (Wang et al., 2019) benchmarks involve fine-tuning on a variety of tasks, e.g. question answering, correct identification of entailment or the extraction of correct co-references. As such, this benchmark is more focused on semantic and pragmatic aspects.

Regarding the (Super)GLUE scores (table 5), a similar picture to the BLiMP scores emerges. Across many of the tasks, our model performs in similar ranges as the baselines, often better than the T5 baseline and more similar to the OPT baseline. Although our models are considerably smaller, they seem to provide similar starting points for fine-tuning on additional data.

Finally, the Mixed Signals Generalization Set (MSGS) introduced by Warstadt et al. (2020b) also contains different ambiguous binary classification tasks. The test sentences are ambiguous in the sense of allowing both surface generalizations and generalizations that require deeper linguistic understanding of structure. Additionally, control experiments are included that test whether a feature is actually encoded. The scores reported in table 6 are correlations, where a value greater than zero denotes a preference for linguistics generalizations, and a value below zero shows a preference for surface generalizations. The performance of our model is (once more) very similar to the baselines. The control tasks show that our model does encode the tested features, but the test tasks show a system-

evaluation-pipeline

	CoLA (MCC)	SST-2	MRPC (F1)	QQP (F1)	MNLI	MNLI-mm	QNLI	RTE	BoolQ	MultiRC	WSC
8k (cu.)	4	80	82	66	60	61	61	60	61	55	60
Maj.	0.0	50.2	82.0	53.1	35.7	35.7	35.4	53.1	50.5	59.9	53.2
OPT	15.2	81.9	72.5	60.4	57.6	60.0	61.5	60.0	63.3	55.2	60.2
RoB.	25.8	87.0	79.2	73.7	73.2	74.0	77.0	61.6	66.3	61.4	61.4
T5	11.3	78.1	80.5	66.2	48.0	50.3	62.0	49.4	66.0	47.1	61.4

Table 5: (Super)GLUE scores (accuracies unless otherwise stated as MCC or F1) for our 8k curriculum GPT-Wee model, the majority baseline and the three provided model baselines

	CR (Control)	LC (Control)	MV (Control)	RP (Control)	SC (Control)	CR_LC	CR_RTP	MV_LC	MV_RTP	SC_LC	SC_RP
8k (cu.)	43	93	37	100	76	0	-74	-99	-99	-57	-73
OPT	50.8	53.6	99.5	99.9	77.2	0.4	-70.3	-72.1	-77.6	13.8	-68.9
RoB.	43.1	100.0	97.7	76.7	86.2	-28.3	-77.7	-99.3	-79.4	16.3	-45.0
T5	21.1	100.0	33.4	82.5	77.6	-78.3	-62.0	-100.0	-79.7	-25.3	-39.4

Table 6: MSGS scores (MCC) for our 8k curriculum GPT-Wee model and the three provided model baselines

atic bias for surface generalizations. However, this behavior is also (with minor deviations) observable in the baseline models. All naïve models fail to generalize based on the linguistic features.

6.4 Age-of-acquisition evaluation

Additionally, the BabyLM evaluation suite provided an age-of-acquisition evaluation (Portelance et al., 2023). The calculated scores (table 7) are Mean Absolute Deviation (MAD) values, measured in months, representing the difference between the actual average age-of-acquisition (AoA) of the tested word among American English-speaking children and the predicted AoA based on our models' average surprisal scores. Lower MAD scores indicate better performance. We calculate these scores for all of our models and find that the individual differences between the models are tiny or nonexistent, and roughly the same as the baseline results provided by the challenge. As such, also here the effect of the choice of a specific language model architecture does not seem to have much of an influence on the evaluation metric.

7 Discussion

The present analysis set out to investigate the influence of a usage-based factors, input ordering, and an architectural factor, model size, on the learning processes (and successes) of language models. We found that both factors have a certain influence on the training process and the model performance. While model size affects the performance in linguistic evaluation, the effect is not linear across tasks. For zero-shot tasks, the majority show improved scores, although a few scores decrease with increasing model size. Compared to much larger baseline models, our models' performance is not considerably worse. Especially the non-linear effects of model size warrant further inspection: it remains unclear which internal factors (context length, vocabulary size, model parameters, number of training epochs, etc.) contribute to which developments, and how these factors interact with each other. For the tasks requiring additional fine-tuning, our 8k curriculum model also performed similarly to the baselines. Especially for the (SUPER)Glue benchmark, a more semantics- and pragmatics-oriented benchmark, the performance was quite in line with the baseline models, hinting at the acquisition of a fair amount of the needed information. The MSGS benchmark, however, showed that our model systematically picks up surface generalizations. Yet, this also applies to the much larger baselines.

The usage-inspired naïve ordering approach to curriculum learning also has no straightforward effects on model performance. Especially during the training process, differences to traditional, randomized learning are observable. Although it appears to be somewhat detrimental to overall performance, certain specific evaluation tasks are positively influenced. The results thus remain inconclusive. From a usage-based viewpoint, Diessel (2013b) stresses the importance of deictic pointing and joint attention as (extralinguistic) language acquisition fac-

	Overall	Nouns	Predicates	Function words
4k	2.07	2.00	1.84	2.65
4k (cu.)	2.06	1.99	1.84	2.64
8k	2.07	2.00	1.82	2.65
8k (cu.)	2.06	2.00	1.82	2.64
16k	2.06	2.00	1.83	2.65
16k (cu.)	2.06	2.00	1.83	2.58
OPT	2.03	1.98	1.81	2.57
RoBERTa	2.06	1.99	1.85	2.65
T5	2.04	1.97	1.82	2.64

Table 7: MAD scores between actual AoA and the predicted AoA, for our GPT-Wee models and the three baselines

tors. Besides, also intention reading, role reversal and imitation (Tomasello, 2003, 21–28) are important acquisition factors that LLMs cannot mirror – they are strictly confined to statistical/frequency-driven aspects of usage-based theory (which are nevertheless very important, as noted by Ambridge et al., 2015). Still, we only have child-directed *speech* for training, and no real child-directed *communication*, which connects speech with such extralinguistic factors and influences utterance prototypicality beyond the modalities that we were able to include in the present experiment.

The non-improvements added by the curriculum approach also further add to the debate on what language models mean for linguistic theory. For example, Pannitto and Herbelot (2022) and Piantadosi (2023) have stressed the anti-Chomskyan evidence provided by the successes of language models. Curriculum learning looks like an obvious choice when trying to implement usage-based findings in the training process for (smaller) language models. However, this does not seem to work with the simple form of curriculum learning based on prototypicality measures that we used in this paper. For that, several explanations are possible: 1) more advanced curriculum approaches are needed, with different and more directed ways of ordering and optimizing the curriculum, 2) curriculum learning may not be the right choice for small models (it seems that, if at all, it was rather the larger models which showed tendencies of improvement. Also, other options for implementing usage-based accounts might just work better (e.g. models with dynamic structures and growing numbers of nodes). After all, real human neural networks grow and mature while they are constantly shaped and re-shaped by linguistic input and processing. As such, it also remains hard to interpret language models, their parts and their performance on various evaluation suites in a coherent way. The integration of more linguistic factors into the training process needs to be tested in this regard. For example, Yehezkel and Pinter (2023) propose a subword tokenization algorithm that incorporates contextual information and creates vocabularies that seem to align more with classical ideas of morphology. It remains an open question whether such alterations and other linguistic experiments in the training process would also improve the linguistic quality of the generated output.

8 Conclusion

The BabyLM challenge set out to test different approaches to language modelling with small data. When looking at the leaderboard[6], we find that our model is located in the lower section of the rankings. However, the best-performing models implement much more complex learning strategies and larger architectures. We, on the other hand, decided on very small architectures. As such, our results can be seen as a success: benchmark performance seems to be much more strongly constrained by the concrete linguistic make-up of the training data and not so much by model size alone, as our downsizing apprach shows. This also confirms earlier findings from BabyBERTa (Huebner et al., 2021) and TinyStories (Eldan and Li, 2023). Our key takeaway is that a *one size fits all* approach to language model architectures should not be adopted without further thought, and that training data quality and make-up should be valued more. Besides, we also tested a usage-based approach to curriculum learning. Although our curriculum models are generally not superior to the regular, randomized

[6]At `https://dynabench.org/babylm`

models, some zero-shot evaluation tasks did benefit from it. Additionally, small model size and the curriculum training did not have a detrimental effect on pre-training for the tasks that require fine-tuning. Still, our results show that a much more fine-grained approach to the evaluation of such factors is needed. As language model engineers, we can choose between a large variety of evaluation suites that test along all levels of linguistic analysis and across many different task set-ups. However, we do not know how the changes in individual, low-level variables (e.g. number of hidden layers, context size) impact specific factors of linguistic performance (e.g. the ability to judge acceptability for island effects, or the ability to correctly predict entailment). To correctly interpret such choices, further systematic analyses are clearly needed.

Acknowledgements

We acknowledge financial support by the project "SAIL: SustAInable Life-cycle of Intelligent Socio-Technical Systems" (Grant ID NW21-059A), which is funded by the program "Netzwerke 2021" of the Ministry of Culture and Science of the State of Northrhine Westphalia, Germany.

References

Ben Ambridge, Evan Kidd, Caroline F. Rowland, and Anna L. Theakston. 2015. The ubiquity of frequency effects in first language acquisition. *Journal of Child Language*, 42(2):239–273.

Emily M. Bender, Timnit Gebru, Angelina McMillan-Major, and Shmargaret Shmitchell. 2021. On the Dangers of Stochastic Parrots: Can Language Models Be Too Big? In *Proceedings of the 2021 ACM Conference on Fairness, Accountability, and Transparency*, pages 610–623, Virtual Event Canada. ACM.

Yoshua Bengio, Jérôme Louradour, Ronan Collobert, and Jason Weston. 2009. Curriculum learning. In *Proceedings of the 26th Annual International Conference on Machine Learning*, pages 41–48, Montreal Quebec Canada. ACM.

Martin D. S. Braine and Melissa Bowerman. 1976. Children's First Word Combinations. *Monographs of the Society for Research in Child Development*, 41(1).

Thea Cameron-Faulkner, Elena Lieven, and Michael Tomasello. 2003. A construction based analysis of child directed speech. *Cognitive Science*, 27(6):843–873.

Thea Cameron-Faulkner and Claire Noble. 2013. A comparison of book text and Child Directed Speech. *First Language*, 33(3):268–279.

Eve V. Clark. 2009. *First Language Acquisition*, 2nd ed edition. Cambridge University Press, Cambridge ; New York.

Holger Diessel. 2013a. Construction Grammar and First Language Acquisition. In Thomas Hoffmann and Graeme Trousdale, editors, *The Oxford Handbook of Construction Grammar*. Oxford University Press, Oxford.

Holger Diessel. 2013b. Where does language come from? Some reflections on the role of deictic gesture and demonstratives in the evolution of language. *Language and Cognition*, 5(2-3):239–249.

Ronen Eldan and Yuanzhi Li. 2023. TinyStories: How Small Can Language Models Be and Still Speak Coherent English?

Jeffrey L. Elman. 1993. Learning and development in neural networks: The importance of starting small. *Cognition*, 48(1):71–99.

Jeffrey L. Elman, Elizabeth L. Bates, Mark H. Johnson, Annette Karmiloff-Smith, Domenico Parisi, and Kim Plunkett. 1996. *Rethinking Innateness: A Connectionist Perspective on Development*. Neural Network Modeling and Connectionism. MIT Press, Cambridge, MA.

Leo Gao, Jonathan Tow, Stella Biderman, Charles Lovering, Jason Phang, Anish Thite, Fazz, Niklas Muennighoff, Thomas Wang, Sdtblck, Tttyuntian, Researcher2, Zdeněk Kasner, Khalid Almubarak, Jeffrey Hsu, Pawan Sasanka Ammanamanchi, Dirk Groeneveld, Eric Tang, Charles Foster, Kkawamu1, Xagi-Dev, Uyhcire, Andy Zou, Ben Wang, Jordan Clive, Igor0, Kevin Wang, Nicholas Kross, Fabrizio Milo, and SilentvOx. 2022. EleutherAI/lm-evaluation-harness: V0.3.0. Zenodo.

Dirk Geeraerts. 1989. Introduction: Prospects and problems of prototype theory. *Linguistics*, 27(4):587–612.

Guy Hacohen and Daphna Weinshall. 2019. On the power of curriculum learning in training deep networks. In *Proceedings of the 36th International Conference on Machine Learning*, volume 97 of *Proceedings of Machine Learning Research*, pages 2535–2544. PMLR.

Philip A. Huebner, Elior Sulem, Fisher Cynthia, and Dan Roth. 2021. BabyBERTa: Learning More Grammar With Small-Scale Child-Directed Language. In *Proceedings of the 25th Conference on Computational Natural Language Learning*, pages 624–646, Online. Association for Computational Linguistics.

Ori Lavi-Rotbain and Inbal Arnon. 2023. Zipfian Distributions in Child-Directed Speech. *Open Mind*, 7:1–30.

Brian MacWhinney. 2000. *The CHILDES Project: Tools for Analyzing Talk*, 3 edition. Lawrence Erlbaum Associates, Mahwah, NJ.

Sanmit Narvekar, Bei Peng, Matteo Leonetti, Jivko Sinapov, Matthew E. Taylor, and Peter Stone. 2020. Curriculum learning for reinforcement learning domains: A framework and survey. *Journal of Machine Learning Research*, 21(1).

Ludovica Pannitto and Aurelie Herbelot. 2022. Can Recurrent Neural Networks Validate Usage-Based Theories of Grammar Acquisition? *Frontiers in Psychology*, 13:741321.

Steven T. Piantadosi. 2023. Modern language models refute Chomsky's approach to language.

Steven T. Piantadosi, Harry Tily, and Edward Gibson. 2011. Word lengths are optimized for efficient communication. *Proceedings of the National Academy of Sciences*, 108(9):3526–3529.

Eva Portelance, Yuguang Duan, Michael C. Frank, and Gary Lupyan. 2023. Predicting age of acquisition for children's early vocabulary in five languages using language model surprisal.

Alec Radford, Jeffrey Wu, Rewon Child, David Luan, Dario Amodei, Ilya Sutskever, et al. 2019. Language models are unsupervised multitask learners. *OpenAI blog*, 1(8):9.

Rachel Ryskin, Roger P. Levy, and Evelina Fedorenko. 2020. Do domain-general executive resources play a role in linguistic prediction? Re-evaluation of the evidence and a path forward. *Neuropsychologia*, 136:107258.

Matthew Saxton. 2009. The Inevitability of Child Directed Speech. In Susan Foster-Cohen, editor, *Language Acquisition*, pages 62–86. Palgrave Macmillan UK, London.

Matthew Saxton. 2017. *Child Language: Acquisition and Development*, 2nd edition edition. SAGE, Los Angeles.

Petru Soviany, Radu Tudor Ionescu, Paolo Rota, and Nicu Sebe. 2022. Curriculum Learning: A Survey. *International Journal of Computer Vision*, 130(6):1526–1565.

Kenneth O. Stanley and Risto Miikkulainen. 2002. Evolving Neural Networks through Augmenting Topologies. *Evolutionary Computation*, 10(2):99–127.

Michael Tomasello. 2000. The item-based nature of children's early syntactic development. *Trends in Cognitive Sciences*, 4(4).

Michael Tomasello. 2003. *Constructing a Language: A Usage-Based Theory of Language Acquisition*. Harvard University Press.

Alex Wang, Yada Pruksachatkun, Nikita Nangia, Amanpreet Singh, Julian Michael, Felix Hill, Omer Levy, and Samuel R. Bowman. 2019. SuperGLUE: A stickier benchmark for general-purpose language understanding systems. In *Proceedings of the 33rd International Conference on Neural Information Processing Systems*. Curran Associates Inc., Red Hook, NY, USA.

Alex Wang, Amanpreet Singh, Julian Michael, Felix Hill, Omer Levy, and Samuel Bowman. 2018. GLUE: A Multi-Task Benchmark and Analysis Platform for Natural Language Understanding. In *Proceedings of the 2018 EMNLP Workshop BlackboxNLP: Analyzing and Interpreting Neural Networks for NLP*, pages 353–355, Brussels, Belgium. Association for Computational Linguistics.

Alex Warstadt, Leshem Choshen, Aaron Mueller, Adina Williams, Ethan Wilcox, and Chengxu Zhuang. 2023a. Call for Papers – The BabyLM Challenge: Sample-efficient pretraining on a developmentally plausible corpus.

Alex Warstadt, Aaron Mueller, Leshem Choshen, Ethan Gotlieb Wilcox, Chengxu Zhuang, Juan Ciro, Rafael Mosquera, Adina Williams, Bhargavi Paranjabe, Tal Linzen, and Ryan Cotterell. 2023b. Findings of the 2023 BabyLM Challenge: Sample-efficient pretraining on developmentally plausible corpora. In *Proceedings of the 2023 BabyLM Challenge*. Association for Computational Linguistics (ACL).

Alex Warstadt, Alicia Parrish, Haokun Liu, Anhad Mohananey, Wei Peng, Sheng-Fu Wang, and Samuel R. Bowman. 2020a. BLiMP: The Benchmark of Linguistic Minimal Pairs for English. *Transactions of the Association for Computational Linguistics*, 8:377–392.

Alex Warstadt, Yian Zhang, Xiaocheng Li, Haokun Liu, and Samuel R. Bowman. 2020b. Learning Which Features Matter: RoBERTa Acquires a Preference for Linguistic Generalizations (Eventually). In *Proceedings of the 2020 Conference on Empirical Methods in Natural Language Processing (EMNLP)*, pages 217–235, Online. Association for Computational Linguistics.

Thomas Wolf, Lysandre Debut, Victor Sanh, Julien Chaumond, Clement Delangue, Anthony Moi, Pierric Cistac, Tim Rault, Remi Louf, Morgan Funtowicz, Joe Davison, Sam Shleifer, Patrick Von Platen, Clara Ma, Yacine Jernite, Julien Plu, Canwen Xu, Teven Le Scao, Sylvain Gugger, Mariama Drame, Quentin Lhoest, and Alexander Rush. 2020. Transformers: State-of-the-Art Natural Language Processing. In *Proceedings of the 2020 Conference on Empirical Methods in Natural Language Processing: System Demonstrations*, pages 38–45, Online. Association for Computational Linguistics.

Xiaoxia Wu, Ethan Dyer, and Behnam Neyshabur. 2021. When do curricula work? In *International Conference on Learning Representations*.

Shaked Yehezkel and Yuval Pinter. 2023. Incorporating context into subword vocabularies. In *Proceedings of the 17th Conference of the European Chapter of the Association for Computational Linguistics*, pages 623–635, Dubrovnik, Croatia. Association for Computational Linguistics.

Jiwen Zhang, zhongyu wei, Jianqing Fan, and Jiajie Peng. 2021. Curriculum learning for vision-and-language navigation. In *Advances in Neural Information Processing Systems*.

George K. Zipf. 1935. *The Psycho-Biology of Language*. Houghton Mifflin, Boston.

A Training losses

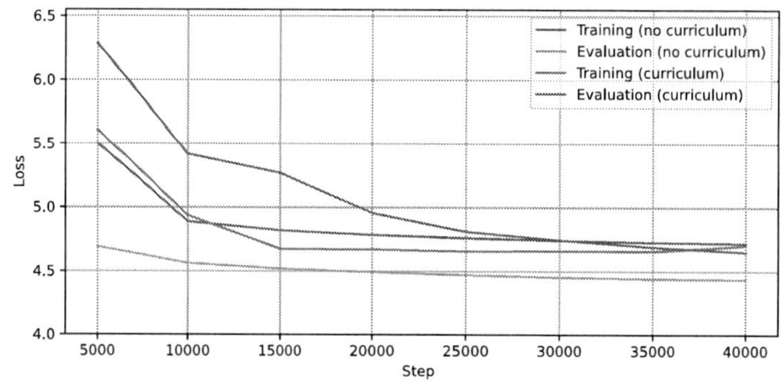

Figure 1: Training and evaluation losses for the 4k vocabulary models, calculated every 5k steps

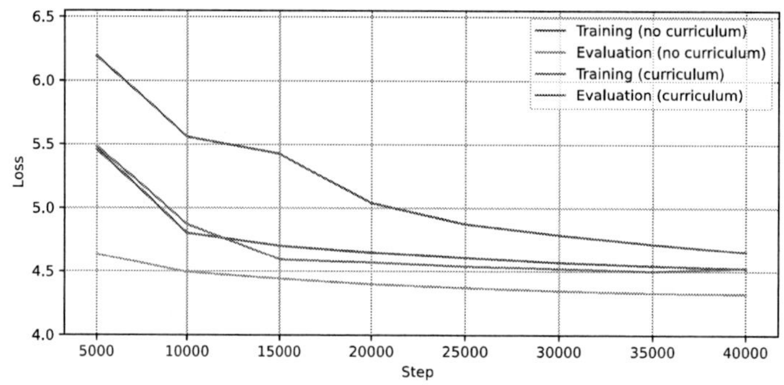

Figure 2: Training and evaluation losses for the 8k vocabulary models, calculated every 5k steps

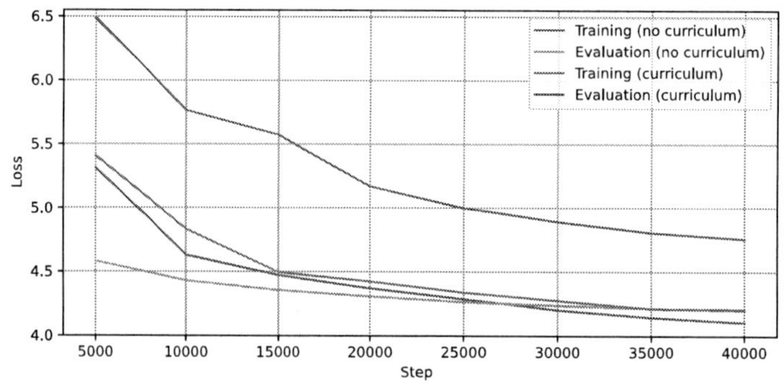

Figure 3: Training and evaluation losses for the 16k vocabulary models, calculated every 5k steps

Tiny Language Models Enriched with Multimodal Knowledge from Multiplex Networks

Clayton Fields claytonfields@u.boisestate.edu
Osama Natouf osamanatouf@u.boisestate.edu
Andrew McMains andrewmcmains@u.boisestate.edu
Catherine Henry catherinehenry@u.boisestate.edu
Casey Kennington caseykennington boisestate.edu

Department of Computer Science
Boise State University

Abstract

Large transformer language models trained exclusively on massive quantities of text are now the standard in NLP. In addition to the impractical amounts of data used to train them, they require enormous computational resources for training. Furthermore, they lack the rich array of sensory information available to humans, who can learn language with much less exposure to language. In this study, performed for submission in the BabyLM challenge, we show that we can improve a small transformer model's data efficiency by enriching its embeddings by swapping the learned word embeddings from a tiny transformer model with vectors extracted from a custom multiplex network that encodes visual and sensorimotor information. Further, we use a custom variation of the ELECTRA model that contains less than 7 million parameters and can be trained end-to-end using a single GPU. Our experiments show that models using these embeddings outperform equivalent models when pretrained with only the small BabyLM dataset, containing only 10 million words of text, on a variety of natural language understanding tasks from the GLUE and SuperGLUE benchmarks and a variation of the BLiMP task.

1 Introduction

The field of natural language processing is now dominated by large-scale transformer models such as GPT-3 (Brown et al., 2020). These models are characterized not only by their enormous size—billions of parameters—but also the huge datasets that are used in their pretraining. The 200 billion text tokens used to train GPT-3 are dwarfed by the 1.4 trillion used to train Chinchilla (Hoffmann et al., 2022). Huge model sizes and enormous pretraining datasets make research on pretraining language models impractical for all but the most lavishly funded industry research groups.

Beyond the practical problems posed by such massive data inputs, the current methods for language modeling require vastly more resources to learn and perform language tasks than human beings do. American children, for example, begin speaking around the age of 1 year on average (Gilkerson et al., 2017), and studies suggest that they have only heard around 5 million words before the onset of recognizable words (i.e., beyond babbling). Even the medium-sized BERT model was trained with a 3.3 billion word corpus (Devlin et al., 2019)—orders of magnitude more than human beings require to begin speaking and reach language proficiency. This disparity suggests that current methods in natural language procession (NLP) are missing crucial aspects of language learning.

One thing which models trained exclusively on text undoubtedly lack is a genuine connection between concrete words, such as *red*, and the physical world they describe. Human beings learn to speak with the aid of their sensory impressions, emotions and a rich environment of social cues (Smith and Gasser, 2005), which is to say that human language is grounded in the human sensory experience (Harnad, 1990). To use the same example, the word *red* is grounded in the visual perception of color. In contrast, transformer NLP models only have access to text and can only define words in terms of other words, following the distributional hypothesis of linguistic meaning. The lack of concrete sensory information is one possible reason why transformers require so much text and compute to learn perform basic human language tasks.

In this study, conducted as part of the BabyLM challenge (Warstadt et al., 2023), we seek to improve a tiny transformer model's data efficiency by providing it with a facsimile of that missing sensory information. Specifically, we follow the approach taken by Kennington (2021) and replace a pretrained model's word embeddings with vector representations that encode visual and sensorimotor information. Our approach differs in that we extract our embeddings from a custom multiplex network

Proceedings of the 27th Conference on Computational Natural Language Learning: Volume 2: The BabyLM Challenge, pages 47–57
December 6-7, 2023

that captures visual and sensorimotor relationships between words. Multiplex networks are multi-layer graphs, and researchers such as Ciaglia et al. (2023) have demonstrated their potential for representing various types of semantic relationships. Our multiplex network consists of two layers: a visual layer and a sensorimotor layer, which we explain below.

As one of the goals of our study, and the BabyLM challenge in general, is to increase a model's data effeciency, we pretrain our models with the cognitively plausible 10M word dataset provided by the BabyLM organizers. Additionally, with the aim of making research on pretraining transformer models more accessible, we use a tiny variation of ELECTRA (Clark et al., 2020) with fewer than 7 million parameters that can be trained on a single modestly priced GPU. This approach allows us to simultaneously address the topics of data efficiency and parameter efficiency. The contributions of our study can be summarized as follows:

- We show that tiny models can be as effective as models twice their size in a scarce pretraining data regime.
- We show that embeddings from a multiplex network that encodes visual and sensorimotor information related to English words can improve the data efficiency of a small transformer model.
- Models using these embeddings can perform as well as similar models that are trained with ten times the amount of pretraining data.

In the following section we present some work related to the topics associated with our modeling approach. In Section 3, we introduce both the pretraining datasets and the data we use to evaluate our models' downstream performance. Section 4 describe the ELECTRA model we use as the basis for our study and the multiplex network from which we extract our novel embeddings. Finally, we describe our experiments in Section 5 and conclude in Section 6.

2 Related Work

Data Efficient Pretraining for Language Models To date, model compression techniques for transformers have recieved more attention than data efficiency. There has, however, been some research directly addressing pretraining data types and sizes for transformers. Micheli et al. (2020) and Martin et al. (2019) experimented with reducing the absolute amount of training data in French language models. They showed that full sized French language transformer models can perform well on select tasks with significantly less pretraining data. Warstadt et al. (2020b) and Zhang et al. (2020) investigated the effect of different pretraining data volumes on the grammatical knowledge of the RoBERTa-base model using probing techniques. Another example is the BabyBERTa model introduced in Huebner et al. (2021). Here the authors used the CHILDES (MacWhinney, 2000), a small dataset of transcribed, child-directed speech to train a variation of RoBERTa (Liu et al., 2019). Notably, the CHILDES dataset is one the components of the dataset used in this study.

Small-Scale Language Models The process of creating transformers with fewer parameters and less computational demands has been an active area of research. A number of techniques for compressing transformers exist, but knowledge distillation is probably the most common. In knowledge distillation, a full-sized teacher model is used to train a smaller student network. DistilBERT (Sanh et al., 2019), TinyBERT (Jiao et al., 2019), MiniLM (Wang et al., 2020) and MobileBERT (Sun et al., 2020) are popular examples of compact transformers distilled using full sized BERT models as teachers. These methods produce effective smaller models, but they can't directly address the amount of input data required, and the training process still requires a using a full-sized teacher model trained with a large text corpus.

Multiplex Networks and Language Multiplex networks have been explored as a way of modeling the language acquisition process in human children (Stella et al., 2017, 2018). Citraro et al. (2023) used a complex network that incorporated phonetic, cooccurance, frequency, length, polysemy, (among others) to explore potential mental strategies for early word learning. Ciaglia et al. (2023) recently brought aspects of NLP into multiplex networks by including word-level embedding knowledge, which we build on here.

3 Data & Benchmarks

In this section we describe the datasets we use both for pretraining and for downstream evaluation of our models. As this paper was intended as part of

Dataset	Domain	Words-10M	Words-100M	Reference
CHILDES	Child-directed speech	0.44M	4.21M	MacWhinney (2000)
British National Corpus (BNC)	Dialogue	0.86M	8.16M	Consortium (2007)
Children's Book Test	Children's books	0.57M	5.55M	Hill et al. (2016)
Children's Stories Text Corpus	Children's books	0.34M	3.22M	Edenbd (2021)
Standardized Project Gutenberg	Written English	0.99M	9.46M	Gerlach and Font-Clos (2018)
OpenSubtitles	Movie subtitles	3.09M	31.28M	Lison and Tiedemann (2016)
QCRI Educational Domain Corpus	Video subtitles	1.04M	10.24M	Abdelali et al. (2014)
Wikipedia	Wikipedia	0.99M	10.08M	Wikimedia
Simple Wikipedia	Wikipedia (Simple)	1.52M	14.66M	Wikimedia
Switchboard Dialog Act Corpus	Dialogue	0.12M	1.18M	Stolcke et al. (2000)

Table 1: Composition of the BabyLM Datasets, from Warstadt et al. (2023).

the BabyLM competition, we use only the datasets provided by the organizers and their evaluation pipeline to assess our results. Although this information is described in Warstadt et al. (2023) and its associated references, we provide a brief summary in the interest of completeness and readability.

BabyLM Datasets The pretraining data provided for the BabyLM competition consists of two datasets with roughly 10 million and 100 million words. We will refer to these as the BabyLM-10M and the BabyLM-100M datasets. These datasets are meant to be developmentally plausible and are inspired by language input for children. The compositions of the datasets are described in Table 1 with references for each source dataset. The 10M word dataset is a uniform sample of the 100M word dataset.

GLUE and SuperGLUE Many of the datasets we use for fine-tuning and evaluation, are drawn from the GLUE (Wang et al., 2018) and SuperGLUE (Wang et al., 2019) benchmarks. Each consists of a suite of natural language understanding tasks and they are among the most commonly used benchmarks for evaluating natural language understanding. From GLUE, we use 7 of the 9 tasks in the suite. COLA, a grammatical acceptability task and SST-2, a sentiment classification task, are both single sentence tasks. QQP and MRPC are both two-sentence paraphrase tasks. Finally, MNLI, QNLI and RTE are natural language inference tasks. From SuperGLUE we use three tasks: BoolQ and MultiRC are both question answering tasks, and WSC is a co-reference task.

BLiMP The Benchmark of Linguistic Minimal Pairs (BLiMP) is a set of 67,000 pairs of sentences designed to test a language model's grasp of English grammar introduced in Warstadt et al. (2020a). The full BLiMP set consists of 67 sets of 1,000 pairs of English sentences covering 12 different grammatical phenomena. The sentences were generated from grammars created by linguists with each pair containing one grammatically correct and one incorrect sentence that differ by only a single edit. On aggregate, the creators found that humans agreed with the labels over 96 percent of the time. For each pair, a language model trained with causal language modeling, e.g. GPT-3, is considered to be successful if it assigns a higher likelihood to the grammatically correct sentence. BLiMP was concieved as a zero-shot task and many popular language models can be evaluated on BLiMP without fine-tuning using either the log-likelihood or the pseudo-log-likelihood scoring method (Wang and Cho, 2019; Salazar et al., 2020). Unfortunately, the ELECTRA model (Clark et al., 2020) that we use in our experiments is not one of them and we therefore adopt a minimal fine-tuning approach to the BLiMP task. To keep with the zero-shot spirit of the task as much as possible, we cast BLiMP as binary choice task with only enough training to remove large variances from run to run. The details of the fine-tuning regime that we used can be found in Section 5.2.

MSGS The MSGS dataset, pronounced *messages*, was introduced in Warstadt et al. (2020b) with the goal of studying the inductive biases of NLP models. The task challenges models to classify sentences based on either surface features, e.g. *Does the sentence contain the word "the"?*, or linguistic features, *Does the sentence contain an irregular past-tensed verb?*. In total the set contains 4 surface features and 5 linguistic features. By pairing a sentences containing a surface feature and a linguistic feature, the task tests a model's preference for surface features versus more meaningful linguistic features. The MSGS dataset contains 20 tasks, one for each possible combination of surface

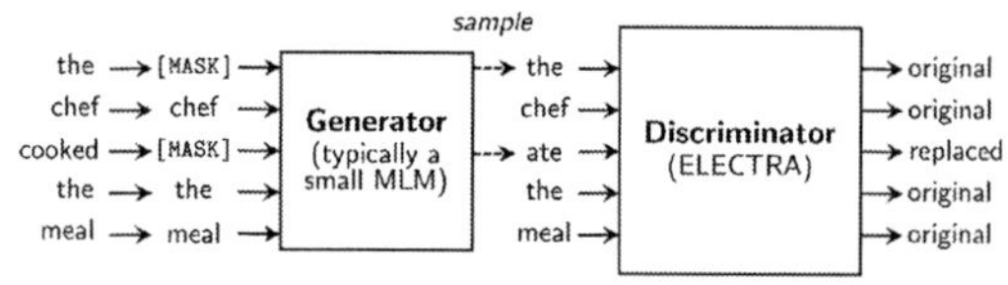

Figure 1: The ELECTRA model is a Generator-Discriminator ensemble. The Discriminator is tasked with determining if the Generator properly guessed a masked word; borrowed from (Clark et al., 2020).

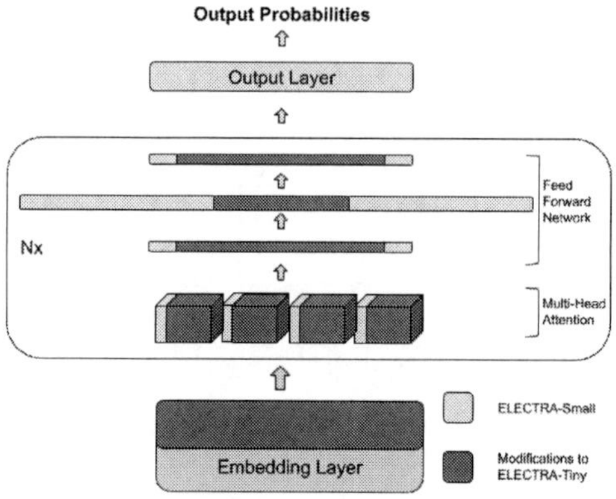

Figure 2: Relative size comparison of ELECTRA-Small (blue) with ELECTRA-Tiny (red). ELECTRA-Tiny has smaller embeddings, hidden size, and intermediate size, but has more hidden layers.

and linguistic features, as well as 9 control tasks whose sentences contain only a surface or linguistic feature being tested. From this set we use 5 control tasks and 6 from the set of combinations. A more detailed description of these tasks can also be found in Section 5.2.

4 Method

4.1 ELECTRA-Tiny

In this subsection we describe ELECTRA (Clark et al., 2020), the language model that forms the basis of our experiments. In place of masked language modeling, ELECTRA pretrains a transformer encoder stack, structurally identical to BERT's, by corrupting some input tokens through replacing them with plausible alternative words sampled from a small generator network. A larger discriminator model then predicts whether each token is corrupted or not. After training, the generator is discarded and the discriminator is used for downstream tasks. See Figure 1 for an illustration of the ELECTRA model. Clark et al. (2020) show that this strategy leads to better results with less data and less compute than causal language modeling or standard masked language modeling, making it a natural choice for use in these experiments.

We make use of two architectural variations of ELECTRA. ELECTRA-Small is a scaled down version of the base model that was also introduced in Clark et al. (2020). This small version of ELECTRA has embedding vectors of dimension 128, 12 layers and a hidden size of 256. Following the original transformer architecture in (Vaswani et al., 2017), the intermediate size of each layer's feed-forward network is 4 times the model's hidden size, or 1024. In total, it contains only 14 million parameters and can be trained end to end using a single GPU. The other model we use is an even smaller variation that we call ELECTRA-Tiny and it was introduced and evaluated in Fields and Kennington (2023). ELECTRA-Tiny is very small, containing only 6.7 million parameters, approximately half as many as ELECTRA-Small. The tiny variation of ELECTRA however, is not simply scaled down with the same proportions. The model has an embedding size of 96, a hidden size of 196 and rather than a 4-fold expansion of the feed-forward network's intermediate layer, reduces the layer's size to 128. Finally, to compensate for the models decreased width, it contains 18 layers. The combination of an efficient pretraining method and small model sizes make these models ideal for our purposes. Figure 2 shows how ELECTRA-Small and ELECTRA-Tiny compare in their underlying sizes.

4.2 Enriching ELECTRA-Tiny with Multimodal Knowledge: Multiplex Networks

A multiplex network is a type of conceptual network that consists of multiple *layers*, where each layer represents a different type of relationship or interaction between nodes. In a multiplex network, the nodes can be the same across layers (which means nodes can be duplicated across different layers), but the relationships between them may vary. Figure 3 shows an example of a multiplex network that has five nodes composed of two layers.

A multiplex network can be represented as a multilayer graph, where the nodes are connected by edges in each layer and potentially across different layers. The layers can capture different aspects or modalities of the interactions between the entities. For example, in Ciaglia et al. (2023), the authors used a small vocabulary of words as the nodes, where the layers of their multiplex network were represented by free association (i.e., when presented with a word, participants were asked to write the first word that comes to mind), visual relationships, sensory relationships, and distributional semantic relationships.

In any weighted multiplex network, the connections between nodes can have different types or strengths, depending on the layer and the weight on the edge. This allows for a more comprehensive representation of the relationships between nodes, as different layers capture different aspects of the relationships. Multiplex networks can provide richer information than a standard network that is made up of only one layer.

Ciaglia et al. (2023)'s network was composed of layers derived from word embeddings, free association, visual and sensorimotor vectors. Their work only included a vocabulary of 531; we extend their work by dramatically increasing the vocabulary covered in the multiplex network. Important for our work here is to only use layers that are cognitively plausible for a language learning child to have as they speak their initial words. As the embedding and free association layers were derived using adult written text and adult participants respectively, we leave them out of our model here and focus only on the visual and sensorimotor layers; modalities that children certainly have access to and from which they build their language learning.

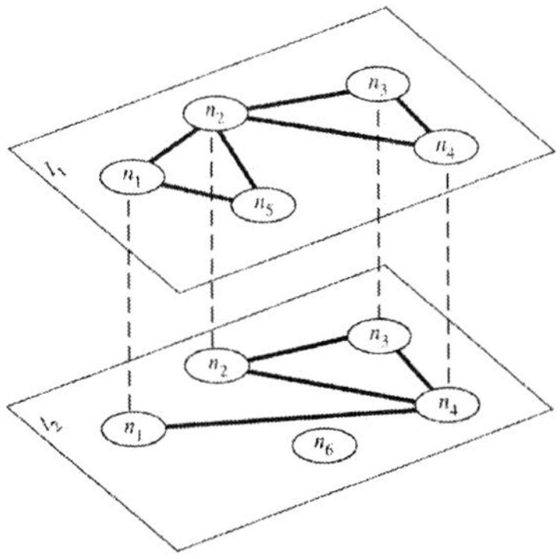

Figure 3: From Bródka et al. (2018). A visual representation of a multiplex network demonstrating interconnected layers. The dotted lines represent the interlayer connections (node relationships across layers) while the solid lines represent intralayer connections (node relationships within a layer).

Visual Layer: Words-as-Classifiers To represent the visual layer, we use the word-as-classifiers (WAC) model of grounded lexical semantics (Kennington and Schlangen, 2015). We train a binary logistic regression classifier that learns the *fitness* of identifying a visual aspect (e.g., *redness*) on images for each vocabulary word (e.g., images of dogs for the word *dog*) and randomly sampled negative images from other words. We use 100 positive images for each word with a ratio of 3 negative examples for each positive example. Each image is encoded as a vector for training using the CLIP model (Radford et al., 2021). Once each classifier for each word is trained, we take the learned coefficients and bias term as the vector (size 513) representing the word.

Sensorimotor Layer: Lancaster Sensorimotor Norms The Lancaster dataset (Lynott et al., 2020) uses the Lancaster Norms rating as a measure of perceptual and action strength on about 40K English words. Sensorimotor information plays a fundamental role in cognition and provides a useful connection between words and understanding. For example, the word *kick* has a strong sensorimotor grounding in leg and foot movement, the word *sour* is grounded in taste, and the word *ping* is grounded in auditory processing. For each word in the dataset, raters were asked to rate how strongly that word is associated with a specific perceptual modality including touch, hearing, smell, taste, vision, and interoception, and five action effectors including mouth/throat, hand/arm, foot/leg, head excluding mouth/throat, and torso. The dataset reports the mean and standard deviation of the ratings, as well as ways of aggregating the ratings, which we use as a vector (size of 39) for each word.

Constructing the Multiplex Network Kennington (2021) used the WAC and Lancaster vectors as the embedding layer for a language model in their experiments. We use the same modalities here, but we first combine the two modalities into a multiplex network and then extract the embeddings from the network to use for the embedding layer. This approach, we argue, is more cognitively plausible because words are associated by vision and sensorimotor modalities at a more categorical level, which is the basis of cognition (Harnad, 2017).

To create the network, we had to determine if two words had a relationship within a layer. To do so, we computed the cosine distance between all possible word pairs in each layer, forming relationships between words (i.e., the nodes) if the cosine

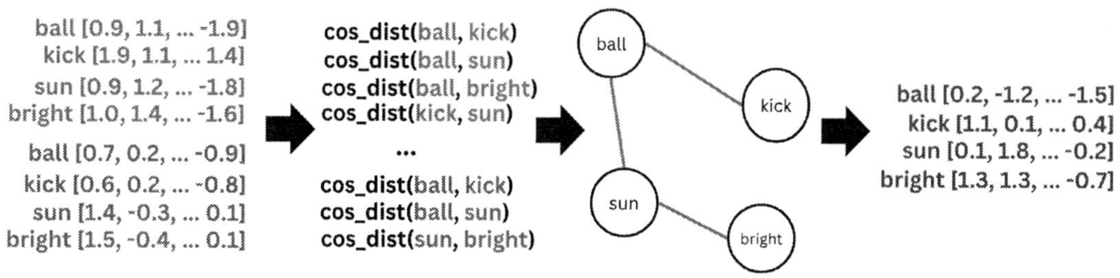

Figure 4: **Our Methodology**: vectors from vision (red, top) and sensorimotor (purple, bottom) are compared to each other using cosine distance. Word pairs that are above a specific threshold are added to the network, where connections from different modalities are retained in a multiple network (e.g., *ball* and *kick* are similar in sensorimotor vectors, whereas *ball* and *sun* are shaped similarly visually). Finally, we use the MultiVERSE algorithm to map from the multiplex network to the vector embeddings used in ELECTRA-Tiny.

distance was above a specific threshold. The selection of these thresholds was motivated by the goal of striking a balance between sparsity and density in the network, taking into account computational constraints associated with extracting the network embeddings. We then used those resulting embeddings in the ELECTRA-Tiny model. The process is depicted visually in Figure 4. In our experiments, we use three networks: visual only (cosine distance threshold of 0.94, vocabulary size of 21,235), sensorimotor only (cosine distance threshold of 0.27, vocabulary size of 22,054), and a multiplex combination of visual and sensorimotor (same thresholds as individual layers, vocabuary size of 35,607).

From Multiplex Network back to Embeddings: MultiVERSE We use the MultiVERSE algorithm, introduced in Pio-Lopez et al. (2021) to map from our multiplex network representation back to embeddings to be used in a language model. MultiVERSE is a network representation learning algorithm tailored for multiplex networks that aims to capture complex interactions by considering interdependencies between layers. By employing a unified framework integrating the multiplex network structure, node attributes, and meta-path-guided random walks, MultiVERSE learns low-dimensional node representations, clustering nodes with similar relationships. Importantly, the Random Walk with Restart algorithm explores different layers in parallel (i.e., the layers are represented as separate *sub*-networks instead of a complete network), retraining multiplex relationships. In contrast, other well-known algorithms that map from networks to embeddings, like node2vec (Grover and Leskovec, 2016), do not adequately retain multiplex information from each individual layer, making MultiVERSE a superior choice for mapping multiplex network representations to meaningful embeddings for downstream language model applications while maintaining the meaning from different relationships in different layers. This resulted in embeddings for many words in the ELECTRA vocabulary, but for the words that were not represented, we simply used zero vectors.

5 Experiments

5.1 Experiment 1: GLUE and SuperGLUE Tasks

In this experiment we determine to what extent embeddings extracted from our multiplex network can improve our small scale models on natural language understanding tasks. We begin by pretraining ELECTRA-Tiny on the BabyLM-10M word dataset described in Section 3 for 10 epochs using the Adam optimizer (Kingma and Ba, 2014), with a lerning rate of 1e-5 and a batch size of 64. Following Kennington (2021), our strategy is to swap the learned word embeddings from the pretrained model with our own embeddings prior to finetuning and evaluation. Using the MultiVERSE algorithm we extract three sets of embeddings from our network corresponding to the WAC visual layer, the Lancaster Norm layer and the multiplex combination of both layers. We then finetune the ELECTRA-Tiny model with each embedding set as well as a control model using ELECTRA's learned word embeddings. We fine-tune each model for ten epochs with a learning rate of 5e-5, and a batch size of 64. For the sake of comparison, we also trained ELECTRA-Tiny on the 100M word dataset and the original ELECTRA-Small (Clark et al., 2020) on the 10M dataset.

Model	Data	COLA	RTE	MultiRC	QQP	QNLI	MNLI	MNLI-mm	SST2	Avg.
Tiny	10M	69.5	48.9	60.4	63.2	56.6	42.2	42.8	81.0	60.7
Tiny-L	10M	69.5	49.5	55.9	63.4	57.4	48.6	49.1	78.0	58.9
Tiny-V	10M	67.1	62.6	59.5	62.4	57.9	49.6	51.2	82.1	63.2
Tiny-LV	10M	67.1	62.6	59.5	62.4	57.9	49.6	51.2	82.1	63.2
Small	10M	69.3	50.5	56.3	62.2	57.0	39.5	39.0	81.3	59.9
Tiny	100M	69.5	54.5	56.0	64.3	58.8	51.5	51.5	81.7	62.8
Maj. Label	10M	69.5	53.1	59.9	53.1	35.4	35.7	35.7	50.2	52.6
OPT-125m	10M	64.6	60.0	55.2	60.4	61.5	60.0	57.6	81.9	63.4
RoBERTa	10M	70.8	61.6	61.4	73.7	77.0	73.2	74.0	87.0	71.4
T5-base	10M	61.2	49.4	47.1	66.2	62.0	48.0	50.3	78.1	60.9

Table 2: **GLUE and SuperGLUE results for the initial datasets on our various models.** Note that the last size models in the table are baselines included for the sake of comparison.

Model	Data	MRPC	RTE	MultiRC	QQP	QNLI	MNLI	MNLI-mm	SST2	Avg.
Tiny	10M	82.0	53.5	56.6	66.3	53.1	62.4	62.0	82.7	64.5
Tiny-L	10M	82.0	49.5	58.1	78.8	53.2	64.9	66.7	82.3	66.9
Tiny-V	10M	82.0	63.6	59.8	76.4	53.1	63.3	65.8	85.2	67.3
Tiny-LV	10M	81.6	54.5	57.0	76.5	59.4	66.3	67.2	84.4	67.1
Small	10M	82.0	50.5	58.1	73.2	53.1	60.3	60.7	81.1	64.5
Tiny	100M	82.0	53.5	50.9	79.3	61.3	67.4	67.6	86.6	67.2

Table 3: **GLUE and SuperGLUE results for our various model using the held-out portion of data.** Note that the last two models in the table are baselines, provided for the sake of comparison.

Results For ease of comparison we present our results for initial datasets and the portion held out by the BabyLM challenge organizers separately. The results for each model on the various tasks are displayed in Tables 2 and 3. Table 2 also includes the baseline values provided by the BabyLM organizers using the 10M dataset. Firstly, we note that the standard ELECTRA-Tiny model performs nearly identically with ELECTRA-Small when trained on the 10M word dataset and the T5-base model that was provided as a baseline by the BabyLM organizers. This indicates that larger models are not necessarily superior when using a very small training corpus. The model using embeddings derived from our Lancaster Norm layer showed little difference over the standard ELECTRA-Tiny model. The model using embeddings from the WAC visual layer, however, performed substantially better. In particular, it produced the highest score that we tested on the RTE textual entailment task. It also performed nearly as well on the MNLI tasks as the ELECTRA-Tiny model trained with ten times as much data.

The model using embeddings extracted from the combined layer performed nearly identically to the model containing embeddings from the visual layer on both data splits. This suggests that the model is better able to use the visual information provided via embeddings from the WAC layer of our multiplex than the embeddings extracted from the multiplex's Lancaster Norm layer on natural language understanding tasks. Whether the model benefits more from visual information than sensorimotor information or whether the disparity comes from the nature of our multiplex network can't be determined within the confines of this study. We can, however, definitively say that the visual information in our multiplex embeddings provide a significant boost to model performance in a low data training regime. These results verify prior work (Kennington, 2021), with some differences, that suggest that mapping the visual and sensorimotor sources of information to a network representation, then back to embeddings provides rich and useful information.

Several of the tasks produced identical scores for each model that we evaluated, even the model that was pretrained on the 100M dataset. Each variation yielded a score of 59.9 on BoolQ and 61.4 on WSC using both the initial and held-out datasets. Using the initial dataset each model scored 82.0 on MRPC. Each model also uniformly scored 69.5 on COLA using the held-out data. These results aren't displayed in the tables though their values contribute to the figures listed in the **Avg.** column of each table. Though this is somewhat surprising, we surmise that these scores would vary with additional data and extending training times.

Model	Data	BLiMP	CR_LC	CR_RP	MV_LC	MV_RP	SC_LC	SC_RP
Tiny	10M	60.1	66.2	66.7	66.6	67.0	67.5	66.6
Tiny-L	10M	63.1	66.0	66.6	66.6	66.8	70.6	58.9
Tiny-V	10M	64.1	66.5	66.9	66.6	66.4	67.5	72.0
Tiny-LV	10M	65.1	66.6	66.7	66.6	67.2	68.0	67.6
Small	10M	61.8	66.0	66.7	66.6	66.4	67.4	63.6
Tiny	100M	64.6	66.0	68.2	66.6	67.6	71.3	68.5
OPT-125m	10M	N/A	66.5	67.0	66.5	67.6	80.2	67.5
RoBERTa	10M	N/A	67.7	68.6	66.7	68.6	84.2	65.7
T5-base	10M	N/A	66.7	69.7	66.6	66.9	73.6	67.8

Table 4: **BLiMP and MSGS results for various models.** Note that the last 5 models are baselines included for the sake of comparison. BLiMP scores are note included for baselines provided by the BabyLM organizers as they are not directly comparable to our scores produced through minimal fine-tuning.

5.2 Experiment 2: BLiMP and MSGS Syntactic Tasks

In this experiment we evaluate our models on a set of tasks devoted to testing their grammatical capacity and their inductive biases. Following the BabyLM guidelines, we use the BLiMP dataset to measure the grammatical capacity of our models. The evaluation pipeline for BabyLM treats BLiMP as a zero-shot task using the method of Wang and Cho (2019) or Salazar et al. (2020). Unfortunately, ELECTRA's novel pretraining task is not compatible with either method and produces scores at chance levels for every model variation. In order to make use of BLiMP, and to do so in the closest way possible to the zero-shot paradigm, we create a minimal fine-tuning regime for BLiMP. We treat BLiMP as a binary choice task and train for 1 epoch with only ten percent of each of BLiMP's 67 data subsets in the training split. We use the ADAM optimizer (Kingma and Ba, 2014), with a learning rate of 2e-5 and a batch size of 32. This allows us to obtain consistent results using minimal finetuning. We use the default methods and hyper-parameters provided and finetune for ten epochs with a learning rate of 5e-5 and a batch size of 64. Per BabyLM, we use 5 control tasks and 6 of the ambiguous evaluation tasks. Of the 5 controls, we have two surface features, Lexical Content (LC) and Relative Position (RP), and three linguistic features, Control Raising (CR), Main Verb (MV) and Syntactic Category (SC). The features are combined to form the MSGS tasks in which our models are measured for preference of linguistic features over surface features via Matthews correlation (Matthews, 1975).

Results As our results for BLiMP are not directly comparable to the zero-shot baselines of the BabyLM submissions, we list only the overall average BLiMP score over all 67 data subsets it contains. In the third column of Table 4 we see the BLiMP results for our various models. In each case, the embeddings derived from our multiplex network improved the results over our baseline ELECTRA-Tiny model trained on the 10M dataset. This result is somewhat surprising in that we had not expected concrete sensory information to benefit an abstract task such a grammatical acceptability. Further, we noticed no similar effect relative to the COLA task, the only grammatical acceptability task conducted in the first experiment. That said, we feel confident in claiming that our models derive definite benefit from multi-modal embeddings in a fine-tuning variation of BLiMP.

The results that we obtain for the various MSGS tasks are less definitive. The results for the main task are displayed in Table 4. None of our embeddings seem to have a significant effect, either positive or negative, on model performance for the main MSGS tasks. The only model that we trained that showed a broad increase in performance was the ELECTRA-Tiny model trained with the 100M word dataset. When considered with our other results, this suggests that a model's tendency to adopt favorable inductive biases may primarily be a function of dataset size.

6 Conclusion

In this study, performed in response to the BabyLM challenge, we have shown that small language models can be made more data efficient by enriching their embeddings with sensory information. In particular, the embeddings derived from the Words as Classifiers layer of our multiplex network improve model performance on a variety of tasks from GLUE, SuperGLUE and a version of BLiMP recast as a fine-tuning task. Embeddings derived from Lancaster Sensorimotor Norms likewise provided useful information for the language models that we evaluated on the BLiMP task, but were less effective on the GLUE and SuperGLUE tasks. Our results from the MSGS evaluations suggest that our models don't gain strong inductive biases toward deep linguistic features as defined by the MSGS task.

Limitations

Our choice to conduct our study on very small models means that our results cannot be assumed to generalize to much larger models. This of course limits the applicability of the findings we have presented. It also stands to reason that multimodal information, like the kind we used to enrich our models, could improve the performance of language models trained on traditional large-scale datasets. Due to the dataset restrictions of the BabyLM challenge, this was also outside the scope of our study and is left to future research.

Acknowledgements

We are grateful to the BabyLM Challenge organizers for making this important challenge happen. Thanks to the anonymous reviewers for their very useful feedback. This material is based upon work supported by the National Science Foundation under Grant No. 2140642.

References

Ahmed Abdelali, Francisco Guzman, Hassan Sajjad, and Stephan Vogel. 2014. The amara corpus: Building parallel language resources for the educational domain. In *LREC*, volume 14, pages 1044–1054.

Piotr Bródka, Anna Chmiel, Matteo Magnani, and Giancarlo Ragozini. 2018. Quantifying layer similarity in multiplex networks: a systematic study. *R Soc Open Sci*, 5(8):171747.

Tom Brown, Benjamin Mann, Nick Ryder, Melanie Subbiah, Jared D Kaplan, Prafulla Dhariwal, Arvind Neelakantan, Pranav Shyam, Girish Sastry, Amanda Askell, et al. 2020. Language models are few-shot learners. *Advances in neural information processing systems*, 33:1877–1901.

Floriana Ciaglia, Massimo Stella, and Casey Kennington. 2023. Investigating preferential acquisition and attachment in early word learning through cognitive, visual and latent multiplex lexical networks. *Physica A: Statistical Mechanics and its Applications*, 612:128468.

Salvatore Citraro, Michael S Vitevitch, Massimo Stella, and Giulio Rossetti. 2023. Feature-rich multiplex lexical networks reveal mental strategies of early language learning. *Sci. Rep.*, 13(1):1474.

Kevin Clark, Minh-Thang Luong, Quoc V Le, and Christopher D Manning. 2020. Electra: Pre-training text encoders as discriminators rather than generators. *arXiv preprint arXiv:2003.10555*.

B N C Consortium. 2007. British national corpus. *Oxford Text Archive Core Collection*.

Jacob Devlin, Ming-Wei Chang, Kenton Lee, and Kristina Toutanova. 2019. Bert: Pre-training of deep bidirectional transformers for language understanding. In *Proceedings of the 2019 Conference of the North American Chapter of the Association for Computational Linguistics: Human Language Technologies, Volume 1 (Long and Short Papers)*, pages 4171–4186.

Edenbd. 2021. Children stories text corpus.

Clayton Fields and Casey Kennington. 2023. Exploring transformers as compact, data-efficient language models. In *Proceedings of the 27th Conference on Computational Natural Language Learning*. Association for Computational Linguistics.

Martin Gerlach and Francesc Font-Clos. 2018. A standardized project gutenberg corpus for statistical analysis of natural language and quantitative linguistics.

Jill Gilkerson, Jeffrey A Richards, Steven F Warren, Judith K Montgomery, Charles R Greenwood, D Kimbrough Oller, John HL Hansen, and Terrance D Paul. 2017. Mapping the early language environment using all-day recordings and automated analysis. *American journal of speech-language pathology*, 26(2):248–265.

Aditya Grover and Jure Leskovec. 2016. node2vec: Scalable feature learning for networks. *KDD*, 2016:855–864.

Stevan Harnad. 1990. The symbol grounding problem. *Physica D*, 42(1-3):335–346.

Stevan Harnad. 2017. To cognize is to categorize: Cognition is categorization. In *Handbook of Categorization in Cognitive Science*, pages 21–54.

Felix Hill, Antoine Bordes, Sumit Chopra, and Jason Weston. 2016. The goldilocks principle: Reading children's books with explicit memory representations.

Jordan Hoffmann, Sebastian Borgeaud, Arthur Mensch, Elena Buchatskaya, Trevor Cai, Eliza Rutherford, Diego de Las Casas, Lisa Anne Hendricks, Johannes Welbl, Aidan Clark, Tom Hennigan, Eric Noland, Katie Millican, George van den Driessche, Bogdan Damoc, Aurelia Guy, Simon Osindero, Karen Simonyan, Erich Elsen, Jack W. Rae, Oriol Vinyals, and Laurent Sifre. 2022. Training compute-optimal large language models.

Philip A Huebner, Elior Sulem, Fisher Cynthia, and Dan Roth. 2021. Babyberta: Learning more grammar with small-scale child-directed language. In *Proceedings of the 25th conference on computational natural language learning*, pages 624–646.

Xiaoqi Jiao, Yichun Yin, Lifeng Shang, Xin Jiang, Xiao Chen, Linlin Li, Fang Wang, and Qun Liu. 2019. Tinybert: Distilling bert for natural language understanding. *arXiv preprint arXiv:1909.10351*.

Casey Kennington. 2021. Enriching language models with visually-grounded word vectors and the Lancaster sensorimotor norms. In *Proceedings of the 25th Conference on Computational Natural Language Learning*, pages 148–157, Online. Association for Computational Linguistics.

Casey Kennington and David Schlangen. 2015. Simple learning and compositional application of perceptually grounded word meanings for incremental reference resolution. In *Proceedings of the 53rd Annual Meeting of the Association for Computational Linguistics and the 7th International Joint Conference on Natural Language Processing (Volume 1: Long Papers)*, pages 292–301, Beijing, China. Association for Computational Linguistics.

Diederik P Kingma and Jimmy Ba. 2014. Adam: A method for stochastic optimization. *arXiv preprint arXiv:1412.6980*.

Pierre Lison and Jörg Tiedemann. 2016. OpenSubtitles2016: Extracting large parallel corpora from movie and TV subtitles. In *Proceedings of the Tenth International Conference on Language Resources and Evaluation (LREC'16)*, pages 923–929, Portorož, Slovenia. European Language Resources Association (ELRA).

Yinhan Liu, Myle Ott, Naman Goyal, Jingfei Du, Mandar Joshi, Danqi Chen, Omer Levy, Mike Lewis, Luke Zettlemoyer, and Veselin Stoyanov. 2019. Roberta: A robustly optimized bert pretraining approach. *arXiv preprint arXiv:1907.11692*.

Dermot Lynott, Louise Connell, Marc Brysbaert, James Brand, and James Carney. 2020. The lancaster sensorimotor norms: multidimensional measures of perceptual and action strength for 40,000 english words. *Behavior Research Methods*, 52:1271–1291.

Brian MacWhinney. 2000. *The CHILDES project: The database*, volume 2. Psychology Press.

Louis Martin, Benjamin Muller, Pedro Javier Ortiz Suárez, Yoann Dupont, Laurent Romary, Éric Villemonte de La Clergerie, Djamé Seddah, and Benoît Sagot. 2019. Camembert: a tasty french language model. *arXiv preprint arXiv:1911.03894*.

Brian W Matthews. 1975. Comparison of the predicted and observed secondary structure of t4 phage lysozyme. *Biochimica et Biophysica Acta (BBA)-Protein Structure*, 405(2):442–451.

Vincent Micheli, Martin d'Hoffschmidt, and François Fleuret. 2020. On the importance of pre-training data volume for compact language models. In *Proceedings of the 2020 Conference on Empirical Methods in Natural Language Processing (EMNLP)*, pages 7853–7858, Online. Association for Computational Linguistics.

Léo Pio-Lopez, Alberto Valdeolivas, Laurent Tichit, Élisabeth Remy, and Anaïs Baudot. 2021. Multiverse: a multiplex and multiplex-heterogeneous network embedding approach. *Scientific reports*, 11(1):8794.

Alec Radford, Jong Wook Kim, Chris Hallacy, Aditya Ramesh, Gabriel Goh, Sandhini Agarwal, Girish Sastry, Amanda Askell, Pamela Mishkin, Jack Clark, Gretchen Krueger, and Ilya Sutskever. 2021. Learning transferable visual models from natural language supervision.

Julian Salazar, Davis Liang, Toan Q. Nguyen, and Katrin Kirchhoff. 2020. Masked language model scoring. In *Proceedings of the 58th Annual Meeting of the Association for Computational Linguistics*, pages 2699–2712, Online. Association for Computational Linguistics.

Victor Sanh, Lysandre Debut, Julien Chaumond, and Thomas Wolf. 2019. Distilbert, a distilled version of bert: smaller, faster, cheaper and lighter. *arXiv preprint arXiv:1910.01108*.

Linda Smith and Michael Gasser. 2005. The development of embodied cognition: Six lessons from babies. *Artif. Life*, (11):13–29.

Massimo Stella, Nicole M Beckage, and Markus Brede. 2017. Multiplex lexical networks reveal patterns in early word acquisition in children. *Sci. Rep.*, 7:46730.

Massimo Stella, Nicole M Beckage, Markus Brede, and Manlio De Domenico. 2018. Multiplex model of mental lexicon reveals explosive learning in humans. *Scientific Reports, Nature*, 8(1):2259.

Andreas Stolcke, Klaus Ries, Noah Coccaro, Elizabeth Shriberg, Rebecca Bates, Daniel Jurafsky, Paul Taylor, Rachel Martin, Carol Van Ess-Dykema, and Marie Meteer. 2000. Dialogue act modeling for automatic tagging and recognition of conversational speech. *Computational linguistics*, 26(3):339–373.

Zhiqing Sun, Hongkun Yu, Xiaodan Song, Renjie Liu, Yiming Yang, and Denny Zhou. 2020. Mobilebert: a compact task-agnostic bert for resource-limited devices. *arXiv preprint arXiv:2004.02984*.

Ashish Vaswani, Noam Shazeer, Niki Parmar, Jakob Uszkoreit, Llion Jones, Aidan N Gomez, Łukasz Kaiser, and Illia Polosukhin. 2017. Attention is all you need. *Adv. Neural Inf. Process. Syst.*, 30.

Alex Wang and Kyunghyun Cho. 2019. BERT has a mouth, and it must speak: BERT as a Markov random field language model. In *Proceedings of the Workshop on Methods for Optimizing and Evaluating Neural Language Generation*, pages 30–36, Minneapolis, Minnesota. Association for Computational Linguistics.

Alex Wang, Yada Pruksachatkun, Nikita Nangia, Amanpreet Singh, Julian Michael, Felix Hill, Omer Levy, and Samuel Bowman. 2019. Superglue: A stickier benchmark for general-purpose language understanding systems. *Advances in neural information processing systems*, 32.

Alex Wang, Amanpreet Singh, Julian Michael, Felix Hill, Omer Levy, and Samuel R Bowman. 2018. Glue: A multi-task benchmark and analysis platform for natural language understanding. *arXiv preprint arXiv:1804.07461*.

Wenhui Wang, Furu Wei, Li Dong, Hangbo Bao, Nan Yang, and Ming Zhou. 2020. Minilm: Deep self-attention distillation for task-agnostic compression of pre-trained transformers. *Advances in Neural Information Processing Systems*, 33:5776–5788.

Alex Warstadt, Aaron Mueller, Leshem Choshen, Ethan Gotlieb Wilcox, Chengxu Zhuang, Juan Ciro, Rafael Mosquera, Adina Williams, Bhargavi Paranjabe, Tal Linzen, and Ryan Cotterell. 2023. Findings of the 2023 BabyLM Challenge: Sample-efficient pretraining on developmentally plausible corpora. In *Proceedings of the 2023 BabyLM Challenge*. Association for Computational Linguistics (ACL).

Alex Warstadt, Alicia Parrish, Haokun Liu, Anhad Mohananey, Wei Peng, Sheng-Fu Wang, and Samuel R Bowman. 2020a. Blimp: The benchmark of linguistic minimal pairs for english. *Transactions of the Association for Computational Linguistics*, 8:377–392.

Alex Warstadt, Yian Zhang, Haau-Sing Li, Haokun Liu, and Samuel R Bowman. 2020b. Learning which features matter: Roberta acquires a preference for linguistic generalizations (eventually). *arXiv preprint arXiv:2010.05358*.

Wikimedia. simplewiki. `https://dumps.wikimedia.org/simplewiki/20230301/`. Accessed: 2023-7-31.

Yian Zhang, Alex Warstadt, Haau-Sing Li, and Samuel R Bowman. 2020. When do you need billions of words of pretraining data? *arXiv preprint arXiv:2011.04946*.

Mini Minds: Exploring Bebeshka and Zlata Baby Models

Irina Proskurina, Guillaume Metzler, Julien Velcin
Université de Lyon, Lyon 2, ERIC UR 3083, France
Correspondence: Irina.Proskurina@univ-lyon2.fr

Abstract

In this paper, we describe the University of Lyon 2 submission to the STRICT-SMALL track of the BabyLM competition. The shared task is created with an emphasis on small-scale language modelling from scratch on limited-size data and human language acquisition. Dataset released for STRICT-SMALL track has 10M words, which is comparable to children's vocabulary size. We approach the task with an architecture search, minimizing masked language modelling loss on the data of the shared task. Having found an optimal configuration, we introduce two small-size language models (LMs) that were submitted for evaluation, a 4-layer encoder with 8 attention heads and a 6-layer decoder model with 12 heads which we term Bebeshka and Zlata, respectively. Despite being half the scale of the baseline LMs, our proposed models achieve comparable performance. We further explore the applicability of small-scale language models in tasks involving moral judgment, aligning their predictions with human values. These findings highlight the potential of compact LMs in addressing practical language understanding tasks. We make our code and models publicly available.[1]

1 Introduction

LMs accurately encode language-specific phenomena required for natural language understanding and generating coherent continuation of text. LMs gain language understanding about morphosyntax and grammar from large corpora during pre-training. However, they demonstrate partial functional linguistic competence when applying grammatical knowledge to novel expressions at inference time, which is caused by memorising the most occurring linguistic patterns from the training corpus and limited generalization ability of learnt linguistic representations (Wu et al., 2022; Tucker et al., 2022; Mahowald et al., 2023).

Recent pre-training dynamics studies revealed that the performance of LMs can be seen as a function of training corpus vocabulary: (1) grammatical knowledge improves with the expansion of the pre-training data vocabulary (van Schijndel et al., 2019) and (2) small-scale LMs can perform on par with RoBERTa if the vocabulary of used tokenizer is close to the actual human and even child's vocabulary (Liu et al., 2019).

In this paper, we introduce small-scale LMs with an architecture optimized for the STRICT-SMALL track data of BabyLM competition (Warstadt et al., 2023). Our objective is to estimate the general performance and capabilities of shallow LMs in downstream tasks beyond the ones suggested in the evaluation pipeline of shared task. That was achieved through two main contributions.

Contribution 1. We determine an optimal architecture of encoder-based LMs using the Tree-structured Parzen Estimator algorithm and minimal perplexity as a minimizing objective function. Our parameter search results suggest that optimal LMs have a ratio of attention heads to layers around 2, while the ratio of previously tested and existing LMs at their base configuration is equal to one. We introduce new small-scale LMs submitted to the shared task: (*i*) 4-layer encoder Bebeshka[2] and (*ii*) 6-layer decoder Zlata.[3] The parameters of the models are presented in Table 1. Our LMs perform on par with the shared task baselines, while they are half the size of those.

Contribution 2. We investigate the alignment of small-scale LMs predictions with shared human values in the context of moral judgment tasks. We find that shallow LMs, yet trained on limited corpora, perform on par with base LMs in commonsense morality scenarios, and, surprisingly outper-

[1]`https://github.com/upunaprosk/small-language-models`

[2]A word used to call a baby in a range of South and East Slavic languages.

[3]From Zlato ("Golden sweetheart") used to call babies in West and East Slavic languages.

Proceedings of the 27th Conference on Computational Natural Language Learning: Volume 2: The BabyLM Challenge, pages 58–68
December 6-7, 2023 ©2023 Association for Computational Linguistics

Parameter	RoBERTa	Bebeshka	GPT-2	Zlata
Pre-training objective	MLM	MLM	CLM	CLM
Vocabulary size	50K	8K	50K	30K
#Parameters	125M	16M	345M	66M
Positional embedding type	absolute	rel. key query	absolute	absolute
Maximum sequence length	512	128	1024	1024
(L, A, H, F)	(12, 12, 64, 3072)	(4, 8, 70, 1412)	(24, 16, 64, 4x 1024)	(6, 12, 64, 4x 768)
Activation function	GELU	New GELU	New GELU	GELU
Dropout probability	0.1	0.15	0.1	0.2
Attention dropout	0.1	0.3	0.1	0.2
Processing	1024x V100	4x IPU-M2000	64x V100	4x IPU-M2000
Processing time	1 day	4h	>30 days	6h
Epochs	>40	10	>40	10

Table 1: Model configurations and pre-training details of Bebeshka and Zlata LMs compared to RoBERTa-base and GPT-2 medium. Our LMs have configurations of optimal architecture determined with an architecture search (§3.2). GPT-2 official training information has not been publicly disclosed; we report GPT-2 pre-training hardware details when using model parallelism specified by Shoeybi et al., 2019. We use Graphcore Intelligence Processing Units (IPUs) for pre-training our LMs (Jia et al., 2019 provide a detailed review on IPUs). MLM=Masked Language modelling, CLM=Causal Language modelling, L=Layers, A=Attention heads, H=Hidden size per head, F=Feed-forward (intermediary) layer size.

forming existing baselines in such tasks as virtue and justice assessment. To the best of our knowledge, our work represents one of the earliest attempts to investigate how predictions made by tiny language models trained on a developmentally plausible corpus correlate with human-shared values.

This paper has the following structure. After a short section dedicated to related work (§2), we first describe tokenizer training (§3.1), architecture search results and optimal model selection (§3.2), and the final architecture of the pre-trained LMs (§3.3). Then, we present scores on datasets included in the shared task (§4), and we present ethics evaluation results (§5).

2 Related Work

Recent large LMs found applications in many NLP tasks, such as grammatical correction, text completion, and question answering; yet, their usage is constrained by their computational cost. Previous works reduce the model size and inference time with knowledge distillation, parameter quantization and other compression techniques (Sanh et al., 2019; Yao et al., 2021; Tao et al., 2022). Other studies investigated the relationship between model parameter count and performance. Kaplan et al., 2020 has introduced scaling laws, showing the power-law dependency between perplexity and the model size, as well as between the training loss and dataset size. The paradigm of scaling laws further formed the basis for recent research examining the behaviour of LMs at a small scale (Fedus et al., 2022; Fu et al., 2023). For instance, Puvis de Chavannes et al., 2021 presented results of *Neural Architecture Search* in limited parameter space, suggesting that optimal LMs are smaller than the existing base configurations.

In parallel, there is numerous research focusing on the efficiency of dataset size, vocabulary and representation that can help to reduce computation cost by minimizing the training steps (van Schijndel et al., 2019; Huebner et al., 2021; Schick and Schütze, 2021; Warstadt and Bowman, 2022). van Schijndel et al., 2019 have demonstrated that LMs trained on a small-volume corpus can reach human performance under some grammatical knowledge evaluation scenarios, questioning the necessity of large datasets for pre-training. Huebner et al., 2021 introduced a small encoder-based LM BabyBERTa with 5M parameters and showcased the efficiency of small training data; that work bridged the gap between earlier studies on model size reduction and optimal data size.

The aforementioned related works mainly analyse the difference between compact LMs and their larger counterparts with throughput time measures and performance on GLUE benchmark (Wang et al., 2018). In this paper, we evaluate LMs at a small scale trained on a 10M size dataset of BabyLM shared tasks and try to complement existing research with additional evaluation on moral judgment tasks. The decision to focus on the moral judgment task is driven by recent studies that reveal human-like biases in the moral acceptability judgments made by large language models trained on extensive corpora (Schramowski et al., 2022). This paper complements existing research by conducting a moral judgment evaluation for small language models.

3 Methodology

We follow pre-training tasks of RoBERTa (Liu et al., 2019) and GPT-2 (Radford et al., 2019) and refer to these as the architecture baselines in this section. We train Bebeshka[4] and Zlata[5] with masked language and causal language modelling objectives, respectively, and compare their vocabularies and architectures with the baselines.

3.1 Vocabulary

Training Data We use data provided within the STRICT-SMALL track of the shared task. We report statistics of the training corpus in Table 6 (Appendix A). The transcribed speech, extracted from recordings of casual speech addressed to children and educational movie subtitles, makes up the bulk of the corpus. The average length of the texts is around 30 tokens; considering that and the maximum text length, we lower the maximum sequence length from the base 512 to 128 tokens for the configuration of our LMs.

Input Representation We follow tokenization models of the baselines (GPT-2, RoBERTa) and BabyBERTa (Huebner et al., 2021) and use byte-level Byte-Pair Encoding (BPE) algorithm (Sennrich et al., 2016); that is, a tokenization method based on iterative merging of the most occurring bytes pairs in a further shared vocabulary. For the encoder Bebeshka, we build a case-insensitive vocabulary[6] of size 8K. We find a few mismatches between Bebeshka and RoBERTa tokenization and provide more details in Appendix B. The decoder Zlata has a 30K vocabulary constructed with default parameter settings of Tokenizers trainer;[7] that value also allows for bypassing the inclusion of onomatopoeic words that prevail in some transcribed texts of the shared task data.

3.2 Model Selection

To determine an optimal configuration of encoder LM, we use an Optuna-implemented Bayesian optimization algorithm (Akiba et al., 2019) and tune parameters listed in Table 2 that determine the architecture. The upper bounds of the numerical parameters in a search space are chosen in accordance with the base RoBERTa configuration. We set the lower bounds to 1, ensuring a thorough exploration of architectural variations to find the optimal configuration for the masked language modelling task. Optuna features efficient implementation of optimization algorithms; in our optimization study, we use a standard Tree-structured Parzen Estimator (TPE) algorithm, which uses tree-structured representations and Parzen windows for modelling the probability distributions of hyper-parameters and their density estimation. We use TPE to sample parameter values from the search space and an automated early-stopping based on pruning runs with an intermediary perplexity higher than the median of preceding runs.

We set masked language modelling loss (perplexity) of RoBERTa initialized with the TPE sampled configuration parameters as a minimizing objective function. The perplexity is calculated on the STRICT-SMALL validation set after training the model for 10 epochs on written English texts sample (Gutenberg and Children's Book Test corpora and Wikipedia) from the training BabyLM corpus (see Table 6). We choose a corpus sample to reduce parameter search executing time since dataset size directly impacts an LM training time at each optimization step. We manually found that training on written texts yields a better score. Optimization study with an upper bound of 100 trial runs ran for roughly two days on a single A100 GPU.

Table 2 reports parameter search results for the best and worst runs according to perplexity on the validation dataset.

The **optimal configuration** for encoder LMs can be summarized as follows: (1) the ratio of the number of attention heads to the number of layers fluctuates within the 1.5-2 range, (2) employing relative key query type positional embeddings, (3) the dropping ratio 0.3 for attention probabilities. We further use these three key configuration attributes to initialize Bebeshka. Parameters other than positional embeddings type, dropout ratio and the number of layers/heads vary significantly across the top 10% runs. Precisely, all types of activation functions, except for ReLU, appear evenly in the best range. When it comes to the hidden size per head, it takes values from 65 to 85, with a mean

[4]https://huggingface.co/iproskurina/bebeshka

[5]https://huggingface.co/iproskurina/zlata

[6]We use BPE implementation available under HuggingFace Tokenizers library (Moi and Patry, 2023).

[7]https://github.com/huggingface/tokenizers

Parameter	Search range	10% Best runs Mean	10% Worst runs Mean
Positional embedding type	(rel. key, rel. key query, absolute)	rel. key query	absolute
# Hidden layers	[1-12]	6.2	10.9
# Attention heads	[1-18]	11.9	7.1
Hidden size per head	[1-100]	81.6	64.1
Feed-forward layer size	[1-3072]	1446.3	2034.5
Activation function	(New GELU, GELU, SiLU, ReLU)	New GELU	ReLU
Dropout probability	[0.1-1.0]	0.16	0.63
Attention dropout	[0.1-1.0]	0.33	0.70
Avg. perplexity	-	24.53	992.27

Table 2: Parameter search space of Optuna study for pre-training encoder LMs on STRICT-SMALL corpus and mean parameter values across 10 best and worst runs sorted by the perplexity. For non-numerical parameters, we report the most common parameter values among study runs.

Model	Loss		Run time	
	Val	Test	Val	Test
	MLM			
RoBERTa (125M)	3.72	4.42	1519	1592
Bebeshka (16M)	**3.54**	**4.30**	**485**	**649**
	CLM			
OPT (125M)	7.11	7.10	1493	1567
Zlata (66M)	4.64	4.69	831	869

Table 3: Pre-training objective loss on validation and test data of Bebeshka and Zlata compared to baseline models and average run time in seconds. We run an evaluation of all LMs on the same V100 GPU and use Hugging Face Trainer API for calculating the scores. The best score is in bold, and the second-best score is underlined.

of 81.6. We also observe a notable deviation of intermediary size from the mean value. Altogether our results show that the best-performing encoder LMs are smaller than the base configuration of RoBERTa, which aligns with Puvis de Chavannes et al., 2021.

3.3 Model Pre-training

We train our models on 4 Graphcore IPUs with two encoder layers trained on each with mixed precision[8] and use STRICT-SMALL training split. Table 1 shows the configuration settings of our LMs.

Bebeshka The 16M parameters model is based on RoBERTa architecture with determined optimal layer sizes (§3.2). We train Bebeshka on the 10M training corpus of the shared task. We decrease the probability for selecting masked tokens from standard 15% to 13.5%, which is one of the equivalents to set RoBERTa unmasking probability to 0 discussed by Huebner et al., 2021.

Zlata That decoder LM is a light 66M version of GPT-2 with 6 layers trained for 10 epochs on the training STRICT-SMALL data. Motivated by the configuration of the best encoder LM, we use the ratio of attention heads to decoder layers equal to 2. We explain parameter choice in Appendix C.

4 Experiments Results

In this section, we report the results submitted for the BabyLM shared task. LMs discussed in this section are pre-trained on the shared task data, including the baselines. We use baselines that were created with existing tokenizers and released by the organizers of the BabyLM competition.[9]

4.1 Pre-training Objective Loss

We present the evaluation results of our LMs in Table 3, where we compare their performance against the shared task baselines and evaluation runtime. While the baselines were trained for 20 epochs, we can observe competitive results by pre-training our small-scale models for ten epochs. One of the main advantages of the introduced models lies in their compact size, which makes them more efficient at inference time, even though they do not outperform the baselines by a large margin, which can be seen from the average run time.

4.2 Linguistic Minimal Pairs

Figure 1 depicts the evaluation results of our LMs on the BLiMP dataset (Warstadt et al., 2020a) in a zero-shot setting. The goal of this evaluation benchmark is to assess a model's ability to distinguish between grammatically acceptable and unacceptable sentences without specific fine-tuning on the task. The dataset consists of minimal pairs annotated

[8]https://www.graphcore.ai/products/ipu

[9]We also report scores for the version of the model trained with full precision weights, which we dub Bebeshka-2. However, we do not discuss those since they were submitted after the leaderboard release.

Model	CoLA MCC	SST-2 Acc.	MRPC F1	QQP F1	MNLI Acc.	MNLI_{mm} Acc.	QNLI Acc.	RTE Acc.	BoolQ Acc.	MultiRC Acc.	WSC Acc.
OPT	15.2	81.9	72.5	60.4	57.6	60.0	61.5	60.0	63.3	55.2	60.2
RoBERTa	**25.8**	**87.0**	79.2	73.7	**73.2**	**74.0**	**77.0**	**61.6**	**66.3**	**61.4**	61.4
T5	11.3	78.1	**80.5**	66.2	48.0	50.3	62.0	49.4	66.0	47.1	61.4
Bebeshka	0.11	81.3	73.5	66.4	58.7	62.0	59.0	45.4	63.9	48.7	61.4
Zlata	0.05	81.7	77.6	65.9	61.9	63.9	61.7	56.6	65.3	53.8	**61.5**
Bebeshka-2	24.5	83.5	77.7	**77.3**	65.4	66.9	64.0	56.6	60.2	46.9	61.4

Table 4: Evaluation results on GLUE and SuperGLUE (BoolQ, MultiRC, WSC) benchmark datasets. We report metrics suggested in the shared task evaluation pipeline and baselines. The best score is in bold, and the second-best score is underlined.

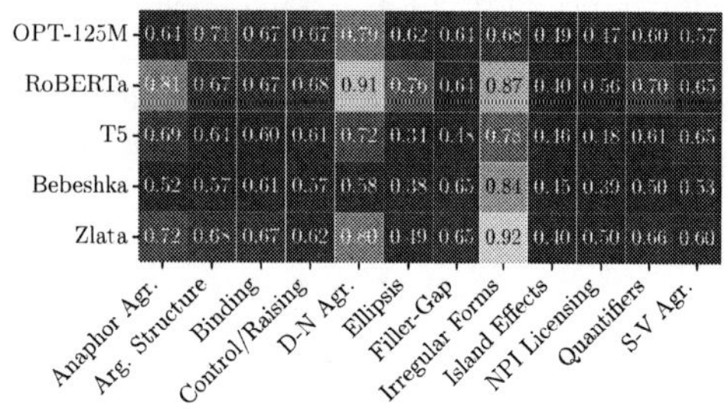

Figure 1: Accuracy on BLiMP tasks of our LMs with RoBERTa-base, OPT-125M, and T5-base baselines. The lighter colours correspond to greater accuracy and, hence, better scores. Morphology: *Anaphor Agr.*, *D-N Agr.*, *Irregular Forms*, *S-V Agr.*. Semantics: *NPI Licensing*, *Quantifiers*. Syntax-Semantics:*Binding*, *Control/Raising*. The rest phenomena correspond to the Syntax category.

with a grammatical phenomenon. We report detailed LMs accuracy scores across various BLiMP tasks in Table 7 (Appendix D). The general trend is that LMs trained on BabyLM data perform well on minimal pairs with morphological tasks, such as *Irregular Forms* and *Determiner-Noun Agreement*.

Zlata achieves the best accuracy (92.1%) on *Irregular Forms* and outperforms OPT-125M baseline on some morphological tasks (*Anaphor Agreement*, *Subject-Verb Agreement*), minimal pairs with a violation in phrasal movements (*Filler Gap*) and other tasks, such as *NPI Licensing*. Bebeshka achieves the second-best accuracy (64.7%) on *Filler Gap* minimal pairs and distinguishes sentences with syntactic errors in pronoun and its antecedent relationship or syntactic islands (*Binding*, *Island Effects*). The results show that LMs trained on the BabyLM corpus have syntactic and morphology understanding which influences their behaviour on downstream tasks discussed next.

4.3 GLUE

Table 4 shows results of fine-tuned LMs evaluation on a variety of tasks present in GLUE and SuperGLUE benchmarks.[10] Submitted to the shared task, Bebeshka and Zlata were fine-tuned for ten epochs on most of the tasks (see Appendix C for more detail). The overall trend is that the introduced small-scale encoder Bebeshka and decoder Zlata demonstrate scores comparable with large baseline LMs on downstream tasks. That highlights that LMs at a small scale can quickly adapt to the fine-tuning task, though may achieve lower performance in a zero-shot evaluation on BliMP. When comparing decoder LMs, we observe that the introduced Zlata outperforms OPT-baseline on paraphrase detection (MRPC & QQP), entailment/contradiction detection (MNLI), and question answering (BoolQ) downstream tasks. As for the encoder LMs, the encoder Bebeshka has moderate scores compared to RoBERTa, which, in general, achieves the best scores on GLUE. However, Bebeshka outperforms OPT-125M baseline on QQP and MRPC tasks with F1 scores of 73.5% and 66.4%, respectively.

The most difficult task for shallow LMs seems to be Recognizing Textual Entailment (RTE). We suppose that LMs trained on STRICT-SMALL corpus with an average length of 28.65 tokens (Table 6, Appendix D) or restricted to the 128 maximum sequence length, can perform well on datasets with short sequences and contexts, which can explain lower results on some fine-tuned tasks; another issue can be the fine-tuning hyper-parameters search: perhaps, shallow LMs require more epochs to improve the submitted scores.

[10] Provided datasets within the shared task were filtered according to the vocabulary of BabyLM STRICT-SMALL corpus.

Model	Justice	Deontology	Virtue	Utilitarianism	Commonsense
RoBERTa-large (355M)	<u>56.7</u>	<u>60.3</u>	53.0	**79.5**	**90.4**
GPT-3 few-shot (175B)	15.2	15.9	18.2	<u>73.7</u>	<u>73.3</u>
Bebeshka (16M)	**64.6**	**71.4**	**74.1**	69.0	-
Zlata few-shot (66M)	50.7	49.6	<u>72.0</u>	50.3	53.3

Table 5: Accuracy scores on ETHICS benchmark. LMs trained on STRICT-SMALL corpus reach results close to the large model baselines reported by Hendrycks et al., 2020. We do not report results for the fine-tuning tasks which require the maximum sequence length exceeding the one of an LM. The best score is in bold, and the second-best score is underlined.

4.4 Mixed Signals Generalization

The MSGS dataset introduced by (Warstadt et al., 2020b) comprises 20 binary classification tasks and is used to test whether a LM has a preference for linguistic or surface generalizations. The evaluation pipeline of the shared task includes 11 MSGS tasks; we report obtained accuracy scores for the fine-tuned LMs in Table 8 (Appendix D). The Matthew's Correlation Coefficient (MCC; Matthews, 1975) scores suggest that all LMs fine-tuned in a controlled setting show better results (>0.9) than those fine-tuned in an ambiguous scenario, with the only exception for *Control Raising* category; the highest scores are achieved on *Lexical content* and *Relative position* tasks. *Lexical Content* is a task of classifying sentences with "the" (*the mouse* vs *a mouse*) when *Relative Position* is a task of determining whether "the" precedes "a" in a sentence. Decoder LMs perform similarly on MSGS tasks chosen for the BabyLM competition, excluding *Syntactic Category-Lexical Content* (SC-LC) classification task, where SC is a task of detecting sentences with adjectives. A decoder LM Zlata seems to adopt surface generalization during fine-tuning on unambiguous data (SC-LC), whereby the baseline model OPT learns to represent linguistic features. Bebeshka behaves likewise on the *Syntactic Category* task and reaches scores close to RoBERTa on *Lexical Content* and *Main Verb* classification problems, suggesting that Bebeshka tends to encode surface features.

4.5 Age of Acquisition

Portelance et al., 2023 introduced a method for measuring the age-of-acquisition in LMs compared to the actual age-of-acquisition by English American children on words set from the CHILDES corpus. Table 9 (Appendix D) illustrates that deviation measured in months for the introduced and baseline LMs. The models Zlata and Bebeshka demonstrate comparable scores to the baselines.

5 Moral Judgments

In this section, we present the results of additional experiments on moral judgements that we conduct outside of the main shared task evaluation.

We evaluate small-scale LM's understanding of fundamental moral principles in various scenarios covered by ETHICS benchmark (Hendrycks et al., 2020). The benchmark consists of 5 morality judgment tasks, including reasonable and fair justice, virtue responses, permitted behaviour depending on context-specified constraints (deontology ethics), pleasant scenario choice (utilitarianism ethics), and commonsense morality. We grid search hyper-parameters for our LMs and use test splits for further evaluation. We fine-tune Bebeshka for ten epochs on each of the tasks and evaluate Zlata in a few-shot setting (see more details in Appendix C). Table 5 outlines the moral judgements classification results. Our small LMs generally outperform existing baselines with respect to accuracy scores on sentence-level tasks, and the best results are achieved on *Virtue* moral judgements.

We suggest that the efficiency of small LMs in these tasks can be explained by some properties of pre-training data, such as lower mean sequence length, transcribed speech prevalence with single-word reactions or responses, children-directed speech, and imperatives. For example, *Virtue* task is a collection of scenario-trait pairs, such as *"Jordan will never do harm to his friends. <sep> caring"*, which have a structure similar to one-word responses in transcribed dialogues.

6 Conclusion and Future Work

In this paper, we present our results for the STRICT-SMALL track of the BabyLM competition. Our submission to the shared task consists of two LMs, namely encoder Bebeshka and decoder Zlata. We first search for an optimal architecture, minimizing perplexity on the released training corpus, and find that the best models have around 6 encoder layers on average, down from 12 layers of existing base models, and have twice as many attention heads. When the number of encoder layers fluctuates among the best models, we find that they all have an attention-heads-to-layers ratio of two, which we further use for building our LMs. Our final LMs, which are scaled-down versions of RoBERTa and GPT-2 with a total of 16M and 66M parameters, perform better than the baseline LMs on development and test BabyLM corpora. Zero-shot evaluation results suggest that our shallow LMs have some basic grammatical knowledge of language syntax and morphology. The introduced LMs also perform better than OPT model on several downstream tasks when having 2 times fewer parameters. We also observe a good performance of our small LMs in a range of ethics judgment tasks, showing that their vocabulary and after-training knowledge can positively contribute to the morality assessment of the described scenarios. These results can serve as baselines for the evaluation of ethical judgment capabilities in small language models. The achieved scores may be attributed to the interplay between ethical and linguistic rules, particularly in encoding action verbs used to describe moral and immoral behaviour. This aspect can be further explored by examining the usage of verbs in various syntactic contexts within the BabyLM corpus and their encoding by trained language models.

In our future work, we plan to determine more capabilities of small LMs, trained on small-size corpora, such as short stories data containing words only 4-year-old children can understand (Eldan and Li, 2023). We also plan to extend our experiments with an analysis of fine-tuning dynamics to investigate how small models adapt to the tasks.

Limitations

Despite achieving good performance on BabyLM test data, our approach has some limitations. We use a variant of Bayesian optimization (TPE algorithm, §3.2) to find an optimal range of parameters that we further use for building our LMs. We predefine constraints for parameters (Table 2) that narrows down the search space and can influence further parameter distributions built with Parzen (kernel density) estimators and, thus, future candidate selection. Future work can benefit from both expanded search space and parameter limits range. The architecture of our small language models, including the number of layers, heads, and hidden layer size, can serve as a minimum lower bound for the parameter search space.

Acknowledgements

This work was funded by the ANR project Diké (grant number ANR-21-CE23-0026-02).

References

Takuya Akiba, Shotaro Sano, Toshihiko Yanase, Takeru Ohta, and Masanori Koyama. 2019. Optuna: A next-generation hyperparameter optimization framework. In *Proceedings of the 25th ACM SIGKDD International Conference on Knowledge Discovery & Data Mining*, KDD '19, page 2623–2631, New York, NY, USA. Association for Computing Machinery.

Ronen Eldan and Yuanzhi Li. 2023. TinyStories: How small can language models be and still speak coherent english? *arXiv preprint arXiv:2305.07759*.

William Fedus, Barret Zoph, and Noam Shazeer. 2022. Switch transformers: Scaling to trillion parameter models with simple and efficient sparsity. *The Journal of Machine Learning Research*, 23(1):5232–5270.

Yao Fu, Hao Peng, Litu Ou, Ashish Sabharwal, and Tushar Khot. 2023. Specializing smaller language models towards multi-step reasoning. *arXiv preprint arXiv:2301.12726*.

Dan Hendrycks, Collin Burns, Steven Basart, Andrew Critch, Jerry Li, Dawn Song, and Jacob Steinhardt. 2020. Aligning AI with shared human values. *arXiv preprint arXiv:2008.02275*.

Philip A. Huebner, Elior Sulem, Fisher Cynthia, and Dan Roth. 2021. BabyBERTa: Learning more grammar with small-scale child-directed language. In *Proceedings of the 25th Conference on Computational Natural Language Learning*, pages 624–646, Online. Association for Computational Linguistics.

Zhe Jia, Blake Tillman, Marco Maggioni, and Daniele Paolo Scarpazza. 2019. Dissecting the graphcore ipu architecture via microbenchmarking. *arXiv preprint arXiv:1912.03413*.

Jared Kaplan, Sam McCandlish, Tom Henighan, Tom B Brown, Benjamin Chess, Rewon Child, Scott Gray, Alec Radford, Jeffrey Wu, and Dario Amodei. 2020. Scaling laws for neural language models. *arXiv preprint arXiv:2001.08361*.

Yinhan Liu, Myle Ott, Naman Goyal, Jingfei Du, Mandar Joshi, Danqi Chen, Omer Levy, Mike Lewis, Luke Zettlemoyer, and Veselin Stoyanov. 2019. RoBERTa: A Robustly Optimized BERT Pretraining Approach. *arXiv preprint arXiv:1907.11692*.

Kyle Mahowald, Anna A Ivanova, Idan A Blank, Nancy Kanwisher, Joshua B Tenenbaum, and Evelina Fedorenko. 2023. Dissociating language and thought in large language models: a cognitive perspective. *arXiv preprint arXiv:2301.06627*.

Brian W Matthews. 1975. Comparison of the predicted and observed secondary structure of t4 phage lysozyme. *Biochimica et Biophysica Acta (BBA)-Protein Structure*, 405(2):442–451.

Anthony Moi and Nicolas Patry. 2023. HuggingFace's Tokenizers.

Eva Portelance, Yuguang Duan, Michael C. Frank, and Gary Lupyan. 2023. Predicting age of acquisition for children's early vocabulary in five languages using language model surprisal.

Lucas Høyberg Puvis de Chavannes, Mads Guldborg Kjeldgaard Kongsbak, Timmie Rantzau, and Leon Derczynski. 2021. Hyperparameter power impact in transformer language model training. In *Proceedings of the Second Workshop on Simple and Efficient Natural Language Processing*, pages 96–118, Virtual. Association for Computational Linguistics.

Alec Radford, Jeffrey Wu, Rewon Child, David Luan, Dario Amodei, Ilya Sutskever, et al. 2019. Language models are unsupervised multitask learners. *OpenAI blog*, 1(8):9.

Victor Sanh, Lysandre Debut, Julien Chaumond, and Thomas Wolf. 2019. DistilBERT, a distilled version of BERT: smaller, faster, cheaper and lighter. *arXiv preprint arXiv:1910.01108*.

Timo Schick and Hinrich Schütze. 2021. It's not just size that matters: Small language models are also few-shot learners. In *Proceedings of the 2021 Conference of the North American Chapter of the Association for Computational Linguistics: Human Language Technologies*, pages 2339–2352, Online. Association for Computational Linguistics.

Patrick Schramowski, Cigdem Turan, Nico Andersen, Constantin A Rothkopf, and Kristian Kersting. 2022. Large pre-trained language models contain human-like biases of what is right and wrong to do. *Nature Machine Intelligence*, 4(3):258–268.

Rico Sennrich, Barry Haddow, and Alexandra Birch. 2016. Neural machine translation of rare words with subword units. In *Proceedings of the 54th Annual Meeting of the Association for Computational Linguistics (Volume 1: Long Papers)*, pages 1715–1725, Berlin, Germany. Association for Computational Linguistics.

Mohammad Shoeybi, Mostofa Patwary, Raul Puri, Patrick LeGresley, Jared Casper, and Bryan Catanzaro. 2019. Megatron-lm: Training multi-billion parameter language models using model parallelism. *arXiv preprint arXiv:1909.08053*.

Chaofan Tao, Lu Hou, Wei Zhang, Lifeng Shang, Xin Jiang, Qun Liu, Ping Luo, and Ngai Wong. 2022. Compression of generative pre-trained language models via quantization. In *Proceedings of the 60th Annual Meeting of the Association for Computational Linguistics (Volume 1: Long Papers)*, pages 4821–4836, Dublin, Ireland. Association for Computational Linguistics.

Mycal Tucker, Tiwalayo Eisape, Peng Qian, Roger Levy, and Julie Shah. 2022. When does syntax mediate neural language model performance? evidence from dropout probes. In *Proceedings of the 2022 Conference of the North American Chapter of the Association for Computational Linguistics: Human Language Technologies*, pages 5393–5408, Seattle, United States. Association for Computational Linguistics.

Marten van Schijndel, Aaron Mueller, and Tal Linzen. 2019. Quantity doesn't buy quality syntax with neural language models. In *Proceedings of the 2019 Conference on Empirical Methods in Natural Language Processing and the 9th International Joint Conference on Natural Language Processing (EMNLP-IJCNLP)*, pages 5831–5837, Hong Kong, China. Association for Computational Linguistics.

Alex Wang, Amanpreet Singh, Julian Michael, Felix Hill, Omer Levy, and Samuel Bowman. 2018. GLUE: A multi-task benchmark and analysis platform for natural language understanding. In *Proceedings of the 2018 EMNLP Workshop BlackboxNLP: Analyzing and Interpreting Neural Networks for NLP*, pages 353–355, Brussels, Belgium. Association for Computational Linguistics.

Alex Warstadt and Samuel R Bowman. 2022. What artificial neural networks can tell us about human language acquisition. *Algebraic Structures in Natural Language*, pages 17–60.

Alex Warstadt, Aaron Mueller, Leshem Choshen, Ethan Gotlieb Wilcox, Chengxu Zhuang, Juan Ciro, Rafael Mosquera, Adina Williams, Bhargavi Paranjabe, Tal Linzen, and Ryan Cotterell. 2023. Findings of the 2023 BabyLM Challenge: Sample-efficient pretraining on developmentally plausible corpora. In *Proceedings of the 2023 BabyLM Challenge*. Association for Computational Linguistics (ACL).

Alex Warstadt, Alicia Parrish, Haokun Liu, Anhad Mohananey, Wei Peng, Sheng-Fu Wang, and Samuel R. Bowman. 2020a. BLiMP: The benchmark of linguistic minimal pairs for English. *Transactions of the Association for Computational Linguistics*, 8:377–392.

Alex Warstadt, Yian Zhang, Xiaocheng Li, Haokun Liu, and Samuel R. Bowman. 2020b. Learning which features matter: RoBERTa acquires a preference for linguistic generalizations (eventually). In *Proceedings of the 2020 Conference on Empirical Methods in Natural Language Processing (EMNLP)*, pages 217–235, Online. Association for Computational Linguistics.

Zhengxuan Wu, Atticus Geiger, Joshua Rozner, Elisa Kreiss, Hanson Lu, Thomas Icard, Christopher Potts, and Noah Goodman. 2022. Causal distillation for language models. In *Proceedings of the 2022 Conference of the North American Chapter of the Association for Computational Linguistics: Human Language Technologies*, pages 4288–4295, Seattle, United States. Association for Computational Linguistics.

Yunzhi Yao, Shaohan Huang, Wenhui Wang, Li Dong, and Furu Wei. 2021. Adapt-and-distill: Developing small, fast and effective pretrained language models for domains. In *Findings of the Association for Computational Linguistics: ACL-IJCNLP 2021*, pages 460–470, Online. Association for Computational Linguistics.

A Experimental Framework

Dataset	# Sentences	Avg. length*	Questions (Proportion)	Proportion
CHILDES	64258	7.17	39%	5%
British National Corpus (BNC)	66100	16.06	17%	8%
Children's Book Test	25946	25.49	3%	6%
Children's Stories Text Corpus	5569	60.58	1%	3%
Standardized Project Gutenberg Corpus	90402	16.22	0%	10%
OpenSubtitles	417984	9.94	17%	31%
QCRI Educational Domain Corpus	91904	16.38	0%	11%
Wikipedia	40876	51.28	0%	10%
Simple Wikipedia	9938	14.57	6%	15%
Switchboard Dialog Act Corpus	5569	60.58	0%	1%
Total	832274	28.65	13.1%	100%

Table 6: Statistics of the training corpus offered in the STRICT-SMALL track of BabyLM competition. *= Average tokenized text length.

B Tokenization Tests

We compare the tokenization of Bebeshka and RoBERTa on the corpus of STRICT-SMALL track and find that the tokenization coincides on 87% of the sequences. We manually analyse a random sample of 100 non-matching tokenization cases and find that those fall on transcribed speech sentences with no more than three words or include two words missing in RoBERTa vocabulary but processed as a whole word by Bebeshka LM (*sweetie* and *duke*). We also found that the RoBERTa tokenizer splits non-capitalised first names or other terms used for addressing (*th-omas*, *m-ister*, *mom-my*) opposed to Bebeshka.

C Training Details

C.1 Pre-training parameters

We experimented with the same configuration for our decoder LM Zlata as we used for Bebeshka, including 4 layers and the same type of positional embeddings; however, that always resulted in gradients underflow and that loss was not decreasing. We manually found the 6-layer and absolute positional embedding configurations by increasing and traversing values of the parameters that were grid searched for Bebeshka (Table 2). We pre-train our LMs using 4x IPUs freely available in Paperspace[11] and use IPU Trainer API. We use auto-loss scaling with an initial value of 16384 and half-precision for training our LMs. Training with IPUs requires specifying IPU configuration, containing instructions for mapping layers between the devices; for Bebeshka, we use one layer per IPU, and for Zlata, we use that parameter equal to 2. For both LMs, we use per-device training batch size equal to 1 and gradient accumulation steps equal to 64. Each batch consists of 1,000 concatenated data examples from the training corpus. The time for the computational graph construction took under 10 minutes for both training both LMs.

C.2 Fine-tuning parameters

BabyLM Evaluation For Bebeshka fine-tuning, we use parameters used by default in the evaluation pipeline of the competition, that is, learning rate equal to 5e-5, batch size equal to 64, and maximum epochs equal to 10. For Zlata fine-tuning, we use the learning rate equal to 1e-4 and fine-tune the tasks for 5 epochs. That allowed us to reduce fine-tuning time. Note that the performance of our LMs can be improved upon the submitted results if grid search the optimal hyper-parameters.

Moral Judgement We use a weighted loss for fine-tuning Bebeshka and grid search optimal parameters using an official implementation by the authors of the dataset.[12] For our GPT-2 based model Zlata, we use an existing evaluation harness benchmark in the k-shot setting with k equal to 15.[13]

[11] https://www.paperspace.com
[12] https://github.com/hendrycks/ethics
[13] https://github.com/EleutherAI/lm-evaluation-harness/

D Evaluation Results

Model	Anaphor Agr.	Arg. Structure	Binding	Control/Raising	D-N Agr.	Ellipsis	Filler-Gap	Irregular Forms	Island Effects	NPI Licensing	Quantifiers	S-V Agr.
OPT-125M	63.8	**70.6**	67.1	<u>66.5</u>	78.5	62.0	63.8	67.5	**48.6**	46.7	59.6	56.9
RoBERTa-base	**81.5**	67.1	<u>67.3</u>	**67.9**	**90.8**	**76.4**	63.5	87.4	39.9	**55.9**	**70.5**	**65.4**
T5-base	68.9	63.8	60.4	60.9	72.2	34.4	48.2	77.6	<u>45.6</u>	47.8	61.2	<u>65.0</u>
Bebeshka	52.0	57.3	61.5	56.8	58.0	37.9	<u>64.7</u>	84.5	44.8	39.2	49.7	53.2
Zlata	72.0	<u>68.1</u>	66.9	61.7	80.0	48.6	**65.4**	<u>92.1</u>	40.3	<u>50.4</u>	66.4	60.3
Bebeshka-2	<u>77.7</u>	60.2	**68.0**	56.2	<u>87.4</u>	<u>68.8</u>	<u>64.7</u>	**92.8**	37.0	45.1	<u>70.2</u>	60.5

Table 7: Model evaluation results on BLiMP dataset. The scores show the model's accuracy in distinguishing between the grammatical and ungrammatical sentences within each minimal pair. The best score is in bold, and the second-best score is underlined.

Model	CR	LC	MV	RP	SC	CR LC	CR RTP	MV LC	MV RTP	SC LC	SC RP
	Control					Ambiguous					
OPT	**50.8**	53.6	**99.5**	**99.9**	77.2	**0.4**	-70.3	<u>-72.1</u>	-77.6	<u>13.8</u>	-68.9
RoBERTa	43.1	**100.0**	97.7	76.7	**86.2**	-28.3	-77.7	-99.3	-79.4	**16.3**	-45.0
T5	21.1	**100.0**	33.4	82.5	<u>77.6</u>	-78.3	**-62.0**	-100.0	-79.7	-25.3	<u>-39.4</u>
Bebeshka	13.0	**100.0**	97.0	72.0	41.0	-95.0	<u>-63.0</u>	-100.0	<u>-66.0</u>	-58.0	-62.0
Zlata	37.0	<u>79.0</u>	90.0	87.0	64.0	<u>-9.0</u>	-85.0	**-70.0**	-94.0	-58.0	**-39.0**
Bebeshka-2	<u>49.4</u>	**100.0**	<u>98.2</u>	<u>88.3</u>	61.5	-28.9	-80.4	-100.0	**-40.8**	-57.2	-46.4

Table 8: Model evaluation results: Matthews Correlation Coefficient (MCC) on the synthetic MSGS dataset, multiplied by 100. CR=*Control Raising*, LC=*Lexical Content*, MV=*Main Verb*, RP=*Relative Position*, SC=*Syntactic Category*, RTP=*Relative Token Position*. Control columns correspond to the control experiments when an LM is trained to classify sentences with certain linguistic and surface features. Ambiguous correspond to the experiments when an LM is tested on a single-feature dataset (for example, LC) after training on a set with labels consistent across both linguistic and surface features (SC LC). The highest score is in bold, and the second-highest score is underlined.

Model	Overall (591 words)	Nouns (322)	Predicates (167)	Function words (102)
OPT-125M	2.03	1.98	1.81	2.57
RoBERTa-base	2.06	1.99	1.85	2.65
T5-base	2.04	1.97	1.82	2.64
Bebeshka	2.06	1.98	1.84	2.66
Zlata	2.07	1.99	1.83	2.67

Table 9: Age-of-acquisition (AoA) predictions on child-directed utterances from CHILDES data. The scores are Mean Absolute Deviation scores in months between the actual average AoA of the words by American English-speaking children and model predicted AoA, measured as a likelihood of the words' usage across all the contexts (surprisal scores). The lower the MAD scores, the better. Top-5 words with the highest surprisal scores for LMs: Zlata: *snowsuit, applesauce, lawn mower, sprinkler, tricycle*; Bebeshka: *snowsuit, hen, turkey, belt, lamb.*

Grammar induction pretraining for language modeling in low resource contexts

Xuanda Chen and **Eva Portelance***
Department of Linguistics, McGill University
Mila - Quebec Artificial Intelligence Institute

Abstract

In the context of the BabyLM challenge, we present a language model which uses pretrained embeddings from a grammar induction model as its first layer. We compare it to one of the challenge's baseline models and a minimally different baseline which uses random embeddings. We find that though our model shows improvement over the challenge's baseline, the model with randomly initialized embeddings performs equally well. Our results suggest that it is not the pretrained embeddings which aided performance, but likely our tokenizer and choice of hyperparameters.

1 Introduction

The BabyLM Challenge (Warstadt et al., 2023)'s goal is to develop language models and training pipelines that can learn reasonable linguistic representations for downstream language modeling task using much more constrained datasets. With this goal in mind, we hypothesized that giving models additional information about syntactic structure may help them learn more generalizable representations of language. As part of the strict track of the challenge, we were not allowed to give additional syntactic labels as part of our training data, so instead we propose to first induce a compound probabilistic context-free grammar (compound-PCFG) over the data using a neural grammar induction model (Kim et al., 2019). There are many ways we can then integrate this syntactic information into a language model. Here, we test a simple method: we initialize a language model using the terminal token embeddings of a trained grammar induction model as its embedding layer. We test the effectiveness of this method on the BabyLM strict-small challenge.[1]

Corresponding author: eva.portelance@mcgill.ca

[1]All code for this project is available in this github repository. The trained models and preprocessed data can be downloaded from this OSF Project repository`this Open Science Framework (OSF) project repository`.

2 Data and preprocessing

In the experiments which follow, we use the 10 Million word BabyLM task dataset (the strict track small dataset) to train our language models. Prior to training, we preprocessed the dataset to remove any blank lines or unecessary formatting punctuation (e.g. '== Title ==' became 'Title'). Additionally, we split paragraphs such that each new line represented a single sentence and removed any sentence that was longer than 40 words.

2.1 Grammar induction data

Since grammar induction algorithms can be quite memory intensive, we use a subset of the 10M BabyLM dataset to train our grammar induction model. We randomly sampled a tenth of the sentences from the corpus, resulting is a smaller grammar induction dataset containing 991,510 words.

2.2 Tokenizer

We trained a custom tokenizer on the 10M BabyLM dataset. To guarantee coverage we created a tokenizer that produces both subwords and word-level tokens. Since previous grammar induction models used word-level tokens, we wanted to maximize the number of word-level tokens and keep subwords and character tokens to only a limited necessary number. We therefore trained a tokenizer using the WordPiece algorithm with a vocabulary size of 10,000 and a maximum alphabet of 72 tokens.

3 Models

3.1 Grammar induction model

We first trained a compound-PCFG grammar (Kim et al., 2019) over our subset of the BabyLM small corpus described above. PCFG embeddings are trained to encode terminal rule information, e.g., reflecting syntactic categories in grammar, which could further improve model's language understanding ability. We used our tokenizer to split

Proceedings of the 27th Conference on Computational Natural Language Learning: Volume 2: The BabyLM Challenge, pages 69–73
December 6-7, 2023 ©2023 Association for Computational Linguistics

Table 1: Overall mean performance on each benchmark

benchmark	baseline	baseline-token	grammar
BLiMP	62.63	**64.78**	64.44
BLiMP suppl.	54.72	54.66	**54.88**
SuperGLUE	63.38	**68.21**	67.93
MSGS	**69.22**	67.45	68.08

sentences into tokens and then induced trees over the corpus[2]. During learning, the model induces embedding representations for the grammar rules and terminals, where the terminals are the token embeddings.[3]

Once the grammar is induced, we extract the token embedding layer of the grammar and use it as the initial embedding layer for an OPT-125m-like [4] language model with a vocabulary size of 10,000 [5]. We then trained this language model on next token prediction using the full BabyLM 10M dataset. The embedding layer is trained with other layers and not frozen during training. We will refer to this model as the *grammar* model in the sections which follow.

3.2 Baseline models

We compare our model results to the OPT-125m baseline model supplied by the BabyLM challenge (*baseline*) and to a baseline OPT-125m language model that we trained using our tokenizer and randomly initialized embeddings (*baseline-token*), thus using a vocabulary size of 10,000 tokens. *Baseline-token* has the exact same hyperparameters as our *grammar* model and only differs in terms of its initial embeddings, here random ones.

4 Results

Results for the *baseline* model were taken directly from the BabyLM evaluation pipeline project page (`github.com/babylm/evaluation-pipeline`). For the *baseline-token* and *grammar* models, these were trained for 3 epochs and tested on validation accuracy every 100,000 sentences; we report the best models found during training based on next token prediction on the validation dataset.

We tested all models on the BabyLM evaluation tasks, which included the Benchmark of Linguistic Minimal Pairs (BLiMP) (Warstadt et al., 2020a), a custom supplementary set of BLiMP-like tasks, 'Super' benchmark for General Language Understanding Evaluation (SuperGLUE) (Wang et al., 2019), and the Mixed Signals Generalization Set evaluation (MSGS) (Warstadt et al., 2020b). Results are reported in Table 1. The complete performance results by individual task are presented in Tables 4-7 in Appendix C.

The *baseline-token* and *grammar* models generally do better than the *baseline* on all benchmarks except MSGS, where they perform slightly worse. Overall, the gains in performance are small, though the *baseline-token* and *grammar* do seem to do quite a lot better on the SuperGLUE benchmark than the *baseline* in particular. Importantly, we do not find that the *grammar* model performs better than the *baseline-token* model, suggesting the the addition of our pretrained embeddings did not help the model perform better on the evaluation pipeline.

5 Discussion

Though our *grammar* model did do better overall than the BabyLM OPT-125m *baseline*, when we compared it to our *baseline-token* model, we did not find that initializing the model with pretrained grammar induction embeddings helped perfomance overall. Instead, it may be our tokenizer and choice of hyperparameters which helped improve performance between the *baseline* and *baseline-token/grammar* models.

Simply using the terminal embedding layer of a grammar induction model to initialize a language model is not be the most effective way to encode syntactic information into the model. In future work, we would like to consider other methods for combining these two types of models, like enriching the training set with copies of induced constituents or more complex architectural modification to condition recurrent states with rule embeddings representing the syntactic rules applied to generate a sub-string at each state.

References

Yoon Kim, Chris Dyer, and Alexander Rush. 2019. Compound probabilistic context-free grammars for grammar induction. In *Proceedings of the 57th Annual Meeting of the Association for Computational*

[2]See Appendix D for example induced parses

[3]Hyperparameters for the grammar induction model are reported in Appendix A.

[4]We refer to these models as as OPT-125M-like since they minimally vary from this baseline, however since their vocabulary size is 10,000, they in fact have 94M parameters.

[5]10,000 was the original vocabulary size used in Kim et al. (2019). Since we did not do hyperparameter search over the grammar induction model, we followed their ideal settings.

Linguistics, pages 2369–2385, Florence, Italy. Association for Computational Linguistics.

Alex Wang, Yada Pruksachatkun, Nikita Nangia, Amanpreet Singh, Julian Michael, Felix Hill, Omer Levy, and Samuel Bowman. 2019. Superglue: A stickier benchmark for general-purpose language understanding systems. *Advances in neural information processing systems*, 32.

Alex Warstadt, Leshem Choshen, Ryan Cotterell, Tal Linzen, Aaron Mueller, Ethan Wilcox, Williams Adina, and Chengxu Zhuang. 2023. Findings of the BabyLM Challenge: Sample-efficient pretraining on developmentally plausible corpora. In *Proceedings of the BabyLM Challenge*. Association for Computational Linguistics (ACL).

Alex Warstadt, Alicia Parrish, Haokun Liu, Anhad Mohananey, Wei Peng, Sheng-Fu Wang, and Samuel R. Bowman. 2020a. BLiMP: The benchmark of linguistic minimal pairs for English. *Transactions of the Association for Computational Linguistics*, 8:377–392.

Alex Warstadt, Yian Zhang, Xiaocheng Li, Haokun Liu, and Samuel R. Bowman. 2020b. Learning which features matter: RoBERTa acquires a preference for linguistic generalizations (eventually). In *Proceedings of the 2020 Conference on Empirical Methods in Natural Language Processing (EMNLP)*, pages 217–235, Online. Association for Computational Linguistics.

A Hyperparameters for Grammar Induction

Table 2: Hyper-parameter setting for grammar induction

parameters	values
latent dimension	64
number of preterminal states	60
number of nonterminal states	30
symbol embedding dimension	256
hidden dim for variational LSTM	768
word embedding dim	768
sentence max length	40
vocab size	10000
number of epochs	15
batch size	5
learning rate	1e-4
random seed	1213

B Hyperparameters for OPT language models

Table 3: Hyper-parameter setting for language modeling

parameters	values
embedding size	10000
number of epochs	3
batch size	20
learning rate	1e-4
warm-up steps	2000
gradient clipping threshold	3
max grad norm for gradient clipping	1.0
random seed	527

Table 4: Compute resources for language modeling

parameters	values
Device	A100
Memory	32G of GPU memory
Training time	12 hours

C Complete evaluation results

Table 5: BLiMP accuracy scores

task	baseline	baseline-token	grammar
Anaphor agr.	63.8	68.6	**69.7**
Arg. structure	**70.6**	65.7	63.4
Binding	67.1	66.5	**67.6**
Control/Raising	**66.5**	62.2	60.4
Det.-Noun agr.	**78.5**	77.8	77.2
Ellipsis	**62**	49.3	51.6
Filler-Gap	**63.8**	62.1	63
Irregular forms	67.5	**81.4**	81.2
Island effects	**48.6**	48.5	47.9
NPI licensing	46.7	**56.3**	55
Quantifiers	59.6	**71.4**	68.9
Subject-verb agr.	56.9	**67.5**	67.4
Overall mean	62.63	**64.78**	64.44

Table 6: BLiMP-Supplement accuracy scores

task	baseline	baseline-token	grammar
Hypernym	50	52.3	**53.3**
QA congr. (easy)	54.7	**57.8**	45.3
QA congr. (tricky)	31.5	**41.8**	40
Subj.-aux. inversion	80.3	67.5	**82.9**
Turn taking	**57.1**	53.9	52.9
Overall mean	54.72	54.66	**54.88**

Table 7: Super(GLUE) accuracy scores

task	baseline	baseline-token	grammar
CoLA	64.6	**69.6**	68.8
SST-2	81.9	**85**	83.3
MRPC (F1)	72.5	**76.1**	73.7
QQP (F1)	60.4	78.9	**79.1**
MNLI	57.6	**66.4**	65.9
MNLI-mm	60	66	**67.8**
QNLI	61.5	**66.5**	**66.5**
RTE	60	**52.5**	**52.5**
BoolQ	63.3	**67.6**	65.8
MultiRC	55.2	60.2	**62.3**
WSC	60.2	**61.5**	**61.5**
Overall mean	63.38	**68.21**	67.93

Table 8: MSGS accuracy scores

task	baseline	baseline-token	grammar
contr.-raising/lex. cat.	66.5	66.7	**68.9**
contr.-raising/rel. tok. pos.	67	**67.2**	**67.2**
main verb/lex. cat.	66.5	**66.8**	66.6
main verb/rel. tok. pos.	67.6	**66.8**	**66.8**
synt. cat./lex. cat.	**80.2**	69	71.3
synt. cat./rel. pos.	67.5	**68.2**	67.7
Overall mean	**69.22**	67.45	68.08

D Example trees from grammar induction model

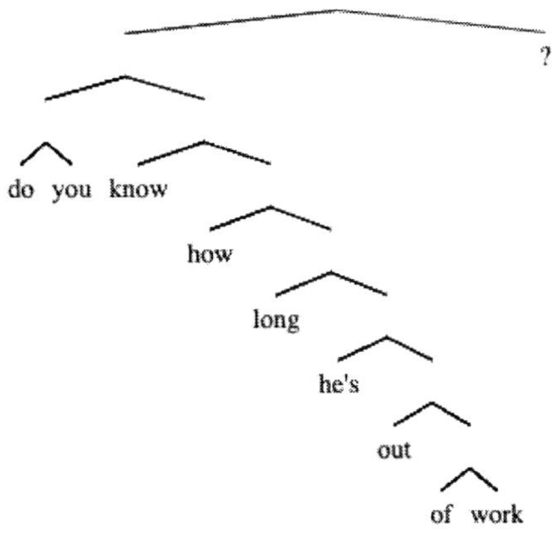

Figure 1: Induced tree for "do you know how long he's out of work?"

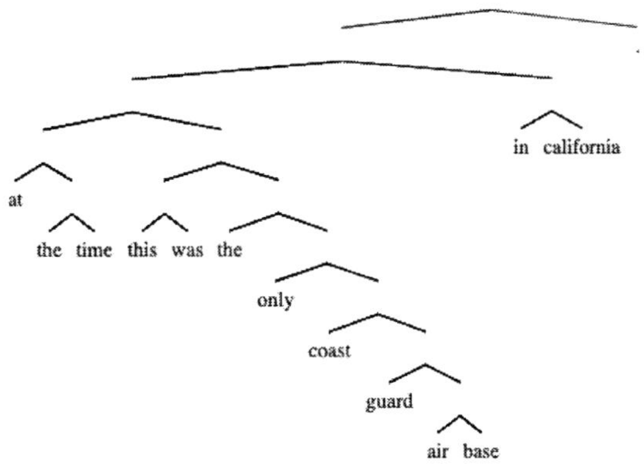

Figure 2: Induced tree for "at the time this was the only coast guard air base in california."

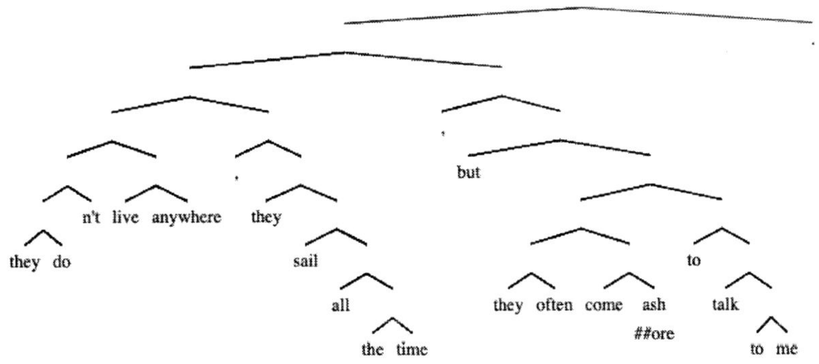

Figure 3: Induced tree for "they don't live anywhere, they sail all the time, but they often come ashore to talk to me."

ChapGTP, ILLC's Attempt at Raising a BabyLM: Improving Data Efficiency by Automatic Task Formation

Jaap Jumelet **Michael Hanna** **Marianne de Heer Kloots**
Anna Langedijk **Charlotte Pouw** **Oskar van der Wal**

Institute for Logic, Language and Computation (ILLC)
University of Amsterdam

Abstract

We present the submission of the ILLC at the University of Amsterdam to the BabyLM challenge (Warstadt et al., 2023), in the `strict-small` track. Our final model, ChapGTP, is a masked language model that was trained for 200 epochs, aided by a novel data augmentation technique called Automatic Task Formation. We discuss in detail the performance of this model on the three evaluation suites: BLiMP, (Super)GLUE, and MSGS. Furthermore, we present a wide range of methods that were ultimately not included in the model, but may serve as inspiration for training LMs in low-resource settings.

1 Introduction

Modern language models (LMs) are trained on datasets that are many orders of magnitude larger than the amount of text a human can read in a single lifetime. Driven by the *scaling law* paradigm, which states that model performance scales as a power law with model and data size, language model training has become increasingly data hungry (Kaplan et al., 2020; Hoffmann et al., 2022). This has raised questions about the *efficiency* of the paradigm: is it possible to train proficient models on amounts of data similar to that what humans process when learning language? The **BabyLM** challenge (Warstadt et al., 2023) proposes a community effort to find efficient training strategies for model training, providing a fixed, "developmentally plausible" training data set.

This paper presents the submission of the Institute of Logic, Language and Computation at the University of Amsterdam to the BabyLM challenge. We participated in the `strict-small` track of the challenge, which limits the amount of training data to a fixed set of 10 million tokens. The usage of any sources trained on external data was not allowed, which forced us to utilize the training data as efficiently as possible. Evaluation is based on various benchmarks, including BLiMP (Warstadt et al., 2020a), (Super)GLUE (Wang et al., 2018, 2019), and MSGS (Warstadt et al., 2020b).

Our final model, **ChapGTP**[1], is a bidirectional masked LM based on the `DeBERTa` architecture (He et al., 2023). Our core contribution is a novel data augmentation technique called **Automatic Task Formation (ATF)**, which generates meaningful textual formulations from the existing training data based on pre-defined templates. These formulations are tailored for learning specific tasks such as question answering and sentiment classification. The procedure relies solely on shallow surface heuristics, and requires no external data or expert labeling.

Besides ATF, we explored many other strategies: prosodic guidance, formal languages, tokenizer and model engineering, emergent language games, and grokking. Although not all of these were included in ChapGTP, many showed potential. Notably, we find that "pre-pre-training" a language model on constituency-labeled text (induced by an unsupervised constituency parser) or on synthetic emergent languages (generated by neural agents in a referential game with real images) can lead to improvements on the final evaluation benchmarks—but more research is needed to explore the practicality and effectiveness of these approaches in more detail. We hope that our discussion of the various strategies for training data-efficient language models will inspire other researchers and engineers working on NLP in low-resource settings.

2 Data-efficient NLP

The exponential growth in computing resources needed to train recent language models has underscored the need for more data-efficient models. Increased model training efficiency would avoid

[1] **Chap**eroned **G**eneralised **T**ask formation and **P**retraining, DynaBench ID 1448. HuggingFace hub link: `https://huggingface.co/mwhanna/ChapGTP`

Proceedings of the 27th Conference on Computational Natural Language Learning: Volume 2: The BabyLM Challenge, pages 74–85
December 6-7, 2023

environmental harms (Schwartz et al., 2020) and ensure the model openness and accountability that is needed to democratize technological development (Ahmed and Wahed, 2020; Liesenfeld et al., 2023). From a cognitive perspective, which aims to model human-like generalization abilities, sample efficiency should be more of priority than is currently reflected in leaderboard-like model comparisons (Linzen, 2020).

Language models' resource consumption can be decreased at all stages of model development, on both the model and data sides; see He et al. (2023) for an overview. On the modeling side, many studies have aimed to improve data-efficiency by injecting neural models with inductive biases that aid generalization. Examples of such work include distilling inductive biases from other neural models (Abnar et al., 2020) or Bayesian learning algorithms (McCoy and Griffiths, 2023). Other work has compared different types of bias by transfer learning to English after "pre-pre-training" models on synthetically generated structures (Papadimitriou and Jurafsky, 2023).

Most relevant to the BabyLM challenge is Huebner et al.'s (2021) work inspired by child language learning abilities, which drastically decreased model parameters as well as training data size. They pre-trained RoBERTa-base from scratch on a developmentally plausible amount of data, resulting in a model with lower grammatical competence than the original, large-scale model (Liu et al., 2019). However, via careful hyperparameter tuning, they developed *BabyBERTa*, which performs well even with acquisition-scale training data. Their model has only 8 million parameters, 8912 vocabulary items and—importantly—does not predict unmasked tokens.

Data-oriented approaches provide a complementary strategy for improving training efficiency. One successful strategy is to *filter* the training data, for example by removing duplicates (Lee et al., 2022), or excluding thematic document clusters that lead to undesirable model behavior (Kaddour, 2023). Mishra and Sachdeva (2020) used human-inspired heuristics to remove irrelevant and redundant data, aiming to select the optimal dataset for learning a specific task. Via a combination of coarse and fine pruning techniques, they achieved competitive results on out-of-distribution NLI datasets with only $\sim$2% of the SNLI training set.

Finally, *data augmentation* has proven to be useful in low-resource settings. Such techniques aim to diversify the set of training examples without collecting more data (Feng et al., 2021); this can lead to task-specific or domain-general improvement on model performance. Fabbri et al. (2020) showed that performance on a downstream question answering (QA) task increased when models' training data was augmented with synthetically generated questions that helped models learn more complex question-context relationships. Their most successful approach used simple templates to generate wh-questions based on sentences retrieved from the original training data.

Jia et al. (2022) showed that including automatically generated question-answer pairs in pre-training data leads to a better encoding of contextual information in token-level representations. They found that this *question-infused pre-training* strategy results in improved model performance on a range of standard NLP tasks beyond QA, including paraphrase detection, named entity recognition, and sentiment analysis.

3 The BabyLM Challenge

The BabyLM Challenge is a shared task that challenges researchers to train a language model from scratch on an amount of linguistic data similar to what is available to a child. The task has two main goals: 1) developing novel techniques for learning efficiently in low-resource settings; and 2) increasing access to cognitively plausible models of language, which could improve our understanding of human language learning.

Training Data The BabyLM Challenge offers a *developmentally plausible* training dataset, drawing inspiration from the linguistic input children typically receive until the age of 13. The dataset contains fewer than 100 million words and predominantly uses transcribed speech, as children are primarily exposed to spoken language during their early years. The data come from various domains: *child-directed speech* (CHILDES; MacWhinney, 2000), *dialogue* (Switchboard Dialog Act Corpus; Stolcke et al., 2000), *subtitles* (OpenSubtitles, Lison and Tiedemann, 2016, and QCRI Educational Domain Corpus (QED), Abdelali et al., 2014), *simple written English* (Simple Wikipedia, Children's Book Test Hill et al., 2015, Children Stories Text Corpus), and *regular written English* (Wikipedia, Standardized Project Gutenberg Corpus Gerlach and Font-Clos, 2018).

The challenge features three participation tracks: `strict`, `strict-small`, and `loose`. In the `strict` track, the training dataset is limited to 100 million written words extracted from the sources above. In the `strict-small` track, the training dataset is further restricted to a subset of merely 10 million words from the `strict` dataset. In the `loose` track, models could additionally be trained on an unlimited amount of non-linguistic data (e.g. symbolic data, audio, images, etc.). For the exact number and proportion of words per data source included in the `strict` and `strict-small` dataset, see Warstadt et al. (2023).

Evaluation The evaluation of BabyLM models is based on various benchmarks, namely BLiMP (Warstadt et al., 2020a), (Super)GLUE (Wang et al., 2018, 2019), and MSGS (Warstadt et al., 2020b). These benchmarks cover a wide range of linguistic phenomena and aim to collectively provide a comprehensive assessment of a model's linguistic capabilities. BabyLM provides filtered versions of the benchmarks, where each example only includes words that have appeared in the `strict-small` training set at least twice.

BLiMP (Benchmark of Linguistic Minimal Pairs for English) targets linguistic acceptability judgments, and contains sentence pairs that differ in grammatical acceptability based on only one distinct linguistic element. The sentence pairs cover 12 phenomena from English morphology, syntax and semantics, such as anaphor agreement, binding and filler-gap constructions. If a language model is sensitive to the linguistic phenomenon under consideration, it should assign higher probability to the acceptable sentence of the minimal pair.

GLUE (General Language Understanding Evaluation) is a collection of diverse natural language understanding tasks, such as sentiment analysis and textual entailment. SuperGLUE is an improvement upon GLUE and additionally includes coreference resolution and question answering tasks. Both GLUE and SuperGLUE are used for BabyLM evaluation, summing to 11 tasks in total.

MSGS (Mixed Signals Generalization Set) aims to test whether a model prefers linguistic or surface generalizations, through a range of binary classification tasks. It contains *unambiguous tasks* that can be solved by relying on either a surface *or* a linguistic feature (not both), and *ambiguous tasks* that can be solved both by relying on a surface feature *and* by relying on a linguistic feature. The unambiguous tasks test whether a model represents the features of interest in the first place. The ambiguous tasks tests the model's preference for linguistic or surface generalization. The BabyLM evaluation includes 5 unambiguous tasks and 6 ambiguous tasks.

Evaluation on BLiMP is performed in a zero-shot setting, by calculating the proportion of minimal pairs for which the model assigns higher probability to the acceptable sentence. For (Super)GLUE and MSGS, evaluation involves fine-tuning models on each task and then calculating accuracy or macro-F1. The task-specific scores are averaged to arrive at a final score for each of the three benchmarks.

4 ChapGTP

In this section we describe the components of our final model, ChapGTP, that we submitted to the `strict-small` track of BabyLM. The results of the model are presented in §6. In §7 we describe various approaches that were not successful, but that may inspire future work on improving data efficiency in language modeling.

Model Architecture In our experiments we initially considered both causal and masked LM architectures; we ultimately chose a masked LM since it outperformed causal LMs on all evaluation tasks. The model is based on the `DeBERTa-small` architecture (He et al., 2023): a 6 layer bidirectional transformer, 12 attention heads, a hidden state size of 768, and intermediate state size of 3072. The final model has 43.5 million parameters.

Data Processing We use a Byte-Pair Encoding tokenizer (Sennrich et al., 2016), which we train on the `strict-small` corpora, limited to a vocabulary size of 10,000 tokens. This relatively small vocabulary size was sufficient for the challenge, and allowed for more compact models and faster model training.

We preprocessed the corpora by appending all sentences together, separated by a special separator token. This ensures that consecutive sentences within a paragraph will occur together in a single batch item, allowing the model to leverage inter-sentential information. It also significantly improves training speed, since all batches are fully filled up, with little to no padding overhead.

Model Training We train the model with a masked token prediction objective, with a token masking probability of 15%. We train for 200 epochs with a batch size of 64 and a maximum sentence length of 128. We investigate the impact of the number of epochs in more detail in §6. We use the `AdamW` optimizer (Loshchilov and Hutter, 2019), with a cosine learning rate scheduler that interpolates from $5 \cdot 10^{-4}$ to 0, weight decay set to 0.1, and gradient accumulation for 8 steps. We train models using the `transformers` library (Wolf et al., 2020).

5 ATF: Automatic Task Formation

The `strict-small` track of the BabyLM challenge did not permit the usage of external data sources to improve the learning procedure. It was therefore vital to use all data in the training corpora as efficiently as possible. To this end, we defined **Automatic Task Formation (ATF)**, a procedure that looks for simple `regex` patterns in the training data that we can use to augment the data. The main goal of ATF was to improve performance on the GLUE tasks: we hoped that if the training data were augmented with patterns that resembled data found in GLUE, the model could already start learning representations useful for GLUE tasks during pre-training.

Question Answering The text in the pre-training corpora already contains questions, such as those found in dialogue. However, most of these questions do not require a retrieval-based approach of finding the answer to the question (e.g. "*How are you doing?*"). To aid the model with retrieval-based question answering, which is vital for GLUE tasks like QNLI (Rajpurkar et al., 2018), we augment the training corpus with question-answer pairs about various topics. The patterns we consider are:

1. **Birth date**
   The (Simple) Wikipedia data contains many patterns of the form '*⟨Name⟩ (born ⟨DD⟩ ⟨Month⟩ ⟨YYYY⟩)*'. For each such instance, we add a question-answer pair of the form '*On what date was ⟨Name⟩ born?* `[SEP]` *⟨DD⟩ ⟨Month⟩ ⟨YYYY⟩*'.

2. **Nationality & Profession**
   The Simple Wikipedia articles describe people in the same template: '*⟨Name⟩ (born X) is a ⟨Profession⟩ from ⟨Nationality⟩*'. We use this pattern to augment the data with question-answer pairs of the form '*Where is ⟨Name⟩ from?*' and '*What is the profession of ⟨Name⟩?*'.

3. **Discovery, Founding & Naming**
   We consider three other patterns, of the form '*⟨Name⟩ was discovered in ⟨Year⟩*', '*⟨Name⟩ was founded in ⟨Year⟩*', and '*$\langle Name_1\rangle$ was named after $\langle Name_2\rangle$*'.

In total this procedure yielded 1663 question-answer pairs that we append to the training corpus.

Sentiment Classification To aid the model with the sentiment classification task of SST-2 (Socher et al., 2013), we augment our dataset by exploiting sentences containing sentiment carrying tokens. After each sentence that contains a token from a list of positive tokens (*great, terrific, etc.*) or negative tokens (*not good, terrible, etc.*)[2], we add a special sentiment token followed by the sentence sentiment. Sentence sentiment is solely based on the presence of a positive or negative token; we skip sentences containing both positive and negative tokens. The procedure yielded 2500 positive and 2500 negative sentences, which we appended to the training corpus.

Note that we do not modify the masked language modeling training objective for this: the prediction of answers (as well as questions) is performed in the same way as any other token prediction. Incorporating the procedure with a separate classification head is something that we leave open for future work.

6 Results

We report the results of our models in Table 1. Results are aggregated over individual subtasks in BLiMP, GLUE, and MSGS. Our final ChapGTP model, trained for 200 epochs with ATF data augmentation, obtained an average score of 77.2. Next to this model we report various alterations to the training regime. To investigate the impact of the ATF procedure, we also train a model without the augmented data. The strongest gains of ATF are achieved in the GLUE tasks (+1.7 points), which is in line with our original goal of aligning the pre-training data more with that of the fine-tuning tasks. Furthermore, prolonging model training has a strong positive impact on both BLiMP and GLUE, but not for the MSGS tasks. In Figure 1 we present a more fine-grained overview of the results split

[2] We report the full lists in Appendix A.

Model	BLiMP	GLUE	MSGS	Avg.
ChapGTP(20E)	73.5	72.3	79.2	75.0
¬ ATF (§5)	73.1	70.6	80.4	74.7
+ 40E	74.8	73.4	80.7	76.3
+ 100E	76.5	73.8	80.0	76.8
+ 200E	**76.6**	**74.0**	80.9	**77.2**
+ FLOTA	57.8	–	–	–
+ BRAK (40E, §7.4)	75.0	72.0	**82.1**	76.4
dGPT-2 (¬ATF, 40E)	68.9	70.2	79.9	73.0
+ OMG (§7.3)	70.8	69.7	80.0	73.5
OPT†	62.6	63.4	79.8	68.6
RoBERTa†	69.5	71.4	80.9	73.9

Table 1: Aggregate results for the ChapGTP model with various configurations on the three evaluation suites. nE denotes a model trained for n epochs. † models are baseline models made available by the BabyLM organisers. Best performing model per suite is in **bold**.

out for each individual task in the evaluation suites, for a subset of models that showcase improvements driven by ATF and prolonged model training.

BLiMP For BLiMP, increasing the amount of epochs has a positive effect on almost all tasks. One clear outlier, however, is the Irregular Forms tasks, where our 200 epoch model performs significantly worse than models trained for shorter. We plot this behavior for models trained on increasing amounts of epochs in Figure 1B, from which it can be seen that this task follows a peculiar *inverse scaling* pattern (McKenzie et al., 2023). Exploring this pattern in more detail could provide an interesting direction for future research, connecting it to the rule learning of irregular forms in LMs (Dankers et al., 2021).

GLUE The impact of training longer is less pronounced on GLUE than for BLiMP, but it still has a positive effect for most tasks. The ATF procedure appears to have a positive effect on only a small number of tasks, especially MultiRC and MRPC. Surprisingly, performance on QNLI and SST2, the tasks targeted by ATF, did not improve significantly.

7 Additional Experiments

Our final ChapGTP model adopted only a small number of the techniques we investigated for the BabyLM challenge. In this section we highlight various approaches that were not entirely successful, but could serve as inspiration for future work. Note that some of these approaches would not be permitted under the `strict-small` conditions of the BabyLM challenge, but would be possible within the `loose` track.

7.1 Model Architecture

FLOTA Our ChapGTP model uses a BPE subword tokenizer, a common tokenizer used by many LMs, such as GPT-3 (Brown et al., 2020). From a linguistic point of view, this tokenization procedure may be sub-optimal: it is based solely on frequency statistics, and takes no morphological information into account (e.g. *undesirable* → *undesi+rable*). The FLOTA tokenizer (Hofmann et al., 2022) addresses this concern, and presents a tokenization procedure that adheres more strongly to the morphological formation of English words (e.g. *undesirable* → *un+desirable*). We incorporated this tokenizer in our pipeline, but unfortunately it resulted in sub-par results on BLiMP (Table 1). A reason for this might be the relatively low vocabulary size (10.000), though it remains surprising that this tokenizer led to such a significant drop in performance.

LLaMA LLaMA (Touvron et al., 2023) is a pretrained model whose performance rivals that of many larger models trained on more data. In order to achieve this performance, it incorporates a variety of architectural tweaks that aim to improve performance or training stability; these include pre-normalization of transformer block inputs using RMSNorm (Zhang and Sennrich, 2019), the SwiGLU activation function (Shazeer, 2020), and rotary embeddings (Su et al., 2022). Unlike our ChapGTP model, LLaMA uses the SentencePiece tokenizer (Kudo and Richardson, 2018).

Motivated by LLaMA's successful training on smaller data using a smarter architecture, we trained our own LLaMA model. We used a variety of scaled-down model architectures, e.g. with a hidden (residual stream) size of 64, an intermediate (MLP) size of 256, 4 layers, 4 attention heads, and a vocabulary size of 10000. However, these models exhibited no performance gains over similarly sized models that used a more traditional, GPT-like architecture.

7.2 Model Training

Prosodic Guidance Information in speech is not only conveyed through which words are said, but also how they are spoken (Wallbridge et al., 2023).

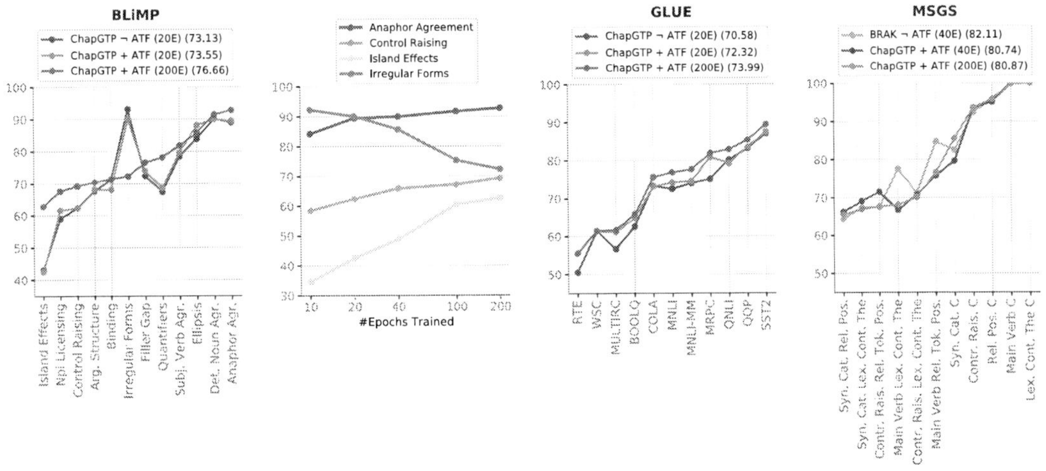

Figure 1: (A) Results for BLiMP on the individual conditions, ordered increasingly by the performance of the final 200E model. (B) Inverse scaling behavior on the Irregular Forms condition, which worsens as the amount of training is increased. For other tasks the opposite is true: training for longer leads to a monotonic improvement. (C) Results for the individual GLUE tasks, ordered similarly to the BLiMP scores in (A). (D) Results for the individual MSGS tasks, including the BRAK model that outperforms the ChapGTP on average.

Hence even models trained on transcribed speech data miss out on the rich auditory cues available in spoken language, which could be informative for learning (Chrupała, 2023). We explored the use prosodic information as one such guiding signal for language model training. Prosody is thought to play an important role in scaffolding human language learning (Gervain et al., 2020), for example in helping infants learn non-adjacent dependencies by highlighting the relevant linguistic elements (Martinez-Alvarez et al., 2023).

One way to provide a text-based language model with a similar learning signal would be to train the model on spoken language transcriptions for which audio recordings are available. Prosodic prominence cues based on properties like pitch and duration, or more advanced scores estimated based on continuous wavelet transforms (Suni et al., 2017), could be extracted from the audio recordings to guide model training. Though we considered this a promising approach to study if language modeling can be improved with access to prosodic information, it was not feasible for us to pursue within the constraints of the BabyLM challenge—curating an audio-aligned text dataset at the 10M- or 100M-word scale poses a significant challenge on its own. We therefore left experiments into using prosodic information for language model training out of our BabyLM submission and hope to work on this idea separately in the future.

Grokking Grokking is a phenomenon in which models seemingly neural networks begin to generalize better after overfitting (Power et al., 2022). In such scenarios, models initially achieve high training performance, but poor held-out (evaluation) performance. Extended training leads models to suddenly generalize, achieving higher evaluation performance. Grokking has been shown to occur not only on toy algorithmic tasks, but also image and sentiment classification (Liu et al., 2022, 2023). More recent work has suggested that transformers can grok hierarchical linguistic structure after extremely prolonged training (Murty et al., 2023).

On the basis of this recent evidence, we conduct experiments to determine if longer training can help language models capture the hierarchical structure of language, even when trained on small data. Our grokking setup is simple: we train a `DistilGPT2` model for 500 epochs on the small (10M word) dataset. We set training hyperparameters as in Murty et al. (2023). We find that grokking does not occur in this scenario: evaluation loss does not improve. Moreover, while our long-training model performed reasonably well on the zero-shot linguistic tasks from BLiMP, performance on the SuperGLUE tasks, which required fine-tuning, is much worse. We conclude that while longer training may not have hurt linguistic knowledge, it may have hurt the model's ability to be fine-tuned.

These results may be surprising, given that in

§6, longer training generally led to better performance on BLiMP and GLUE. Unfortunately, differences in model architecture and training procedure (particularly ATF) could have led to different training dynamics, making direct comparison difficult. Moreover, prior work suggests that the occurrence of grokking is reliant on specific conditions such as a large initial weight norm, or specific adaptive optimizers (Thilak et al., 2022; Liu et al., 2023). More controlled and extensive study is needed to shed light on grokking in LMs.

7.3 OMG: Data from Object Mediated Games

Simulating cooperative games with deep neural agents that need to communicate about objects in their environment is an active area of research; the communication protocols emerging in these settings have been studied extensively in previous works (Havrylov and Titov, 2017; Kottur et al., 2017; Bouchacourt and Baroni, 2018; Lazaridou and Baroni, 2020; Luna et al., 2020, i.a.).

An important motivation for these experiments is to simulate conditions under which certain natural language properties may develop (e.g. Kirby, 2002; Kirby et al., 2015). Others suggest that these settings may enable language models to learn aspects of human communication difficult to acquire from passive language modeling alone (e.g. Lazaridou et al., 2020).

Interestingly, Yao et al. (2022) show that pre-pre-training LMs on synthetic emergent languages generated in referential games with images can in fact improve their performance in low-resource settings. We aim to reproduce the findings of Yao et al. with our particular setup; as such, compare the performance of `DistilGPT2` trained on BabyLM with and without first pre-pre-training on their synthetic emergent languages.

Approach We pre-pre-train `DistilGPT2` on a synthetic emergent language coming from a referential game played with neural agents, as provided by Yao et al. (2022).[3] In this referential game, deep neural agents successfully communicate about images from the Conceptual Captions dataset (Sharma et al., 2018). We use the set of messages with vocabulary size 4035 and maximum message length 15, sampling $2,721,927$ messages for the training data, and $143,260$ for the development set (split in roughly 95% and 5%, respectively).[4]

We pre-pre-train on the emergent language for 8 epochs, after which we continue pre-training on the BabyLM 10M dataset ($\neg$ ATF) for 40 epochs. We compare this to the baseline where we do not pre-pre-train `DistilGPT2` on the emergent messages.[5]

Task	OMG	$\Delta_{baseline}$	BRAK	$\Delta_{baseline}$
BLiMP	70.8	+0.7	75.0	-0.6
GLUE	69.7	+1.4	72.0	-0.7
MSGS	80.0	-0.1	82.1	+3.2

Table 2: Aggregate results for pre-pretraining DistilGPT2 with text from object mediated games (OMG) and ChapGTP with constituency labelled text (BRAK). We also show the difference with their respective baselines ($\Delta_{baseline}$) as discussed in §7.3 and §7.4, where + indicates an improvement. All models shown here are further trained on the BabyLM dataset for 40 epochs *without* the ATF data augmentation (§5).

Results Table 2 shows the aggregate results of pre-pre-training on synthetic emergent languages (OMG). Curiously, OMG pre-pre-training seems to result in a better performance on BLiMP and GLUE compared to the baseline. In our experiments, we also noticed that the loss curves converge faster during training, indicating that OMG pre-pre-training may be a viable strategy for initializing language models in low-resource settings; this is in line with the findings of the original authors (Yao et al., 2022).

7.4 BRAK: Bracketed pre-pre-training

Can initially pre-training on texts where the structure is explicitly marked be used to improve the LM's performance later on? To test this approach, we train the *Deep Inside-Outside Recursive Autoencoders* model (`DIORA`, Drozdov et al., 2019), to augment a portion of the training data with *bracketing* that indicate the constituents of the sentences. The general idea is that the bidirectional ChapGTP can use this extra training signal to quickly learn the syntactic structures of the data—bootstrapping its further language modeling.

Approach We pre-pre-train ChapGTP for 4 epochs on a subset of $15,030$ sentences from the

[3] `https://github.com/ysymyth/ec-nl/`

[4] An example of an emergent message (before tokenization and converting to integers) is: `1019 3876 601 2194 3360 3360 3360 3360 3360 3360 3360 3360 3360 3360 0`.

[5] Note that the results for this baseline are slightly different from Table 1 but comparable, as we used another random seed for training the 40E DistilGPT2.

BabyLM 10M dataset, where the constituents of each sentence is marked using the "[" and "]" tokens.[6] After this, pre-training continued on the entirety of the unbracketed BabyLM dataset (without ATF) for 40 epochs.

To obtain the constituents for the 15,030 sentences, we trained a DIORA model with a hidden dimension of 50 and batch size of 128 for a maximum of 5 epochs. We initialized its embeddings using GloVe (Pennington et al., 2014) (embedding size 16) trained on the same corpus as DIORA. Since DIORA requires sentences as input, we use the dot (".") to split the documents in the datasets into individual sentences, which are then split into words using the space token. We lower-cased each token and removed all punctuation from the sentences. This approach is deliberately kept simple to avoid using any techniques requiring non-trivial expert knowledge. From this set, we labeled 15,030 sentences with a minimum length of three with the trained DIORA model. As a baseline, we pre-pre-train ChapGTP on the same 15,030 sentences, but without the bracketing.

Results The aggregate results of the bracketed pre-pre-training (BRAK) are shown in Table 1 and compared to the baseline in Table 2. While BRAK ChapGTP performs slightly worse on BLiMP and GLUE, it performs considerably better on the MSGS tasks, as seen in Figure 1D. BRAK's main gains stem from two tasks: '*Main Verb Lexical Control The*', and '*Main Verb Relative Token Position*'. We encourage future work on how including inductive biases can improve the performance of language models in low-resource settings.

8 Conclusion

In this paper, we introduced our submission to the `strict-small` track of the BabyLM challenge. ChapGTP is a DeBERTa-based masked LM, trained for 200 epochs with help of our novel data augmentation technique: Automatic Task Formation (ATF). We proposed ATF as a means of creating more task-specific textual formulations based on the existing training data. In particular, we focused on improving representations for question answering and sentiment classification. The idea behind these specific ATF augmentations was that they might lead our model to learn useful representations for the retrieval- and classification-based GLUE tasks during pre-training; such representations could be harder to learn from the primarily spoken language data in the BabyLM `strict-small` training set alone.

Our results show that the ATF procedure indeed improved performance on GLUE tasks, especially for the paraphrase detection (MRPC) and multi-sentence reading comprehension (MultiRC) subtasks. The QNLI and SST2 tasks targeted by the Sentiment Classification component of ATF did not improve significantly. Our experiments with prolonged training of ChapGTP up to 200 epochs resulted in increased performance for most evaluation benchmarks, but we also found *inverse scaling* behavior for the *Irregular Forms* BLiMP task. Based on this result, exploring how prolonged training affects LM's memorization of linguistic patterns beyond generalizable rules seems an interesting direction for future research.

ChapGTP outperforms the baseline models provided by the BabyLM challenge, and our ATF augmentation technique proved successful at improving performance on specific targeted tasks. Jia et al. (2022) motivated their QA-infused pre-training approach by the intuition that phrase representations should encode all questions that the phrase can answer in context. Such relational information integration might be encouraged by the addition of ATF question-answer pairs in our augmented training data as well, and could potentially result in more human-like encodings of contextual knowledge.

Nevertheless, the performance of ChapGTP on BabyLM admittedly does not present significant advances in terms of cognitive plausibility. We believe that promising approaches for stimulating more human-like learning in language models incorporate some form of human-like inductive biases in model training. Since humans presumably come to the language learning task from much less of a "blank slate" state than randomly-initialized masked language models, this area leaves much potential for further research. Our use of unsupervised constituency parsers for BRAK ChapGTP (§7.4) was an attempt to make use of such inductive biases in the syntactic domain, and resulted in notable performance gains on hierarchical generalization tasks (MSGS), although ideally such biases would be integrated into LMs more holistically.

Finally, ChapGTP is only trained only on text,

[6] An example of a constituency-labeled sentence is: `[ [ [ they are ] placed ] into ] [ [ [ one [ character [ and [ it is ] ] ] ] [ [ mostly [ used with ] ] [ east asian ] ] ] fonts ] ]`.

while children rely on many other modalities to learn language (e.g. audition and vision). Although we made efforts to indirectly incorporate multimodal cues through speech prosody and object-mediated referential games, we only scratched the surface of what is possible. The BabyLM challenge provided an inspiring start to explore such possibilities, and we hope that our range of experiments presented here will usefully inform future work on data-efficient and cognitively plausible NLP.

Limitations

There are various aspects in our setup that could have been addressed more rigorously. For reproducibility, the number of random seeds should be increased to obtain more robust insights into the impact of various training enhancements. The optimality of our hyperparameter setup is not guaranteed, a wider hyperparameter search sweep would be necessary for this.

Acknowledgements

The authors gratefully acknowledge Sarenne Wallbridge for insightful discussions about prosody-enhanced LM training, and Jelle Zuidema for useful feedback during the project.

References

Ahmed Abdelali, Francisco Guzman, Hassan Sajjad, and Stephan Vogel. 2014. The amara corpus: Building parallel language resources for the educational domain. In *LREC*, volume 14, pages 1044–1054.

Samira Abnar, Mostafa Dehghani, and Willem Zuidema. 2020. Transferring Inductive Biases through Knowledge Distillation. ArXiv:2006.00555 [cs, stat].

Nur Ahmed and Muntasir Wahed. 2020. The De-democratization of AI: Deep Learning and the Compute Divide in Artificial Intelligence Research. ArXiv:2010.15581 [cs].

Diane Bouchacourt and Marco Baroni. 2018. How agents see things: On visual representations in an emergent language game. In *Proceedings of the 2018 Conference on Empirical Methods in Natural Language Processing*, pages 981–985.

Tom Brown, Benjamin Mann, Nick Ryder, Melanie Subbiah, Jared D Kaplan, Prafulla Dhariwal, Arvind Neelakantan, Pranav Shyam, Girish Sastry, Amanda Askell, Sandhini Agarwal, Ariel Herbert-Voss, Gretchen Krueger, Tom Henighan, Rewon Child, Aditya Ramesh, Daniel Ziegler, Jeffrey Wu, Clemens Winter, Chris Hesse, Mark Chen, Eric Sigler, Mateusz Litwin, Scott Gray, Benjamin Chess, Jack Clark, Christopher Berner, Sam McCandlish, Alec Radford, Ilya Sutskever, and Dario Amodei. 2020. Language models are few-shot learners. In *Advances in Neural Information Processing Systems*, volume 33, pages 1877–1901. Curran Associates, Inc.

Grzegorz Chrupała. 2023. Putting Natural in Natural Language Processing. In *Findings of the Association for Computational Linguistics: ACL 2023*, pages 7820–7827, Toronto, Canada. Association for Computational Linguistics.

Verna Dankers, Anna Langedijk, Kate McCurdy, Adina Williams, and Dieuwke Hupkes. 2021. Generalising to German plural noun classes, from the perspective of a recurrent neural network. In *Proceedings of the 25th Conference on Computational Natural Language Learning*, pages 94–108, Online. Association for Computational Linguistics.

Andrew Drozdov, Pat Verga, Mohit Yadav, Mohit Iyyer, and Andrew McCallum. 2019. Unsupervised latent tree induction with deep inside-outside recursive autoencoders. In *North American Association for Computational Linguistics*.

Alexander Fabbri, Patrick Ng, Zhiguo Wang, Ramesh Nallapati, and Bing Xiang. 2020. Template-Based Question Generation from Retrieved Sentences for Improved Unsupervised Question Answering. In *Proceedings of the 58th Annual Meeting of the Association for Computational Linguistics*, pages 4508–4513, Online. Association for Computational Linguistics.

Steven Y. Feng, Varun Gangal, Jason Wei, Sarath Chandar, Soroush Vosoughi, Teruko Mitamura, and Eduard Hovy. 2021. A Survey of Data Augmentation Approaches for NLP. In *Findings of the Association for Computational Linguistics: ACL-IJCNLP 2021*, pages 968–988, Online. Association for Computational Linguistics.

Martin Gerlach and Francesc Font-Clos. 2018. A standardized project gutenberg corpus for statistical analysis of natural language and quantitative linguistics. *CoRR*, abs/1812.08092.

Judit Gervain, Anne Christophe, and Reiko Mazuka. 2020. Prosodic Bootstrapping. In Carlos Gussenhoven and Aoju Chen, editors, *The Oxford Handbook of Language Prosody*. Oxford University Press.

Serhii Havrylov and Ivan Titov. 2017. Emergence of language with multi-agent games: Learning to communicate with sequences of symbols. *Advances in neural information processing systems*, 30.

Pengcheng He, Jianfeng Gao, and Weizhu Chen. 2023. Debertav3: Improving deberta using electra-style pre-training with gradient-disentangled embedding sharing. In *The Eleventh International Conference on Learning Representations, ICLR 2023, Kigali, Rwanda, May 1-5, 2023*. OpenReview.net.

Felix Hill, Antoine Bordes, Sumit Chopra, and Jason Weston. 2015. The goldilocks principle: Reading children's books with explicit memory representations. *arXiv preprint arXiv:1511.02301*.

Jordan Hoffmann, Sebastian Borgeaud, Arthur Mensch, Elena Buchatskaya, Trevor Cai, Eliza Rutherford, Diego de Las Casas, Lisa Anne Hendricks, Johannes Welbl, Aidan Clark, et al. 2022. An empirical analysis of compute-optimal large language model training. *Advances in Neural Information Processing Systems*, 35:30016–30030.

Valentin Hofmann, Hinrich Schuetze, and Janet Pierrehumbert. 2022. An embarrassingly simple method to mitigate undesirable properties of pretrained language model tokenizers. In *Proceedings of the 60th Annual Meeting of the Association for Computational Linguistics (Volume 2: Short Papers)*, pages 385–393, Dublin, Ireland. Association for Computational Linguistics.

Philip A. Huebner, Elior Sulem, Fisher Cynthia, and Dan Roth. 2021. BabyBERTa: Learning more grammar with small-scale child-directed language. In *Proceedings of the 25th Conference on Computational Natural Language Learning*, pages 624–646, Online. Association for Computational Linguistics.

Robin Jia, Mike Lewis, and Luke Zettlemoyer. 2022. Question Answering Infused Pre-training of General-Purpose Contextualized Representations. In *Findings of the Association for Computational Linguistics: ACL 2022*, pages 711–728, Dublin, Ireland. Association for Computational Linguistics.

Jean Kaddour. 2023. The minipile challenge for data-efficient language models. *arXiv preprint arXiv:2304.08442*.

Jared Kaplan, Sam McCandlish, Tom Henighan, Tom B. Brown, Benjamin Chess, Rewon Child, Scott Gray, Alec Radford, Jeffrey Wu, and Dario Amodei. 2020. Scaling laws for neural language models. *CoRR*, abs/2001.08361.

Simon Kirby. 2002. Natural language from artificial life. *Artificial life*, 8(2):185–215.

Simon Kirby, Monica Tamariz, Hannah Cornish, and Kenny Smith. 2015. Compression and communication in the cultural evolution of linguistic structure. *Cognition*, 141:87–102.

Satwik Kottur, José Moura, Stefan Lee, and Dhruv Batra. 2017. Natural language does not emerge 'naturally'in multi-agent dialog. In *Proceedings of the 2017 Conference on Empirical Methods in Natural Language Processing*, pages 2962–2967.

Taku Kudo and John Richardson. 2018. SentencePiece: A simple and language independent subword tokenizer and detokenizer for neural text processing. In *Proceedings of the 2018 Conference on Empirical Methods in Natural Language Processing: System Demonstrations*, pages 66–71, Brussels, Belgium. Association for Computational Linguistics.

Angeliki Lazaridou and Marco Baroni. 2020. Emergent multi-agent communication in the deep learning era. *arXiv preprint arXiv:2006.02419*.

Angeliki Lazaridou, Anna Potapenko, and Olivier Tieleman. 2020. Multi-agent communication meets natural language: Synergies between functional and structural language learning. In *Proceedings of the 58th Annual Meeting of the Association for Computational Linguistics*, pages 7663–7674.

Katherine Lee, Daphne Ippolito, Andrew Nystrom, Chiyuan Zhang, Douglas Eck, Chris Callison-Burch, and Nicholas Carlini. 2022. Deduplicating Training Data Makes Language Models Better. In *Proceedings of the 60th Annual Meeting of the Association for Computational Linguistics (Volume 1: Long Papers)*, Dublin, Ireland. Association for Computational Linguistics.

Andreas Liesenfeld, Alianda Lopez, and Mark Dingemanse. 2023. Opening up ChatGPT: Tracking openness, transparency, and accountability in instruction-tuned text generators. In *Proceedings of the 5th International Conference on Conversational User Interfaces*, CUI '23, pages 1–6, New York, NY, USA. Association for Computing Machinery.

Tal Linzen. 2020. How Can We Accelerate Progress Towards Human-like Linguistic Generalization? In *Proceedings of the 58th Annual Meeting of the Association for Computational Linguistics*, pages 5210–5217, Online. Association for Computational Linguistics.

Pierre Lison and Jörg Tiedemann. 2016. Opensubtitles2016: Extracting large parallel corpora from movie and tv subtitles.

Yinhan Liu, Myle Ott, Naman Goyal, Jingfei Du, Mandar Joshi, Danqi Chen, Omer Levy, Mike Lewis, Luke Zettlemoyer, and Veselin Stoyanov. 2019. Roberta: A robustly optimized bert pretraining approach.

Ziming Liu, Ouail Kitouni, Niklas Nolte, Eric J Michaud, Max Tegmark, and Mike Williams. 2022. Towards understanding grokking: An effective theory of representation learning. In *Advances in Neural Information Processing Systems*.

Ziming Liu, Eric J Michaud, and Max Tegmark. 2023. Omnigrok: Grokking beyond algorithmic data. In *The Eleventh International Conference on Learning Representations*.

Ilya Loshchilov and Frank Hutter. 2019. Decoupled weight decay regularization. In *7th International Conference on Learning Representations, ICLR 2019, New Orleans, LA, USA, May 6-9, 2019*. OpenReview.net.

Diana Rodríguez Luna, Edoardo Maria Ponti, Dieuwke Hupkes, and Elia Bruni. 2020. Internal and external pressures on language emergence: least effort, object constancy and frequency. In *Findings of the Association for Computational Linguistics: EMNLP 2020*, pages 4428–4437.

Brian MacWhinney. 2000. *The CHILDES project: The database*, volume 2. Psychology Press.

Anna Martinez-Alvarez, Judit Gervain, Elena Koulaguina, Ferran Pons, and Ruth de Diego-Balaguer. 2023. Prosodic cues enhance infants' sensitivity to nonadjacent regularities. *Science Advances*, 9(15):eade4083. Publisher: American Association for the Advancement of Science.

R. Thomas McCoy and Thomas L. Griffiths. 2023. Modeling rapid language learning by distilling Bayesian priors into artificial neural networks. ArXiv:2305.14701 [cs].

Ian R. McKenzie, Alexander Lyzhov, Michael Pieler, Alicia Parrish, Aaron Mueller, Ameya Prabhu, Euan McLean, Aaron Kirtland, Alexis Ross, Alisa Liu, Andrew Gritsevskiy, Daniel Wurgaft, Derik Kauffman, Gabriel Recchia, Jiacheng Liu, Joe Cavanagh, Max Weiss, Sicong Huang, The Floating Droid, Tom Tseng, Tomasz Korbak, Xudong Shen, Yuhui Zhang, Zhengping Zhou, Najoung Kim, Samuel R. Bowman, and Ethan Perez. 2023. Inverse scaling: When bigger isn't better.

Swaroop Mishra and Bhavdeep Singh Sachdeva. 2020. Do we need to create big datasets to learn a task? In *Proceedings of SustaiNLP: Workshop on Simple and Efficient Natural Language Processing*, pages 169–173, Online. Association for Computational Linguistics.

Shikhar Murty, Pratyusha Sharma, Jacob Andreas, and Christopher Manning. 2023. Grokking of hierarchical structure in vanilla transformers. In *Proceedings of the 61st Annual Meeting of the Association for Computational Linguistics (Volume 2: Short Papers)*, pages 439–448, Toronto, Canada. Association for Computational Linguistics.

Isabel Papadimitriou and Dan Jurafsky. 2023. Pretrain on just structure: Understanding linguistic inductive biases using transfer learning. ArXiv:2304.13060 [cs].

Jeffrey Pennington, Richard Socher, and Christopher D Manning. 2014. Glove: Global vectors for word representation. In *Proceedings of the 2014 conference on empirical methods in natural language processing (EMNLP)*, pages 1532–1543.

Alethea Power, Yuri Burda, Harri Edwards, Igor Babuschkin, and Vedant Misra. 2022. Grokking: Generalization beyond overfitting on small algorithmic datasets.

Pranav Rajpurkar, Robin Jia, and Percy Liang. 2018. Know what you don't know: Unanswerable questions for SQuAD. In *Proceedings of the 56th Annual Meeting of the Association for Computational Linguistics (Volume 2: Short Papers)*, pages 784–789, Melbourne, Australia. Association for Computational Linguistics.

Roy Schwartz, Jesse Dodge, Noah A. Smith, and Oren Etzioni. 2020. Green AI. *Commun. ACM*, 63(12):54–63.

Rico Sennrich, Barry Haddow, and Alexandra Birch. 2016. Neural machine translation of rare words with subword units. In *Proceedings of the 54th Annual Meeting of the Association for Computational Linguistics (Volume 1: Long Papers)*, pages 1715–1725, Berlin, Germany. Association for Computational Linguistics.

Piyush Sharma, Nan Ding, Sebastian Goodman, and Radu Soricut. 2018. Conceptual captions: A cleaned, hypernymed, image alt-text dataset for automatic image captioning. In *Proceedings of the 56th Annual Meeting of the Association for Computational Linguistics (Volume 1: Long Papers)*, pages 2556–2565.

Noam Shazeer. 2020. Glu variants improve transformer.

Richard Socher, Alex Perelygin, Jean Wu, Jason Chuang, Christopher D. Manning, Andrew Ng, and Christopher Potts. 2013. Recursive deep models for semantic compositionality over a sentiment treebank. In *Proceedings of the 2013 Conference on Empirical Methods in Natural Language Processing*, pages 1631–1642, Seattle, Washington, USA. Association for Computational Linguistics.

Andreas Stolcke, Klaus Ries, Noah Coccaro, Elizabeth Shriberg, Rebecca Bates, Daniel Jurafsky, Paul Taylor, Rachel Martin, Carol Van Ess-Dykema, and Marie Meteer. 2000. Dialogue act modeling for automatic tagging and recognition of conversational speech. *Computational linguistics*, 26(3):339–373.

Jianlin Su, Yu Lu, Shengfeng Pan, Ahmed Murtadha, Bo Wen, and Yunfeng Liu. 2022. Roformer: Enhanced transformer with rotary position embedding.

Antti Suni, Juraj Šimko, Daniel Aalto, and Martti Vainio. 2017. Hierarchical representation and estimation of prosody using continuous wavelet transform. *Computer Speech & Language*, 45:123–136.

Vimal Thilak, Etai Littwin, Shuangfei Zhai, Omid Saremi, Roni Paiss, and Joshua Susskind. 2022. The slingshot mechanism: An empirical study of adaptive optimizers and the grokking phenomenon.

Hugo Touvron, Thibaut Lavril, Gautier Izacard, Xavier Martinet, Marie-Anne Lachaux, Timothée Lacroix, Baptiste Rozière, Naman Goyal, Eric Hambro, Faisal Azhar, Aurelien Rodriguez, Armand Joulin, Edouard Grave, and Guillaume Lample. 2023. Llama: Open and efficient foundation language models.

Sarenne Wallbridge, Peter Bell, and Catherine Lai. 2023. Quantifying the perceptual value of lexical and non-lexical channels in speech. In *Interspeech 2023: 24th Annual Conference of the International Speech Communication Association.*

Alex Wang, Yada Pruksachatkun, Nikita Nangia, Amanpreet Singh, Julian Michael, Felix Hill, Omer Levy, and Samuel R. Bowman. 2019. *SuperGLUE: A Stickier Benchmark for General-Purpose Language Understanding Systems*. Curran Associates Inc., Red Hook, NY, USA.

Alex Wang, Amanpreet Singh, Julian Michael, Felix Hill, Omer Levy, and Samuel Bowman. 2018. GLUE: A multi-task benchmark and analysis platform for natural language understanding. In *Proceedings of the 2018 EMNLP Workshop BlackboxNLP: Analyzing and Interpreting Neural Networks for NLP*, pages 353–355, Brussels, Belgium. Association for Computational Linguistics.

Alex Warstadt, Leshem Choshen, Ryan Cotterell, Tal Linzen, Aaron Mueller, Ethan Wilcox, Williams Adina, and Chengxu Zhuang. 2023. Findings of the BabyLM Challenge: Sample-efficient pretraining on developmentally plausible corpora. In *Proceedings of the BabyLM Challenge*. Association for Computational Linguistics (ACL).

Alex Warstadt, Alicia Parrish, Haokun Liu, Anhad Mohananey, Wei Peng, Sheng-Fu Wang, and Samuel R. Bowman. 2020a. BLiMP: The benchmark of linguistic minimal pairs for English. *Transactions of the Association for Computational Linguistics*, 8:377–392.

Alex Warstadt, Yian Zhang, Xiaocheng Li, Haokun Liu, and Samuel R. Bowman. 2020b. Learning which features matter: RoBERTa acquires a preference for linguistic generalizations (eventually). In *Proceedings of the 2020 Conference on Empirical Methods in Natural Language Processing (EMNLP)*, pages 217–235, Online. Association for Computational Linguistics.

Thomas Wolf, Lysandre Debut, Victor Sanh, Julien Chaumond, Clement Delangue, Anthony Moi, Pierric Cistac, Tim Rault, Remi Louf, Morgan Funtowicz, Joe Davison, Sam Shleifer, Patrick von Platen, Clara Ma, Yacine Jernite, Julien Plu, Canwen Xu, Teven Le Scao, Sylvain Gugger, Mariama Drame, Quentin Lhoest, and Alexander Rush. 2020. Transformers: State-of-the-art natural language processing. In *Proceedings of the 2020 Conference on Empirical Methods in Natural Language Processing: System Demonstrations*, pages 38–45, Online. Association for Computational Linguistics.

Shunyu Yao, Mo Yu, Yang Zhang, Karthik R Narasimhan, Joshua B Tenenbaum, and Chuang Gan. 2022. Linking emergent and natural languages via corpus transfer. *arXiv preprint arXiv:2203.13344*.

Biao Zhang and Rico Sennrich. 2019. *Root Mean Square Layer Normalization*. Curran Associates Inc., Red Hook, NY, USA.

A Sentiment Tokens

To augment the training corpus with sentiment classification we use the following lists of negative and positive tokens.

Negative: { *"not good", "not great", "not like", "didn't like", "not [a-z]+ great", "not [a-z]+ good", "horrible", "terrible", "hate", "hated", "bad", "disliked", "annoying", "frustrating", "worst"* }

Positive: { *"loved", "not bad", "not [a-z]+ bad", "great", "fantastic", "incredible", "terrific", "gorgeous", "enjoyed", "enjoy", "beautiful"* }

Penn & BGU BabyBERTa+ for Strict-Small BabyLM Challenge

Yahan Yang
University of Pennsylvania
yangy96@seas.upenn.edu

Elior Sulem
Ben-Gurion University
eliorsu@bgu.ac.il

Insup Lee
University of Pennsylvania
lee@cis.upenn.edu

Dan Roth
University of Pennsylvania
danroth@seas.upenn.edu

Abstract

The BabyLM Challenge aims at pre-training a language model on a small-scale dataset of inputs intended for children. In this work, we adapted the architecture and masking policy of BabyBERTa (Huebner et al., 2021) to solve the strict-small track of the BabyLM challenge. Our model, Penn & BGU BabyBERTa+, was pre-trained and evaluated on the three benchmarks of the BabyLM Challenge. Experimental results indicate that our model achieves higher or comparable performance in predicting 17 grammatical phenomena, compared to the RoBERTa baseline. [1]

1 Introduction

With the emergence of deep-learning techniques (Liu et al., 2019; Vaswani et al., 2017), large language models pre-trained on massive datasets containing billions or trillions of words have achieved remarkable performance across various downstream tasks. However, the BabyLM challenge (Warstadt et al., 2023) highlights the importance of investigating the impact of small-scale pretraining and cognitive modeling. BabyBERTa (Huebner et al., 2021), a variant of the RoBERTa architecture in a smaller size, demonstrated superior performance and data efficiency in learning grammar phenomena with child-directed inputs compared to RoBERTa-base (Liu et al., 2019). Inspired by this work, we propose a model named Penn & BGU BabyBERTa+[2] (encoder-only), which shares the architecture and pretraining policies, for the BabyLM challenge with BabyBERTa. In this work, we consider the strict-small challenge which contains approximately 10M words for small-scale pretraining. We provide the details of our BabyBERTa+ in Section 2 and show the result of the BabyLM challenge in Section 3.

2 Methodology

In this section, we provide the descriptions of our BabyBERTa+ model including the architectures, tokenizers, training objectives and so on. As shown in Table 1, our model is much smaller compared to RoBERTa-base in terms of depth and width but uses a different masking policy[3]. The pre-training hyperparameters are the same as in the RoBERTa baseline as used in Warstadt et al. (2023) if not specified in Table 1 and the architecture choices are based on (Huebner et al., 2021). The model is pre-trained on the dataset ($\sim$ 10M words) provided in the strict-small track of the challenge. In other words, BabyBERTa+ differs from BabyBERTa (Huebner et al., 2021) by its vocabulary size and training corpus.

	RoBERTa-base	BabyBERTa+
layers	12	8
attention heads	12	8
hidden size	768	256
intermediate size	3072	1024
vocabulary size	50265	30000
epochs	20	100

Table 1: Comparison of RoBERTa and BabyBERTa+ in terms of their architectures.

2.1 Tokenizer

Following previous work (Liu et al., 2019; Huebner et al., 2021), our model utilizes Byte-Pair Encoding to create a vocabulary containing both words and subwords. We create a tokenizer with a vocabulary size of 30,000 and train it on the strict-small dataset.

2.2 Unmasking Removal Policy

To train the masked language model, the standard RoBERTa masking strategy replaces 80% of the corrupted tokens with the "<mask>" token, while 10% of the tokens are replaced with random tokens, and the remaining 10% are left unchanged. The

[1] Our Dynabench submission ID is 1372. The link to access the model is https://huggingface.co/yangy96/BabyLM_strict_small_Penn-BGU-BabyBERTa/tree/main.

[2] In our paper, we use Penn & BGU BabyBERTa+ and BabyBERTa+ interchangeably.

[3] Our implementation of the model is based on the Huggingface transformer library (Wolf et al., 2020).

Proceedings of the 27th Conference on Computational Natural Language Learning: Volume 2: The BabyLM Challenge, pages 86–88
December 6-7, 2023 ©2023 Association for Computational Linguistics

Acc.	Ana Agr.	Agr. Str	Binding	C/R	D-N Agr.	Ellipsis	Filler-Gap	Irregular	Isl. Eff
R	81.5	67.1	67.3	67.9	90.8	76.4	63.5	87.4	39.9
B+	83.6	68.2	66.9	65.9	92.4	82.5	65.8	92.1	39.7
	NPI	Quan.	S-V Agr.	Hypernym	QA (easy)	QA (tricky)	Subj.-Aux.	Turn Taking	
R	55.9	70.5	65.4	49.4	31.3	32.1	71.7	53.2	
B+	68.8	75.9	68.1	50.2	71.9	40.6	87.6	67.5	

Table 2: Zeroshot performance of RoBERTa (R) and BabyBERTa+ (B+) on the BLiMP benchmark. The performances were reported in terms of accuracy.

Acc.	CoLA	SST-2	MRPC	QQP	MNLI	MNLI-mm	QNLI	RTE	BoolQ	MultiRC	WSC
R	70.8	87	79.2	73.7	73.2	74	77	61.6	66.3	61.4	61.4
B+	69.48	86.42	82	81.08	70.39	71.18	69.29	51.52	61.69	60.02	61.45

Table 3: Comparison of RoBERTa (R) and BabyBERTa+ (B+) on the SuperGLUE benchmark. The performances were reported in terms of accuracy, except for MRPC and QQP, where the F1 score was used instead.

Acc.	CR_C	LC_C	MV_C	RP_C	SC_C	CR_LC	CR_RTP	MV_LC	MV_RTP	SC_LC	SC_RP
R	84.1	100	99.4	93.5	96.4	67.7	68.6	66.7	68.6	84.2	65.7
B+	85.6	100.0	98.7	96.2	87.3	66.3	66.7	66.6	66.9	67.4	64.2

Table 4: Comparison of RoBERTa (R) and BabyBERTa+ (B+) on the MSGS benchmark. The performances were reported in terms of accuracy.

unmasking removal policy proposed in Huebner et al. (2021) takes a different approach by removing the prediction for unchanged tokens. In this case, 90% of the corrupted tokens are masked with the "<mask>", and the remaining are replaced with random tokens. We utilize the same masking policy when pre-training BabyBERTa+.

3 BabyBERTa+ on downstream tasks of BabyLM challenge

In this section, we evaluate our pre-trained models on the tasks in BabyLM challenges of the strict-small tracks. There are three different evaluation benchmarks: BLiMP test suites (Warstadt et al., 2020a), SuperGLUE (Wang et al., 2019) and Mixed Signals Generalization Set (MSGS) (Warstadt et al., 2020b). The BLiMP test suite evaluates the ability of language models to handle grammar. MSGS is a syntactic dataset to test the inductive bias for downstream tasks. SuperGLUE is a standard benchmark to evaluate the capabilities of the pre-trained language models on natural language understanding downstream tasks. We presented the detailed performance of predicting grammatical phenomena in Table 2 and downstream tasks in Table 3 and 4. We use the default hyperparameters as defined in (Warstadt et al., 2023) to fine-tune our system on BabyLM challenges. Our model gets 6% improvement on BLiMP test suite compared to the baseline RoBERTa (69.86% vs 63.02%). The average score on all SuperGLUE tasks in Table 3 is 69.50% while the performance of the baseline model is 71.42%. The average score on MSGS is 78.72% while the RoBERTa-base's score is 81.35%.[4]

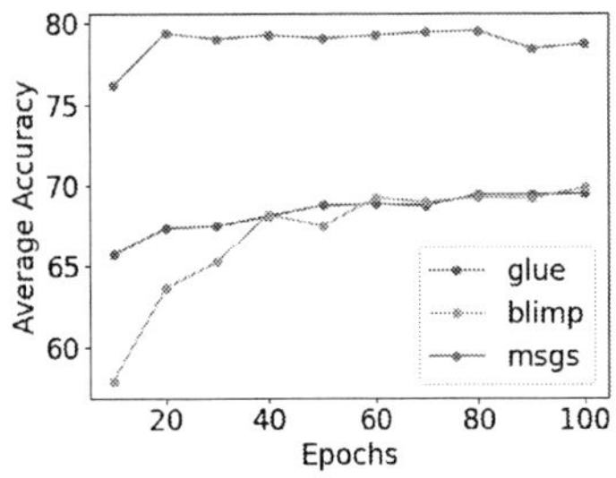

Figure 1: Average accuracy of BabyBERTa+ on three tasks versus the number of pre-training epochs.

We additionally plot the average accuracy on grammaticality tests and downstream tasks versus the number of pre-training epochs in Figure 1. We observe that when continually pre-training with more epochs, both grammatical phenomena prediction and SuperGLUE downstream task performance improve.

4 Conclusion

In this study, we propose a model named BabyBERTa+ by adapting BabyBERTa (Huebner et al., 2021) for the BabyLM challenge (Warstadt et al., 2023) on strict-small tasks and demonstrate the effectiveness of pre-training a smaller model in learning grammatical phenomena compared to RoBERTa (Liu et al., 2019) and other baselines. However, while our model exhibits promising results in learning grammatical features, its performance on downstream tasks remains lower than larger models like RoBERTa. In the future, we aim to explore the impact of the various pre-training factors when pre-training the small model on a limited size of child-directed data corpora and enhance the small model's performance on downstream tasks.

[4]The RoBERTa's results are provided in the BabyLM challenge.

Acknowledgements

Research was sponsored by the Army Research Office and was accomplished under Grant Number W911NF-20-1-0080. It was also supported by Contracts FA8750-19-2-0201 and FA8750-19-2-1004 with the US Defense Advanced Research Projects Agency (DARPA) as well as by grants from the Israeli Ministry of Innovation, Science & Technology (#000519) and the BGU/Philadelphia Academic Bridge (The Sutnick/Zipkin Endowment Fund). Approved for Public Release, Distribution Unlimited. The views expressed are those of the authors and do not reflect the official policy or position of the Army Research Office, the Department of Defense or the U.S. Government. The U.S. Government is authorized to reproduce and distribute reprints for Government purposes notwithstanding any copyright notation herein. This research was also supported by a gift from AWS AI for research in Trustworthy AI.

References

Philip A. Huebner, Elior Sulem, Fisher Cynthia, and Dan Roth. 2021. BabyBERTa: Learning more grammar with small-scale child-directed language. In *Proceedings of the 25th Conference on Computational Natural Language Learning*, pages 624–646, Online. Association for Computational Linguistics.

Yinhan Liu, Myle Ott, Naman Goyal, Jingfei Du, Mandar Joshi, Danqi Chen, Omer Levy, Mike Lewis, Luke Zettlemoyer, and Veselin Stoyanov. 2019. Roberta: A robustly optimized bert pretraining approach. *arXiv preprint arXiv:1907.11692*.

Ashish Vaswani, Noam Shazeer, Niki Parmar, Jakob Uszkoreit, Llion Jones, Aidan N Gomez, Łukasz Kaiser, and Illia Polosukhin. 2017. Attention is all you need. *Advances in neural information processing systems*, 30.

Alex Wang, Yada Pruksachatkun, Nikita Nangia, Amanpreet Singh, Julian Michael, Felix Hill, Omer Levy, and Samuel Bowman. 2019. Superglue: A stickier benchmark for general-purpose language understanding systems. *Advances in neural information processing systems*, 32.

Alex Warstadt, Aaron Mueller, Leshem Choshen, Ethan Gotlieb Wilcox, Chengxu Zhuang, Juan Ciro, Rafael Mosquera, Adina Williams, Bhargavi Paranjabe, Tal Linzen, and Ryan Cotterell. 2023. Findings of the 2023 BabyLM Challenge: Sample-efficient pretraining on developmentally plausible corpora. In *Proceedings of the 2023 BabyLM Challenge*. Association for Computational Linguistics (ACL).

Alex Warstadt, Alicia Parrish, Haokun Liu, Anhad Mohananey, Wei Peng, Sheng-Fu Wang, and Samuel R. Bowman. 2020a. BLiMP: The Benchmark of Linguistic Minimal Pairs for English. *Transactions of the Association for Computational Linguistics*, 8:377–392.

Alex Warstadt, Yian Zhang, Haau-Sing Li, Haokun Liu, and Samuel R Bowman. 2020b. Learning which features matter: Roberta acquires a preference for linguistic generalizations (eventually). In *Proceedings of the 2020 Conference on Empirical Methods in Natural Language Processing*, Punta Cana, Dominican Republic. Association for Computational Linguistics.

Thomas Wolf, Lysandre Debut, Victor Sanh, Julien Chaumond, Clement Delangue, Anthony Moi, Pierric Cistac, Tim Rault, Remi Louf, Morgan Funtowicz, Joe Davison, Sam Shleifer, Patrick von Platen, Clara Ma, Yacine Jernite, Julien Plu, Canwen Xu, Teven Le Scao, Sylvain Gugger, Mariama Drame, Quentin Lhoest, and Alexander Rush. 2020. Transformers: State-of-the-art natural language processing. In *Proceedings of the 2020 Conference on Empirical Methods in Natural Language Processing: System Demonstrations*, pages 38–45, Online. Association for Computational Linguistics.

Too Much Information: Keeping Training Simple for BabyLMs

Lukas Edman **Lisa Bylinina**
Center for Language and Cognition
University of Groningen
j.l.edman@rug.nl, e.g.bylinina@rug.nl

Abstract

This paper details the work of the University of Groningen for the BabyLM Challenge (Warstadt et al., 2023). We follow the idea that, like babies, language models should be introduced to simpler concepts first and build off of that knowledge to understand more complex concepts. We examine this strategy of simple-then-complex through a variety of lenses, namely context size, vocabulary, and overall linguistic complexity of the data. We find that only one, context size, is truly beneficial to training a language model. However this simple change to context size gives us improvements of 2 points on average on (Super)GLUE tasks, 1 point on MSGS tasks, and 12% on average on BLiMP tasks. Our context-limited model outperforms the baseline that was trained on 10× the amount of data.

1 Introduction

The pretraining of language models has traditionally relied on large amounts of data, which, for many languages, is readily available. However there exist several low-resource languages in which even unlabeled data is not so readily available. While transferring knowledge from other languages is often an effective way to achieve better performance, there may be implicit biases also transferred from the text of the higher-resource language, which could be potentially harmful. Additionally, given that a 13 year old sees less than 100 million words in their lifetime (orders of magnitude less than the amount used in LM pretraining), there ought to be methods that more efficiently learn from limited data.

Such is the motivation for the BabyLM Challenge and subsequently our work. We focus on the `strict-small` track, which limits the training data to only 10 million words, from a selection of domains with varying complexity (from child speak up to Wikipedia articles).

In our work, we investigate different methods for introducing the model to varying levels of complexity. Namely we ramp up the difficulty of the pretraining along 3 avenues:

1. Context length
2. Dataset complexity
3. Vocabulary size

Concerning context length, we adopt the strategy of starting with a small number of tokens per input and increasing this over the course of training, with the intuition that a human typically learns a language starting with short sentences with limited cross-sentential context, and builds up from there to longer contexts.

In addition, the sentences initially learned by a human are also simpler conceptually, starting with frequently-used words and building up to rarer words. To this end, we develop a strategy to filter the dataset such that the model starts training on simpler data and later trains on more complex data.

Similarly, we also follow the intuition that a human develops a vocabulary over time, originating from the chunking of characters within the words, and as such we start with a character-level vocabulary and introduce a transfer method to give a good initialization for a larger subword vocabulary.

2 Related Work

Concerning context size, prior work (Edman et al., 2022) has shown that in low-resource language modeling, using a lower context size can greatly help with model convergence. The concept of increasing context size is not novel: BERT (Devlin et al., 2018) was initially trained on a smaller context size of 128 tokens before being increased to 512, though, to our knowledge, this was done for efficiency reasons. There have been several works on internally reducing the scope of contextualization by limiting attention to local patches (Beltagy

Proceedings of the 27th Conference on Computational Natural Language Learning: Volume 2: The BabyLM Challenge, pages 89–97
December 6-7, 2023

et al., 2020; Zaheer et al., 2020), thereby decreasing the complexity of self-attention. These works were done with processing long documents in mind, however, and can have a negative impact on model speed given an extra layer of complexity in calculating self-attention.

Concerning vocabulary size, there is ample work on character-level models, where they have been shown to require less data for pretraining while achieving the same or better performance at the cost of training and inference speed (Xue et al., 2022). Character models also can greatly outperform subword models on out-of-domain tasks (Boukkouri et al., 2020), low-resource translation (Edman et al., 2023), and tasks which require morphology or character-level perturbations (Xue et al., 2022; Ingólfsdóttir et al., 2023). Their performance in these scenarios has been largely attributed to their non-static vocabulary, allowing for good initializations to unseen or rarely-seen words. All of this points to character-informed models being potentially useful for this shared task.

Concerning lexical complexity, (Eldan and Li, 2023) has shown that using a synthetic dataset of children's stories, written for a 3 or 4 year old to understand, one can train a small (<10M parameter) Transformer model and generate stories near the quality of much larger models.

Another group of NLP approaches that condition learning on linguistic complexity is a branch of curriculum learning, exploring potential benefits from exposing models to training samples in a meaningful order, from easy to hard (Bengio et al. 2009; Kocmi and Bojar 2017; Zhang et al. 2018 among many others). These approaches show conceptual promise but are complicated by the choice of appropriate complexity measures and the pacing function.[1]

3 Method

3.1 Model Choice

We opted to use encoder-only models. We initially experimented with encoder-decoder models, but found that the evaluation metrics for this shared task being non-generative gave encoder-only models an advantage, as it allows for full attention, rather than only causal attention. In terms of specific model selection, we opted for RoBERTa-base (Liu et al., 2019) in order to directly compare with the provided baseline. We also experimented with (and ultimately submitted) DeBERTa-large (He et al., 2021) as it is a larger model and considered state-of-the-art for encoder-only models.

3.2 Training and Evaluation

Our pretraining uses the standard MLM scheme (Liu et al., 2019), which proved most effective initial tests.[2] Table 1 shows the hyperparameters we used for our pretraining experiments. For finetuning, we use the default hyperparameters provided by the shared task organizers.

Hyperparameter	Value
Learning rate	1e-4
Decay	0.01
Warmup steps	10000
Optimizer	AdamW
Batch size	256
Epochs	50

Table 1: Hyperparameters used.

We primarily evaluate with BLiMP (Warstadt et al., 2020a), due to its speed of evaluation and not requiring a fine-tuning step. We also report results of our best models for the BLiMP supplement, (Super-)GLUE (Wang et al., 2018, 2019), and MSGS (Warstadt et al., 2020b) tasks.

3.3 Vocabulary size

We first experiment with vocabulary size. For creating the vocabulary, we use SentencePiece's Unigram model (Kudo and Richardson, 2018; Kudo, 2018). We found that a vocabulary size of 40k provided the best standalone performance on BLiMP (we report this in Appendix A).

We further experiment with a character-level vocabulary, and transferring to a subword vocabulary (of size 40k). To enable this transfer, we copy over all character-only embeddings, and initialize subword embeddings as the sum of their respective character embeddings. The main body of the transformer model is also directly copied. The language modelling head is simply re-trained from scratch.

[1]Pacing function is a broad term used by Soviany et al. (2022), describing the method for ramping up difficulty across the course of training.

[2]We also varied masking amounts to 20% and 40% following Wettig et al. (2022), but did not see any increased performance on BLiMP.

3.4 Context size

We also experiment with context sizes in powers of 2, from 16 to 256. To achieve a consistent and coherent context size, we split the data into n-token examples (with n being the context size), prior to shuffling. Our initial experiments with determining the optimal vocabulary size use a context size of 64, although we later find that a context size of 32 performs slightly better.

3.5 Curriculum learning

We explored potential gains from different order of exposure of the model to training data, inspired by curriculum learning approaches (see Bengio et al. 2009 and much subsequent work; for a recent comprehensive survey of the field of curriculum learning, see Soviany et al. 2022).

The basic motivating intuition is to start the training with subsets of data that are 'simpler' than others in some relevant sense, gradually increasing the complexity of data the model is trained on. Hopefully, simple data can give the model a head start that would also form a foundation for linguistic generalization. To try out this idea, we formulate a **complexity measure** that we use in data reordering. The measure is a combination of the following features:

- **Type/Token Ratio**: The number of unique words in a text divided by the length of the text in words. The feature targets lexical diversity of the text per text unit.
- **Mean word rarity**: The mean of rarity scores across all words in the text (word rarity score is 1 - normalized log-frequency; it ranges from 0 to 1, the higher the rarer). This is another measure of text complexity via lexical diversity – this time, based on how rare the words used in the text are, as judged based on the whole training dataset.
- **Max word rarity**: The maximum of word rarity scores in the text. Same as above, but picking out the maximum – the peak of complexity-as-rarity reached in the text.
- **Punctuation density**: The proportion of punctuation marks in the union of words and punctuation marks in the text. This proportion is used as a proxy to syntactic complexity.
- **Mean sentence length** in the text, in words.
- **Mean word length** in the text, in characters. These last two scores approximate syntactic and morphological/lexical complexity, respectively.

Features like these and their different combinations are often used to measure text complexity and/or readability (Bengio et al., 2009; Spitkovsky et al., 2009; Cirik et al., 2016; Kocmi and Bojar, 2017; Zhang et al., 2018; Platanios et al., 2019; Chang et al., 2021).

In our experiments, we scale all these features to fit into the [0,1] interval (with MinMax scaler) and use their mean as our complexity measure.

To assess the role of data ordering along the complexity scale based on the measure above, we trained triples of minimally different models, keeping everything apart from the data ordering fixed:

- **Curriculum model**: All training data is ordered by increasing complexity.
- **No-curriculum model**: No particular order is imposed on the training data.
- **Reversed-curriculum model**: Training data is ordered by **decreasing** complexity.

All models in this set of experiments are RoBERTa-base models trained following the two-stage procedure described in Section 4.1 – first, the models are trained on context size 32, then the context is increased to 128. Unlike in other experiments, however, each of the stages was further divided into three consecutive phases:

- **Phase 1**: The first 1/3 of the data is used in training, the other 2/3 are withheld. The curriculum model just sees the 'easiest' data here; the reversed-curriculum model sees the 'most difficult' portion; the baseline, no-curriculum model sees 1/3 of data without any particular selection;
- **Phase 2**: Another 1/3 of the data is unlocked. Now all models are being trained on 2/3 of all training data. Both the curriculum model and the reversed-curriculum model now have access to the middle of the complexity range.
- **Phase 3**: The final 1/3 of data is unlocked. Now all models are being trained on the whole range of complexity.

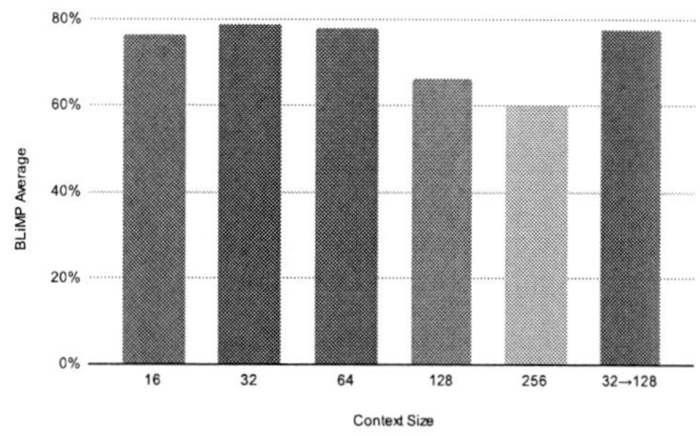

Figure 1: Average BLiMP score for models trained using various context sizes. 32→128 indicates a model trained initially on context size 32, then trained again on 128.

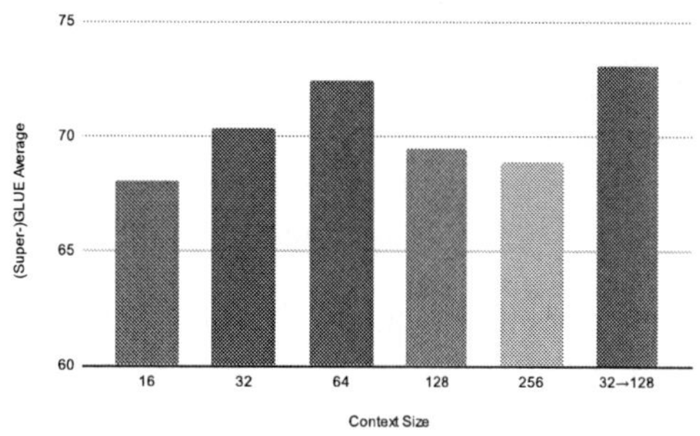

Figure 2: Average (Super-)GLUE score for models trained using various context sizes. 32→128 indicates a model trained initially on context size 32, then trained again on 128.

The data-unlocking procedure above happens twice: first, on a small context size (32 tokens), and later when the context size is increased (128 tokens).

Using the taxonomy of curriculum learning in (Soviany et al., 2022), we can describe our approach as vanilla data-level curriculum learning with easy-then-hard iterative schedule.

4 Results

4.1 Context Size

The vast majority of our improvement comes from limiting the context size. We show this in Figures 1 and 2. Here we can see that a context size of 32 gives the best performance on BLIMP, whereas 64 gives the best performance on GLUE. The overall shift in trend between the two benchmarks fits with the fact that the average input length is longer in GLUE than in BLIMP. There is a substantial drop in performance using a context size of greater than 64. To our understanding, the baselines provided by the task organizers use a context size of 128, which may explain their relatively poorer performance (as shown later in Figure 4).

However, if we simply first train with a context size of 32, then increase the context size to 128, we see a substantial gain over training on 128 from the beginning. In the case of GLUE, we see that increasing the context size from 32 to 128 increases the performance beyond what simply training on 32 *or* 128 alone can accomplish. This suggests that a larger context size is indeed necessary for performance on (Super-)GLUE, but pretraining initially on a smaller context can guide the model to more efficient training on larger context sizes.

4.2 Vocabulary Expansion

Next, we look at the performance of our models which were initially trained on a character-level vocabulary, then transferred to our 40k subword vocabulary. We show the results in Table 2.

		Vocabulary size	
		40k	Char→40k
Context size	32	**78.6**	77.1
	64	77.8	**78.6**

Table 2: Average performance on BLiMP across context and vocabulary sizes.

As we can see, the performance is mixed and depends on the context size. For context size 64, there appears to be an improvement, however for context size 32, the performance drops. The lack of improvement for context size 32 led us to leave out this technique in our final model, as the potential gains are inconsistent and training first on the character level adds a costly extra pretraining step.

As for the use of characters in low-resource pretraining, we suspect that there are better ways of integrating rather than via an extra initial pretraining step. Using our method, the model is susceptible to forgetting what it has learned during the character-level pretraining when it is pretraining for the second time.

Additionally, the evaluation metrics chosen for this shared task do not stand out as tasks where character models would be particularly beneficial. Other tasks where character-level models have been shown to greatly outperform subword-level models such as morphological inflection would be perhaps

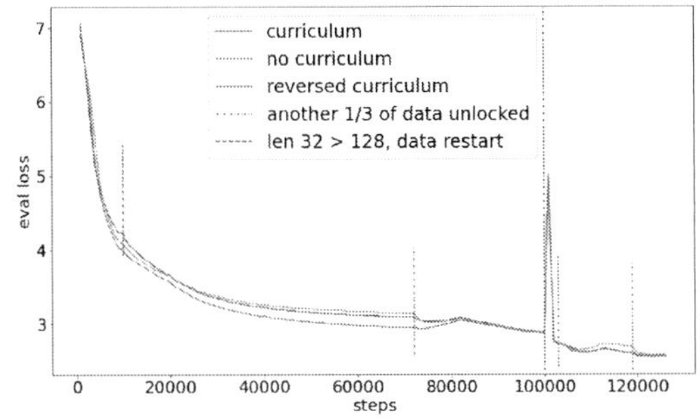

Figure 3: Loss dynamics for three minimally different models: curriculum; no curriculum; reversed curriculum.

more suitable for assessing the potential benefits of our character-informed model.

4.3 Curriculum learning

We evaluate the results of data ordering from simple to complex against two alternatives: no data ordering and reversed data ordering (from difficult to simple). We train triples of models that minimally differ from each other – everything apart from the order of data is kept constant.

Figure 3 shows evaluation loss dynamics of one typical model triples during training (we set up several training experiments, varying the number of epochs per phase, without qualitative change in results, so here we only report one of them).

While there are stages in training where the loss seems to indicate an advantage of the curriculum model against the baseline one, the no-curriculum model eventually catches up. Perhaps more surprisingly, the reversed-curriculum model shows systematically lower loss during longer phases of training.

Targeted linguistic evaluation also shows mixed results. Table 3 lists BLiMP scores for the model triple:

We don't see a clear pattern in what types of linguistic phenomena benefit from a particular order of data exposure and can't conclude whether the observed effects are robust and systematic.

The lack of a clear benefit from the curriculum might be traced back to at least one of the following:

- Low quality of the complexity metric;
- Inadequacy of the complexity metric for the training objective;
- Interfering data noise;

BLiMP Scores	Cur.	Rev. cur.	No cur.
Anaph. agree.	89.4	89.4	**90.1**
Arg. struct.	**73.6**	71.3	72.5
Binding	69.3	**70.7**	68.8
Control raising	**71.1**	71.0	70.5
Det. noun agree.	**95.3**	94.0	**95.3**
Ellipsis	**86.2**	82.2	83.7
Filler gap	**75.9**	70.7	72.8
Irregular forms	83.7	83.0	**86.5**
Island effects	54.9	**62.1**	53.5
NPI licensing	67.1	66.8	**70.5**
Quantifiers	68.9	**69.3**	66.2
SV agree.	81.2	**81.8**	78.8
Average	**76.4**	76.0	75.8

Table 3: The effect of data ordering on linguistic generalization.

- Non-optimal pacing function;
- The genuine lack of advantage from data reordering.

To illustrate some of these considerations, we pick three typical samples from the ordered dataset for context size 32 – from the 'simplest' end, from the middle, and from the 'most complex' end, respectively:

(a)
```
down!
up up up up up up up up up
up up up up up down!
```

(b)
```
the flared skirt of the cone yet to
be combed, and this provide
```

(c)
```
p;amp;gt;&amp;amp;gt;Exactly.
&amp;amp;gt;&amp;amp;gt;Combining
```

The easiest samples are indeed linguistically simple – they contain a lot of repetitions, very simple syntactic structures and very frequent words. At the same time they are not very representative of the rest of the dataset, both grammatically and lexicaly. The typical sample from the main body of the dataset – samples like (b) – do not show the characteristic repetitive pattern and a large proportion of the lexical material across the dataset falls outside of what the simplest samples contain. The simplest data defined the way we do it is useful for generalization to the rest of the data only to a very limited degree: the model does see the most frequent words, but the contexts of their use are pretty different from how they are typically used elsewhere. For a model with non-character-level tokenization, it might not be particularly helpful.

On the other side of the complexity scale, a lot of samples are indeed difficult, but in a way that does not necessarily reflect true linguistic complexity: vocabulary and punctuation features push up samples that contain elements of HTML, have collapsed space symbols, are lists or are written in languages that are not the main language of the dataset.

In a sense, both extreme ends of the complexity scale contain samples that are probably not good grounds for linguistic generalization given the MLM training objective, but in different ways.

4.4 Model Size

Table 4 shows the performances of the two models we used, as well as DeBERTa-base to control for the differences in model architecture between RoBERTa and DeBERTa. We can see that DeBERTa-large generally performs best. Interestingly, we see that switching from RoBERTa to DeBERTa seems to account for the difference in GLUE scores, but scaling up to large accounts for the increase in BLiMP scores. This shows that when limiting the context size, we can potentially scale up to larger models even when data is scarce.

	Ro-base	De-base	De-large
BLiMP	78.6	79.0	**81.0**
BLiMP supp.	**63.8**	59.8	**63.8**
MSGS	-70.7	-62.2	**-53.7**
GLUE	70.3	**72.5**	**72.5**

Table 4: RoBERTa-base versus DeBERTA-base and large on all tasks. MSGS is the average Matthew's Correlation Coefficient multiplied by 100. Best in bold.

We also experimented with training a Deberta-XL model, which is identical to Deberta-Large except with 48 layers rather than 24. Our results on BLiMP were however not better (roughly 2% worse than the comparable `large` model), so it would seem that there is a limit to how much one can simply scale up model size and see performance improvements when it comes to pretraining on limited data.

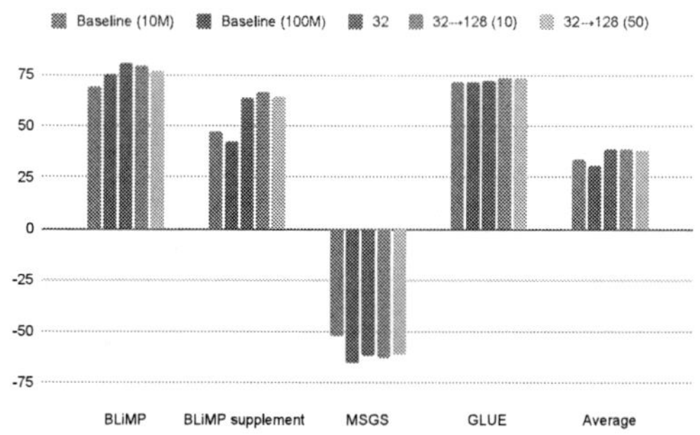

Figure 4: Average scores for submitted models compared to baselines. 32→128 indicates a model trained initially on context size 32, then trained again on 128. The number in parentheses indicates the number of epochs trained on for the second iteration of pretraining. MSGS scores are the average Matthew's Correlation Coefficient, multiplied by 100.

4.5 Submission

In Figure 4, we show the overall results for our best models, compared to the baselines. We also report results on each individual sub-task in Appendix B. Our final models include a model trained only on context size 32, and two trained again on context size 128, one for 10 epochs and one for 50 epochs. As our one trained with 10 additional epochs performed best on average, this was our final submission. We can see the trade-off for context size between the GLUE and BLiMP scores, as BLiMP favors models trained on a shorter context while GLUE favors models trained on a longer context. MSGS appears to also have some slight preference for models trained on a shorter context, though the differences between all models is comparatively small. Interestingly, the 10M baseline is better on average than the 100M baseline on MSGS, as well as the BLiMP supplement. We see the largest difference in the BLiMP supplement, where our models outperform the baselines by around 20 points on average. Much of this improvement comes from the `qa_congruence_easy` set, where our best model achieved a score of 81%, compared to the baseline score of 31%.

5 Conclusion

Our conclusion is very simple: if you want to pretrain a model on little data, train with a smaller context size. This can greatly aid in model convergence such that no specific hyperparameter tuning or complex methods need to be used for superior performance.

In fact, both of our more "complex" approaches concerning initialization with a character vocabulary and curriculum learning proved to be unreliable, where gains paled in comparison to the gains realized from simply lowering context size.

If a larger context size is eventually needed, such as for some GLUE tasks, continuing training with a larger context size can provide some benefit. We do think that there may be a smarter way to control context size, such as a gradual increasing during training, which could lead to smoother and faster training. Additionally we expect that there are other potential ways to implicitly limit context size, such as limiting self-attention, which may achieve a similar effect.

Acknowledgements

We thank the Center for Information Technology of the University of Groningen for their support and for providing access to the Hábrók high performance computing cluster.

References

Iz Beltagy, Matthew E Peters, and Arman Cohan. 2020. Longformer: The long-document transformer. *arXiv preprint arXiv:2004.05150*.

Yoshua Bengio, Jérôme Louradour, Ronan Collobert, and Jason Weston. 2009. Curriculum learning. In *Proceedings of the 26th annual international conference on machine learning*, pages 41–48.

Hicham El Boukkouri, Olivier Ferret, Thomas Lavergne, Hiroshi Noji, Pierre Zweigenbaum, and Junichi Tsujii. 2020. Characterbert: Reconciling elmo and bert for word-level open-vocabulary representations from characters. *arXiv preprint arXiv:2010.10392*.

Ernie Chang, Hui-Syuan Yeh, and Vera Demberg. 2021. Does the order of training samples matter? Improving neural data-to-text generation with curriculum learning. In *Proceedings of the 16th Conference of the European Chapter of the Association for Computational Linguistics: Main Volume*, pages 727–733.

Volkan Cirik, Eduard Hovy, and Louis-Philippe Morency. 2016. Visualizing and understanding curriculum learning for long short-term memory networks. *arXiv preprint arXiv:1611.06204*.

Jacob Devlin, Ming-Wei Chang, Kenton Lee, and Kristina Toutanova. 2018. Bert: Pre-training of deep bidirectional transformers for language understanding. *arXiv preprint arXiv:1810.04805*.

Lukas Edman, Antonio Toral, and Gertjan van Noord. 2022. The importance of context in very low resource language modeling. *arXiv preprint arXiv:2205.04810*.

Lukas Edman, Antonio Toral, and Gertjan van Noord. 2023. Are character-level translations worth the wait? An extensive comparison of character-and subword-level models for machine translation. *arXiv preprint arXiv:2302.14220*.

Ronen Eldan and Yuanzhi Li. 2023. Tinystories: How small can language models be and still speak coherent english? *arXiv preprint arXiv:2305.07759*.

Pengcheng He, Jianfeng Gao, and Weizhu Chen. 2021. Debertav3: Improving deberta using electra-style pretraining with gradient-disentangled embedding sharing. *arXiv preprint arXiv:2111.09543*.

Svanhvít Lilja Ingólfsdóttir, Pétur Orri Ragnarsson, Haukur Páll Jónsson, Haukur Barri Símonarson, Vilhjálmur Þorsteinsson, and Vésteinn Snæbjarnarson. 2023. Byte-level grammatical error correction using synthetic and curated corpora. *arXiv preprint arXiv:2305.17906*.

Tom Kocmi and Ondrej Bojar. 2017. Curriculum learning and minibatch bucketing in neural machine translation. *arXiv preprint arXiv:1707.09533*.

Taku Kudo. 2018. Subword regularization: Improving neural network translation models with multiple subword candidates. *arXiv preprint arXiv:1804.10959*.

Taku Kudo and John Richardson. 2018. Sentencepiece: A simple and language independent subword tokenizer and detokenizer for neural text processing. *arXiv preprint arXiv:1808.06226*.

Yinhan Liu, Myle Ott, Naman Goyal, Jingfei Du, Mandar Joshi, Danqi Chen, Omer Levy, Mike Lewis, Luke Zettlemoyer, and Veselin Stoyanov. 2019. Roberta: A robustly optimized bert pretraining approach. *arXiv preprint arXiv:1907.11692*.

Emmanouil Antonios Platanios, Otilia Stretcu, Graham Neubig, Barnabás Poczós, and Tom Mitchell. 2019. Competence-based curriculum learning for neural machine translation. In *Proceedings of the 2019 Conference of the North American Chapter of the Association for Computational Linguistics: Human Language Technologies, Volume 1 (Long and Short Papers)*, pages 1162–1172.

Petru Soviany, Radu Tudor Ionescu, Paolo Rota, and Nicu Sebe. 2022. Curriculum learning: A survey. *International Journal of Computer Vision*, 130(6):1526–1565.

Valentin I Spitkovsky, Hiyan Alshawi, and Daniel Jurafsky. 2009. Baby steps: How "less is more" in unsupervised dependency parsing.

Alex Wang, Yada Pruksachatkun, Nikita Nangia, Amanpreet Singh, Julian Michael, Felix Hill, Omer Levy, and Samuel Bowman. 2019. Superglue: A stickier benchmark for general-purpose language understanding systems. *Advances in neural information processing systems*, 32.

Alex Wang, Amanpreet Singh, Julian Michael, Felix Hill, Omer Levy, and Samuel R Bowman. 2018. Glue: A multi-task benchmark and analysis platform for natural language understanding. *arXiv preprint arXiv:1804.07461*.

Alex Warstadt, Aaron Mueller, Leshem Choshen, Ethan Gotlieb Wilcox, Chengxu Zhuang, Juan Ciro, Rafael Mosquera, Adina Williams, Bhargavi Paranjabe, Tal Linzen, and Ryan Cotterell. 2023. Findings of the 2023 BabyLM Challenge: Sample-efficient pretraining on developmentally plausible corpora. In *Proceedings of the 2023 BabyLM Challenge*. Association for Computational Linguistics (ACL).

Alex Warstadt, Alicia Parrish, Haokun Liu, Anhad Mohananey, Wei Peng, Sheng-Fu Wang, and Samuel R Bowman. 2020a. Blimp: The benchmark of linguistic minimal pairs for english. *Transactions of the Association for Computational Linguistics*, 8:377–392.

Alex Warstadt, Yian Zhang, Haau-Sing Li, Haokun Liu, and Samuel R Bowman. 2020b. Learning which features matter: Roberta acquires a preference for linguistic generalizations (eventually). In *Proceedings of the 2020 Conference on Empirical Methods in Natural Language Processing*, Punta Cana, Dominican Republic. Association for Computational Linguistics.

Alexander Wettig, Tianyu Gao, Zexuan Zhong, and Danqi Chen. 2022. Should you mask 15% in masked language modeling? *arXiv preprint arXiv:2202.08005*.

Linting Xue, Aditya Barua, Noah Constant, Rami Al-Rfou, Sharan Narang, Mihir Kale, Adam Roberts, and Colin Raffel. 2022. Byt5: Towards a token-free future with pre-trained byte-to-byte models. *Transactions of the Association for Computational Linguistics*, 10:291–306.

Manzil Zaheer, Guru Guruganesh, Kumar Avinava Dubey, Joshua Ainslie, Chris Alberti, Santiago Ontanon, Philip Pham, Anirudh Ravula, Qifan Wang, Li Yang, et al. 2020. Big bird: Transformers for longer sequences. *Advances in neural information processing systems*, 33:17283–17297.

Xuan Zhang, Gaurav Kumar, Huda Khayrallah, Kenton Murray, Jeremy Gwinnup, Marianna J Martindale, Paul McNamee, Kevin Duh, and Marine Carpuat. 2018. An empirical exploration of curriculum learning for neural machine translation. *arXiv preprint arXiv:1811.00739*.

A Vocabulary Size

We experiment with vocabulary size, as shown in Table 5. Here, we initially chose a context size of 64, which we later show to be a close to optimal. The results favor a vocabulary size of 40k, however we note that certain aspects of the character model, namely its performance on quantifiers, indicates that it could complement the subword vocabulary.

B Final Full Results

We report the results for the baselines and our submitted models in Table 6.

	Vocabulary Size							
BLiMP Scores (%)	Char	8k	16k	24k	32k	40k	48k	64k
Anaphor agreement	44.0	88.3	90.1	**92.9**	92.6	91.8	92.8	91.3
Argument structure	59.4	69.0	73.8	73.6	73.6	74.6	74.4	**74.7**
Binding	61.5	69.2	69.3	70.4	69.3	**71.5**	68.9	68.3
Control raising	60.0	63.0	68.2	69.1	69.6	70.9	**71.7**	69.5
Determiner noun agreement	89.2	89.5	88.0	89.8	94.5	95.4	**96.6**	96.5
Ellipsis	42.4	85.8	84.9	87.1	86.4	**88.6**	84.5	87.3
Filler gap	70.3	**73.9**	73.0	73.7	73.0	72.0	74.0	73.5
Irregular forms	78.9	84.4	89.6	89.3	89.6	**92.6**	85.8	88.8
Island effects	43.9	44.4	46.8	48.9	51.8	50.9	53.0	**53.4**
NPI licensing	55.0	56.0	63.5	68.3	70.2	**73.0**	67.0	67.1
Quantifiers	**80.4**	66.5	70.8	68.3	69.0	70.9	71.0	68.5
Subject verb agreement	71.4	78.2	79.3	80.3	**83.5**	81.3	81.7	81.1
Average	63.0	72.3	74.8	76.0	76.9	**77.8**	76.8	76.7

Table 5: BLiMP scores for each vocabulary size tested. "Char" refers to a character-level model. Best in bold.

		Baseline (10M)	Baseline (100M)	32	32→128 (10)	32→128 (50)
BLiMP	Anaphor agreement	81.5	89.5	**94.5**	93.0	88.0
	Argument structure	67.1	71.3	**76.3**	74.5	72.9
	Binding	67.3	71.0	**77.0**	76.3	74.9
	Control raising	67.9	67.1	**75.5**	74.2	72.8
	Determiner noun agreement	90.8	93.1	**95.6**	94.4	91.0
	Ellipsis	76.4	83.8	**84.1**	78.5	77.4
	Filler gap	63.5	68.0	**80.0**	78.8	76.0
	Irregular forms	87.4	89.6	**87.9**	85.8	83.2
	Island effects	39.9	54.5	68.4	**70.7**	68.8
	NPI licensing	55.9	66.3	72.5	**73.2**	69.9
	Quantifiers	70.5	70.3	**70.8**	66.4	66.0
	Subject verb agreement	65.4	76.2	**89.0**	87.8	84.3
BLiMP Supp.	hypernym	49.4	**50.8**	46.9	49.1	45.4
	qa_congruence_easy	31.3	34.4	76.6	**81.3**	73.4
	qa_congruence_tricky	32.1	34.5	45.5	**49.1**	46.7
	subject_aux_inversion	71.7	45.6	82.8	**84.3**	83.3
	turn_taking	53.2	46.8	67.1	68.9	**73.6**
GLUE	CoLA	70.8	75.9	**76.8**	**76.8**	77.4
	SST-2	87.0	**88.6**	87.8	**88.6**	88.0
	MRPC (F1)	79.2	**80.5**	70.6	72.9	73.5
	QQP (F1)	73.7	78.5	86.6	86.6	**87.1**
	MNLI	73.2	68.7	76.4	76.2	**77.1**
	MNLI-mm	74.0	**78.0**	77.3	76.3	77.0
	QNLI	77.0	82.3	83.2	**83.5**	79.7
	RTE	**61.6**	51.5	50.5	55.6	56.6
	BoolQ	66.3	59.9	65.2	**67.9**	67.2
	MultiRC	61.4	61.3	61.9	62.0	**64.4**
	WSC	61.4	61.4	**61.5**	**61.5**	**61.5**
MSGS	CR_LC	**-0.28**	-0.89	-0.98	-0.92	-0.49
	CR_RTP	-0.78	-0.91	**-0.52**	-0.85	-0.84
	MV_LC	**-0.99**	-1.00	-1.00	-1.00	-1.00
	MV_RTP	-0.79	-0.15	-0.32	**-0.18**	-0.60
	SC_LC	**0.16**	-0.58	-0.38	-0.29	-0.18
	SC_RP	-0.45	**-0.39**	-0.51	-0.53	-0.55
AoA	Overall	2.06	2.06	2.06	**2.05**	**2.05**
	Nouns	**1.99**	**1.99**	2.00	**1.99**	2.00
	Predicates	1.85	**1.82**	1.85	1.85	1.83
	Function words	2.65	2.66	2.60	2.58	**2.55**

Table 6: All individual results for our final models, versus the baselines. Best in bold.

Can training neural language models on a curriculum with developmentally plausible data improve alignment with human reading behavior?

Aryaman Chobey
Colgate University
achobey@colgate.edu

Oliver Smith
Colgate University
osmith@colgate.edu

Anzi Wang
Colgate University
awang1@colgate.edu

Grusha Prasad
Colgate University
gprasad@colgate.edu

Abstract

The use of neural language models to model human behavior has met with mixed success. While some work has found that the surprisal estimates from these models can be used to predict a wide range of human neural and behavioral responses, other work studying more complex syntactic phenomena has found that these surprisal estimates generate incorrect behavioral predictions. This paper explores the extent to which the misalignment between empirical and model-predicted behavior can be minimized by training models on more developmentally plausible data, such as in the BabyLM Challenge. We trained teacher language models on the BabyLM "strict-small" dataset and used sentence level surprisal estimates from these teacher models to create a curriculum. We found tentative evidence that our curriculum made it easier for models to acquire linguistic knowledge from the training data: on the subset of tasks in the BabyLM challenge suite evaluating models' grammatical knowledge of English, models first trained on the BabyLM data curriculum and then on a few randomly ordered training epochs performed slightly better than models trained on randomly ordered epochs alone. This improved linguistic knowledge acquisition did not result in better alignment with human reading behavior, however: models trained on the BabyLM dataset (with or without a curriculum) generated predictions that were as misaligned with human behavior as models trained on larger less curated datasets. This suggests that training on developmentally plausible datasets alone is likely insufficient to generate language models capable of accurately predicting human language processing.

1 Introduction

The rapidly increasing success of neural language models has resulted in a corresponding increase the use of these models to model human neural and behavioral responses. This research direction has yielded mixed success — while the surprisal estimates from these language models (i.e., the negative log probability of words given their preceding context) can certainly predict a wide range of neural and behavioral responses (Schrimpf et al., 2021), there are cases where surprisal estimates from these models generate quantitiatively (Huang et al., 2023; Van Schijndel and Linzen, 2021) and even qualitatively (Arehalli and Linzen, 2020) incorrect predictions.

To what extent are these incorrect predictions a consequence of the fact that these models are trained on orders of magnitude more data than an average human is exposed to in their lifetime (Linzen, 2020)? Can training these models on more developmentally plausible datasets, such as in the BabyLM challenge (Warstadt et al., 2023), bridge the gap between empirical and predicted behavior? Does increased alignment with human behavior come at the cost of success on other NLP tasks? We explore these questions in this paper by training models on the the "strict-small" dataset of the BabyLM Challenge ($\sim$10M tokens) and evaluating the models on two types of tasks: first, tasks from the BabyLM challenge designed to test these models' linguistic abilities; second, a large scale reading time dataset of syntactically complex sentences designed to evaluate models' ability to capture aspects of human language processing (SAP benchmark; Huang et al., 2023).

Concretely, we explored whether training models on an easy-to-difficult curriculum (Elman, 1993) could result in improved performance on the BabyLM suite of challenge tasks and/or an improved fit to human reading behavior in the SAP Benchmark. To design the curriculum, we used the Cross-Review method (Xu et al., 2020): we trained teacher language models on different subsets of the training dataset and then generated sentence level surprisal estimates for held out sentences from each of the teacher models. For every sentence, the surprisal estimates from multiple teachers were av-

Proceedings of the 27th Conference on Computational Natural Language Learning: Volume 2: The BabyLM Challenge, pages 98–111
December 6-7, 2023

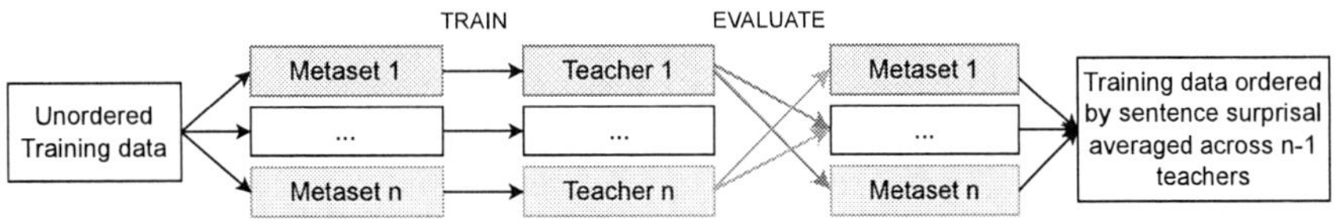

Figure 1: Schematic for how Cross-Review can be used to generate an easy-to-difficult order for the training dataset.

eraged together to compute a "difficulty" score, which was then used to generate an ordered sequence of training sentences (or "curriculum").

To foreshadow our results, we found that models trained on our curriculum alone performed *worse* on the BabyLM suite of challenge tasks compared to models trained for the same number of steps without a curriculum. However, for a subset of the challenge tasks evaluating models' grammatical knowledge, models which were trained on the curriculum followed by a few randomly ordered training epochs performed better than models trained on the randomly ordered epochs alone. This suggests that while training on the curriculum alone was not sufficient to acquire relevant linguistic knowledge, it might have induced useful biases in the models which made it easier for the models to acquire linguistic knowledge from the training data.

However, any useful biases that training on the the curriculum might have induced did not result in improved alignment with human reading behavior: models trained on the BabyLM data (with or without the curriculum) had nearly identical performance on the SAP benchmark to each other and to models trained on larger and less curated datasets. This result, along with prior work on training models on child directed speech (Yedetore et al., 2023), suggests that merely training on developmentally plausible data is likely insufficient for bridging the gap between human behavior and language-model predicted behavior.

2 Background

Curriculum learning (Bengio et al., 2009) refers to training models through a difficulty-based ordering of training examples (i.e. a curriculum), most often "starting small" (Elman, 1993) from easy examples before progressing to increasingly difficult sentences. In NLP, curriculum learning has been widely used for Machine Translation (e.g., Platanios et al., 2019), but has also been applied more recently to other natural language understanding tasks (Xu et al., 2020). For a survey see Soviany et al. (2022); Wang et al. (2021).

There are two steps involved in designing a curriculum: assigning a difficulty score to every training example ("difficulty measurer") and using these difficulty scores to determine the order in which training examples are presented to the model ("training scheduler") (Wang et al., 2021).

2.1 Difficulty measurer

Prior work exploring the efficacy of curriculum learning for NLU tasks has used a wide range of properties to compute sentence difficulty such as sentence length, word frequency (or rarity), tree depth, diversity and understandability (for a review, see Soviany et al., 2022). None of these properties by themselves can comprehensively capture what makes one sentence more difficult to process or acquire than another. For example, while long sentences are in general more difficult than short sentences, a shorter ambiguous sentence ("the horse raced past the barn fell") is more difficult to process than a longer unambiguous one ("the horse which was raced past the barn is the same horse that fell"). Given the complex ways in which all of the individual properties can interact, a holistic way of combining these properties is likely necessary to generate good measures of sentence difficulty.

A natural way of combining these properties to compute a difficulty measure is to use a "teacher" language model to compute the predictability of words in a sentence: given some context, a good language model will assign lower probabilities to words that result in long continuations with infrequent words and structures and/or continuations that describe improbable or hard-to-understand events. Concretely, in this work we define difficulty of a sentence as the mean surprisal of words in the sentence, as given in equation 1, where $\mathcal{D}$ is difficulty, L is the model being used to compute difficulty, s_k is the k-th sentence, and n is the number of words in s_k.

$$\mathcal{D}(s_k, L) = -\frac{1}{n}\sum_{i=0}^{n} \log P(w_i \mid w_0...w_{i-1}, L) \tag{1}$$

There are two issues with estimating sentence difficulty in this manner. First, the difficulty estimates can be inaccurate if the teacher language model is trained on the same data for which difficulty scores are being computed. Second, the difficulty estimates can be affected by noisy idiosyncrasies if they are computed from just one teacher language model. To avoid these two issues, we use the Cross-Review method proposed by Xu et al. (2020). In this method each teacher is trained on a subset of the data, and then evaluated on all subsets other than the one it was trained on. Therefore if there are n teachers, there are n-1 difficulty scores for each sentence which can then be averaged together for a final difficulty score for the sentence (see Equation 2 and Figure 1).

$$\mathbf{D}(s_k) = \frac{1}{M} \sum_{m=1}^{M} \mathcal{D}(s_k, m) \tag{2}$$

2.2 Training scheduler

Given a training dataset E in which examples are ordered by difficulty and a training time step t, the training scheduler determines the subset of E that the model can be exposed to at t. At a broad level there are two types of schedulers: discrete and continuous (see Wang et al., 2021 for a more detailed taxonomy of training schedulers). In discrete schedulers, the training proceeds in stages with m training time steps; at all training time steps in a stage $t_i ... t_{i+m}$, the model is exposed to the same subset of E.[1] In continuous schedulers on the other hand, the subset of E that the model is exposed to changes at every training time step.

In this work we use a continuous scheduler proposed by Platanios et al. (2019), in which the proportion of E that the model can be exposed to at t, $c_{root-p}(t)$, is given by the formula below, where T is the maximum number of training time steps and c_0 is the proportion of sentences that the model is exposed in the first time step:

$$c_{root-p}(t) = \min\left(1, \sqrt[p]{t\frac{1-c_0^p}{T} + c_0^p}\right) \tag{3}$$

Our primary reason for using the scheduler above is that it has only three hyperparameters: c_0, T and p. The authors demonstrate that hyperparameters like warmup steps, which are normally very highly tuned, do not have to be tuned with their scheduler. Given our compute limitations, hyperparameter tuning was infeasible, thus making this approach appealing.

3 Designing the curriculum

3.1 Datasets

We trained our random baselines and designed our curriculum using the datasets provided in the "strict-small" track of the BabyLM challenge. The data for this track was made up of 10 datasets, with a total of about ~10M tokens and ~920K sentences (where sentences were defined as sequences separated by a new line character). As specified in the BabyLM call for papers, the relative distribution of the ten datasets at the token level was intended to be developmentally plausible – for example, about 55% of all the tokens in the "strict-small" dataset comes from transcribed speech, and another 19% of the tokens come from stories (see Table 1).

While the BabyLM challenge datasets were constructed at the *token level*, we designed our curriculum at the *sentence level*, where we defined sentences as sequences separated by a new line character. We did this because it was more straightforward to sort the training dataset based on the difficulty of entire sentences; creating a token-level curriculum would require specifying an additional mechanism for ensuring that contextual integrity was maintained. The relative distribution of the ten datasets at the sentence level was very different from the relative distribution of tokens (see Table 1). Specifically, the proportion of more "complex" datasets (such as Wikipedia and Simple Wikipedia) was much lower at the sentence level than at the token level. We discuss the consequence of these distributional differences in § 7.

3.2 Computing sentence difficulty

As discussed in § 2.1, we used the Cross-Review method proposed by Xu et al. (2020) to compute the difficulty of every sentence in the training dataset. We divided the training dataset into five metasets, each with approximately the same number of tokens and number of sentences. Then, we used the neural-complexity codebase (van Schijndel and Linzen, 2018)[2] to train five LSTM teachers on each of these metasets.

Our LSTM teachers each had two hidden layers with 200 units in each layer. Training sentences

[1]This is equivalent to saying that the at any given training stage, the model is trained on m epochs of a subset of E.

[2]https://github.com/vansky/neural-complexity

Dataset	Speech?	# tokens	Proportion	# sentences	Proportion
CHILDES	Yes	0.44 M	4%	80K	9%
BNC Spoken	Yes	0.84 M	9%	73.41 K	8%
Children's book test	No	0.57 M	6%	26 K	3%
Children stories	No	0.34 M	3%	5.72 K	1%
Project Gutenberg	No	0.99 M	10%	91.81 K	10%
Open Subtitles	Yes	3.03 M	31%	470.89 K	51%
QED	Yes	1.03M	10%	91.91 K	10%
Simple Wikipedia	No	1.51 M	15%	48.80 K	5%
Switchboard	Yes	0.11 M	1%	11.09 K	1%
Wikipedia	No	0.99 M	10%	19.35 K	2%
Total		9.87 M		918.98 K	

Table 1: Number of tokens and sentences in each of the sub-datasets in the BabyLM "strict-small" datasets. The number of tokens are based on a BPE tokenizer we trained and we exlcude tokens from lines with just a tab or space. Therefore the numbers are slightly different from those in the BabyLM call for papers.

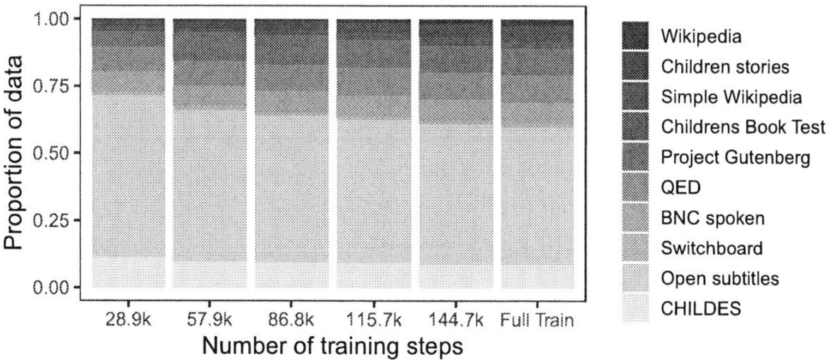

Figure 2: Proportion of sentences from each of the sub-datasets in our training curriculum for every 28937 training steps (i.e. equivalent to 1 epoch in the random models), as well as the proportions in the entire training dataset.

were pre-tokenized using a BPE tokenizer that we trained (described in § 4.2) and were passed to the teacher models in 20 batches. They were trained until their validation loss did not improve for three epochs, or until they reached 100 epochs. All teachers converged within 67 epochs, with the fastest teacher converging in 54 epochs.

We then evaluated each of the teacher LSTMs on all metasets except the one they were trained on, and then used the resulting surprisal values to compute the difficulty of every sentence in the training dataset (see Equation 2 and Figure 1).

Why use LSTM teachers? We trained LSTM language models instead of transformers because prior work has demonstrated that for datasets with 4 million tokens or less, such as our metasets, LSTM language models outperform their transformer counterparts (Hu et al., 2020), and therefore would make better "teachers". Note, we did not use state-of-the-art language models as our teachers because of the constraints of the *strict-small track* of the BabyLM challenge.

3.3 Creating the training dataset

As discussed in § 2.2, we use the training scheduler proposed by Platanios et al. (2019) which has three hyperparameters (see Equation 3): the initial competence (c_0), the total number of training steps (T) and the root value (p). Following Platanios et al. (2019), we set the value of c_0 to 0.01. We set the value of T to be 150001 because our random baseline (described in § 4.3) achieved the highest validation perplexity after 144685 training steps (i.e., after 5 epochs).[3] We set the value of p to be 10 after some experimentation because for values of p lower than that, the complex domains in our training dataset (such as Wikipedia) were very underrepresented (see Figure 5 in the Appendix). Then, for every batch, we sampled 32 sentences

[3]It was 150001 instead of 150000 because of an error.

from the subset of sentences that the model can be exposed to at the current time step as determined by Equation 3.

4 Training

4.1 Model architecture

For our target models we use the OPT 125M architecture (Zhang et al., 2022). This decoder-only transformer architecture consists of 12 layers with 12 attention heads each, an embedding size of 768 and a context length of 2048 tokens. We additionally use a final 0.2M layer with a causal language modeling head.

4.2 Tokenization and batching

Since the BabyLM challenge does not permit the use of pretrained tokenizer, we trained a BPE tokenizer on the training dataset with a vocabulary size of 50272 (the same as was used in the original OPT models). Like in the GPT-2 (Radford et al., 2019) tokenizer implementation, we do not significantly normalize or pre-tokenize the tokenizer training data. For the batching process, the tokenizer truncates sequences longer than 128 tokens, and returns the overflowing tokens as a separate sequence; only about 2% of our training examples were truncated. We used batch size of 32 with dynamic padding. The entire training dataset was divided into 28937 batches or training steps per epoch.

4.3 Model types

Random baseline: A randomly initialized OPT 125M model trained on our training dataset without any curriculum for up to 8 epochs. We present results from two baselines: the checkpoint after the 5th epoch (RandOPT 5ep; 144685 training steps) which had the best validation loss, and the last checkpoint (RandOPT 8 ep; 231496 training steps).

Curriculum only model: A randomly initialized OPT 125M model trained on our entire curriculum (CurrOPT; 150001 training steps).

Curriculum + Finetuning: The checkpoint of the CurrOPT model after it was trained on 144685 steps (i.e., same number of steps as the RandOPT 5ep model) further "finetuned" on the entire randomly ordered training dataset for upto 5 additional epochs. We present results from the checkpoint after 3 finetuning epochs (CurrOPT_ft 3ep; 231496 training steps, same as RandOPT 8ep) and the checkpoint after 5 finetuning epochs (CurrOPT_ft 5ep; 289370 training steps).

4.4 Training procedure

We use an AdamW optimizer (Loshchilov and Hutter, 2017) with β_1 and β_2 set to 0.9 and 0.95 respectively. We use a weight decay and dropout of 0.1, and clip gradient norms at 1.0. For our random baseline we use a linear learning rate schedule and use a warmup of $\sim$5% of our maximum training steps. As discussed in § 2.2 we do not use warmup for our curriculum models. Due to our considerably smaller pre-training corpus we do not implement the several mid-flight changes to learning rate and gradient clipping employed by Zhang et al. (as an adhoc response to training instability) over the course of their significantly longer training run.

5 Evaluation

We evaluate our models on the three challenge sets included in the BabyLM challenge – BLiMP (Warstadt et al., 2020a), (Super)GLUE (Wang et al., 2018, 2019) and MSGS (Warstadt et al., 2020b) — as well as on the SAP Benchmark (Huang et al., 2023).

BLiMP and BLiMP supplement The Benchmark of Linguistic Minimal Pairs (BLiMP) probes the linguistic knowledge that a language model encodes by measuring how often the model accurately assigns higher probabilities to words in minimally different grammatical and ungrammatical sentences. The original dataset contains minimal pairs for 12 different linguistic phenomena probing English morphology, syntax and semantics. The BabyLM challenge supplements this dataset with five additional linguistic phenomena targeting discourse level acceptability as well as other syntactic phenomena (such as question formation).

SuperGLUE The General language Understanding Evaluation (GLUE) benchmark and its successor SuperGLUE are challenge sets that are designed to evaluate models' general purpose natural language understanding. The BabyLM challenge includes tasks from GLUE (COLA, SST2, MRPC, QQP, MNLI, QNLI, RTE), three tasks from SuperGLUE (BoolQ, RTE and WSC), as well as an additional task (Multimodal NLI). Unlike BLiMP which largely evaluates grammatical knowledge, the SuperGLUE tasks are designed to evaluate higher level linguistic abilities such as sentiment analysis, inference, causal reasoning, coreference resolution, question answering, paraphrasing, etc.

MSGS The Mixed Signals Generalization Set is a diagnostic set used to evaluate how models solve an ambiguous classification task that can be solved using either linguistic features or surface features. The MSGS set contains five surface features and four linguistic features, resulting in 20 ambiguous classification tasks. There are also 9 control tasks to evaluate how well models can classify each of the features in an unambiguous context. The BabyLM challenge uses three linguistic features (syntactic position, syntactic construction, and syntactic category) and two surface features (lexical content and relative position), thus resulting in six ambiguous classification tasks.

SAP Benchmark The Syntactic Ambiguity Processing (SAP) benchmark is a large scaled reading time dataset for seven different types of syntactically complex sentences. Unlike the other datasets which measure models' linguistic knowledge and ability, this dataset measures whether the models process information as humans do; specifically, whether models and humans are equally surprised by sentences that are grammatical but have complex and infrequent syntactic structures. The data processing pipeline of the SAP benchmark involves three steps: first, estimating *empirical* effects of interest using Bayesian mixed effects models; second, generating predicted reading times from language model surprisal (i.e. negative log probability) values and fitting mixed effects models to estimate *predicted* effects of interest;[4]and third, comparing empirical and predicted effects of interest. The surprisal estimates and reading times are measured at specific *target* words and the following two spillover words. Further details about the different constructions are included in the Supplementary materials.

6 Results

6.1 What curriculum was learned?

The datasets with transcribed speech had the lowest average sentence difficulty scores. Even within transcribed speech, datasets with informal speech (such as child directed speech and subtitles) had lower average difficulty scores than datasets with more formal speech (such as BNC). Additionally, as expected the proportion of transcribed speech steadily decreased over time, as the proportion of written text increased. By the last "epoch", the distribution of datasets was very similar to the true distribution (see Figure 2), suggesting that the cross-review method we used as our difficulty-measurer was effective, as was the root-10 training scheduler.

Agreement between LSTM teachers For any given sentence, there was a lot of variance in the surprisal estimates across the teachers: the average standard deviation was 113 bits of surprisal; the mean Spearman rank correlation between any two pairs of teachers was only 0.0009. This highlights the importance of averaging the surprisal estimates across different teachers to avoid over-fitting to idiosyncrasies of any particular teacher model.

Other difficulty measures Figure 7 plots the correlation between our difficulty measure computed using the cross-review method and two other simpler difficulty measures: average unigram frequency of the words in a sentence and sentence length. Our difficulty measure is moderately correlated with unigram frequency ($R = 0.27$, $p < 0.0001$) and highly correlated with sentence length ($R = 0.89$, $p < 0.0001$). We also predicted our difficulty measure as a function of unigram frequency and sentence length in a linear regression model and found that unigram frequency explains variance in our difficulty measure over and above sentence length, and together they explain most of the variance in the difficulty measure (adjusted R-squared = 0.93). This suggests that for the specific BabyLM datasets, using cross-review, while effective, might not be necessary: using faster-to-compute measures such as sentence length would have likely resulted in a comparable curriculum.

6.2 Training time

Since our difficulty measure was highly correlated with sentence length, in early stages of training the average sentence length in our curriculum was lower than the average sentence length in early epochs of model training without a curriculum. Since we dynamically padded our sequences, the model trained on our curriculum (CurrOPT) was initially trained on batches consisting of fewer total tokens than the model trained on the unordered data (RandOPT). As a result, in early stages of training, the time taken to train CurrOPT was less than half the amount of time taken to train RandOPT. As

[4]SAP Benchmark uses Bayesian mixed effects models. We use linear mixed effects models because they are less resource intensive to fit and yield nearly identical model estimates.

Dataset	Task	RandOPT 5 ep	RandOPT 8 ep	CurrOPT	CurrOPT_ft 3 ep	CurrOPT_ft 5 ep
		114685 steps	231496 steps	150001 steps	231496 steps	289370 steps
BLiMP	Anaphor Agr.	75.72	**86.71**	70.35	72.59	75.05
	Agr. structure	66.09	67.85	67.8	**70.44**	70.04
	Binding	69.19	66.83	69.23	69.29	**72.72**
	Control/Raising	63.65	65.89	63.57	66.81	**68.58**
	D-N Agr.	72.33	74.64	72.05	76.58	**78.6**
	Ellipsis	52.71	52.89	53	**61.66**	55.43
	Filler-gap	72.84	73.5	72.74	74.4	**75.18**
	Irregular forms	**82.39**	71.04	82.34	80.97	81.27
	Island effects	52.06	57.21	57.1	**64.13**	62.48
	NPI licensing	47.46	41.59	38.76	45.52	**48.25**
	Quantifiers	55.69	64.4	52.81	67.03	**67.34**
	Subj-Verb Agr	63.92	64.43	58.84	64.73	**65.55**
BLIMP Supplement	Hypernym	**50.58**	49.19	48.95	47.91	47.21
	Congr. (easy)	48.44	51.56	50	**53.12**	**53.12**
	Congr. (tricky)	**36.97**	**36.97**	36.36	36.36	36.36
	Subj-Aux Inv.	84.92	**86.53**	72.55	84.58	85.02
	Turn taking	55	**60.71**	51.43	55.71	57.5
SuperGlue	COLA	3.2	9.35	3.2	**9.77**	8.91
	SST2	83.07	83.86	83.27	**85.43**	83.86
	MRPC	73.64	75.59	65.50	72.07	**80.14**
	QQP	76.86	77.27	74.78	**77.33**	76.83
	MNLI	65.75	**67.07**	64.63	65.18	65.3
	MNLI-MM	65.88	**66.31**	65.58	66.2	66.22
	QNLI	60.63	59.84	59.54	**61.33**	60.98
	RTE	51.51	45.46	47.48	**53.54**	48.49
	BoolQ	65.15	**67.50**	66.53	60.30	66.81
	MultiRC	55.53	48.85	**56.74**	46.55	47.54
	WSC	56.63	**61.45**	**61.45**	**61.45**	**61.45**
MSGS	MV lexical	-100	-100	-100	-100	-100
	MV position	-99.95	-98.39	-99.75	**-88.76**	-97.62
	SC lexical	**0.18**	-57.66	-58.62	-62.46	-69.88
	SC position	**-62.68**	-66.39	-62.82	-76.28	-62.88
	CR lexical	**0**	-4.17	-1.7	-2.4	-1.2
	CR position	**-69.49**	-95.59	-87.47	-70.38	-98.53

Table 2: Results for the tasks included in the BabyLM challenge set. Most of the numbers in the table indicate accuracy except for the following cases: MSGS tasks and COLA numbers are Matthew's Correlation Coefficient; MRPC and QQP numbers are F1 scores. Light green cells indicate cases in which CurrOPT and CurrOPT_ft 3ep performed better than their random counterpart trained on the same number of steps: RandOPT 5ep and RandOPT 8ep respectively. Similarly, red cells indicate cases in which CurrOPT and CurrOPT_ft 3ep perform worse. Orange cells indicate tasks in which one of the random models ultimately had the best performance. Teal cells indicate tasks in which training the random model on more epochs led to *worse* performance. Bolded numbers indicate the best performance in a task across all five models. For MSGS we interpret "best performance" as having the weakest surface bias (i.e., the least negative numbers).

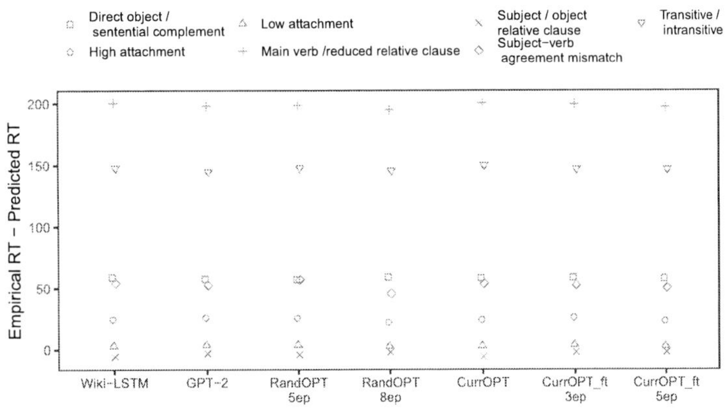

Figure 3: Difference between empirical and model-predicted reading times for the different constructions in the SAP Benchmark. Wiki-LSTM and GPT-2 estimates were from the original paper.

the curriculum progressed, the number of tokens in each batch of CurrOPT approached those in RandOPT causing the training time for CurrOPT to be similar to that of RandOPT.

6.3 BabyLM challenge tasks

On almost all of the tasks, the performance of the model trained on our curriculum (CurrOPT) was worse than the random baseline trained on fewer training examples (RandOPT 5ep). However, when we continued to train CurrOPT on more epochs of the entire training data, the resulting model (CurrOPT_ft 3ep) performed better than the random baseline trained on the same number of training examples (RandOPT 8ep) on some tasks (see Table 2). Specifically, CurrOPT_ft 3ep performed better than RandOPT 8ep on most tasks that evaluated models' knowledge of English grammar (e.g., BLiMP, COLA). However, additional training did not seem to help the curriculum models' performance on tasks that required specific lexical knowledge (e.g., irregular forms and hypernyms) or on tasks that required the model to learn more factual information (e.g., MNLI, MNLI-MM and BoolQ). Taken together these results suggest that while training on our curriculum by itself is insufficient to impart the necessary grammatical knowledge, it might induce biases in the model that make it easier for the model to acquire this knowledge from training data. However, there may be limits to the usefulness of these induced biases: training on our curriculum seemed to have some negative impact on the models' ability to acquire nuanced lexical or factual information required to solve more complex tasks like inference or question answering.

6.4 SAP Benchmark

We compared reading times predicted from the surprisal estimates of each of our models, as well as two baselines that were used in the original paper (GPT-2 (Radford et al., 2019) and an LSTM model trained on Wikipedia) to the empirical reading times. The difference between predicted and empirical reading times is nearly identical across all models, and very high (greater than 25 ms) for five out of the seven constructions (see Figure 3). This difference is not just a result of an incorrect conversion from surprisal to RTs — we observe qualitatively similar patterns when we look at raw surprisal values (see Figure 8 in the Appendix). Thus training on developmentally plausible data (with or without a curriculum) does not result in more human-like processing compared to models trained on less curated written text from the internet. This result aligns with the finding that training on child directed speech does not result in human-like generalization (Yedetore et al., 2023). Taken together these results suggest that merely modifying the training data of language models is unlikely to result in better cognitive models of human language acquisition and processing.

7 Discussion

In this paper we explored whether training on a developmentally plausible dataset can improve alignment with human behavior, and whether the improved alignment (if any) comes at the cost of performance on other NLP tasks evaluating different aspects of linguistic competence. We trained models with and without a curriculum on the BabyLM "strict-small" dataset and evaluated them on the BabyLM suite of evaluation tasks as well as on a large scale benchmark of reading behavior for syntactically complex sentences (SAP benchmark).

Drawing on prior work on curriculum learning, we created an easy-to-difficult ordering of the sentences in the training dataset using surprisal values from LSTM teacher language models in a Cross-Review paradigm (Xu et al., 2020), and then used this ordering with a root-10 scheduler (Platanios et al., 2019) to design the training curriculum. This learned curriculum aligned with intuitive expectations for our curriculum — for example, the proportion of transcribed speech decreased over time, whereas the proportion of written text increased.

An OPT125M causal language model trained on our curriculum (CurrOPT) performed *worse* on most of the tasks in the BabyLM challenge set compared to baselines trained without a curriculum, suggesting that the models were unable to acquire relevant linguistic knowledge from the curriculum alone. Continuing to train CurrOPT on epochs of randomly ordered training data improved performance on most tasks targeting grammatical knowledge, but not on tasks that required more fine-grained knowledge about lexical or factual content.

Why did training on the curriculum lead to worse performance on some tasks? Domains with complex sentences (e.g., Wikipedia) were underrepresented in our curriculum because of our sentence level curriculum: domains like Wikipedia had fewer but longer sentences, and were therefore were less likely to be sampled than sentences from domains with many short sentences (e.g., Open Subtitles). As a consequence there might not have been enough signal in the training data for the models to acquire factual information (which might explain their poor performance on tasks like MNLI and BoolQ) or nuanced lexical representations (which might explain their poor performance on tasks like irregular forms and hypernyms).

Can training on developmentally plausible data improve alignment with human behavior? Crucial to our question, we found that our models which were trained on developmentally plausible data (with or without a curriculum) had nearly identical performance to models trained on less curated larger datasets — all of the models severely under-predicted the magnitude of processing difficulty in syntactically complex sentences. This suggests that training on developmentally plausible data alone is likely insufficient to bridge the gap between human and model-predicted behavior.

Limitations and future work All of the performance increases that we've discussed were very modest and based on just one model architecture. Therefore further work with additional random runs of the model is required to ensure that the improvements in performance were not just random noise. Similarly repeating the experiments with different architectures for the target and teacher models can shed light on the generalizability of our conclusions. In a similar vein, the conclusions about SAP benchmark results also need to be validated in future work. Specifically, it is necessary to more carefully define what "developmentally plausible" means, develop concrete hypotheses about why training on specific datasets might result in better alignment with reading behavior, and test these hypotheses with controlled experiments.

8 Conclusion

We designed a surprisal-based curriculum using the developmentally plausible data in the BabyLM strict-small dataset. We found that a model which was first trained on this curriculum and then trained on several additional epochs of the unordered training dataset performed slightly better than a random baseline trained on the same number of examples across a range of NLP tasks. When these models were evaluated on the SAP benchmark, their performance was nearly identical to each other and to that of models trained on larger and less curated datasets. This suggests that merely altering the training data to be more developmentally plausible is unlikely to improve alignment with human behavior.

Acknowledgements

This work was supported in part through the Colgate University's ITS HPC resources, services, and staff expertise. We would also like to thank Tom McCoy and Suhas Arehalli and NYU's ITS HPC resources for their assistance with evaluating our models on the BabyLM evaluation tasks, as well as Suhas Arehalli and Forrest Davis for their valuable feedback.

References

Suhas Arehalli and Tal Linzen. 2020. Neural language models capture some, but not all, agreement attraction effects. In *Proceedings of the 42nd Annual Conference of the Cognitive Science Society*, pages 370–376.

Yoshua Bengio, Jérôme Louradour, Ronan Collobert, and Jason Weston. 2009. Curriculum learning. In *Proceedings of the 26th annual international conference on machine learning*, pages 41–48.

Jeffrey L Elman. 1993. Learning and development in neural networks: The importance of starting small. *Cognition*, 48(1):71–99.

Jennifer Hu, Jon Gauthier, Peng Qian, Ethan Wilcox, and Roger Levy. 2020. A systematic assessment of syntactic generalization in neural language models. In *Proceedings of the 58th Annual Meeting of the Association for Computational Linguistics*, pages 1725–1744, Online. Association for Computational Linguistics.

Kuan-Jung Huang, Suhas Arehalli, Mari Kugemoto, Christian Muxica, Grusha Prasad, Brian Dillon, and Tal Linzen. 2023. Surprisal does not explain syntactic disambiguation difficulty: evidence from a large-scale benchmark.

Tal Linzen. 2020. How can we accelerate progress towards human-like linguistic generalization? In *Proceedings of the 58th Annual Meeting of the Association for Computational Linguistics*, Seattle, Washington. Association for Computational Linguistics.

Ilya Loshchilov and Frank Hutter. 2017. Decoupled weight decay regularization. *arXiv preprint arXiv:1711.05101*.

Emmanouil Antonios Platanios, Otilia Stretcu, Graham Neubig, Barnabas Poczos, and Tom M Mitchell. 2019. Competence-based curriculum learning for neural machine translation. *arXiv preprint arXiv:1903.09848*.

Alec Radford, Jeffrey Wu, Rewon Child, David Luan, Dario Amodei, Ilya Sutskever, et al. 2019. Language models are unsupervised multitask learners. *OpenAI blog*, 1(8):9.

Martin Schrimpf, Idan Asher Blank, Greta Tuckute, Carina Kauf, Eghbal A Hosseini, Nancy Kanwisher, Joshua B Tenenbaum, and Evelina Fedorenko. 2021. The neural architecture of language: Integrative modeling converges on predictive processing. *Proceedings of the National Academy of Sciences*, 118(45):e2105646118.

Petru Soviany, Radu Tudor Ionescu, Paolo Rota, and Nicu Sebe. 2022. Curriculum learning: A survey. *International Journal of Computer Vision*, 130(6):1526–1565.

Marten van Schijndel and Tal Linzen. 2018. A neural model of adaptation in reading. In *Proceedings of the 2018 Conference on Empirical Methods in Natural Language Processing*, pages 4704–4710, Brussels, Belgium. Association for Computational Linguistics.

Marten Van Schijndel and Tal Linzen. 2021. Single-stage prediction models do not explain the magnitude of syntactic disambiguation difficulty. *Cognitive science*, 45(6):e12988.

Alex Wang, Yada Pruksachatkun, Nikita Nangia, Amanpreet Singh, Julian Michael, Felix Hill, Omer Levy, and Samuel Bowman. 2019. Superglue: A stickier benchmark for general-purpose language understanding systems. *Advances in neural information processing systems*, 32.

Alex Wang, Amanpreet Singh, Julian Michael, Felix Hill, Omer Levy, and Samuel Bowman. 2018. GLUE: A multi-task benchmark and analysis platform for natural language understanding. In *Proceedings of the 2018 EMNLP Workshop BlackboxNLP: Analyzing and Interpreting Neural Networks for NLP*, pages 353–355, Brussels, Belgium. Association for Computational Linguistics.

Xin Wang, Yudong Chen, and Wenwu Zhu. 2021. A survey on curriculum learning. *IEEE Transactions on Pattern Analysis and Machine Intelligence*, 44(9):4555–4576.

Alex Warstadt, Aaron Mueller, Leshem Choshen, Ethan Gotlieb Wilcox, Chengxu Zhuang, Juan Ciro, Rafael Mosquera, Adina Williams, Bhargavi Paranjabe, Tal Linzen, and Ryan Cotterell. 2023. Findings of the 2023 BabyLM Challenge: Sample-efficient pretraining on developmentally plausible corpora. In *Proceedings of the 2023 BabyLM Challenge*. Association for Computational Linguistics (ACL).

Alex Warstadt, Alicia Parrish, Haokun Liu, Anhad Mohananey, Wei Peng, Sheng-Fu Wang, and Samuel R. Bowman. 2020a. BLiMP: The benchmark of linguistic minimal pairs for English. *Transactions of the Association for Computational Linguistics*, 8:377–392.

Alex Warstadt, Yian Zhang, Xiaocheng Li, Haokun Liu, and Samuel R. Bowman. 2020b. Learning which features matter: RoBERTa acquires a preference for linguistic generalizations (eventually). In *Proceedings of the 2020 Conference on Empirical Methods in Natural Language Processing (EMNLP)*, pages 217–235, Online. Association for Computational Linguistics.

Benfeng Xu, Licheng Zhang, Zhendong Mao, Quan Wang, Hongtao Xie, and Yongdong Zhang. 2020. Curriculum learning for natural language understanding. In *Proceedings of the 58th Annual Meeting of the Association for Computational Linguistics*, pages 6095–6104.

Aditya Yedetore, Tal Linzen, Robert Frank, and R. Thomas McCoy. 2023. How poor is the stimulus? evaluating hierarchical generalization in neural networks trained on child-directed speech. In *Proceedings of the 61st Annual Meeting of the Association for Computational Linguistics (Volume 1: Long Papers)*, pages 9370–9393, Toronto, Canada. Association for Computational Linguistics.

Susan Zhang, Stephen Roller, Naman Goyal, Mikel Artetxe, Moya Chen, Shuohui Chen, Christopher Dewan, Mona Diab, Xian Li, Xi Victoria Lin, et al. 2022. Opt: Open pre-trained transformer language models. *arXiv preprint arXiv:2205.01068*.

Main verb / reduced relative clause garden path

The little girl fed the lamb remained relatively calm ...

The little girl who was fed the lamb remained relatively calm ...

Direct object / sentential complement garden path

The little girl found the lamb remained relatively calm ...

The little girl found that the lamb remained relatively calm ...

Transitive / intransitive garden path

When the little girl attacked the lamb remained relatively calm ...

When the little girl attacked, the lamb remained relatively calm ...

Subject / object relative clause

The bus driver that the kids followed ...

The bus driver that followed the kids ...

Relative clause modifiers recent noun (low attachment)

Janet charmed the executives of the assistant who decides almost everything ...

Janet charmed the executive of the assistant who decides almost everything ...

Relative clause modifiers distant noun (high attachment)

Janet charmed the executive of the assistants who decides almost everything ...

Janet charmed the executive of the assistant who decides almost everything ...

Subject-verb agreement mismatch

Whenever the nurse calls, the doctors stops working immediately ...

Whenever the nurse calls, the doctor stops working immediately ...

Figure 4: Figure and caption adapted from (Huang et al., 2023). Each sentence pair illustrates a construction tested in SAP Benchmark. An effect of interest is defined as the difference in reading times associated with a disambiguating or ungrammatical word, marked in green, minus the reading time associated with that same word in a context where it is grammatical and does not disambiguate the structure of the sentence, marked in turquoise.

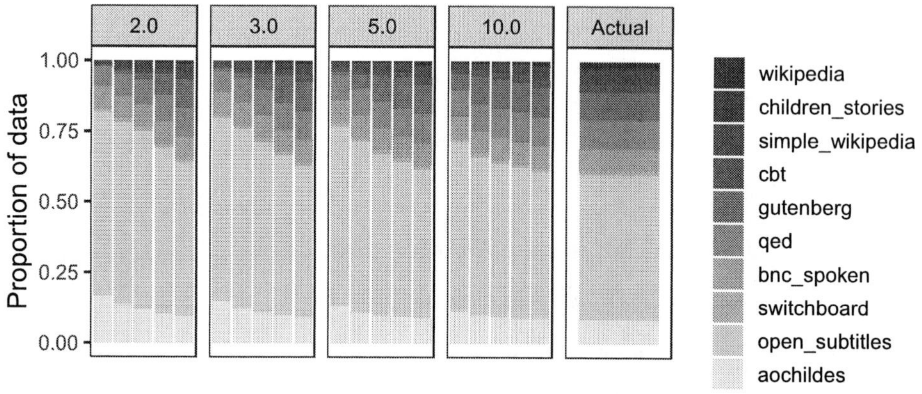

Figure 5: Proportion of sentences from each of the sub-datasets in training curricula with different root values for every 28937 training steps (i.e. equivalent to 1 epoch in the random models), as well as the proportions in the entire training dataset. The curriculum used this is paper is root 10.

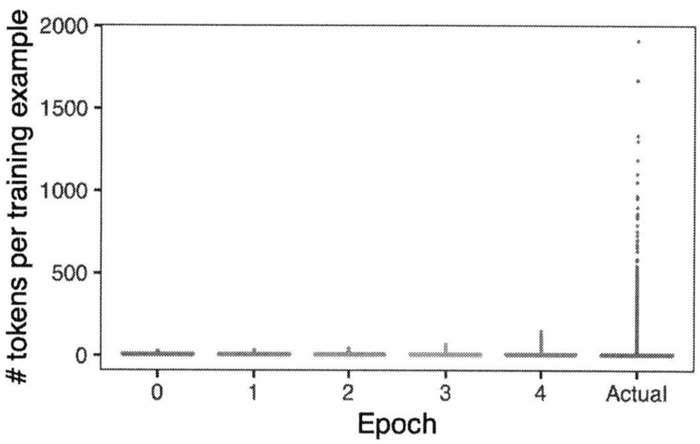

Figure 6: Caption

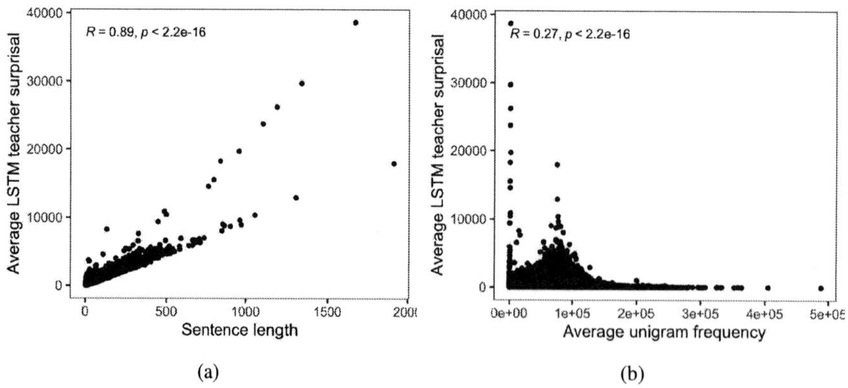

Figure 7: Relationship between the order average LSTM teacher surprisal and other difficulty measures. R values indicate the Spearman rank correlation coefficients.

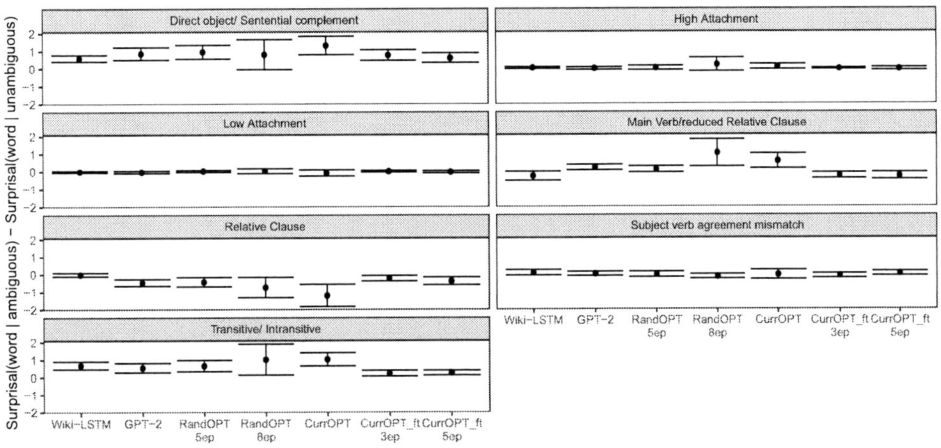

Figure 8: Difference in surprisal value at the target word in ambiguous and unambiguous sentences averaged across all sentences in a construction. Error bars represent 2 standard errors from the mean.

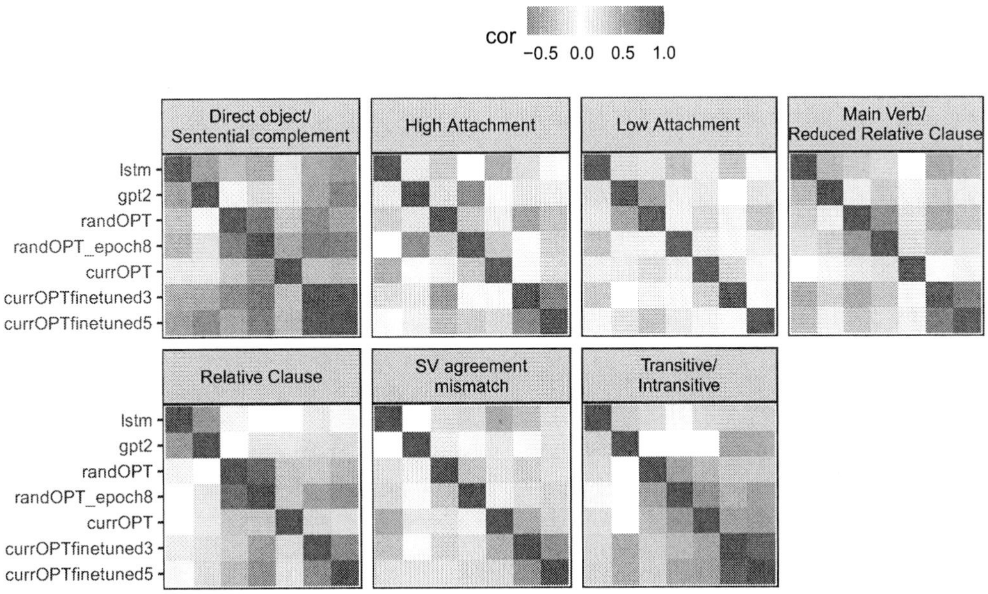

Figure 9: Correlation between model surprisal estimates at the item level. For each model, an item level difference in surprisal at the target word in the ambiguous and unambiguous conditions was computed. This item-level difference was correlated between models using Pearsons's correlation. The relatively weak correlations suggest that even though the models have the same aggregate behavior on the SAP benchmark, their behavior differs at the item level.

CLIMB – Curriculum Learning for Infant-inspired Model Building

Richard Diehl Martinez Zébulon Goriely* Hope McGovern*
Christopher Davis Andrew Caines Paula Buttery Lisa Beinborn
Department of Computer Science & Technology, University of Cambridge, U.K.
ALTA Institute, University of Cambridge, U.K.
Vrije Universiteit Amsterdam, Netherlands
firstname.secondname@cl.cam.ac.uk
l.beinborn@vu.nl

Abstract

We describe our team's contribution to the STRICT-SMALL track of the BabyLM Challenge (Warstadt et al., 2023). The challenge requires training a language model from scratch using only a relatively small training dataset of ten million words. We experiment with three variants of cognitively-motivated curriculum learning and analyze their effect on the performance of the model on linguistic evaluation tasks. In the **vocabulary curriculum**, we analyze methods for constraining the vocabulary in the early stages of training to simulate cognitively more plausible learning curves. In the **data curriculum** experiments, we vary the order of the training instances based on i) infant-inspired expectations and ii) the learning behaviour of the model. In the **objective curriculum**, we explore different variations of combining the conventional masked language modelling task with a more coarse-grained word class prediction task to reinforce linguistic generalization capabilities. Our results did not yield consistent improvements over our own non-curriculum learning baseline across a range of linguistic benchmarks; however, we do find marginal gains on select tasks. Our analysis highlights key takeaways for specific combinations of tasks and settings which benefit from our proposed curricula. We moreover determine that careful selection of model architecture, and training hyper-parameters yield substantial improvements over the default baselines provided by the BabyLM challenge. Our code is publicly available at https://github.com/codebyzeb/CLIMB.

1 Introduction

Children acquire language skills from being exposed to an estimated two to seven million words per year (Gilkerson et al., 2017). The current learning regimes of large language models require disproportionately larger sizes of training data to acquire linguistic generalization capabilities (Zhang et al., 2021). State-of-the-art LMs are typically trained on gigabytes of data gleaned from the World Wide Web, on multiple GPUs continuously for days at a time (Zhao et al., 2023). For example, the Chinchilla language model was trained on a dataset of 1.4 trillion words (Hoffmann et al., 2022). Such large-scale training regimes are economically and ecologically unsustainable, and access to the required computing resources remains out of reach for most academic groups and industry start-ups (Izsak et al., 2021).

To enable language models to still perform well with limited data, recent work has looked at utilizing smaller, well-curated, and representative corpora (Samuel et al., 2023; Gao et al., 2020) and careful selection of training and model hyper-parameters (Geiping and Goldstein, 2023). 'Zero-shot' and 'few-shot' learning are other data-efficient approaches which can perform well in certain settings but rely on large pre-trained language models (Brown et al., 2020; Wei et al., 2021). These approaches, however, provide engineering solutions to the problem rather than a cognitively-inspired, compute-efficient framework for training language models from scratch.

Conventional pre-training of large language models remains far removed from human language learning: models operate on a predetermined static vocabulary and optimize a monotonous training objective on a randomly shuffled dataset. We conducted experiments to explore more dynamic learning processes that are motivated by the psycholinguistic and language acquisition literature and are set within the machine learning paradigm of curriculum learning (Bengio et al., 2009). Our

*Equal contribution

Proceedings of the 27th Conference on Computational Natural Language Learning: Volume 2: The BabyLM Challenge, pages 112–127
December 6-7, 2023 ©2023 Association for Computational Linguistics

models are implemented and evaluated within the 'BabyLM Challenge' framework, a shared task in which the stated goal is "to incentivize researchers with an interest in pretraining and/or cognitive modeling to focus their efforts on optimizing pretraining given data limitations inspired by human development" (Warstadt et al., 2023). Our goal in participating in the BabyLM Challenge is two fold: First, we aim to contribute toward democratizing language modelling research and move towards this goal by training smaller language models that are still well-performing on NLP tasks. Second, we establish a computational framework based on curriculum learning for simulating aspects of human language acquisition. We participate in the strictest track of the challenge, limiting the training data to only 10 million words of text extracted from various pre-existing corpora.

Initially, we train our own BabyBERTa-style vanilla model [1] (Huebner et al., 2021) and find that simply tuning model size and vocabulary size in itself leads to substantial performance gains on some of the BabyLM test sets compared to the shared task baselines. We furthermore carried out a number of pre-processing steps on the training data to further improve performance, including concatenating input sequences to make the most of the available input length.

In our own approach, which we term CLIMB – Curriculum Learning for Infant-inspired Model Building – we explore three different curriculum strategies for language modelling: gradually increasing the size of the vocabulary (**vocabulary curriculum**), the difficulty of the training instances (**data curriculum**), or the specificity of the objective function (**objective curriculum**) over the course of training. Within the context of the BabyLM Challenge, Curriculum Learning establishes a framework through which we attempt to replicate key facets of child language acquisition. Counter-intuitively, we find that all of our curriculum learning approaches under-perform our BabyBERTa-style (non curriculum learning) vanilla models. Our contribution to the Baby LM Challenge builds upon this negative finding in three main ways:

1. Our paper establishes a novel framework through which to categorize and implement curriculum learning methods that simulate human language acquisition. We open-source our accompanying code-base for future research to study how curriculum learning replicates the language learning dynamics in humans.

2. We conduct a comprehensive evaluation of our three main curriculum approaches; our results show that the curriculum learning settings we tested did not provide consistent improvements over a baseline on linguistic benchmarks. Instead, we provide a set of recommendations for specific combinations of tasks and settings which may benefit from our proposed curricula.

3. We highlight the importance of careful data, model and hyper-parameter selection to establish a well performing fully supervised baseline for the BabyLM shared task. Our vanilla models outperform the shared task baseline models on tasks involving grammatical knowledge (BLiMP: The Benchmark of Linguistic Minimal Pairs (Warstadt et al., 2020a)) and all the shared-task baselines except RoBERTa (Liu et al., 2019) on tasks involving natural language understanding (SuperGLUE (Wang et al., 2019)).

2 Curriculum Learning

Curriculum learning (Bengio et al., 2009) is a machine-learning paradigm which optimizes a model's performance by gradually increasing the difficulty of training over time according to a set schedule (a 'curriculum') – based on the idea that learning should proceed from easy to hard, inspired by the way that humans learn (Elman, 1993). Within the context of curriculum learning, one of the central questions is how to define and manipulate the difficulty of the learning process over the course of training. In a recent survey, Soviany et al. (2022) decompose this challenge into two main sub-problems: determining a sorting mechanism to assess the difficulty of instances and developing a pacing function for increasing difficulty over time.

2.1 Determining Difficulty

Previous work in curriculum learning typically focuses on difficulty from a data-centric perspective, however, we note that difficulty can arise from (at least) three major elements of training a neural

[1] We refer to our non-curriculum learning baselines as 'vanilla' models in order to differentiate these models from the baselines that were provided by the workshop organizers.

model: the input representation, the data sampling, and the training process. We explore curriculum learning strategies across three distinct dimensions: the vocabulary, the order of training data, and the objective function.

For machine learning models, instance difficulty is in part influenced by the choice of instance representation. For language models, the representational space is constrained by the vocabulary. We propose a new **vocabulary curriculum** inspired by Soviany et al. (2022), who discuss linking the curriculum criteria to the observed vocabulary sizes in child development. To the best of our knowledge, this is the first attempt at manipulating the vocabulary available to a language model through curriculum learning.

In natural language processing models, the order of the training instances can have a strong effect on performance (Schluter and Varab, 2018). Existing approaches to instance-level curriculum learning determine the difficulty of each instance according to a pre-defined static difficulty assessment according to linguistic criteria (Campos, 2021; Kocmi and Bojar, 2017; Liu et al., 2018; Platanios et al., 2019). It has been shown that humans pay more attention to stimuli that are in just the right zone of difficulty for them: neither too easy nor too hard (Kidd et al., 2012). This so-called 'Goldilocks effect' can be modelled by assessing the difficulty of an instance dynamically based on model behaviour (Sachan and Xing, 2016; Lalor and Yu, 2020). Static and dynamic difficulty assessment can be mapped to teacher-centric and learner-centric educational approaches and we compare both variants in our **data curriculum** experiments.

Human language learning is guided and enabled to some extent by other agents in the learner's environment (e.g., adult caregivers, siblings) who interact with the learner. In machine learning, such interactions are modelled by the objective function that guides the weight optimization process. The typical 'masked language modelling' (MLM) objective function requires that a model predicts a target token from a pre-defined vocabulary of size N given the surrounding context. Thus standard MLM defines an N-way token classification task.

Curriculum learning can be leveraged within this context to attenuate the difficulty of the classification task during training. One natural starting point for doing so is to redefine the classification task to be over a smaller set of items, K, such that $K << N$. Bai et al. (2022) map rare words with hypernyms of that word to simplify the classification task in training. A related line of research suggests replacing certain words with either part-of-speech tags (Wang et al., 2022) or syntactic dependency relations (Cui et al., 2022). Since the number of syntactic tags is substantially smaller than the number of vocabulary items, these approaches greatly reduce the difficulty of the objective. Moreover, by varying the amount of syntactic tags that the model should classify over, the difficulty of the task can be dynamically adapted (Wang et al., 2022). We take inspiration from this latter line of work in defining our own **objective curriculum**.

2.2 Pacing Functions

Once a notion of difficulty is set, a pacing function is needed to govern how quickly the model will progress from training on easier examples to training on harder ones (Wu et al., 2021). We experiment with two different pacing functions: linear and logarithmic. Linear pacing functions involve a steady and consistent advancement through the curriculum. This approach ensures a gradual increase in difficulty over time. Logarithmic pacing functions, on the other hand, emphasize early exposure to "easier" concepts, with diminishing increments as the model's capabilities are assumed to increase. Both pacing functions have been proposed in the broader curriculum learning literature (Bai et al., 2022; Li et al., 2021; Wu et al., 2021).

3 Methodology

All of our models are based on an 8-layer Transformer language model (Section 3.2) comparable to the BabyBERTa model (Huebner et al., 2021). For all experiments, we use the Hugging Face Transformers library (Wolf et al., 2020), Weights & Biases for performance tracking (Biewald, 2020), Hydra to define experiment configurations (Yadan, 2019), and a high performance computing cluster. We introduce curriculum learning to three of the primary components of language model pre-training: the vocabulary (Section 3.3), the data sampling approach (Section 3.4), and the selection of the objective function (Section 3.5). For each of these aspects, we attempt to simulate facets of human language learning by dynamically increasing the difficulty of the language modelling task over the course of training. Table 1 provides an overview of our experiment variables.

Curriculum Type	Parameter	Variants
Vocabulary	Selection Pacing	frequency, word class, mixed linear, logarithmic
Data	Difficulty Pacing Initial Perplexity	source, unigram perplexity, self-perplexity linear, logarithmic unigram, random
Objective	Tasks Learning Setup	noun-verb prediction, POS prediction, MLM sequential, multitask

Table 1: Curriculum learning experiments overview

3.1 Training Data

We use only the training data provided in the STRICT-SMALL track of the BabyLM challenge, which is limited to 10 million words and combined from 10 individual corpora. Given the variety of data sources (including books, subtitles, transcripts and articles) we carefully curated the data to ensure consistency across corpora. These steps include lowercasing, normalizing punctuation, standardizing typographical conventions using regular expressions, and removing extraneous lines (such as page numbers, bibliography entries, plain text tables , and one-word on-screen actions). We also concatenated contiguous sections of five lines into a single data instance in the transcribed speech corpora (except the BNC) due to the relatively short sequence lengths. In addition, we join data at the point of passing input to the models, in order to make full use of the available input sequence length (128 subtokens).

According to the rules of the STRICT-SMALL track, we were not permitted to make use of external resources, including supervised part-of-speech (POS) taggers. Therefore, we attempted to cluster the words in the training data into word classes by applying the `anchor-features` algorithm of the unsupervised POS-tagger by Stratos et al. (2016) on our cleaned data. The algorithm yields 30 clusters which we manually mapped to the 12 universal speech tags (Petrov et al., 2012) by choosing the POS-tag that best represents the anchor word of each cluster. We were only able to identify 10 of the 12 universal POS tags in the 30 clusters: no cluster neatly coincided with 'ADV' or 'X' tags. We provide further detail on our data preprocessing and unsupervised POS-tagging in the Appendix.

We provide our cleaned and tagged versions of the 10M word dataset on Hugging Face, along with the scripts used.[2] Our pre-processing procedure reduces the data down to 335,858 instances (corresponding to roughly 9.4 million words) from the initial 1,058,740 newline-delineated samples.[3] Our models, tokenizers and part-of-speech taggers were trained on this pre-processed data; however, we actually noticed an increase in performance when training on the raw data, as discussed in Section 5.

3.2 Vanilla Models

We investigate three different sizes of a vanilla Pre-Layer Norm RoBERTa model (Liu et al., 2019; Ott et al., 2019) based on the BabyBERTa model (Huebner et al., 2021): 'small', 'medium', and 'large' – Table 2 lists the model configurations and presents the results for the different model sizes evaluated by perplexity, on BLiMP (Warstadt et al., 2020a) and on the supplementary BLiMP-like tasks issued by the BabyLM organizers ('Blimp.Supp'). We found the medium model with a small vocabulary size performed the best overall; however, the small model achieved similar results, and so to save on compute and keep to the restrained intentions of the STRICT-SMALL track, we used the small model in our curriculum learning experiments. We use Byte Pair Encoding (BPE) tokenization (Gage, 1994) with a vocabulary of 8,192 because it yields better overall performance compared to a larger vocabulary of 16,384. The tokenizers we use in our experiments were trained on the cleaned data that we processed using the steps outlined in 3.1. In pilot experiments, we did not observe the benefits reported by Huebner et al. (2021) from removing the unmasking procedure that is a standard component of the MLM objective (Devlin et al., 2019), and therefore did not investigate this option further.

All of the curriculum learning methods in the following sections were applied on top of our small vanilla BabyBERTa-style baseline – to isolate the effect of the curriculum-learning training process,

[2] `https://huggingface.co/cambridge-climb`

[3] The word count is estimated by whitespace splitting; the same metric used by the organizers of the task to derive the estimate of 10 million words. When applying a tokenizer, the pre-processed dataset is more accurately split into 11.7 million words (including punctuation) or 13.6 million subwords

Model	Layers	Heads	Hidden	Intermediate	Vocab	Train.steps	BLiMP	BLiMP.Supp	Perplexity
Small	8	8	256	2,048	8,192	250K	75.43	61.14	9.46
Medium	10	10	500	2,000	8,192	156K	76.45	63.28	9.05
Large	12	12	768	3,072	8,192	94K	75.80	60.83	9.34
Small	8	8	256	2,048	16,384	250K	76.16	60.85	13.80
Medium	10	10	500	2,000	16,384	94K	76.09	60.03	13.80
Large	12	12	768	3,072	16,384	62K	75.08	63.45	14.22

Table 2: Our vanilla BabyBERTa-style models evaluated on original BLiMP and the BLiMP-like tasks prepared for BabyLM (BLiMP.Supp). Models are grouped by their vocabulary sizes.

we fixed the architecture of the model and the model hyper-parameters. We use an AdamW optimizer with linear scheduling (Loshchilov and Hutter, 2019).

3.3 Vocabulary Curriculum

During the early stages of language acquisition, children start with a small vocabulary that rapidly expands at a rate of eight to ten words per day (Weizman and Snow, 2001). In this process, children prioritize learning verbs and nouns before progressing to other parts of speech (Bergelson and Swingley, 2015). Large language models, on the other hand, tend to begin training with a full, fixed vocabulary available to them.

To represent a child's growing vocabulary, we select a limited vocabulary in the initial stages of learning and map all other input tokens into the representation for the unknown token (UNK). We consider three strategies for selecting tokens. In the first strategy, tokens are selected according to frequency. We approximate the frequency of a token by the identifier the BPE tokenizer assigns to it as lower IDs are assigned to tokens that are merged first (i.e., sequences of characters that occur more frequently in the corpus). In the second strategy, tokens are selected by their word class. We approximate the word class of a token by the cluster that the unsupervised POS-tagger assigns to it. We order the word classes as follows, progressing from lexical to functional classes per Bergelson and Swingley (2015): NOUN, VERB, ADJ, PRON, DET, ADP, NUM, CONJ, PRT, PNCT. In this strategy, all words with the respective part-of-speech tag are included in the vocabulary at the same step during learning. To smooth this process, we combine the frequency and the word class constraint in the third strategy. We sort words by their frequency (approximated by the token ID) within each part-of-speech category. Note that the same word may be available in some instances and not others if it is assigned a more difficult POS tag.

During the initial steps of training, only 10% of the tokens are available while the rest are replaced with UNK. The vocabulary curriculum regime begins after 25,000 training steps and ends at 350,000 steps, during which time, the vocabulary gradually increases according to a pacing function. We experiment with linear and logarithmic pacing functions. After the end of the curriculum regime, there remain 50,000 training steps before the end of training during which all of the vocabulary tokens are available to the model. Figure 5 in the Appendix shows a plot of the percentage of unmasked vocabulary over the course of training according to our pacing functions.

3.4 Data Curriculum

Conventional masked language modelling approaches train a given neural network on a large amount of crawled internet data. The resulting text sequences are usually not curated beyond basic cleaning and are presented to the model in random order, in contrast to the way that human children learn a language.

We attempt to carefully optimize the way data is sampled and presented to the language model over the course of training. We experiment with theory-driven and model-driven approaches to determine the 'relative difficulty' of a certain example and train the model on instances with progressively increasing difficulty.

Source Difficulty We order the available datasets based on their sources so that spoken samples are considered 'easier' and purely written texts 'harder', following the findings of Huebner et al. (2021). Within this ordering, we place the mostly child-directed speech from CHILDES before adult-to-adult dialogues in the Switchboard Corpus, and

Difficulty Level	Corpora
1	AO-CHILDES
2	BNC Spoken, Switchboard
3	Open Subtitles, QED
4	CBT, Children's Stories
5	Simple Wikipedia
6	Wikipedia, Gutenberg

Table 3: Difficulty level assigned to each dataset.

Simple Wikipedia before Wikipedia, see Table 3.[4]

Model Difficulty Determining the difficulty of an instance based on its data source is a relatively naive heuristic that ignores the variation of instance difficulty within one corpus. As a more fine-grained alternative, we determine the difficulty of each instance individually using the model-intrinsic metric of perplexity which determines the likelihood of a sentence. We experiment with two variants: a static unigram language model and a more dynamic self-evaluation. With the unigram model, perplexity for each instance is only determined once at the beginning of training. Alternatively, we evaluate the perplexity of the remaining training data using the model that has been trained so far – from model checkpoints saved at regular intervals in training (every 25K steps).

One challenge with the latter approach is the lack of exposure to training data at the beginning, leading to random perplexity scores for each sample. To address this, we propose two ideas: 1) using a separately trained unigram model to initially evaluate perplexity, or 2) initially sample training instances randomly. After 25,000 training steps, we switch to using the current model for perplexity evaluation. Every 25,000 steps thereafter, we re-evaluate perplexity to identify samples categorized as relatively difficult or relatively easy by the model.

3.5 Objective Curriculum

The MLM objective has proven tremendously successful in training Transformer networks as language models (Devlin et al., 2019). Psycholinguistic research, however, suggests that MLM is not a cognitively plausible approximation of language acquisition processes in children (Caucheteux et al., 2023). Curriculum learning establishes a framework for varying the difficulty of the learning process over the course of training. The MLM objective is a very challenging discriminative classification task because the identity of the masked token needs to be determined over the entire vocabulary. We experiment with using more coarse-grained tasks at the initial stages of training to facilitate generalization and leverage syntactic information. Research in cognitive linguistics has shown that one-year-old infants are sensitive to distributional aspects of language and from two years of age begin to recognize lexical categories such as nouns and verbs Alishahi (2010); Gleitman (1990). We therefore experiment with predicting only the word class of a masked token at the start of training rather than predicting its exact target token ID.

The psycholinguistic literature remains divided on the question of how exactly word learning proceeds from memorizing a small set of fixed lexical items to a more generalized representation of word classes (Clark and Casillas, 2015). Our framework provides a flexible approach to vary the difficulty of objective functions during the course of training, and to enable systematic studies of the effect of objective functions on the acquisition of linguistic knowledge by a model. Here we propose estimating the word class using the unsupervised POS tagger and we vary the number of POS tags which are being classified over. The masked word is classified into 1) one of VERB, NOUN, or OTHER, or 2) one of 10 universal POS tags.

We examine activating the tasks in sequential order (first word class prediction then MLM) or optimizing them in parallel, comparable to a multi-task learning setting. For each objective function, we learn a separate task head with its own linear task classifier and separate optimizer.

4 Results

Multiple evaluation metrics are employed in BabyLM. In this paper we focus on BLiMP (Warstadt et al., 2020a) and the supplementary BLiMP-style tests provided by the shared task organizers. We also report our results on the natural language understanding benchmark, SuperGLUE (Wang et al., 2019), and the ambiguous subset of MSGS (the Mixed Signals Generalization Set) (Warstadt et al., 2020b). In brief, BLiMP evaluates specific linguistic abilities, MSGS evaluates linguistic preference over surface generalisation and SuperGLUE evaluates downstream task performance. For all scores, we report the average score across all categories, rather than test instances, as provided by the BabyLM evaluation

[4] There is likely some adult-to-adult dialogue included in CHILDES as well.

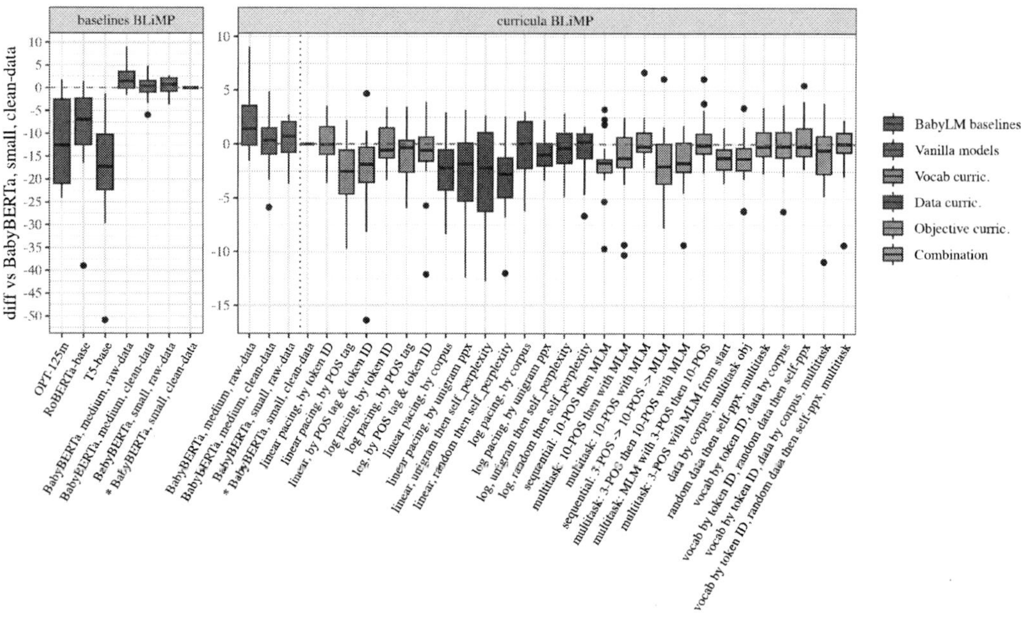

Figure 1: Comparison of the BabyLM baselines with our BabyBERTa-style vanilla models (left), and our vanilla models against our curriculum learning models (right) – using BabyBERTa-small trained on clean data as a reference point (asterisked) to show the difference in scores on BLiMP and BLiMP-supplement tasks. For combination models, all pacing is logarithmic, and 'multitask' refers to the 2-task objective curriculum, 10 POS-tags and MLM from the outset. Absolute values may be found in Appendix Tables 5–9.

pipeline.[5] All of our curriculum learning models are small BabyBERTa-style ones using the parameters shown in Table 2 and the cleaned training dataset of 9.4M words (reduced from the 10M word dataset for the STRICT-SMALL track) and their results can be found in Tables 5, 6 and 7.

In the tables we compare to our small BabyBERTa-style vanilla model also trained on the clean data (Section 3.2). Figure 1 visualizes these comparisons for the BLiMP tasks; there are similar plots for SuperGLUE in the Appendix (Figure 4). Furthermore, we experimented with some combinations of different curricula to see how they would interact (Table 8), and compare the official BabyLM shared-task baselines with our shared task entries – a number of our own BabyBERTa-style vanilla models and curriculum learning models (Table 9). For all of our runs, we use the same set of hyper-parameters that we report in Table 10. We also report the average amount of compute used for each type of curriculum learning setting (Table 11).

We find notable gains for our own vanilla models over the shared-task baselines, and, while we do not identify further large improvements in our curriculum learning models, we do notice some modest gains which suggest possibilities for future research and experimentation over variables. While the differences in performance between most of our experimental conditions are small, the large number of ablations we run enables us to provide a comprehensive set of recommendations for how and when different curriculum learning strategies may offer improved performance on linguistic tasks. Below we summarize our observations over the full results tables.

In general, log pacing works at least as well as linear pacing across different curricula learning strategies. In our data curriculum experiments, models using the log pacing function outperform their linear counterparts in 4/4 settings on BLiMP, and 3/4 settings for BLiMP-supplement and SuperGLUE (Table 6). This indicates that rapidly increasing the difficulty of training instances in the early stages brings downstream benefits on grammaticality and NLU tasks.

In our vocabulary curriculum experiments on

[5] For instance, there are 12 categories in BLiMP but 50+ individual tests. We average over the scores given for each category, rather than the scores given for each test.

the other hand, there is not such a clear picture. Log pacing outperforms linear in 2/3 settings on BLiMP and 3/3 on SuperGLUE, but 0/3 for BLiMP-supplement (Table 5). Presumably this is a reflection of the different vocabulary required by each set of evaluation tasks, which could be a matter for future investigation but also indicates that we do not yet have a clear generalizable pacing function for the vocabulary curriculum. There are of course other pacing functions to be tried.

Different representations of vocabulary difficulty work better for different tasks. When representing difficulty in the vocabulary curriculum experiments, token ID – our proxy for frequency – appears to work better than word classes (POS tags) or a combination of token ID and POS tags on the BLiMP evaluation tasks, but worse than POS tags on SuperGLUE and MSGS (Table 5).

In multi-corpora datasets, ordering by difficulty is a good first step. Training data requirements have grown so much in modern NLP that usually training a language model from scratch will involve multiple datasets, or multiple domains. The results of our data curriculum experiments indicate that a good first step is to put these sub-corpora into some order of intuitive difficulty, as we did (Table 6). In the case of BLiMP this approach outperforms our perplexity-based data curricula, and with log pacing our vanilla model. The same is true of MSGS (with log pacing), as well as BLiMP-supplement and SuperGLUE (though the last two do not beat our vanilla model). Amongst the perplexity-driven models, the picture is less positive: out of 24 tests, only one model outperforms our vanilla model (log pacing, random initialisation + model perplexity in Table 6).

Multitask learning holds sway over sequentially swapping objective functions for now. In our experiments with curricula for the objective function, we compare training on simultaneous tasks – known as multitask learning (Caruana, 1997) – with predefined sequences of objective functions which swap from one to another at set thresholds in the training process. We set up two sequential curricula: one with 2 tasks (predicting the 10 universal POS tags found in our dataset, and MLM) and the other with 3 (like the 2 task curriculum, additionally with noun/verb/other prediction). We compare these against multitasking alternatives. In general the sequential curricula are outperformed by the multitasking ones, though the 3-task sequential curriculum outperforms our BabyBERTa-style vanilla model on SuperGLUE and is second only marginally to our best-performing multitask model (Table 7). The multitask learning model with 10-class universal POS-tag prediction and MLM in place from the outset performs best on BLiMP and SuperGLUE. However, our best model on BLiMP-supplement – a multitask one – has an element of sequential task scheduling in that the two POS-tag prediction tasks are lined up one after the other, with a switch from 3-class to 10-class after 6.25% of training steps. In Figure 2, we visualize this result for each task in BLiMP-supplement, illustrating that our curriculum learning model improves over our vanilla model in 5/6 tasks. Altogether, these results suggest that sequential objective function curricula do hold some potential for performance gains if further tuning of the tasks and scheduling can be carried out.

Combining all three curricula shows potential on BLiMP. While each individual curriculum learning experiment did not result in consistent improvements across tasks, we investigated whether combining aspects from the different curricula would, together, improve the model. We do find that a combination of all three curricula outperforms any single curriculum model on BLiMP, but the same is not true for BLiMP-supplement and SuperGLUE (Table 8). This is another matter for future investigation, as it seems that improving each of the three curricula we investigate may lead to further gains if they are all combined.

In small data settings, filtering data which we intuitively think is noisy is in fact counter-productive. Perhaps surprisingly, we find that the vanilla models trained on the raw data outperform those trained on the pre-processed data on BLiMP and MSGS. We surmise that models can learn even from linguistically non-standard datapoints.

4.1 Submitted models

Table 9 in the Appendix compares our submissions to the shared task baselines. We submitted our best curriculum learning models from each individual curriculum learning setting, and four different vanilla models: two small and two medium models, where each pair additionally varies by whether it was trained on the pre-processed dataset or the raw dataset. We find our curriculum learning models are comparable to our BabyBERTa-style vanilla models, and we think that in most cases some continued experimentation with configurations may yield larger gains for CL approaches.

For interest, we also trained a BabyBERTa-style large vanilla model on the 100M training set made available in the BabyLM STRICT track ('large-100M' in the table). The improvements over smaller models trained on less data are evident and finally provide an advantage over the RoBERTa baseline on SuperGLUE. It remains to be seen how well curriculum learning methods, and our preprocessing methods, would work with this larger dataset.

5 Discussion

We set out to investigate a number of curriculum learning approaches to language model training, motivated by findings from the human language acquisition process and by the wish to successfully train smaller models for smaller budgets. We first of all implemented a stronger model of our own, based on BabyBERTa (Huebner et al., 2021) and found that a small 8-layer vanilla model could outperform the provided BabyLM baselines on the BLiMP grammaticality tests and get close to the best RoBERTa shared-task baseline on SuperGLUE. This underlines the findings reported in the BabyBERTa paper: that with smaller datasets, it makes sense to use smaller models and a smaller vocabulary size.

The results of our curriculum learning experiments, trained with a small BabyBERTa-style vanilla model, suggest that we can further improve performance in certain linguistic tasks by careful application of a pacing function, how we represent and grow the model's vocabulary during training, select the next training instances according to their difficulty, and vary the objective function. Specifically, we find that a logarithmic pacing function works better for the data curriculum than a linear one, but the findings for the vocabulary curriculum are less clear. Other pacing functions might be tried in the future, including those that reflect acquisition theory around non-monotonic or 'U-shaped' development trajectories.

It is apparent that ordering the subcorpora within a training set may be worthwhile, and that perplexity-based approaches to data selection hold potential even though we have not found a clear-cut best method for perplexity calculation as yet. As shown in other NLP work, multitask learning can be a beneficial approach, though MLM or next-word prediction remain preeminent as singular tasks used in language modelling. We find multitask learning models hard to beat in the objective curriculum, but do find good performance in our sequential settings. We believe that future work varying the timing of task switches and introducing more tasks could be worthwhile.

On a more general note, the Baby LM challenge evaluates a language model only on its final downstream performance on a set of tasks – i.e. at a finite point in time. The challenge does not directly measure whether a given model is learning in a 'human-like' fashion. Our contribution to the BabyLM challenge is to provide a set of curriculum learning strategies which are motivated by the language learning dynamics of infants and children. We encourage future research to study how to quantitatively evaluate whether the learning trajectory of a model parallels that of a human language learner and how similarities to human language learning results in downstream NLU performance.

6 Conclusions

We use child-like language learning as inspiration to investigate and implement three types of curriculum learning for language modelling: gradually increasing the size of the vocabulary (**vocabulary curriculum**), the difficulty of the training instances (**data curriculum**), or the specificity of the objective function (**objective curriculum**).

We find that our BabyBERTa-style vanilla models outperform the BabyLM baselines on BLiMP and MSGS, and get close on SuperGLUE. Our various curriculum learning models at times offer further gains over our vanilla models, and indicate the potential for curriculum learning methods given further exploration. We list out a set of recommendations for when and how to optimally apply our proposed curriculum learning strategies.

Additionally, training our vanilla model trained on unprocessed data outperforms a 'cleaned' version – suggesting that retaining as much data as possible, in low-resource settings, is more important than standardizing it according to linguistic norms.

Finally, our work establishes a computational framework for how to categorise and implement curricula learning strategies that simulate human language learning dynamics.

Acknowledgements

This paper reports on work supported by Cambridge University Press & Assessment. It was performed using resources provided by the Cambridge Service for Data Driven Discovery (CSD3) operated by the University of Cambridge Research Computing Service, provided by Dell EMC and Intel using Tier-2 funding from the Engineering and Physical Sciences Research Council (capital grant EP/T022159/1), and DiRAC funding from the Science and Technology Facilities Council. Richard Diehl Martinez is supported by the Gates Cambridge Trust (grant OPP1144 from the Bill & Melinda Gates Foundation). Hope McGovern's work is supported by The Cambridge Trust and the Woolf Institute for Interfaith Relations. Zébulon Goriely's work is supported by The Cambridge Trust. Lisa Beinborn's work is supported by the Dutch National Science Organisation (NWO) through the VENI program (Vl.Veni.211C.039).

References

Afra Alishahi. 2010. *Computational modeling of human language acquisition*. Morgan & Claypool Publishers.

He Bai, Tong Wang, Alessandro Sordoni, and Peng Shi. 2022. Better language model with hypernym class prediction. In *Proceedings of the 60th Annual Meeting of the Association for Computational Linguistics (Volume 1: Long Papers)*, pages 1352–1362, Dublin, Ireland. Association for Computational Linguistics.

Yoshua Bengio, Jérôme Louradour, Ronan Collobert, and Jason Weston. 2009. Curriculum learning. In *Proceedings of the 26th Annual International Conference on Machine Learning*, pages 41–48.

Elika Bergelson and Daniel Swingley. 2015. Early word comprehension in infants: Replication and extension. *Language Learning and Development*, 11(4):369–380.

Lukas Biewald. 2020. Experiment tracking with Weights and Biases.

Steven Bird, Ewan Klein, and Edward Loper. 2009. *Natural language processing with Python: analyzing text with the natural language toolkit*. " O'Reilly Media, Inc.".

Tom Brown, Benjamin Mann, Nick Ryder, Melanie Subbiah, Jared D Kaplan, Prafulla Dhariwal, Arvind Neelakantan, Pranav Shyam, Girish Sastry, Amanda Askell, Sandhini Agarwal, Ariel Herbert-Voss, Gretchen Krueger, Tom Henighan, Rewon Child, Aditya Ramesh, Daniel Ziegler, Jeffrey Wu, Clemens Winter, Chris Hesse, Mark Chen, Eric Sigler, Mateusz Litwin, Scott Gray, Benjamin Chess, Jack Clark, Christopher Berner, Sam McCandlish, Alec Radford, Ilya Sutskever, and Dario Amodei. 2020. Language models are few-shot learners. In *Advances in Neural Information Processing Systems*, volume 33, pages 1877–1901. Curran Associates, Inc.

Daniel Campos. 2021. Curriculum learning for language modeling. arXiv:2108.02170.

Rich Caruana. 1997. Multitask learning. *Machine learning*, 28:41–75.

Charlotte Caucheteux, Alexandre Gramfort, and Jean-Rémi King. 2023. Evidence of a predictive coding hierarchy in the human brain listening to speech. *Nature human behaviour*, 7(3):430–441.

Eve V Clark and Marisa Casillas. 2015. *First language acquisition*. Routledge.

Yiming Cui, Wanxiang Che, Shijin Wang, and Ting Liu. 2022. Lert: A linguistically-motivated pre-trained language model. arXiv:2211.05344.

Jacob Devlin, Ming-Wei Chang, Kenton Lee, and Kristina Toutanova. 2019. BERT: Pre-training of deep bidirectional transformers for language understanding. In *Proceedings of the 2019 Conference of the North American Chapter of the Association for Computational Linguistics: Human Language Technologies, Volume 1 (Long and Short Papers)*, pages 4171–4186, Minneapolis, Minnesota. Association for Computational Linguistics.

Jeffrey L. Elman. 1993. Learning and development in neural networks: the importance of starting small. *Cognition*, 48(1):71–99.

Philip Gage. 1994. A new algorithm for data compression. *C Users Journal*, 12(2):23–38.

Leo Gao, Stella Biderman, Sid Black, Laurence Golding, Travis Hoppe, Charles Foster, Jason Phang, Horace He, Anish Thite, Noa Nabeshima, Shawn Presser, and Connor Leahy. 2020. The pile: An 800gb dataset of diverse text for language modeling.

Jonas Geiping and Tom Goldstein. 2023. Cramming: Training a language model on a single GPU in one day. In *International Conference on Machine Learning*, pages 11117–11143. PMLR.

Jill Gilkerson, Jeffrey A Richards, Steven F Warren, Judith K Montgomery, Charles R Greenwood, D Kimbrough Oller, John H L Hansen, and Terrance D Paul. 2017. Mapping the early language environment using all-day recordings and automated analysis. *American Journal of Speech-Language Pathology*, 26:248–265.

Lila Gleitman. 1990. The structural sources of verb meanings. *Language acquisition*, 1(1):3–55.

Jordan Hoffmann, Sebastian Borgeaud, Arthur Mensch, Elena Buchatskaya, Trevor Cai, Eliza Rutherford, Diego de Las Casas, Lisa Anne Hendricks, Johannes Welbl, Aidan Clark, Tom Hennigan, Eric Noland, Katie Millican, George van den Driessche, Bogdan Damoc, Aurelia Guy, Simon Osindero, Karen Simonyan, Erich Elsen, Jack W. Rae, Oriol Vinyals, and Laurent Sifre. 2022. Training compute-optimal large language models. In *Proceedings of the 36th Conference on Neural Information Processing Systems (NeurIPS)*.

Philip A. Huebner, Elior Sulem, Fisher Cynthia, and Dan Roth. 2021. BabyBERTa: Learning more grammar with small-scale child-directed language. In *Proceedings of the 25th Conference on Computational Natural Language Learning*, pages 624–646, Online. Association for Computational Linguistics.

Peter Izsak, Moshe Berchansky, and Omer Levy. 2021. How to train BERT with an academic budget. In *Proceedings of the 2021 Conference on Empirical Methods in Natural Language Processing*, pages 10644–10652, Online and Punta Cana, Dominican Republic. Association for Computational Linguistics.

Celeste Kidd, Steven T. Piantadosi, and Richard N. Aslin. 2012. The Goldilocks Effect: Human infants allocate attention to visual sequences that are neither too simple nor too complex. *PLOS ONE*, 7(5):1–8.

Tom Kocmi and Ondřej Bojar. 2017. Curriculum learning and minibatch bucketing in neural machine translation. In *Proceedings of the International Conference on Recent Advances in Natural Language Processing, RANLP 2017*, pages 379–386.

John P. Lalor and Hong Yu. 2020. Dynamic data selection for curriculum learning via ability estimation. In *Findings of the Association for Computational Linguistics: EMNLP 2020*, pages 545–555, Online. Association for Computational Linguistics.

Conglong Li, Minjia Zhang, and Yuxiong He. 2021. Curriculum learning: A regularization method for efficient and stable billion-scale gpt model pre-training.

Cao Liu, Shizhu He, Kang Liu, Jun Zhao, et al. 2018. Curriculum learning for natural answer generation. In *IJCAI*, pages 4223–4229.

Yinhan Liu, Myle Ott, Naman Goyal, Jingfei Du, Mandar Joshi, Danqi Chen, Omer Levy, Mike Lewis, Luke Zettlemoyer, and Veselin Stoyanov. 2019. RoBERTa: A robustly optimized BERT pretraining approach. arXiv:1907.11692.

Ilya Loshchilov and Frank Hutter. 2019. Decoupled weight decay regularization. arXiv:1711.05101.

Myle Ott, Sergey Edunov, Alexei Baevski, Angela Fan, Sam Gross, Nathan Ng, David Grangier, and Michael Auli. 2019. fairseq: A fast, extensible toolkit for sequence modeling. In *North American Chapter of the Association for Computational Linguistics*.

Slav Petrov, Dipanjan Das, and Ryan McDonald. 2012. A universal part-of-speech tagset. In *Proceedings of the Eighth International Conference on Language Resources and Evaluation (LREC'12)*, pages 2089–2096, Istanbul, Turkey. European Language Resources Association (ELRA).

Emmanouil Antonios Platanios, Otilia Stretcu, Graham Neubig, Barnabás Poczós, and Tom Mitchell. 2019. Competence-based curriculum learning for neural machine translation. In *Proceedings of the 2019 Conference of the North American Chapter of the Association for Computational Linguistics: Human Language Technologies, Volume 1 (Long and Short Papers)*, pages 1162–1172.

Mrinmaya Sachan and Eric Xing. 2016. Easy questions first? a case study on curriculum learning for question answering. In *Proceedings of the 54th Annual Meeting of the Association for Computational Linguistics (Volume 1: Long Papers)*, pages 453–463, Berlin, Germany. Association for Computational Linguistics.

David Samuel, Andrey Kutuzov, Lilja Øvrelid, and Erik Velldal. 2023. Trained on 100 million words and still in shape: BERT meets British National Corpus. In *Findings of the Association for Computational Linguistics: EACL 2023*, pages 1954–1974, Dubrovnik, Croatia. Association for Computational Linguistics.

Natalie Schluter and Daniel Varab. 2018. When data permutations are pathological: the case of neural natural language inference. In *Proceedings of the 2018 Conference on Empirical Methods in Natural Language Processing*, pages 4935–4939, Brussels, Belgium. Association for Computational Linguistics.

Petru Soviany, Radu Tudor Ionescu, Paolo Rota, and Nicu Sebe. 2022. Curriculum learning: A survey. *International Journal of Computer Vision*, pages 1–40.

Karl Stratos, Michael Collins, and Daniel Hsu. 2016. Unsupervised part-of-speech tagging with anchor hidden Markov models. *Transactions of the Association for Computational Linguistics*, 4:245–257.

Alex Wang, Yada Pruksachatkun, Nikita Nangia, Amanpreet Singh, Julian Michael, Felix Hill, Omer Levy, and Samuel Bowman. 2019. SuperGLUE: A stickier benchmark for general-purpose language understanding systems. *Advances in Neural Information Processing Systems*, 32.

Yile Wang, Yue Zhang, Peng Li, and Yang Liu. 2022. Language model pre-training with linguistically motivated curriculum learning.

Alex Warstadt, Aaron Mueller, Leshem Choshen, Ethan Gotlieb Wilcox, Chengxu Zhuang, Juan Ciro, Rafael Mosquera, Adina Williams, Bhargavi Paranjabe, Tal Linzen, and Ryan Cotterell. 2023. Findings of the 2023 BabyLM Challenge: Sample-efficient pretraining on developmentally plausible corpora. In

Proceedings of the 2023 BabyLM Challenge. Association for Computational Linguistics (ACL).

Alex Warstadt, Alicia Parrish, Haokun Liu, Anhad Mohananey, Wei Peng, Sheng-Fu Wang, and Samuel R Bowman. 2020a. BLiMP: The benchmark of linguistic minimal pairs for english. *Transactions of the Association for Computational Linguistics*, 8:377–392.

Alex Warstadt, Yian Zhang, Xiaocheng Li, Haokun Liu, and Samuel R. Bowman. 2020b. Learning which features matter: RoBERTa acquires a preference for linguistic generalizations (eventually). In *Proceedings of the 2020 Conference on Empirical Methods in Natural Language Processing (EMNLP)*, pages 217–235, Online. Association for Computational Linguistics.

Jason Wei, Maarten Bosma, Vincent Y. Zhao, Kelvin Guu, Adams Wei Yu, Brian Lester, Nan Du, Andrew M. Dai, and Quoc V. Le. 2021. Finetuned language models are zero-shot learners. arXiv:2109.01652.

Zehava Oz Weizman and Catherine E Snow. 2001. Lexical output as related to children's vocabulary acquisition: Effects of sophisticated exposure and support for meaning. *Developmental psychology*, 37(2):265.

Thomas Wolf, Lysandre Debut, Victor Sanh, Julien Chaumond, Clement Delangue, Anthony Moi, Pierric Cistac, Tim Rault, Remi Louf, Morgan Funtowicz, Joe Davison, Sam Shleifer, Patrick von Platen, Clara Ma, Yacine Jernite, Julien Plu, Canwen Xu, Teven Le Scao, Sylvain Gugger, Mariama Drame, Quentin Lhoest, and Alexander Rush. 2020. Transformers: State-of-the-art natural language processing. In *Proceedings of the 2020 Conference on Empirical Methods in Natural Language Processing: System Demonstrations*, pages 38–45, Online. Association for Computational Linguistics.

Xiaoxia Wu, Ethan Dyer, and Behnam Neyshabur. 2021. When do curricula work? In *International Conference on Learning Representations*.

Omry Yadan. 2019. Hydra – a framework for elegantly configuring complex applications. Github.

Yian Zhang, Alex Warstadt, Xiaocheng Li, and Samuel R. Bowman. 2021. When do you need billions of words of pretraining data? In *Proceedings of the 59th Annual Meeting of the Association for Computational Linguistics and the 11th International Joint Conference on Natural Language Processing (Volume 1: Long Papers)*, pages 1112–1125, Online. Association for Computational Linguistics.

Wayne Xin Zhao, Kun Zhou, Junyi Li, Tianyi Tang, Xiaolei Wang, Yupeng Hou, Yingqian Min, Beichen Zhang, Junjie Zhang, Zican Dong, et al. 2023. A survey of large language models. arXiv:2303.18223.

Appendix

Unsupervised POS-tagging. The strict-small track we enter does not allow using any external dataset. This restriction disallows usage of any third-party POS taggers, as these tend to be trained with a supervised corpus. To still be able to use POS information we train our own POS tagger using the unsupervised `anchor-features` part-of-speech algorithm by Stratos et al. (2016). This algorithm learns a hidden Markov model (HMM) under the assumption that certain tags are associated with words that have no other tags (the anchor words) and uses additional features to improve the estimation process.

We used the default parameters for this algorithm but learn 30 clusters instead of 12. These clusters are lexicalized, labelled only by the anchor word found for each by the algorithm so must be mapped to POS tags for our usage. Unsupervised POS taggers are typically evaluated by mapping each cluster to the most frequently coinciding gold POS tag. However, since this would be taking advantage of supervised data, we instead map each cluster by inspection, choosing the universal part-of-speech tag (Petrov et al., 2012) most representative of the anchor word for each cluster. This mapping is many-to-one, with several clusters mapping to the same tag, but no clusters mapped to ADV (adverb) or X (unknown), suggesting that the unsupervised approach failed to coherently group adverbs into a single cluster.

POS Tag	Precision	Recall	F1
NOUN	0.786	0.790	0.788
DET	0.820	0.772	0.795
CONJ	0.969	0.821	0.895
NUM	0.592	0.799	0.681
PRON	0.592	0.962	0.733
VERB	0.816	0.823	0.819
PRT	0.501	0.701	0.584
ADJ	0.673	0.554	0.608
ADP	0.842	0.888	0.864
PUNC	0.944	0.960	0.952

Table 4: Accuracy of our unsupervised POS tagger on a per-tag level.

We also evaluate how well our POS tagger predicts POS tags, compared to the supervised POS tagging system that is part of the NLTK Python package (Bird et al., 2009). Table 4 summarizes these results. Interestingly, we observe a large difference in our ability to correctly predict different types of POS tokens.

Objective curriculum models on BLiMP Supplement and (Super)GLUE. Figures 2 and 3 compare our small BabyBERTa-style vanilla model to our best objective-curriculum model – a multi-task trained model with sequential POS-tag prediction – on each task in BLiMP Supplement and (Super)GLUE. We find our curriculum-learning (CL) model outperforms our vanilla model on 5/6 tasks in BLiMP Supplement. While on (Super)GLUE, our CL model outperforms our baseline on 4/10 tasks and obtains comparable performance on another 4/10 tasks. This results illustrate the potential to further explore objective-curricula settings.

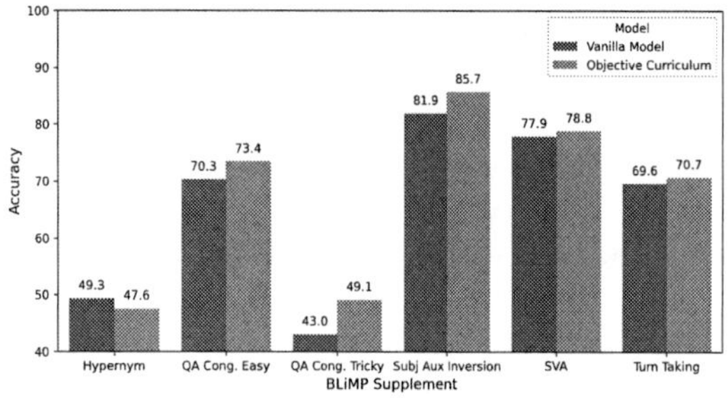

Figure 2: Comparison between our vanilla model and the best objective curriculum learning setting on the BLiMP supplementary tasks.

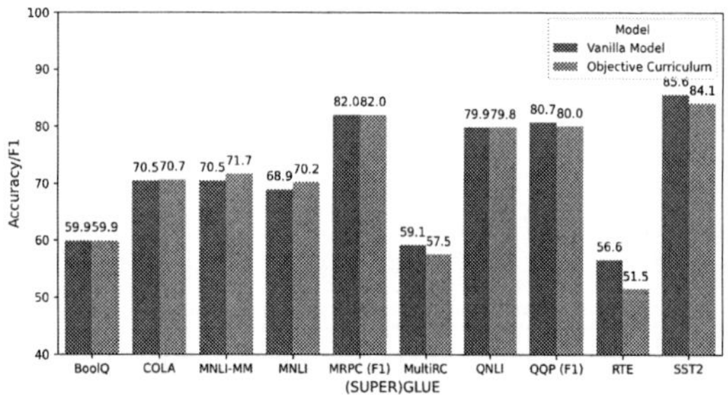

Figure 3: Comparison between our vanilla model and the best objective curriculum learning setting on the (Super)GLUE tasks.

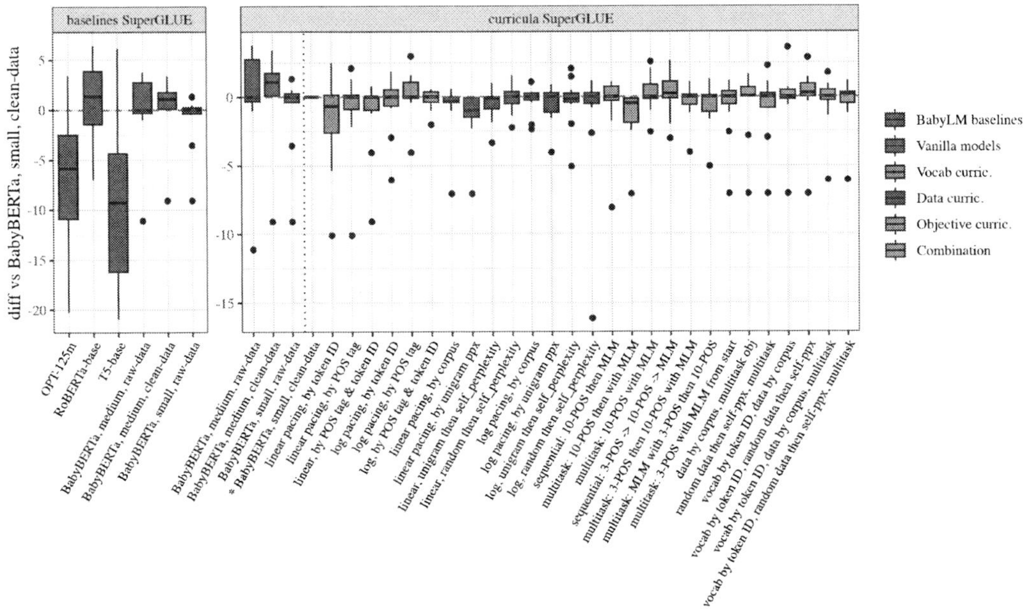

Figure 4: Comparison of the BabyLM baselines with our BabyBERTa-style vanilla models (left), and our vanilla models against our curriculum learning models (right) – using BabyBERTa-small trained on clean data as a reference point (asterisked) to show the difference in scores on SuperGLUE tasks. For combination models, all pacing is logarithmic, and 'multitask' refers to the 2-task objective curriculum, 10 POS-tags and MLM from the outset.

Pacing	Difficulty	Perplexity	BLiMP	BLiMP.Supp	(Super)GLUE	MSGS Ambig
†Linear	Token ID	9.70	75.09	**66.43**	68.71	68.61
Linear	POS	10.17	72.06	63.44	69.50	66.91
Linear	POS + Token ID	10.21	73.37	66.11	69.22	66.61
Log	Token ID	9.26	74.97	64.63	69.94	66.82
Log	POS	9.29	74.12	62.06	**70.66**	**70.52**
Log	POS + Token ID	9.29	74.74	63.62	70.29	66.42
Vanilla Model		**9.21**	**75.48**	65.34	70.47	68.30

Table 5: Results for vocabulary curriculum models (Section 3.3). All models score above 90 in the MSGS Control tasks. † indicates the model we submitted to BabyLM, 'CLIMB-tokens'.

Pacing	Difficulty	Perplexity	BLiMP	BLiMP.Supp	(Super)GLUE	MSGS Ambig
Linear	Source	10.41	73.32	61.99	69.68	66.22
Linear	Unigram ppx	12.51	72.45	61.67	69.10	66.90
Linear	Unigram + model ppx	11.88	72.62	62.57	69.86	66.64
Linear	Random + model ppx	10.82	71.88	63.10	70.37	67.48
†Log	Source	**9.21**	**75.87**	64.29	70.20	**70.99**
Log	Unigram ppx	9.39	75.03	63.78	69.90	66.69
Log	Unigram + model ppx	9.35	74.83	64.24	70.09	66.89
Log	Random + model ppx	**9.21**	75.81	63.03	68.93	66.64
Vanilla Model		**9.21**	75.48	**65.34**	**70.47**	68.30

Table 6: Results for data curriculum models (Section 3.4). All models score above 92 in the MSGS Control tasks. † indicates the model we submitted to BabyLM, 'CLIMB-data-split'.

Task Order	Task duration (% of training steps) 3 POS	10 POS	MLM	PPX	BLiMP	BLiMP.Supp	(Super)GLUE	MSGS Ambig
Sequential	–	0 - 12.5	12.5 - 100	9.58	73.87	62.98	69.85	66.70
Multitask	–	0 - 100	12.5 - 100	9.78	74.60	62.17	69.12	66.64
Multitask	–	0 - 100	0 - 100	9.30	**75.82**	65.77	**70.74**	66.58
Sequential	0 - 6.25	6.25 - 12.5	12.5 - 100	9.49	74.03	63.02	70.71	66.93
Multitask	0 - 6.25	6.25 - 100	12.5 - 100	9.72	73.68	63.89	70.07	67.00
†Multitask	0 - 6.25	6.25 - 100	0 - 100	9.30	74.80	**67.55**	69.89	67.65
Multitask	0 - 100	–	0 - 100	9.25	74.48	63.98	69.77	67.72
Vanilla Model				**9.21**	75.48	65.34	70.47	**68.30**

Table 7: Results for objective curriculum models (Section 3.5). All models score above 94 in the MSGS Control tasks. Task duration defines when an objective function was active during training, as a percentage of the total number of training steps. † indicates the model we submitted to BabyLM, 'CLIMB-multitask'.

Vocab Curric.	Data Curric.	Obj. Curric.	PPX	BLiMP	BLiMP.Supp	(Super)GLUE	MSGS Ambig
–	Source	Multitask	9.29	74.06	64.06	70.02	66.90
–	Random + model ppx	Multitask	9.44	75.89	64.63	69.72	67.78
Token ID	Source	–	9.27	75.89	64.62	70.24	67.90
Token ID	Random + model ppx	–	9.30	75.88	**65.79**	70.42	66.63
Token ID	Source	Multitask	9.22	74.86	62.82	70.09	66.68
Token ID	Random + model ppx	Multitask	9.46	**75.92**	63.68	69.98	**71.30**
Vanilla Model			**9.21**	75.48	65.34	**70.47**	68.30

Table 8: Results for the combination curriculum models. The multitask objective curriculum refers to the 2-task 10-POS and MLM model shown in Table 7.

Type	Model	PPX	BLiMP	BLiMP.Supp	(Super)GLUE	MSGS Ambig
Official Baseline	OPT-125m	–	63.16	55.08	63.38	69.22
	RoBERTa-base	–	69.84	50.52	71.42	70.25
	T5-base	–	58.27	47.55	60.93	68.55
Vanilla Models	CLIMB-base (medium)	9.01	75.66	66.13	70.75	67.62
	CLIMB-base-small	9.21	75.48	65.34	70.47	68.30
	CLIMB-raw (medium)	8.47	77.97	66.16	70.63	69.44
	CLIMB-small-raw	8.64	76.42	64.60	69.46	70.65
	large-100M	4.35	81.03	75.56	72.93	74.17
Vocab Curriculum	CLIMB-tokens	9.70	75.09	66.43	68.71	68.61
Data Curriculum	CLIMB-data-split	9.21	75.87	64.29	70.20	70.99
Objective Curriculum	CLIMB-multitask	9.30	74.80	67.55	69.89	67.65

Table 9: Comparison between the official shared task baselines, our BabyBERTa-style vanilla models, and our submitted curriculum learning models on the main evaluation tasks: BLiMP, (Super)GLUE, and MSGS. Our *small and *medium models are defined in Section 3.2. All models are trained on pre-processed data except for those labelled with *-raw, which are trained on mostly unprocessed data (except we join the input sentences). The 'large-100M' model was a larger BabyBERTa-style model trained on the 100M BabyLM training set (all others have been trained on the 10M dataset available in the STRICT-SMALL track).

Parameter	Value
Layer Norm EPS	1e-5
Tie Word Embeddings	False
Learning Rate	0.001
Optimizer	AdamW
Scheduler Type	Linear
Max Steps	400,000
Warm-up Steps	100,000
Per Device Batch Size	32

Table 10: Hyperparameter settings which are constant across our vanilla models described in 3.2. Table 2 reports variations to the architectures to create the 'small', 'medium' and 'large' versions of the vanilla model. Where values are not reported, they may be assumed to be default values.

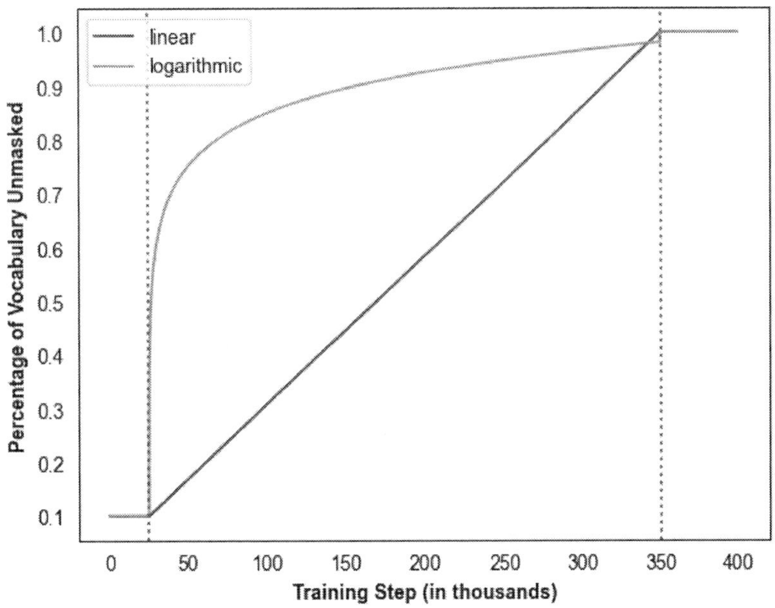

Figure 5: Illustration of the linear and logarithmic pacing functions used in our vocabulary curriculum experiments. The red dotted lines denote the curriculum regime, during which the percentage of unmasked words available to the model grows according to the respective function.

Type	Model	Training Time
Vanilla Models	CLIMB-small-raw	12h
	CLIMB-raw (medium)	17h40m
Data Curriculum	Log Source	12h30m
	Log Random + model ppl	17h10m
Objective Curriculum	Sequential All POS	11h40m
	Multitask All POS	15h30m
Vocabulary Curriculum	Linear POS	11h50m
	Log Token ID	12h10m
Combination	Log Data Split + Log Token ID	12h30m
	Log Random + model ppl + Log Token ID	17h10m

Table 11: Compute required to train our models. We report the model with the shortest and longest runtime for each experiment type. Each model is trained for 400,000 steps with 4 A100 GPUs.

Acquiring Linguistic Knowledge from Multimodal Input

Theodor Amariucai
ETH Zürich
tamariucai@ethz.ch

Alex Warstadt
ETH Zürich
awarstadt@ethz.ch

Abstract

In contrast to children, language models (LMs) exhibit considerably inferior data efficiency when acquiring language. In this submission to the BabyLM Challenge (Warstadt et al., 2023), we test the hypothesis that this data efficiency gap is partly caused by a lack of multimodal input and grounding in the learning environment of typical language models. Although previous work looking into this question found that multimodal training can even harm language-only performance, we speculate that these findings can be attributed to catastrophic forgetting of complex language due to fine-tuning on captions data. To test our hypothesis, we perform an ablation study on FLAVA (Singh et al., 2022), a multimodal vision-and-language model, independently varying the volume of text and vision input to quantify how much text data (if any) can be offset by vision at different data scales. We aim to limit catastrophic forgetting through a multitask pretraining regime that includes unimodal text-only tasks and data sampled from WiT, the relatively diverse Wikipedia-based dataset (Srinivasan et al., 2021). Our results are largely negative: Multimodal pretraining does not harm our models' language performance but does not consistently help either. That said, our conclusions are limited by our having been able to conduct only a small number of runs. While we must leave open the possibility that multimodal input explains some of the gap in data efficiency between LMs and humans, positive evidence for this hypothesis will require better architectures and techniques for multimodal training.

1 Introduction

Children can learn language from a relatively small amount of linguistic input: at most 100 million words (Gilkerson et al., 2017). By contrast, the quantity of training data a language model needs to achieve strong grammar and language performance is on the order of billions or tens of billions of words (Zhang et al., 2021). This data efficiency gap may be due, in part, to innate differences in learning mechanisms between models and humans, but environmental differences likely play a role as well (Warstadt and Bowman, 2022). This work tests the hypothesis that the lack of visual grounding in language models accounts for some of the gap in data efficiency.

The likelihood of finding evidence for this hypothesis rests largely on two factors: (1) its cognitive plausibility and (2) its technological viability. If vision does help children learn language, then there ought to be some way of incorporating vision into text-only language models that improves their learning ability. However, whether or not we can find this approach depends on the present technological capabilities of multimodal models.

To address the first point, one cognitively-motivated mechanism for how children integrate nonlinguistic sensory data in language learning is cross-situational learning (XSL) (Smith and Smith, 2012). This theoretical mechanism holds that the learner accumulates statistical evidence about word meanings by observing multiple instances of co-occurring word-object pairs across many different real-world situations (Smith et al., 2011; Kachergis et al., 2014; Zhang et al., 2019). Encouragingly, Nikolaus and Fourtassi (2021) find that, in a highly constrained visual-linguistic domain, computational multimodal models *do* benefit from cross-situational learning.

To address the second point, prior evidence that vision will improve language models given current technologies is, at best, mixed. Recent approaches have successfully trained Transformer-based multimodal language models using self-supervised objectives resembling those developed originally for the training of unimodal models (Tan and Bansal, 2019). Nevertheless, in comparison to the unimodal models, multimodal LMs often perform relatively poorly on language-only tasks (Iki and

Proceedings of the 27th Conference on Computational Natural Language Learning: Volume 2: The BabyLM Challenge, pages 128–141
December 6-7, 2023

Aizawa, 2021). We hypothesize that these shortcomings may be due to the common practice of training multimodal models by fine-tuning pretrained language models on captions data.

Our approach addresses these limitations in two ways that differ from most previous pretraining recipes. First, we use the FLAVA architecture and follow its multitask training procedure (Singh et al., 2022). Second, we train on the Wikipedia-based WiT dataset (Srinivasan et al., 2021), which pairs images with a mixture of strongly aligned (but formulaic) captions and weakly aligned (but syntactically complex) articles. Despite these efforts, our results show that the addition of image data and multimodal training objectives leads to no reliable improvement over text-only baselines on benchmarks for grammar (BLiMP; Warstadt et al., 2020a), understanding (GLUE; Wang et al., 2018), and generalization (MSGS; Warstadt et al., 2020b). We conclude that, to the extent that multimodality is partly responsible for the data-efficiency gap, present multimodal (and multitask) pretraining methods do not benefit from this richer learning signal.

To summarize, this work brings forward three main contributions:

1. We develop a robust codebase[1] for pretraining (from scratch) large multimodal LMs under varying text and vision input configurations.
2. We evaluate, in this controlled environment, the effects of the visual signal on the model's textual encoder (hence, its linguistic ability).
3. We investigate plausible mechanisms for how incorporating visual input into the pretraining procedure might affect linguistic behavior.

2 Background

Prior work on multimodal language model training can be roughly differentiated by whether the main objectives are cognitively-oriented or engineering-oriented. So far, neither of these directions has produced clear evidence supporting the hypothesis that multimodality aids language learning at the scale of human language acquisition. Many cognitively oriented contributions are limited by a small data scale or a restricted domain. By contrast, engineering-oriented contributions using state-of-the-art Transformer-based architectures achieve more developmentally plausible scale and diversity but emphasize multimodal performance over language learning.

2.1 Cognitively Oriented Approaches

Infants enter a diverse and abundant visual world where they develop mental models to comprehend and mimic the patterns they encounter. These mental models empower them to grasp and anticipate their surroundings and accomplish objectives by incrementally improving their communicative abilities (Roy and Pentland, 2002). Relatedly, the impact of vision on specific aspects of human language learning has been an important question in human development for decades.

Contemporary research has tried to answer this question through computational simulations of cognitive processes involved in language acquisition. Multimodal models trained on visual question answering or reference games can use cross-situational learning to learn grounded meanings of words (Mao et al., 2019; Wang et al., 2021; Nikolaus and Fourtassi, 2021; Portelance et al., 2023). Nonetheless, computational models show different learning biases than humans in many cases, at least in the absence of specific training or architectural interventions (Gauthier et al., 2018; Vong and Lake, 2022). Ultimately, however, all of these studies are limited in their cognitive plausibility and language learning by a reliance on supervised training on small, artificial datasets in which texts and images correspond to arrangements of a limited set of objects in a simple, usually static scene.

Other studies aim for more naturalistic training. Lazaridou et al. (2017) and Chrupała et al. (2015) are notable for pioneering self-supervised training objectives for multimodal models several years before the advent of Transformer architectures trained on masking objectives. Wang et al. (2023) train LMs on data from the SAYCam dataset (Sullivan et al., 2021), pairing (written) child-directed utterances with visual data from the child's point of view. While this data domain is nearly ideal from a developmental plausibility perspective, the available data is too small to model anything past the first month of development.

Finally, we note that most of the studies in this area focus primarily on word learning. However, the data efficiency gap applies more broadly to language learning. Recent studies evaluating contemporary Transformer-based models have largely re-

[1]https://github.com/amariucaitheodor/acquiring-linguistic-knowledge

ported negative results for the effect of multimodality on semantics (Shahmohammadi et al., 2022), commonsense reasoning (Yun et al., 2021), and learning biases (Kuribayashi, 2023). To the best of our knowledge, ours is the first work to perform targeted syntactic evaluation (Marvin and Linzen, 2018; Warstadt et al., 2020a; Hu et al., 2020) on multimodal models.

2.2 Engineering Oriented Approaches

The most effective recent approaches for training multimodal language models generalize the self-supervised objectives (and Transformer-based architectures) that have become dominant for unimodal language models such as BERT (Devlin et al., 2019) to the vision-and-language domain (Li et al., 2020, 2019; Zhou et al., 2020; Tan and Bansal, 2019; Chen et al., 2020; Yu et al., 2021; Lu et al., 2019; Bugliarello et al., 2021; Pramanick et al., 2022).

These studies, for the most part, share many aspects of a typical recipe: First, they initialize all or some of the model parameters with the pretrained weights of a model such as BERT. Second, they fine-tune (using one or more self-supervised objectives) on a dataset of image-caption pairs.[2] Finally, the model is evaluated on multimodal tasks such as visual question answering or image captioning.

While the ability to perform such grounded tasks is the key advantage of multimodal models over unimodal ones, it is critical for our research question to examine whether this advantage comes at the cost of language ability. Unfortunately, few of the works that train new multimodal models evaluate on language-only tasks. Some works perform this evaluation post hoc. Iki and Aizawa (2021) study five multimodal architectures, all initialized with BERT and fine-tuned using identical data and training objectives by Bugliarello et al. (2021). Evaluating on the GLUE benchmark (Wang et al., 2018), they find that, in nearly all cases, the original pretrained BERT outperforms the models with additional multimodal fine-tuning. Similar results are reported by Madasu and Lal (2023) and Yun et al. (2021).

From a human development perspective, it may seem unintuitive that additional supervision on images harms language performance. However, from a machine learning perspective, this finding is easy to explain as an example of domain mismatch (Yun et al., 2021), catastrophic forgetting (McCloskey and Cohen, 1989), under-parameterization (Amariucai, 2023), or other similar technical reasons.

BERT's original training data (Wikipedia and books) is diverse in terms of writing style and subject matter. By contrast, captions datasets commonly used to train multimodal LMs, such as MS COCO (Chen et al., 2015) or Visual Genome (Krishna et al., 2017), consist entirely of short formulaic physical descriptions of objects or scenes. Hence, the text domain that the models were trained on most recently bears little resemblance to the texts in the GLUE tasks, for example. Furthermore, the multimodal tasks incentivize using the models' limited parameters for both text *and* image processing, potentially sacrificing language ability.

Our experiments, which we describe in Section 3, are designed to address these issues through two complementary approaches: First, we prevent catastrophic forgetting by multitask-training on the language-only masked language modeling (MLM) objective jointly with the multimodal objectives. Second, we lessen the impact of domain mismatch by training on data that pairs images, not just with captions, but also with longer and more complex texts.

3 Methods

We conduct experiments to uncover differences in how language models' linguistic abilities change as the amount of visual input varies. We pretrain and evaluate multimodal LMs in eight conditions, derived by independently varying the volume of text data (10M or 100M words) and image data (none, 40K, 400K, or 4M images). We perform only one training run for each of the eight conditions due to computing constraints (see Limitations, Section 5). The text quantities are compatible with both human-scale linguistic exposure (Gilkerson et al., 2017) and the BabyLM strict-small and strict tracks (Warstadt et al., 2023).

3.1 Dataset

All the data for our experiments comes from WiT, a large, multimodal dataset entirely sourced from Wikipedia (Srinivasan et al., 2021). Our choice

[2] For example, in the masked multimodal modeling task (MMM; Tan and Bansal, 2019), regions of an aligned image-text pair are randomly masked before being input into the model and then predicted. As the information from the image presumably helps reconstruct the masked text (Frank et al., 2021), this objective encourages learning text representations that encode information from the visual modality (and vice-versa).

of WiT was motivated by its size and the diversity and complexity of its text data. English WiT includes 5.5M image–text pairs,[3] making it one of the largest public datasets of its kind. It contains extended passages from Wikipedia articles, offering a more representative sample of sentence types than typical multimodal datasets sourced from captions. Furthermore, WiT features multiple types of text aligned with a given image. From most strongly aligned to most weakly aligned, these include alt text, captions, article text from the same section as the image, and article text from the lead section. Together with the fact that Wikipedia covers many different concepts and real-world entities, we hypothesize that WiT provides an adequately rich environment for supporting cross-situational learning while maintaining strong grammar and language understanding performance.

We subsample from the English portion of WiT to reach the desired data volume for each modality. For training purposes, we use either one (when either modality is 0%) or three (when both modalities are non-zero) data loaders. For example, when training on 100M words and 40K images, we sample the first 10% of the pairs for the text unimodal data loader, the first 1% for the vision unimodal data loader, and the first $1\% = \min(10\%, 1\%)$ for the multimodal data loader (containing paired images and text). Hence, all images in this configuration will be paired with some text, but not all texts will be paired with an image. This logic also implies that some images and texts will be seen both in the multimodal and their corresponding unimodal data loaders.

3.2 Model

For our experiments, we use the FLAVA model architecture and training objectives (Singh et al., 2022). We choose to study FLAVA for two reasons: First, Singh et al. (2022) conduct a controlled comparison between a unimodally trained FLAVA text encoder and a fully multimodal FLAVA, and they report improved performance on language-only tasks from the multimodal model. As such, FLAVA is the only example of a large multimodal model for which prior (anecdotal) evidence supports our hypothesis that vision can help language learning. Second, FLAVA is trained in a multitask setting on a combination of unimodal text, unimodal vision, and multimodal objectives. This methodology addresses our concern (Section 2.2) that other common multimodal training recipes can lead to catastrophic forgetting of linguistic ability.

FLAVA's architecture combines three modality-specific encoders: Text and vision embeddings are fed into unimodal text and vision encoders, respectively, and the hidden states output by these encoders are concatenated before being fed into a multimodal encoder. For the unimodal objectives, task-specific heads can be placed after the corresponding unimodal encoder. All encoders are based on the ViT-B/16 encoder (Dosovitskiy et al., 2021).[4]

Following the original work, we pretrain models from scratch using multitask learning with the following five objectives: masked image modeling, masked language modeling, masked multimodal modeling for both text and vision, image-text matching, and cross-modal contrastive learning. More details on each objective, as well as the encoder architecture itself, can be found in the original paper (Singh et al., 2022).

3.3 Training Details

Hyperparameters We perform a hyperparameter search and empirically settle on the following values:

- Warmup steps: 10^4
- Batch size: 4096 effective $= 32 \times 2$ GPUs $\times$ 64 accumulation steps
- Learning rate (text encoder): 7.5×10^{-4}
- Learning rate (other encoders): 10^{-3}
- Precision: bf16 mixed
- Seed: 5501650
- Adam optimizer:
  - Epsilon: 10^{-8}
  - Weight decay: 0.1
  - Betas: [0.9, 0.999]

We use two distinct learning rates because a lower value is commonly recommended for text-only pretraining (Liu et al., 2019; Devlin et al., 2019), while a higher one was originally used for

[3]WiT is also multilingual, containing over 30M pairs in over 100 languages. During preprocessing, however, we only sample English text.

[4]*B/16* refers to a base-sized architecture with 86M total parameters using a patch resolution of 16x16. We opt for this version of the encoder based on the authors' observation that ViT-B/16 performs just as well as the larger alternatives when pretraining on smaller datasets of under 300M images (such as WiT).

multimodally pretraining FLAVA. Multiple strategies for correctly choosing modality-specific learning rates are treated extensively in Yao and Mihalcea (2022), where the *"Keep" Strategy* (ours) is among the most straightforward of them. While simple, it outperforms (in the authors' empirical study) the global learning rate strategy as it ensures that each unimodal subpart still has effective gradients when training the fusion model.

Software We use `Pytorch Lightning` (Falcon and The PyTorch Lightning team, 2019) as the main training framework and `Weights and Biases` (Biewald, 2020) to track relevant metrics in real time. We use the Huggingface `datasets` library (Lhoest et al., 2021) to interleave the modality-specific datasets, and the HuggingFace `transformers` library (Wolf et al., 2020) to access and train randomly-initialized FLAVA models.

Hardware We run each training job in Distributed Data-Parallel mode, across two NVIDIA Tesla A100 Ampere 40 GB graphics cards, on the same node, in ETH Zürich's Euler datacenter. For each of the two GPUs, there are 4 CPU workers loading data (this number was empirically found to be optimal), with each CPU worker having 10GB of RAM available. The average runtime for our jobs running on 100M words was six days, and for 10M words, it was three days. Thus, we count a total of (2 GPUs) * (8 jobs) * (108 hours / job) = 1728 GPU hours used to train the models reported in this study, not counting our hyperparameter search.

Dataloader Sampling Weights During multimodal pretraining, we alternate samples from three data loaders with independent weights, initialized (and normalized) proportional to their sizes. For example, for the condition with 100M words and 40K images (hence, all images and 10M words of text are paired), we would have the following initial sampling weights: 0.833 (text), 0.083 (vision), 0.083 (multimodal). For maximal text encoder performance, we perform a hyperparameter search and determine a simple rule-based approach to further improve the distribution of the sampling weights: If text is not the predominant modality, we change it to the uniform distribution; otherwise, we leave the initial weights unchanged.

Modality-Specific Early Stopping We develop custom logic to prevent the models from overfitting on any given modality. For example, when the

Words \ Images	None	40K	400K	4M
10M	4604	5346	4876	4876
100M	23818	12267	16344	16542

Table 1: Model checkpoints (training step #) chosen for evaluation based on the masked language modeling validation loss (Figure 4).

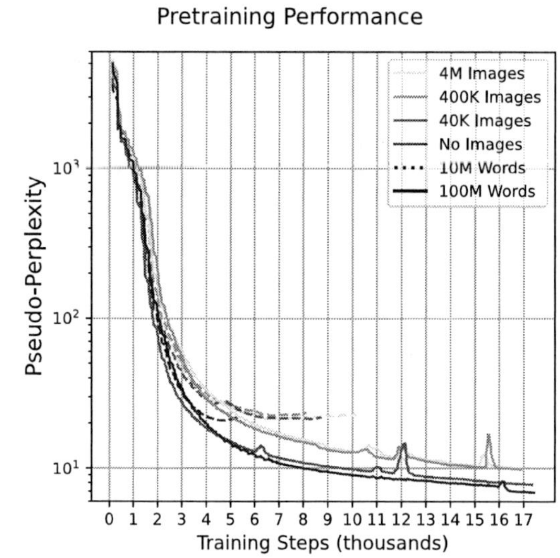

Figure 1: PPPL performance for the two data volumes of 10M and 100M words. The training steps on the x-axis are counted across all objectives.

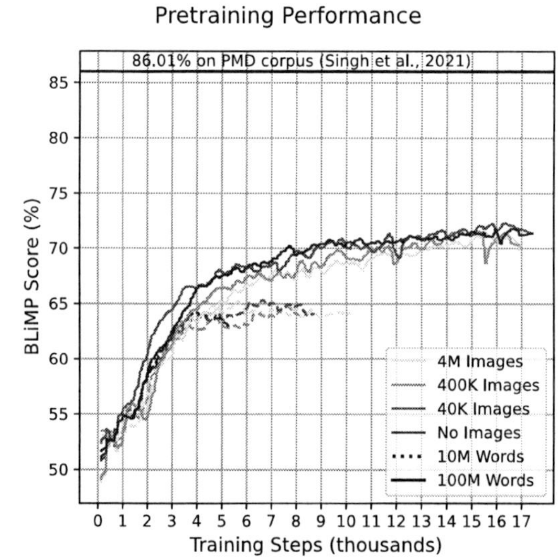

Figure 2: BLiMP performance for the two data volumes of 10M and 100M words. The training steps on the x-axis are counted across all objectives.

Tasks	10M Words				100M Words			
	None	40K	400K	40M	None	40K	400K	40M
(Super)GLUE (Acc., F1, MCC)	65.49	64.68	65.17	65.76	70.42	69.24	68.9	69.07
BLiMP (Acc.)	63.96	63.98	63.31	64.53	71.32	70.45	71.9	70.93
MSGS (MCC)	-12.88	-12.16	-8.84	-18.62	-8.66	-6.18	-7.41	-7.47

Table 2: Performance for each of the eight models on the BabyLM test suites (detailed version in Table 3).

sampling rate is 0.083 for the multimodal and text data loaders yet 0.833 for the vision data loader, the former two modalities will likely begin to overfit well before the latter. To avoid this, we detect increases in validation loss and (each time) halve the corresponding task's sampling weight. If the validation loss continues to steadily increase after three validation steps, we set the task weight to 0. To prevent catastrophic forgetting of the multimodal input, we allow the models to restart training on vision and multimodal data after a certain period of inactivity (here, 10 validation phases).

Model Selection For each of the eight input configurations, we select the best model checkpoints for evaluation based on the lowest recorded masked language modeling loss on the validation set (see Figure 4 for validation losses for every training objective and model). Table 1 shows the number of training steps for the selected checkpoints from each configuration. For additional information, we also regularly evaluate the models' pseudo-perplexity on a held-out test set (see Figure 1).

4 Results

We evaluate the selected checkpoints from all eight training configurations on the BabyLM evaluation pipeline (Warstadt et al., 2023), including evaluations on benchmarks for grammar (BLiMP; Warstadt et al., 2020a), language understanding (GLUE and SuperGLUE; Wang et al., 2018, 2019), and linguistic generalization (MSGS; Warstadt et al., 2020b). For BLiMP and pseudo-perplexity (Wang et al., 2018), we also report intermediate results for all of the training checkpoints.

Our overall results in Table 2 largely confirm earlier work finding that vision is, at best, not consistently helpful to language performance. With a data volume of 10M words, FLAVA does sometimes perform marginally better on grammar-oriented tasks in the presence of visual cues. For other evaluations and with a data volume of 100M words, we also find no consistent advantages in our experimental setting. Of those improvements we do observe, our tests deem it unlikely that they are due to cross-situational learning (see Section 4.4).

4.1 Pseudo-perplexity

For validation, Figure 1 shows the pseudo-perplexity (PPPL; Wang and Cho, 2019) per token on a held-out evaluation subset of WIT throughout training. Unsurprisingly, PPPL is lower (better) for the 100M word models compared to the 10M word models. Additionally, the metric appears to converge for the 10M word models, while it may still be decreasing for 100M word models.[5] The most unexpected finding is that PPPL is consistently worse as the amount of image data increases for a given amount of text data throughout training. This degradation may suggest that our multitask training procedure causes the models to sacrifice MLM performance in favor of other objectives as the proportion of visual and multimodal samples increases.

4.2 Grammaticality

We evaluate linguistic knowledge using BLiMP (Warstadt et al., 2020a), which tests the ability of models to distinguish grammatical sequences from minimally different ungrammatical ones in a zero-shot setting.

Table 2 shows the overall BLiMP performance from each condition. We notice that text quantity makes a big difference in performance. Changes in vision, on the other hand, are associated with small amounts of variation that are sometimes positive or negative. Hence, due to the lack of a consistent pattern and the small number of runs, we cannot confidently conclude that vision causes an increase or decrease in performance.

Figure 2 shows the BLiMP results for each val-

[5] Our scheduler triggered early stopping based on validation loss despite the apparent possibility that longer training might have been beneficial. More generally, there are many potential improvements to task scheduling and early stopping for multitask learning that we leave to future work.

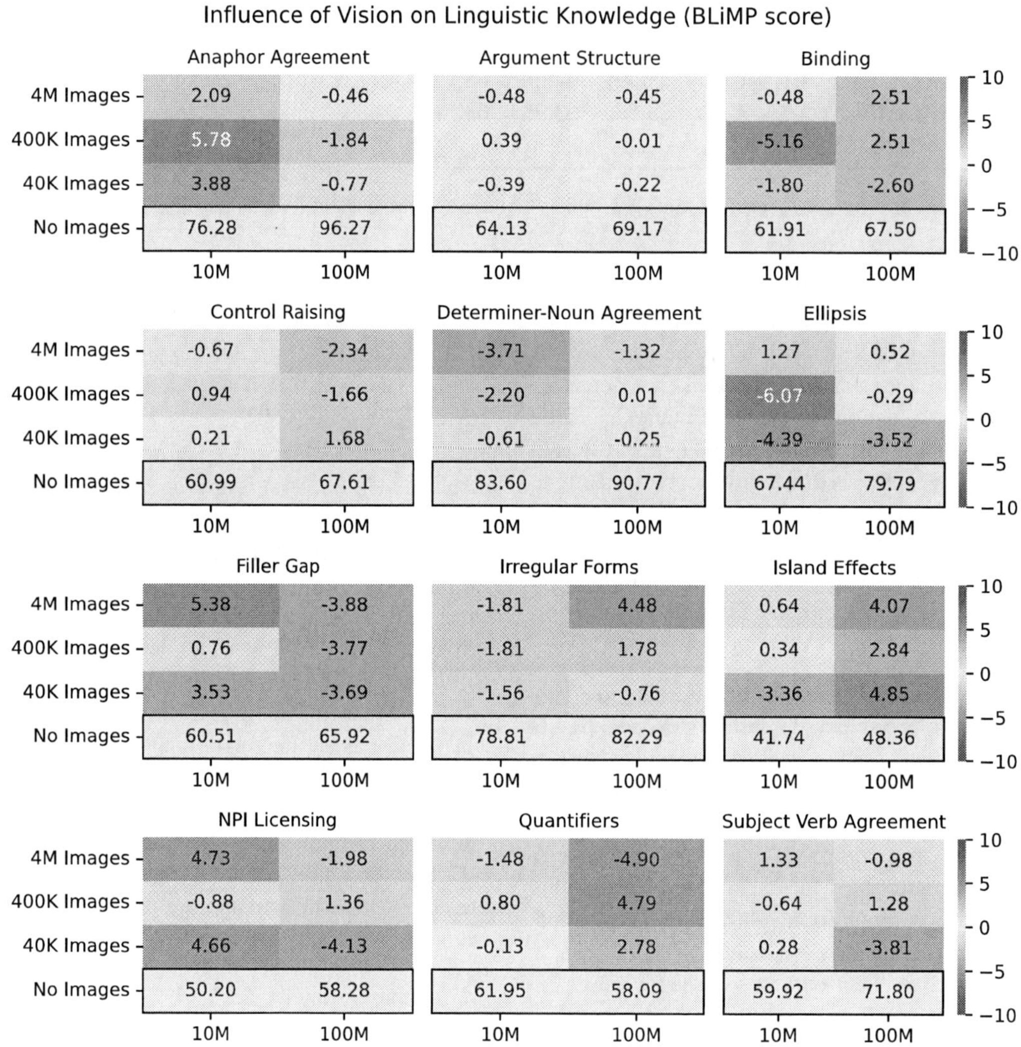

Figure 3: Zero-shot accuracies, in percentages, obtained on the BLiMP task for each grammatical category (x12) and FLAVA run configuration of input text volume (10M and 100M words) and input vision volume (0, 40K, 400K and 4M images). The model checkpoints used to generate these results were selected as described in Table 1.

idation step throughout training. For most of the duration of training, particularly for the 100M word models, models with less image data perform better. This behavior mostly matches the pattern we observe for pseudo-perplexity, except that the differences seemingly disappear by the end of training. This result confirms earlier findings that (pseudo-)perplexity is not entirely predictive of grammatical knowledge (Hu et al., 2020).

Individual BLiMP categories are more closely compared in Figure 3. Previous work shows that phenomena related to agreement have the steepest learning curves at the 10M word scale (Zhang et al., 2021). Therefore, if the hypothesis that vision accelerates LM learning is correct, we might expect to see the greatest signs of improvement for 10M word models on this subset of test suites. Figure 3, however, shows conflicting and inconclusive results, with improvements in *anaphor agreement* but a slight degradation for *determiner-noun agreement*, and little change for *subject-verb agreement*.

We observe that multimodal pretraining may have a regularizing effect at smaller data scales: BLiMP performance improves at times although the pseudo-perplexity (i.e., test loss) is consistently higher (by 1-3 units) for the vision-infused models. Moreover, the vision-infused models run for almost twice as long before starting to overfit (8k v.s. 4k steps), gaining accuracy in areas such as *anaphor agreement*, *filler gap dependencies*, and *NPI licensing*, although not so on test suites such as *argument structure* and *subject-verb agreement*.

4.3 Fine-Tuning Evaluations

In addition to the above, we also use GLUE/SuperGLUE (Wang et al., 2018, 2019) and MSGS (Warstadt et al., 2020b) to fine-tune and evaluate all eight models on a selection of downstream tasks that focus on language understanding and linguistic generalization.

As expected, the results in Table 2 show that overall GLUE performance increases (by around 5%) at higher text data scales. Within each of the two text volume groups, however, there is no reliable improvement due to the addition of vision, though vision-infused models appear to be slightly better (relatively) at lower data scales, of up to 10M words. Generally, the models perform similarly on the selected downstream tasks (performance after fine-tuning), in line with BLiMP results.

Scores on MSGS are negative for all models, for all ambiguous subtasks (i.e., those subtasks not in the control condition), as shown in Table 3. This indicates that all of our models are consistently biased towards generalizing based on shallow surface cues rather than linguistic features.

4.4 Cross-Situational Learning

To assess the *symbolic grounding* of our models, for every input configuration checkpoint in Table 1, we evaluate the multimodal text retrieval zero-shot accuracy on ImageNet-1k (Russakovsky et al., 2015). The goal is to select, for every given *query* image, the best-fitting text caption from a pool of 1000 options. To this end, we compute cosine similarities as matching scores between the queried image's representation and the representations of 1000 template-averaged[6] potential captions. Lastly, we retrieve the text caption with the highest matching score for each image query. We follow Radford et al. (2021) to calculate the zero-shot accuracy.

As a baseline, we assess FLAVA pretrained on the PMD corpus and obtain *top1* and *top5* accuracies of 32% and 60%, respectively. The models we pretrain, however, obtain average *top1* and *top5* accuracies of 0.1% and 0.5%, respectively. Some of the possible factors responsible for this random guess performance could be: 1) the multitask scheduler described in Appendix 3.3 was misconfigured (this aligns with findings in Amariucai (2023)), 2) the smaller magnitude of the training data (WiT is a subset of PMD), 3) the weak alignment between some of the text (full paragraphs) and the corresponding images (Imagenet-1k only evaluates caption alignments), or 4) the fact that we do not pretrain the vision encoder unimodally on ImageNet-1k, as in Singh et al. (2022).

5 Conclusion

We perform an ablation study on a state-of-the-art, multimodal language model under varying text and vision configurations. Our training recipe avoids the problem of catastrophic forgetting of complex language, which previous approaches fell prey to, by performing multitask training on both multimodal and unimodal tasks in a more diverse domain. Nonetheless, our results largely confirm earlier work finding that vision is (at best) not consistently helpful to language performance. During pretraining at the small 10M word scale, the FLAVA architecture (Singh et al., 2022) does sometimes appear to perform marginally better on grammar-oriented tasks in the presence of visual cues. However, for other evaluations and with a data volume of 100M words, we find no consistent advantages in our experimental setting.

At the small data scales that we pretrain our models in this study (up to 100M words and the corresponding images), our tests in Section 4.4 deem it unlikely that the models are benefiting from cross-situational learning. Alternatively, the extra parameters in the multimodal encoder could simply be increasing FLAVA's modeling capacity, a hypothesis that we leave for future work. Regardless, multimodal pretraining seems to exhibit a regularizing effect: although pseudo-perplexity is consistently worse for the vision-infused models, grammatical performance fluctuates and is often at least as good.

We conclude that the lack of visual input alone does little to explain the large data efficiency gap between LMs and humans observed in grammar learning, though we leave open the possibility that this conclusion will change with better architectures and techniques for integrating vision and language at training time.

[6]Since the captions for even a specific entity can vary, e.g., *a doodle of a car*, *a photo of a large car*, etc. we compute an average over ~80 such templates for each entity.

Limitations

The robustness of the observations made in this report is limited by the fact that each configuration (text/vision input volume) was only run once. Future work should provide at least 5 re-runs per configuration (with different seeds), as there can be considerable variance even in different models with the same configuration (McCoy et al., 2020). Due to the computational intensity of performing re-runs, this was not possible in time for this submission.

Significant GPU resources are required to effectively train large language models, partly because of the large batch sizes and the scale of the datasets. In this work, we use $\approx$ 1728 GPU hours on very recent hardware (further details in Section 3.3).

Finally, there is an architectural difference between the unimodal and multimodal models in our experiments. The unimodal models are trained entirely without the visual or multimodal encoders. Although these parameters are not used by the multimodal model during evaluation on language-only tasks, they are used during training, and so they may have an indirect effect on what the language encoder learns. To test whether the potential performance improvements in grammaticality and language understanding can indeed be attributed to the visual cues or rather simply to the increased number of parameters in the multimodal encoder, future work should conduct additional baseline experiments, e.g., where the images are replaced with random noise pixels.

References

Theodor Amariucai. 2023. Acquiring linguistic knowledge from multimodal input. Master thesis, ETH Zürich, Zürich.

Lukas Biewald. 2020. Experiment tracking with weights and biases. Software available from wandb.com.

Emanuele Bugliarello, Ryan Cotterell, Naoaki Okazaki, and Desmond Elliott. 2021. Multimodal pretraining unmasked: A meta-analysis and a unified framework of vision-and-language BERTs. *Transactions of the Association for Computational Linguistics*, 9:978–994.

Xinlei Chen, Hao Fang, Tsung-Yi Lin, Ramakrishna Vedantam, Saurabh Gupta, Piotr Dollar, and C. Lawrence Zitnick. 2015. Microsoft COCO Captions: Data Collection and Evaluation Server. In *European conference on computer vision*, pages 740–755. Springer. ArXiv: 1504.00325.

Yen-Chun Chen, Linjie Li, Licheng Yu, Ahmed El Kholy, Faisal Ahmed, Zhe Gan, Yu Cheng, and Jingjing Liu. 2020. UNITER: UNiversal Image-TExt Representation Learning. In *Computer Vision – ECCV 2020: 16th European Conference, Glasgow, UK, August 23–28, 2020, Proceedings, Part XXX*, page 104–120, Berlin, Heidelberg. Springer-Verlag.

Grzegorz Chrupała, Àkos Kádár, and Afra Alishahi. 2015. Learning language through pictures. In *Proceedings of the 53rd Annual Meeting of the Association for Computational Linguistics and the 7th International Joint Conference on Natural Language Processing (Volume 2: Short Papers)*, pages 112–118, Beijing, China. Association for Computational Linguistics.

Jacob Devlin, Ming-Wei Chang, Kenton Lee, and Kristina Toutanova. 2019. BERT: Pre-training of deep bidirectional transformers for language understanding. In *Proceedings of the 2019 Conference of the North American Chapter of the Association for Computational Linguistics: Human Language Technologies, Volume 1 (Long and Short Papers)*, pages 4171–4186, Minneapolis, Minnesota. Association for Computational Linguistics.

Alexey Dosovitskiy, Lucas Beyer, Alexander Kolesnikov, Dirk Weissenborn, Xiaohua Zhai, Thomas Unterthiner, Mostafa Dehghani, Matthias Minderer, Georg Heigold, Sylvain Gelly, Jakob Uszkoreit, and Neil Houlsby. 2021. An image is worth 16x16 words: Transformers for image recognition at scale. In *International Conference on Learning Representations*.

William Falcon and The PyTorch Lightning team. 2019. PyTorch Lightning.

Stella Frank, Emanuele Bugliarello, and Desmond Elliott. 2021. Vision-and-language or vision-for-language? on cross-modal influence in multimodal transformers. In *Proceedings of the 2021 Conference on Empirical Methods in Natural Language Processing*, pages 9847–9857, Online and Punta Cana, Dominican Republic. Association for Computational Linguistics.

Jon Gauthier, Roger Levy, and Joshua B. Tenenbaum. 2018. Word learning and the acquisition of syntactic–semantic overhypotheses. In *Proceedings of the 40th annual meeting of the cognitive science society*, Madison, Wisconsin.

Jill Gilkerson, Jeffrey A. Richards, Steven F. Warren, Judith K. Montgomery, Charles R. Greenwood, D. Kimbrough Oller, John H. L. Hansen, and Terrance D. Paul. 2017. Mapping the Early Language Environment Using All-Day Recordings and Automated Analysis. *American Journal of Speech-Language Pathology*, 26(2):248–265.

Jennifer Hu, Jon Gauthier, Peng Qian, Ethan Wilcox, and Roger Levy. 2020. A Systematic Assessment of

Syntactic Generalization in Neural Language Models. In *Proceedings of the 58th Annual Meeting of the Association for Computational Linguistics*, pages 1725–1744, Online. Association for Computational Linguistics.

Taichi Iki and Akiko Aizawa. 2021. Effect of Visual Extensions on Natural Language Understanding in Vision-and-Language Models. In *Proceedings of the 2021 Conference on Empirical Methods in Natural Language Processing*, pages 2189–2196, Online and Punta Cana, Dominican Republic. Association for Computational Linguistics.

George Kachergis, Chen Yu, and Richard M. Shiffrin. 2014. Cross-situational word learning is both implicit and strategic. *Frontiers in Psychology*, 5.

Ranjay Krishna, Yuke Zhu, Oliver Groth, Justin Johnson, Kenji Hata, Joshua Kravitz, Stephanie Chen, Yannis Kalantidis, Li-Jia Li, David A. Shamma, Michael S. Bernstein, and Li Fei-Fei. 2017. Visual Genome: Connecting Language and Vision Using Crowdsourced Dense Image Annotations. *International Journal of Computer Vision*, 123(1):32–73.

Tatsuki Kuribayashi. 2023. Does Vision Accelerate Hierarchical Generalization of Neural Language Learners? ArXiv:2302.00667 [cs].

Angeliki Lazaridou, Marco Marelli, and Marco Baroni. 2017. Multimodal Word Meaning Induction From Minimal Exposure to Natural Text. *Cognitive Science*, 41(S4):677–705.

Quentin Lhoest, Albert Villanova del Moral, Patrick von Platen, Thomas Wolf, Mario Šaško, Yacine Jernite, Abhishek Thakur, Lewis Tunstall, Suraj Patil, Mariama Drame, Julien Chaumond, Julien Plu, Joe Davison, Simon Brandeis, Victor Sanh, Teven Le Scao, Kevin Canwen Xu, Nicolas Patry, Steven Liu, Angelina McMillan-Major, Philipp Schmid, Sylvain Gugger, Nathan Raw, Sylvain Lesage, Anton Lozhkov, Matthew Carrigan, Théo Matussière, Leandro von Werra, Lysandre Debut, Stas Bekman, and Clément Delangue. 2021. Datasets: A Community Library for Natural Language Processing. In *Proceedings of the 2021 Conference on Empirical Methods in Natural Language Processing: System Demonstrations*, pages 175–184. Association for Computational Linguistics.

Gen Li, Nan Duan, Yuejian Fang, Ming Gong, and Daxin Jiang. 2020. Unicoder-VL: A universal encoder for vision and language by cross-modal pretraining. *Proceedings of the AAAI Conference on Artificial Intelligence*, 34:11336–11344.

Liunian Harold Li, Mark Yatskar, Da Yin, Cho-Jui Hsieh, and Kai-Wei Chang. 2019. VisualBERT: A simple and performant baseline for vision and language.

Yinhan Liu, Myle Ott, Naman Goyal, Jingfei Du, Mandar Joshi, Danqi Chen, Omer Levy, Mike Lewis, Luke Zettlemoyer, and Veselin Stoyanov. 2019. RoBERTa: A Robustly Optimized BERT Pretraining Approach.

Jiasen Lu, Dhruv Batra, Devi Parikh, and Stefan Lee. 2019. ViLBERT: Pretraining task-agnostic visiolinguistic representations for vision-and-language tasks. In *Advances in Neural Information Processing Systems*, volume 32. Curran Associates, Inc.

Avinash Madasu and Vasudev Lal. 2023. Is multimodal vision supervision beneficial to language?

Jiayuan Mao, Chuang Gan, Pushmeet Kohli, Joshua Tenenbaum, and Jiajun Wu. 2019. The Neuro-Symbolic Concept Learner: Interpreting Scenes, Words, and Sentences from Natural Supervision. In *Proceedings of ICLR*.

Rebecca Marvin and Tal Linzen. 2018. Targeted Syntactic Evaluation of Language Models. In *Proceedings of the 2018 Conference on Empirical Methods in Natural Language Processing*, pages 1192–1202.

Michael McCloskey and Neal J. Cohen. 1989. Catastrophic Interference in Connectionist Networks: The Sequential Learning Problem. In *Psychology of Learning and Motivation*, volume 24, pages 109–165. Elsevier.

R. Thomas McCoy, Junghyun Min, and Tal Linzen. 2020. BERTs of a feather do not generalize together: Large variability in generalization across models with similar test set performance. In *Proceedings of the Third BlackboxNLP Workshop on Analyzing and Interpreting Neural Networks for NLP*, pages 217–227, Online. Association for Computational Linguistics.

Mitja Nikolaus and Abdellah Fourtassi. 2021. Evaluating the acquisition of semantic knowledge from cross-situational learning in artificial neural networks. In *Proceedings of the Workshop on Cognitive Modeling and Computational Linguistics*, pages 200–210, Online. Association for Computational Linguistics.

Eva Portelance, Michael C. Frank, and Dan Jurafsky. 2023. Learning the meanings of function words from grounded language using a visual question answering model. ArXiv:2308.08628 [cs].

Shraman Pramanick, Li Jing, Sayan Nag, Jiachen Zhu, Hardik Shah, Yann LeCun, and Ramalingam Chellappa. 2022. VoLTA: Vision-language transformer with weakly-supervised local-feature alignment. *ArXiv*, abs/2210.04135.

Alec Radford, Jong Wook Kim, Chris Hallacy, Aditya Ramesh, Gabriel Goh, Sandhini Agarwal, Girish Sastry, Amanda Askell, Pamela Mishkin, Jack Clark, Gretchen Krueger, and Ilya Sutskever. 2021. Learning transferable visual models from natural language supervision. In *Proceedings of the 38th International Conference on Machine Learning*, volume 139 of *Proceedings of Machine Learning Research*, pages 8748–8763. PMLR.

Deb K Roy and Alex P Pentland. 2002. Learning words from sights and sounds: a computational model. *Cognitive Science*, 26(1):113–146.

Olga Russakovsky, Jia Deng, Hao Su, Jonathan Krause, Sanjeev Satheesh, Sean Ma, Zhiheng Huang, Andrej Karpathy, Aditya Khosla, Michael Bernstein, Alexander C. Berg, and Li Fei-Fei. 2015. ImageNet Large Scale Visual Recognition Challenge. *International Journal of Computer Vision (IJCV)*, 115(3):211–252.

Hassan Shahmohammadi, Maria Heitmeier, Elnaz Shafaei-Bajestan, Hendrik P. A. Lensch, and Harald Baayen. 2022. Language with vision: a study on grounded word and sentence embeddings.

A. Singh, R. Hu, V. Goswami, G. Couairon, W. Galuba, M. Rohrbach, and D. Kiela. 2022. FLAVA: A foundational language and vision alignment model. In *2022 IEEE/CVF Conference on Computer Vision and Pattern Recognition (CVPR)*, pages 15617–15629, Los Alamitos, CA, USA. IEEE Computer Society.

Andrew D. M. Smith and Kenny Smith. 2012. *Cross-Situational Learning*, pages 864–866. Springer US, Boston, MA.

Kenny Smith, Andrew D. M. Smith, and Richard A. Blythe. 2011. Cross-Situational Learning: An Experimental Study of Word-Learning Mechanisms. *Cognitive Science*, 35(3):480–498.

Krishna Srinivasan, Karthik Raman, Jiecao Chen, Michael Bendersky, and Marc Najork. 2021. WIT: Wikipedia-based image text dataset for multimodal multilingual machine learning. In *Proceedings of the 44th International ACM SIGIR Conference on Research and Development in Information Retrieval*, SIGIR '21, page 2443–2449, New York, NY, USA. Association for Computing Machinery.

Jessica Sullivan, Michelle Mei, Andrew Perfors, Erica Wojcik, and Michael C. Frank. 2021. SAYCam: A Large, Longitudinal Audiovisual Dataset Recorded From the Infant's Perspective. *Open Mind*, 5:20–29.

Hao Tan and Mohit Bansal. 2019. LXMERT: Learning cross-modality encoder representations from transformers. In *Proceedings of the 2019 Conference on Empirical Methods in Natural Language Processing and the 9th International Joint Conference on Natural Language Processing (EMNLP-IJCNLP)*, pages 5100–5111, Hong Kong, China. Association for Computational Linguistics.

Wai Keen Vong and Brenden M. Lake. 2022. Cross-Situational Word Learning With Multimodal Neural Networks. *Cognitive Science*, 46(4):e13122.

Alex Wang and Kyunghyun Cho. 2019. BERT has a Mouth, and It Must Speak: BERT as a Markov Random Field Language Model. In *Proceedings of the Workshop on Methods for Optimizing and Evaluating Neural Language Generation*, pages 30–36, Minneapolis, Minnesota. Association for Computational Linguistics.

Alex Wang, Yada Pruksachatkun, Nikita Nangia, Amanpreet Singh, Julian Michael, Felix Hill, Omer Levy, and Samuel R. Bowman. 2019. SuperGLUE: A stickier benchmark for general-purpose language understanding systems. In *33rd Conference on Neural Information Processing Systems*. Journal Abbreviation: arXiv preprint arXiv:1905.00537.

Alex Wang, Amanpreet Singh, Julian Michael, Felix Hill, Omer Levy, and Samuel Bowman. 2018. GLUE: A multi-task benchmark and analysis platform for natural language understanding. In *Proceedings of the 2018 EMNLP Workshop BlackboxNLP: Analyzing and Interpreting Neural Networks for NLP*, pages 353–355, Brussels, Belgium. Association for Computational Linguistics.

Ruocheng Wang, Jiayuan Mao, Samuel Gershman, and Jiajun Wu. 2021. Language-Mediated, Object-Centric Representation Learning. In *Findings of the Association for Computational Linguistics: ACL-IJCNLP 2021*, pages 2033–2046, Online. Association for Computational Linguistics.

Wentao Wang, Wai Keen Vong, Najoung Kim, and Brenden M. Lake. 2023. Finding Structure in One Child's Linguistic Experience. *Cognitive Science*, 47(6):e13305.

Alex Warstadt and Samuel R Bowman. 2022. What artificial neural networks can tell us about human language acquisition. In Shalom Lappin and Jean-Philippe Bernardy, editors, *Algebraic Structures in Natural Language*, pages 17–60. CRC Press. Publisher: CRC Press.

Alex Warstadt, Aaron Mueller, Leshem Choshen, Ethan Gotlieb Wilcox, Chengxu Zhuang, Juan Ciro, Rafael Mosquera, Adina Williams, Bhargavi Paranjabe, Tal Linzen, and Ryan Cotterell. 2023. Findings of the 2023 BabyLM Challenge: Sample-efficient pretraining on developmentally plausible corpora. In *Proceedings of the 2023 BabyLM Challenge*. Association for Computational Linguistics (ACL).

Alex Warstadt, Alicia Parrish, Haokun Liu, Anhad Mohananey, Wei Peng, Sheng-Fu Wang, and Samuel R. Bowman. 2020a. BLiMP: The Benchmark of Linguistic Minimal Pairs for English. *Transactions of the Association for Computational Linguistics*, 8:377–392. _eprint: https://doi.org/10.1162/tacl_a_00321.

Alex Warstadt, Yian Zhang, Xiaocheng Li, Haokun Liu, and Samuel R. Bowman. 2020b. Learning which features matter: RoBERTa acquires a preference for linguistic generalizations (eventually). In *Proceedings of the 2020 conference on empirical methods in natural language processing (EMNLP)*, pages 217–235, Online. Association for Computational Linguistics.

Thomas Wolf, Lysandre Debut, Victor Sanh, Julien Chaumond, Clement Delangue, Anthony Moi, Pierric Cistac, Tim Rault, Remi Louf, Morgan Funtowicz, Joe Davison, Sam Shleifer, Patrick von Platen, Clara Ma, Yacine Jernite, Julien Plu, Canwen Xu, Teven

Le Scao, Sylvain Gugger, Mariama Drame, Quentin Lhoest, and Alexander Rush. 2020. Transformers: State-of-the-Art Natural Language Processing. In *Proceedings of the 2020 Conference on Empirical Methods in Natural Language Processing: System Demonstrations*, pages 38–45, Online. Association for Computational Linguistics.

Yiqun Yao and Rada Mihalcea. 2022. Modality-specific learning rates for effective multimodal additive late-fusion. In *Findings of the Association for Computational Linguistics: ACL 2022*, pages 1824–1834, Dublin, Ireland. Association for Computational Linguistics.

Fei Yu, Jiji Tang, Weichong Yin, Yu Sun, Hao Tian, Hua Wu, and Haifeng Wang. 2021. ERNIE-ViL: Knowledge Enhanced Vision-Language Representations Through Scene Graph. *Proceedings of the AAAI Conference on Artificial Intelligence*, 35(4):3208–3216.

Tian Yun, Chen Sun, and Ellie Pavlick. 2021. Does Vision-and-Language Pretraining Improve Lexical Grounding? In *Findings of the Association for Computational Linguistics: EMNLP 2021*, pages 4357–4366, Punta Cana, Dominican Republic. Association for Computational Linguistics.

Yayun Zhang, Chi hsin Chen, and Chen Yu. 2019. Chapter Two - Mechanisms of Cross-situational Learning: Behavioral and Computational Evidence. volume 56 of *Advances in Child Development and Behavior*, pages 37–63. JAI.

Yian Zhang, Alex Warstadt, Xiaocheng Li, and Samuel R. Bowman. 2021. When do you need billions of words of pretraining data? In *Proceedings of the 59th Annual Meeting of the Association for Computational Linguistics and the 11th International Joint Conference on Natural Language Processing (Volume 1: Long Papers)*, pages 1112–1125, Online. Association for Computational Linguistics.

Luowei Zhou, Hamid Palangi, Lei Zhang, Houdong Hu, Jason Corso, and Jianfeng Gao. 2020. Unified Vision-Language Pre-Training for Image Captioning and VQA. *Proceedings of the AAAI Conference on Artificial Intelligence*, 34(07):13041–13049.

A Pretraining Validation Losses

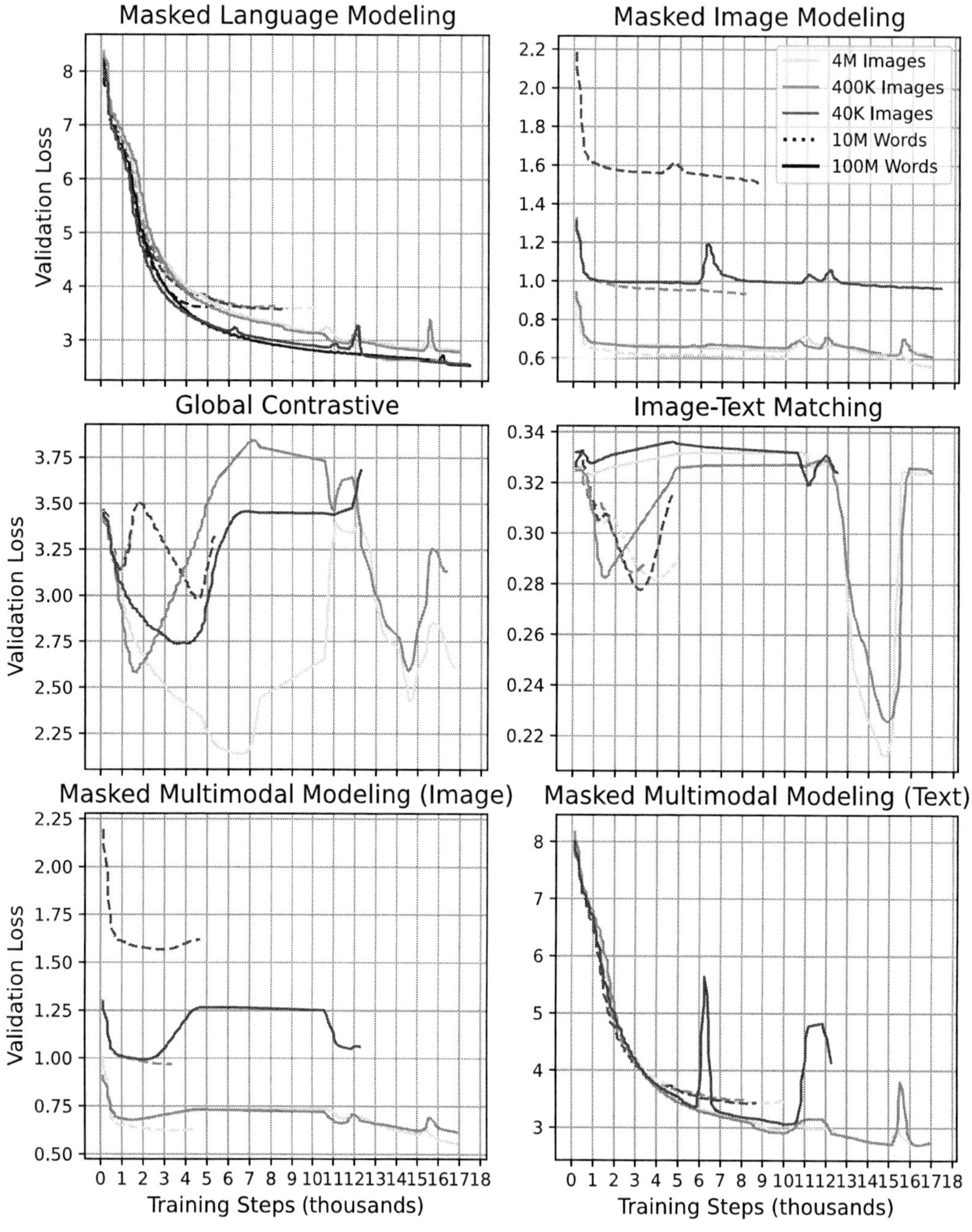

Figure 4: Validation losses for every training objective on a held-out set. While the MLM – and to a certain extent, also the MMM (Text) – losses are closely proportional to the pseudo-perplexity metric in Figure 1 (including some occasional spikes associated with checkpoint loading), the other losses are less stable. We point out some issues with the scheduler mechanism in Sections 4.1 and 4.4.

B Fine-tuning Performance

Task	Subtask	10M Words None	10M Words 40K	10M Words 400K	10M Words 40M	100M Words None	100M Words 40K	100M Words 400K	100M Words 40M
(Super)GLUE	BoolQ (accuracy)	64.32	65.70	65.98	66.8	69.43	67.08	65.70	66.25
	CoLA (MCC)	4.21	-4.16	0.00	0.00	28.43	21.56	20.00	20.93
	MNLI (accuracy)	73.27	72.46	70.07	71.98	74.63	71.85	74.57	74.11
	MNLI-mm (accuracy)	72.5	73.71	73.98	73.74	78.06	77.83	76.78	75.84
	MRPC (F1)	81.61	83.10	81.61	82.00	82.99	85.51	84.78	84.98
	MultiRC (accuracy)	59.58	60.35	61.45	62.32	67.47	62.76	64.62	67.25
	QNLI (accuracy)	80.88	79.40	80.31	79.97	83.90	82.76	82.55	81.98
	QQP (F1)	81.76	82.28	82.49	82.57	82.99	84.30	82.91	82.43
	RTE (accuracy)	57.58	53.54	53.54	55.56	53.54	57.58	58.59	56.57
	SST-2 (accuracy)	83.27	83.66	84.84	87.01	91.73	88.98	87.20	87.99
	WSC (accuracy)	61.45	61.45	62.65	61.45	61.45	61.45	60.24	61.45
BLiMP (Acc.)	Anaphor Agreement	76.84	79.55	76.99	77.04	94.89	95.35	91.10	96.27
	Argument Structure	64.14	62.38	62.55	62.45	69.58	69.77	68.15	68.38
	Binding	62.07	63.79	64.00	60.98	68.91	66.62	65.67	67.99
	Control/Raising	61.4	62.06	64.54	63.10	67.96	69.64	67.63	67.87
	Determiner Noun Agreement	82.91	80.42	82.11	83.00	90.27	91.94	88.45	89.49
	Ellipsis	68.48	65.76	61.61	66.22	81.12	78.12	80.60	77.37
	Filler Gap Dependencies	59.52	59.73	57.91	60.85	67.24	65.41	64.19	61.92
	Irregular Forms	83.51	75.98	78.73	74.45	84.17	84.12	83.66	84.89
	Island Effects	40.43	44.13	40.28	48.02	51.83	53.10	48.47	48.65
	NPI Licensing	52.49	54.43	54.66	49.53	61.24	64.79	60.04	54.68
	Quantifiers	58.55	57.86	64.76	57.73	60.10	58.40	57.16	58.50
	Subject Verb Agreement	60.29	61.72	61.81	61.37	75.34	72.65	70.19	69.18
MSGS (MCC)	Control Raising (control)	21.90	27.36	31.42	22.24	46.21	45.25	46.85	55.00
	Control Raising–Lexical Content	-46.54	-18.71	-13.17	-72.82	-61.04	-66.26	-63.65	-88.49
	Contro Raising–Relative Position	-98.69	-97.82	-98.33	-100.00	-99.90	-89.06	-97.74	-99.34
	Lexical Content (control)	100.00	100.00	100.00	100.00	100.00	100.00	100.00	100.00
	Main Verb (control)	86.84	96.84	93.24	86.92	99.85	99.40	96.54	98.08
	Main Verb–Lexical Content	-100.00	-100.00	-100.00	-100.00	-100.00	-100.00	-100.00	-100.00
	Main Verb–Relative Position	-86.73	-88.78	-91.56	-95.32	-98.41	-86.56	-95.64	-93.18
	Relative Position (control)	96.78	81.47	90.28	89.14	99.98	99.47	100.00	99.98
	Syntactic Category (control)	57.04	13.15	38.77	28.12	72.40	73.32	77.37	89.29
	Syntactic Category–Lexical Content	-100.00	-81.37	-77.31	-95.49	-81.08	-74.66	-79.96	-78.53
	Syntactic Category–Relative Position	-72.34	-65.91	-70.53	-67.61	-73.29	-68.86	-65.26	-64.96

Table 3: Detailed fine-tuning performance for each of the eight models. F1 denotes macro-F1, MCC denotes Matthew's correlation coefficient, and random chance accuracy on all BLiMP tasks (i.e., the second group) is 50.

Large GPT-like Models are Bad Babies: A Closer Look at the Relationship between Linguistic Competence and Psycholinguistic Measures

Julius Steuer **Marius Mosbach** **Dietrich Klakow**
Department of Language Science and Technology
Saarland University
{jsteuer,mmosbach,dietrich.klakow}@lsv.uni-saarland.de

Abstract

Research on the cognitive plausibility of language models (LMs) has so far mostly concentrated on modelling psycholinguistic response variables such as reading times, gaze durations and N400/P600 EEG signals, while mostly leaving out the dimension of what Mahowald et al. (2023) described as formal and functional linguistic competence, and developmental plausibility. We address this gap by training a series of GPT-like language models of different sizes on the strict version of the BabyLM pretraining corpus, evaluating on the challenge tasks (BLiMP, GLUE, MSGS) and an additional reading time prediction task. We find a positive correlation between LM size and performance on all three challenge tasks, with different preferences for model width and depth in each of the tasks. In contrast, a negative correlation was found between LM size and reading time fit of linear mixed-effects models using LM surprisal as a predictor, with the second-smallest LM achieving the largest log-likelihood reduction over a baseline model without surprisal. This suggests that modelling processing effort *and* linguistic competence may require an approach different from training GPT-like LMs on a developmentally plausible corpus.

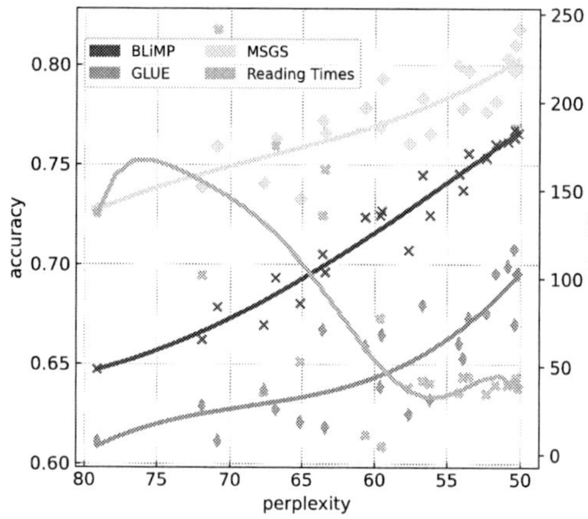

Figure 1: Our results show that LM performance on the BabyLM challenge tasks is negatively correlated with perplexity on the development set of the BabyLM corpus (lower perplexity leads to higher performance). In contrast, a *positive* correlation (Spearman's $\rho = 0.4784$, $p < 0.05$) was found between LM perplexity and the fit of LM surprisal to self-paced reading times from the Natural Stories corpus (Futrell et al., 2021) in terms of the difference in log-likelihood between a basline linear mixed-effects model and a model using LM surprisal as a predictor. Lines were fitted with 3 (challenge tasks) or 6 (reading times) degrees of freedom to the LMs' average performance on the task. See Section 6 for detailed results.

1 Introduction

In recent years several approaches have been taken to test LMs for cognitive plausibility. This is usually done by using output probabilities of the LM as a predictor for a model's preference towards certain linguistic structures (Roark et al., 2009; Wilcox et al., 2020). Another strain of research uses the output probabilities as a correlate of psycholinguistic measures, e.g., N400 and P600 EEG signals (Heilbron et al., 2019 and recently Li and Futrell, 2023) and (self-paced) reading times (Fernandez Monsalve et al., 2012). A natural question that arises is whether cognitive plausibility should be attributed to the model architecture itself, or to the training regime in combination with the training dataset. Little research has been done on the actual neurological plausibility of large LMs (LLMs), but Schrimpf et al. (2021) showed that the architecture of BERT-like models is already plausible for the next word prediction task before training: model predictions with only the language modelling head trained are already predictive of human brain activity during reading *and* correlate well with the predictions of the fully trained model. In contrast, no correlation between brain activity and model predictions was found for models trained on GLUE (Wang et al., 2019), a natural language understand-

Proceedings of the 27th Conference on Computational Natural Language Learning: Volume 2: The BabyLM Challenge, pages 142–157
December 6-7, 2023 ©2023 Association for Computational Linguistics

ing (NLU) benchmark. This finding may mirror an underlying difference in language processing between *formal* and *functional linguistic competence* as introduced by Mahowald et al. (2023):

Formal linguistic competence is defined as the "capacity required to produce and comprehend a given language, i.e., the ability to distinguish grammatically correct from incorrect formations, based either on "knowledge of and flexible use of linguistic rules" or "non-rule-like statistical regularities" (Mahowald et al., 2023). An example for the former mechanism would be the regular formation of past tense verbs in English (*look*:*looked*), and for the latter the formation of irregular or ablauting past tense verbs (*go*:*went*,*tread*:*trod*).

Functional linguistic competence is defined as "non-language-specific cognitive functions that are required when we use language in real-world circumstances" (Mahowald et al., 2023) , i.e., the ability to perform cognitive tasks *with* language. GLUE is an example for a benchmark that test this dimension of linguistic competence, with some if its tasks (CoLA (Warstadt et al., 2019)) also testing for aspects of *formal linguistic competence*.

The dichotomy between formal and functional linguistic competence can be understood in terms of Wittgenstein's definition of the meaning of a word as its use in a language (Wittgenstein (1953), §43). The debate on whether statistical learners (i.e. LMs) can learn the meaning of a linguistic unit (word, phrase, text, etc.) in Wittgenstein's sense is still ongoing, with much division between positions that strongly deny that LMs can have such a property (Bender and Koller, 2020) and positions that advocate that they might have it, e.g., under the condition that the LM's predictions are grounded in extralinguistic reality (Bisk et al., 2020). Our study does not attempt to find arguments in favour of either position, but to study the implications of this dichotomy for the paradigm of cognitive modelling.

As stated earlier, the output probabilities of LMs lie at the basis of the application of LMs to cognitive language modelling, usually in the form of a probability distribution over a vocabulary of word forms given either surrounding words (masked language modelling) or preceding words (causal language modelling). Evidence for the use of surprisal (a word's negative logarithmic probability in context) instead of the actual probablity comes from logarithmic effects of contextual probabilities on processing difficulty (Shain et al., 2022). Another approach is to evaluate the output probabilities of a LM over a number of classes that may or may not apply to the input sequence, usually after finetuning the LM. The reliance of research in this direction on the output probabilities of LMs has already been criticized from multiple sides. There is a growing body of evidence that the performance of a LM in the typical language modelling task, next word prediction, and measures of formal linguistic competence are not correlated. Hu et al. (2020) found no correlation between LM perplexity and measures of formal linguistic competence, while Huang et al. (2023) argue that LM surprisal should not be assumed to be a good predictor of psycholinguistic measures of processing difficulty that require more than just lexical information. This lack of correlation with psycholinguistic measures becomes more prominent with the increasing size of LMs (Oh and Schuler, 2022), and especially so in extreme cases of human processing difficulty: Arehalli et al. (2022) showed that surprisal from LSTM-based LMs underestimates garden-path effects on reading times, while successfully predicting reading times for most non-garden-path sentences. This finding has been corroborated for transformer-based LMs such as GPT-2 (Jurayj et al., 2022) and BERT (Irwin et al., 2023).

2 BabyLM

The BabyLM challenge (Warstadt et al., 2023) introduces a novel constraint to cognitively plausible language modelling by limiting the token budget for LM pretraining to 100 million (100M) tokens, roughly the same amount of tokens a 13-year old child has seen during language acquisition (Gilkerson et al., 2017). While the focus of the challenge is on the pretraining procedure, the evaluation pipeline consists of the BLiMP (Warstadt et al., 2020a), MSGS (Warstadt et al., 2020b) and GLUE benchmarks, each of which aims to test for a specific dimension of linguistic competence.

BLiMP BLiMP tests for *formal linguistic competence* by comparing model predictions at a critical word in pairs of grammatically acceptable and unacceptable sentences, with the sentence pair only differing with respect to a single feature, e.g., whether a determiner agrees with its antecedent in gender or not. A model succeeds at the task if it assigns a higher probability to the critical word in the acceptable sentence.

GLUE GLUE is a benchmark that requires fine-tuning[1] of the LM. It tests for a wide range of NLU problems, e.g., question answering, natural language inference and linguistic acceptability judgements, and hence can be regarded as a proxy for the *functional linguistic competence* of a LM.

MSGS MSGS is a benchmark of binary classification tasks that tests whether a LM prefers *surface generalizations* over *syntactic generalization* by first fine-tuning on data consistent with both types of generalization. At inference time, items are consistent with only one type, potentially revealing a bias towards either generalization type.

Previous studies mainly provided insights into the relationship of pretraining token budget and measures of formal and functional linguistic competence. Zhang et al. (2021) showed that encoder-only LMs already perform well on formal tasks such as BLiMP at a budget of 10-100M tokens, while requiring substantially larger token budgets to perform well on functional tasks such as GLUE. While this research established correlations for pretraining token budgets, similar relationships for *model size* at a fixed token budget have not yet been investigated. This study is dedicated to finding a relationship between model size and performance on these tasks, while simultaneously addressing the dimension of *processing effort*, which is not covered by the challenge tasks. This is done using the **strict** version of the BabyLM corpus, mainly because there is evidence that the fit with psycholinguistic measures profits from token budgets far larger than the 100M tokens in the corpus (Oh and Schuler, 2023).However, we also implicity evaluate on models that are trained on token budgets of 10M tokens, corresponding rather to the **strict-small** track in Section 7.

3 Research questions

The starting point of our work is Zhang et al. (2021)'s finding of an earlier saturation effect (in terms of pretraining tokens) for BLiMP as opposed to (Super)GLUE. If performance on BLiMP is already close to the optimum after pretraining for 100M tokens, we suspect that a model with relatively small capacity is sufficient to reliably learn the required syntactic and semantic features. In contrast, the larger pretraining token budget and model size needed for GLUE should also require a model with higher capacity.

Studies on reading time prediction generally use causal LMs trained on a next-word prediction task instead of masked LMs (Oh and Schuler, 2022; Arehalli et al., 2022; Jurayj et al., 2022) because of their closer similarity to human language processing. Although masked LMs such as BERT show some word order effects (Papadimitriou et al., 2022) and even garden-path effects (Irwin et al., 2023), they are cognitively implausible in the sense that they process all words in a sequence simultaneously when predicting a word at a masked position, rather than processing language sequentially. This *autoregressive* property mirrors human language processing, and is therefore desirable in studies with the primary goal of modelling human reading behaviour. We therefore employ decoder-only, GPT-like LMs (Radford et al., 2019) in our study, i.e., we want to answer the following research questions:

Research question A

Are GPT-like models cognitively plausible in the sense that they are able to acquire (a degree of) formal and functional linguistic competence, while being also predictive of human processing effort?

Research question B

Can such LMs be trained on the same data as a child has available during language acquisition (100M tokens)?

4 Previous work

Do we need transformers for cognitive plausibility? Despite promising findings by Hosseini et al. (2021), it has yet to be determined whether transformers, and decoder-only transformer LMs in particular, are cognitively plausible in the sense that they are data-efficient enough to acquire human-like[2] linguistic competence. Indeed, there are results that seem to partially contradict the necessity

[1]During fine-tuning, we train all parameters of the pretrained LM as well as a randomly initialized classifier on top of the LM.

[2]Here, we do not use "human-like" to imply human-level performance, but rather that the model is *subject to similar processing constraints* as a human.

of LLMs with wide context windows in order for a model to exhibit human-like processing behaviour. Kuribayashi et al. (2022) showed that *reducing* context length of LLMs improves the fit of a linear mixed-effects model (LME) on gaze durations, with surprisal from a bigram GPT-2 model as a predictor yielding the largest log-likelihood reduction over the baseline model. Wilcox et al. (2020) failed to identify a relationship between psychometric predictive power (Δ log-likelihood) and syntactic generalization, concluding that different models are needed for modelling human processing effort versus syntactic generalization.

Linguistic competence vs. psycholinguistic measures It has long been clear that LM capacity, and subsequently LM perplexity, does not necessarily correlate with human-likeness (Kuribayashi et al., 2021). LLMs such as GPT-3 in particular were found to have considerable disadvantages when it comes to predicting psycholinguistic measures from their next-word predictions: Oh and Schuler (2022) found an inverse relationship between both perplexity and LLM capacity, versus fit to human reading times. The authors of this study hypothesize that this is because transformers have access to the full sequence context, and are trained on large enough corpora to make use of the information that they contain. This relationship between model perplexity and reading times is however not intrinsic to transformer-based LMs: Hu et al. (2020) found a similar relationship for LSTM LMs, though small GPT-like models have an advantage over recurrent models.

The impact of LM size on linguistic competence was investigated by Eldan and Li (2023), who found that relatively small GPT2-like models (<10M parameters) manage to produce fluent English and can be trained on relatively small corpora with a reduced vocabulary. Their study also shows that the relationship still holds for small models, while also identifying trade-offs between model width (hidden size) and depth (number of decoder layers).

As for training dataset size, Oh and Schuler (2023) found that surprisal from transformer-based LLMs gives the best fit to reading times at about 2B train tokens, across a wide range of model sizes. The corpus used in their study is very large (300B tokens), allowing for extensive training of a model without repeating any data. Reaching the same number of update steps with the much smaller BabyLM corpus would require training for multiple epochs.

Single- vs. multi-epoch training Since the BabyLM training data is substantially smaller than the 2B tokens suggested by Oh and Schuler (2023), training our models in a multi-epoch setting cannot be avoided. Previous research has shown that repeating the training data can have adverse effects: Xue et al. (2023) compared single-epoch vs. multi-epoch training in a limited data setting and show that multi-epoch training leads to overfitting, with little performance being gained after the first epoch. They also find that regularization can only partially alleviate the overfitting problem, with dropout having the largest effect. Not having to repeat the training data is advantageous for downstream tasks and psycholinguistic modelling, if a certain amount of training data is available: Oh and Schuler (2023) found that reading time fit deteriorates after 2B tokens over a wide range of model sizes. However, it is not clear if repeating the training data would lead to an even stronger deterioration. If the corpus is substantially smaller than 2B tokens, repeating the training data could have a different effect, especially if the optimum of the reading time fit depends on the availability of the 2B tokens.

5 Methodology

Modelling We use the OPT architecture by Zhang et al. (2022) with a language modelling head for pretraining. Following our intuition that BLiMP should require much smaller model sizes than MSGS and GLUE, we train a series of OPT models of different sizes, varying only model width (hidden size) and model depth (number of decoder layers). In total we train 24 models varying over 4 hidden sizes $l_{hidden} \in \{192, 384, 768, 1536\}$ and 6 numbers of decoder layers ($l_{decoder} \in \{1, 2, 4, 8, 16, 24\}$). We also adjust the dimension of the feedforward layers such that the size of the output vector $l_{forward} = 3 \times l_{hidden}$. Table 1 in Appendix A shows the resulting model sizes. The models and all code for pretraining are implemented with PyTorch (Paszke et al., 2019) and HuggingFace transformers (Wolf et al., 2020), starting from their implementation of OPT. We also trained a new tokenizer on the training set of the BabyLM corpus, using the same vocabulary size $|V| = 50272$ as the original OPT tokenizer. We report all results as averages over 3 random seeds (see Appendix D for full results and standard error).

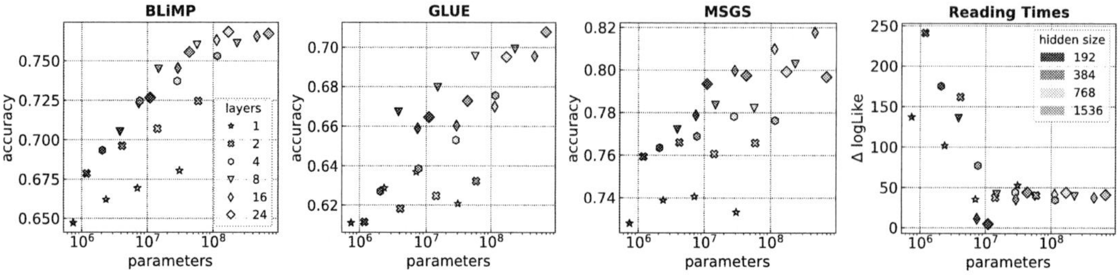

Figure 2: Task performance by model size (higher numbers are better). Baselines can be found in Appendix D.

Training Following the Shortformer pipeline (Press et al., 2021), each model is trained for one epoch with an initial sequence length of 64, followed by 4 epochs with the full sequence length of 256. The full sequence length of 256 was chosen as a compromise between the relatively short test items in the challenge tasks (up to 128 tokens) In order to ensure that the model generalizes to longer sequences we use ALiBI (Press et al., 2022) instead of learned positional embeddings. This also ensures that our models generalize to the longer sequences in the Natural Stories corpus. We trained each model on a A100 GPU with 40 GB VRAM and an effective batch size of 128, using gradient accumulation for models that could not fit the full batch size. We used AdamW (Loshchilov and Hutter, 2019) as our optimizer with an initial learning rate of 0.001 and weight decay of 0.001 with 2000 linear warm-up steps. We use a dropout of 0.1 following the default HuggingFace transformers parameters for OPT.

Pretraining experiments We also experimented with changes to the pretraining regime. We trained models on multiple permutations of the training dataset: ordering sequences according to length (number of words), word length (number of characters), sequence-level perplexity from a 3-gram LM trained on the same data, and different orderings of the subcorpora as in Mueller and Linzen (2023). None of these approaches resulted in significant performance gains in terms of perplexity and performance on the challenge tasks over a baseline model trained on the concatenated BabyLM corpus with subsequent shuffling of the sequences.

Evaluation We evaluated all models on the downstream tasks of the BabyLM challenge. While these three tasks test for the linguistic competence of a model, they do not quantify the cognitive effort associated with language processing. We therefore also evaluate all models on a reading time prediction task. For each model, we calculated surprisal on the items of the Natural Stories Corpus (Futrell et al., 2021). This corpus was chosen because its domain is close to at least one of the BabyLM subcorpora (Children's Stories). We fitted linear mixed-effects (LME) models with random intercepts for subject, word and item (the id of the story); surprisal, word frequency, word length and sentence position as predictors and log-normalized reading times as the response variable. The exact formula is

```
log(reading_time) ~
  word_surprisal + len(word)
  + log(word_frequency) + position
  + (1|word) + (1|subject) + (1|item)
```

For the reading time analysis we report the difference in log-likelihood between the models with surprisal as a predictor over a baseline model with only the control predictors. For all other tasks we report accuracy.

Code We used the evaluation code provided by the organizers of the BabyLM challenge[3], with some modifications to load custom models. The evaluation pipeline is based on the LM-Eval framework by Gao et al. (2021). Fine-tuning on GLUE and MSGS was done with the default hyperparameter settings, but we reduced the number of fine-tuning epochs to 3 as we did not observe any improvements after 3 epochs. The LME models were fitted using the lmerTest R library (Kuznetsova et al., 2017) via the pymer4 Python package (Jolly, 2018). The code to pretrain and evaluate all models is publicly available on GitHub[4]. The model with the highest BLiMP accuracy and detailed results for the LME models are made available at the same

[3]https://github.com/BabyLM/evaluation-pipeline

[4]https://github.com/uds-lsv/babylm

location, alongside instructions on how to run the training and evaluation pipelines.

6 Results

Fine-tuning GLUE Fine-tuning on GLUE was overall very unstable and often failed to outperform the baseline. This was mainly due to the one-size-fits-all approach to the fine-tuning hyperparameters; we repeated several more fine-tuning runs with different hyperparameter settings on some of the GLUE tasks, and found that, e.g., RTE profited from a longer warm-up period (which is in line with the findings of Mosbach et al. (2021) for BERT-like models), but most other sub-tasks fine-tuned with the same hyperparameters showed a drop in performance. While we could have optimized hyperparameters for all sub-tasks, the main objective of the BabyLM challenge is to improve the pretraining part of the NLP pipeline. Thus, we decided to fine-tune with the default hyperparameters, only adjusting the number of epochs as we found that the fine-tuning runs already converged after a few epochs.

Model size Figure 2 shows the relationship between model size and task performance: While GLUE (Spearman's $\rho = 0.7739$, $p < 1^{-4}$) and MSGS ($\rho = 0.7148$, $p < 1^{-4}$) performance scales with model size, BLiMP performance plateaus after reaching a model size of about 50M parameters ($\rho = 0.8835$, $p < 1^{-4}$). In contrast, reading time fit was negatively correlated with model size ($\rho = -51.39$, $p < 0.05$). All correlations are statistically significant with $p < 1^{-4}$. No single model performed best on all three challenge tasks, with large differences in the size of the best model. Figure 1 shows that similar correlations hold for model perplexity and task performance (BLiMP: $\rho = -0.9765$, $p < 1^{-4}$, GLUE: $\rho = -0.8287$, $p < 1^{-4}$, MSGS: $\rho = -0.8661$, $p < 1^{-4}$); negative correlations mean that lower perplexity leads to higher performance. We found strong positive correlations (pictured in Figure 7 in Appendix D) between performance on the challenge tasks (BLiMP and GLUE ($\rho = 0.8784$), BLiMP and MSGS ($\rho = 0.9182$) and GLUE and MSGS ($\rho = 0.815$) generally with $p < 1^{-4}$).

Model width vs. depth While BLiMP performance was not found to be strongly correlated with either the number of decoder layers or hidden size, GLUE and MSGS showed some variability based on the number of layers. For GLUE the only configuration that showed a monotonic improvement in performance was a hidden size of 1536, with models with more decoder layers achieving higher accuracy in this setting. For MSGS we observed a drop in performance for the models with 24 decoder layers at the largest hidden sizes (384, 768). Overall, the effect of hidden size and number of layers was minor when compared to overall model size. In contrast, the best fit on the reading time data was achieved with the second smallest model with only 2 decoder layers and a hidden size of 192. Figure 3 illustrates this trend: for the challenge tasks, performance increases with the number of layers (though not monotonically), whereas Δ log-likelihood of the LME models decreases with the number of layers at $l_{hidden} = 192$ and, to a lesser extent, at $l_{hidden} = 384$, while deeper models with more decoder layers and larger hidden sizes perform considerably worse.

Possible confounds The reading time analysis suffers from several potential confounding factors: Firstly, the domain of the training data differs considerably from the data in the Natural Stories corpus. While the training data also contains some longer texts (Wikipedia, Children's Stories), most of the corpora are more representative of spoken language (Open Subtitles, BNC Spoken, CHILDES). In addition, most sequences are relatively short, with a median sequence length of 8 in the Open Subtitles corpus, which accounts for $>50\%$ of the training data. This is considerably less than the median sequence length of 22 in the Natural Stories corpus. Another confounding factor might be the difference in exposure to language data of the model and that of the participants of the original reading time study. Futrell et al. (2021) do not provide demographic data of their participants, but since data collection was done via Amazon Mechanical Turk we can safely assume that the mean age of the participants was higher than 13, meaning that they were exposed to considerably more language data than the 100M tokens in the BabyLM corpus. Although a recent study by Oh and Schuler (2023) showed that reading time fit (in terms of Δ log-likelihood) from transformer models still profits from pretraining data multiple orders of magnitude larger than our corpus, with an optimum at 2B tokens, this is partially alleviated in this study by the multiple-epoch training regime, totalling about 500M tokens seen by each of our

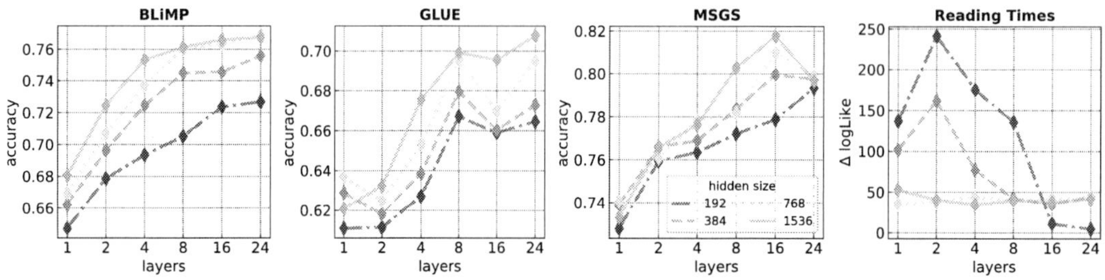

Figure 3: Task performance by hidden size, number of layers and task.

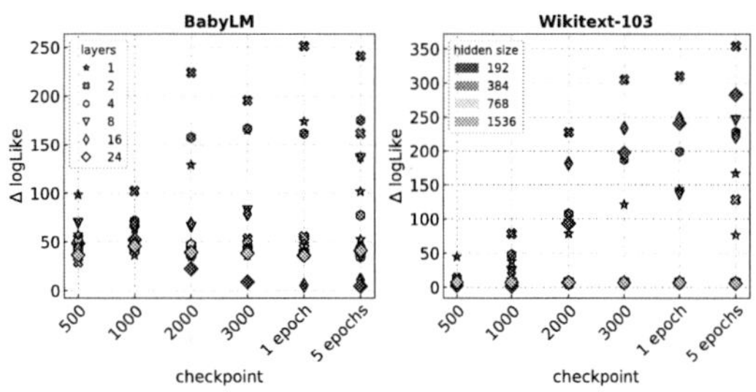

Figure 4: Reading time fit in terms of Δ log-likelihood over a base model without surprisal as a predictor, on the BabyLM and Wikitext-103 data after 500, 1000, 2000 and 3000 training steps (1/8, 1/4, 1/2 and 3/4 of an epoch) and 1 and 5 epochs.

models. Since Oh and Schuler (2023) found that training on more *unseen* tokens after reaching the optimum leads to a quick deterioration of reading time fit proportional to model size, it is unclear what impact repeating the training data would have on the reading time fit.

7 Reading time prediction in a multi-epoch setting

Experimental setup In order to evaluate whether the negative correlation is an artifact of the domain mismatch between the BabyLM corpus and the items in the Natural Stories corpus or the repetition of the training data before reaching the optimal token budget, we conduct two additional experiments: First, we retrain all models on the BabyLM corpus for a single epoch, saving intermediate checkpoints at 100, 500, 1000, 2000 and 3000 training steps. Then, we use the intermediate models to fit LME models to the reading time data, using the same formula as given in Section 5. Second, we replicate these experiments on Wikitext-103, a corpus of similar size that does not have the same limitations of the BabyLM corpus (i.e. an average sequence length and a domain closer to the Natural Stories corpus). The models trained on Wikitext-103 serve as a control for the experiments on the BabyLM corpus and were not included in the final submission. Since the results indicate that larger models yield a worse reading time fit, we restrict the experiment to small models (1-4 layers, all hidden sizes) and larger models with the smallest and largest hidden size (192 and 1536). The models are trained with the same hyperparameter settings as the original models, but sequence length is not reduced in the first epoch.

Results Figure 4 shows a somewhat different picture for the models trained on Wikitext-103, with reading time fit of smaller models increasing over the whole pretraining procedure, while models with $l_{hidden} > 192$ almost never improve over the baseline model. In contrast, the reading time fit of the LMs trained on the BabyLM data improves significantly over the baseline for shallower models ($<$ 2 decoder layers), while staying roughly constant for deeper and wider models (16, 24 decoder layers). However, the relationship between the number of training steps and reading time fit is not monotonic, with a slight decrease after training for 4 more epochs for the best model. While the models trained on the Wikitext-103 dataset yield a better fit to reading times in terms of Δ log-likelihood, the basic finding on the BabyLM data is corroborated: exposing a transformer model to multiple repetitions of the training data before reaching the optimal token budget does not lead to a decrease in reading time fit, but also does not improve over the single epoch setting in a meaningful way. The results also show that the improved reading time fit for $l_{hidden} = 192$ cannot be attributed to smaller model size alone, as the deepest model with that hidden size, 24*192 shows an improved fit over the baseline, while 1*384, a model with a comparable number of parameters, but a larger hidden size, does not. In conclusion, we did not find a degradation of reading time fit when repeating the training data, with similar effects of LM size on reading time fit for Wikitext-103 and the BabyLM corpus (see Table 2 in Appendix C for Spearman's ρ's and p-values). We also found The BabyLM corpus to be advantageous for this task in the sense that – in contrast to Wikitext-103 – reading time fit from all models improved over the baseline LME model.

8 Discussion

Correlation between BLiMP, GLUE & MSGS The experiments presented in Section 6 provide evidence for a correlation between LM performance on BLiMP, GLUE and MSGS tasks when pretraining on the BabyLM corpus. This correlation is in accordance with established effects of training dataset size (Zhang et al., 2021), and interactions of train corpus size and model capacity (Eldan and Li, 2023, Kaplan et al., 2020). However, no single model achieves the highest score on all three tasks: BLiMP shows diminishing returns for model sizes larger than 50M tokens, while the best model on MSGS (16*1536) is substantially smaller than the best model on GLUE (24*1536). This discrepancy between the best model on the BabyLM challenge tasks and on the reading times prediction task is illustrated by Figure 5. The correlation between BLiMP/MSGS and GLUE may be an artifact of the sub-optimal fine-tuning on GLUE, failing to outperform the baseline model. It cannot be ruled out that the results would change when determining the optimal hyperparameters for each sub-task individually. However, even if the correlation were an artifact of the pretraining data, the findings of a negative correlation between model size and reading time fit would still hold.

Cognitive plausibility of GPT-like models The best fit on self-paced reading times from the Natural Stories corpus was obtained with the second-smallest model, with models with $l_{hidden} > 192$ only slightly improving over the baseline. The second suite of experiments in Section 7 confirms that this is not solely caused by the multi-epoch training regime necessitated by the small token budget. The reason for the mismatch between measures of cognitive plausibility (reading times) and measures of formal (BLiMP, MSGS) and functional linguistic competence (GLUE) is rooted in the interaction of pretraining regime and model size: While it is feasible to train a model that performs comparatively well on all four tasks on a budget of 100M tokens, the sweet spot for model size and dataset size is reached much earlier for the reading time prediction task than for the BabyLM challenge tasks. This problem could easily be resolved by using one model when modelling reading times (or any other psycholinguistic measure), and another model when either of the forms of linguistic competence is the aim. This might be a valid and promising approach in a situation where the understanding of the research object does not depend on the connectedness of its experimental analoga. In the case of our research object – the human language faculty – it may not be necessary to find a single analogon that accounts for all its components, but since we *know* that the human language faculty is part of a unified cognitive system (with specialized sub-units) performing the tasks which the modern language modelling pipeline of pretraining and fine-tuning splits up into individual modules, it would be worthwile to move in the direction of a unified approach that accounts for both forms of linguistic competence and empirical evidence of processing effort. This could be achieved through adjustments to the pretraining regime (in terms of data, modelling objective etc.), as suggested by the BabyLM challenge, or through adjustments to the model architecture.

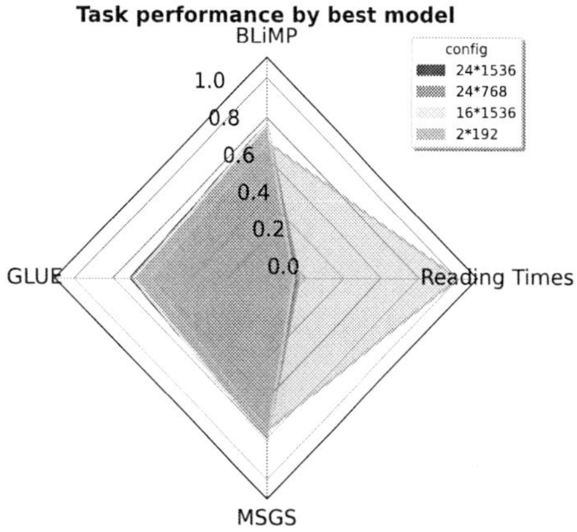

Figure 5: Performance of the best models by task. Reading times Δ log-likelihoods are normalized in the interval $[0, 1]$.

Size of transformer models The results of the reading time prediction study on the BabyLM corpus indicate that it in fact has an *advantage* over

Wikitext-103, although the LMs trained on the latter achieve larger Δ log-likelihoods on average: Since the largest models fail to improve over the baseline model if trained on Wikitext-103, it is possible that some properties of the language in the BabyLM corpus facilitate the learning mechanism that actuates the correlation of LM surprisal and reading times. The reason for the worse fit of surprisal from the larger models may be that both Wikitext-103 and the BabyLM corpus are not large enough to induce the learning bias needed to give good predictions of reading times in larger models, with Figure 4 showing that the results on the BabyLM corpus are much less stable than on Wikitext-103 and the improvements over the baseline much less sharply linear. In summary, our results lead to the following answers to our research questions:

Result: Research question A

GPT-like LMs can be cognitively plausible and display formal and functional linguistic competence, although not both at the same time...

Result: Research question B

...under the constraint of a developmentally plausible training dataset.

9 Conclusion

Our study highlights the challenges of training a LM that performs well on tasks requiring some degree of formal and functional linguistic competence as defined by Mahowald et al. (2023), while also being predictive of the psycholinguistic measure of reading times. We find that small, shallow models of less than 5M parameters yield the best fit to the psycholinguistic measure, while performance on BLiMP, GLUE and MSGS improves with increasing model size, although to a different degree for each of the tasks. This has implications for research on cognitively or developmentally plausible models of human language processing: in the case of a small, domain-specific training corpus it is not feasible to pretrain an LLM that displays formal linguistic competence and performs well on a reading time prediction tasks, a conclusion also drawn by Wingfield and Connell (2022). Consequently, research in this direction has concentrated on fine-tuning pretrained LLMs on domain-specific data, e.g., Škrjanec et al. (2023). A promising approach to a unified architecture could be relegating special tasks (such as classifying a sequence as in GLUE) to adapters (Houlsby et al., 2019), sub-networks within a pretrained LM. This approach is common in multilingual language modelling (Pfeiffer et al., 2022; Alabi et al., 2022), where its success is partially attributed to its ability to separate general linguistic knowledge from language-specific information. A similar modelling decision may be necessary for cognitively plausible language models.

Acknowledgements

The authors thank Iza Škranjec for helping with the training and interpretation of LME models, and Vagrant Gautam, Michael Hahn, Benedict Schneider, Iza Škranjec and for their helpful comments. This research was supported by the Deutsche Forschungsgemeinschaft (DFG, German Research Foundation), Project ID 232722074 – SFB 1102.

Limitations

The results of the paper mainly hold for decoder-only transformer LMs. While these LMs are closer to human language processing in the sense that they process language incrementally, this has some disadvantages for reading time predictions, since humans do not attribute equal importance to each word, skipping some words in the process, and typically integrate words from the left- *and* right-hand context of a fixated word. While the first point can be addressed by explicitly modelling skipping behaviour (Hahn and Keller, 2016), the second could require a solution closer to masked language models.

A second limitation is the focus on self-paced reading time as the psycholinguistic response variable. Since the setup of self-paced reading studies, with the participants observing a single word at a time, distorts the natural reading process, the measure itself may be not that cognitively plausible. This could be addressed by repeating the experiments on corpora from eye-tracking studies such as the Dundee corpus (Kennedy and Pynte, 2005). There is evidence that much larger models than those tested in the current study still improve the fit to total reading times in less restricted experimental settings (de Varda and Marelli, 2023). The latter study also shows that the fit to psycholinguistic measures varies over languages and writing systems.

Another option is modelling brain activity patterns directly by predicting N400 and P600 EEG signals, which have the additional advantage of providing a means of decomposing LM surprisal without the proxy of linguistic structure, as shown by Li and Futrell (2023).

Ethics Statement

The authors foresee no ethical concerns about the work presented in the paper.

References

Jesujoba O. Alabi, David Ifeoluwa Adelani, Marius Mosbach, and Dietrich Klakow. 2022. Adapting pre-trained language models to African languages via multilingual adaptive fine-tuning. In *Proceedings of the 29th International Conference on Computational Linguistics*, pages 4336–4349, Gyeongju, Republic of Korea. International Committee on Computational Linguistics.

Suhas Arehalli, Brian Dillon, and Tal Linzen. 2022. Syntactic Surprisal From Neural Models Predicts, But Underestimates, Human Processing Difficulty From Syntactic Ambiguities. In *Proceedings of the 26th Conference on Computational Natural Language Learning (CoNLL)*, pages 301–313, Abu Dhabi, United Arab Emirates (Hybrid). Association for Computational Linguistics.

Emily M. Bender and Alexander Koller. 2020. Climbing towards NLU: On meaning, form, and understanding in the age of data. In *Proceedings of the 58th Annual Meeting of the Association for Computational Linguistics*, pages 5185–5198, Online. Association for Computational Linguistics.

Yonatan Bisk, Ari Holtzman, Jesse Thomason, Jacob Andreas, Yoshua Bengio, Joyce Chai, Mirella Lapata, Angeliki Lazaridou, Jonathan May, Aleksandr Nisnevich, Nicolas Pinto, and Joseph Turian. 2020. Experience grounds language. In *Proceedings of the 2020 Conference on Empirical Methods in Natural Language Processing (EMNLP)*, pages 8718–8735, Online. Association for Computational Linguistics.

Andrea de Varda and Marco Marelli. 2023. Scaling in cognitive modelling: a multilingual approach to human reading times. In *Proceedings of the 61st Annual Meeting of the Association for Computational Linguistics (Volume 2: Short Papers)*, pages 139–149, Toronto, Canada. Association for Computational Linguistics.

Ronen Eldan and Yuanzhi Li. 2023. TinyStories: How Small Can Language Models Be and Still Speak Coherent English?

Irene Fernandez Monsalve, Stefan L. Frank, and Gabriella Vigliocco. 2012. Lexical surprisal as a general predictor of reading time. In *Proceedings of the 13th Conference of the European Chapter of the Association for Computational Linguistics*, pages 398–408, Avignon, France. Association for Computational Linguistics.

Richard Futrell, Edward Gibson, Harry J. Tily, Idan Blank, Anastasia Vishnevetsky, Steven T. Piantadosi, and Evelina Fedorenko. 2021. The Natural Stories corpus: A reading-time corpus of English texts containing rare yyntactic constructions. *Language Resources and Evaluation*, 55(1):63–77.

Leo Gao, Jonathan Tow, Stella Biderman, Sid Black, Anthony DiPofi, Charles Foster, Laurence Golding, Jeffrey Hsu, Kyle McDonell, Niklas Muennighoff, Jason Phang, Laria Reynolds, Eric Tang, Anish Thite, Ben Wang, Kevin Wang, and Andy Zou. 2021. A framework for few-shot language model evaluation.

Jill Gilkerson, Jeffrey A. Richards, Steven F. Warren, Judith K. Montgomery, Charles R. Greenwood, D. Kimbrough Oller, John H. L. Hansen, and Terrance D. Paul. 2017. Mapping the Early Language Environment Using All-Day Recordings and Automated Analysis. *American Journal of Speech-Language Pathology*, 26(2):248–265.

Michael Hahn and Frank Keller. 2016. Modeling human reading with neural attention. In *Proceedings of the 2016 Conference on Empirical Methods in Natural Language Processing*, pages 85–95, Austin, Texas. Association for Computational Linguistics.

Micha Heilbron, Benedikt Ehinger, Peter Hagoort, and Floris de Lange. 2019. Tracking Naturalistic Linguistic Predictions with Deep Neural Language Models. In *2019 Conference on Cognitive Computational Neuroscience*, Berlin, Germany. Cognitive Computational Neuroscience.

Kasra Hosseini, Kaspar Beelen, Giovanni Colavizza, and Mariona Coll Ardanuy. 2021. Neural Language Models for Nineteenth-Century English. ArXiv:2105.11321 [cs].

Neil Houlsby, Andrei Giurgiu, Stanislaw Jastrzebski, Bruna Morrone, Quentin de Laroussilhe, Andrea Gesmundo, Mona Attariyan, and Sylvain Gelly. 2019. Parameter-efficient transfer learning for nlp.

Jennifer Hu, Jon Gauthier, Peng Qian, Ethan Wilcox, and Roger P. Levy. 2020. A Systematic Assessment of Syntactic Generalization in Neural Language Models. Publisher: arXiv Version Number: 2.

Kuan-Jung Huang, Suhas Arehalli, Mari Kugemoto, Christian Muxica, Grusha Prasad, Brian Dillon, and Tal Linzen. 2023. Surprisal does not explain syntactic disambiguation difficulty: evidence from a large-scale benchmark. preprint, PsyArXiv.

Tovah Irwin, Kyra Wilson, and Alec Marantz. 2023. BERT Shows Garden Path Effects. In *Proceedings of the 17th Conference of the European Chapter of the Association for Computational Linguistics*, pages 3220–3232, Dubrovnik, Croatia. Association for Computational Linguistics.

Eshin Jolly. 2018. Pymer4: Connecting R and Python for Linear Mixed Modeling. *Journal of Open Source Software*, 3(31):862.

William Jurayj, William Rudman, and Carsten Eickhoff. 2022. Garden-Path Traversal in GPT-2. ArXiv:2205.12302 [cs].

Jared Kaplan, Sam McCandlish, Tom Henighan, Tom B. Brown, Benjamin Chess, Rewon Child, Scott Gray, Alec Radford, Jeffrey Wu, and Dario Amodei. 2020. Scaling Laws for Neural Language Models. ArXiv:2001.08361 [cs, stat].

Alan Kennedy and Joël Pynte. 2005. Parafoveal-on-foveal effects in normal reading. *Vision Research*, 45(2):153–168.

Tatsuki Kuribayashi, Yohei Oseki, Ana Brassard, and Kentaro Inui. 2022. Context Limitations Make Neural Language Models More Human-Like. In *Proceedings of the 2022 Conference on Empirical Methods in Natural Language Processing*, pages 10421–10436, Abu Dhabi, United Arab Emirates. Association for Computational Linguistics.

Tatsuki Kuribayashi, Yohei Oseki, Takumi Ito, Ryo Yoshida, Masayuki Asahara, and Kentaro Inui. 2021. Lower Perplexity is Not Always Human-Like. In *Proceedings of the 59th Annual Meeting of the Association for Computational Linguistics and the 11th International Joint Conference on Natural Language Processing (Volume 1: Long Papers)*, pages 5203–5217, Online. Association for Computational Linguistics.

Alexandra Kuznetsova, Per B. Brockhoff, and Rune H. B. Christensen. 2017. lmerTest package: Tests in linear mixed effects models. *Journal of Statistical Software*, 82(13):1–26.

Jiaxuan Li and Richard Futrell. 2023. A decomposition of surprisal tracks the N400 and P600 brain potentials. *Proceedings of the Annual Meeting of the Cognitive Science Society*, 45(45).

Ilya Loshchilov and Frank Hutter. 2019. Decoupled weight decay regularization.

Kyle Mahowald, Anna A. Ivanova, Idan A. Blank, Nancy Kanwisher, Joshua B. Tenenbaum, and Evelina Fedorenko. 2023. Dissociating language and thought in large language models: a cognitive perspective.

Marius Mosbach, Maksym Andriushchenko, and Dietrich Klakow. 2021. On the stability of fine-tuning bert: Misconceptions, explanations, and strong baselines.

Aaron Mueller and Tal Linzen. 2023. How to Plant Trees in Language Models: Data and Architectural Effects on the Emergence of Syntactic Inductive Biases. Publisher: arXiv Version Number: 1.

Byung-Doh Oh and William Schuler. 2022. Why Does Surprisal From Larger Transformer-Based Language Models Provide a Poorer Fit to Human Reading Times? Publisher: arXiv Version Number: 1.

Byung-Doh Oh and William Schuler. 2023. Transformer-Based LM Surprisal Predicts Human Reading Times Best with About Two Billion Training Tokens. ArXiv:2304.11389 [cs].

Isabel Papadimitriou, Richard Futrell, and Kyle Mahowald. 2022. When classifying grammatical role, BERT doesn't care about word order... except when it matters. ArXiv:2203.06204 [cs].

Adam Paszke, Sam Gross, Francisco Massa, Adam Lerer, James Bradbury, Gregory Chanan, Trevor Killeen, Zeming Lin, Natalia Gimelshein, Luca Antiga, Alban Desmaison, Andreas Kopf, Edward Yang, Zachary DeVito, Martin Raison, Alykhan Tejani, Sasank Chilamkurthy, Benoit Steiner, Lu Fang, Junjie Bai, and Soumith Chintala. 2019. Pytorch: An imperative style, high-performance deep learning library. In H. Wallach, H. Larochelle, A. Beygelzimer, F. d'Alché-Buc, E. Fox, and R. Garnett, editors, *Advances in Neural Information Processing Systems 32*, pages 8024–8035. Curran Associates, Inc.

Jonas Pfeiffer, Naman Goyal, Xi Lin, Xian Li, James Cross, Sebastian Riedel, and Mikel Artetxe. 2022. Lifting the Curse of Multilinguality by Pre-training Modular Transformers. In *Proceedings of the 2022 Conference of the North American Chapter of the Association for Computational Linguistics: Human Language Technologies*, pages 3479–3495, Seattle, United States. Association for Computational Linguistics.

Ofir Press, Noah A. Smith, and Mike Lewis. 2021. Shortformer: Better Language Modeling using Shorter Inputs. In *Proceedings of the 59th Annual Meeting of the Association for Computational Linguistics and the 11th International Joint Conference on Natural Language Processing (Volume 1: Long Papers)*, pages 5493–5505, Online. Association for Computational Linguistics.

Ofir Press, Noah A. Smith, and Mike Lewis. 2022. Train Short, Test Long: Attention with Linear Biases Enables Input Length Extrapolation. ArXiv:2108.12409 [cs].

Alec Radford, Jeffrey Wu, Rewon Child, David Luan, Dario Amodei, and Ilya Sutskever. 2019. Language Models are Unsupervised Multitask Learners.

Brian Roark, Asaf Bachrach, Carlos Cardenas, and Christophe Pallier. 2009. Deriving lexical and syntactic expectation-based measures for psycholinguistic modeling via incremental top-down parsing. In *Proceedings of the 2009 Conference on Empirical Methods in Natural Language Processing*, pages 324–333, Singapore. Association for Computational Linguistics.

Martin Schrimpf, Idan Asher Blank, Greta Tuckute, Carina Kauf, Eghbal A. Hosseini, Nancy Kanwisher, Joshua B. Tenenbaum, and Evelina Fedorenko. 2021. The neural architecture of language: Integrative modeling converges on predictive processing. *Proceedings of the National Academy of Sciences*, 118(45):e2105646118.

Cory Shain, Clara Meister, Tiago Pimentel, Ryan Cotterell, and Roger Philip Levy. 2022. Large-Scale Evidence for Logarithmic Effects of Word Predictability on Reading Time. preprint, PsyArXiv.

Iza Škrjanec, Frederik Y. Broy, and Vera Demberg. 2023. Expert-adapted language models improve the fit to reading times.

Alex Wang, Amanpreet Singh, Julian Michael, Felix Hill, Omer Levy, and Samuel R. Bowman. 2019. GLUE: A Multi-Task Benchmark and Analysis Platform for Natural Language Understanding. ArXiv:1804.07461 [cs].

Alex Warstadt, Aaron Mueller, Leshem Chohen, Ethan Gotlieb Wilcox, Chengxu Zhuang, Juan Ciro, Rafael Mosquera, Adina Williams, Bhargavi Paranjabe, Tal Linzen, and Ryan Cotterell. 2023. Findings of the 2023 BabyLM Challenge: Sample-efficient pretraining on developmentally plausible corpora. In *Proceedings of the 2023 BabyLM Challenge*. Association for Computational Linguistics (ACL).

Alex Warstadt, Alicia Parrish, Haokun Liu, Anhad Mohananey, Wei Peng, Sheng-Fu Wang, and Samuel R. Bowman. 2020a. BLiMP: The Benchmark of Linguistic Minimal Pairs for English. *Transactions of the Association for Computational Linguistics*, 8:377–392.

Alex Warstadt, Amanpreet Singh, and Samuel R. Bowman. 2019. Neural network acceptability judgments.

Alex Warstadt, Yian Zhang, Xiaocheng Li, Haokun Liu, and Samuel R. Bowman. 2020b. Learning Which Features Matter: RoBERTa Acquires a Preference for Linguistic Generalizations (Eventually). In *Proceedings of the 2020 Conference on Empirical Methods in Natural Language Processing (EMNLP)*, pages 217–235, Online. Association for Computational Linguistics.

Ethan Gotlieb Wilcox, Jon Gauthier, Jennifer Hu, Peng Qian, and Roger Levy. 2020. On the Predictive Power of Neural Language Models for Human Real-Time Comprehension Behavior. Publisher: arXiv Version Number: 1.

Cai Wingfield and Louise Connell. 2022. Understanding the role of linguistic distributional knowledge in cognition. volume 37, pages 1220–1270. Routledge.

Ludwig Wittgenstein. 1953. *Philosophische Untersuchungen*. Suhrkamp Verlag, Frankfurt am Main.

Thomas Wolf, Lysandre Debut, Victor Sanh, Julien Chaumond, Clement Delangue, Anthony Moi, Pierric Cistac, Tim Rault, Remi Louf, Morgan Funtowicz, Joe Davison, Sam Shleifer, Patrick von Platen, Clara Ma, Yacine Jernite, Julien Plu, Canwen Xu, Teven Le Scao, Sylvain Gugger, Mariama Drame, Quentin Lhoest, and Alexander Rush. 2020. Transformers: State-of-the-art natural language processing. In *Proceedings of the 2020 Conference on Empirical Methods in Natural Language Processing: System Demonstrations*, pages 38–45, Online. Association for Computational Linguistics.

Fuzhao Xue, Yao Fu, Wangchunshu Zhou, Zangwei Zheng, and Yang You. 2023. To Repeat or Not To Repeat: Insights from Scaling LLM under Token-Crisis.

Susan Zhang, Stephen Roller, Naman Goyal, Mikel Artetxe, Moya Chen, Shuohui Chen, Christopher Dewan, Mona Diab, Xian Li, Xi Victoria Lin, Todor Mihaylov, Myle Ott, Sam Shleifer, Kurt Shuster, Daniel Simig, Punit Singh Koura, Anjali Sridhar, Tianlu Wang, and Luke Zettlemoyer. 2022. OPT: Open Pretrained Transformer Language Models. Publisher: arXiv Version Number: 4.

Yian Zhang, Alex Warstadt, Xiaocheng Li, and Samuel R. Bowman. 2021. When do you need billions of words of pretraining data? In *Proceedings of the 59th Annual Meeting of the Association for Computational Linguistics and the 11th International Joint Conference on Natural Language Processing (Volume 1: Long Papers)*, pages 1112–1125, Online. Association for Computational Linguistics.

A OPT models

$l_{decoder}$	l_{hidden}	**Parameters (non-embedding)**
1	192	0.74
2	192	1.19
4	192	2.07
8	192	3.85
16	192	7.41
24	192	10.9
1	384	2.37
2	384	4.14
4	384	7.69
8	384	14.79
16	384	28.99
24	384	43.18
1	768	7.09
2	768	14.18
4	768	28.35
8	768	56.70
16	768	113.41
24	768	170.11
1	1536	30.69
2	1536	59.00
4	1536	115.69
8	1536	229.01
16	1536	455.67
24	1536	682.32

Table 1: OPT models sizes in million parameters by hidden size and number of decoder layers. The number of parameters does not include the embedding table, which is always of the size $l_{emb} \times |V| = 768 \times 50272 = 38.608.896$, as in OPT-128m.

B Validation perplexity

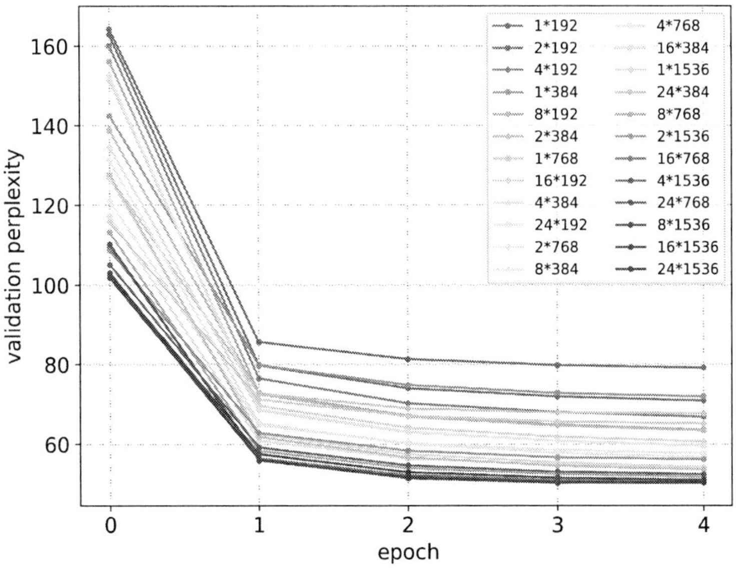

Figure 6: Validation perplexity by configuration and epoch on the development set of the BabyLM corpus.

C Detailed resutls: Reading time experiments

Corpus	Step	Spearman's ρ	p-value
babylm	500	-0.5913	0.0097
babylm	1000	-0.6285	0.0052
babylm	2000	-0.7833	0.0001
babylm	3000	-0.7874	0.0001
babylm	1	-0.7915	0.0001
babylm	5	-0.614	0.0067
wikitext-103	500	0.0815	0.7478
wikitext-103	1000	-0.4241	0.0794
wikitext-103	2000	-0.7482	0.0004
wikitext-103	3000	-0.7441	0.0004
wikitext-103	1	-0.7172	0.0008
wikitext-103	5	-0.7523	0.0003

Table 2: Spearman's ρ of model size (in terms of number of parameters) and Δ log-likelihood over the baseline LME model. Steps 1 and 5 refer to the first and fifth epoch.

D Detailed results: BabyLM challenge tasks

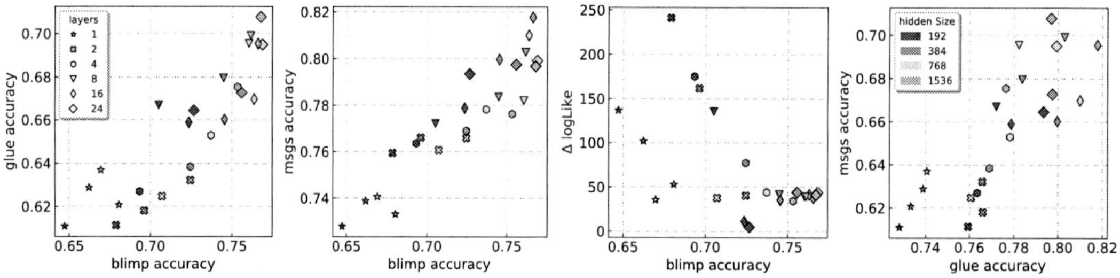

Figure 7: Correlation of LM performance on BLiMP vs. GLUE, BLiMP vs. MSGS, GLUE vs. MSGS.

Table 3: BLiMP accuracy by task and model

Task	1*192	1*384	1*768	1*1536	2*192	2*384	2*768	2*1536	4*192	4*384	4*768	4*1536	8*192	8*384	8*768	8*1536	16*192	16*384	16*768	16*1536	24*192	24*384	24*768	24*1536	OPT-125m (baseline)
anaphor-agreement	0.95 ± 0.01	0.96 ± 0.00	0.94 ± 0.01	0.95 ± 0.00	0.94 ± 0.01	0.96 ± 0.00	0.97 ± 0.00	0.97 ± 0.00	0.96 ± 0.00	0.97 ± 0.00	0.97 ± 0.00	0.98 ± 0.00	0.95 ± 0.01	0.97 ± 0.01	0.99 ± 0.00	0.98 ± 0.00	0.96 ± 0.01	0.97 ± 0.00	0.98 ± 0.00	0.97 ± 0.00	0.96 ± 0.01	0.97 ± 0.01	0.98 ± 0.00	0.98 ± 0.00	94.9
argument-structure	0.70 ± 0.00	0.71 ± 0.00	0.72 ± 0.00	0.72 ± 0.00	0.76 ± 0.00	0.76 ± 0.00	0.77 ± 0.00	0.77 ± 0.00	0.76 ± 0.00	0.78 ± 0.00	0.79 ± 0.00	0.79 ± 0.00	0.77 ± 0.00	0.79 ± 0.00	0.79 ± 0.00	0.79 ± 0.00	0.78 ± 0.00	0.80 ± 0.00	0.80 ± 0.00	0.80 ± 0.00	0.79 ± 0.00	0.80 ± 0.00	0.80 ± 0.00	0.79 ± 0.01	73.8
binding	0.67 ± 0.00	0.67 ± 0.00	0.68 ± 0.01	0.68 ± 0.00	0.69 ± 0.00	0.69 ± 0.02	0.72 ± 0.00	0.71 ± 0.02	0.72 ± 0.02	0.74 ± 0.01	0.74 ± 0.00	0.72 ± 0.00	0.72 ± 0.00	0.74 ± 0.00	0.74 ± 0.01	0.75 ± 0.00	0.73 ± 0.03	0.72 ± 0.00	0.76 ± 0.00	0.76 ± 0.01	0.74 ± 0.00	0.74 ± 0.00	0.76 ± 0.01	0.77 ± 0.01	73.8
control-raising	0.64 ± 0.01	0.66 ± 0.00	0.68 ± 0.01	0.67 ± 0.00	0.67 ± 0.00	0.69 ± 0.00	0.72 ± 0.00	0.73 ± 0.00	0.69 ± 0.00	0.70 ± 0.00	0.73 ± 0.00	0.73 ± 0.00	0.73 ± 0.00	0.74 ± 0.00	0.74 ± 0.01	0.74 ± 0.00	0.73 ± 0.00	0.74 ± 0.01	0.72 ± 0.00	0.75 ± 0.00	0.72 ± 0.00	0.75 ± 0.00	0.74 ± 0.00	0.76 ± 0.01	72.2
determiner-noun-agreement	0.85 ± 0.00	0.85 ± 0.01	0.87 ± 0.00	0.88 ± 0.00	0.91 ± 0.00	0.91 ± 0.00	0.92 ± 0.00	0.93 ± 0.00	0.90 ± 0.00	0.93 ± 0.00	0.93 ± 0.01	0.94 ± 0.00	0.92 ± 0.00	0.95 ± 0.00	0.94 ± 0.00	0.95 ± 0.00	0.93 ± 0.00	0.94 ± 0.00	0.94 ± 0.00	0.95 ± 0.00	0.94 ± 0.00	0.95 ± 0.00	0.94 ± 0.00	0.94 ± 0.00	93.1
ellipsis	0.57 ± 0.01	0.62 ± 0.01	0.63 ± 0.00	0.64 ± 0.01	0.62 ± 0.02	0.63 ± 0.00	0.70 ± 0.00	0.72 ± 0.01	0.66 ± 0.01	0.69 ± 0.01	0.75 ± 0.01	0.78 ± 0.02	0.71 ± 0.00	0.76 ± 0.01	0.82 ± 0.01	0.82 ± 0.01	0.75 ± 0.01	0.80 ± 0.00	0.82 ± 0.01	0.82 ± 0.03	0.76 ± 0.01	0.81 ± 0.00	0.84 ± 0.02	0.82 ± 0.01	80.5
filler-gap	0.64 ± 0.01	0.65 ± 0.00	0.65 ± 0.00	0.65 ± 0.01	0.67 ± 0.00	0.68 ± 0.00	0.70 ± 0.01	0.72 ± 0.00	0.68 ± 0.00	0.71 ± 0.00	0.73 ± 0.00	0.75 ± 0.00	0.70 ± 0.01	0.72 ± 0.00	0.74 ± 0.00	0.74 ± 0.00	0.72 ± 0.00	0.74 ± 0.01	0.75 ± 0.00	0.75 ± 0.01	0.73 ± 0.00	0.74 ± 0.00	0.76 ± 0.00	0.75 ± 0.01	73.6
irregular-forms	0.88 ± 0.01	0.90 ± 0.01	0.89 ± 0.01	0.89 ± 0.01	0.93 ± 0.00	0.93 ± 0.00	0.92 ± 0.01	0.93 ± 0.00	0.92 ± 0.00	0.91 ± 0.01	0.91 ± 0.00	0.90 ± 0.00	0.91 ± 0.02	0.90 ± 0.01	0.92 ± 0.01	0.92 ± 0.01	0.93 ± 0.00	0.92 ± 0.02	0.92 ± 0.01	0.92 ± 0.00	0.89 ± 0.03	0.90 ± 0.02	0.92 ± 0.00	0.87 ± 0.02	80.8
island-effects	0.54 ± 0.01	0.55 ± 0.01	0.56 ± 0.01	0.61 ± 0.02	0.50 ± 0.03	0.55 ± 0.01	0.52 ± 0.01	0.57 ± 0.02	0.56 ± 0.03	0.60 ± 0.01	0.63 ± 0.00	0.65 ± 0.01	0.55 ± 0.03	0.64 ± 0.02	0.66 ± 0.02	0.67 ± 0.00	0.61 ± 0.02	0.65 ± 0.01	0.65 ± 0.00	0.69 ± 0.01	0.62 ± 0.02	0.65 ± 0.01	0.68 ± 0.00	0.70 ± 0.00	51.6
npi-licensing	0.53 ± 0.01	0.52 ± 0.00	0.52 ± 0.00	0.56 ± 0.00	0.57 ± 0.00	0.64 ± 0.01	0.60 ± 0.02	0.63 ± 0.01	0.58 ± 0.04	0.65 ± 0.00	0.67 ± 0.01	0.72 ± 0.00	0.63 ± 0.00	0.65 ± 0.01	0.68 ± 0.00	0.71 ± 0.00	0.63 ± 0.01	0.69 ± 0.03	0.72 ± 0.01	0.70 ± 0.02	0.66 ± 0.02	0.75 ± 0.00	0.70 ± 0.01	0.70 ± 0.01	51.6
quantifiers	0.71 ± 0.01	0.71 ± 0.01	0.74 ± 0.01	0.73 ± 0.02	0.75 ± 0.01	0.71 ± 0.01	0.69 ± 0.01	0.71 ± 0.02	0.73 ± 0.01	0.75 ± 0.00	0.71 ± 0.03	0.74 ± 0.02	0.72 ± 0.02	0.76 ± 0.01	0.73 ± 0.01	0.70 ± 0.00	0.69 ± 0.02	0.71 ± 0.02	0.74 ± 0.00	0.74 ± 0.00	0.66 ± 0.00	0.69 ± 0.01	0.77 ± 0.01	0.75 ± 0.00	74.5
subject-verb-agreement	0.62 ± 0.00	0.64 ± 0.00	0.65 ± 0.00	0.67 ± 0.00	0.71 ± 0.00	0.76 ± 0.00	0.79 ± 0.01	0.81 ± 0.01	0.75 ± 0.00	0.83 ± 0.00	0.85 ± 0.00	0.87 ± 0.00	0.81 ± 0.00	0.86 ± 0.00	0.87 ± 0.00	0.88 ± 0.01	0.84 ± 0.01	0.88 ± 0.00	0.87 ± 0.00	0.88 ± 0.00	0.84 ± 0.00	0.87 ± 0.01	0.87 ± 0.00	0.88 ± 0.01	77.3
hypernym	0.51 ± 0.00	0.50 ± 0.01	0.49 ± 0.00	0.48 ± 0.00	0.49 ± 0.00	0.48 ± 0.00	0.47 ± 0.01	0.48 ± 0.00	0.49 ± 0.01	0.48 ± 0.00	0.50 ± 0.00	0.48 ± 0.01	0.48 ± 0.00	0.48 ± 0.01	0.48 ± 0.00	0.48 ± 0.00	0.49 ± 0.01	0.48 ± 0.00	0.46 ± 0.00	0.46 ± 0.00	0.48 ± 0.00	0.48 ± 0.00	0.47 ± 0.01	0.46 ± 0.00	46.3
qa-congruence-easy	0.47 ± 0.03	0.55 ± 0.02	0.52 ± 0.01	0.59 ± 0.00	0.50 ± 0.02	0.58 ± 0.02	0.60 ± 0.01	0.66 ± 0.00	0.58 ± 0.01	0.64 ± 0.02	0.67 ± 0.04	0.71 ± 0.01	0.59 ± 0.03	0.66 ± 0.01	0.69 ± 0.01	0.68 ± 0.03	0.59 ± 0.02	0.66 ± 0.02	0.71 ± 0.01	0.70 ± 0.04	0.62 ± 0.01	0.69 ± 0.03	0.72 ± 0.00	0.68 ± 0.03	76.5
qa-congruence-tricky	0.29 ± 0.00	0.36 ± 0.01	0.35 ± 0.05	0.42 ± 0.02	0.35 ± 0.01	0.39 ± 0.02	0.42 ± 0.01	0.41 ± 0.01	0.33 ± 0.04	0.41 ± 0.04	0.45 ± 0.01	0.46 ± 0.00	0.32 ± 0.00	0.48 ± 0.02	0.52 ± 0.01	0.48 ± 0.01	0.39 ± 0.03	0.40 ± 0.01	0.50 ± 0.00	0.51 ± 0.00	0.38 ± 0.03	0.50 ± 0.04	0.46 ± 0.00	0.53 ± 0.04	47.9
subject-aux-inversion	0.83 ± 0.02	0.81 ± 0.00	0.83 ± 0.01	0.81 ± 0.00	0.83 ± 0.02	0.82 ± 0.01	0.80 ± 0.00	0.86 ± 0.01	0.84 ± 0.00	0.82 ± 0.02	0.80 ± 0.02	0.82 ± 0.02	0.81 ± 0.01	0.83 ± 0.01	0.84 ± 0.01	0.86 ± 0.01	0.85 ± 0.02	0.83 ± 0.01	0.84 ± 0.00	0.85 ± 0.02	0.86 ± 0.01	0.83 ± 0.02	0.87 ± 0.02	0.88 ± 0.01	85.3
turn-taking	0.61 ± 0.02	0.60 ± 0.01	0.65 ± 0.01	0.61 ± 0.01	0.66 ± 0.01	0.65 ± 0.02	0.71 ± 0.02	0.71 ± 0.00	0.64 ± 0.01	0.71 ± 0.01	0.71 ± 0.01	0.75 ± 0.02	0.66 ± 0.02	0.73 ± 0.01	0.78 ± 0.01	0.79 ± 0.01	0.69 ± 0.01	0.74 ± 0.01	0.80 ± 0.01	0.77 ± 0.01	0.72 ± 0.01	0.73 ± 0.00	0.78 ± 0.01	0.78 ± 0.00	82.9
Average	0.65 ± 0.03	0.66 ± 0.03	0.67 ± 0.03	0.68 ± 0.02	0.68 ± 0.03	0.7 ± 0.03	0.71 ± 0.03	0.72 ± 0.03	0.69 ± 0.03	0.72 ± 0.02	0.74 ± 0.02	0.75 ± 0.02	0.71 ± 0.03	0.74 ± 0.02	0.76 ± 0.02	0.76 ± 0.02	0.72 ± 0.03	0.75 ± 0.03	0.76 ± 0.02	0.77 ± 0.02	0.73 ± 0.03	0.76 ± 0.02	0.77 ± 0.02	0.77 ± 0.02	73.11

Table 4: GLUE accuracy by task and model

Task	1*192	1*384	1*768	1*1536	2*192	2*384	2*768	2*1536	4*192	4*384	4*768	4*1536	8*192	8*384	8*768	8*1536	16*192	16*384	16*768	16*1536	24*192	24*384	24*768	24*1536	OPT-125m (baseline)
boolq	0.59 ± 0.00	0.60 ± 0.00	0.59 ± 0.00	0.60 ± 0.00	0.58 ± 0.00	0.60 ± 0.00	0.59 ± 0.00	0.60 ± 0.00	0.59 ± 0.00	0.60 ± 0.00	0.60 ± 0.01	0.59 ± 0.00	0.60 ± 0.00	0.60 ± 0.01	0.60 ± 0.00	0.61 ± 0.00	0.60 ± 0.00	0.59 ± 0.00	0.59 ± 0.01	0.61 ± 0.01	0.60 ± 0.00	0.60 ± 0.00	0.60 ± 0.00	0.64 ± 0.01	66.0
cola	0.69 ± 0.00	0.70 ± 0.00	0.69 ± 0.00	0.70 ± 0.00	0.69 ± 0.00	0.69 ± 0.00	0.69 ± 0.00	0.69 ± 0.00	0.69 ± 0.00	0.69 ± 0.00	0.70 ± 0.00	0.70 ± 0.00	0.69 ± 0.00	0.69 ± 0.00	0.70 ± 0.00	0.74 ± 0.00	0.70 ± 0.00	0.70 ± 0.00	0.71 ± 0.00	0.74 ± 0.00	0.70 ± 0.00	0.71 ± 0.00	0.75 ± 0.00	0.76 ± 0.00	36
mnli	0.55 ± 0.00	0.56 ± 0.00	0.58 ± 0.00	0.53 ± 0.00	0.52 ± 0.01	0.54 ± 0.00	0.55 ± 0.00	0.57 ± 0.00	0.54 ± 0.01	0.59 ± 0.02	0.64 ± 0.00	0.65 ± 0.00	0.67 ± 0.00	0.71 ± 0.00	0.72 ± 0.00	0.74 ± 0.00	0.63 ± 0.00	0.66 ± 0.00	0.67 ± 0.00	0.74 ± 0.00	0.64 ± 0.00	0.66 ± 0.00	0.74 ± 0.00	0.75 ± 0.00	70.1
mnli-mm	0.56 ± 0.00	0.57 ± 0.00	0.57 ± 0.00	0.54 ± 0.00	0.53 ± 0.00	0.54 ± 0.00	0.55 ± 0.00	0.58 ± 0.01	0.56 ± 0.01	0.61 ± 0.02	0.67 ± 0.00	0.68 ± 0.00	0.69 ± 0.00	0.72 ± 0.00	0.73 ± 0.00	0.74 ± 0.00	0.65 ± 0.00	0.68 ± 0.00	0.70 ± 0.00	0.76 ± 0.00	0.67 ± 0.00	0.69 ± 0.00	0.75 ± 0.00	0.76 ± 0.00	71.9
mrpc	0.69 ± 0.00	0.69 ± 0.00	0.69 ± 0.00	0.69 ± 0.00	0.69 ± 0.00	0.69 ± 0.00	0.69 ± 0.00	0.69 ± 0.00	0.69 ± 0.00	0.69 ± 0.00	0.69 ± 0.00	0.69 ± 0.00	0.69 ± 0.00	0.69 ± 0.00	0.69 ± 0.00	0.69 ± 0.00	0.70 ± 0.00	0.69 ± 0.00	0.69 ± 0.00	0.70 ± 0.01	0.69 ± 0.00	0.69 ± 0.00	0.69 ± 0.00	0.68 ± 0.01	82.1
multirc	0.50 ± 0.00	0.52 ± 0.00	0.51 ± 0.00	0.51 ± 0.01	0.50 ± 0.01	0.49 ± 0.02	0.51 ± 0.01	0.52 ± 0.01	0.51 ± 0.01	0.51 ± 0.02	0.52 ± 0.01	0.53 ± 0.00	0.51 ± 0.01	0.50 ± 0.01	0.53 ± 0.01	0.51 ± 0.00	0.52 ± 0.01	0.48 ± 0.01	0.50 ± 0.01	0.52 ± 0.02	0.50 ± 0.00	0.50 ± 0.01	0.50 ± 0.00	0.51 ± 0.01	61.1
qnli	0.60 ± 0.00	0.61 ± 0.00	0.60 ± 0.00	0.60 ± 0.00	0.60 ± 0.00	0.61 ± 0.00	0.61 ± 0.00	0.62 ± 0.00	0.62 ± 0.00	0.69 ± 0.05	0.78 ± 0.00	0.80 ± 0.00	0.74 ± 0.02	0.79 ± 0.00	0.81 ± 0.00	0.82 ± 0.01	0.78 ± 0.00	0.80 ± 0.00	0.81 ± 0.00	0.82 ± 0.00	0.78 ± 0.00	0.80 ± 0.00	0.82 ± 0.00	0.83 ± 0.00	80.1
qqp	0.76 ± 0.00	0.76 ± 0.00	0.77 ± 0.00	0.74 ± 0.00	0.71 ± 0.00	0.73 ± 0.00	0.74 ± 0.00	0.75 ± 0.00	0.73 ± 0.01	0.75 ± 0.01	0.78 ± 0.00	0.80 ± 0.00	0.81 ± 0.00	0.83 ± 0.00	0.84 ± 0.00	0.85 ± 0.00	0.77 ± 0.00	0.79 ± 0.00	0.80 ± 0.00	0.85 ± 0.00	0.78 ± 0.00	0.79 ± 0.00	0.84 ± 0.00	0.86 ± 0.00	77.8
rte	0.47 ± 0.00	0.57 ± 0.00	0.61 ± 0.00	0.56 ± 0.04	0.53 ± 0.01	0.50 ± 0.01	0.55 ± 0.01	0.52 ± 0.02	0.49 ± 0.00	0.51 ± 0.02	0.50 ± 0.00	0.58 ± 0.04	0.56 ± 0.01	0.53 ± 0.04	0.56 ± 0.02	0.51 ± 0.00	0.51 ± 0.00	0.53 ± 0.00	0.53 ± 0.02	0.52 ± 0.01	0.52 ± 0.01	0.56 ± 0.01	0.56 ± 0.04	0.54 ± 0.01	67.7
sst2	0.82 ± 0.00	0.83 ± 0.00	0.85 ± 0.00	0.84 ± 0.01	0.85 ± 0.00	0.85 ± 0.00	0.86 ± 0.00	0.86 ± 0.00	0.86 ± 0.00	0.85 ± 0.00	0.86 ± 0.00	0.86 ± 0.01	0.86 ± 0.00	0.86 ± 0.00	0.88 ± 0.00	0.87 ± 0.00	0.84 ± 0.00	0.85 ± 0.00	0.87 ± 0.00	0.89 ± 0.00	0.85 ± 0.00	0.87 ± 0.00	0.88 ± 0.00	0.89 ± 0.00	86.6
wsc	0.48 ± 0.00	0.52 ± 0.00	0.54 ± 0.00	0.53 ± 0.03	0.52 ± 0.03	0.55 ± 0.03	0.53 ± 0.01	0.55 ± 0.03	0.61 ± 0.01	0.52 ± 0.00	0.46 ± 0.00	0.55 ± 0.03	0.51 ± 0.04	0.56 ± 0.00	0.59 ± 0.02	0.61 ± 0.00	0.57 ± 0.01	0.49 ± 0.01	0.49 ± 0.01	0.50 ± 0.02	0.58 ± 0.00	0.52 ± 0.02	0.51 ± 0.02	0.57 ± 0.00	59.0
Average	0.61 ± 0.03	0.63 ± 0.03	0.64 ± 0.03	0.62 ± 0.02	0.61 ± 0.02	0.62 ± 0.02	0.62 ± 0.02	0.63 ± 0.02	0.63 ± 0.02	0.64 ± 0.02	0.65 ± 0.03	0.68 ± 0.02	0.67 ± 0.02	0.68 ± 0.02	0.7 ± 0.02	0.7 ± 0.03	0.66 ± 0.02	0.66 ± 0.03	0.67 ± 0.03	0.7 ± 0.03	0.66 ± 0.02	0.67 ± 0.02	0.7 ± 0.03	0.71 ± 0.03	68.95

Table 5: MSGS accuracy by task and model

Task	1*192	1*384	1*768	1*1536	2*192	2*384	2*768	2*1536	4*192	4*384	4*768	4*1536	8*192	8*384	8*768	8*1536	16*192	16*384	16*768	16*1536	24*192	24*384	24*768	24*1536
main-verb-control	0.63 ± 0.01	0.66 ± 0.01	0.65 ± 0.00	0.66 ± 0.00	0.78 ± 0.04	0.90 ± 0.01	0.91 ± 0.00	0.93 ± 0.01	0.92 ± 0.00	0.95 ± 0.01	0.99 ± 0.00	0.99 ± 0.00	0.99 ± 0.00	1.00 ± 0.00	1.00 ± 0.00	1.00 ± 0.00	0.99 ± 0.00	0.99 ± 0.00	1.00 ± 0.00	1.00 ± 0.00	0.99 ± 0.00	1.00 ± 0.00	1.00 ± 0.00	1.00 ± 0.00
control-raising-control	0.82 ± 0.01	0.85 ± 0.00	0.84 ± 0.02	0.90 ± 0.00	0.88 ± 0.01	0.91 ± 0.01	0.93 ± 0.00	0.93 ± 0.00	0.92 ± 0.00	0.94 ± 0.01	0.94 ± 0.01	0.96 ± 0.01	0.92 ± 0.00	0.93 ± 0.01	0.96 ± 0.01	0.96 ± 0.00	0.93 ± 0.01	0.95 ± 0.01	0.97 ± 0.00	0.97 ± 0.00	0.94 ± 0.01	0.95 ± 0.01	0.96 ± 0.01	0.96 ± 0.00
syntactic-category-control	0.82 ± 0.02	0.82 ± 0.00	0.84 ± 0.00	0.79 ± 0.01	0.90 ± 0.01	0.88 ± 0.01	0.82 ± 0.02	0.83 ± 0.01	0.81 ± 0.01	0.78 ± 0.01	0.83 ± 0.01	0.80 ± 0.01	0.83 ± 0.01	0.86 ± 0.00	0.83 ± 0.00	0.84 ± 0.01	0.83 ± 0.00	0.84 ± 0.01	0.87 ± 0.02	0.78 ± 0.00	0.83 ± 0.01	0.84 ± 0.02	0.83 ± 0.00	0.82 ± 0.01
lexical-content-the-control	0.79 ± 0.01	0.79 ± 0.00	0.80 ± 0.02	0.76 ± 0.00	0.80 ± 0.02	0.76 ± 0.00	0.75 ± 0.00	0.75 ± 0.00	0.81 ± 0.01	0.83 ± 0.00	0.79 ± 0.01	0.76 ± 0.00	0.79 ± 0.01	0.80 ± 0.03	0.77 ± 0.01	0.76 ± 0.00	0.78 ± 0.01	0.77 ± 0.01	0.76 ± 0.00	0.76 ± 0.00	0.88 ± 0.04	0.78 ± 0.00	0.76 ± 0.01	0.75 ± 0.00
relative-position-control	0.96 ± 0.01	0.98 ± 0.00	0.95 ± 0.01	0.92 ± 0.00	0.97 ± 0.00	0.97 ± 0.00	0.96 ± 0.00	0.97 ± 0.00	0.98 ± 0.00	0.98 ± 0.00	0.97 ± 0.01	0.99 ± 0.00	0.99 ± 0.00	1.00 ± 0.00	0.99 ± 0.00	0.99 ± 0.00	0.98 ± 0.01	1.00 ± 0.00	1.00 ± 0.00	0.99 ± 0.00	0.99 ± 0.00	0.98 ± 0.01	1.00 ± 0.00	0.99 ± 0.00
main-verb-lexical-content-the	0.67 ± 0.00	0.66 ± 0.00	0.66 ± 0.00	0.67 ± 0.00	0.67 ± 0.00	0.67 ± 0.00	0.67 ± 0.00	0.67 ± 0.00	0.68 ± 0.00	0.67 ± 0.00	0.68 ± 0.01	0.69 ± 0.01	0.67 ± 0.00	0.69 ± 0.00	0.68 ± 0.01	0.73 ± 0.02	0.69 ± 0.01	0.75 ± 0.00	0.71 ± 0.00	0.81 ± 0.01	0.71 ± 0.01	0.73 ± 0.01	0.77 ± 0.02	0.76 ± 0.01
main-verb-relative-token-position	0.66 ± 0.00	0.66 ± 0.00	0.66 ± 0.00	0.67 ± 0.00	0.67 ± 0.00	0.66 ± 0.00	0.67 ± 0.00	0.67 ± 0.00	0.67 ± 0.00	0.67 ± 0.00	0.69 ± 0.01	0.68 ± 0.00	0.66 ± 0.00	0.68 ± 0.01	0.70 ± 0.01	0.75 ± 0.01	0.69 ± 0.01	0.76 ± 0.01	0.74 ± 0.01	0.78 ± 0.01	0.72 ± 0.02	0.74 ± 0.01	0.77 ± 0.00	0.78 ± 0.02
syntactic-category-lexical-content-the	0.67 ± 0.03	0.70 ± 0.00	0.73 ± 0.01	0.71 ± 0.00	0.70 ± 0.01	0.67 ± 0.03	0.67 ± 0.03	0.70 ± 0.07	0.62 ± 0.02	0.65 ± 0.00	0.68 ± 0.01	0.64 ± 0.01	0.66 ± 0.02	0.65 ± 0.02	0.65 ± 0.02	0.68 ± 0.02	0.67 ± 0.02	0.67 ± 0.03	0.68 ± 0.01	0.63 ± 0.00	0.64 ± 0.01	0.67 ± 0.01	0.66 ± 0.00	0.66 ± 0.01
syntactic-category-relative-position	0.66 ± 0.00	0.66 ± 0.00	0.68 ± 0.00	0.66 ± 0.00	0.65 ± 0.01	0.67 ± 0.01	0.66 ± 0.00	0.63 ± 0.00	0.65 ± 0.01	0.63 ± 0.00	0.65 ± 0.00	0.64 ± 0.00	0.64 ± 0.01	0.64 ± 0.00	0.63 ± 0.00	0.64 ± 0.01	0.63 ± 0.01	0.62 ± 0.00	0.63 ± 0.00	0.63 ± 0.00	0.62 ± 0.00	0.62 ± 0.00	0.62 ± 0.01	0.61 ± 0.00
control-raising-lexical-content-the	0.66 ± 0.00	0.67 ± 0.00	0.67 ± 0.00	0.66 ± 0.00	0.67 ± 0.00	0.67 ± 0.00	0.66 ± 0.00	0.67 ± 0.00	0.67 ± 0.00	0.67 ± 0.00	0.68 ± 0.01	0.70 ± 0.01	0.68 ± 0.00	0.68 ± 0.00	0.70 ± 0.02	0.79 ± 0.01	0.68 ± 0.00	0.75 ± 0.00	0.82 ± 0.05	0.91 ± 0.01	0.72 ± 0.00	0.75 ± 0.03	0.71 ± 0.02	0.82 ± 0.01
control-raising-relative-token-position	0.67 ± 0.00	0.67 ± 0.00	0.67 ± 0.00	0.68 ± 0.00	0.67 ± 0.00	0.67 ± 0.00	0.67 ± 0.00	0.67 ± 0.00	0.67 ± 0.00	0.67 ± 0.00	0.69 ± 0.01	0.69 ± 0.00	0.67 ± 0.00	0.69 ± 0.01	0.69 ± 0.00	0.69 ± 0.00	0.68 ± 0.01	0.69 ± 0.00	0.73 ± 0.01	0.74 ± 0.01	0.69 ± 0.01	0.71 ± 0.01	0.72 ± 0.00	0.71 ± 0.00
Average	0.73 ± 0.02	0.74 ± 0.02	0.74 ± 0.02	0.73 ± 0.02	0.76 ± 0.02	0.77 ± 0.03	0.76 ± 0.02	0.77 ± 0.03	0.76 ± 0.03	0.77 ± 0.03	0.78 ± 0.03	0.78 ± 0.03	0.77 ± 0.03	0.78 ± 0.03	0.78 ± 0.03	0.8 ± 0.03	0.78 ± 0.03	0.8 ± 0.03	0.81 ± 0.03	0.82 ± 0.03	0.79 ± 0.03	0.8 ± 0.03	0.8 ± 0.03	0.8 ± 0.03

Baby's CoThought: Leveraging Large Language Models for Enhanced Reasoning in Compact Models

Zheyu Zhang[*♣] **Han Yang**[*♣,◇] **Bolei Ma**[*♠] **David Rügamer**[♠,♡] **Ercong Nie**[†♣,♡]

[♣]Center for Information and Language Processing, LMU Munich
[◇]GESIS - Leibniz Institute for the Social Sciences, Cologne
[♠]Department of Statistics, LMU Munich [♡]Munich Center for Machine Learning

zheyu.zhang@campus.lmu.de han.yang@gesis.org
{bolei.ma, david.ruegamer}@stat.uni-muenchen.de
nie@cis.lmu.de

Abstract

Large Language Models (LLMs) demonstrate remarkable performance on a variety of natural language understanding (NLU) tasks, primarily due to their in-context learning ability. This ability could be applied to building baby-like models, i.e. models at small scales, improving training efficiency. In this paper, we propose a "**CoThought**" pipeline, which efficiently trains smaller "baby" language models (BabyLMs) by leveraging the **C**hain **o**f **Thought** prompting of LLMs. Our pipeline restructures a dataset of less than 100M in size using GPT-3.5-turbo, transforming it into task-oriented, human-readable texts that are comparable to the school texts for language learners. The BabyLM is then pretrained on this restructured dataset in a RoBERTa fashion. In evaluations across 4 benchmarks, our BabyLM outperforms the vanilla RoBERTa in 10 linguistic, NLU, and question-answering tasks by more than 3 points, showing a superior ability to extract contextual information. These results suggest that compact LMs pretrained on small, LLM-restructured data can better understand tasks and achieve improved performance.[1]

1 Introduction

Recent advances in language modeling of Large Language Models (LLMs) have shown great performance potential on diverse NLP tasks. A large number of work has been proposed towards enhancing LLMs pretraining at massive scales (Devlin et al., 2019; Radford and Narasimhan, 2018; Brown et al., 2020). However, less attention has been paid to language model (LM) pretraining at smaller human-like data scales, i.e. smaller data scales, which are similar to the amount of language data for human language acquisition.

Studies in language acquisition demonstrate that humans predominantly acquire language in early life stages by observing their environment. Significant progress in language communication and usage is typically achieved by early childhood (Tomasello, 2003; Saxton, 2010). Previous studies show that language modeling is to some extent similar to children's language acquisition, as they both require input data from the outside world and learn the data by updating knowledge about the outside world repeatedly (Nikolaus and Fourtassi, 2021; Chang and Bergen, 2022; Evanson et al., 2023). It is reasonable to apply this human cognitive process to LM pretraining by using relatively small sets of pretraining data that are comparable to the text data for human language acquisition.

While a child learns a piece of knowledge by continuously obtaining relevant examples from the outside world and updating its knowledge base, pretrained LLMs have the capacity to learn and complete previously unknown tasks when given several task samples or instructions already from the inside of their context, the process of which is known as "*In-Context Learning*" (ICL) (Brown et al., 2020). A more recent advance of ICL called "*Chain of Thought*" (CoT) (Wei et al., 2022) significantly enhances the reasoning abilities of LLMs. CoT enables LLMs to perform a series of intermediate reasoning steps by providing a few CoT demonstrations as examples during the training process. This method has been found to be very effective, especially in complex reasoning tasks.

The LLM is like a teacher who is able to transfer knowledge by reformulating raw data from the outside world into a task-like text format by CoT prompting, making the data more suitable for teaching. The BabyLM is like a student who is trained

[*] Equal contribution.
[†] Corresponding author.
[1]The code for data processing and model training is available at: https://github.com/oooranz/Baby-CoThought.

Proceedings of the 27th Conference on Computational Natural Language Learning: Volume 2: The BabyLM Challenge, pages 158–170
December 6-7, 2023 ©2023 Association for Computational Linguistics

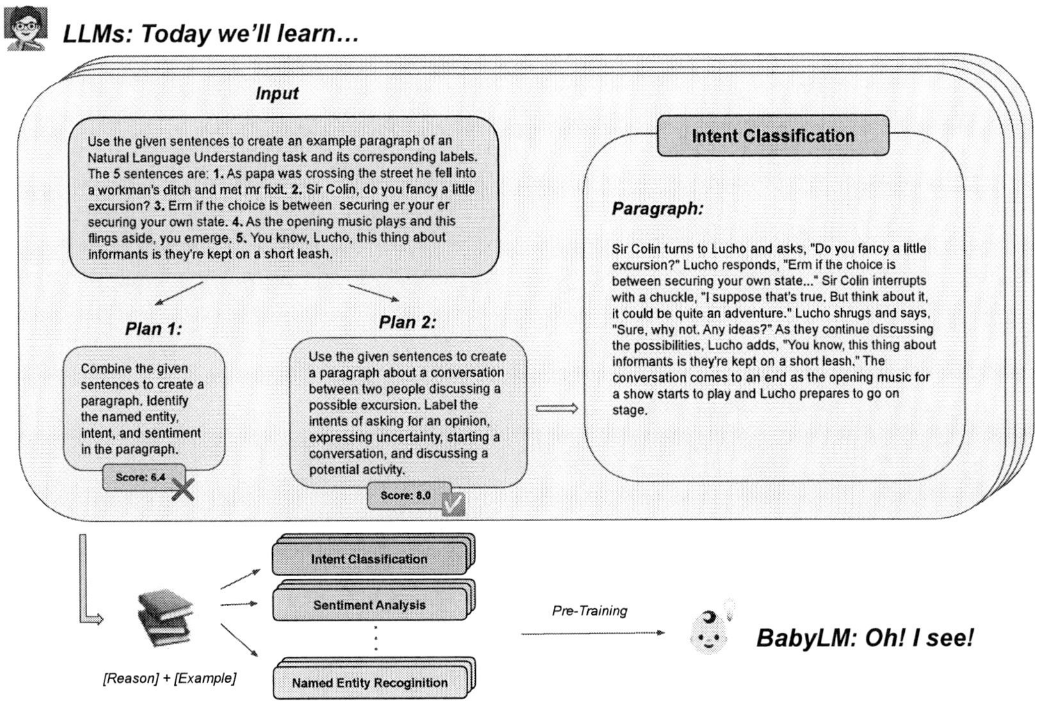

Figure 1: Overview of the "CoThought" pipeline. We propose to generate NLU examples from discrete short sentences using CoT prompting and an automatic scoring mechanism. This constructs a pretraining dataset in a *[Reason] + [Example]* format, which is then used to pretrain smaller models.

based on this generated text. In this work, we propose "**CoThought**" pipeline to pretrain a BabyLM with human-like smaller corpus data, by leveraging the LLM's **Chain of Thought** feature and the child's cognitive learning ability. In this way, the LLM and the child are "co-thinking" during the training process. We use the "CoThought" approach to train our BabyLM, combining the productivity of the LLM with the effectiveness of human language acquisition for LM pretraining.

Our overall framework is illustrated in Figure 1. The raw pretraining data is provided by Warstadt et al. (2023) in the BabyLM Challenge, which has the goal of sample-efficient pretraining on a developmentally plausible corpus at a small human-like data scale. We choose the loose track of the BabyLM Challenge, where we apply our "CoThought" pipeline and use the LLM GPT-3.5-turbo[2] to preprocess the raw data. For every 5 sentences of the raw data, the GPT-3.5-turbo uses CoT prompting to propose different NLU tasks and selects the best task. Then, it combines these 5 sentences into a task-like text based on the best task for our BabyLM to learn. The BabyLM is pretrained on the augmented data in a RoBERTa (Liu et al., 2019) fashion. Our BabyLM pretrained in the CoThought pipeline notably outperforms the original RoBERTa model on common benchmarks.

Our work makes contributions in

1) proposing the CoThought pretraining pipeline fitting the human-like data scenarios,

2) pretraining a BabyLM model of the RoBERTa-base architect in the CoThought pipeline surpassing the original RoBERTa model on several tasks, and

3) providing insights of the CoThought pipeline by conducting linguistic case analysis on representative tasks.

2 Related Work

Language Acquisition and Modelling The language acquisition of children is a widely studied topic in linguistics. The empiricism of language acquisition contends that language ability is a component of social cognitive ability and children acquire

[2]https://platform.openai.com/docs/models/gpt-3-5

language through language communication and language use (Bybee, 2001; Pullum and Scholz, 2002; Tomasello, 2003; Saxton, 2010). According to the Universal Grammar (Chomsky, 1957), language norms and parameters are hard-wired within every single person, and learning a language is just a matter of adjusting those parameters (Gegov et al., 2014). In this way, child language acquisition and language modeling are similar, as the neural language models such as BERT (Devlin et al., 2019) and GPT (Radford and Narasimhan, 2018) are pretrained based on big corpora with their model parameters tuned during pretaining. Recent studies show the applicability of language models to child language development tracking. Nikolaus and Fourtassi (2021) propose an integrated perception- and production-based learning and highlight that children are not only understood as passively absorbing the input but also as actively participating in the construction of their linguistic knowledge in language learning. Chang and Bergen (2022) study the factors that predict words' ages of acquisition in contemporary language models compared to word acquisition in children. Evanson et al. (2023) compare the sequence of learning stages of language models with child language acquisition.

In-Context Learning (ICL) LLMs like GPT-3 (Brown et al., 2020) make "*In-Context Learning*" possible, which means the model makes predictions by learning from a natural language prompt describing the language task or learning from (only a few) examples. Based on the concept of ICL, recent research has demonstrated that LLMs can be used to extract relevant knowledge from the content. Liu et al. (2022) propose to use GPT-3 to generate pertinent contexts and then supply those contexts as extra input in order to answer a commonsense question. Yu et al. (2023) employ a generate-then-read pipeline which first prompts a large language model to generate contextual documents based on a given question, and then reads the generated documents to produce the final answer.

Chain of Thought (CoT) Wei et al. (2022) introduced "*Chain of Thought*", which is a series of intermediate reasoning steps a few chain of thought demonstrations are provided as exemplars in prompting, in order to improve the ICL ability of LLMs to perform complex reasoning. Kojima et al. (2023) demonstrate the zero-shot performance of CoT. Paranjape et al. (2023) introduces a framework that uses frozen LLMs to automatically generate intermediate reasoning steps as a program. Yao et al. (2023) put forward a "*Tree of Thoughts*" (ToT) framework, which generalizes over CoT to prompting language models and enables exploration over coherent units of text ("thoughts") that serve as intermediate steps toward problem solving. A more recent study (Gu et al., 2023) proposes a pretraining for ICL framework which pretrains the model on a set of "intrinsic tasks" in the general plain-text corpus using the simple language modeling objective to enhance the language models' ICL ability.

3 Method

In the realm of cognitive learning, the teacher's thought process greatly influences the way instructional content is delivered, which in turn impacts the students' understanding (Chew and Cerbin, 2021). Our method attempts to mimic this process. The LLMs, in the role of the teacher, use CoT prompting to reinterpret the raw data, generating task-like text that incorporates the context of the sentences and enriches the learning materials.

We first introduce an overview of our CoThought pipeline (see Figure 1 for an illustration) and then describe the details in the following sections.

3.1 Problem Statement

The genesis of our research lies in addressing a significant problem within the context of the BabyLM Challenge as proposed by Warstadt et al. (2023). The goal of this challenge is to conduct sample-efficient pretraining on a developmentally plausible corpus at a small human-like data scale, which we previously introduced. Nevertheless, the majority of the training data provided consists of discrete short sentences. As an illustration, below are some of the provided sentences:

```
- You want your book back, don't you?
- Let's see, do you want to see who this is?
- This is Big Bird.
- Enough with that.
- Can you read your book again? You like the
  book?
```

These sentences, albeit contextually rich, are sampled from a wide range of sources including dialogues, scripted content, fiction, nonfiction, and child-directed materials. Due to the diverse and fragmented nature of this dataset, the sentences often lack strong semantic ties with each other, making it difficult for models to learn contextual and coherent representations.

In response, we propose a method that transforms these fragmented sentences into cohesive units using LLMs, subsequently enabling more effective learning for the smaller models. The succeeding sections will provide a succinct outline of our pipeline and process.

3.2 Creative NLU-Example Generation

Inspired by recent studies that demonstrate the capability of LLMs to generate rationales supporting their predictions, we invent a novel task called Creative NLU-Example Generation (CNLU-EG), inspired by the Creative Writing task proposed by the "*Tree of Thought*" (Yao et al., 2023). Instead of creating coherent paragraphs from random sentences, CNLU-EG employs the provided sentences to generate coherent paragraphs, which define a plausible intrinsic NLU task and its corresponding labels. In this task, we employ the reasoning capability of LLMs to generate rationales for training smaller baby models.

We first remove any duplicate sentences from the BabyLM_100M (Warstadt et al., 2023) D. After the cleaning process, we randomly sample five unique sentences $\{x_i\}_{i \in D}$ from the cleaned dataset D. We initiate the task by providing a specific CoT prompt p to the LLM. This prompt instructs the LLM to first create a plan, then use the provided sentences to compose an example paragraph that illustrates a possible intrinsic NLU task, and finally generate the corresponding labels for this task. Given the creative nature of the task, we use a zero-shot prompt here. The prompt is structured such that it encourages the LLM to present the output in four distinct sections: the plan, the paragraph, the task, and the labels.

Once the LLM receives the prompt p, for each sentence $x_i, i \in D$, the LLM generates an execution plan $\hat{r}_i$, a paragraph $\hat{e}_i$ embodying an example of a possible NLU task, the task name $\hat{t}_i$, and the corresponding labels $\hat{y}_i$.

CNLU-EG essentially transforms the original, discrete sentences into a structured task, anchoring the sentences to a common theme or question. This 'taskification' process helps to create a more cohesive narrative, enabling the baby model to gain a more contextual and comprehensive understanding of the sentences.

We also incorporate a scoring mechanism, to assess the coherence of the generated content. We use a separate simple zero-shot prompt, p_s, to instruct the LLM to analyze the composed paragraph and assign a coherence score ranging from 1 to 10. For each task output, the LLM generates five such coherence scores from the same scoring prompt p_s, and these scores are then averaged to produce a final coherence score. According to our settings, we explicitly direct the LLM to generate two distinct plans for each task. Each plan is independently scored, and the one that achieves a higher coherence score is selected for subsequent steps.

In this way, the LLM functions as a teacher, generating examples of possible NLU tasks, providing insights into how these examples were created, and supplying the corresponding labels. This collection of generated plans and example paragraphs forms the training data for the smaller model to learn from.

3.3 Training Data Construction

Our objective is to construct a high-quality dataset for pretraining our small model, ensuring the instances included in the training set are coherent and task-relevant. As previously discussed, each instance in our data comprises a tuple: an example e and a corresponding plan r, denoted as $[e, r]$. However, not all generated instances meet the quality criteria necessary for effective learning.

To filter out lower-quality instances, we employ the coherency score obtained through the p_s prompt. We set a threshold, stipulating that only instances with a coherency score of $s \geq 7.0$ are included in the training data. This threshold was empirically established based on extensive manual analysis to ensure a satisfactory level of coherence and quality in the dataset. Mathematically, this can be represented as:

$$D_{select} = [e_i, r_i] : i \in D, s_i \geq 7.0 \quad (1)$$

Here, D denotes the initial set of generated instances and D_{select} represents the selected high-quality instances that are used for training.

Another important aspect of our methodology is leveraging the correlation between segments with similar intrinsic tasks. Studies indicate that such segments when grouped together, provide valuable information for ICL (Gu et al., 2023). Therefore, we aim to collate instances with similar tasks, denoted as T, into grouped sets, which we denote as

G_T.

$$G_T = [e_i, r_i] : i \in D_{select}, t_i = T \qquad (2)$$

In the equation above, t_i represents the task type of the i-th instance, and G_T denotes the set of instances from D_{select} that are associated with task type T.

In the end, we amalgamate these grouped sets to create a comprehensive pretraining dataset containing N instances.

$$D_{pretrain} = \bigcup_{T \in \mathcal{T}} G_T \qquad (3)$$

Here, $\mathcal{T}$ represents the set of all task types and G_T denotes the set of instances corresponding to each task type T in D_{select}.

Through these rigorous steps, we ensure that the final training data is both high-quality and task-relevant, optimally structured to facilitate effective learning in our small model.

4 Experimental Setups

We conducted our experiments in three parts, the generation of the additional data used for training, the pretraining of the language model, and the evaluation.

4.1 Data Generation via CoT Prompting

We generated first our extended data based on the dataset `babylm_100M` (Warstadt et al., 2023), which contains subsets including AOCHILDES, BNC spoken, cbt, children stories, Gutenberg, pen subtitles, qed, simple Wikipedia, switchboard, and Wikipedia.[3]

We leveraged the API of GPT-3.5-turbo from OpenAI and provided CoT prompt with the format:

```
- Use the given sentences to create an example
  paragraph of an NLU task and its corresponding
  labels. The 5 sentences are: input.

- Make a plan then write and determine. Your
  output should be of the following format:

- Plan:

- Your plan here.

- Paragraph:

- Your paragraph here.

- Task:

- [Only the task name here, without additional
  information.]

- Labels:

- [Only the labels here, without additional
  information.]
```

The GPT will generate the corresponding answers in the defined format. To evaluate the generated task plans, we prompt the GPT again with the score prompt in the format:

```
- Analyze the following paragraph, then at the
  last line conclude "Thus the coherency score
  is s", where s is an integer from 1 to 10.
```

We filter out the generated texts with a score lower than 7. The additional data will be generated by the GPT with the selected proposals as prompts.

4.2 Pretraining

We then trained a RoBERTa model with the extended dataset using `RobertaForMaskedLM` provided by the `huggingface` library [4], which uses the default settings of `RobertaConfig` library and is also the same settings as the hyperparameter of the baseline provided by the organizers. In the training phase, we trained 5 epochs using the Trainer provided by the `huggingface`. We refer §C for detailed hyperparameters in Appendix.

4.3 Benchmarks and Evaluation

We evaluated the model using the evaluation pipeline tools[5] also provided by the organizer (Warstadt et al., 2023; Gao et al., 2021). This tool automatically performs experiments on 4 benchmarks:

1) Benchmark of Linguistic Minimal Pairs (BLiMP) (Warstadt et al., 2020a);

2) BLiMP Supplement[6], including Hypernym, QA Congruence Easy, QA Congruence Tricky, Subject Aux Inversion, and Turn Taking datasets;

3) General Language Understanding Evaluation (GLUE) (Wang et al., 2019), and

[3] The full datasets could be downloaded here: https://github.com/babylm/babylm.github.io/raw/main/babylm_data.zip

[4] https://huggingface.co/docs/transformers/model_doc/roberta

[5] https://github.com/babylm/evaluation-pipeline

[6] The relevant paper for this benchmark had not been published at the time of this project, and the relevant data can be found here https://github.com/babylm/evaluation-pipeline/blob/main/filter_data.zip

4) Mixed Signals Generalization Set (MSGS) (Warstadt et al., 2020b).

The detailed documentation of each benchmark can be found in §D. The organizer (Warstadt et al., 2023) also provided 3 models as baselines, including OPT-125M, RoBERTa-base, and T5-base, trained on the `babylm_100M` data.

5 Results

We compare the performance of our BabyLM (trained in the RoBERTa way) to the original RoBERTa-base (baseline). Table 1 shows our selected experimental results with: i) performance improvement by at least 3 points (+3), and ii) performance reduction over 3 points (-3). We report the performance with absolute performance difference of our BabyLM over baseline on the selected tasks, as well as the overall performance of the whole tasks. The full results are available in §D.

Tasks	Models		Diff.
	Ours	Baseline	
BLiMP			
Filler Gap	**78.52**	68	**10.52**
Sub.-Verb Agr.	**85.17**	76.2	**8.97**
Arg. Structure	**78.06**	71.3	**6.76**
Det.-Noun Agr.	**97.75**	93.1	**4.65**
Anaphor Agr.	**93.61**	89.5	**4.11**
Ellipsis	77.02	83.8	-6.78
Island Effects	45.85	54.5	-8.65
BLiMP Supplement			
Sub. Aux Inversion	**77.73**	45.6	**32.13**
QA Cong. Easy	**62.5**	34.4	**28.1**
Turn Taking	**62.5**	46.8	**15.7**
GLUE			
BoolQ	**65.84**	59.9	**5.94**
MNLI	**73.73**	68.7	**5.03**
MNLI-mm	74.76	78	-3.24
QNLI	76.86	82.3	-5.44
RTE	45.45	51.5	-6.05
AVG. (overall)	**73.95**	71.75	**2.2**

Table 1: Selected results of our BabyLM and the RoBERTa (baseline), where the performance of BabyLM improved by at least 3 points (in **bold**), or reduced (-) over 3. The metric in this table is all accuracy score.

We noticed that on the BLiMP benchmark, 5 indicators increased by more than 3 points, namely Filler Gap (+10.52), Subject-Verb Agreement (+8.97), Argument Structure (+6.76), Determiner Noun Agreement (+4.65) and Anaphor Agreement (+4.11), while two tasks dropped by more than 3 points, namely Ellipsis (-6.78) and Island Effects (-8.65). The average performance on this benchmark has also increased by 2.24.

On the GLUE benchmark, BoolQ and MNLI showed an improvement of 5.94 and 5.03, respectively, while MNLI-mm, QNLI, and RTE showed a decrease of -3.24, -5.44, and -6.05 respectively.

On top of that, we surprisingly find significant improvements in 3 tasks of the BLiMP Supplement benchmark: Subject Aux Inversion (+32.13), QA Congruence Easy (+28.10), and Turn Taking (+15.70). The average performance on this benchmark improved by 14.85 points.

The overall average performance is increased by 2.2, which shows that our model, pretrained with our reinterpreted small data, already demonstrates a great improvement.

6 Discussion

6.1 Augmented Dataset via CoT Prompting

We generated our data via the above-mentioned CoT prompting and the GPT-3.5-turbo for nearly 700, 000 lines, we show a case study of a part of the generated data here.

```
- Paragraph:
    - We have a few topics to cover in this
      paragraph. Firstly, a possible I.D. has
      been found in one of Gina's snapshots.
      Secondly, there is a new technology
      in development called autostereoscopic
      3D that will allow people to watch
      3D movies without glasses. This is
      great news for those who find wearing
      3D glasses uncomfortable and causes eye
      strain. Unfortunately, the narrator
      regrets not asking Jean for the details
      about something. Lastly, the police
      are seen moving down the main street
      of Atenco, and we are tracking their
      movements.

- Plan:

-   1. Introduce the topic of the paragraph
    2. Mention the possible I.D. from Gina's
       snapshots
    3. Talk about the new technology called
       autostereoscopic 3D
    4. Mention the difficulty of wearing 3D
       glasses
    5. Mention the regret of not asking Jean
       for details
    6. Talk about the police and their movement
       down the main street of Atenco
```

```
- Task:
    - Text Classification
- Labels:
-   1. I.D. Mentioned
    2. Technology Mentioned
    3. Regret Expressed
    4. Police Mentioned
```

As we can see from the script, the paragraph is an extension of the input sentences sampled from the original dataset, while the plan and labels generated by the language model are the outlines, where the scenes also are the critical information from the generated paragraph. It means that our approach augmented the original data with interpretation, emphasis, and simplification, with which the model is possible to learn about a story with different versions and sizes and finally get a clearer understanding.

6.2 Performance in QA Congruence Easy

We analyzed the most noticeable improvement of the QA Congruence Easy dataset from the BLiMP Supplement benchmark, and dived deep into each case. This dataset consists of 64 single-choice questions with 20 *what*-questions, 25 *who*-questions, and 19 *where*-questions. Each question contains a question mark, and each answer ends with a period. Each question corresponds to 2 candidate answers, and the boundary of the candidate answers is clear, i.e., for the *what*- and *who*-questions, the answers contain an inanimate or an animate, and for the *where*-questions the answer is a location or a noun phrase. Obviously, the answer to the what-questions should be inanimate, like *a car*, the answer to the who-question should be animate, like *a doctor* or person's name *Sarah*, and the answer to the where-question should be location, like *at home*. The model is expected to select the answer that matches the question. For example, a question is "*Who did you see?*" and the candidate answers are 1. "*A doctor*", 2. "*A car*", and it is clear that the answer should be "*A doctor*". The final metric for the evaluation is accuracy.

6.2.1 Influence of the 3 Types of Questions

In these three kinds of questions, our model is better at answering the *what*-questions, where the accuracy is 75. Besides, it obtains an accuracy of 64 for the *who*-questions, and 47 for the *where*-questions.

6.2.2 Influence of the 2 Types of Answers

We also note that there are two forms of the answers:

1) *sentence*, where the answer is a complete sentence that includes at least the verb, e.g. "*I sent the package to europe*";

2) *fragment*, where the answer is a single word or a simple phrase, and does not include the verb, e.g. "*a car*".

The form of the two candidates' answers to each question is consistent, i.e., both candidates' answers are either sentences or fragments. The dataset contains 27 question-answer pairs in the form of sentences (42%) and 37 cases in fragments (57%). We also counted the accuracy on the above two forms, where the accuracy is 77.78 for sentences and 51.35 for fragments. Additionally, we also counted the accuracy with the different forms of the three questions i.e. *what*-, *who*-, and *where*-questions. The accuracy of the sentence labels on the *what*-questions is 80, while the fragment is 70. The accuracy on the who-question with sentence answers was 71 and 61 with fragment answers. On *where*-questions, the tasks with sentence answers obtained an accuracy of 80, however, it was only 11 with the fragment answers. Thus we can observe that our model is better at deciding with complete answers rather than fragments.

6.2.3 Influence of the 3 Types of Dialogues

Besides, we also notice that there are three types of dialogues for each question,

1) *direct* dialogues, where the question is started by a question word directly and the answer is direct with the answer, e.g., question: "*What did you get?*", candidate answers: "*I got a chair*", "*I got a doctor*";

2) *A-B* dialogues, where the letters *A* and *B* are used as names for both sides of the conversation before proposing the question and the candidate answers respectively, e.g. question "*A*: What did you sell?", candidate answers: "*B*: A chair.", "*B*: A doctor.";

3) *David-Sarah* dialogues, the person's name *David* is used as the questioner's name before the question, and *Sarah* is used as the answerer's name before the answer.

The dataset comprises 21 direct dialogues (32%), 22 *A-B* dialogues (34%), and 21 *David-Sarah* dialogues (32%), with the model's accuracy consistently ranging between 61-63% across these types.

We then explored the proportionality between these three forms of dialogue and the three kinds of questions. Of the 20 *what*-questions, 7 are written in *direct* dialogues, 6 are in *A-B* dialogues, and 7 are *David-Sarah* dialogues. we notice a difference in the accuracy, where the accuracy with *direct* dialogues is 100, the *A-B* dialogues have an accuracy of 83, and the David-Sarah dialogues reached only 45.

Of the 25 *who*-questions, 8 *direct* dialogues obtained an accuracy only of 25, while 7 *A-B* dialogues gained 85 accuracy and the accuracy of the 10 *David-Sarah* dialogues is 80. Out of the 19 *where*-questions, the accuracy of the 6 direct dialogues is 66%, 33% of *A-B* dialogues are correct, and the accuracy of the 4 *David-Sarah* dialogues is 50%.

From the above results, we can see that our model is good at selecting answers from *direct* and *A-B* dialogues on the *what*-questions. In contrast, for the *who*-questions, our model is good at selecting animates from the *David-Sarah* dialogues and the *A-B* dialogues, but not good at selecting the animate from the direct dialogues. It might be positively affected by the presence of the person's name. In the *where*-questions, the form of dialogues has a more limited effect on the performance.

6.3 Performance in QA Congruence Tricky

We compared the performance on the QA Congruence Tricky dataset, on which we have a very similar performance (35) to the baseline model. It contains 165 tricky questions including *who-*, *where-*, *when-*, *why-*, and *how many*-questions, where the proportions of the *who-* and the *where*-questions are 15% and 16% respectively. The accuracy of the *who-* and *where*-questions are only 37 and 30 respectively, differ from the accuracies in the QA Congruence Easy dataset.

We also notice that, in this dataset, our model is better at selecting fragment answers rather than answers in the form of sentences, where the accuracy with fragments is 62, while the accuracy of the sentences is only 10. On both *who-* and *where*-questions, our model is better at finding the answer in the *David-Sarah* dialogues (55 and 45 respectively in accuracy), and the accuracies of both questions in the other two dialogue forms are under 30. Similar to the fact shown in the easy dataset, the presence of people's names probably provides a sign to the animate and thus influences the performance, especially on the *who*-questions.

We analyzed the questions-candidate answers pairs from the tricky dataset, where both the questions and the candidate answers are generally shorter, e.g., the question is "*Who ate?*", and the candidate answers are "*A teacher ate.*", and "*Pasta ate.*", where the question only contains the *wh-*word, a verb, and a question mark, and the candidate answers contain only a subjective and a verb. The answers in the form of fragments are even shorter, e.g. to a question "*Who cooked?*", the candidate answers are "*Sarah*", and "*A sandwich*".

Besides the questions being more varied and complex, this dataset is more tricky, because the context is short. The candidate answers written in sentences are generally very similar to the fragments with only an additional verb, where the verb has been mentioned in the questions, which means the form of sentence possibly doesn't provide additional information, but may confuse the model to understand the answers.

7 Conclusion

In this work, we proposed the CoThought pipeline for training a BabyLM at a small scale, combining the LLMs' productivity with the concept of a child's cognitive learning ability. We let the raw training data for the BabyLM be reformulated by the LLM's CoT prompting (i.e. let the teacher think) and then train a BabyLM in a pretraining fashion based on the newly structured data (i.e. let the child co-think and learn). We compare the performance results of our BabyLM to another vanilla pretrained LM RoBERTa and demonstrate that our model achieves higher performance in many tasks including linguistic, question and answer, especially congruence tasks. This suggests that data processed by LLMs based on their contextual reasoning is more natural and efficient in the learning process, just as text revised by experienced teachers in the school is more suitable for students to learn and understand. And when we use data restructured by LLMs, even in the case of small data volume, the model is able to achieve the effect of a model trained from a large amount of data, or to be even better.

Limitations

One limitation of our work is the exclusive use of a specific LLM for data generation. It would be insightful to explore how performance varies when using different LLMs to generate the pre-training data. Different LLMs may introduce variability and diversity in the generated data, which could influence the effectiveness of the pre-training process. This aspect, while not explored in our current work, presents a promising avenue for future research to understand the impact of various LLMs on data generation and subsequent model performance.

Another limitation of our work is that our primary focus is on data generation, leaving potential improvements or optimizations in this domain unexplored.

Additionally, our model training exclusively utilized the RoBERTa architecture. Other architectures, including causal language models and various transformer variants, also showed potential research value. Therefore, exploring our approach across a broader range of architectures and identifying pretraining methods most compatible with our generated data remains an important area for future research.

By acknowledging these limitations, we hope to spur further research in this area, encouraging the exploration of data generation techniques, model architectures, and extended data methods in the context of small-scale language modeling.

Ethics Statement

This research was conducted in accordance with the ACM Code of Ethics. The datasets that we use are publicly available (Warstadt et al., 2023). We report only aggregated results in the main paper. We have not intended or do not intend to share any Personally Identifiable Data with this paper.

Acknowledgements

We thank the anonymous reviewers and the organizing committee for their efforts and helpful advice. E.N. was supported by MCML and CSC.

References

Luisa Bentivogli, Peter Clark, Ido Dagan, and Danilo Giampiccolo. 2009. The fifth pascal recognizing textual entailment challenge. *TAC*, 7:8.

Tom B. Brown, Benjamin Mann, Nick Ryder, Melanie Subbiah, Jared Kaplan, Prafulla Dhariwal, Arvind Neelakantan, Pranav Shyam, Girish Sastry, Amanda Askell, Sandhini Agarwal, Ariel Herbert-Voss, Gretchen Krueger, Tom Henighan, Rewon Child, Aditya Ramesh, Daniel M. Ziegler, Jeffrey Wu, Clemens Winter, Christopher Hesse, Mark Chen, Eric Sigler, Mateusz Litwin, Scott Gray, Benjamin Chess, Jack Clark, Christopher Berner, Sam McCandlish, Alec Radford, Ilya Sutskever, and Dario Amodei. 2020. Language models are few-shot learners. *CoRR*, abs/2005.14165.

Joan Bybee. 2001. *Phonology and Language Use*. Cambridge Studies in Linguistics. Cambridge University Press.

Tyler A. Chang and Benjamin K. Bergen. 2022. Word acquisition in neural language models. *Transactions of the Association for Computational Linguistics*, 10:1–16.

Stephen L Chew and William J Cerbin. 2021. The cognitive challenges of effective teaching. *The Journal of Economic Education*, 52(1):17–40.

Noam Chomsky. 1957. *Syntactic Structures*. The Hague: Mouton and Co.

Christopher Clark, Kenton Lee, Ming-Wei Chang, Tom Kwiatkowski, Michael Collins, and Kristina Toutanova. 2019. Boolq: Exploring the surprising difficulty of natural yes/no questions. *arXiv preprint arXiv:1905.10044*.

Ido Dagan, Oren Glickman, and Bernardo Magnini. 2005. The pascal recognising textual entailment challenge. In *Machine learning challenges workshop*, pages 177–190. Springer.

Jacob Devlin, Ming-Wei Chang, Kenton Lee, and Kristina Toutanova. 2019. BERT: Pre-training of deep bidirectional transformers for language understanding. In *Proceedings of the 2019 Conference of the North American Chapter of the Association for Computational Linguistics: Human Language Technologies, Volume 1 (Long and Short Papers)*, pages 4171–4186, Minneapolis, Minnesota. Association for Computational Linguistics.

William B. Dolan and Chris Brockett. 2005. Automatically constructing a corpus of sentential paraphrases. In *Proceedings of the Third International Workshop on Paraphrasing (IWP2005)*.

Linnea Evanson, Yair Lakretz, and Jean Rémi King. 2023. Language acquisition: do children and language models follow similar learning stages? In *Findings of the Association for Computational Linguistics: ACL 2023*, pages 12205–12218, Toronto, Canada. Association for Computational Linguistics.

Leo Gao, Jonathan Tow, Stella Biderman, Sid Black, Anthony DiPofi, Charles Foster, Laurence Golding, Jeffrey Hsu, Kyle McDonell, Niklas Muennighoff, Jason Phang, Laria Reynolds, Eric Tang, Anish Thite, Ben Wang, Kevin Wang, and Andy Zou. 2021. A framework for few-shot language model evaluation.

Emil Gegov, Fernand Gobet, Mark Atherton, Daniel Freudenthal, and Julian Pine. 2014. Modelling language acquisition in children using network theory. In *European Perspectives on Cognitive Science*.

Danilo Giampiccolo, Bernardo Magnini, Ido Dagan, and William B Dolan. 2007. The third pascal recognizing textual entailment challenge. In *Proceedings of the ACL-PASCAL workshop on textual entailment and paraphrasing*, pages 1–9.

Yuxian Gu, Li Dong, Furu Wei, and Minlie Huang. 2023. Pre-training to learn in context. In *Proceedings of the 61st Annual Meeting of the Association for Computational Linguistics (Volume 1: Long Papers)*, pages 4849–4870, Toronto, Canada. Association for Computational Linguistics.

R Bar Haim, Ido Dagan, Bill Dolan, Lisa Ferro, Danilo Giampiccolo, Bernardo Magnini, and Idan Szpektor. 2006. The second pascal recognising textual entailment challenge. In *Proceedings of the Second PASCAL Challenges Workshop on Recognising Textual Entailment*, volume 7, pages 785–794.

Daniel Khashabi, Snigdha Chaturvedi, Michael Roth, Shyam Upadhyay, and Dan Roth. 2018. Looking beyond the surface:a challenge set for reading comprehension over multiple sentences. In *Proceedings of North American Chapter of the Association for Computational Linguistics (NAACL)*.

Vid Kocijan, Thomas Lukasiewicz, Ernest Davis, Gary Marcus, and Leora Morgenstern. 2020. A review of winograd schema challenge datasets and approaches. *arXiv preprint arXiv:2004.13831*.

Takeshi Kojima, Shixiang Shane Gu, Machel Reid, Yutaka Matsuo, and Yusuke Iwasawa. 2023. Large language models are zero-shot reasoners.

HJ Levesque. 2011. The winograd schema challenge. aaai spring symposium: Logical formalizations of commonsense reasoning. *Palo Alto CA*.

Jiacheng Liu, Alisa Liu, Ximing Lu, Sean Welleck, Peter West, Ronan Le Bras, Yejin Choi, and Hannaneh Hajishirzi. 2022. Generated knowledge prompting for commonsense reasoning. In *Proceedings of the 60th Annual Meeting of the Association for Computational Linguistics (Volume 1: Long Papers)*, pages 3154–3169, Dublin, Ireland. Association for Computational Linguistics.

Yinhan Liu, Myle Ott, Naman Goyal, Jingfei Du, Mandar Joshi, Danqi Chen, Omer Levy, Mike Lewis, Luke Zettlemoyer, and Veselin Stoyanov. 2019. Roberta: A robustly optimized BERT pretraining approach. *CoRR*, abs/1907.11692.

Mitja Nikolaus and Abdellah Fourtassi. 2021. Modeling the interaction between perception-based and production-based learning in children's early acquisition of semantic knowledge. In *Proceedings of the 25th Conference on Computational Natural Language Learning*, pages 391–407, Online. Association for Computational Linguistics.

Bhargavi Paranjape, Scott Lundberg, Sameer Singh, Hannaneh Hajishirzi, Luke Zettlemoyer, and Marco Tulio Ribeiro. 2023. Art: Automatic multi-step reasoning and tool-use for large language models.

Geoffrey K Pullum and Barbara C Scholz. 2002. Empirical assessment of stimulus poverty arguments. *The Linguistic Review*, 19(1-2):9–50.

Alec Radford and Karthik Narasimhan. 2018. Improving language understanding by generative pre-training. *OpenAI*.

Matthew Saxton. 2010. *Child Language: Acquisition and Development*. Sage Publications.

Richard Socher, Alex Perelygin, Jean Wu, Jason Chuang, Christopher D. Manning, Andrew Ng, and Christopher Potts. 2013. Recursive deep models for semantic compositionality over a sentiment treebank. In *Proceedings of the 2013 Conference on Empirical Methods in Natural Language Processing*, pages 1631–1642, Seattle, Washington, USA. Association for Computational Linguistics.

Michael Tomasello. 2003. *Constructing a Language: A Usage-Based Theory of Language Acquisition*. Harvard University Press.

Alex Wang, Amanpreet Singh, Julian Michael, Felix Hill, Omer Levy, and Samuel R. Bowman. 2019. GLUE: A multi-task benchmark and analysis platform for natural language understanding. In *7th International Conference on Learning Representations, ICLR 2019, New Orleans, LA, USA, May 6-9, 2019*. OpenReview.net.

Alex Warstadt, Aaron Mueller, Leshem Choshen, Ethan Gotlieb Wilcox, Chengxu Zhuang, Juan Ciro, Rafael Mosquera, Adina Williams, Bhargavi Paranjabe, Tal Linzen, and Ryan Cotterell. 2023. Findings of the 2023 BabyLM Challenge: Sample-efficient pretraining on developmentally plausible corpora. In *Proceedings of the 2023 BabyLM Challenge*. Association for Computational Linguistics (ACL).

Alex Warstadt, Alicia Parrish, Haokun Liu, Anhad Mohananey, Wei Peng, Sheng-Fu Wang, and Samuel R. Bowman. 2020a. BLiMP: The benchmark of linguistic minimal pairs for English. *Transactions of the Association for Computational Linguistics*, 8:377–392.

Alex Warstadt, Amanpreet Singh, and Samuel R Bowman. 2018. Neural network acceptability judgments. *arXiv preprint arXiv:1805.12471*.

Alex Warstadt, Yian Zhang, Xiaocheng Li, Haokun Liu, and Samuel R. Bowman. 2020b. Learning which features matter: Roberta acquires a preference for linguistic generalizations (eventually). In *Proceedings of the 2020 Conference on Empirical Methods in Natural Language Processing, EMNLP 2020, Online, November 16-20, 2020*, pages 217–235. Association for Computational Linguistics.

Jason Wei, Xuezhi Wang, Dale Schuurmans, Maarten Bosma, Ed H. Chi, Quoc Le, and Denny Zhou. 2022. Chain of thought prompting elicits reasoning in large language models. *CoRR*, abs/2201.11903.

Adina Williams, Nikita Nangia, and Samuel Bowman. 2018. A broad-coverage challenge corpus for sentence understanding through inference. In *Proceedings of the 2018 Conference of the North American Chapter of the Association for Computational Linguistics: Human Language Technologies, Volume 1 (Long Papers)*, pages 1112–1122. Association for Computational Linguistics.

Shunyu Yao, Dian Yu, Jeffrey Zhao, Izhak Shafran, Thomas L. Griffiths, Yuan Cao, and Karthik Narasimhan. 2023. Tree of thoughts: Deliberate problem solving with large language models.

Wenhao Yu, Dan Iter, Shuohang Wang, Yichong Xu, Mingxuan Ju, Soumya Sanyal, Chenguang Zhu, Michael Zeng, and Meng Jiang. 2023. Generate rather than retrieve: Large language models are strong context generators. In *International Conference for Learning Representation (ICLR)*.

A Code and Model

The code for data processing and model training is available at: `https://github.com/oooranz/Baby-CoThought`.

Our BabyLM is available at: `https://huggingface.co/yaanhaan/Baby-CoThought`.

B Pretraining Data Statistics

The generated dataset for LM pretraining is available at: `https://huggingface.co/datasets/yaanhaan/Baby-CoThought-Data`.

We present a statistical analysis of the generated dataset. Given that our task revolves around creative NLU example generation, the dataset inherently encompasses a wide variety of tasks. This diversity is reflective of the creative nature of the task, allowing for a richer and more comprehensive pretraining process. Each example in the dataset includes an NLU example and its corresponding reason.

We plot the task distribution of the pretraining dataset in Figure 2. Tasks that appeared only once in the dataset are categorized as others.

The average number of words in the paragraphs across all examples in the dataset is approximately 115.25 words.

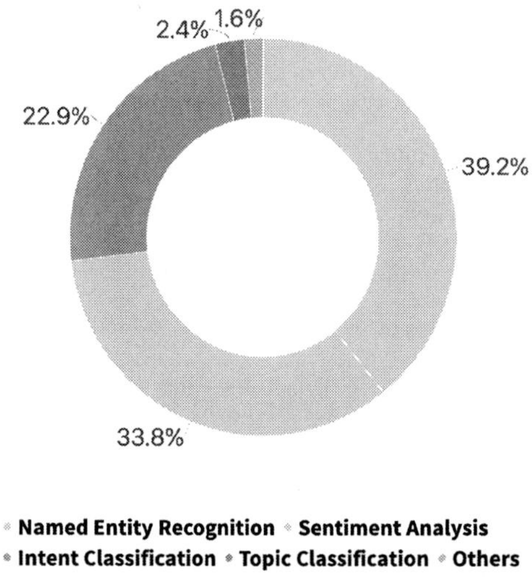

Figure 2: The distribution of the different NLU task examples in the pretraining dataset.

C Hyperparameter

We followed the instruction[7] and trained the tokenizers separately for the original dataset and our enhanced dataset via the `ByteLevelBPETokenizer` library with the hyperparameters shown in Table 2. Other hyperparameters were set to default and can be found in the document [8].

Hyperparameter	Value
vocab_size	52000
min_frequency	2
special_tokens	<s>, <pad>, </s>, <unk>,<mask>

Table 2: Hyperparameters used for tokenizers

Besides, we report our hyperparameters during the pretraining of our RoBERTa models in Table 3. We used the default settings from the `RobertaConfig` library. More default values and technical details can be found in the documents 3111[9].

Additionally, the evaluation process was done automatically via the evaluation tool provided by the organizer, without changing the hyperparameters, which can be found on the webpage [10].

[7] `https://huggingface.co/blog/how-to-train`

[8] `https://github.com/huggingface/tokenizers/blob/main/bindings/python/py_src/tokenizers/implementations/byte_level_bpe.py`

[9] `https://huggingface.co/docs/transformers/model_doc/roberta#transformers.RobertaConfig`

[10] `https://github.com/babylm/`

Hyperparameter	Value
attention_probs_dropout_prob	0.1
bos_token_id	0
classifier_dropout	null
eos_token_id	2
hidden_act	gelu
hidden_dropout_prob	0.1
hidden_size	768
initializer_range	0.02
intermediate_size	3072
layer_norm_eps	1.00E-12
max_position_embeddings	512
model_type	roberta
num_attention_heads	12
num_hidden_layers	12
pad_token_id	1
position_embedding_type	absolute
torch_dtype	float32
transformers_version	4.17.0
type_vocab_size	1
use_cache	TRUE
vocab_size	52000

Table 3: Hyperparameters used for pretraining

D Full Results

We used 4 benchmarks:

1) Benchmark of Linguistic Minimal Pairs (BLiMP) (Warstadt et al., 2020a), including Anaphor Agreement, Argument Structure, Binding, Control Raising, Determiner Noun Agreement, Ellipsis, Filler Gap, Irregular Forms, Island Effects, NPI Licensing, Quantifiers, and Subject Verb Agreement;

2) BLiMP Supplement[11], including Hypernym, QA Congruence Easy, QA Congruence Tricky, Subject Aux Inversion, and Turn Taking;

3) General Language Understanding Evaluation (GLUE) (Wang et al., 2019), including CoLA (Warstadt et al., 2018), SST-2 (Socher et al., 2013), MRPC (F1) (Dolan and Brockett, 2005), QQP[12] (F1), MNLI (Williams et al., 2018), MNLI-mm, QNLI (Levesque, 2011), RTE (Dagan et al., 2005; Haim et al., 2006; Giampiccolo et al., 2007; Bentivogli et al., 2009), BoolQ (Clark et al., 2019), MultiRC (Khashabi et al., 2018) and WSC (Kocijan et al., 2020);

4) Mixed Signals Generalization Set (MSGS) (Warstadt et al., 2020b), including Control Raising Control (CR Control), Lexical Content The Control (LC Control), Main Verb Control (MV Control), Relative Position Control (RP Control), Syntactic Category Control (SC Control), Control Raising Lexical Content The (CR LC), Control Raising Relative Token Position (CR RTP), Main Verb Lexical Content The (MV LC), Main Verb Relative Token Position (MV RTP), Syntactic Category Lexical Content The (SC LC), Syntactic Category Relative Position (SC RP).

to process our evaluation.

The organizer provided three baseline models, including OPT-125M[13] , RoBERTa-base[14] , and T5-base[15]. We show our full results in Table 4.

evaluation-pipeline#hyperparameters

[11]https://github.com/babylm/evaluation-pipeline/blob/main/filter_data.zip

[12]https://quoradata.quora.com/First-Quora-Dataset-Release-Question-Pairs

[13]https://huggingface.co/facebook/opt-125m

[14]https://huggingface.co/roberta-base

[15]https://huggingface.co/t5-base

Tasks	Models				Difference	
	Ours	OPT-125m	RoBERTa-base	T5-base	in abs	in rel.
BLiMP						
Anaphor Agreement	93.61	**94.90**	89.50	66.70	4.11	4.59%
Argument Structure	**78.06**	73.80	71.30	61.20	6.76	9.48%
Binding	72.84	**73.80**	71.00	59.40	1.84	2.59%
Control Raising	69.55	**72.20**	67.10	59.80	2.45	3.65%
Determiner Noun Agreement	**97.75**	93.10	93.10	53.80	4.65	4.99%
Ellipsis	77.02	80.50	**83.80**	49.10	-6.78	-8.09%
Filler Gap	**78.52**	73.60	68.00	70.00	10.52	15.47%
Irregular Forms	**91.25**	80.80	89.60	75.50	1.65	1.84%
Island Effects	45.85	**57.80**	54.50	43.60	-8.65	-15.87%
NPI Licensing	**67.35**	51.60	66.30	45.60	1.05	1.58%
Quantifiers	70.58	**74.50**	70.30	34.20	0.28	0.40%
Subject Verb Agreement	**85.17**	77.30	76.20	53.20	8.97	11.77%
BLiMP Supplement						
Hypernym	49.07	46.30	50.80	**51.10**	-1.73	-3.41%
QA Congruence Easy	62.50	**76.50**	34.40	45.30	28.10	81.69%
QA Congruence Tricky	34.55	**47.90**	34.50	25.50	0.05	0.14%
Subject Aux Inversion	**77.73**	85.30	45.60	69.20	32.13	70.46%
Turn Taking	62.50	**82.90**	46.80	48.90	15.70	33.55%
GLUE						
CoLA	74.09	73.70	75.90	**76.30**	-1.81	-2.38%
SST-2	**88.78**	86.60	88.60	88.00	0.18	0.20%
MRPC (F1)	80.45	82.10	80.50	**85.90**	-0.05	-0.06%
QQP (F1)	**81.20**	77.80	78.50	79.70	2.70	3.44%
MNLI	**73.73**	70.10	68.70	71.50	5.03	7.32%
MNLI-mm	74.76	71.90	**78.00**	74.00	-3.24	-4.15%
QNLI	76.86	80.10	82.30	**83.10**	-5.44	-6.61%
RTE	45.45	**67.70**	51.50	60.60	-6.05	-11.74%
BoolQ	65.84	66.00	59.90	**69.00**	5.94	9.91%
MultiRC	62.21	61.10	61.30	**62.40**	0.91	1.49%
WSC	**61.45**	59.00	61.40	60.20	0.05	0.07%
MSGS						
CR (Control)	83.96	**97.20**	93.00	95.10	-9.04	-9.72%
LC (Control)	94.49	82.60	**100.00**	**100.00**	-5.51	-5.51%
MV (Control)	99.98	**100.00**	**100.00**	**100.00**	-0.02	-0.02%
RP (Control)	**100.00**	99.80	**100.00**	99.80	0.00	0.00%
SC (Control)	88.44	88.10	**89.00**	88.70	-0.56	-0.62%
CR LC	67.07	75.30	68.30	**76.70**	-1.23	-1.80%
CR RTP	**70.71**	67.10	66.80	69.40	3.91	5.86%
MV LC	66.61	66.30	66.60	**67.00**	0.01	0.01%
MV RTP	67.59	66.80	**80.20**	67.70	-12.61	-15.72%
SC LC	75.47	**84.80**	67.40	72.70	8.07	11.98%
SC RP	**70.90**	62.00	67.40	68.00	3.50	5.19%

Table 4: Full results, with difference of our BabyLM over RoBERTa-base (baseline). Metric of MRPC and QQP from GLUE is F_1, in other tasks the metric is accuracy. The best results of the four models are marked in **bold**.

ToddlerBERTa: Exploiting BabyBERTa for Grammar Learning and Language Understanding

Ömer Veysel Çağatan
Koç University
Rumelifeneri, Sarıyer Rumeli Feneri Yolu
34450 Sarıyer/İstanbul,Turkey
ocagatan19@ku.edu.tr

Abstract

We present ToddlerBERTa, a scaled BabyBERTa language model, exploring its capabilities through five different models with varied hyperparameters. We obtain our best model named ToddlerBERTa by meticulously optimizing our models on the BLiMP benchmark. Despite training on a smaller dataset, ToddlerBERTa demonstrates commendable performance, outperforming the baselines provided by a significant margin in the overall evaluation that include BLiMP, SuperGLUE, MSGS and BLiMP supplement. ToddlerBERTa showcases robust language understanding, even with single-sentence pretraining, and competes with baselines that leverage broader contextual information. Our work provides insights into hyperparameter choices, and data utilization, contributing to the advancement of low-resource language models.

1 Introduction

Over the past few years, there has been a lot of effort put into improving the pretraining of large language models (LLMs) on a large scale (Brown et al., 2020; Raffel et al., 2019; Chowdhery et al., 2022; Hoffmann et al., 2022). While there is often a focus on increasing the number of parameters, there has also been significant growth in dataset size. However, there has been minimal progress in pretraining on smaller data scales that are comparable to how humans learn language.

Exploring pretraining on a smaller scale can serve as a trial area for developing original techniques that boost data effectiveness. These techniques can be scaled up to larger datasets utilized and employed to enhance current methods for modelling low-resource languages.

The BabyLM challenge (Warstadt et al., 2023) has been created to address the gap in research on pretraining for small-scale language models. Our focus will be on a limited corpus of approximately 10 million words, which includes child-directed speech, transcribed speech from various sources, children's books, and Wikipedia data.

We trained more than 180 BabyBERTa (Huebner et al., 2021) models in different sizes and hyperparameters to determine how well language models learn grammar and understand language. Our findings showed that scaling the model and data resulted in significantly better outcomes compared to baseline models which underscores the low utilisation of both the data and architecture we currently have. All in all, our work demonstrates that well-known and widely used (Liu et al., 2019; Devlin et al., 2019; Vaswani et al., 2017) architectures can be enhanced with moderate modifications to their training recipes.

2 Related Work

There has been a significant amount of research on data-efficient language models. These models aim to achieve high accuracy in language tasks while using less training data than their larger counterparts. One way to create data-efficient language models is to reduce the number of model parameters while maintaining high performance. For instance, DistilBERT (Sanh et al., 2019) is a smaller and faster version of the popular BERT model. It was trained by distilling knowledge from the larger model into a smaller version. TinyBERT (Jiao et al., 2019), on the other hand, was designed for low-resource environments, such as mobile devices. It was trained using a combination of teacher-student learning and knowledge distillation techniques.

Another example of a data-efficient language model is ALBERT (Lan et al., 2019) which reduces the number of parameters of the BERT model by using factorization techniques and sharing parameters across different layers. This results in a more data-efficient model that can achieve similar or better performance than the larger BERT model.

GPT-Neo (Black et al., 2021) is another data-efficient language model that was trained on a large

Proceedings of the 27th Conference on Computational Natural Language Learning: Volume 2: The BabyLM Challenge, pages 171–179
December 6-7, 2023

dataset of text, but it can be fine-tuned on smaller datasets with good results. It has demonstrated competitive performance on various natural language processing tasks, including language generation, summarization, and question-answering.

ELECTRA (Clark et al., 2020) is a novel pre-training approach for language models that is designed to be more data-efficient than traditional models like BERT. Instead of using a traditional masked language modelling task, ELECTRA uses a discriminator network to predict whether a given input is real or generated by another model. This approach allows for more efficient training and can achieve similar or better performance than traditional models.

TinyStories (Eldan and Li, 2023) is an artificial collection of short stories, specifically designed with words understandable to 3 to 4-year-olds. These stories are generated using GPT-3.5 and GPT-4 (OpenAI, 2023).TinyStories can effectively serve as a training and evaluation dataset for language models (LMs) that are considerably smaller than the current state-of-the-art models (less than 10 million parameters) or have simpler architectures (with just one transformer block). Despite their reduced size and simplicity, these LMs are capable of producing coherent and consistent stories spanning multiple paragraphs. The stories are diverse, exhibit nearly flawless grammar, and showcase impressive reasoning abilities.

BabyBERTa is a lightweight model for language acquisition (Huebner et al., 2021). BabyBERTa is similar to RoBERTa (Liu et al., 2019), but it is much smaller and simpler. BabyBERTa was trained on a dataset of 5M words of American-English child-directed input, and it can be run on a single desktop with a single GPU.BabyBERTa was able to achieve comparable performance to RoBERTa on a number of language acquisition tasks, including grammatical knowledge acquisition, generalization to novel grammatical contexts, syntactic structure learning, and semantic word and phrase learning. These results suggest that BabyBERTa could be a valuable tool for language acquisition research.

Small size: BabyBERTa is much smaller than RoBERTa, with only 8 layers, 8 attention heads, 256 hidden units, and an intermediate size of 1024. This makes it much faster and easier to train and use than RoBERTa.

Comparable performance: Despite its smaller size and simpler training regime, BabyBERTa was able to achieve comparable performance to RoBERTa on a number of language acquisition tasks. This suggests that BabyBERTa could be a valuable tool for language acquisition research.

BabyBERTa makes a number of contributions to the field. First, it demonstrates that a small, lightweight model can be used to acquire grammatical knowledge from child-directed input. Second, it shows that BabyBERTa can generalize to novel grammatical contexts. Third, it shows that BabyBERTa is able to learn the syntactic structure of sentences. Fourth, it shows that BabyBERTa is able to learn the semantics of words and phrases

3 Experiment Settings

We embrace BabyBERTa (Huebner et al., 2021) as the foundational model for our research endeavour. Building upon this foundation, our investigation sets forth to explore an array of model sizes and diverse hyperparameters in a systematic and rigorous manner.

We construct five different models to validate and then further exploit the performance of BabyBERTa. All hyperparameters are kept the same except, hidden size, intermediate size, number of attention heads and number of layers. Models configurations can be found in Table 1.

Our study closely follows the established hyperparameters of BabyBERTa but with three key variations: number of mask patterns{1, 5, 10, 20, 50}, epochs{1,5,10}, and batch size {16,32,64,128}. Due to computational limitations, we are limited to having 36 different configurations per model.

4 Evaluation Setup

We adopt the official evaluation pipeline of the BabyLM Challenge (Warstadt et al., 2023; Gao et al., 2021), which combines BLiMP (Warstadt et al., 2019), SuperGLUE (Wang et al., 2019), MSGS (Warstadt et al., 2020), and a Supplement benchmark. Our best model is evaluated on all benchmarks, while other models are evaluated on BLiMP due to limited computing resources. This approach ensures a rigorous assessment of our model's performance across diverse tasks while optimizing resource allocation.

4.1 Baselines

The competition organizers supply baseline models extracted from well-known language models, including OPT (Zhang et al., 2022), RoBERTa (Liu

Table 1: Model Configurations of ToddlerBERTa.

	Hidden Size	Inter. Size	# Heads	# Layers	# Parameters
ToddlerBERTa-xs	64	256	4	4	0.75 M
ToddlerBERTa-s	128	512	4	4	1.8 M
ToddlerBERTa-base	256	1024	8	8	8.5 M
ToddlerBERTa-l	512	2048	8	8	29.7 M
ToddlerBERTa-xl	768	3072	12	12	92.0 M

et al., 2019), and T5 (Raffel et al., 2019). These baselines are trained from scratch on the competition's exclusive dataset. Since no external models are available, we use these baseline models as references to assess our models' performance within the competition's context.

5 Results and Analysis

As stipulated earlier, a substantial portion of our model evaluations is conducted under BLiMP (Warstadt et al., 2019), encompassing comparisons across various linguistic tasks. Additionally, we undertake a comprehensive evaluation of our best-performing model using the entire prescribed evaluation pipeline. As a result, we present our findings as two distinct sets of results: BLiMP results and main results.

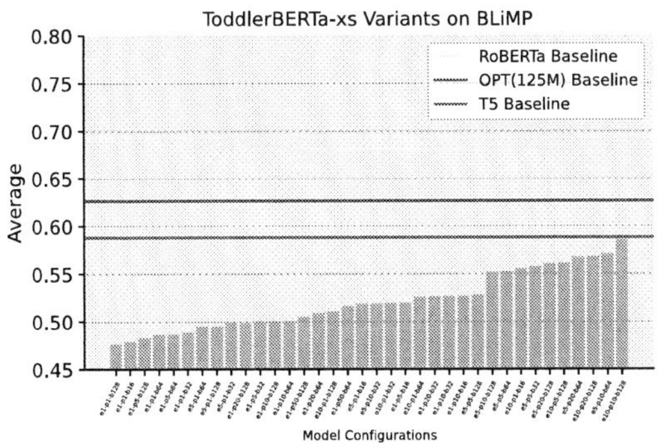

Figure 1: Average scores of the ToddlerBERTa-xs models on BLiMP are reported. We shorten the different configuration names as number of epochs: e, number of dynamic patterns: p and batch size: b.

5.1 BliMP Results

5.1.1 ToddlerBERTa-xs

Our ToddlerBERTa-xs model, with approximately 750 thousand parameters, achieves competitive performance compared to the larger T5 baseline on the BLiMP benchmark, in Figure 1. This data scaling behaviour highlights the potential benefits of optimizing smaller architectures for specific tasks, showcasing efficient language modelling approaches.

5.1.2 ToddlerBERTa-s

ToddlerBERTa-s model, consisting of 1.8 million parameters, exhibits superior performance compared to the OPT baseline across various configurations. Remarkably, experimental results demonstrate that even with smaller parameter sizes, these models can outperform larger counterparts in the low data regime when leveraging the BabyBERTa training and preprocessing recipes.

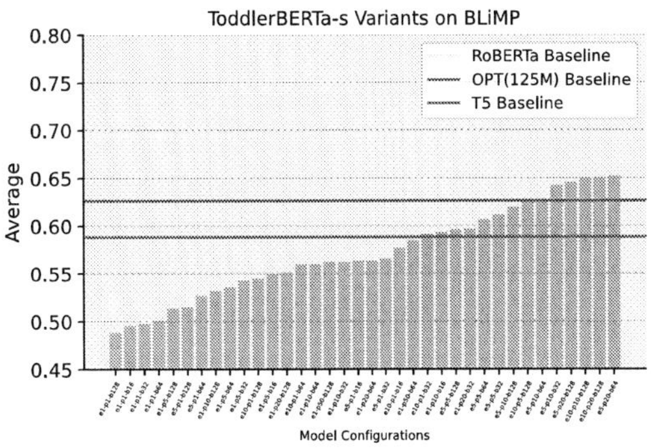

Figure 2: Average scores of the ToddlerBERTa-s models on BLiMP are reported. We shorten the different configuration names as number of epochs: e, number of dynamic patterns: p and batch size: b.

5.1.3 ToddlerBERTa-base

The ToddlerBERTa-base and BabyBERTa (Huebner et al., 2021) have the same number of parameters, which is 8.5 million. However, the best-performing model of ToddlerBERTa-base scores 0.7407 with more epochs and mask patterns than the original, as shown in Figure 3. On the other hand, the original BabyBERTa (Huebner et al., 2021) configuration achieves 0.6660.

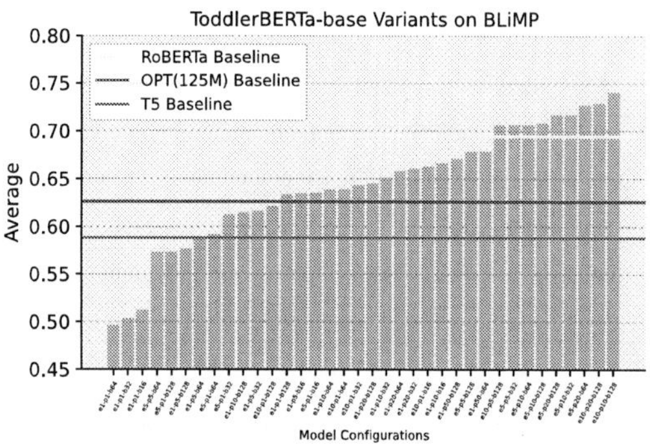

Figure 3: Average scores of the ToddlerBERTa-base models on BLiMP are reported. We shorten the different configuration names as number of epochs: e, number of dynamic patterns: p and batch size: b.

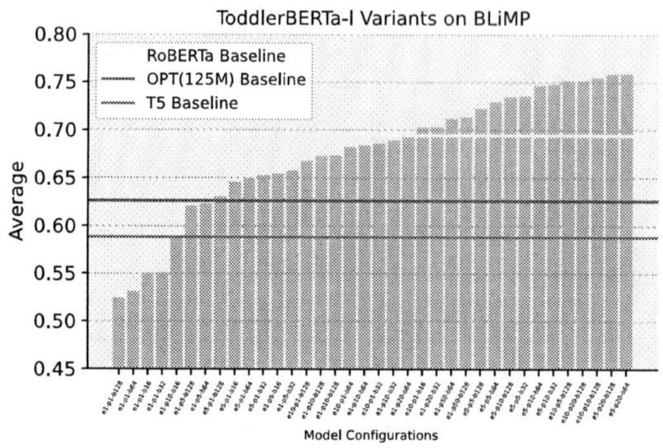

Figure 4: Average scores of the ToddlerBERTa-l models on BLiMP are reported. We shorten the different configuration names as number of epochs: e, number of dynamic patterns: p and batch size: b.

5.1.4 ToddlerBERTa-l

The utilization of data scaling techniques is evidently advantageous in enhancing model performance for grammar learning tasks. However, our research findings demonstrate that surpassing the RoBERTa baseline is achievable through the increase of model parameters. This observation prompts an inquiry into the sustainability of this trend. In order to address this question, we developed ToddlerBERTa-l, featuring a substantial parameter count of approximately 30 million. Our experimental results emphasize the indispensability of model size, despite the relatively modest increase in the top score, Figure 4. Notably, a significant performance boost is observed in the majority of models when larger architectures are employed. These findings underscore the critical role of model size in optimizing grammar learning capabilities.

5.1.5 ToddlerBERTa-xl

To further explore the capabilities of BabyBERTa within the strict-small portion of BabyLM, we introduce ToddlerBERTa-xl, a language model equipped with 92 million parameters similar to RoBERTa (Liu et al., 2019). Our prior experiments have highlighted the significance of both data and model size; however, these studies have predominantly employed relatively smaller model sizes compared to baseline models, which exhibit exceptional results when trained on extended corpora over extended periods. Such large models excel under substantial data volumes but tend to perform inadequately in low-data scenarios. Consequently, previous investigations (Eldan and Li, 2023; Huebner et al., 2021) have often opted for smaller model sizes. Nonetheless, to thoroughly evaluate the boundaries of this approach, we undertake the training of larger models in order to affirm our hypothesis which is that performance will improve with the model scaling. Figure 5 verifies our hypothesis by achieving remarkable results on BLiMP with a significant margin to baselines which share a similar number of parameters.

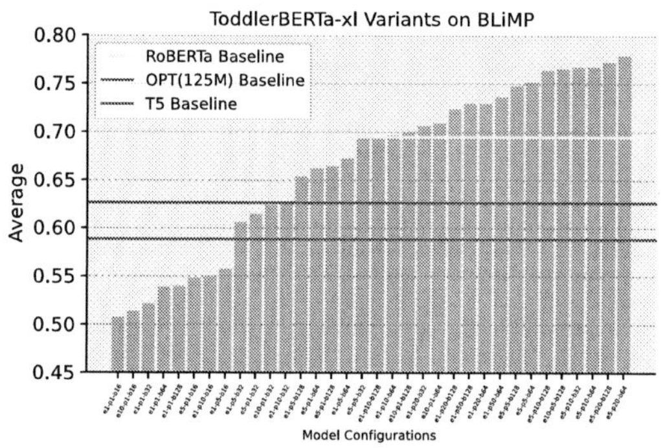

Figure 5: Average scores of the ToddlerBERTa-xl models on BLiMP are reported. We shorten the different configuration names as number of epochs: e, number of dynamic patterns: p and batch size: b.

5.1.6 BLiMP Summary

Our extensive experiments show that improving the BabyBERTa methodology involves using numerous different mask patterns to augment the data, processing single sentences, and using smaller context and vocabulary sizes with limited batch sizes and epochs. However, to achieve superior performance with larger models, we increase batch sizes

Models	Overall	ANA. AGR	ARG. STR	BINDING	CTRL. RAIS.	D-N AGR	ELLIPSIS	FILLER GAP	IRREGULAR	ISLAND	NPI	QUANTIFIERS	S-V AGR
OPT-125m(baseline)	**62.63**	63.75	70.56	67.10	66.48	78.47	62.01	63.83	67.53	48.58	46.71	59.61	56.87
RoBERTa-base(baseline)	**69.47**	81.54	67.12	67.26	67.85	90.75	76.44	63.48	87.43	39.87	55.92	70.53	65.42
T5(baseline)	**57.70**	68.92	63.82	60.40	60.87	72.21	34.41	48.24	77.56	45.59	47.80	56.72	55.81
ToddlerBERTa	**76.68**	87.68	70.62	71.82	69.07	93.44	76.27	81.68	82.80	58.07	63.59	82.64	82.51
Roberta-base	**85.4**	97.30	83.50	77.80	81.9	97.00	91.40	90.10	96.20	80.70	81.00	69.80	91.90

Table 2: BLiMP(Warstadt et al., 2019) benchmark results, baseline scores are taken from the leaderboard page of the competition , RoBERTa-base results from (Huebner et al., 2021).

Models	Overall	HYPERNYM	QA CONGR.(EASY)	QA CONGR.(TRICKY)	SUBJ.-AUX. INVER.	TURN TAKING
OPT-125m(baseline)	**52.72**	50.00	54.69	31.52	70.26	57.14
RoBERTa-base(baseline)	**42.42**	50.80	34.40	34.50	45.60	46.80
T5(baseline)	**43.96**	48.02	40.63	21.21	64.92	45.00
ToddlerBERTa	**57.12**	48.02	62.50	35.76	79.65	59.64

Table 3: BLiMP Supplement benchmark results, baseline scores are taken from the GitHub page of evaluation pipeline.

and the number of epochs. Larger batch sizes enhance training stability, while more epochs help models learn better. Consequently, our best model outperforms the original BabyBERTa model by a substantial 10 point in BLiMP, highlighting the effectiveness of these changes.

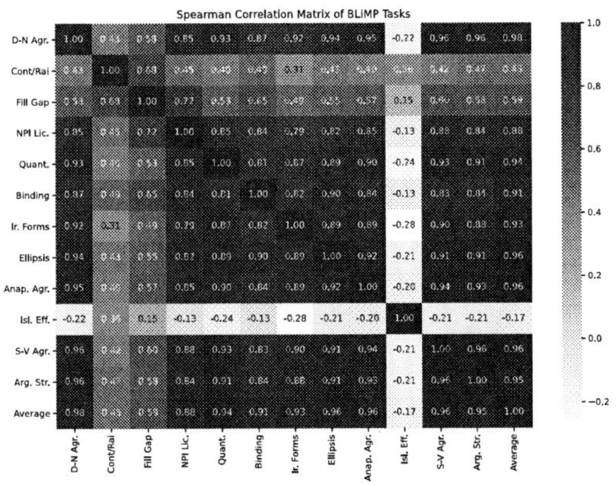

Figure 6: Spearman correlation matrix on the scores of BLiMP tasks.

To refine our models based on BLiMP evaluation, we carefully consider the average results while remaining aware of potential outliers that could have an implicit impact on the reliability of the approach that we take while optimizing the models. To thoroughly explore relationships among the nearly 180 results of our models, we use a Spearman correlation matrix as a robust analytical tool, providing insights into potential patterns and dependencies. See Figure 6 for the correlation matrix

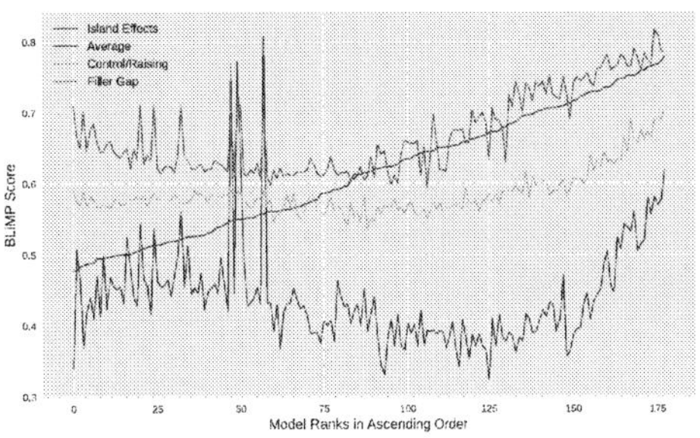

Figure 7: Models are ranked by the average BLiMP score in ascending order, in the Blue time series plot. Other time series plots represent how task scores vary while the average score consistently improves.

The majority of the tasks exhibit a strong positive correlation with the average, with the exception of Island Effects, Filler Gap, and Control/Raising. In order to gain insights into the underlying reasons behind this anomaly, we present a visual analysis by plotting the scores of these specific tasks in ascending order based on their respective average scores, as illustrated in Figure 7. The plot reveals that all task scores either improve slightly or stay around a fixed interval. This observation leads us to postulate that these particular tasks may be inherently more challenging, demanding a larger volume

Models	Overall	CR	LC	MV	RP	SC	CR_LC	CR_RTP	MV_LC	MV_RTP	SC_LC	SC_RP
OPT-125m(baseline)	**9.63**	50.77	53.55	99.47	99.91	77.15	0.37	-70.33	-72.14	-77.60	13.76	-68.92
RoBERTa-base(baseline)	**8.22**	43.08	100.00	97.67	76.73	86.24	-28.28	-77.69	-99.30	-79.36	16.28	-45.02
T5(baseline)	**-6.38**	21.11	100.00	33.36	82.54	77.58	-78.33	-62.04	-100.00	-79.70	-25.28	-39.43
ToddlerBERTa	**2.51**	51.61	80.00	99.95	71.23	45.90	2.32	-72.15	-85.73	-82.68	-34.41	-49.60

Table 4: MSGS (Warstadt et al., 2020) benchmark results, baseline scores are taken from the GitHub page of evaluation pipeline

Models	Overall	CoLA(MCC)	SST-2	MRPC(F1)	QQP(F1)	MNLI	MNLI-MM	QNLI	RTE	BoolQ	MultiRC	WSC
OPT-125m(baseline)	**62.38**	15.22	84.25	74.13	78.89	67.66	69.43	65.40	55.26	65.28	51.37	59.04
RoBERTa-base(baseline)	**67.38**	25.75	87.60	77.27	82.76	73.15	77.27	81.54	53.54	65.70	61.23	57.83
T5(baseline)	**58.34**	11.26	80.91	78.49	72.19	52.80	56.70	63.91	50.51	63.49	48.85	62.65
ToddlerBERTa	**64.94**	37.37	86.02	79.29	74.53	70.28	70.34	64.83	54.55	67.77	47.97	61.45

Table 5: SuperGLUE (Wang et al., 2019) benchmark results, baseline scores are taken from the GitHub page of evaluation pipeline

of data and more complex model architectures for optimal performance.

5.2 Main Results

After evaluating various models on BLiMP (Warstadt et al., 2019), we select the best one as our final model which is a ToddlerBERTa-xl that is trained for 5 epochs with 20 different mask patterns and 64 as the batch size. We then assess its performance on Blimp Supplement and fine-tune it on (Wang et al., 2019) and MSGS (Warstadt et al., 2020) using the evaluation pipeline (Warstadt et al., 2023).

BLiMP: In our investigation, we focus on evaluating our models compared to baselines during iterative training. We also include results of RoBERTa-base (Liu et al., 2019) from Huebner et al. (2021) for a more comprehensive analysis in Table 2. RoBERTa-base outperforms our ToddlerBERTa model, largely due to its extensive 3-billion-word training data, while ToddlerBERTa is trained on a smaller 10-million-word dataset.

To narrow the performance gap, we increase mask patterns in ToddlerBERTa's training, improving data utilization despite the 1-billion-word exposure constraint. Our results show that ToddlerBERTa, with limited data, can perform relatively well compared to RoBERTa-base, highlighting the effectiveness of data augmentation by employing different masks for enhancing language model training.

SuperGLUE: In the SuperGLUE benchmark, our models face a challenge due to their exclusive focus on single sentences while the dataset often includes inputs with multiple sentences. However, even with this constraint, our model competes remarkably well with baselines trained on multiple sentences. Our results in Table 5, highlight our model's ability to grasp complex linguistic relationships and reasoning, aligning its performance with state-of-the-art baselines that use broader contextual information. This showcases our model's potential for robust language understanding, even in scenarios with multi-sentence inputs.

MSGS: The Mixed Signals Generalization Set (MSGS) evaluates language models' generalization capabilities for both linguistic and surface features. Our analysis in Table 4 suggests that the poor performance may be due in part to overexposure. To enhance training, we add more mask patterns and use them for numerous epochs, which can lead to repeated patterns and examples in the training data. This overexposure may affect the model's learning process, causing a preference for specific features. As a result, the model might struggle to adapt to novel patterns in the MSGS. On the other hand, baseline models also suffer from poor performance. Considering the worst score is -100 and the best is 100, their performances are no better than ours which points out that undertraining is another drawback for generalization.

BLiMP Supplement: The challenge has been enriched with an extra benchmark, the details of which have not been published yet, but it is presumed to be connected to the BLiMP evaluation framework. Analysis of the results presented in Table 3 leads us to speculate that the performance gains in BLiMP are still relevant whereas insufficient to truly accomplish a major performance. ToddlerBERTa achieves better scores than the baselines however performance of OPT-125m (Zhang et al., 2022) and T5 (Raffel et al., 2019) compared to RoBERTa (Liu et al., 2019) can be explained by the presence of the decoder in T5 and OPT architectures. Further analysis will be ineffective given that details of benchmark are non-disclosed yet.

6 Conclusion

We undertake a systematic and rigorous exploration of language models, building upon the foundational work of BabyBERTa. Through the development and evaluation of five distinct ToddlerBERTa models, we have demonstrated the significance of hyperparameter choices and model sizes in the context of natural language processing.

Our experiments have revealed the potential benefits of optimizing smaller architectures for specific linguistic tasks, showcasing the efficiency of language modelling techniques in tackling various challenges. Additionally, our best-performing ToddlerBERTa models have exhibited competitive performance compared to established baselines, showcasing their adaptability and capacity to excel in diverse language understanding tasks.

The comprehensive evaluations conducted on BLiMP, SuperGLUE, MSGS, and the new BLiMP Supplement benchmark have provided valuable insights into the strengths and limitations of our approach. While our research has shed light on the impact of different hyperparameters, we acknowledge that further exploration of model architectures and training methodologies may yield additional advancements in language modelling.

By contributing to the collective understanding of transformer-based models and their potential for natural language processing, our research aims to inspire future investigations and innovations in the field. As the quest for advancements in language modelling continues, we emphasize the importance of replicability and reproducibility in research to facilitate the development of robust and reliable language models.

7 Limitations

Despite the contributions of our research, it is essential to acknowledge its limitations. Firstly, the exploration of hyperparameters and model sizes may not have encompassed all possible configurations due to computational constraints. This leaves room for potential superior settings to be uncovered. Secondly, the evaluation framework's focus on transformer-based models may limit the comparability with other non-transformer architectures. Additionally, the fixed dataset used for training and evaluation may restrict the model's exposure to diverse linguistic patterns and contexts. Furthermore, the reliance on single-sentence processing during pretraining could impact the model's performance on tasks requiring broader contextual understanding. Lastly, our study did not extensively explore architectural innovations or novel training methodologies. Despite these limitations, our research provides valuable insights into language modeling, calling for further investigations to address these constraints and advance the field.

Ethics Statement

The model under consideration, ToddlerBERTa, is devoid of generative capabilities, thereby ensuring that it cannot engender unfair, biased, or harmful content. The datasets employed in this study have been sourced from widely acknowledged repositories with an established reputation for safety in research applications, being meticulously selected to preclude the inclusion of personal information or offensive material.

Acknowledgements

We would like to express our gratitude to the KUIS AI Center for their generous provision of computing resources for this project. We would also like to extend our appreciation to Gözde Gül Şahin for her valuable feedback and insightful discussions.

Implementation and Hardware Details

We use the official repository of the BabyBERTa (Huebner et al., 2021). We use the transformers (Wolf et al., 2019) to train our tokenizer and host our best model. We use the Tesla T4 and Tesla A100 provided by KUIS AI Center.

References

Sid Black, Leo Gao, Phil Wang, Connor Leahy, and Stella Rose Biderman. 2021. Gpt-neo: Large scale autoregressive language modeling with mesh-tensorflow.

Tom B. Brown, Benjamin Mann, Nick Ryder, Melanie Subbiah, Jared Kaplan, Prafulla Dhariwal, Arvind Neelakantan, Pranav Shyam, Girish Sastry, Amanda Askell, Sandhini Agarwal, Ariel Herbert-Voss, Gretchen Krueger, T. J. Henighan, Rewon Child, Aditya Ramesh, Daniel M. Ziegler, Jeff Wu, Clemens Winter, Christopher Hesse, Mark Chen, Eric Sigler, Mateusz Litwin, Scott Gray, Benjamin Chess, Jack Clark, Christopher Berner, Sam McCandlish, Alec Radford, Ilya Sutskever, and Dario Amodei. 2020. Language models are few-shot learners. *ArXiv*, abs/2005.14165.

Aakanksha Chowdhery, Sharan Narang, Jacob Devlin, Maarten Bosma, Gaurav Mishra, Adam Roberts, Paul Barham, Hyung Won Chung, Charles Sutton, Sebastian Gehrmann, Parker Schuh, Kensen Shi, Sasha Tsvyashchenko, Joshua Maynez, Abhishek Rao, Parker Barnes, Yi Tay, Noam M. Shazeer, Vinodkumar Prabhakaran, Emily Reif, Nan Du, Benton C. Hutchinson, Reiner Pope, James Bradbury, Jacob Austin, Michael Isard, Guy Gur-Ari, Pengcheng Yin, Toju Duke, Anselm Levskaya, Sanjay Ghemawat, Sunipa Dev, Henryk Michalewski, Xavier García, Vedant Misra, Kevin Robinson, Liam Fedus, Denny Zhou, Daphne Ippolito, David Luan, Hyeontaek Lim, Barret Zoph, Alexander Spiridonov, Ryan Sepassi, David Dohan, Shivani Agrawal, Mark Omernick, Andrew M. Dai, Thanumalayan Sankaranarayana Pillai, Marie Pellat, Aitor Lewkowycz, Erica Moreira, Rewon Child, Oleksandr Polozov, Katherine Lee, Zongwei Zhou, Xuezhi Wang, Brennan Saeta, Mark Díaz, Orhan Firat, Michele Catasta, Jason Wei, Kathleen S. Meier-Hellstern, Douglas Eck, Jeff Dean, Slav Petrov, and Noah Fiedel. 2022. Palm: Scaling language modeling with pathways. *ArXiv*, abs/2204.02311.

Kevin Clark, Minh-Thang Luong, Quoc V. Le, and Christopher D. Manning. 2020. Electra: Pre-training text encoders as discriminators rather than generators. *ArXiv*, abs/2003.10555.

Jacob Devlin, Ming-Wei Chang, Kenton Lee, and Kristina Toutanova. 2019. Bert: Pre-training of deep bidirectional transformers for language understanding. *ArXiv*, abs/1810.04805.

Ronen Eldan and Yuan-Fang Li. 2023. Tinystories: How small can language models be and still speak coherent english? *ArXiv*, abs/2305.07759.

Leo Gao, Jonathan Tow, Stella Biderman, Sid Black, Anthony DiPofi, Charles Foster, Laurence Golding, Jeffrey Hsu, Kyle McDonell, Niklas Muennighoff, Jason Phang, Laria Reynolds, Eric Tang, Anish Thite, Ben Wang, Kevin Wang, and Andy Zou. 2021. A framework for few-shot language model evaluation.

Jordan Hoffmann, Sebastian Borgeaud, Arthur Mensch, Elena Buchatskaya, Trevor Cai, Eliza Rutherford, Diego de Las Casas, Lisa Anne Hendricks, Johannes Welbl, Aidan Clark, Tom Hennigan, Eric Noland, Katie Millican, George van den Driessche, Bogdan Damoc, Aurelia Guy, Simon Osindero, Karen Simonyan, Erich Elsen, Jack W. Rae, Oriol Vinyals, and L. Sifre. 2022. Training compute-optimal large language models. *ArXiv*, abs/2203.15556.

Philip A. Huebner, Elior Sulem, Cynthia Fisher, and Dan Roth. 2021. Babyberta: Learning more grammar with small-scale child-directed language. In *Conference on Computational Natural Language Learning*.

Xiaoqi Jiao, Yichun Yin, Lifeng Shang, Xin Jiang, Xiao Chen, Linlin Li, Fang Wang, and Qun Liu. 2019. Tinybert: Distilling bert for natural language understanding. In *Findings*.

Zhenzhong Lan, Mingda Chen, Sebastian Goodman, Kevin Gimpel, Piyush Sharma, and Radu Soricut. 2019. Albert: A lite bert for self-supervised learning of language representations. *ArXiv*, abs/1909.11942.

Yinhan Liu, Myle Ott, Naman Goyal, Jingfei Du, Mandar Joshi, Danqi Chen, Omer Levy, Mike Lewis, Luke Zettlemoyer, and Veselin Stoyanov. 2019. Roberta: A robustly optimized bert pretraining approach. *ArXiv*, abs/1907.11692.

OpenAI. 2023. Gpt-4 technical report. *ArXiv*, abs/2303.08774.

Colin Raffel, Noam M. Shazeer, Adam Roberts, Katherine Lee, Sharan Narang, Michael Matena, Yanqi Zhou, Wei Li, and Peter J. Liu. 2019. Exploring the limits of transfer learning with a unified text-to-text transformer. *ArXiv*, abs/1910.10683.

Victor Sanh, Lysandre Debut, Julien Chaumond, and Thomas Wolf. 2019. Distilbert, a distilled version of bert: smaller, faster, cheaper and lighter. *ArXiv*, abs/1910.01108.

Ashish Vaswani, Noam M. Shazeer, Niki Parmar, Jakob Uszkoreit, Llion Jones, Aidan N. Gomez, Lukasz Kaiser, and Illia Polosukhin. 2017. Attention is all you need. In *NIPS*.

Alex Wang, Yada Pruksachatkun, Nikita Nangia, Amanpreet Singh, Julian Michael, Felix Hill, Omer Levy, and Samuel R. Bowman. 2019. Superglue: A stickier benchmark for general-purpose language understanding systems. *ArXiv*, abs/1905.00537.

Alex Warstadt, Aaron Mueller, Leshem Choshen, Ethan Gotlieb Wilcox, Chengxu Zhuang, Juan Ciro, Rafael Mosquera, Adina Williams, Bhargavi Paranjabe, Tal Linzen, and Ryan Cotterell. 2023. Findings of the 2023 BabyLM Challenge: Sample-efficient pretraining on developmentally plausible corpora. In *Proceedings of the 2023 BabyLM Challenge*. Association for Computational Linguistics (ACL).

Alex Warstadt, Alicia Parrish, Haokun Liu, Anhad Mohananey, Wei Peng, Sheng-Fu Wang, and Samuel R. Bowman. 2019. Blimp: A benchmark of linguistic minimal pairs for english. *Transactions of the Association for Computational Linguistics*, 8:377–392.

Alex Warstadt, Yian Zhang, Haau-Sing Li, Haokun Liu, and Samuel R. Bowman. 2020. Learning which features matter: Roberta acquires a preference for linguistic generalizations (eventually). In *Conference on Empirical Methods in Natural Language Processing*.

Thomas Wolf, Lysandre Debut, Victor Sanh, Julien Chaumond, Clement Delangue, Anthony Moi, Pierric Cistac, Tim Rault, Rémi Louf, Morgan Funtowicz, and Jamie Brew. 2019. Huggingface's transformers: State-of-the-art natural language processing. *ArXiv*, abs/1910.03771.

Susan Zhang, Stephen Roller, Naman Goyal, Mikel Artetxe, Moya Chen, Shuohui Chen, Christopher Dewan, Mona Diab, Xian Li, Xi Victoria Lin, Todor Mihaylov, Myle Ott, Sam Shleifer, Kurt Shuster, Daniel Simig, Punit Singh Koura, Anjali Sridhar, Tianlu Wang, and Luke Zettlemoyer. 2022. Opt: Open pre-trained transformer language models. *ArXiv*, abs/2205.01068.

CogMemLM: Human-Like Memory Mechanisms Improve Performance and Cognitive Plausibility of LLMs

Lukas Thoma[⋆,∘,•], **Ivonne Weyers**[∘], **Erion Çano**[⋆], **Stefan Schweter**[⋄], **Jutta L. Mueller**[∘], **Benjamin Roth**[⋆,△]
[⋆]Faculty of Computer Science, University of Vienna, Vienna, Austria
[∘]Department of Linguistics, University of Vienna, Vienna, Austria
[•]UniVie Doctoral School Computer Science, Vienna, Austria
[△]Faculty of Philological and Cultural Studies, University of Vienna, Vienna, Austria
{lukas.thoma, ivonne.weyers, erion.cano, jutta.mueller, benjamin.roth}@univie.ac.at
[⋄]schweter.ml, stefan@schweter.eu

1 Introduction

Current large language models (LLMs) demonstrate impressive NLP performance, but they require massive amounts of training data. RoBERTa (Liu et al., 2019), for instance, sees 30 billion words during pre-training, which amounts to roughly 300x as many words as a human child hears until the age of 12 (Warstadt and Bowman, 2022). It is one of the explicit aims of the BabyLM challenge (Warstadt et al., 2023) to address this issue by training models on developmentally-plausible quantities and types of data (for similar approaches, see Hosseini et al., 2022; Huebner et al., 2021), in order to ultimately develop more cognitively plausible models that can inform research into human language acquisition (Keller, 2010; Dupoux, 2018).

In the present contribution to the BabyLM STRICT track, we take a threefold approach: firstly, we implement a simple curriculum learning approach and split the provided BabyLM dataset into four sub-datasets by increasing complexity, to broadly structure the data such that it better reflects what kind of input is available to infants and children throughout development (see 2.1). Secondly, we simulate a memory-based vocabulary learning inspired by psycholinguistic work (Perruchet and Vinter, 1998). Starting with a set of single characters, larger linguistics units (sub-words, words, and multi-words) are created based on the core memory mechanisms *activation* and *forgetting*. Possible units are limited in size, imitating working-memory constraints, but become larger across development (see 2.2). Thirdly, we implement redundant text representations to make the compositional aspect of language more salient: The lexicons that emerge from our curriculum learning steps, respectively, shape the (token) encoding of the given input text (see 2.3).

We pre-trained a RoBERTa-base architecture with masked language modeling and our CogMemLM-s model achieves improved results compared to the BabyLM RoBERTa baseline model in 27 out of 39 evaluation tasks. Although the so far integrated mechanisms have been implemented in a simplified form with regard to cognitive plausibility, it is intriguing that our pre-training method already improved performance considerably.

2 Methodology

2.1 Curriculum Learning

Child-directed speech typically consists of shorter and less syntactically complex sentences, more repetitions and limited vocabulary compared to adult-directed speech (Foushee et al., 2016; Kirchhoff and Schimmel, 2005). As the child's language competence increases, the linguistic input received from the environment becomes both more complex and diverse (Kunert et al., 2011). In an attempt to reflect this trajectory, we subdivided the provided 98M word corpus into four approximately equally-sized datasets of increasing linguistic complexity and lexical diversity (for details see Appendix A Table 1). The division was based mainly on the domains which the original corpora stem from and a subjective rating of their linguistic complexity and diversity; i.e. Dataset 1 (least complex) included materials mainly from child-speech contexts, whereas Dataset 4 (most complex) comprised the Wikipedia and Written English corpora. Although this split is rather coarse, it is only a first attempt at a curriculum learning approach, which may be followed-up by more fine-grained analyses and sub-divisions of the available materials.

2.2 Lexicon Creation

Because of computational and memory limitations in humans, any type of input, including language input, has to be "chunked" into units that can be stored and further manipulated (Archibald, 2017;

Proceedings of the 27th Conference on Computational Natural Language Learning: Volume 2: The BabyLM Challenge, pages 180–185
December 6-7, 2023

Baddeley, 2003). For infants, the additional challenge consists in learning to chunk the perceived language input such that the resulting memorized chunks align with word boundaries, which allows for words to be stored in and retrieved from the lexicon. Inspired by the PARSER model for word segmentation (Perruchet and Vinter, 1998), we used a memory-based, variable parsing algorithm for lexicon creation. We start with a set of single characters and from these, larger linguistics units (sub-words, words, and multi-words) are created based on the core memory mechanisms *activation* and *forgetting*. The text data is processed sentence by sentence. Sentences are split into linguistic sub-units (percepts), which vary in size (see Appendix A). If a percept already exists, its activation value is increased by 1, strengthening its representation, if not, an entry is created and receives an activation of 1. After each processed sentence, forgetting is applied by subtracting 1/1000 from all activations. Any percept that is not re-activated within 1000 sentences (activation = 0) is removed from the lexicon. In curriculum 1 (C 1), lexicon creation starts with an empty lexicon, C 2 builds upon the lexicon of C 1 and so on. A 10 % sample of each data set was processed to create the lexicons which resulted in the following number of percepts: 13,444 after C 1, 22,740 after C 2, 25,887 after C 3 and 39,126 after C 4. We used the lexicon information to roughly dimension the vocabulary size of the respective curriculum tokenizers (see A.3) and to re-represent the training data for the perception shaping (see 2.3).

2.3 Perception Shaping

The BabyLM dataset was given in three different representations during pre-training: original text, coarse re-representation, and fine re-representation. For the coarse re-representation, text was processed left-to-right and the lexicon was searched for the longest fitting percept. Following this percept, an additional whitespace was added. For the fine re-representation, the identified percepts were split up further based on smaller units in the lexicon. The representation with the highest activation on average was used to split the coarse percept. Again, whitespaces were added after identified percepts. In the final step, whitespaces were normalized (multiple spaces to one). Usually, an existing token for e.g., the word "ended" would always be encoded with the corresponding token ID. In our training, however, linguistic units would also be encoded in two alternative representations, which increases the likelihood of "ended" also being encoded as "end" and "ed".

3 Results and Conclusion

Building on psycholinguistic work on memory-based word learning, we simulated lexicon creation given the BabyLM dataset as input. We used this information in a four step curriculum learning approach to guide the encoding of text, thereby increasing the cognitive plausibility in the following aspects: the language acquisition trajectory is reflected in the (increasing) number and quality of available linguistic units (percepts), which are not static, as usual in modern NLP, but change over time in our pre-training method. These percepts are further used to create redundant representations of text, based on the assumption that elements in memory shape perception in humans. Our CogMemLM-s model shows increased performance in 27 out of 39 tasks compared to the BabyLM RoBERTa baseline model, which is a significant result ($p = 0.0071$, for details see Appendix A, all results are based on the BabyLM Evaluation Pipeline Warstadt et al. (2023); Gao et al. (2021)). The most striking improvement was archived in the BLiMP and BLiMP Supplement task sets, for which the relative change is 54 % and 46 %, respectively (better performance in 16/17 tasks).

Although these results suggest that implementing human-like cognitive mechanisms in LLMs is a promising avenue for future research and can result in substantial gains in performance also for small training datasets, a few limitations should be addressed. The memory processes as implemented here are relatively simplistic and do not yet consider that forgetting, as observed in humans, is non-linear (Ebbinghaus, 1885; Vlach and Sandhofer, 2012). Nor have we considered interference, which may have a substantial impact in lexicon creation (James et al., 2023). Furthermore, the chunk size of units that infants segment from language input and that subsequently enter the lexicon remains a topic of considerable debate (Grimm et al., 2017). Finally, many aspects of our approach are so far only integrated at text level, however, the lexical information could also be directly implemented in the tokenizer. Planned ablation studies will allow a more detailed evaluation of these first results and provide direction for future extensions of the present implementations.

Acknowledgements

The present research was funded by the Go!Digital 3.0 grant program of the Austrian Academy of Sciences (GD3.0 2021-18 CogML). We thank our intern student Célestin Eve for assisting us in this project. Furthermore, we would like to thank Google's TPU Research Cloud (TRC) program for giving us access to TPUs that were used for training our BabyLM models. We would also like to thank Hugging Face for providing the ability to host and perform inferencing of our models on the Hugging Face Model Hub.

References

Lisa MD Archibald. 2017. Slp-educator classroom collaboration: A review to inform reason-based practice. *Autism & Developmental Language Impairments*, 2:2396941516680369.

Alan D. Baddeley. 2003. Working memory: looking back and looking forward. *Nature Reviews Neuroscience*, 4:829–839.

Nelson Cowan. 2016. Working memory maturation: Can we get at the essence of cognitive growth? *Perspectives on Psychological Science*, 11(2):239–264. PMID: 26993277.

Emmanuel Dupoux. 2018. Cognitive science in the era of artificial intelligence: A roadmap for reverse-engineering the infant language-learner. *Cognition*, 173:43–59.

Hermann Ebbinghaus. 1885. *Über das Gedächtnis: Untersuchungen zur experimentellen Psychologie*. Duncker & Humblot.

Ruthe Foushee, Thomas L. Griffiths, and Mahesh Srinivasan. 2016. Lexical complexity of child-directed and overheard speech: Implications for learning. In *Proceedings of the 38th Annual Meeting of the Cognitive Science Society, CogSci 2016*, Proceedings of the 38th Annual Meeting of the Cognitive Science Society, CogSci 2016, pages 1697–1702. The Cognitive Science Society.

Leo Gao, Jonathan Tow, Stella Biderman, Sid Black, Anthony DiPofi, Charles Foster, Laurence Golding, Jeffrey Hsu, Kyle McDonell, Niklas Muennighoff, Jason Phang, Laria Reynolds, Eric Tang, Anish Thite, Ben Wang, Kevin Wang, and Andy Zou. 2021. A framework for few-shot language model evaluation.

Robert Grimm, Giovanni Cassani, Steven Gillis, and Walter Daelemans. 2017. Facilitatory Effects of Multi-Word Units in Lexical Processing and Word Learning: A Computational Investigation. *Frontiers in Psychology*, 8.

Eghbal A. Hosseini, Martin Schrimpf, Yian Zhang, Samuel Bowman, Noga Zaslavsky, and Evelina Fedorenko. 2022. Artificial neural network language models align neurally and behaviorally with humans even after a developmentally realistic amount of training. *bioRxiv*.

Philip A. Huebner, Elior Sulem, Fisher Cynthia, and Dan Roth. 2021. BabyBERTa: Learning more grammar with small-scale child-directed language. In *Proceedings of the 25th Conference on Computational Natural Language Learning*, pages 624–646, Online. Association for Computational Linguistics.

Emma James, M. Gareth Gaskell, Gráinne Murphy, Josie Tulip, and Lisa M. Henderson. 2023. Word learning in the context of semantic prior knowledge: evidence of interference from feature-based neighbours in children and adults. *Language, Cognition and Neuroscience*, 38(2):157–174. Publisher: Routledge _eprint: https://doi.org/10.1080/23273798.2022.2102198.

Frank Keller. 2010. Cognitively plausible models of human language processing. In *Proceedings of the ACL 2010 Conference Short Papers*, pages 60–67, Uppsala, Sweden. Association for Computational Linguistics.

Katrin Kirchhoff and Steven Schimmel. 2005. Statistical properties of infant-directed versus adult-directed speech: Insights from speech recognition. *The Journal of the Acoustical Society of America*, 117(4):2238–2246.

Richard Kunert, Raquel Fernandez, and Willem Zuidema. 2011. Adaptation in Child Directed Speech: Evidence from Corpora.

Yinhan Liu, Myle Ott, Naman Goyal, Jingfei Du, Mandar Joshi, Danqi Chen, Omer Levy, Mike Lewis, Luke Zettlemoyer, and Veselin Stoyanov. 2019. Roberta: A robustly optimized bert pretraining approach. Cite arxiv:1907.11692.

Pierre Perruchet and Annie Vinter. 1998. Parser: A model for word segmentation. *Journal of Memory and Language*, 39:246–263.

Haley Vlach and Catherine Sandhofer. 2012. Fast Mapping Across Time: Memory Processes Support Children's Retention of Learned Words. *Frontiers in Psychology*, 3.

Alex Warstadt and Samuel R. Bowman. 2022. What artificial neural networks can tell us about human language acquisition. *CoRR*, abs/2208.07998.

Alex Warstadt, Aaron Mueller, Leshem Choshen, Ethan Gotlieb Wilcox, Chengxu Zhuang, Juan Ciro, Rafael Mosquera, Adina Williams, Bhargavi Paranjabe, Tal Linzen, and Ryan Cotterell. 2023. Findings of the 2023 BabyLM Challenge: Sample-efficient pretraining on developmentally plausible corpora. In *Proceedings of the 2023 BabyLM Challenge*. Association for Computational Linguistics (ACL).

A Appendix

A.1 Schematic Overview of CogMemLM-s

Figure 1 shows the basic concept of our approach: Based on the RoBERTa architecture, CogMemLM-s is first trained on the Curriculum 1 Data Set. In the Tokenizer C 1 only 10 000 elements of the (final) Tokenizer are available, a number that is influenced by the size of the Lexicon C 1. Also based on Lexicon C 1 two alternative representations are created for every original sample in the Curriculum 1 Data Set: a coarse and a fine re-representation, as for the following example sentence:
Original: *She was a beautiful girl.*
Coarse: *She was a be aut if ul girl .*
Fine: *She was a be au t if ul gi rl .*

For curriculum 2, the RoBERTa architecture is initialized based on the resulting ComMemLM-s_c1, and the process descried for C 1 is repeated. The same applies to C 3 and C 4. The number of available elements in the respective tokenizers grows for each curriculum and in C 4 the full model vocabulary is available (see A.3 for further details).

A.2 Percept Lengths in Lexicon Creation

We assume that the mean length of sub-units is three and that initially, there are four working memory slots available for these sub-units. In order to account for cognitive growth throughout infancy and childhood (Cowan, 2016), we increase the number of available working memory slots and thereby the possible length of percepts across curriculum training steps: curriculum 1 (C 1): 4 slots, percepts of length 2-12 characters; C 2: 5, 2-15; C 3: 6, 2-18; C 4: 7, 2-21.

A.3 Tokenizer

We trained byte-level BPE tokenizers on the curriculum datasets as follows: Tokenizer C1 (model vocabulary 10 000) on C 1 dataset, tokenizer C 2 (model vocabulary 20 000) on datasets C 1 and C 2, tokenizer C 3 (model vocabulary 30 000) on datasets C 1, C 2, and C 3, and tokenizer C 4 (model vocabulary 40 000) on the full BabyLM dataset. The intersection of all model vocabularies was used as the final tokenizer (vocabulary size 41 130). In the curriculum training, however, only the tokens of the respective curriculum tokenizer were available (using the IDs of the final tokenizer).

A.4 Model Training

We used the same RoBERTa base model provided by the BabyML organizers for all model instances that we trained. The detailed model parameters are specified at Liu et al. (2019). The training data were organized in four sets of growing complexity, as illustrated in Table 1. The vocabulary size of the full training data is 41130. For each curriculum, the models were trained for 100 epochs, with maximal sequence length 512, learning rate 0.0001 and batch size 256.

A.5 BabyLM Leaderboard Results

Table 2-5 show the results of the official BabyLM model leader board `https://dynabench.org/tasks/baby_strict` for our model and the comparable BabyLM RoBERTa baseline model.

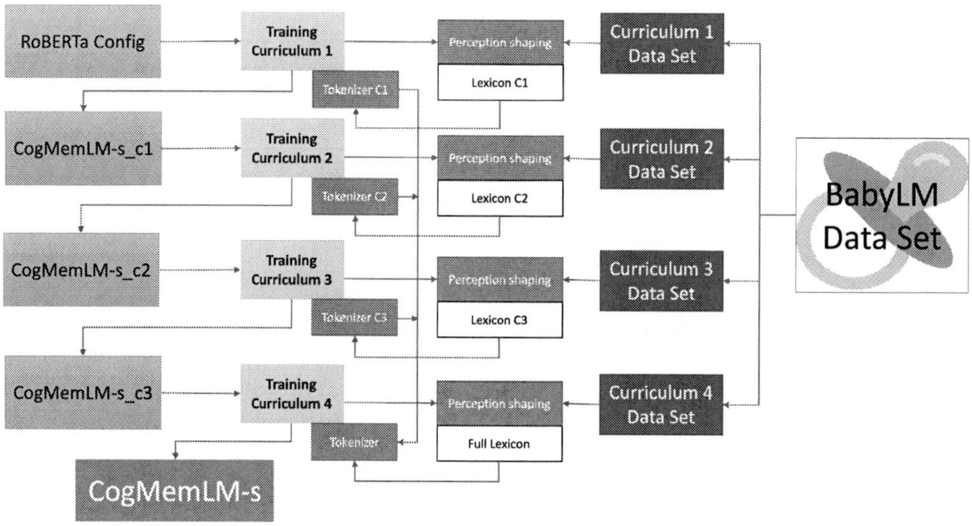

Figure 1: Schematic overview of CogMemLM-s.

	Corpus	Domain	# Words
C 1	CHILDES (MacWhinney, 2000)	Child-directed speech	4.21 M
	Children's Book Test (Hill et al., 2016)	Children's books	5.55 M
	Children's Stories Text Corpus	Children's books	3.22 M
	OpenSubtitles (Lison and Tiedemann, 2016)	Movie subtitles	31.28 M/4
C 2	Switchboard Dialog Act Corpus (Stolcke et al., 2000)	Dialogue	1.18 M
	British National Corpus (BNC), dialogue portion	Dialogue	8.16 M
	Simple Wikipedia	Wikipedia (Simple EN)	14.66 M/2
	OpenSubtitles (Lison and Tiedemann, 2016)	Movie subtitles	31.28 M/4
C 3	QCRI Educational Domain Corpus (QED; Abdelali et al., 2014)	Educational video subtitles	10.24 M
	Simple Wikipedia	Wikipedia (Simple EN)	14.66 M/2
	OpenSubtitles (Lison and Tiedemann, 2016)	Movie subtitles	31.28 M/4
C 4	Wikipedia	Wikipedia (English)	10.08 M
	Standardized Project Gutenberg Corpus (Gerlach and Font-Clos, 2018)	Written English	9.46 M
	OpenSubtitles (Lison and Tiedemann, 2016)	Movie subtitles	31.28 M/4

Table 1: Split of the BabyLM-STRICT dataset into curriculum subsets (C 1–C 4). The open subtitles corpus is represented in all curricula, as this type of language input is assumed to be constant across all developmental stages.

Model	ANA. AGR	AGR. STR	BINDING	CTRL. RAIS.	D-N AGR	ELLIPSIS	FILLER. GAP	IRREG. FORMS	ISLAND	NPI	QUANTIFIERS	S-V AGR
BLM RoBERTa	59.2	62.05	48.03	54.90	49.76	41.05	56.26	51.76	40.21	38.79	49.10	51.49
CogMemLM-s	88.75	73.31	73.24	71.06	93.65	89.09	73.09	85.24	61.81	70.15	69.65	78.28
change	*49.92*	*18.15*	*52.49*	*29.44*	*88.20*	*117.03*	*29.91*	*64.68*	*53.72*	*80.85*	*41.85*	*52.03*

Table 2: Results of our model compared with BabyLM RoBERTa-base on the BLiMP benchmark. The accuracy of the two models and the relative change between them are reported in percent.
Avg. BLiMP: baseline 50.22, ours 77.27.

Model	HYPERNYM	QA CONGR. (EASY)	QA CONGR. (TRICKY)	SUBJ.-AUX. INVERSION	TURN TAKING
BabyLM RoBERTa	50.81	34.38	34.55	45.60	46.79
CogMemLM-s	50.12	67.19	46.06	80.63	65.71
change	*-1.36*	*95.43*	*33.31*	*76.82*	*40.44*

Table 3: Results of our model compared with BabyLM RoBERTa-base on the BLiMP Supplement benchmark. The accuracy of the two models and the relative change between them are reported in percent.
Avg. BLiMP Suppl.: baseline 42.43, ours 61.94.

Model	COLA	SST-2	MRPC (F1)	QQP (F1)	MNLI	MNLI-MM	QNLI	RTE	BOOLQ	MULTIRC	WSC
BabyLM RoBERTa	45.30	87.80	82.00	84.54	77.10	77.94	84.08	54.55	59.89	67.58	61.45
CogMemLM-s	44.93	89.57	82.52	85.84	78.16	79.34	85.39	53.54	68.33	66.59	60.24
change	*-0.82*	*2.02*	*0.63*	*1.54*	*1.37*	*1.80*	*1.56*	*-1.85*	*14.09*	*-1.46*	*-1.97*

Table 4: Results of our model compared with BabyLM RoBERTa-base on the SuperGLUE benchmark. The accuracy and F1 score of the two models and the relative change between them are reported in percent.
Avg. (Super)GLUE: baseline 71.11, ours 72.22.

Model	CR (CONTROL)	LC (CONTROL)	MV (CONTROL)	RP (CONTROL)	SC (CONTROL)	CR_LC	CR_RTP	MV_LC	MV_RTP	SC_LC	SC_RP
BabyLM RoBERTa	74.68	100.00	99.93	99.98	59.23	-89.04	-91.24	-99.84	-15.30	-57.74	-39.17
CogMemLM-s	91.30	100.00	99.88	86.84	65.81	-68.19	-75.12	-99.97	-86.83	-65.29	-49.54
change	*22.25*	*0.00*	*-0.05*	*-13.14*	*11.11*	*23.42*	*17.67*	*-0.13*	*-467.52*	*-13.08*	*-26.47*

Table 5: Results of our model compared with BabyLM RoBERTa-base on the MSGS benchmark. The Matthew correlation coefficients of the two models and the relative change between them are reported in percent (negative correlation scores indicate surface generalisations, positive correlation scores linguistic generalizations).
Avg. MSGS: baseline 3.77, ours -0.10.

BabyStories: Can Reinforcement Learning Teach Baby Language Models to Write Better Stories?

Xingmeng Zhao, Tongnian Wang, Sheri Osborn, and **Anthony Rios**
Department of Information Systems and Cyber Security
The University of Texas at San Antonio
{xingmeng.zhao, tongnian.wang, sheri.osborn, anthony.rios}@utsa.edu

Abstract

Language models have seen significant growth in the size of their corpus, leading to notable performance improvements. Yet, there has been limited progress in developing models that handle smaller, more human-like datasets. As part of the BabyLM shared task, this study explores the impact of reinforcement learning from human feedback (RLHF) on language models pretrained from scratch with a limited training corpus. Comparing two GPT-2 variants, the larger model performs better in storytelling tasks after RLHF fine-tuning. These findings suggest that RLHF techniques may be more advantageous for larger models due to their higher learning and adaptation capacity, though more experiments are needed to confirm this finding. These insights highlight the potential benefits of RLHF fine-tuning for language models within limited data, enhancing their ability to maintain narrative focus and coherence while adhering better to initial instructions in storytelling tasks. The code for this work is publicly at https://github.com/Zephyr1022/BabyStories-UTSA.

1 Introduction

The recent growth in the size of large language models (LLMs) has enhanced natural language processing capabilities, from information extraction (Agrawal et al., 2022) to language generation (Stiennon et al., 2020). However, the majority of research has been concentrated on environments with high computational power and a large number of parameters, leaving the emergence of these capabilities largely uninvestigated in low data and low resource settings (Brown et al., 2020; Fedus et al., 2022). Although some studies have looked into the relationship between model size, training volume, and performance for LLMs, they have primarily focused on scaling laws in high-compute settings (Hoffmann et al., 2022). Investigations into the effects of pretraining at a smaller scale have been limited (Huebner et al., 2021; Deshpande et al., 2023). Therefore, it would be interesting to explore strategies that maximize the efficiency of pretraining, especially considering the constraints of limited data availability.

Storytelling is a fundamental human activity used to share information, impart lessons, and keep loved ones informed about our daily lives (Bietti et al., 2019). Teachers leverage children's love for stories and their desire to tell them, using storytelling to promote cognitive and literacy development. Storytelling is a critical bridge between the oral language skills of early childhood and the more mature language skills associated with reading and writing. The recent BabyLM shared task aims to address these challenges (Warstadt et al., 2023). Hence, we report our submission to the shared task in this paper. Specifically, our study aims to understand whether we can pretrain a language model from scratch on the same amount of linguistic data available to a child, modeling a smaller, reduced-vocabulary language. We are interested in assessing a particular model's effectiveness and potential for enhancement. Specifically, we investigate whether the model can demonstrate high performance and if its performance can be further improved using reinforcement learning techniques from human feedback (RLHF) (Fernandes et al., 2023). This process is analogous to how teachers instruct children in storytelling, providing feedback to encourage them to develop more coherent and reasonable narratives. Implementing RLHF has shown promising results in aligning foundation models with human preferences. By using RLHF, models can undergo subtle yet significant improvements, such as refining tone (Liu, 2023), reducing biases and toxic elements (Bai et al., 2022), and enabling domain-specific content generation (Bang et al., 2023). The primary goal of this research is to explore whether the small pretrained model, with its limited data size, can also benefit from RLHF,

Proceedings of the 27th Conference on Computational Natural Language Learning: Volume 2: The BabyLM Challenge, pages 186–197
December 6-7, 2023

thus potentially improving its overall performance.

The performance of small language models (SLMs) trained on large datasets has been observed to be poor, generating incoherent and repetitive text. Training large language models on limited data can lead to overfitting, making smaller models a potential solution to prevent overfitting (Warstadt et al., 2020c). Inspired by how humans acquire language and the BabyLM shared task, we explore downsizing the language used in models to observe the effects of pretraining. The main questions are whether small language models can generate coherent English text and if this ability is limited to larger, more complex models. It is also questioned whether the limited capacity of small models to memorize linguistic features—such as syntax, semantics, morphology, and phonology—leads to less creative outputs compared to larger models. For example, linguistic features are crucial for understanding and generating text, with a broader grasp potentially enabling more creative language use. Larger models, with their increased capacity, might capture a wider range of these features, possibly leading to more creative and nuanced language outputs. Conversely, small models might only learn basic or frequent linguistic patterns, potentially limiting their creative language generation capabilities. Previous research indicates that models can learn linguistic features with limited pretraining data but need more data to prioritize linguistic generalizations over superficial ones (Warstadt et al., 2020c). Some models fail to effectively use the linguistic features they learn during fine-tuning for natural language understanding tasks. The study aims to investigate whether GPT-2 models of varying sizes can acquire specific language patterns when fine-tuned with reinforcement learning and human feedback, aiming to enhance the model's storytelling abilities.

In summary, in this paper, we pretrain GPT-2-base model with a parameter of 125M from scratch and compare it with the larger GPT2-Large model, which has a parameter of 774M, making it approximately six times larger. Both models are trained using a limited dataset provided from the BabyLM Challenge, which consists of approximately 100M words (Warstadt et al., 2023). The dataset encompasses various sources, including child-directed speech, transcribed speech from multiple sources, children's books, and Wikipedia. Subsequently, we use the RLHF technique to fine-tune both models and evaluate their ability to acquire new linguistic features through human feedback and also perform human evaluation on generated stories.

2 Related Work

Research has shown that smaller models tend to underperform when trained on large datasets, making the study of model downscaling a non-trivial (Turc et al., 2019). Previous investigations into smaller models have primarily centered around distillation processes (Sanh et al., 2019), with the aim of maximizing performance while reducing the number of parameters involved. Huebner et al. (2021) is one of the most relevant papers to our work, where they found that a small language model trained on child-directed speech can yield results comparable to larger language models when used in specific probing tasks. And another study, Deshpande et al. (2023) trained several models to explore scaling in low-compute environments, assessing their performance on a modified version of GLUE.

Our research, however, is driven by a desire to understand if small pretrained models can benefit from Reinforcement Learning from Human Feedback (RLHF), potentially improving their overall performance despite their limited data size. Two previous studies have a direct relation to this work: the first employed human ranking feedback to train summarization models using reinforcement learning (RL) (Stiennon et al., 2020), and the second used stories to generate a value-aligned reward signal for RL agents, aimed at mitigating hallucination behavior (Riedl and Harrison, 2016).

3 Data

In this section, we describe the pertaining data used for the language models and the data used for the reinforcement model.

3.1 Pretraining Data

We pretrain GPT-2 models using the dataset from the STRICT track in the BabyLM Challenge (Warstadt et al., 2023), which includes various types of corpora, both spoken-based and written-based. Examples of the spoken-based corpus include CHILDES (MacWhinney, 2000), the British National Corpus (BNC) dialogue section, OpenSubtitles (Lison and Tiedemann, 2016), the QCRI Educational Domain Corpus (Abdelali et al., 2014), and the Switchboard Dialog Act Corpus

(Stolcke et al., 2000). The written-based corpus includes the Children's Book Test (Hill et al., 2016), the Children's Stories Text Corpus, the Standardized Project Gutenberg Corpus (Gerlach and Font-Clos, 2020), Wikipedia, and Simple Wikipedia. For example, the Children's Book Story and Wikipedia corpora stand in contrast to dialogue or subtitle-based corpora, which mostly consist of transcribed speech, the primary language input for children. Wikipedia, in particular, is a compilation of written language rather than spoken dialogues. Most of its articles are composed by professionals who possess subject-matter expertise and adhere to rigorous standards of grammatical correctness. These corpora contain a variety of sources with approximately 100 million words, corresponding to the linguistic competence expected at the onset of adolescence (around 13 years old).

3.2 Reward Model Data

In this paper, we construct a reward model dataset for reinforcement learning by selecting 100 sentences from the STRICT track of the Babylm Challenge dataset. These sentences, serving as prompts, are derived from two subsets in the Babylm dataset: the Standardized Project Gutenberg and the Simple Wikipedia corpus development sets, with a prerequisite that each sentence includes characters and plots. These prompts are then used to generate two short stories each from the GPT-2 Base and GPT-2 Large models, beginning with the prefix "write me a story starting with". To enhance story diversity, we set a maximum length of 128 tokens and enforce a minimum of 10 new tokens in the generated stories. The generation code incorporates a beam size of 7 to optimize the story quality by exploring various potential continuations.

The purpose of collecting feedback is to align the model's behavior with some goal behavior. For example, we aim for the model to generate stories consistent with the background plot, coherent, non-repetitive, devoid of nonsensical sentences, and maintain a clear topic or logical structure. Rating the quality of a story accurately presents challenges due to its potentially subjective nature and the varying expectations of readers regarding emotional connection and engagement. Rather than directly estimating a generated story quality through scale-based annotation, we treat it as a latent variable to be inferred from relative comparisons. Following prior work in NLP on annotating social aspects of language (Pei and Jurgens, 2020), we adopt a method similar to Best-Worst Scaling (BWS) (Louviere et al., 2015; Kiritchenko and Mohammad, 2016) to generate comparison data on people's preferences. Intuitively, it is easier for annotators to identify the best and worst stories from a set of stories than it is for them to provide numerical assessments. The process involves asking two student annotators to choose from sets of stories, identifying the best (most preferred) and worst (least preferred) stories in each choice set. We provide four stories for the annotators to choose from. This method provides more information per choice set than traditional preference methods and enables a more precise ranking of items in terms of preference. For instance, if we have stories A, B, C, and D, and A is ranked as the best while D is ranked as the worst, then we create the following pairs: A $>$ B, A $>$ C, A $>$ D, B $>$ D, and C $>$ D, resulting in a total of 500 additional pairs for reward model training from 100 best-worst annotations. A $>$ B means that the model should learn to provide a higher score to A because it was ranked higher than B. This is inferred because A was marked as the best story.

3.2.1 Agreement for Reward Model Data Annotation

Krippendorff's alpha, introduced by Krippendorff (1970), is a statistical measure commonly used for assessing the level of agreement between two or more annotators across various categories. Its advantage lies in its versatility, as it can be applied to not only nominal data but any measurement scale, such as Best-Worst Scaling.

In our case, two graduate student annotators were designated to annotate human feedback data., which yielded a Krippendorff's alpha agreement score of .4657. To address disagreements, the two annotators discuss each story example together. They reconcile differences through discussion and unanimously select the best and worst stories based on the given story prompt.

4 Method

This section discusses pretraining data, the development of the data tokenizer, language model configuration, the objective of pretraining from scratch, and the process of fine-tuning using reinforcement learning with human feedback.

4.1 Tokenizer

Our model uses a sub-word vocabulary built with Byte-Pair Encoding (BPE) (Sennrich et al., 2016), an approach initially developed for text compression. Later, this technique was applied by OpenAI for tokenization during the pretraining stage of the GPT model (Radford et al., 2019). Rather than maintaining the original vocabulary size of 50,257 used in the GPT-2 model, we developed a custom tokenizer based on a vocabulary size of 32,001. This custom tokenizer is trained on the collective set of all training corpora from STRICT track in the BabyLM Challenge, applying the ByteLevelBPETokenizer from the Hugging Face Tokenizers library[1].

Prior research informed our decision to significantly reduce the vocabulary size. Studies suggest a vocabulary size of about 32,000 tokens is a good balance for a single-language model (Kudo, 2018). This size carefully balances the model's proficiency in handling less common words while preserving its computational efficiency.

4.2 Model Architecture and Configuration

Models we pretrained in our experiments using the default configuration setting of GPT-2 (Radford et al., 2019). In these settings, we employed a context length of 1042 tokens and set the maximum training epoch limit to 15. The restriction to 15 epochs was primarily due to constraints on training time and GPU resources. We conducted the training of the GPT-2 Base model on an NVIDIA GeForce GTX 1080 Ti, while the GPT-2 Large model was trained on an NVIDIA RTX A6000 GPU. The training time for the base model was approximately 72 hours, while it extended to around 216 hours for the large model. To train, we used the Lion optimizer (Chen et al., 2023), configured with a learning rate of 1e-5 and a weight decay of 1e-2. We also integrated Triton, a GPU programming language detailed by (Tillet and Cox, 2019), to optimize hardware performance and implemented mixed-precision computations using the 'bfloat16' format for efficient resource utilization (Wang and Kanwar, 2019).

For model selection, we chose the best model across all epochs based on the average score on two datasets: the Question-answering Natural Language Inference (QNLI) (Demszky et al., 2018) and the SST-2 Binary Classification Benchmark (Socher et al., 2013). We evaluated the models' performances on these benchmarks using the F1 score. Additionally, the perplexity scores on the validation dataset for our models were recorded as 24.10 for the GPT-2 Base model and 22.73 for the GPT-2 Large model.

4.3 Reward Model

The reward model (RM) is designed to capture human preferences, and ideally, we could fine-tune it using Reinforcement Learning and human annotations for every output returned by the language model. However, due to practical constraints like workload and time limitations, it is not feasible for humans to provide enough feedback for each optimization iteration. As an alternative, a more effective approach is to train a reward model that simulates the evaluation process carried out by humans. This RM will evaluate any text and assign a scalar reward value to the sentences, where higher values indicate high-quality samples. Following Stiennon et al. (2020), training reward models often involve using a paired comparison dataset between two responses generated for the same input.

To train our reward models, We initialize the weights of the reward model by leveraging a pretrained GPT-2 Large model as described above, then we add a randomly initialized linear head that outputs a scalar value to form the reward model $r_\theta(x, y)$. We train this model to predict which generated story $y \in \{y_0, y_1\}$, where y_0 is the chosen (good) response to the prompt as labeled by our annotators and y_1 is the rejected (bad) response. In practice, this is where our annotators ranked $y_0 > y_1$. The model is trained using the loss function

$$loss(r_\theta) = -E_{(x,y_0,y_1,i)\sim D}\Big[\log(\sigma(r_\theta(x^i, y_0^i) - r_\theta(x^i, y_1^i))\Big]$$

where σ is the sigmoid function and D is the set of all training triplets in our dataset, i denotes the index of a specific data point in the dataset D. Intuitively, the model learns to give a larger score to the prompts with a higher rank. We have configured the reward model to run for a maximum of 10 epochs, with a set learning rate of 1e-5.

4.3.1 Proximal Policy Optimization

After we train the reward model, we treat the logit output of the reward model as a reward that we optimize policy model outputs using reinforcement

[1] https://github.com/huggingface/tokenizers

learning, specifically with the Proximal Policy Optimization (PPO) algorithm (Schulman et al., 2017). During the RL fine-tuning with PPO phase, we use the learned reward function to provide feedback to the language model. In particular, we formulate the following optimization problem

$$\max_{\pi^{RL}(y|x)} E_{x\sim D, y\sim\pi^{RL}(y|x)}\Big[r(x,y)\Big] - \beta D_{KL} \log\left[\frac{\pi^{RL}(y|x)}{\pi^{SFT}(y|x)}\right]$$

where $r(x, y)$ is the reward model's output, β is a hyper-parameter controlling the deviation from the initial policy. Our optimization focuses on the policy $\pi^{RL}(y|x)$ using Proximal Policy Optimization (PPO), with initialization based on the pretrained language model policy $\pi^{SFT}(y|x)$ (Stiennon et al., 2020; Rafailov et al., 2023).

To encourage exploration and prevent the policy from getting stuck in a single mode, the optimization uses the Kullback-Leibler (KL) divergence term. This term also discourages the policy from generating outputs that differ significantly from those seen by the reward model during training, thereby maintaining coherence in the generated text. Without this penalty, the optimization might generate gibberish text that tricks the reward model into providing a high reward. In our implementation, we used the trlX library with its default settings[2]. The algorithm was executed with a maximum of 5 epochs and a sequence length of 512, and the run spanned around 208 hours. In our approach, we used the default hyperparameter provided by the trlX library, which employs Ray Tune for hyperparameter tuning. This choice was primarily driven by the significant time and GPU resource constraints associated with training the PPO model, making it a pragmatic decision to leverage the preconfigured settings of trlX. Although we experimented with random modifications to some hyperparameters, the outcomes were less satisfactory as compared to the default settings of trlX. Hence, the decision to restrict the training to 5 epochs was in alignment with these considerations, ensuring a balance between computational feasibility and the pursuit of meaningful reward training.

4.4 Evaluation Metrics and Datasets

To assess the performance of our models, we employed various automated evaluation metrics used in the BabyLM shared task and our own human evaluation. The BabyLM shared task had two major sets of evaluations: zero-shot evaluation and fine-tuned evaluation. We describe each evaluation task below.

Zero-shot Evaluation. BLiMP, introduced by Warstadt et al. (2020a), is a series of zero-shot tasks included in the evaluation. BLiMP assesses the ability of language models to handle category membership, provide congruent answers to specific types of questions, and recognize grammatical questions. It serves as a behavioral probe, containing pairs of test sentences that isolate particular phenomena in syntax and morphology, such as island effects and determiner-noun agreement. Essentially, BLiMP is a challenge set designed to evaluate the linguistic knowledge of language models, focusing on major grammatical phenomena in English. The BLiMP Supplement benchmark consists of BLiMP-style minimal pairs that specifically focus on aspects not covered by BLiMP. These additional aspects include discourse-level acceptability across multiple speakers and question formation.

Fine-tuned Evaluation. Two datasets are used for the fine-tuned evaluation: SuperGLUE and the Mixed Signals Generalization Set (MSGS). SuperGLUE (Wang et al., 2019), an advanced version of GLUE (Wang et al., 2018), is a benchmark for assessing progress in general-purpose language understanding technologies. It comprises a public leaderboard and a single-number performance metric for various tasks. These include CoLA, which evaluates the grammatical acceptability of English sentences; SST-2, which predicts the sentiment of movie review sentences; MRPC, which determines semantic equivalence between sentence pairs; QQP, another task focused on semantic equivalence; MNLI and MNLI-mm, which predict the relationship between a premise and a hypothesis sentence; QNLI, which matches a question to a paragraph containing the answer; RTE, which determines if a sentence entails a given hypothesis; BoolQ, which answers yes/no questions about a text passage; MultiRC, which identifies true and false answers given a context paragraph and a question; and WSC, a coreference resolution task. These tasks, designed to be challenging, represent a broad spectrum of language understanding capabilities, making SuperGLUE a robust tool for evaluating language models.

[2]https://github.com/CarperAI/trlx

Model	AA	AS	BD	CR	DNA	E	FG	IF	IE	NL	Q	SV	H	QACe	QACt	SAI	TT	AVG
Baselines																		
OPT-125m	94.9	73.8	73.8	**72.2**	**93.1**	80.5	73.6	80.8	57.8	51.6	74.5	77.3	46.3	**76.5**	47.9	85.3	**82.9**	73.1
RoBERTa-base	89.5	71.3	71.0	67.1	**93.1**	**83.8**	68.0	89.6	54.5	66.3	70.3	76.2	50.8	34.4	34.5	45.6	46.8	65.5
T5-base	66.7	61.2	59.4	59.8	53.8	49.1	70.0	75.5	43.6	45.6	34.2	53.2	**51.1**	45.3	25.5	69.2	48.9	53.7
Ours																		
GPT2-Base	95.4	75.5	74.0	67.0	90.8	77.7	70.0	**87.7**	53.6	57.6	**79.0**	75.8	**50.2**	60.9	41.8	85.0	67.9	71.2
GPT2-Base-PPO	95.5	75.4	73.6	67.0	90.8	78.3	70.2	86.7	54.4	58.0	77.7	75.2	49.9	59.4	40.0	**85.7**	68.2	70.9
GPT2-Large	96.9	78.7	**74.1**	**71.0**	92.0	79.0	73.8	87.2	**60.8**	**60.9**	75.9	**81.1**	49.2	**71.9**	49.7	79.8	**73.6**	**73.9**
GPT2-Large-PPO	**97.0**	**78.8**	**74.1**	**71.0**	**92.1**	**79.3**	**73.7**	87.1	60.7	60.8	75.9	**81.1**	49.4	**71.9**	**50.3**	79.6	73.2	**73.9**

Table 1: Performance on BLiMP benchmarks. Evaluation tasks map accordingly: Anaphor Agr.:AA, Agr. Structure: AS, Binding: BD, Control/Raising: CR, D-N Agr.: DNA, Ellipsis: E, Filler-Gap: FG, Irregular Forms: IF, Island Effects: IE, NPI Licensing: NL, Quantifiers: Q, S-V Agr.: SV, Hypernym: H, QA Congruence (easy): QAC(e), QA Congruence (tricky): QAC(t), Subj.-Aux. Inversion: SAI, Turn Taking: TT. The overall largest scores are in bold.

The MSGS dataset, introduced by Warstadt et al. (2020b), is a diagnostic tool designed to evaluate the preferences of language models for either linguistic features, such as specific syntactic constructions, or surface features, like the presence of a word in a certain position. The primary objective of the MSGS tasks is to determine whether a pretrained model leans more toward linguistic or surface generalizations during the fine-tuning process. Fine-tuning on self-supervised linguistic tasks proves effective because it equips models with features beneficial for language understanding. Furthermore, pretrained models are not only capable of representing these linguistic features but also tend to use them preferentially during fine-tuning.

To maintain consistency and ensure fair comparisons, we adopted the default hyperparameter settings recommended by Gao et al. (2021). Our only modification was adjusting the batch size to 32 due to GPU limitations. These evaluation procedures allowed us to thoroughly assess the models' capabilities and compare their performance across different tasks. Our experiments report the average scores of all performance metrics across tasks.

Human Evaluation. Inspired by the TinyStories (Eldan and Li, 2023), we assess the four key story generation outcome metrics of grammar (how grammatically correct the story is), creativity (how original and inventive the story is), consistency with the story's beginning (how well the story adheres to the given prompts), and plot coherence (whether the plot of the story makes sense). We randomly selected 100 prompts from the ROCStories dataset (Mostafazadeh et al., 2016). Each prompt was composed of a story title and the first sentence. We fed these prompts to the model, and it generated short stories based on the given prompts. To assess the quality of the generated stories, we enlisted the help of a graduate student evaluator. The evaluator was presented with the story's beginning (title + first sentence) and the completed story generated by the model. They were then asked to rate the completed story on a scale of 1 to 10, considering aspects such as grammar, creativity, consistency with the story's beginning, and plot coherence. This human evaluation process provided valuable insights into the model's performance across these critical dimensions.

5 Results

In this section, we report the results of the automated BabyLM metrics and our human evaluation for story generation.

Performance on BLiMP benchmarks. Shown in Table 1, the GPT2-Large and GPT2-Large-PPO models outperform the GPT-base variants on the BLiMP task with an average score of 73.9, excelling in many specific tasks. For example, GPT2-Large does well in tasks like Island Effects, NPI Licensing, and Subject-Verb Agreement, whereas GPT2-Large-PPO stands out in the QA Congruence (tricky) task. The GPT2-Base and GPT2-Base-PPO models score lower with averages of 71.2 and 70.9, respectively, suggesting that model size (base versus large) plays a crucial role in determining performance. However, for the BLiMP benchmark, PPO training has little impact on model performance. However, more experiments on different architecture could potentially point in a different direction.

Performance on SuperGLUE benchmarks. In Table 2, we report the performance of the models on the SuperGLUE benchmarks, which assess

Model	CoLA	SST-2	MRPC (F1)	QQP (F1)	MNLI	MNLI-mm	QNLI	RTE	BoolQ	MultiRC	WSC	AVG
					Baselines							
Majority label	69.5	50.2	82.0	53.1	35.7	35.7	35.4	53.1	50.5	59.9	53.2	52.6
OPT-125m	73.7	86.6	82.1	77.8	70.1	71.9	80.1	**67.7**	66.0	61.1	59.0	72.4
RoBERTa-base	75.9	**88.6**	80.5	78.5	68.7	**78.0**	82.3	51.5	59.9	61.3	61.4	71.5
T5-base	**76.3**	88.0	**85.9**	**79.7**	**71.5**	74.0	**83.1**	60.6	**69.0**	**62.4**	60.2	**73.7**
					Ours							
GPT2-Base	69.5	83.3	78.1	**72.2**	60.0	61.3	57.0	49.5	59.9	46.8	42.2	61.8
GPT2-Base-PPO	69.5	81.3	82.0	67.3	60.9	61.7	61.4	45.5	59.9	46.8	39.8	61.5
GPT2-Large	69.5	82.7	**83.0**	32.4	**61.4**	62.2	54.4	**58.6**	66.8	46.8	**61.5**	61.7
GPT2-Large-PPO	69.5	**84.3**	82.3	66.7	59.5	**64.0**	**79.6**	53.5	**67.4**	46.8	**61.5**	**66.8**

Table 2: Performance on (Super)GLUE benchmarks. The task shortcuts correspond to the following datasets: Corpus of Linguistic Acceptability (CoLA), the Stanford Sentiment Treebank (SST-2), the Microsoft Research Paraphrase Corpus (MRPC), the Quora Question Pairs (QQP), the Multi-Genre Natural Language Inference (MNLI), the mismatched version of MNLI (MNLI-mm), the Question Natural Language Inference (QNLI), the Recognizing Textual Entailment (RTE), the BoolQ, the Multi-Sentence Reading Comprehension (MultiRC), and the Winograd Schema Challenge (WSC). The overall largest scores are in bold.

Model	CR_C	LC_C	MV_C	RP_C	SC_C	CR_LC	CR_RTP	MV_LC	MV_RTP	SC_LC	SC_RP	AVG
						Baselines						
OPT-125m	**97.2**	82.6	**100.0**	99.8	88.1	75.3	67.1	66.3	66.8	**84.8**	62.0	80.9
RoBERTa-base	93.0	**100.0**	**100.0**	**100.0**	89.0	68.3	66.8	66.6	**80.2**	67.4	67.4	81.7
T5-base	95.1	**100.0**	**100.0**	99.8	88.7	**76.7**	**69.4**	**67.0**	67.7	72.7	68.0	82.3
						Ours						
GPT2-Base	**96.7**	**99.8**	99.7	**100.0**	95.5	68.2	68.3	66.6	**67.0**	**74.6**	**76.5**	**83.0**
GPT2-Base-PPO	85.9	**99.8**	**99.9**	99.9	93.3	**71.7**	67.9	66.6	**67.0**	68.4	70.5	81.0
GPT2-Large	91.2	98.5	**99.9**	**100.0**	94.0	67.3	**68.5**	66.6	66.8	71.9	69.4	81.3
GPT2-Large-PPO	93.6	**99.8**	99.4	**100.0**	**96.2**	70.0	66.7	66.6	66.9	73.1	68.1	81.9

Table 3: Performance on MSGS benchmarks. The MSGS shortcuts correspond to the respective tasks as follows: CR_RTP maps to control_raising_relative_token_position, CR_LC maps to control_raising_lexical_content_the, SC_RP maps to syntactic_category_relative_position, SC_LC maps to syntactic_category_lexical_content_the, MV_RTP maps to main_verb_relative_token_position, MV_LC maps to main_verb_lexical_content_the. The shortcuts RP_C, LC_C, SC_C, CR_C, and MV_C correspond to the tasks relative_position_control, lexical_content_the_control, syntactic_category_control, control_raising_control, and main_verb_control, respectively. The overall largest scores are in bold.

a range of language understanding abilities. The GPT2-Large-PPO model stands out with the highest average score of 66.8, underlining the potential for enhanced performance using larger models fine-tuned with PPO. Other models present comparable average scores across the SuperGLUE tasks. Compared to the Majority Label baseline, the GPT-2 models exhibit varied levels of performance enhancement across different tasks. Specifically, the GPT2-Base model outperforms the baseline in SST-2, QQP (F1), MNLI, MNLI-mm, QNLI, and BoolQ. Similarly, the GPT2-Base-PPO model surpasses the baseline in the same tasks: SST-2, QQP (F1), MNLI, MNLI-mm, QNLI, and BoolQ. The GPT2-Large model demonstrates superior performance over the baseline in SST-2, MRPC (F1), MNLI, MNLI-mm, QNLI, BoolQ, and WSC. While, the GPT2-Large-PPO model outperforms the majority baseline in all tasks except for CoLA and MultiRC, marking significant performance improvement in SST-2, MNLI-mm, and QNLI, with an increase of 34.1, 28.3, and 44.2 respectively.

The performance across various models and tasks exhibits considerable variability, showing that different models may excel in distinct language understanding domains. The superior scores of the GPT2-Large-PPO model suggest that larger models fine-tuned with PPO could enhance performance, yet further examination reveals inconsistencies. Finally, we note that the PPO training only improves the performance of the GPT2-Large model, suggesting that PPO training may require a model with a minimum number of parameters to work in the limited data setting. However, more experiments

Model	Overall	Nouns	Predicates	Function words
GPT2-Base	2.05	1.98	1.84	2.62
GPT2-Base-PPO	2.06	1.99	1.83	2.66
GPT2-Large	2.05	1.98	1.83	2.63
GPT2-Large-PPO	2.05	1.98	1.82	2.63

Table 4: Performance on the Age-of-acquisition benchmarks. This table presents Mean Absolute Deviation (MAD) scores in months, comparing the actual average age-of-acquisition (AoA) of words by American English speaking children with the predicted AoA based on the model's average surprisal scores. A lower MAD score indicates a better fit between the actual and predicted AoA.

Model	Gram.	Creat.	Consist.	PCoh
GPT2-Base	7.84	6.11	3.49	1.94
GPT2-Base-PPO	6.82***	5.66**	3.37	1.89
GPT2-Large	7.65	6.23	3.94	2.35
GPT2-Large-PPO	7.62	6.21	4.48**	2.87*

Table 5: Performance on Human Evaluation. Gram. (Grammar), Creativity (Creat.), Consistency (Consist.), and Plot Coherence (PCoh). Significant differences based on a paired t-test are marked with * (p-value < .1), ** (p-value < .05), and *** (p-value <.001).

are needed to confirm this finding.

Performance on MSGS benchmarks Table 3 shows the results of testing GPT2 models of different sizes on the MSGS benchmark. These results help us understand how well the models use and generalize different language and surface features. Among the models, the GPT2-Base model outperforms other models with the highest average score of 83.0. This suggests that GPT2-Base, despite being a smaller model, has effectively learned to generalize across a range of linguistic and surface features. This might be due to the model's efficient use of its limited parameters. Instead of overfitting to less important details in the training data.

Performance on Age-of-acquisition benchmarks According to Portelance et al. (To Appear), a smaller mean absolute deviation (MAD) score indicates a better alignment between the model's predictions and the actual average age-of-acquisition (AoA) of words in children. Table 4 shows similar MAD scores across all models for all word categories (Overall, Nouns, Predicates, and Function words). This suggests that all models exhibit similar levels of accuracy in predicting the AoA of words, and their word-learning sequences align closely with the natural language acquisition patterns observed in children.

Performance on Human Evaluation. In Table 5, we report the results of our human evaluation. The findings indicate that the GPT2-Base and GPT2-Large models exhibit comparable average grammar scores. However, the GPT2-Base-PPO model performs significantly worse (p-value < 0.001) than the GPT2-Base in grammar and creativity evaluations. The result is consistent with the BablyLM automated evaluation metrics, where the GPT-Base-PPO generally underperforms GPT-Base. Table 6 shows several examples from our TinyStory analysis. Specifically, the GPT2-Base-PPO tends to generate repetitive and lengthy stories, likely contributing to its poorer grammar and creativity performance. Furthermore, when comparing the GPT2-Large and GPT2-Large-Base models in Table 5, their performance levels for Grammar and Creativity are similar, showing that PPO had minimal impact on the Large model for both metrics.

We also find significant differences in Consistency (Const.) and Plot Coherence (PCoh) between GPT-Large and GPT2-Large-PPO. Intuitively, these metrics evaluate generative models' capability in following the beginning of the story background rather than just content creation. Our findings indicate that the performance scores for GPT2-Base and GPT2-Base-PPO models are fairly similar, but both are lower than those of the GPT2-Large model variants. Again, this indicates that the large models outperform the smaller models, even though we trained on a relatively small dataset. Moreover, the GPT2-Large-PPO model significantly improves consistency and plot coherence scores compared to the standard GPT2-Large model. This suggests that large models (at least GPT2-Large in our case) can integrate the reward model to generate better outputs than the GPT2-base (smaller model).

We analyze the large model outputs in Table 6. Specifically, in the second story from Table 6, the beginning of the story is set as "Awkward I was driving into the McDonald's beside school." Distinct differences can be seen when comparing the narrative continuations generated by the GPT2-Large and GPT2-Large-PPO models. For example, the GPT2-Large model diverges from the initial context, transitioning abruptly from the act of driving into McDonald's to a sudden need to return to

Prompt	gpt2-base	gpt2-base-ppo	gpt2-Large	gpt2-large-ppo
Aquarium closed Yesterday I went to the aquarium.	It was on the way to the museum and there was a lot of fish in it. (10/7/7/7)	It was one of the most important things I've ever seen in my life. The first thing I want to tell you is that we are not going to be able to help each other. The first thing I want to tell you is that we are not going to be able to help each other. We are going to be able to help each other. (6/6/1/1)	" It was full of fish, and there were so many different kinds of things to eat. " (10/8/8/7)	" It was full of fish. He looked at it and he said, ""I'm going to tell you a story."" (10/9/8/7)
Awkward I was driving into the McDonald's beside school.	I'm going to tell you something,"" he said. ""You're going to have to do it, don't you? " (9/7/4/1)	"I don't know what to do,"" he said. ""I'm not going to tell anyone about it."" " (9/7/4/1)	It was about two-and-a-half hours ahead of my time. It was then that I realized that I had to get back to work. (9/7/4/1)	"I didn't know how to drive, but I thought it was great fun. " (10/7/7/7)
Tie Game The teams were tied and this was the last inning.	It was also the first time that Tie Game would be able to play the part of the game. (6/2/9/8)	" ""Tie Game"" was released on August 26, 2010. It is the second single from Tie Game." (8/7/8/1)	It's hard to imagine how easy it would have been for them to come up with us. (9/6/2/1)	" That's what I'm trying to figure out, so let's try it again. " (9/6/2/1)

Table 6: Performance comparison of various models on grammar, creativity, consistency with the beginning of the story, and plot coherence. The scores in the parentheses represent the evaluations for Grammar, Creativity, Consistency, and Plot, respectively.

work. This abrupt shift disrupts the narrative flow and doesn't seamlessly connect with the story's beginning. On the other hand, the GPT2-Large-PPO model manages to retain focus on the primary activity of driving in its generated story. Although it introduces an inconsistency by stating the character doesn't know how to drive, it maintains the plot around the theme of a character recklessly driving without knowing how to do so. This suggests that the GPT2-Large-PPO model has a stronger adherence to the initial instructions and makes a better attempt at following them.

Summary of Findings and Limitations. Overall, we found that the **GPT-2-Large generally works better than GPT-2-base *with* and *without* PPO**. Also, **PPO made significant improvements to the model's consistency and plot coherence on the storytelling task when used with the large model**. However, PPO generally hurts performance with the smaller GPT-2-Base model.

There were several limitations to our study. First, a major limitation of this work is the lack of comparison with architectures beyond GPT-2. Moreover, comparisons to even larger models should be made in the future. We were limited by the computational resources required for large-scale testing during the BabyLM shared task timeline. Next, we had a limited-size reward model dataset. Future work should explore the impact of reward model dataset size and variety. Future work should explore the impact of reward model dataset size and variety. Additionally, the study did not explore the hyperparameter tuning for the reward model and the loss function in depth. Exploring different settings for hyperparameters and examining alternative methods for reward training, such as varying the weighting of the loss terms, could yield different results and improve the model's performance in the storytelling task. Finally, we only had one annotator for the human evaluation and were limited in size. A more extensive human study could find more intricate differences between the models.

6 Conclusion

In this study, we investigated whether the small pretrained model, with its limited data size, can also benefit from RLHF, thus potentially improving its overall performance. We evaluate the two variants of the GPT-2 model: the GPT-2 Base model with 125M parameters and the larger GPT-2 Large model with 774M parameters. Both variants are pretrained on the 100M words BabyLM Challenge dataset. We then fine-tune both models using RLHF and evaluate their ability to acquire new linguistic patterns and storytelling ability, including generating coherent and creative English text while adhering to the story background. We observe that RLHF has a little or negative effect on the smaller model. However, a substantial increase in model parameters noticeably enhances the larger model's performance in storytelling tasks. In summary, our experiments shed light on the behavior of small language models fine-tuned using RLHF to perform storytelling tasks in a limited dataset setting.

References

Ahmed Abdelali, Francisco Guzman, Hassan Sajjad, and Stephan Vogel. 2014. The amara corpus: Building parallel language resources for the educational domain. In *LREC*, volume 14, pages 1044–1054.

Monica Agrawal, Stefan Hegselmann, Hunter Lang, Yoon Kim, and David Sontag. 2022. Large language models are zero-shot clinical information extractors. *arXiv preprint arXiv:2205.12689*.

Yuntao Bai, Andy Jones, Kamal Ndousse, Amanda Askell, Anna Chen, Nova DasSarma, Dawn Drain, Stanislav Fort, Deep Ganguli, Tom Henighan, et al. 2022. Training a helpful and harmless assistant with reinforcement learning from human feedback. *arXiv preprint arXiv:2204.05862*.

Yejin Bang, Samuel Cahyawijaya, Nayeon Lee, Wenliang Dai, Dan Su, Bryan Wilie, Holy Lovenia, Ziwei Ji, Tiezheng Yu, Willy Chung, et al. 2023. A multitask, multilingual, multimodal evaluation of chatgpt on reasoning, hallucination, and interactivity. *arXiv preprint arXiv:2302.04023*.

Lucas M Bietti, Ottilie Tilston, and Adrian Bangerter. 2019. Storytelling as adaptive collective sensemaking. *Topics in cognitive science*, 11(4):710–732.

Tom Brown, Benjamin Mann, Nick Ryder, Melanie Subbiah, Jared D Kaplan, Prafulla Dhariwal, Arvind Neelakantan, Pranav Shyam, Girish Sastry, Amanda Askell, et al. 2020. Language models are few-shot learners. *Advances in neural information processing systems*, 33:1877–1901.

Xiangning Chen, Chen Liang, Da Huang, Esteban Real, Kaiyuan Wang, Yao Liu, Hieu Pham, Xuanyi Dong, Thang Luong, Cho-Jui Hsieh, et al. 2023. Symbolic discovery of optimization algorithms. *arXiv preprint arXiv:2302.06675*.

Dorottya Demszky, Kelvin Guu, and Percy Liang. 2018. Transforming question answering datasets into natural language inference datasets. *arXiv preprint arXiv:1809.02922*.

Vijeta Deshpande, Dan Pechi, Shree Thatte, Vladislav Lialin, and Anna Rumshisky. 2023. Honey, i shrunk the language: Language model behavior at reduced scale. *arXiv preprint arXiv:2305.17266*.

Ronen Eldan and Yuanzhi Li. 2023. Tinystories: How small can language models be and still speak coherent english? *arXiv preprint arXiv:2305.07759*.

William Fedus, Barret Zoph, and Noam Shazeer. 2022. Switch transformers: Scaling to trillion parameter models with simple and efficient sparsity. *The Journal of Machine Learning Research*, 23(1):5232–5270.

Patrick Fernandes, Aman Madaan, Emmy Liu, António Farinhas, Pedro Henrique Martins, Amanda Bertsch, José GC de Souza, Shuyan Zhou, Tongshuang Wu, Graham Neubig, et al. 2023. Bridging the gap: A survey on integrating (human) feedback for natural language generation. *arXiv preprint arXiv:2305.00955*.

Leo Gao, Jonathan Tow, Stella Biderman, Sid Black, Anthony DiPofi, Charles Foster, Laurence Golding, Jeffrey Hsu, Kyle McDonell, Niklas Muennighoff, Jason Phang, Laria Reynolds, Eric Tang, Anish Thite, Ben Wang, Kevin Wang, and Andy Zou. 2021. A framework for few-shot language model evaluation.

Martin Gerlach and Francesc Font-Clos. 2020. A standardized project gutenberg corpus for statistical analysis of natural language and quantitative linguistics. *Entropy*, 22(1):126.

Felix Hill, Antoine Bordes, Sumit Chopra, and Jason Weston. 2016. The goldilocks principle: Reading children's books with explicit memory representations. In *4th International Conference on Learning Representations, ICLR 2016*.

Jordan Hoffmann, Sebastian Borgeaud, Arthur Mensch, Elena Buchatskaya, Trevor Cai, Eliza Rutherford, Diego de Las Casas, Lisa Anne Hendricks, Johannes Welbl, Aidan Clark, et al. 2022. Training compute-optimal large language models. *arXiv preprint arXiv:2203.15556*.

Philip A Huebner, Elior Sulem, Fisher Cynthia, and Dan Roth. 2021. Babyberta: Learning more grammar with small-scale child-directed language. In *Proceedings of the 25th conference on computational natural language learning*, pages 624–646.

Svetlana Kiritchenko and Saif Mohammad. 2016. Capturing reliable fine-grained sentiment associations by crowdsourcing and best–worst scaling. In *Proceedings of the 2016 Conference of the North American Chapter of the Association for Computational Linguistics: Human Language Technologies*, pages 811–817.

Klaus Krippendorff. 1970. Estimating the reliability, systematic error and random error of interval data. *Educational and psychological measurement*, 30(1):61–70.

Taku Kudo. 2018. Subword regularization: Improving neural network translation models with multiple subword candidates. In *Proceedings of the 56th Annual Meeting of the Association for Computational Linguistics (Volume 1: Long Papers)*, pages 66–75, Melbourne, Australia. Association for Computational Linguistics.

Pierre Lison and Jörg Tiedemann. 2016. Opensubtitles2016: Extracting large parallel corpora from movie and tv subtitles.

Gabrielle Kaili-May Liu. 2023. Perspectives on the social impacts of reinforcement learning with human feedback. *arXiv preprint arXiv:2303.02891*.

Jordan J Louviere, Terry N Flynn, and Anthony Alfred John Marley. 2015. *Best-worst scaling: Theory, methods and applications*. Cambridge University Press.

Brian MacWhinney. 2000. *The CHILDES project: The database*, volume 2. Psychology Press.

Nasrin Mostafazadeh, Nathanael Chambers, Xiaodong He, Devi Parikh, Dhruv Batra, Lucy Vanderwende, Pushmeet Kohli, and James Allen. 2016. A corpus and cloze evaluation for deeper understanding of commonsense stories. In *Proceedings of the 2016 Conference of the North American Chapter of the Association for Computational Linguistics: Human Language Technologies*, pages 839–849, San Diego, California. Association for Computational Linguistics.

Jiaxin Pei and David Jurgens. 2020. Quantifying intimacy in language. In *Proceedings of the 2020 Conference on Empirical Methods in Natural Language Processing (EMNLP)*, pages 5307–5326.

Eva Portelance, Yuguang Duan, Michael C. Frank, and Gary Lupyan. To Appear. Predicting age of acquisition for children's early vocabulary in five languages using language model surprisal. *Cognitive Science*.

Alec Radford, Jeffrey Wu, Rewon Child, David Luan, Dario Amodei, Ilya Sutskever, et al. 2019. Language models are unsupervised multitask learners. *OpenAI blog*, 1(8):9.

Rafael Rafailov, Archit Sharma, Eric Mitchell, Stefano Ermon, Christopher D Manning, and Chelsea Finn. 2023. Direct preference optimization: Your language model is secretly a reward model. *arXiv preprint arXiv:2305.18290*.

Mark O Riedl and Brent Harrison. 2016. Using stories to teach human values to artificial agents. In *AAAI Workshop: AI, Ethics, and Society*.

Victor Sanh, Lysandre Debut, Julien Chaumond, and Thomas Wolf. 2019. Distilbert, a distilled version of bert: smaller, faster, cheaper and lighter. *arXiv preprint arXiv:1910.01108*.

John Schulman, Filip Wolski, Prafulla Dhariwal, Alec Radford, and Oleg Klimov. 2017. Proximal policy optimization algorithms. *arXiv preprint arXiv:1707.06347*.

Rico Sennrich, Barry Haddow, and Alexandra Birch. 2016. Edinburgh neural machine translation systems for wmt 16. In *Proceedings of the First Conference on Machine Translation: Volume 2, Shared Task Papers*, pages 371–376.

Richard Socher, Alex Perelygin, Jean Wu, Jason Chuang, Christopher D Manning, Andrew Y Ng, and Christopher Potts. 2013. Recursive deep models for semantic compositionality over a sentiment treebank. In *Proceedings of the 2013 conference on empirical methods in natural language processing*, pages 1631–1642.

Nisan Stiennon, Long Ouyang, Jeffrey Wu, Daniel Ziegler, Ryan Lowe, Chelsea Voss, Alec Radford, Dario Amodei, and Paul F Christiano. 2020. Learning to summarize with human feedback. *Advances in Neural Information Processing Systems*, 33:3008–3021.

Andreas Stolcke, Klaus Ries, Noah Coccaro, Elizabeth Shriberg, Rebecca Bates, Daniel Jurafsky, Paul Taylor, Rachel Martin, Carol Van Ess-Dykema, and Marie Meteer. 2000. Dialogue act modeling for automatic tagging and recognition of conversational speech. *Computational linguistics*, 26(3):339–373.

Philippe Tillet and David Cox. 2019. Triton: an intermediate language and compiler for tiled neural network computations. In *Proceedings of the 3rd ACM SIGPLAN International Workshop on Machine Learning and Programming Languages*, pages 10–19.

Iulia Turc, Ming-Wei Chang, Kenton Lee, and Kristina Toutanova. 2019. Well-read students learn better: On the importance of pre-training compact models. *arXiv preprint arXiv:1908.08962*.

Alex Wang, Yada Pruksachatkun, Nikita Nangia, Amanpreet Singh, Julian Michael, Felix Hill, Omer Levy, and Samuel Bowman. 2019. Superglue: A stickier benchmark for general-purpose language understanding systems. *Advances in neural information processing systems*, 32.

Alex Wang, Amanpreet Singh, Julian Michael, Felix Hill, Omer Levy, and Samuel Bowman. 2018. Glue: A multi-task benchmark and analysis platform for natural language understanding. In *Proceedings of the 2018 EMNLP Workshop BlackboxNLP: Analyzing and Interpreting Neural Networks for NLP*, pages 353–355.

Shibo Wang and Pankaj Kanwar. 2019. Bfloat16: The secret to high performance on cloud tpus. *Google Cloud Blog*, 4.

Alex Warstadt, Aaron Mueller, Leshem Choshen, Ethan Gotlieb Wilcox, Chengxu Zhuang, Juan Ciro, Rafael Mosquera, Adina Williams, Bhargavi Paranjabe, Tal Linzen, and Ryan Cotterell. 2023. Findings of the 2023 BabyLM Challenge: Sample-efficient pretraining on developmentally plausible corpora. In *Proceedings of the 2023 BabyLM Challenge*. Association for Computational Linguistics (ACL).

Alex Warstadt, Alicia Parrish, Haokun Liu, Anhad Mohananey, Wei Peng, Sheng-Fu Wang, and Samuel R Bowman. 2020a. Blimp: The benchmark of linguistic minimal pairs for english. *Transactions of the Association for Computational Linguistics*, 8:377–392.

Alex Warstadt, Yian Zhang, Xiaocheng Li, Haokun Liu, and Samuel Bowman. 2020b. Learning which features matter: Roberta acquires a preference for linguistic generalizations (eventually). In *Proceedings of the 2020 Conference on Empirical Methods in Natural Language Processing (EMNLP)*, pages 217–235.

Alex Warstadt, Yian Zhang, Xiaocheng Li, Haokun Liu, and Samuel R. Bowman. 2020c. Learning which features matter: RoBERTa acquires a preference for linguistic generalizations (eventually). In *Proceedings of the 2020 Conference on Empirical Methods in Natural Language Processing (EMNLP)*, pages 217–235, Online. Association for Computational Linguistics.

Byte-ranked Curriculum Learning for BabyLM Strict-small Shared Task 2023

Justin DeBenedetto
Villanova University

Abstract

The size of neural language models has increased rapidly over the past several years. This increase in model size has been accompanied by using larger and larger amounts of language data to train them. As these models and training data sizes have grown, the computational resources required to train them has surpassed what is available to many researchers. This work is part of a shared task called the BabyLM Challenge which requires language models to be trained using a restricted amount of training data a small fraction of the size of what large models use. In addition, no pretrained tools can be used. This work presents a curriculum learning approach to this data restricted setting by applying a bytes per line ordering to provided datasets. Throughout training, the average bytes per line is gradually increased by including more datasets as training data. Overall, there is an increase in performance on downstream tasks when using this curriculum learning approach, which provides a basis for potential further exploration of byte-based curriculum learning approaches.

1 Introduction

Large language models (LLMs) have received much attention from researchers and the general public in recent years (Devlin et al., 2018; Liu et al., 2019; Brown et al., 2020; Chowdhery et al., 2022; Hoffmann et al., 2022). One distinguishing aspect of these recent models is an explosion in the size of the models and a corresponding massive increase in training data to train these large models. In particular, the Chinchilla (Hoffmann et al., 2022) work suggests that model size and training tokens should be scaled at the same rate. To demonstrate the importance of the amount of training data used to train a model, Chinchilla was trained with 1.4 trillion training tokens, nearly five times the size of the training data for other LLMs at the time. The result was an improvement on a number of downstream tasks.

While large models perform very well on a large variety of tasks, they also come with many drawbacks. These models require large amounts of computing resources beyond what is available to many researchers. Additionally, the amount of data used to train these models is not currently available in the majority of the world's languages. In an effort to investigate language modeling abilities and training strategies in data-limited situations, the BabyLM challenge restricts the amount of data available to models (Warstadt et al., 2023).

One approach to improve training speed and improve downstream performance is by providing training data in a specific order. In particular, gradually increasing the difficulty of the training samples provided to the model is known as curriculum learning (Elman, 1993). Human children learning language follow a similar exposure to language. Speech directed at babies is far simpler than speech directed at adults and written language data follows the same trend. The motivation behind curriculum learning is to treat a neural network in a similar manner and allow it to learn from easier training samples before being presented with more difficult training samples.

The approach taken in this current work is to apply curriculum learning in a data restricted setting, without incorporating outside knowledge or data, to see its impact on training. The preprocessing steps are kept the same across models presented to reduce their effect on the ability to compare across training runs. A byte-level byte-pair-encoding tokenization is used across all models presented. Inspired by the byte-level approach to encoding, bytes per line is used as the measure of "difficulty" for a given portion of the dataset. The data used to train the model came from several different datasets. The bytes per line "difficulty" is used to determine the order in which training datasets are provided to the models as part of a curriculum learning approach. While no additional or outside information is required to apply this approach to data, the result for this challenge was that transcribed speech was used as training data

Proceedings of the 27th Conference on Computational Natural Language Learning: Volume 2: The BabyLM Challenge, pages 198–206
December 6-7, 2023 ©2023 Association for Computational Linguistics

before any of the written text data. This provides another parallel to human language acquisition as speech comes before literacy in children.

Given that the limitations motivating this work and this challenge include data limitations as well as computational resources, we train each model for a set number of epochs. Models trained using the curriculum learning approach outperformed a traditional training approach baseline across several benchmark downstream tasks. When computational resources are less limited, the models also continue to improve when the model size is increased and when trained longer.

2 Related Work

There is much existing work on language models, including methods to work with them in computational or data constrained settings. One approach that has been used is model distillation. A well-known example of this is DistilBERT (Sanh et al., 2019). DistilBERT, and other distillation trained models, require a larger pretrained model to act as a teacher when a smaller model is trained. While the end result is a smaller model which can perform quite well. This approach can be applied to systems which require a small final model, but does not work for data or computationally constrained settings for training such as ours.

A similar approach is to use a large language model and simply finetune on the data-restricted task. Since this requires a pretrained large language model, this approach also does not work for constrained training settings with no such pretrained model available. While finetuning is used as part of the evaluation process for this challenge, this approach violates the restrictions of this challenge. As such, this solution to data-restricted settings is not used here. When there is a domain mismatch between the data used to pretrain an existing language model and the training data for a desired domain, some work suggests that training a new language model may be beneficial. For example, Gu et al. (2021) find that training a new language model specifically on in-domain biomedical data produced a better result for in-domain downstream tasks. This is more similar to the setting of this work as a language model is trained from scratch.

Another area of research within Natural Language Processing that is similar to this strict-small track is work with low-resource languages. While many of the largest language models are built for English with large quantities of data, there have been efforts to improve language modeling in lower resource language as well. Some of these, such as multilingual BERT (Devlin et al., 2018), are themselves large language models which combine many languages into one model. These models still require a large amount of resources (data and computational) and are larger than what is presented in the challenge.

Since curriculum learning relies upon increasing the difficulty of training samples as training continues, determining what makes a training sample more difficult than another is centrally important. For language input, some proposed measures of difficulty include presence of rare words (Bengio et al., 2009), block size (Nagatsuka et al., 2021), and length (Nagatsuka et al., 2023). When viewed in relation to these approaches, this work represents an exploration of a new, related measure of difficulty of training samples.

The learning schedule used in this work which determines at what rate new samples are added to the training set shares a similar motivation to work by Amiri et al. (2017). Their work applies findings from psychology that human learners learn effectively when the same information is reviewed with increasing lengths of time between reviews. These findings suggest that human learners ability to learn information is impacted not only by repetition of material, but also by the interval of time between those repetitions. The work by Amiri et al. (2017) uses this as a basis for a curriculum learning schedule. That work created a scheduler which spends more time on difficulty training instances and less time on easy instances. This work, by contrast, by gradually increasing the size of the training set, also gradually increases the time between repetitions of the easiest training samples while saving the more difficulty samples for later in training.

As this work was part of a shared task BabyLM challenge, there will be other related works published at the same time as this work. While those works cannot be discussed here, they will also provide good comparisons of other possible approaches.

3 Data

The dataset provided for this challenge came from ten sources. These sources were chosen to represent the type of language that a human child may be exposed to when learning English and includes both written text and transcribed speech. For the strict-small track, the total training data available was just under 10 million words.

Given the variety of sources, the text format was not consistent across the provided data and required some preprocessing.

3.1 Preprocessing

Due to the strict nature of the challenge, no preprocessing steps which were pretrained on outside data were allowed. This restriction ruled out the use of many off-the-shelf preprocessing tools. In many

Dataset	Domain	Words	Size (MB)	Lines	Bytes/line
CHILDES	Child-directed speech	0.44M	1.9	80K	24
OpenSubtitles	Movie subtitles	3.09M	16.0	527K	30
Switchboard Dialog Act Corpus	Dialogue	0.12M	0.6	16K	37
British National Corpus, dialogue portion	Dialogue	0.86M	4.3	89K	48
QCRI Educational Domain Corpus (QED)	Educational video subtitles	1.04M	5.6	100K	56
Simple Wikipedia	Wikipedia (Simple English)	1.52M	8.7	120K	72
Children's Book Test	Children's books	0.57M	2.6	26K	100
Standardized Project Gutenberg Corpus	Written English	0.99M	5.5	54K	102
Children's Stories Text Corpus	Children's books	0.34M	1.8	16K	112
Wikipedia	Wikipedia (English)	0.99M	5.8	50K	117
Total		9.96M	52.8	1078K	49

Table 1: Dataset provided for the strict-small track of the BabyLM challenge. Dataset names, domain descriptions, and word counts provided in Warstadt et al. (2023). Bytes, line counts, and bytes per line all measured after preprocessing was completed. See section 3.1 for details.

low-resource settings there may be no or limited existing pretrained tools to use for preprocessing. While such tools are useful when available, in this challenge those tools are off-limits.

We used a rule-based sentence splitter. Sentences are automatically split by punctuation unless they are preceded by one of the listed prefixes (for example, "Dr" followed by punctuation does not signify a sentence split).[1] This approach was selected since it was not trained on any outside data and provides decent sentence breaks.

Additional preprocessing included removal of blank lines, and lower casing the entire "QED" dataset, which came in all capital letters.

3.2 Tokenizer

In order for the model to train on the data, a tokenizer must convert the input sentences into tokens. Word-level tokenizers replace any words not seen in the training data with an unknown token. Given the small amount of training data available in this challenge, this would result in many words marked as unknown. At the other extreme, character-level tokenization breaks every input into characters in order to eliminate any unknown tokens from occurring. This also has the advantage of having a small vocabulary size, since it consists only of characters. A major drawback of this approach is that, unlike words, characters may not have meaning by themselves. A popular and successful approach sits between these two by merging frequent pairs of characters together iteratively to create a vocabulary of characters and merged tokens. This approach is known as byte-pair encoding (BPE) (Sennrich et al., 2015). Despite its name, byte-pair encoding applied to natural language models typically does not operate at the byte level. A more recent approach used in language models such as GPT-2 (Radford et al., 2019) is byte-level byte-pair encoding. This is similar to earlier BPE, but operates directly on the byte representations and has been effective in language models.

After preprocessing, a byte-level byte-pair-encoding tokenizer was trained on the data. The vocabulary size was set to 52,000 with special tokens added for sentence beginning and end, padding, masking, and an unknown token in case any bytes were never seen in the training data. The maximum length was set to 128 (126+beginning and end tokens). Once trained, this tokenizer was used across models for consistency.

4 Model and Training

Our model is a RoBERTa (Liu et al., 2019) model. RoBERTa improves upon the BERT (Devlin et al., 2018) model, increasing performance across a range of benchmarks. While the architecture of both models is nearly identical, there are a number of smaller changes made in RoBERTa. Among the most relevant for his work is the removal of next sentence prediction task during pretraining and modifying the masked language mod-

[1]https://github.com/mediacloud/sentence-splitter

eling pretraining task by re-selecting the masks each training epoch. The architecture underlying these models is the Transformer model (Vaswani et al., 2017). The "base" model and the "CL-sm" model are the same size and number of parameters, differing only in how they were trained. The "CL-lrg" model is trained in the same way as "CL-sm" but is a slightly larger model. More details of the models are discussed in section 5.1. The "CL-sm" model trained for 5 epochs was submitted to the BabyLM Challenge[2]. The "CL-lrg" model trained for 10 epochs is also available for download[3]. Since we do not significantly modify this underlying architecture, we leave the details of these models to their respective papers. Code to train our model can be found on GitHub [4].

4.1 Masked Language Modeling

The pretraining objective used to train our models was masked language modeling. In masked language modeling (MLM), tokens are randomly replaced with a special ¡mask¿ token. Given the surrounding context, the model predicts the masked token and the loss is used to train the model. As mentioned above, MLM as a pretraining task for language modeling has been used successfully in many existing models such as BERT and RoBERTa. Following RoBERTa, masks were computed dynamically for each training instance and were not retained across epochs.

4.2 Curriculum Learning

Our models used curriculum learning to gradually increase the difficulty of the training set. As discussed earlier, there are ten datasets that were combined to create the training data. Each of these datasets were added one at a time to increase the training data. The way "difficulty" was measured, avoiding applying outside knowledge to the data, was by dividing each of the ten data files' size by the number of lines in that file. This gave an approximate bytes per line ranking of the ten training files. This was computed after all preprocessing was done, including the additional line splits and blank line removals.

A number of epochs is chosen prior to pretraining. After that number of epochs of training, another dataset was added to the training data. The model weights from the end of the previous epochs were used, but the learning rate and other hyperparameters were reset. As there was more data in the training set as training continued, the epochs contained more updates the further the training went. The final set of epochs included all of the training data.

The order in which datasets were added by following this approach was:

1. CHILDES (MacWhinney, 2000)
2. OpenSubtitles (Lison and Tiedemann, 2016)
3. Switchboard Dialog Act Corpus (Stolcke et al., 2000)
4. British National Corpus, dialogue portion[5]
5. QCRI Educational Domain Corpus (QED) (Abdelali et al., 2014)
6. Simple Wikipedia[6]
7. Children's Book Test (Hill et al., 2016)
8. Standardized Project Gutenberg Corpus (Gerlach and Font-Clos, 2020)
9. Children's Stories Text Corpus[7]
10. Wikipedia[8]

This ordering also orders spoken, transcribed datasets before written datasets. This follows the language acquisition and exposure ordering that human children encounter. The exact ordering differs from an ordering based on when children would be exposed to these particular datasets, in particular Children's Stories Test Corpus would come much earlier in the order. One benefit of our approach is that it can be applied to any datasets without prior knowledge of what the datasets contain.

Unlike many other works which combine data from all sources into one pool before assigning an order to samples, this work places the ordering on the data sources themselves. This approach is fitting for settings such as this one in which the data from different sources can differ widely in their complexity. Datasets which contain more similar sources may not benefit from this approach, but that is outside the scope of this current work.

Since our tokenizer uses byte level byte pair encoding, we chose to explore a byte-based ranking for the dataset complexities.

5 Results

Here we examine the results of models on the provided evaluation benchmarks (Gao et al., 2021).

[2]https://huggingface.co/jdebene/BabyLM-jde-5/tree/main
[3]https://huggingface.co/jdebene/BabyLM-jde-larger-10/tree/main
[4]https://github.com/jdebened/BabyLM2023

Model	Ana. Agr.	Agr. Str.	Bind.	Ctrl. Rais.	D-N Agr.	Ellip.	Fill. Gap	Irreg.	Isl.	NPI	Quan.	S-V Agr.	Avg.
Base													
5 ep	72.65	66.59	64.84	60.96	85.12	51.39	63.60	90.69	34.19	57.52	78.77	57.85	65.35
10 ep	79.35	70.42	68.06	64.85	94.76	65.65	65.66	**92.32**	34.68	59.57	**79.01**	62.48	69.73
20 ep	84.25	72.65	68.60	65.11	96.55	70.44	68.04	91.09	32.21	55.86	72.23	67.37	70.37
CL-sm													
5 ep	81.65	72.77	**71.40**	67.34	96.38	71.94	68.32	81.63	33.48	65.87	69.22	71.29	70.94
10 ep	86.50	72.81	69.46	68.91	94.79	**75.87**	71.68	80.46	39.05	62.22	67.95	72.68	71.87
CL-lrg													
5 ep	84.92	**73.44**	70.36	**69.07**	**97.14**	74.31	74.07	85.70	34.87	64.14	74.91	72.86	72.98
10 ep	**87.88**	71.40	70.04	68.94	94.75	75.75	**74.56**	84.17	**44.25**	**67.86**	66.18	**77.76**	**73.63**

Table 2: Comparison of models on BLiMP tasks. Average shown is macro-average across all tasks. Models trained using curriculum learning surpassed baseline (all data, no curriculum learning) and improved further when more epochs were used for training. **Bolded** values show best in column.

5.1 BLiMP

Distributed as part of the BabyLM challenge was an evaluation pipeline. This pipeline included zero-shot evaluation on tasks from the BLiMP benchmark (Warstadt et al., 2020a). The BLiMP data was filtered to only include words which appeared at least twice in our training dataset (strict-small track) [9]. BLiMP (The Benchmark of Linguistic Minimal Pairs) provides a pretrained language model with a pair of sentences to score. The sentence pairs have small differences designed to assess whether a language model can select the correct sentence. If the language model assigns a higher score to the correct sentence in the pair, it is marked as correct. The tasks within BLiMP test different phenomena spanning syntax, semantics, and morphology. Since the sentences come in pairs, a random guessing baseline would achieve around 50% accuracy across all tasks.

Table 2 shows the results on BLiMP tasks. All models shown used the same preprocessing, tokenization, and are RoBERTa models. The base model had six attention heads and four hidden layers. All data was used for every epoch of training the base model. The "CL-sm" model also had six attention heads and four hidden layers, thus maintaining the same architecture. The curriculum learning technique described above was applied at training time, gradually increasing the amount of available training data. The "CL-lrg" model is a larger version with twelve attention heads and six hidden layers. The curriculum learning technique is the same as was used for the smaller model.

As can be seen in Table 2, even with the limited amount of training data available in this challenge, the language models were able to improve on most BLiMP tasks. The models trained using a curriculum learning approach all had higher average scores across the BLiMP tasks. The only two tasks in which the base model outperformed the curriculum learning models were irregular forms and quantifiers. The irregular forms task focuses on irregular forms of words in English for past particles. The example given in the BLiMP paper for the irregular forms task is: "Aaron broke the unicycle" compared to "Aaron broken the unicycle". For the quantifiers task, grammatical use of quantifiers is tested as shown in the example from the BLiMP paper: "No boy knew fewer than six guys" compared to "No boy knew at most six guys".

Upon further inspection of the training data, this drop in performance on the irregular forms makes sense given the order in which the curriculum learning datasets were used. Initially, the model trains exclusively on the CHILDES dataset. After the specified number of epochs, the OpenSubtitles data is added and additional training is done. As this process continues, the model appears to be heavily influenced by the improper use of irregular forms within the CHILDES dataset. For example, "you broken the trains ?" is a sentence in the dataset in which the speaker is likely repeating a statement made by the child. By contrast, the model is exposed to every dataset during every epoch in the base model. The training data coming from sources such as Wikipedia, simple Wikipedia, Project Gutenberg, and others is much less likely to feature many improper uses of irregular forms.

The performance drop on the quantifiers task is not as obvious in the data, nor is the drop in performance as dramatic. Even within the base model itself, performance on the quantifier task dropped when moving from 10 epochs of training to 20 epochs of training. Training models on larger portions of the datasets included in this challenge

[5] http://www.natcorp.ox.ac.uk

[6] https://dumps.wikimedia.org/simplewiki/20221201/

[7] https://www.kaggle.com/datasets/edenbd/children-stories-text-corpus

[8] https://dumps.wikimedia.org/enwiki/20221220/

[9] See https://github.com/babylm/evaluation-pipeline for more details

may provide more insight into which datasets contribute positively or negatively toward each task in the benchmark. This is left to future work outside of this challenge.

Another task of note is the island effects task. This task assesses how well the language model learns that certain syntactic structures prevent syntactic dependencies across them. This phenomenon is investigated in works such as by Kush et al. (2018). An example of this, given in the BLiMP paper, is: "Whose hat should Tonya wear?" compared to "Whose should Tonya wear hat?". It is noted in the BLiMP paper that this is the hardest task in the benchmark for models they tested. Our models not only did not do better than random chance (50%), they actually consistently preferred the wrong option. Similar to quantifiers, there may be interesting results from uncovering why these models prefer the sentences which violate the island effects, but that is left to future work outside the scope of this challenge.

5.2 SuperGLUE

The GLUE benchmark (Wang et al., 2018) was designed to assess natural language systems on language understanding tasks. There were nine tasks aimed at testing different aspects of the language understanding problem. About a year after its release, in response to rapid improvements on the benchmark by natural language systems, SuperGLUE was published as a more challenging supplement or replacement (Wang et al., 2019).

Since these tasks require more than just a language model score to make predictions, the provided evaluation scripts finetuned a model for each task. The finetuning process involves a small amount of additional, task-specific training of a pretrained model in order to boost performance or add a suitable encoder or decoder layer for the specific task. The initial learning rate was set to 5e-5, the batch size set to 64, and the model trained for up to 10 epochs.

The results for tasks from GLUE and SuperGLUE can be seen in Table 3. The models trained with curriculum learning had higher average scores than those trained conventionally. While the curriculum learning models improved on most tasks, there were three tasks worth examining further: QNLI, BoolQ, and WSC.

The task labeled QNLI (Question-answering NLI) comes from the Stanford Question Answering Dataset (SQuAD) (Rajpurkar et al., 2016). In SQuAD, systems were provided with a question and a paragraph which contained a sentence answering the question. The task was to pick out which sentence answered the given question. This was converted into the QNLI task by pairing the question with each sentence in the given paragraph and asking a natural language system to classify whether the answer to the question is contained in the given sentence.

In our results, we can see that the curriculum learning approach has the highest score of any of our models after its shortest training set of 5 epochs. However, performance dropped when the pretraining within the curriculum learning framework was increased to 10 epochs per set of data. Performance degraded even further when the model size was increased and the curriculum remained the same.

For the task labeled BoolQ (Boolean Questions) (Clark et al., 2019), the task is to provide a boolean response (yes/no) to a question. The system is provided with the question and a paragraph from a Wikipedia article which contains the answer to the question. Here we see a similar phenomenon to the trend with QNLI. The curriculum learning models' performance decreases when allowed more epochs for pretraining. Increasing model size had a less noticeable drop in performance.

The WSC (Winograd Schema Challenge) task (Levesque et al., 2012) requires a system to pick to which noun phrase in a sentence a pronoun is referring. The system is provided with a sentence which includes a pronoun and noun phrases. The pronoun refers to one of the noun phrases. The drop in performance for models which trained for more epochs is fairly consistent across models, regardless of whether curriculum learning was applied for pretraining or not.

Despite these three tasks, average performance across the benchmark does improve when using curriculum learning, when increasing the number of pretraining epochs, and when increasing the model size.

5.3 MSGS

The MSGS (Mixed Signals Generalization Set) (Warstadt et al., 2020b) was designed to test for inductive biases in pretrained language models. The aim of these tests are to not only find whether a language model represents certain phenomena, but more importantly whether it has learned to prefer them when generalizing. As was done for the SuperGLUE tasks, finetuning is done for each model to find its performance on each task. Our finetuning hyperparameter setup is unchanged for MSGS.

The results shown in Table 4 show that the performance across our models was relatively similar. The conventional training method used for the base model had nearly identical average performance across all three different training lengths with the exception of poor performance on the SC-LC task for the model trained for 20 epochs. Given the consistency across other tasks, it is possible that retraining would not replicate this drop, though

Model	CoLA	SST-2	MRPC (F1)	QQP (F1)	MNLI	MNLI-mm	QNLI	RTE	BoolQ	Multi RC	WSC	Avg
Base 5 ep	70.76	84.84	76.92	77.07	67.02	67.84	62.20	48.48	63.35	57.94	61.45	67.08
10 ep	71.05	85.63	74.05	77.30	67.65	69.67	62.64	44.44	63.07	50.82	59.04	65.94
20 ep	70.36	86.61	78.63	77.77	68.07	69.37	65.27	44.44	65.70	58.38	59.04	67.60
CL-sm 5 ep	71.34	84.84	73.90	77.69	65.79	66.52	66.54	46.46	67.36	59.04	61.45	67.36
10 ep	72.33	87.99	76.45	78.47	70.05	71.23	64.22	45.45	64.73	59.58	56.63	67.92
CL-lrg 5 ep	72.33	87.01	79.38	78.60	70.71	72.15	63.87	47.47	65.42	57.28	61.45	68.70
10 ep	74.39	88.19	79.41	78.57	70.05	70.56	63.17	51.52	64.87	59.58	59.04	69.03

Table 3: Comparison of models on (super) GLUE tasks. Average shown is macro-average across all tasks. Models trained using curriculum learning surpassed baseline in average performance.

Model	CR-ctrl	LC-ctrl	MV-ctrl	RP-ctrl	SC-ctrl	CR-LC	CR-RTP	MV-LC	MV-RTP	SC-LC	SC-RP	Avg
Base 5 ep	82.13	100	97.76	99.29	95.25	66.46	66.64	66.61	66.38	88.69	69.75	81.72
10 ep	84.36	100	97.77	98.64	93.46	69.11	66.81	66.61	66.72	89.53	65.07	81.64
20 ep	89.94	100	97.98	99.98	89.92	66.60	66.92	66.61	66.79	67.39	64.56	79.70
CL-sm 5 ep	91.14	100	97.45	99.74	86.71	66.49	67.15	66.61	66.87	63.84	62.34	78.94
10 ep	88.37	100	97.93	100	89.96	66.38	67.29	66.61	66.78	70.10	65.72	79.92
CL-lrg 5 ep	84.57	100	99.36	98.94	94.39	66.35	67.01	66.61	66.62	72.69	70.33	80.62
10 ep	89.56	100	99.87	100	92.21	67.00	66.76	66.61	66.65	75.54	69.30	81.22

Table 4: Comparison of models on MSGS benchmark tasks. Average shown is macro-average across all tasks. Models trained using curriculum learning performed slightly worse than baseline model, but improved with more epochs. The base model, by contrast, had worse performance with more training epochs.

that would need to be tested to be confirmed. The models trained with curriculum learning had slight improvements when pretrained for more epochs as well as when the model size was larger. Overall, the techniques used in this work showed little impact on the MSGS tasks.

6 Conclusion

Large language models have been highly successful across a wide variety of tasks in Natural Language Processing. Due to the rapidly increasing model size and training data size, however, the cost to train new models is prohibitively expensive for many researchers. The BabyLM Challenge is a shared task designed to highlight methods for training language models at a smaller scale. These methods may lead to improvements in scaling up training more efficiently, training language models in low-resource settings, and drawing upon the way human children acquire language.

In this work, the strict-small track allowed our models to use a given dataset containing around ten million words from data sources that a child may encounter when learning language. No tools which used outside data for pretraining were allowed, reducing the ability to use many existing pipelines. This restriction is realistic for many low-resource scenarios in which these tools are lacking.

This work explores ordering training data by bytes per line for a curriculum learning approach. This measure of difficulty is inspired by the use of byte-based byte-pair-encoding tokenization and is easy to apply without needing any domain knowledge of the dataset. The results show that curriculum learning with this setup obtains improved results on benchmark evaluations when training for a set number of epochs. In settings in which additional tools, data, or computational resources are available, this curriculum setup is easy to apply and further evaluation in those settings is a potential area for future work.

This work used the Augie High-Performance Computing cluster, funded by award NSF 2018933, at Villanova University.

Limtations

This work was completed as part of the BabyLM Challenge. As such, additional testing would be required to determine how well the results generalize outside of this data setting. In a similar way, pretraining settings in which some pre-existing tools which are trained on outside data are available may produce different results. Additionally, if more computational resources are available, the benefit to the models when trained for more epochs remains to be seen. Other work on curriculum learning found faster convergence, but models in this work were trained for a set number of epochs and not to convergence. The results outperform the baseline model at the set number of epochs used, but training to convergence may lead to better or worse results.

References

Ahmed Abdelali, Francisco Guzman, Hassan Sajjad, and Stephan Vogel. 2014. The amara corpus: Building parallel language resources for the educational domain. In *LREC*, volume 14, pages 1044–1054.

Hadi Amiri, Timothy Miller, and Guergana Savova. 2017. Repeat before forgetting: Spaced repetition for efficient and effective training of neural networks. In *Proceedings of the 2017 Conference on Empirical Methods in Natural Language Processing*, pages 2401–2410.

Yoshua Bengio, Jérôme Louradour, Ronan Collobert, and Jason Weston. 2009. Curriculum learning. In *Proceedings of the 26th annual international conference on machine learning*, pages 41–48.

Tom Brown, Benjamin Mann, Nick Ryder, Melanie Subbiah, Jared D Kaplan, Prafulla Dhariwal, Arvind Neelakantan, Pranav Shyam, Girish Sastry, Amanda Askell, et al. 2020. Language models are few-shot learners. *Advances in neural information processing systems*, 33:1877–1901.

Aakanksha Chowdhery, Sharan Narang, Jacob Devlin, Maarten Bosma, Gaurav Mishra, Adam Roberts, Paul Barham, Hyung Won Chung, Charles Sutton, Sebastian Gehrmann, et al. 2022. Palm: Scaling language modeling with pathways. *arXiv preprint arXiv:2204.02311*.

Christopher Clark, Kenton Lee, Ming-Wei Chang, Tom Kwiatkowski, Michael Collins, and Kristina Toutanova. 2019. Boolq: Exploring the surprising difficulty of natural yes/no questions. *arXiv preprint arXiv:1905.10044*.

Jacob Devlin, Ming-Wei Chang, Kenton Lee, and Kristina Toutanova. 2018. Bert: Pre-training of deep bidirectional transformers for language understanding. *arXiv preprint arXiv:1810.04805*.

Jeffrey L Elman. 1993. Learning and development in neural networks: The importance of starting small. *Cognition*, 48(1):71–99.

Leo Gao, Jonathan Tow, Stella Biderman, Sid Black, Anthony DiPofi, Charles Foster, Laurence Golding, Jeffrey Hsu, Kyle McDonell, Niklas Muennighoff, Jason Phang, Laria Reynolds, Eric Tang, Anish Thite, Ben Wang, Kevin Wang, and Andy Zou. 2021. A framework for few-shot language model evaluation.

Martin Gerlach and Francesc Font-Clos. 2020. A standardized project gutenberg corpus for statistical analysis of natural language and quantitative linguistics. *Entropy*, 22(1):126.

Yu Gu, Robert Tinn, Hao Cheng, Michael Lucas, Naoto Usuyama, Xiaodong Liu, Tristan Naumann, Jianfeng Gao, and Hoifung Poon. 2021. Domain-specific language model pretraining for biomedical natural language processing. *ACM Transactions on Computing for Healthcare (HEALTH)*, 3(1):1–23.

Felix Hill, Antoine Bordes, Sumit Chopra, and Jason Weston. 2016. The goldilocks principle: Reading children's books with explicit memory representations. arxiv 2015. *arXiv preprint arXiv:1511.02301*.

Jordan Hoffmann, Sebastian Borgeaud, Arthur Mensch, Elena Buchatskaya, Trevor Cai, Eliza Rutherford, Diego de Las Casas, Lisa Anne Hendricks, Johannes Welbl, Aidan Clark, et al. 2022. Training compute-optimal large language models. *arXiv preprint arXiv:2203.15556*.

Dave Kush, Terje Lohndal, and Jon Sprouse. 2018. Investigating variation in island effects: A case study of norwegian wh-extraction. *Natural language & linguistic theory*, 36:743–779.

Hector Levesque, Ernest Davis, and Leora Morgenstern. 2012. The winograd schema challenge. In *Thirteenth international conference on the principles of knowledge representation and reasoning*.

Pierre Lison and Jörg Tiedemann. 2016. Opensubtitles2016: Extracting large parallel corpora from movie and tv subtitles.

Yinhan Liu, Myle Ott, Naman Goyal, Jingfei Du, Mandar Joshi, Danqi Chen, Omer Levy, Mike Lewis, Luke Zettlemoyer, and Veselin Stoyanov. 2019. Roberta: A robustly optimized bert pretraining approach. *arXiv preprint arXiv:1907.11692*.

Brian MacWhinney. 2000. *The CHILDES project: The database*, volume 2. Psychology Press.

Koichi Nagatsuka, Clifford Broni-Bediako, and Masayasu Atsumi. 2021. Pre-training a bert with curriculum learning by increasing block-size of input text. In *Proceedings of the International Conference on Recent Advances in Natural Language Processing (RANLP 2021)*, pages 989–996.

Koichi Nagatsuka, Clifford Broni-Bediako, and Masayasu Atsumi. 2023. Length-based curriculum learning for efficient pre-training of language models. *New Generation Computing*, 41(1):109–134.

Alec Radford, Jeffrey Wu, Rewon Child, David Luan, Dario Amodei, Ilya Sutskever, et al. 2019. Language models are unsupervised multitask learners. *OpenAI blog*, 1(8):9.

Pranav Rajpurkar, Jian Zhang, Konstantin Lopyrev, and Percy Liang. 2016. Squad: 100,000+ questions for machine comprehension of text. *arXiv preprint arXiv:1606.05250*.

Victor Sanh, Lysandre Debut, Julien Chaumond, and Thomas Wolf. 2019. Distilbert, a distilled version of bert: smaller, faster, cheaper and lighter. *arXiv preprint arXiv:1910.01108*.

Rico Sennrich, Barry Haddow, and Alexandra Birch. 2015. Neural machine translation of rare words with subword units. *arXiv preprint arXiv:1508.07909*.

Andreas Stolcke, Klaus Ries, Noah Coccaro, Elizabeth Shriberg, Rebecca Bates, Daniel Jurafsky, Paul Taylor, Rachel Martin, Carol Van Ess-Dykema, and Marie Meteer. 2000. Dialogue act modeling for automatic tagging and recognition of conversational speech. *Computational linguistics*, 26(3):339–373.

Ashish Vaswani, Noam Shazeer, Niki Parmar, Jakob Uszkoreit, Llion Jones, Aidan N Gomez, Łukasz Kaiser, and Illia Polosukhin. 2017. Attention is all you need. *Advances in neural information processing systems*, 30.

Alex Wang, Yada Pruksachatkun, Nikita Nangia, Amanpreet Singh, Julian Michael, Felix Hill, Omer Levy, and Samuel Bowman. 2019. Superglue: A stickier benchmark for general-purpose language understanding systems. *Advances in neural information processing systems*, 32.

Alex Wang, Amanpreet Singh, Julian Michael, Felix Hill, Omer Levy, and Samuel R Bowman. 2018. Glue: A multi-task benchmark and analysis platform for natural language understanding. *arXiv preprint arXiv:1804.07461*.

Alex Warstadt, Aaron Mueller, Leshem Choshen, Ethan Gotlieb Wilcox, Chengxu Zhuang, Juan Ciro, Rafael Mosquera, Adina Williams, Bhargavi Paranjabe, Tal Linzen, and Ryan Cotterell. 2023. Findings of the 2023 BabyLM Challenge: Sample-efficient pretraining on developmentally plausible corpora. In *Proceedings of the 2023 BabyLM Challenge*. Association for Computational Linguistics (ACL).

Alex Warstadt, Alicia Parrish, Haokun Liu, Anhad Mohananey, Wei Peng, Sheng-Fu Wang, and Samuel R Bowman. 2020a. Blimp: The benchmark of linguistic minimal pairs for english. *Transactions of the Association for Computational Linguistics*, 8:377–392.

Alex Warstadt, Yian Zhang, Xiaocheng Li, Haokun Liu, and Samuel R. Bowman. 2020b. Learning which features matter: RoBERTa acquires a preference for linguistic generalizations (eventually). In *Proceedings of the 2020 Conference on Empirical Methods in Natural Language Processing (EMNLP)*, pages 217–235, Online. Association for Computational Linguistics.

McGill BabyLM Shared Task Submission: The Effects of Data Formatting and Structural Biases

Ziling Cheng[1,2] **Rahul Aralikatte**[1,2] **Ian Porada**[1,2]
Cesare Spinoso-Di Piano[1,2] **Jackie Chi Kit Cheung**[1,2,3]
[1]Mila – Quebec Artificial Intelligence Institute [2]McGill University
[3]Canada CIFAR AI Chair
{ziling.cheng, ian.porada, cesare.spinoso-dipiano}@mail.mcgill.ca,
rahul.aralikatte@mila.quebec, jackie.cheung@mcgill.ca

Abstract

In this study, we describe our submission to the 2023 BabyLM shared-task's *strict-small* track. Our findings demonstrate the feasibility of training high-performing models within the constraints of limited data, computational resources, and time. We provide evidence that the formatting of input can significantly impact downstream performance. Furthermore, the induction of structural biases into the models through the use of part-of-speech trees yields modest benefits. Our most successful model achieves 79% on the BLiMP evaluations and 72% on the SuperGLUE evaluations. All models trained during this study can be found at `https://huggingface.co/mcgill-babylm`.[1][2]

1 Introduction

The pretraining of large language models (LLMs) is a resource-intensive process, requiring substantial computational power, time, and particularly, data. Contemporary LLMs are trained on billions, if not trillions, of tokens to achieve satisfactory performance (Kaplan et al., 2020; Hoffmann et al., 2022). This approach is not ideal, given that humans can learn to perform more complex tasks with data that are smaller by orders of magnitude (Linzen, 2020). Consequently, there is a burgeoning interest within the NLP community to identify and implement more data-efficient pretraining regimes.

The 2023 BabyLM challenge (Warstadt et al., 2023) seeks to unify research in this domain by formalizing the constraints and providing common pretraining and evaluation corpora. This shared task involves pretraining LLMs from scratch using data at a scale comparable to what a thirteen-year-old human child would have been exposed to. This approach enables researchers to concentrate their efforts on developing data-efficient pretraining techniques, potentially drawing inspiration from human cognitive development. The "strict-small" track, which limits the amount of pretraining data to 10M words, is of particular interest, and will be the focus of this study. An additional constraint of not being able to use any tools trained on external data further increases the difficulty. The pretraining corpus comprises multiple datasets, primarily consisting of transcribed conversations and other forms of simple language text. The evaluation of pretrained models includes zero-shot linguistic benchmark (Warstadt et al., 2020a, BLiMP) as well as finetuning the models for both standard Natural Language Understanding (NLU) tasks (Wang et al., 2019a, SuperGLUE) and evaluations of linguistic generalization (Warstadt et al., 2020c, MSGS). Brief descriptions of these datasets are provided in Section 3.

In this study, we limit our experiments to a modest computational and time budget of one GPU and 24 hours, respectively. This constraint compels us to focus on incorporating better inductive biases into model pretraining, rather than resorting to the more straightforward, but costlier, approach of extensive hyperparameter tuning. We adhere to standard transformer architectures (Vaswani et al., 2017) and pretraining strategies: masked language modeling (Devlin et al., 2019, MLM) and left-to-right, causal language modeling (Radford et al., 2018, CLM). We first explore the formatting of the data. We also attempt to induce structural biases using part-of-speech (POS) tags. While we did not include our models that incorporate POS tags in our official submission, as this contravenes the rules of the two tracks we are interested in, we believe it represents a promising research direction.

Findings Our findings indicate that within our

[1] Corresponding author: Ziling Cheng (ziling.cheng@mail.mcgill.ca).

[2] The code is available at `https://github.com/ziling-cheng/babylm`.

Proceedings of the 27th Conference on Computational Natural Language Learning: Volume 2: The BabyLM Challenge, pages 207–220
December 6-7, 2023

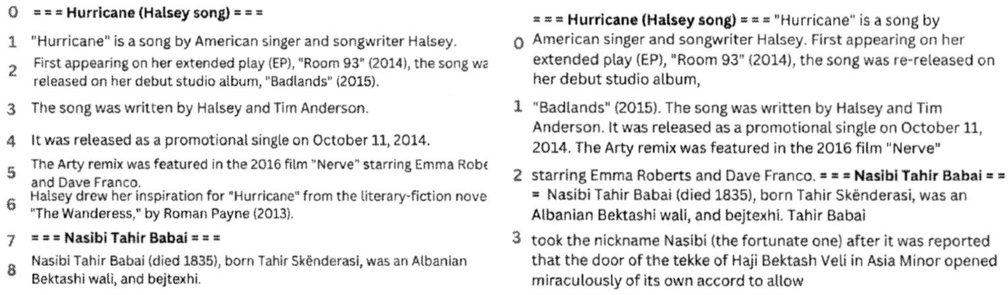

(a) (b)

Figure 1: Visualization of sentence-level training examples employing different grouping strategies, with a maximum sequence length of 32 words. The numbers on the left denote the i-th training example. (a) **sentence-level ungrouped**: any portion exceeding 32 words will be truncated. (b) **sentence-level grouped**: different documents/sentences could be grouped into a single training example, each totaling 32 words.

constrained setting, *data formatting* has the most significant impact on downstream performance. By data formatting, we specifically mean the formats of individual examples (e.g. sentence, document) and the methods of configuring multiple examples into a training minibatch (e.g. data grouping, or truncation). We observe that models pretrained with grouped data perform considerably worse than models pretrained with ungrouped data (62% vs. 79% on BLiMP). We also discover that inducing structural biases using POS trees modestly improves the downstream performance of the models (~1% on BLiMP).

2 Related Work

Existing research, particularly that conducted before the advent of LLMs, has explored the training of language models on relatively small datasets. For instance, Bengio et al. (2003) trained a neural language model on a corpus of approximately 1 million words. Additionally, Penn Treebank (Marcus et al., 1993) and WikiText (Merity et al., 2017) have been commonly used datasets for training language models.

In recent work, Samuel et al. (2023) have examined architectural enhancements to BERT when training on 100 million words, focusing on aspects such as position embeddings or layer normalization. Other studies have trained standard model architectures on limited data and evaluated syntactic or linguistic competency (Warstadt et al., 2020c; Yedetore et al., 2023; Pérez-Mayos et al., 2021). However, these studies have not thoroughly examined the data formatting and syntactic biases that we consider in our experiments.

Previous research has proposed syntactically-motivated inductive biases in the training of language models to enhance performance. These include the ON-LSTM (Shen et al., 2019), Tree Transformer (Wang et al., 2019b), and StructFormer (Shen et al., 2021). These studies have aimed to induce syntactic dependency and constituency parses.

3 Data

In this section, we first introduce the pretraining and evaluation data used, we then explain how we preprocess them (Section 3.1), along with some analysis (Section 3.2).

Pretraining Corpus The pretraining corpus released by the organizers contains ten different carefully selected sub-datasets from different domains, inspired by the typical input children would receive (Warstadt et al., 2023). About 55% and 45% of the pretraining corpus is transcribed-spoken English and written English, respectively.

Evaluation Corpora The shared evaluation pipeline scores models on both syntactic evaluations and semantic (NLU) benchmarks. The benchmarks have been filtered according to the vocabulary of the STRICT-SMALL dataset such that each word in each example should appear in the training set at least twice.

Zero-shot linguistic abilities of the model is assessed mainly using the BLiMP dataset (Warstadt

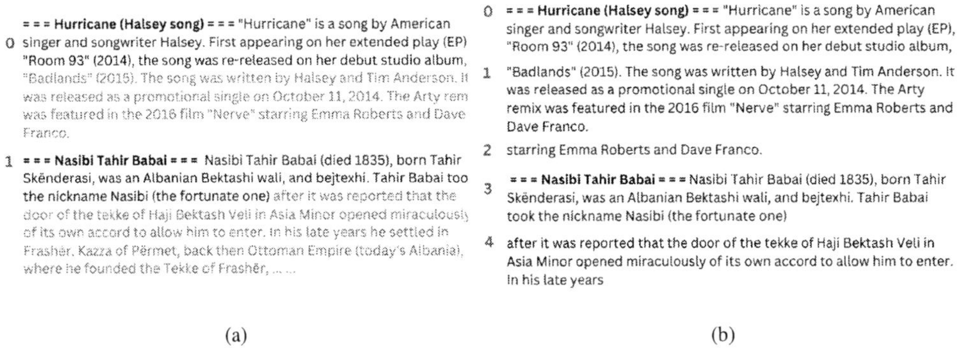

Figure 2: Visualization of document-level training examples employing different grouping strategies, with a maximum sequence length of 32 words. The numbers on the left denote the i-th training example. (a) **document-level ungrouped**: truncated text is shown in blue. (b) **document-level ungrouped without truncation**: document boundary is preserved. The **document-level grouping** strategy is omitted due to its similarity to sentence-level grouping strategy.

et al., 2020a). BLiMP consists of minimally different sentence pairs based on grammatical phenomenon where a model is expected to assign higher probability to the grammatically correct sentence. The sentence pairs were generated from expert-crafted grammars. This evaluation includes 12 phenomena from BLiMP, and also five supplemental phenomena not included in the original BLiMP dataset.

Fine-tuning evaluation is based on 11 canonical NLP tasks from the (Super)GLUE(Wang et al., 2018, 2019a) collections as well as MSGS (Warstadt et al., 2020c) which evaluates the extent to which a fine-tuned model favors linguistic generalizations as compared to spurious surface patterns.

3.1 Data Preprocessing

The pretraining corpus is a collection of sub-corpora and was released as one file for each sub-corpus. Each file consists of multiple documents from the sub-corpus which have been concatenated and then delimited by new line characters. We refer to each file as a sub-dataset, and we refer to each line in a given sub-dataset as a sentence. For each sub-dataset, in addition to training with these sentence-level examples, we also experiment with transforming the sub-dataset into "document-level" examples motivated by Liu et al. (2019) who have shown that formatting inputs as individual sentences negatively affects downstream task performance.

We thus consider two dataset formats in our experiments: *sentence-level* and *document-level*. More specifically, sentence-level refers to the case where each line in a corpus file is considered an independent training example. Document-level refers to the case where we approximately recover the original document boundaries (e.g. a chapter in the book corpus, a wikipedia article, a conversation) using heuristics and take each reconstructed document to be an independent training example. The heuristics we use to approximate document boundaries are based on corpus-specific, keyword-based rules (e.g. the keyword "Chapter" is a sign of a change of document for book corpora). In the case of speech corpora, it is impossible to reconstruct the conversation boundary because of the formatting of the released sub-dataset; therefore, for speech corpora we still consider each line (utterance) to be an independent training example, even for document-level experiments.

Both dataset variants are divided into train, validation, and test splits. We only use the train split to pretrain the models (80% of the original data).

3.2 Data Analysis

In this section, we provide some statistics of the pretraining data and BLiMP evaluation datasets, as well as some analysis of lexical overlap between the two.[3] We first compute the number of unique and total unigrams and bigrams in the data. To understand the extent of syntactic commonality between the datasets, we also examine the ratio of

[3] In this work, we mainly use BLiMP for all analyses, experimentations, and ablations, unless noted otherwise.

10M	Avg. Words			Avg. Tokens		
	train	test	dev	train	test	dev
sent.	9.41	9.74	9.16	14.41	14.99	14.28
doc.	47.22	48.10	46.76	64.33	66.13	64.66

Table 1: Average number of words (split on white space) and tokens (split using WordPiece tokenizer) in the sentences and documents of the BabyLM *strict-small* data.

the overlap of unigrams, bigrams, and linearized dependency graphs between the pretraining corpus and BLiMP data.[4] This allows us to reason about the diversity of the data and what fraction of linguistic structures present in the evaluation is seen by the model during pretraining.

Pretraining Data Table 1 shows that, on average, there are approximately 9 words per sentence and 48 words per document, in the STRICT-SMALL corpus. When measured with a WordPiece tokenizer (pretrained on the 10M data with a vocabulary size of 32,768), each sentence and document contain around 14 and 65 tokens, respectively. The training set of the pretraining corpus contains approximately 181.3K unique unigrams (words) and 2.07M unique bigrams.

BLiMP As we primarily use zero-shot BLiMP task performance to evaluate the model quality, we report the counts of unique unigrams and bigrams in the BLiMP task datasets in Table 2. The total unique vocabulary size is small: 2334 is only around 15% of the simple sum of unigrams of each task dataset, which suggests a considerable vocabulary overlap across different task datasets. Conversely, sentence structures, as characterized by dependency graphs, are remarkably diverse, with 97.6% of the BLiMP data points across tasks featuring unique linearized dependency graphs.

Lexical Overlap 98.67% of the unigrams in BLiMP are seen by models during pretraining. This is expected as the organizers filter the evaluation data based on the vocabulary in the training set. However, only 19% of the bigrams are found in the pretraining data, and more importantly, there is just 2% overlap of linearized dependency trees, suggesting that BLiMP tasks are really 'zero-shot' for BabyLM-trained models.

[4] We use SpaCy for dependency parsing and NLTK to linearize the trees.

BLiMP Phenomenon	Unigram	Bigram	Dep. G.
Anaphor Agreement	0.64K	3.52K	0.06K
Argument Structure	1.80K	19.50K	1.67K
Binding	1.07K	20.16K	2.01K
Control Raising	1.79K	14.10K	4.20K
D-N Agreement	1.17K	13.74K	0.70K
Ellipsis	1.16K	11.51K	3.28K
Filler Gap	1.44K	20.83K	8.36K
Irregular Forms	0.70K	4.29K	0.20K
Island Effects	1.01k	14.52K	3.52K
Npi Licensing	1.82K	19.20K	4.34K
Quantifiers	1.28K	10.08K	1.33K
Subject Verb Agreement	1.82K	17.60K	1.84K
Sum	15.68K	169.06K	31.52K
Total (unique)	2.33K	106.38K	30.78K

Table 2: BLiMP task statistics: number of unique and total unigrams, bigrams, and linearized dependency graphs are reported with respect to the dataset of each task. (Dep. G. stands for Dependency Graphs)

4 Methods

We experiment with two kinds of pretraining: (i) Vanilla pretraining: where we use standard processes as described in the original works that introduced the models (Liu et al., 2019; Radford et al., 2019), and where we only ablate on the way we format the input data. (ii) Structurally biased pretraining: where we induce some syntactic structure into the model either by explicitly augmenting the inputs with POS tags, or by allowing the models to implicitly induce dependency and constituency structures in an unsupervised manner (Shen et al., 2021).

4.1 Input Formatting

To efficiently utilize available compute resources during pretraining, multiple input examples can be 'grouped' together to form a bigger single example. By grouping, we mean that multiple sentences/documents are first concatenated, and then divided into training examples of maximum sequence length supported by the model. If the grouped input examples are not related to each other, the learning might be sub-optimal since the model attends to unrelated tokens. There are two ways to solve this problem: (i) do not group examples – this will require us to generally pad the examples, which brings the compute efficiency down, or (ii) build a dynamic mask such that each token only attends to other relevant tokens – this is harder to implement. We choose to continue with method (i) since the size of the pretraining data is small and the loss of efficiency is manageable, and

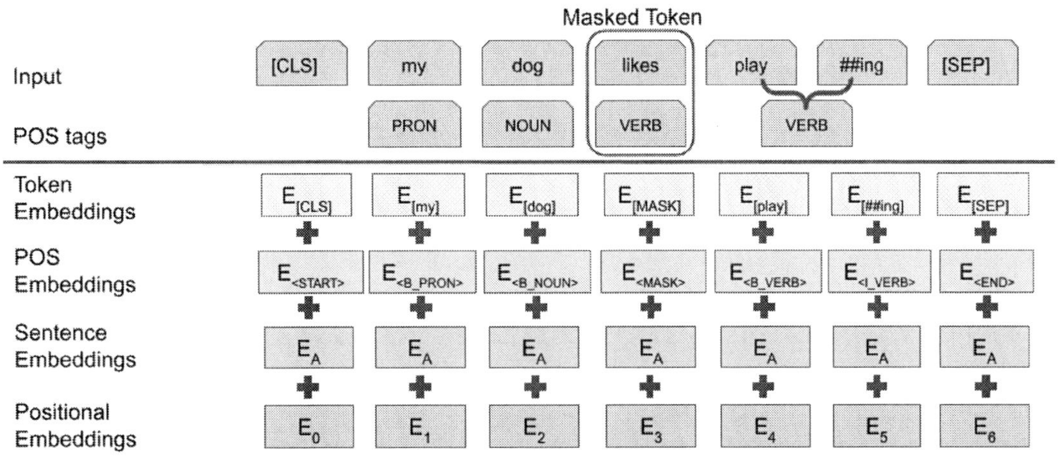

Figure 3: Part-of-Speech augmentation: the input embeddings are the sum of the token embeddings, the sentence type embeddings, the positional embeddings, and the POS embeddings. In Sentence Embeddings, E_A denotes the embedding for the token type A. When a sentence B follows sentence A, the tokens in sentence B will have token type B. In Positional Embeddings, E_i refers to the absolute positional embeddings for a token at position i.

refer to this strategy as 'ungrouping'.

We ablate vanilla pretraining methods in both grouped and ungrouped setups and assess how they impact BabyLM pretraining on both sentence-level and document-level formats. Examples of different grouping strategies with sentence-level and document-level data are shown in Fig. 1 and Fig. 2, respectively. There is a general consensus that the benefits of grouping outweighs its disadvantages, but since the lengths of our pretraining data is small (because a large fraction of them are conversation data), the general consensus might not hold. Note that as the document distribution's extreme tail significantly exceeds the model's context size, we also explore an 'ungrouping without truncation' approach specifically for document-level data. This allows a single lengthy document to be divided into multiple examples without discarding extensive data, ensuring a fair comparison between different strategies. We test these strategies with three maximum sequence lengths: 32, 128, and 512.

4.2 Structurally Biased Pretraining

Part-of-Speech Augmentation We first study the effect of introducing POS tags as additional inputs during pretraining. We embed POS tags of each token in the input and combine them with the token and positional embeddings to form the initial token representation, as illustrated in Fig.3. We first use NLTK's POS tagger[5] to automatically label the inputs using the universal tagset[6]. Since this tagging is done at the word-level, if a word is split into multiple subtokens by WordPiece tokenizers, we further process the label and decompose them into BIO style token-level tags.

This introduction of POS tags results in a slight change in the model architecture: a new embedding matrix for BIO style POS tags is added, and therefore the number of learnable parameters increases. During pretraining, when an input token is masked, we also mask its corresponding POS token to avoid any signal leakage.

StructFormer In contrast with the previous method, Structformer (Shen et al., 2021) allows us to induce structure implicitly. This encoder-only transformer uses dependency-constrained self-attention. This type of self-attention derives from unsupervised induction of constituency and dependency structures, allowing tokens to only attend to other tokens which are part of these structures. More concretely, it utilizes a parser network which learns to predict the syntactic distance between two tokens and the syntatic height of a token in an unsupervised manner, to generate dependency distributions. For more details, please see

[5] https://www.nltk.org/api/nltk.tag.html#nltk.tag.pos_tag

[6] NOUN (nouns), VERB (verbs), ADJ (adjectives), ADV (adverbs), PRON (pronouns), DET (determiners and articles), ADP (prepositions and postpositions), NUM (numerals), CONJ (conjunctions), PRT (particles), . (punctuation marks), X (other)

Model	BLiMP												
	Avg.	Ana. Agr	Arg. Str	Bind.	Ctrl. Rais.	D-N Agr	Ellip.	Filler Gap	Irreg. Form	Island Effect	NPI	Quant.	S-V Agr
GPT-2	**84.59**	99.70	84.00	79.00	80.00	95.90	85.10	80.90	95.80	78.30	76.50	71.90	88.00
RoBERTa	**86.03**	97.70	83.05	79.22	81.93	97.28	92.15	89.39	95.67	79.71	82.60	70.84	91.47
Human (Warstadt et al., 2020b)	**88.60**	97.00	90.00	87.30	83.90	92.20	85.00	86.90	97.00	84.90	88.10	86.60	90.90
OPT-125m (Warstadt et al., 2023)	**62.60**	63.80	70.60	67.10	66.50	78.50	62.00	63.80	67.50	48.60	46.70	59.60	56.90
RoBERTa-base (Warstadt et al., 2023)	**69.50**	81.50	67.10	67.30	67.90	90.80	76.40	63.50	87.40	39.90	55.90	70.50	65.40
T5-base (Warstadt et al., 2023)	**58.80**	68.90	63.80	60.40	60.90	72.20	34.40	48.20	77.60	45.60	47.80	61.20	65.00

Table 3: Ceiling and pre-released baseline model performance on BLiMP: the first three rows compare strong models with human performance, while the last three rows are pre-released BabyLM baselines.

BERT Base			BLiMP												
L	Format	Strategy	Avg.	Ana. Agr	Arg. Str	Bind.	Ctrl. Rais.	D-N Agr	Ellip.	Filler Gap	Irreg. Form	Island Effect	NPI	Quant.	S-V Agr
128	sent.	group	**62.57**	80.06	60.35	61.09	62.31	74.49	62.64	62.11	78.17	40.84	45.08	66.23	57.43
128	sent.	ungroup	**79.08**	94.68	74.03	72.10	73.66	94.27	77.77	78.63	89.72	59.90	74.05	74.65	85.47
128	doc.	group	**62.04**	84.00	57.52	66.84	60.30	58.68	56.76	64.61	71.96	53.21	46.25	71.02	53.37
128	doc.	ungroup	**69.38**	85.48	64.86	67.38	63.50	88.49	74.48	67.96	85.95	47.50	47.78	71.23	67.97
128	doc.	ungr. w/o trun.	**75.39**	92.28	71.02	68.83	69.02	95.01	83.89	75.16	84.78	49.66	63.36	70.09	81.52
32	sent.	group	**77.18**	92.23	72.41	70.21	70.97	94.05	84.76	74.68	91.50	53.18	72.12	67.80	82.26
32	sent.	ungroup	**78.38**	93.61	74.26	70.24	73.64	95.00	73.67	77.68	84.38	61.66	76.18	74.78	85.40
32	doc.	group	**74.90**	92.38	71.42	71.15	69.73	93.54	81.47	72.02	86.92	45.40	68.22	65.12	81.48
32	doc.	ungroup	**67.92**	76.28	63.62	64.37	64.47	88.66	71.02	68.60	83.16	44.73	55.44	64.99	69.68
32	doc.	ungr. w/o trun.	**76.75**	91.67	72.10	68.74	70.06	94.86	80.72	76.28	80.10	53.33	72.61	76.97	83.54
512	sent.	ungroup	**78.00**	94.02	73.90	72.35	72.80	94.97	76.50	77.76	87.48	57.25	71.00	73.03	84.99
512	doc.	ungr. w/o trun.	**73.04**	88.70	70.00	70.26	66.86	94.31	81.18	70.65	84.12	45.59	58.82	69.89	76.04

Table 4: Vanilla pretraining: effects of grouping strategies (Strategy), input formats (Format) and maximum sequence length (L) on BLiMP tasks using the BERT-base model. *Ungr. w/o trun.*, *sent.* and *doc.* denote ungrouped without truncation, sentence-level data, and document-level data, respectively. The metric for all tasks is accuracy.

the original paper.

5 Experimental Setup

Model Architecture Language models usually come in three flavours: encoder-only, decoder-only, and encoder-decoder architectures. Since all the BabyLM downstream tasks are classification-based, we mainly focus our experiments on encoder-only models (BERT (Devlin et al., 2018) and Structformer), whose bidirectionality is more suitable for such tasks (Devlin et al., 2018; Tay et al., 2022). We train decoder-only models (GPT-2) (Radford et al., 2018) only for data grouping experiments, and do not consider encoder-decoder models in this work. Unless otherwise stated, all experiments will use BERT-base as the standard encoder-only model, and GPT-2 as the standard decoder-only model.

Tokenizer We use the same tokenizer for both encoder-only and decoder-only models: an uncased WordPiece tokenizer (Wu et al., 2016) with a vocabulary size of 32,768 (i.e., 2^{15}), trained on *strict-small* pretraining data. For the StructFormer, we follow the original work and train a word-level tokenizer with a vocabulary size of 184,192.

Training Objective We do not make changes to the training objective of any models. We use MLM for encoder-only (including StructFormer) models with a masking rate of 15%, and next token prediction for decoder-only models.

Implementation All models are optimized with AdamW (Loshchilov and Hutter, 2017), with a peak learning rate of 1e-4, a warmup of 2000 steps, and linear decay. All models are trained with a dropout rate of 0.1, and with GELU activations (Hendrycks and Gimpel, 2016). GPT-2 and BERT models are trained with bfloat16[7] on a single NVIDIA A100-SXM4-80GB GPU, and StructFormer is trained in half precision on a single RTX 8000 GPU. All models are pretrained for 30 epochs with a maximum sequence length $L \in \{32, 128, 512\}$. Unless otherwise mentioned, the effective batch size is 128 examples for all experiments.

[7] https://cloud.google.com/tpu/docs/bfloat16

GPT-2 Base		BLiMP												
L	Strategy	AVG.	ANA. AGR	ARG. STR	BIND.	CTRL. RAIS.	D-N AGR	ELLIP.	FILLER GAP	IRREG. FORM	ISLAND EFFECT	NPI	QUANT.	S-V AGR
128	group	**71.30**	92.38	72.49	70.85	65.69	86.99	65.99	67.99	84.68	43.95	57.96	79.52	67.06
128	ungroup	**72.71**	94.33	74.09	69.15	67.06	91.98	60.85	70.53	89.57	46.97	63.68	68.11	76.24
512	group	**67.37**	88.80	70.64	66.90	64.60	83.02	60.85	63.34	88.70	45.48	43.74	68.57	63.83
512	ungroup	**73.18**	92.94	73.33	69.95	68.36	90.92	64.55	69.39	91.09	44.77	63.06	71.92	77.89

Table 5: Vanilla pretraining: effects of grouping strategies (Strategy) and maximum sequence length (L) on BLiMP tasks using the GPT-2 base model with sentence-level data. The metric for all tasks is accuracy.

		BLiMP												
Model	#H	AVG.	ANA. AGR	ARG. STR	BIND.	CTRL. RAIS.	D-N AGR	ELLIP.	FILLER GAP	IRREG. FORM	ISLAND EFFECT	NPI	QUANT.	S-V AGR
VANILLA	768	**77.29**	91.56	73.91	69.72	70.92	94.63	79.62	76.74	89.41	52.43	72.75	72.44	83.29
POS	768	**78.07**	93.76	73.33	71.36	70.97	94.11	83.08	77.23	89.82	53.44	70.97	73.57	85.19
RANDPOS	768	**73.92**	91.00	71.46	69.65	69.77	93.24	82.16	66.54	86.51	41.89	67.99	62.52	84.34
VANILLA	1152	**77.40**	93.10	74.64	70.24	71.39	95.60	78.00	78.14	88.35	52.20	70.06	72.41	84.72
POS	1152	**78.87**	93.66	74.90	68.76	71.96	95.00	84.93	77.90	89.77	55.53	73.69	74.37	86.00
RANDPOS	1152	**74.34**	91.46	71.59	70.39	70.00	94.39	80.37	66.15	86.87	41.70	69.91	64.27	84.97

Table 6: Part-of-Speech augmented pre-training: effect of POS augmentation on BLiMP tasks using BERT models. VANILLA, POS and RANDPOS denote vanilla BERT model, BERT model augmented with POS tags, and BERT model augmented with random POS tags. #H denotes the hidden size of the model. Metric for all tasks is accuracy.

6 Experiments & Results

In this section, we describe the various experiments we conducted, and their results obtained from the BabyLM evaluation pipeline (Warstadt et al., 2023; Gao et al., 2021). All models are evaluated on BLiMP and the best models from each category are further evaluated on SuperGLUE and MSGS tasks.

6.1 BLiMP

To get the ceiling performance of the models, we use the publicly available checkpoints (GPT-2, RoBERTa) which are pretrained on much larger datasets. These results along with the human-level performance is shown in Table 3. We see that the performance of these two models is only 2-3 points below human performance. In addition, we include the pre-released OPT, RoBERTa and T5 baselines, which were trained on the BabyLM data in Table 3. Unlike the publicly available GPT-2 and RoBERTa models, these baselines display a substantial gap with human performance.

6.1.1 Input Formatting

To investigate the impact of grouping strategies, we pretrain the standard BERT model on a variety of combinations.

Grouping Strategy From Table 4, we see that *ungrouped* [8]models consistently outperform the *grouped* models, across all sequence lengths. We postulate that this happens due to the nature of pretraining data. Since a large fraction of the data is conversation-based, the sentence lengths are generally short, and each utterance need not always be a logical continuation of the previous ones. This might cause confusion while learning grouped data since we do not impose any attention masking to stop the model from attending to unrelated tokens. This finding is not limited to encoder-only models. We see a similar pattern in decoder-only models as well, in Table 5. Also, encoder-only models demonstrate superior zero-shot generalization on BLiMP tasks in comparison to decoder-only models. This strengthens our hypothesis in Section 5 that bidirectionality is helpful for classification tasks. Therefore, all other experiments are conducted on encoder-only models.

Truncation on Documents As expected, the performance of *ungrouped* model lags behind the *grouped* model when using document-level data. This discrepancy is primarily due to the truncation, which discards extreme tails of the document distribution. However, when truncation is disabled, the performance of the model improves by 6-13

[8] Here, on document-level data, 'ungrouped' refers to 'ungrouped without truncation' for fair comparison.

points on average. It even surpasses the *grouped* model by approximately 2 points, confirming our conclusion drawn in the preceding paragraph.

Maximum Sequence Length Despite the additional parameters introduced, extending the maximum sequence length does not yield additional performance boost. Interestingly, there seems to be a negative correlation between the two. To make this point clear, we reduce the maximum sequence length to an extremely low value of 32. We see that there is no significant drop in performance among the models. In fact, even the document-level models perform well in this setting. This is because the smaller inputs are now similar to the sentence-level inputs. We also see that the difference between the *grouped* and *ungrouped* models also reduce from 13 points to 1 point, which further shows that sentence-level inputs provide better performance for BabyLM pretraining.

In summary, we see that the sentence-level *ungrouped* model with a sequence length of 128 performs the best with an average BLiMP score of 79.08. This is around 10 points higher than the pre-released Roberta-base baseline. Furthermore, this is only 5-6 points behind the ceiling performance of GPT-2 and RoBERTa-base models trained on much larger datasets. However it is difficult to conclude that these models learn efficiently since we have not yet evaluated them on semantic downstream tasks which require the models to capture long-range dependencies. But we can safely say that 10M words and sentence-level training is enough for models to learn simple linguistic phenomena as tested by BLiMP. Henceforth, we will perform subsequent experiments using only the most effective configurations identified, i.e., sentence-level *ungrouped* models.

6.1.2 POS Augmentation

To test whether explicitly inducing POS tree structures during pretraining improves downstream performance, we embed POS tags and add them to the input representations. To make sure that any improvement is not only due to the increase in the number of parameters,[9] we run two ablations with an effective batch size of 512:[10] (i) randomly shuffle the POS tags of a sentence before adding them to the input – this will make sure that the model gets no signal from the POS tags, and (ii) increase the hidden size of the models – this will contain signals from POS and further increase the number of learnable parameters.

Table 6 illustrates that the encoder-only models, when augmented with POS tags, exhibit a marginal performance improvement of approximately one point compared to the vanilla models, regardless of the hidden size. However, models with shuffled POS tags lag behind by approximately 4-5 points, suggesting that it is indeed beneficial to induce structures during pretraining. Next, we see that boosting the hidden size enhances model performance across all settings. However, on closer inspection we see that the benefit to the standard model is minor, $\sim$0.1 points. This is surprising since the number of learnable parameters in the model with the expanded hidden size is almost an order of magnitude larger than the model with just the additional POS embedding matrix. This result further underscores the benefits of inducing POS tree structures into the pretraining process.

6.1.3 StructFormer

All StructFormer experiments are all conducted using sentence-level ungrouped data, with a maximum sequence length of 512.

Though StructFormer outperforms vanilla BERT when the models are scaled down (Tiny), it fails to do so on larger model sizes. In fact, we see in Table 7 that BERT-Mini outperforms a StructFormer-Base model. We hypothesize: (i) that 10M words are not enough to learn good representations of 180K words present in the StructFormer vocabulary, and (ii) that 10M words are not big enough to fully train the unsupervised parsing network which in-turn affects the downstream performance. This model undertraining is evident from the fact that BERT performance jumps up by 14 points when its size is increased from Tiny to Base, whereas StructFormer's performance only increases by 5 points.

6.2 Other Evaluations

We select the best performing models of each setting mentioned in the previous section and perform a full evaluation on SuperGLUE, BLiMP

[9] This model has an additional embedding matrix for POS tags.

[10] We increase the batch size to improve the runtime of the experiments. But this causes slight discrepancies in the result of our vanilla models between Tables 4 and 6

Model	Size	BLiMP												
		AVG.	ANA. AGR	ARG. STR	BIND.	CTRL. RAIS.	D-N AGR	ELLIP.	FILLER GAP	IRREG. FORM	ISLAND EFFECT	NPI	QUANT.	S-V AGR
BERT	tiny	**63.92**	73.52	64.05	64.16	62.84	80.35	53.29	62.18	91.96	42.53	49.42	63.14	59.62
STRUCTFORMER	tiny	**64.89**	68.51	63.07	61.61	63.52	81.42	48.38	63.26	88.80	51.64	53.31	72.62	62.53
BERT	base	**78.00**	94.02	73.90	72.35	72.80	94.97	76.50	77.76	87.48	57.25	71.00	73.03	84.99
STRUCTFORMER	base	**69.79**	79.09	67.01	67.81	67.26	92.50	62.64	64.47	89.72	46.11	57.41	78.80	64.66
BERT	mini	**70.27**	88.09	69.63	68.76	65.20	91.49	74.65	68.07	92.67	34.87	56.18	67.31	66.29

Table 7: StructFormer: comparison between BERT and StructFormer architectures on tiny and base sizes. Metric for all tasks is accuracy.

Model	L	Format	Strategy	DYNABENCH	BLIMP	BLIMP SUPPL.	SUPERGLUE	MSGS
BERT	128	sent.	ungroup	**69**	79.08	58.19	72.37	81.51
BERT	128	doc.	ungr. w/o trun.	**68**	75.39	61.33	72.28	81.00
BERT-POS	512	sent.	ungroup	**68**	79.67	56.81	71.85	79.64
GPT-2	512	sent.	ungroup	**67**	73.18	55.47	69.23	82.14

Table 8: Results of other benchmarks for the top-performing models evaluated by BLiMP tasks: the score for each benchmark is reported as an average, detailed scores are in Appendix. Dynabench score aggregates all benchmarks and is provided by the model submission platform. *Ungr. w/o trun.*, *sent.* and *doc.* denote ungrouped without truncation, sentence-level data and doc. denotes document-level data, respectively. Metric for all tasks is accuracy.

supplement, and MSGS benchmarks[11]. In Table 8, we report average scores for each benchmark, and the final score computed by the model submission platform (Kiela et al., 2021, Dynabench), for each model. Detailed performance of each task for all benchmarks, as well as the pre-released baselines is given in Table 9, 10, 11, 12, 13, 14, and 15 in Appendix A.

We see in Table 8, which summarizes the results and provides the aggregated scores, that only slight differences exist among the models. The BERT-Base model, trained on sentence-level data, demonstrates superior performance overall, surpassing other models by 1-2 points, consistent with our BLiMP evaluations. Remarkably, the model trained with document-level inputs displays a substantial superiority in BLiMP supplement tasks, achieving a lead of nearly 3 points over models trained on sentences. Surprisingly, the GPT-2 model, despite underperforming in all other tasks, exhibits a robust performance on the MSGS tasks. The BERT model augmented with POS trees, despite its best performance on BLiMP tasks, fails to replicate the success across other benchmarks which suggests that it might have learned some specific structural patterns helpful only in certain cases as pointed out in Warstadt et al. (2020c).

[11] The last two benchmarks were released towards the end of the shared task.

7 Conclusion

In this work, we investigate the effects of data formatting and the induction of structural biases in data-efficient pretraining settings. These experiments were performed under the constrains of limited data, computational resources, and training time. Our findings indicate data grouping is the most significant factor affecting downstream performance due to the nature of the pretraining data. We also see that when the best data format considered is employed, inducing structural biases into the models enhances their downstream performance on BLiMP performance by approximately 1%.

Acknowledgements

We would like to thank the anonymous reviewers for their comments and suggestions. This work was supported in part by the Natural Sciences and Engineering Research Council of Canada (NSERC), and in part by the McGill's Science Undergraduate Research Awards (SURA 2023) during Summer 2023. The authors acknowledge the material support of NVIDIA in the form of computational resources.

References

Yoshua Bengio, Réjean Ducharme, Pascal Vincent, and Christian Janvin. 2003. A neural probabilistic language model. *J. Mach. Learn. Res.*, 3(null):1137–1155.

Jacob Devlin, Ming-Wei Chang, Kenton Lee, and Kristina Toutanova. 2018. Bert: Pre-training of deep bidirectional transformers for language understanding. *arXiv preprint arXiv:1810.04805*.

Jacob Devlin, Ming-Wei Chang, Kenton Lee, and Kristina Toutanova. 2019. BERT: Pre-training of deep bidirectional transformers for language understanding. In *Proceedings of the 2019 Conference of the North American Chapter of the Association for Computational Linguistics: Human Language Technologies, Volume 1 (Long and Short Papers)*, pages 4171–4186, Minneapolis, Minnesota. Association for Computational Linguistics.

Leo Gao, Jonathan Tow, Stella Biderman, Sid Black, Anthony DiPofi, Charles Foster, Laurence Golding, Jeffrey Hsu, Kyle McDonell, Niklas Muennighoff, Jason Phang, Laria Reynolds, Eric Tang, Anish Thite, Ben Wang, Kevin Wang, and Andy Zou. 2021. A framework for few-shot language model evaluation.

Dan Hendrycks and Kevin Gimpel. 2016. Gaussian error linear units (gelus). *arXiv preprint arXiv:1606.08415*.

Jordan Hoffmann, Sebastian Borgeaud, Arthur Mensch, Elena Buchatskaya, Trevor Cai, Eliza Rutherford, Diego de las Casas, Lisa Anne Hendricks, Johannes Welbl, Aidan Clark, Tom Hennigan, Eric Noland, Katherine Millican, George van den Driessche, Bogdan Damoc, Aurelia Guy, Simon Osindero, Karen Simonyan, Erich Elsen, Oriol Vinyals, Jack William Rae, and Laurent Sifre. 2022. An empirical analysis of compute-optimal large language model training. In *Advances in Neural Information Processing Systems*.

Jared Kaplan, Sam McCandlish, Tom Henighan, Tom B. Brown, Benjamin Chess, Rewon Child, Scott Gray, Alec Radford, Jeffrey Wu, and Dario Amodei. 2020. Scaling laws for neural language models.

Douwe Kiela, Max Bartolo, Yixin Nie, Divyansh Kaushik, Atticus Geiger, Zhengxuan Wu, Bertie Vidgen, Grusha Prasad, Amanpreet Singh, Pratik Ringshia, Zhiyi Ma, Tristan Thrush, Sebastian Riedel, Zeerak Waseem, Pontus Stenetorp, Robin Jia, Mohit Bansal, Christopher Potts, and Adina Williams. 2021. Dynabench: Rethinking benchmarking in NLP. In *Proceedings of the 2021 Conference of the North American Chapter of the Association for Computational Linguistics: Human Language Technologies*, pages 4110–4124, Online. Association for Computational Linguistics.

Tal Linzen. 2020. How can we accelerate progress towards human-like linguistic generalization? In *Proceedings of the 58th Annual Meeting of the Association for Computational Linguistics*, pages 5210–5217, Online. Association for Computational Linguistics.

Yinhan Liu, Myle Ott, Naman Goyal, Jingfei Du, Mandar Joshi, Danqi Chen, Omer Levy, Mike Lewis, Luke Zettlemoyer, and Veselin Stoyanov. 2019. Roberta: A robustly optimized bert pretraining approach. *arXiv preprint arXiv:1907.11692*.

Ilya Loshchilov and Frank Hutter. 2017. Decoupled weight decay regularization. *arXiv preprint arXiv:1711.05101*.

Mitchell P. Marcus, Beatrice Santorini, and Mary Ann Marcinkiewicz. 1993. Building a large annotated corpus of English: The Penn Treebank. *Computational Linguistics*, 19(2):313–330.

Stephen Merity, Caiming Xiong, James Bradbury, and Richard Socher. 2017. Pointer sentinel mixture models. In *International Conference on Learning Representations*.

Laura Pérez-Mayos, Miguel Ballesteros, and Leo Wanner. 2021. How much pretraining data do language models need to learn syntax? In *Proceedings of the 2021 Conference on Empirical Methods in Natural Language Processing*, pages 1571–1582, Online and Punta Cana, Dominican Republic. Association for Computational Linguistics.

Alec Radford, Karthik Narasimhan, Tim Salimans, Ilya Sutskever, et al. 2018. Improving language understanding by generative pre-training.

Alec Radford, Jeffrey Wu, Rewon Child, David Luan, Dario Amodei, Ilya Sutskever, et al. 2019. Language models are unsupervised multitask learners. *OpenAI blog*, 1(8):9.

David Samuel, Andrey Kutuzov, Lilja Øvrelid, and Erik Velldal. 2023. Trained on 100 million words and still in shape: BERT meets British National Corpus. In *Findings of the Association for Computational Linguistics: EACL 2023*, pages 1954–1974, Dubrovnik, Croatia. Association for Computational Linguistics.

Yikang Shen, Shawn Tan, Alessandro Sordoni, and Aaron Courville. 2019. Ordered neurons: Integrating tree structures into recurrent neural networks. In *International Conference on Learning Representations*.

Yikang Shen, Yi Tay, Che Zheng, Dara Bahri, Donald Metzler, and Aaron Courville. 2021. StructFormer: Joint unsupervised induction of dependency and constituency structure from masked language modeling. In *Proceedings of the 59th Annual Meeting of the Association for Computational Linguistics and the 11th International Joint Conference on Natural Language Processing (Volume 1: Long Papers)*, pages 7196–7209, Online. Association for Computational Linguistics.

Yi Tay, Mostafa Dehghani, Vinh Q Tran, Xavier Garcia, Jason Wei, Xuezhi Wang, Hyung Won Chung, Dara Bahri, Tal Schuster, Steven Zheng, et al. 2022. Ul2: Unifying language learning paradigms. In *The Eleventh International Conference on Learning Representations*.

Ashish Vaswani, Noam Shazeer, Niki Parmar, Jakob Uszkoreit, Llion Jones, Aidan N Gomez, Łukasz Kaiser, and Illia Polosukhin. 2017. Attention is all you need. *Advances in neural information processing systems*, 30.

Alex Wang, Yada Pruksachatkun, Nikita Nangia, Amanpreet Singh, Julian Michael, Felix Hill, Omer Levy, and Samuel Bowman. 2019a. Superglue: A stickier benchmark for general-purpose language understanding systems. *Advances in neural information processing systems*, 32.

Alex Wang, Amanpreet Singh, Julian Michael, Felix Hill, Omer Levy, and Samuel R Bowman. 2018. Glue: A multi-task benchmark and analysis platform for natural language understanding. In *International Conference on Learning Representations*.

Yaushian Wang, Hung-Yi Lee, and Yun-Nung Chen. 2019b. Tree transformer: Integrating tree structures into self-attention. In *Proceedings of the 2019 Conference on Empirical Methods in Natural Language Processing and the 9th International Joint Conference on Natural Language Processing (EMNLP-IJCNLP)*, pages 1061–1070, Hong Kong, China. Association for Computational Linguistics.

Alex Warstadt, Aaron Mueller, Leshem Choshen, Ethan Gotlieb Wilcox, Chengxu Zhuang, Juan Ciro, Rafael Mosquera, Adina Williams, Bhargavi Paranjabe, Tal Linzen, and Ryan Cotterell. 2023. Findings of the 2023 BabyLM Challenge: Sample-efficient pretraining on developmentally plausible corpora. In *Proceedings of the 2023 BabyLM Challenge*. Association for Computational Linguistics (ACL).

Alex Warstadt, Alicia Parrish, Haokun Liu, Anhad Mohananey, Wei Peng, Sheng-Fu Wang, and Samuel R. Bowman. 2020a. BLiMP: The benchmark of linguistic minimal pairs for English. *Transactions of the Association for Computational Linguistics*, 8:377–392.

Alex Warstadt, Alicia Parrish, Haokun Liu, Anhad Mohananey, Wei Peng, Sheng-Fu Wang, and Samuel R Bowman. 2020b. Blimp: The benchmark of linguistic minimal pairs for english. *Transactions of the Association for Computational Linguistics*, 8:377–392.

Alex Warstadt, Yian Zhang, Xiaocheng Li, Haokun Liu, and Samuel R. Bowman. 2020c. Learning which features matter: RoBERTa acquires a preference for linguistic generalizations (eventually). In *Proceedings of the 2020 Conference on Empirical Methods in Natural Language Processing (EMNLP)*, pages 217–235, Online. Association for Computational Linguistics.

Yonghui Wu, Mike Schuster, Zhifeng Chen, Quoc V Le, Mohammad Norouzi, Wolfgang Macherey, Maxim Krikun, Yuan Cao, Qin Gao, Klaus Macherey, et al. 2016. Google's neural machine translation system: Bridging the gap between human and machine translation. *arXiv preprint arXiv:1609.08144*.

Aditya Yedetore, Tal Linzen, Robert Frank, and R. Thomas McCoy. 2023. How poor is the stimulus? evaluating hierarchical generalization in neural networks trained on child-directed speech. In *Proceedings of the 61st Annual Meeting of the Association for Computational Linguistics (Volume 1: Long Papers)*, pages 9370–9393, Toronto, Canada. Association for Computational Linguistics.

A Appendix

In this section, we provide detailed performance of the top-performing models mentioned in Section 6.2 on each evaluation benchmarks. BLiMP, BLiMP supplement, SuperGLUE, and MSGS results are in Table 9, 11, 13 , and 15, respectively. Pre-released baseline performance for BLiMP supplement, SuperGLUE, and MSGS tasks are in Table 10, 12 , and 14, respectively.

Model	L	Format	Strategy	BLiMP												
				AVG.	ANA. AGR	ARG. STR	BIND.	CTRL. RAIS.	D-N AGR	ELLIP.	FILLER GAP	IRREG. FORM	ISLAND EFFECT	NPI	QUANT.	S-V AGR
BERT	128	sent.	ungroup	**79.08**	94.68	74.03	72.1	73.66	94.27	77.77	78.63	89.72	59.9	74.05	74.65	85.47
BERT	128	doc.	ungr. w/o trun.	**75.39**	92.28	71.02	68.83	69.02	95.01	83.89	75.16	84.78	49.66	63.36	70.09	81.52
BERT-POS	512	ungroup	sent.	**79.67**	94.73	75.36	72.32	73.95	96.15	82.04	78.51	89.21	59.57	71.50	74.57	88.06
GPT	512	sent.	ungroup	**73.18**	92.94	73.33	69.95	68.36	90.92	64.55	69.39	91.09	44.77	63.06	71.92	77.89

Table 9: BLiMP results: *Ungr. w/o trun.*, *sent.* and *doc.* denote ungrouped without truncation, sentence-level data and doc. denotes document-level data, respectively. Metric for all tasks is accuracy.

MODEL	BLiMP Supplement					
	AVG.	HYPERNYM	QA CONGR. (EASY)	QA CONGR. (TRICKY)	SUBJ.-AUX. INVERSION	TURN TAKING
OPT-125M (Warstadt et al., 2023)	54.72	50.00	54.70	31.50	80.30	57.10
ROBERTA-BASE (Warstadt et al., 2023)	47.54	49.40	31.30	32.10	71.70	53.20
T5-BASE (Warstadt et al., 2023)	43.94	48.00	40.60	21.20	64.90	45.00

Table 10: BLiMP supplement pre-released baseline results: Metric for all tasks is accuracy.

Model	L	Format	Strategy	BLiMP Supplement					
				AVG.	HYPERNYM	QA CONGR. (EASY)	QA CONGR. (TRICKY)	SUBJ.-AUX. INVERSION	TURN TAKING
BERT	128	sent.	ungroup	**58.19**	49.07	70.31	29.70	79.39	62.50
BERT	128	doc.	ungr. w/o trun.	**61.33**	50.23	73.44	36.36	77.70	68.93
BERT-POS	512	ungroup	sent.	**56.81**	49.42	64.06	29.09	80.41	61.07
GPT	512	sent.	ungroup	**55.47**	50	53.12	29.7	85.95	58.57

Table 11: BLiMP supplement results: *Ungr. w/o trun.*, *sent.* and *doc.* denote ungrouped without truncation, sentence-level data and doc. denotes document-level data, respectively. Metric for all tasks is accuracy.

Model	SuperGLUE											
	AVG.	CoLA (MCC)	SST-2	MRPC (F1)	QQP (F1)	MNLI	MNLI-MM	QNLI	RTE	BOOLQ	MULTIRC	WSC
Majority label (Warstadt et al., 2023)	46.3	0.0	50.2	82.0	53.1	35.7	35.7	35.4	53.1	50.5	59.9	53.2
OPT-125m (Warstadt et al., 2023)	58.9	15.2	81.9	72.5	60.4	57.6	60.0	61.5	60.0	63.3	55.2	60.2
RoBERTa-base (Warstadt et al., 2023)	67.3	25.8	87.0	79.2	73.7	73.2	74.0	77.0	61.6	66.3	61.4	61.4
T5-base (Warstadt et al., 2023)	56.4	11.3	78.1	80.5	66.2	48.0	50.3	62.0	49.4	66.0	47.1	61.4

Table 12: GLUE pre-released baseline results: Metric for all tasks unless otherwise stated.

Model	L	Format	Strategy	SuperGLUE											
				AVG.	BOOLQ	COLA	MNLI	MNLI-MM	MRPC (F1)	MULTIRC	QNLI	QQP (F1)	RTE	SST-2	WSC
BERT	128	sent.	ungroup	**72.37**	66.39	74.78	74.15	74.79	80.29	63.20	78.74	81.79	51.52	88.98	61.45
BERT	128	doc.	ungr. w/o trun.	**72.28**	66.11	72.33	75.36	76.29	77.78	59.58	82.50	84.13	51.52	87.99	61.45
BERT-POS	512	sent.	ungroup	**71.85**	67.22	75.76	73.80	75.03	77.22	60.24	78.70	83.10	49.49	88.39	61.45
GPT	512	sent.	ungroup	**69.23**	64.87	71.44	72.14	72.69	71.84	62.43	64.22	81.71	50.51	88.19	61.45

Table 13: GLUE results: *Ungr. w/o trun.*, *sent.* and *doc.* denote ungrouped without truncation, sentence-level data and doc. denotes document-level data, respectively. Metric for all tasks except MRPC and QQP is accuracy.

Model	MSGS											
	AVG.	CR CTRL.	LC CTRL.	MV CTRL.	RP CTRL.	SC CTRL.	CR LC	CR RTP	MV LC	MV RTP	SC LC	SC RP
OPT-125m (Warstadt et al., 2023)	80.9	97.2	82.6	100.0	99.8	88.1	75.3	67.1	66.3	66.8	84.8	62.0
RoBERTa-base (Warstadt et al., 2023)	81.7	93.0	100.0	100.0	100.0	89.0	68.3	66.8	66.6	80.2	67.4	67.4
T5-base (Warstadt et al., 2023)	82.3	95.1	100.0	100.0	99.8	88.7	76.7	69.4	67.0	67.7	72.7	68.0

Table 14: MSGS pre-released baseline results: Metric for all tasks is accuracy.

				MSGS											
Model	**L**	**Format**	**Strategy**	AVG.	CR CTRL.	LC CTRL.	MV CTRL.	RP CTRL.	SC CTRL.	CR LC	CR RTP	MV LC	MV RTP	SC LC	SC RP
BERT	128	sent.	ungroup	**81.51**	96.30	100.00	99.94	100.00	83.47	72.67	72.52	66.61	68.65	68.32	68.08
BERT	128	doc.	ungr. w/o trun.	**81.00**	92.32	100.00	99.89	98.26	95.59	67.17	67.14	66.61	68.04	69.73	66.22
BERT-POS	512	sent.	ungroup	**79.64**	91.08	100.00	99.87	99.99	89.70	71.79	67.05	66.77	68.80	63.30	57.64
GPT	512	sent.	ungroup	**82.14**	92.11	100.00	99.94	100.00	95.51	70.23	69.86	66.61	67.78	75.62	65.91

Table 15: MSGS results: *Ungr. w/o trun.*, *sent.* and *doc.* denote ungrouped without truncation, sentence-level data and doc. denotes document-level data, respectively. Metric for all tasks is accuracy.

Mean BERTs make erratic language teachers: the effectiveness of latent bootstrapping in low-resource settings

David Samuel
University of Oslo, Language Technology Group

Abstract

This paper explores the use of latent bootstrapping, an alternative self-supervision technique, for pretraining language models. Unlike the typical practice of using self-supervision on discrete subwords, latent bootstrapping leverages contextualized embeddings for a richer supervision signal. We conduct experiments to assess how effective this approach is for acquiring linguistic knowledge from limited resources. Specifically, our experiments are based on the BabyLM shared task, which includes pretraining on two small curated corpora and an evaluation on four linguistic benchmarks.

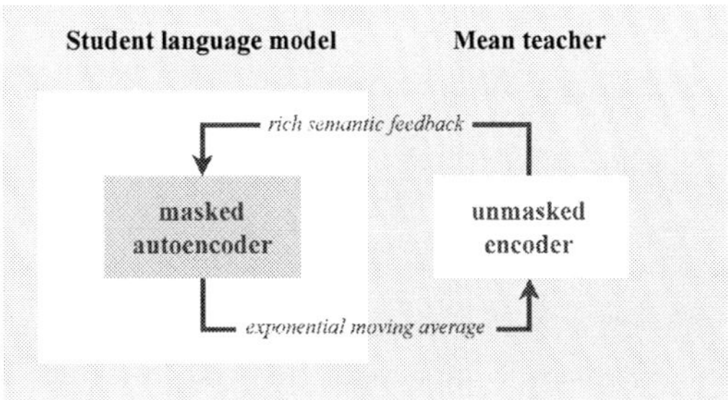

Figure 1: The self-supervision feedback loop of latent bootstrapping: a student model improves by aligning with its teacher's latent outputs and the teacher improves by maintaining the exponential moving average of the student.

1 Introduction

All modern language models are trained with a general self-supervised learning (SSL) paradigm (Radford et al., 2018; Devlin et al., 2019; Raffel et al., 2020). Recently, the field of visual representation learning has seen a growing usage of self-supervision on *latent embeddings* (Grill et al., 2020; Chen et al., 2020; Chen and He, 2020; Assran et al., 2023). While this type of self-supervision has been recently proposed as an integral part of a human-like machine intelligence system (LeCun, 2022), language models are still mostly self-supervised on hard targets, typically on subword tokens.

The concept of *latent bootstrapping* (Grill et al., 2020) offers a promising alternative, as the latent vectors provide a deep and semantically rich representation of the input. This, in turn, delivers a more valuable supervision signal compared to the conventional method of supervision on discrete subword indices. Data2vec (Baevski et al., 2022) showed that latent bootstrapping performs on par with traditional self-supervised language modeling when pretrained on a large text corpus. We argue that, intuitively, the rich training signal from contextualized embeddings should be particularly effective in low-resource data settings.

In this paper, our aim is to test this hypothesis and identify possible drawbacks of the bootstrapping method. We base our experiments on the *BabyLM challenge* (Warstadt et al., 2023b), a shared task that uses two carefully curated, sample-efficient pretraining corpora, mimicking the English language exposure to young children. In addition, this challenge employs four benchmarks to evaluate different aspects of linguistic knowledge and understanding learned by language models.

We introduce BootBERT, a novel masked autoencoder language model (Meng et al., 2023) that harnesses latent bootstrapping (Grill et al., 2020) between a mean teacher (Tarvainen and Valpola, 2017) and its student. Through a positive feedback loop, the student and the teacher iteratively learn from each other, as illustrated in Figure 1. The student is trained to match the teacher's outputs while the *mean* teacher is defined as the exponential moving average of the student. Once pretraining is complete, only the student language model is used for evaluation and the teacher is discarded. We assess its performance on the BabyLM challenge, contrasting it with conventional language models. The source code and pretrained models are available online at `https://github.com/ltgoslo/boot-bert`.

Proceedings of the 27th Conference on Computational Natural Language Learning: Volume 2: The BabyLM Challenge, pages 221–237
December 6-7, 2023 ©2023 Association for Computational Linguistics

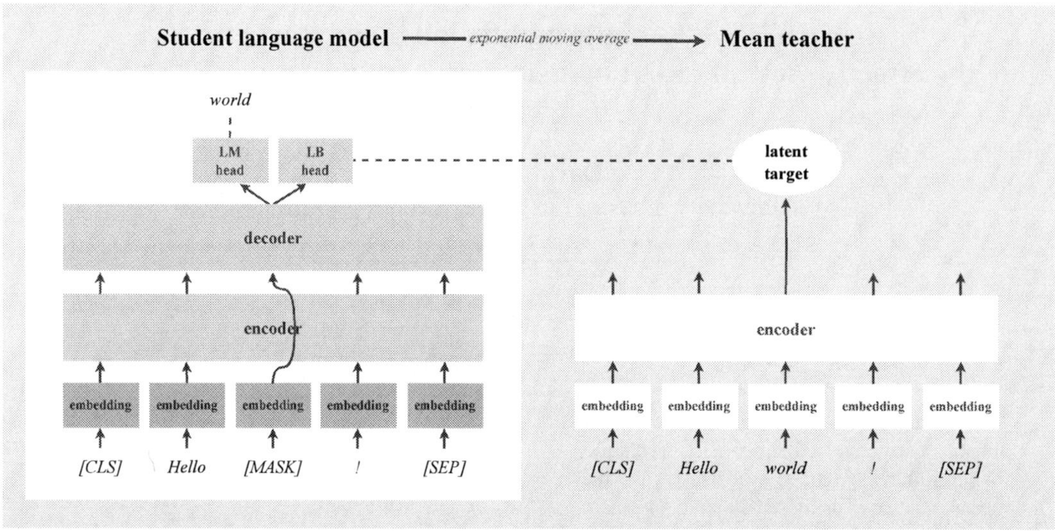

Figure 2: A detailed overview of the self-supervised feedback loop. The left side illustrates the student language model, a masked autoencoder network, that targets two training objectives: 1) conventional masked language modeling, aiming to predict the masked token (e.g., the word 'world'), and 2) aligning the contextualized embedding of the masked tokens to their unmasked counterparts. The embeddings for the unmasked tokens are produced by a mean teacher network (on the right), computed as an exponential moving average of the student parameters.

2 Method

In this section, we outline our proposed model, BootBERT, delving into its neural architecture and the latent bootstrapping training objective. In order to allow for language-modeling-based evaluation, the bootstrapping objective operates alongside conventional masked language modeling. The diagram in Figure 2 illustrates the general idea of this approach.

Masked autoencoder architecture. BootBERT diverges slightly from the standard 'encoder-only' architecture often found in masked language models (Devlin et al., 2019). Instead, following the method of Meng et al. (2023), we employ a masked autoencoder (MAE; He et al., 2022) framework for the text domain. This approach distinguishes the *encoding* of contextualized embeddings from the *decoding* of masked subwords. These two functionalities are separated by dividing the model into an encoder and a decoder module, as illustrated in Figure 2 on the left.

The encoder's role is to create a bidirectional contextualized embedding of input tokens. Unlike traditional masked language models, the encoder does not process any `[MASK]` tokens, thus eliminating the need to allocate parameters for representing them (Meng et al., 2023).

The `[MASK]` tokens are processed and denoised by the decoder module. The decoder is supplied with the full input – the unmasked tokens are represented by their contextualized embeddings (provided by the encoder) and the masked tokens are represented by a static `[MASK]` embedding. Note that the decoder in this type of model is bidirectional and purely self-attentive, differing from the original definition of a transformer decoder by Vaswani et al. (2017).

Teacher-student feedback loop. Conceptually, the training process can be divided into optimization of a student model and optimization of a teacher model. Here, the masked student autoencoder model is trained to match the contextualized embeddings of the *unmasked* tokens, produced by the mean teacher network. In line with Tarvainen and Valpola (2017), the teacher parameters ϕ are not optimized via gradient descent, but rather through a slow exponential moving average (EMA) of the student parameters θ:

$$\phi = \tau\phi + (1 - \tau)\theta.$$

This moving average not only stabilizes the latent targets but also prevents representation collapse (Grill et al., 2020).

Loss. We optimize two objectives during training the student model: a traditional masked language modeling objective with hard targets, symbolized by $\mathcal{L}_{\text{LM}}$, and a latent bootstrapping objective using teacher's latent targets $\mathcal{L}_{\text{LB}}$. The final loss function combines these objectives with a weighted sum:

$$\mathcal{L} = \mathcal{L}_{\text{LB}} + \beta \mathcal{L}_{\text{LM}}.$$

Here, $\mathcal{L}_{\text{LM}}$ is calculated simply as negative log-likelihood of the true targets. Its purpose is two-fold: allowing for a MLM-based evaluation (for example BLiMP), and preventing representation collapse of unconstrained latent bootstrapping (Grill et al., 2020).

The second objective is computed as a smooth L1 loss between student predictions y_s and teacher's contextualized embeddings y_t, This works mostly like a standard mean-squared error but prevents exploding gradients from outliers (Girshick, 2015):

$$\mathcal{L}_{\text{LB}}(y_t, y_s) = \begin{cases} 0.5(y_t - y_s)^2 & |y_t - y_s| \leq 1 \\ |y_t - y_s| - 0.5 & \text{otherwise.} \end{cases}$$

LTG-BERT transformer backbone. As for more low-level architectural and training choices, we adopt the approach of LTG-BERT by Samuel et al. (2023a). This method was optimized for low-resource masked language modeling on a similar corpus to the corpora provided in BabyLM. The key improvements of the LTG-BERT transformer architecture include the use of the NormFormer layer normalization (Shleifer and Ott, 2022), an alternative disentangled attention mechanism with relative positions (He et al., 2021) and gated-linear activation function (GEGLU; Shazeer, 2020); as illustrated in Figure 3. On top of these architectural changes, the authors also employ masking of random subword spans (Joshi et al., 2020). More details about these choices can be found in Samuel et al. (2023a).

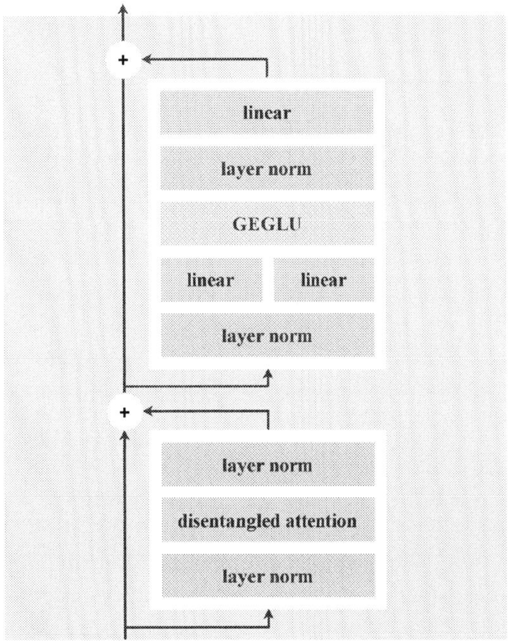

Figure 3: We base our model on LTG-BERT. This simplified diagram shows one layer from that transformer architecture, it illustrates the self-attention module (bottom) and the feed-forward module (top). Both modules utilize a modified NormFormer-like layer normalization placement and the feed-forward module contains a gated-linear activation function.

BabyLM challenge. This challenge provides a share ground for experiments on small-scale language modeling. It consists of three tracks: STRICT, STRICT-SMALL and LOOSE. For the first two tracks, the submissions have to be pretrained solely on a fixed corpus provided by the organizers. This corpus contains about 100M words in the STRICT track and about 10M words in the STRICT-SMALL track. As for the LOOSE track, the submissions are still limited to pretrained on 100M words, but this data can come from any source and the models can utilize an unlimited amount of non-linguistic data in addition. As detailed in Section 3.2, the submissions are compared on a shared evaluation set consisting of syntactic and natural language understanding tasks.

3 Experiments

The main goal of this paper is to evaluate how well language models trained with latent bootstrapping acquire language and if it makes a viable training objective for language representation learning. We base the experiments on the BabyLM challenge (Warstadt et al., 2023b). First, we describe the pretraining process of two BabyLM tracks and second, the evaluation of pretrained models using the BabyLM evaluation pipeline.

3.1 Pretraining

The pretraining is done on corpora provided by the BabyLM challenge. These texts are curated specifically to be of the same type and quantity that children learn from. Thus, it allows us to assess (to some degree) whether latent bootstrapping is a more plausible cognitive model of human language acquisition (Warstadt et al., 2023b).

Training corpus. Specifically, we consider the STRICT and STRICT-SMALL tracks and pretrain the models on their respective 100-million-word and 10-million-word corpora. Both datasets contain child-directed speech, transcribed speech, children's books and Wikipedia, among other sources. The content of these datasets is detailed in Appendix B, together with our simple preprocessing pipeline, which unifies the typographical features of the BabyLM subcorpora.

Pretraining process. Generally speaking, we adopt the training recipe of LTG-BERT (Samuel et al., 2023a), which was optimized for pretraining on another low-resource 100 million English corpus. The pretraining process is the same for both tracks, except for using a smaller vocabulary and a smaller model for the STRICT-SMALL track.

As for the STRICT track, we use a BASE-size language model – 12 encoder layers and 4 decoder layers with hidden size of 768 and with 12 attention heads. We train a case-sensitive WordPiece tokenizer (Wu et al., 2016) with a vocabulary size of $2^{14} = 16\,384$, using solely texts from the STRICT corpus. As per Samuel et al. (2023a), we pretrain the models with 1/2 of the BERT training budget, as it has been shown to be sufficient for a relatively small 100-million-word corpus. The tokens are masked with continuous span masking (Joshi et al., 2020; Raffel et al., 2020). In particular, the masks are iteratively sampled until 15% of tokens are masked and the length of each span is sampled from the geometric distribution Geo(p), with $p = 1/3$.

The STRICT-SMALL track is tackled by a SMALL-size language model – 12 encoder layers and 4 decoder layers with hidden size of 384 and with 6 attention heads. The subword vocabulary is reduced to $2^{12} = 4\,096$ items.[1]

The full list of hyperparameters and implementation details are provided in Appendix C and in the released source code.[2]

3.2 Evaluation

We utilize the language modeling benchmark suite from the BabyLM challenge (Gao et al., 2021; Warstadt et al., 2023b),[3] which relies on three conceptually different evaluation tasks:

1. The GLUE and SuperGLUE datasets test the ability of a pretrained model to adapt to various language understanding tasks.

2. BLiMP and BLiMP supplement tasks test the affinity of a model towards grammatical sentences in a completely zero-shot manner.

3. MSGS measures how much does a pretrained model prefer linguistic generalizations (over surface ones) during finetuning.

We further elaborate on each of these evaluation suites below.

(Super)GLUE benchmark. General Language Understanding Evaluation benchmarks (GLUE and SuperGLUE; Wang et al., 2018, 2019) are arguably the most common ways of evaluating the language-understanding and transfer-learning capabilities of language models. The BabyLM challenge uses a subset of 10 (Super)GLUE tasks, detailed in Appendix F. We employ the standard way of finetuning masked language models on these datasets, as introduced in BERT (Devlin et al., 2019). More details about the finetuning processes are given in Appendix C.

As we use the BabyLM version of GLUE, our results cannot be directly compared with previous literature – the dataset samples are filtered to not contain out-of-vocabulary words and some of the employed metrics differ from the original recommendations (Wang et al., 2018, 2019). We opted to adhere to the BabyLM version to be compatible with other works in this challenge. However, in order to reliably compare our models, we decided to depart from BabyLM and to divide the training set in 90:10 ratio into a new training and development split; the former validation set is then used as a held-out split.[4]

BLiMP. When using any finetuning approach, it is unclear how to disentangle the innate language

[1]This choice is selected according to Gowda and May (2020) who recommend to '*... use the largest possible vocabulary such that at least 95% of classes have 100 or more examples in training.*'

[2]`https://github.com/ltgoslo/boot-bert`

[3]`https://github.com/babylm/evaluation-pipeline`

[4]The BabyLM pipeline unfortunately uses identical validation and test sets, which might yield overly optimistic results due to overfitting during hyperparameter optimization.

understanding from the knowledge learned during the second-stage supervised finetuning (Belinkov, 2022). In contrast, the Benchmark of Linguistic Minimal Pairs (BLiMP; Warstadt et al., 2020a) attempts to measure the linguistic knowledge of a language model in a zero-shot manner – without any additional training. Each pair of sentences in BLiMP differs minimally on the surface level, but only one of the sentences is grammatically valid. We can use the intrinsic ability of language models to assign a probability to every sentence and test how often a language model assigns a higher probability to the correct sentence (Wang and Cho, 2019; Salazar et al., 2020).

As detailed in Appendix A, the results on BLiMP greatly depend on temperature scaling (Guo et al., 2017a). Thus, to fairly compare different types of language models, we employ an alternative approach to evaluating BLiMP: we report the accuracies that are achieved with the optimal temperature for every language model; the reasoning is explained in Appendix A.

The BabyLM challenge also comes with an additional 'BLiMP supplement' held-out set with five additional diagnostic tasks. To comply with the held-out spirit of these tasks, we keep the temperature values calibrated for BLiMP, even though this results in suboptimal performance (Appendix A).

MSGS. The diagnostic dataset called Mixed Signals Generalization Set (MSGS; Warstadt et al., 2020b) measures whether a pretrained model prefers linguistic or surface generalizations. The experiments follow *the poverty of the stimulus design* (Wilson, 2006) – to first finetune a model on ambiguous data (consistent with both linguistic and surface explanations) and then test it on non-ambiguous data to see if it prefers the linguistic generalization.

We use the filtered MSGS datasets with no *inoculation* in the training set, as provided by the BabyLM challenge. Similarly to (Super)GLUE, we avoid the BabyLM approach that validates and tests on the same split – instead, to obtain a reliable comparison, we roughly follow the original work (Warstadt et al., 2020b) and use three learning rates: ($1 \cdot 10^{-5}$, $2 \cdot 10^{-5}$, and $3 \cdot 10^{-5}$), five random seeds, batch size of 16 and finetune for 5 epochs without early-stopping; then we report the mean and standard deviation statistics on the 6 non-ambiguous and non-control test datasets, measuring the Matthew's correlation coefficient (Matthews, 1975, which is renamed to the Linguistic Bias Score (LBS) in MSGS).

Model	GLUE	MSGS	BLiMP	Supplement
STRICT (100M words)				
OPT_{125m}	$73.0^{\pm 3.9}$	$-44.4^{\pm 8.5}$	77.8	67.5
$RoBERTa_{base}$	$74.3^{\pm 0.6}$	$-66.4^{\pm 26.6}$	76.2	63.8
$T5_{base}$	$75.3^{\pm 1.1}$	$-56.5^{\pm 6.7}$	83.6	71.8
$LTG\text{-}BERT_{base}$	$77.8^{\pm 1.4}$	$\mathbf{-43.2}^{\pm 11.0}$	**87.2**	**77.6**
$BootBERT_{base}$	$\mathbf{79.2}^{\pm 1.5}$	$-67.9^{\pm 12.6}$	86.3	72.2
STRICT-SMALL (10M words)				
OPT_{125m}	$68.3^{\pm 3.3}$	$-63.8^{\pm 9.6}$	69.2	60.2
$RoBERTa_{base}$	$72.2^{\pm 1.9}$	$-66.7^{\pm 11.9}$	68.1	60.5
T5-base	$64.7^{\pm 1.3}$	$-68.4^{\pm 7.1}$	59.9	48.6
$LTG\text{-}BERT_{small}$	$74.5^{\pm 1.5}$	$\mathbf{-42.6}^{\pm 34.8}$	80.9	**70.3**
$BootBERT_{small}$	$\mathbf{74.9}^{\pm 3.4}$	$-76.6^{\pm 10.2}$	**82.2**	65.6

Table 1: The overall average scores for the four evaluation suites: (Super)GLUE, MSGS, BLiMP and BLiMP supplement. The (Super)GLUE and MSGS columns show the mean and standard deviation statistics across multiple runs. The best results for each track are typeset in bold. For a more complete view, the full distribution of the MSGS results is plotted in Figure 4.

3.3 Results

The overall averaged results for all four evaluation suits are given in Table 1. Apart from evaluating masked autoencoders trained with latent bootstrapping (BootBERTs), as described in Section 2, we evaluate the three baseline language models provided by the organizers of BabyLM challenge: decoder-only OPT (Zhang et al., 2022), encoder-decoder T5 (Raffel et al., 2020) and encoder-only RoBERTa language models (Liu et al., 2019). As we base our models on the LTG-BERT architecture (Samuel et al., 2023a), we follow recommendations of the authors and also pretrain LTG-BERTs to get a strong and comparable baseline.

In addition to the averaged results, we also provide fine-grained (Super)GLUE scores in Table 2 and a visualization of the full distribution of MSGS scores in Figure 4 and in Appendix D (given the high variation of the aggregated MSGS results). The tables contain the mean and standard deviation statistics over 5 (respectively 15) runs. More details about the BLiMP and BLiMP supplement scores are given in Appendix A.

Model	BoolQ	CoLA	$MNLI_m$	$MNLI_{mm}$	MRPC	MultiRC	QNLI	QQP	RTE	SST-2	WSC	All
STRICT (100M words)												
OPT_{125m}	$66.4^{\pm0.7}$	$74.9^{\pm0.6}$	$75.7^{\pm0.3}$	$77.0^{\pm0.3}$	$81.9^{\pm0.7}$	$61.5^{\pm0.8}$	$82.8^{\pm0.8}$	$84.3^{\pm0.1}$	$58.6^{\pm2.9}$	$87.7^{\pm0.7}$	$52.3^{\pm12.5}$	$73.0^{\pm3.9}$
$RoBERTa_{base}$	$67.7^{\pm0.7}$	$75.6^{\pm0.3}$	$77.4^{\pm0.4}$	$78.3^{\pm0.3}$	$84.0^{\pm0.5}$	$64.3^{\pm0.5}$	$83.6^{\pm0.2}$	$85.5^{\pm0.2}$	$50.7^{\pm1.5}$	$88.3^{\pm0.6}$	$\mathbf{61.4}^{\pm0.0}$	$74.3^{\pm0.6}$
$T5_{base}$	$67.7^{\pm1.5}$	$76.7^{\pm0.9}$	$77.9^{\pm0.3}$	$78.7^{\pm0.3}$	$85.2^{\pm1.1}$	$65.7^{\pm0.8}$	$84.7^{\pm0.9}$	$86.2^{\pm0.1}$	$55.4^{\pm2.2}$	$89.0^{\pm0.8}$	$61.0^{\pm1.1}$	$75.3^{\pm1.1}$
$LTG\text{-}BERT_{base}$	$68.1^{\pm0.4}$	$\mathbf{82.8}^{\pm0.4}$	$83.4^{\pm0.3}$	$83.1^{\pm0.2}$	$84.3^{\pm0.7}$	$\mathbf{71.2}^{\pm0.9}$	$89.3^{\pm0.3}$	$87.9^{\pm0.2}$	$55.2^{\pm2.7}$	$\mathbf{91.9}^{\pm0.6}$	$58.6^{\pm3.5}$	$77.8^{\pm1.4}$
$BootBERT_{base}$	$\mathbf{72.4}^{\pm1.2}$	$81.6^{\pm0.6}$	$\mathbf{84.7}^{\pm0.3}$	$\mathbf{84.7}^{\pm0.3}$	$\mathbf{89.1}^{\pm0.3}$	$70.7^{\pm1.2}$	$\mathbf{91.2}^{\pm0.4}$	$\mathbf{88.1}^{\pm0.1}$	$\mathbf{57.2}^{\pm3.5}$	$91.8^{\pm0.8}$	$60.2^{\pm2.7}$	$\mathbf{79.2}^{\pm1.5}$
STRICT-SMALL (10M words)												
OPT_{125m}	$66.2^{\pm1.5}$	$69.0^{\pm0.5}$	$69.5^{\pm0.2}$	$71.0^{\pm0.5}$	$80.0^{\pm1.8}$	$56.5^{\pm2.0}$	$71.5^{\pm0.7}$	$80.3^{\pm0.3}$	$51.3^{\pm2.1}$	$85.4^{\pm0.9}$	$50.8^{\pm10.3}$	$68.3^{\pm3.3}$
$RoBERTa_{base}$	$65.8^{\pm2.9}$	$70.4^{\pm0.4}$	$72.5^{\pm0.4}$	$74.4^{\pm0.3}$	$82.2^{\pm0.4}$	$61.2^{\pm1.5}$	$80.3^{\pm0.7}$	$83.5^{\pm0.2}$	$\mathbf{56.8}^{\pm5.5}$	$85.6^{\pm0.3}$	$\mathbf{61.7}^{\pm0.5}$	$72.2^{\pm1.9}$
$T5_{base}$	$63.4^{\pm1.6}$	$69.4^{\pm0.1}$	$57.3^{\pm0.8}$	$58.6^{\pm1.1}$	$81.4^{\pm0.6}$	$48.4^{\pm1.4}$	$64.3^{\pm0.9}$	$76.8^{\pm0.3}$	$52.7^{\pm2.4}$	$79.4^{\pm1.0}$	$60.0^{\pm2.2}$	$64.7^{\pm1.3}$
$LTG\text{-}BERT_{small}$	$64.8^{\pm2.1}$	$\mathbf{77.6}^{\pm0.8}$	$78.0^{\pm0.2}$	$78.8^{\pm0.4}$	$82.3^{\pm0.4}$	$64.1^{\pm0.3}$	$85.0^{\pm0.2}$	$85.8^{\pm0.2}$	$53.7^{\pm4.1}$	$\mathbf{88.8}^{\pm0.8}$	$60.5^{\pm1.0}$	$74.5^{\pm1.5}$
$BootBERT_{small}$	$\mathbf{67.6}^{\pm2.7}$	$75.3^{\pm1.4}$	$\mathbf{79.2}^{\pm0.3}$	$\mathbf{80.0}^{\pm0.2}$	$\mathbf{83.2}^{\pm1.5}$	$\mathbf{65.2}^{\pm0.9}$	$\mathbf{86.2}^{\pm0.4}$	$\mathbf{86.6}^{\pm0.1}$	$54.7^{\pm5.3}$	$88.2^{\pm0.8}$	$57.3^{\pm9.2}$	$\mathbf{74.9}^{\pm3.4}$

Table 2: The BabyLM-flavored (Super)GLUE results of language models in the STRICT track and STRICT-SMALL track. We present the mean and standard deviation statistics over 5 finetuning runs (initialized with different random seeds) and boldface the best mean-result.

4 Discussion

LTG-BERT performance. Our results confirm the findings by Samuel et al. (2023a) who introduced the improved language modeling architecture called LTG-BERT. These models perform drastically better than the OPT, RoBERTa and T5 baselines pretrained on the same low-resource BabyLM corpus; the performance is improved across all evaluation suites – GLUE, MSGS, BLiMP as well as the BLiMP supplemental data – and across both STRICT and STRICT-SMALL tracks. LTG-BERT has also been used as the backbone of recent Norwegian language models trained on large amounts of data (Samuel et al., 2023b), which demonstrates that LM methods developed for efficient training are also beneficial for large-scale training.

Self-supervised learning. When we compare BootBERT to the LTG-BERT baseline, we can see that the latent bootstrapping approach leads to a substantially better performance when finetuned on (Super)GLUE in the STRICT track and to a slightly better performance in the STRICT-SMALL track. Specifically on the biggest and arguably most robust GLUE task, MNLI, the accuracy is better by 1.3/1.6 percentage points in the STRICT track and by 1.2/1.2pp in the STRICT-SMALL track. The overall average (Super)GLUE score is better by 1.4pp and by 0.4pp, respectively. This shows that language models pretrained with this approach are a good option for downstream tasks.

The ability of linguistic generalization, as measured by the linguistic bias scores in MSGS, is substantially worse in BootBERT than in the LTG-BERT baseline, as evident from Figure 4. A more detailed analysis in Appendix D reveals that this holds for both BabyLM tracks – but the difference is mainly due to the fact that LTG-BERT reliably prefers the linguistic feature 'is the main verb in "ing" form?', other tests are relatively similar for both types of models. It is unclear what part of latent bootstrapping causes this difference.

The results on the BLiMP-based benchmarks are mixed but overall worse when comparing BootBERT with the LTG-BERT baseline. This is possibly because of the utilization of two conflicting training objectives in BootBERT – intuitively, pure language-modeling-based training should have an advantage on benchmarks that rely on sentence likelihood.

In conclusion, these low-resource experiments suggest that **the advantage of latent bootstrapping for natural language is not as great as the advantage that has been previously demonstrated for computer vision**. We believe that this is because the atomic units of text, subword tokens, can provide much more semantically rich signal when compared to the atomic units of images, pixels. Thus there is not a large need for bootstrapping a rich signal from a teacher; instead, the standard language modeling comes with a training objective that is simple and provides enough signal, while suffering from issues like representation collapse.

The shared task results. The official DynaBench results for BabyLM can be found in Appendix E. Our system ranks high when evaluated on GLUE (first and second place) and on BLiMP (second and first place) in the STRICT and STRICT-SMALL tracks, respectively. As discussed earlier, BootBERT strongly prefers the surface features over the linguistic features and thus places low on the MSGS benchmark (third and last place), which also hurts the overall ranking of our system (third an seventh). Note however that this evaluation is not using a proper train/development/test split and it does not account for high variation of some metrics (MSGS in particular), which is why we have used an alternative evaluation in the rest of this paper.

Computational cost of latent bootstrapping. It is important to note that latent bootstrapping comes with an increased computational cost because of an additional forward pass through the mean teacher; which roughly equates to a 50% increase in pretraining time. Thus, it should be carefully considered whether the potential benefits of bootstrapping are worth this cost. That being said, this method does not bear any additional cost during finetuning nor inference, which might justify it in some cases.

5 Related work

Self-supervised learning. Our work is greatly inspired by the 'bootstrap your own latent' approach (BYOL; Grill et al., 2020), which introduced the bootstrapping feedback loop between a student and a mean teacher network. BYOL by itself can be considered an example of contrastive learning (Hjelm et al., 2019; van den Oord et al., 2019; Chen et al., 2020; He et al., 2020) without negative instances. Another important aspect of BYOL is the usage of a 'mean teacher', a slow-moving average of a student network, which is a term coined by Tarvainen and Valpola (2017).

Many methods of visual representation learning adopted the bootstrapping approach and further improved its parts (Chen and He, 2021; Zbontar et al., 2021; Bardes et al., 2022; He et al., 2022). In particular, our work bears similarities with the recently introduces 'image-based joint-embedding predictive architecture' (I-JEPA; Assran et al., 2023), which also trains a masked autoencoder student network to predict the contextualized embeddings of an unmasked mean teacher. While mostly used for the image domain, *data2vec* method showed that latent bootstrapping can also be successfully applied to text (Baevski et al., 2022).

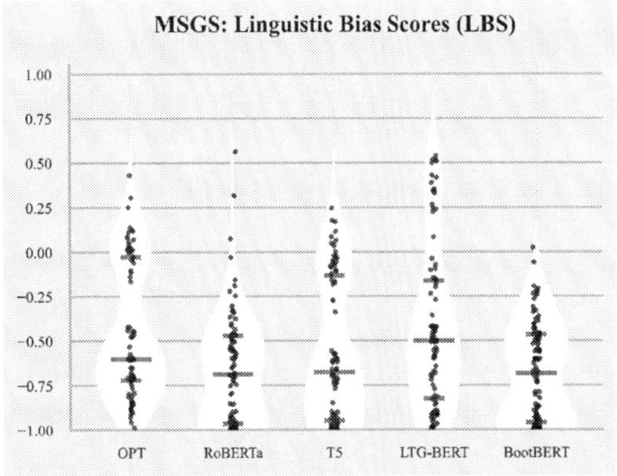

Figure 4: The Linguistic Bias Scores (LBS) of language models pretrained on the STRICT dataset. These plots show the distribution of the LBS scores across 15 evaluation runs (3 learning rates $\times$ 5 random seeds) for each of the 6 non-ambiguous test datasets (90 values in total for each model). The red horizontal lines highlight the first, second (median) and third quartile. The overall negative scores show that none of the tested models prefers linguistic features over the surface ones.

Efficient language modeling. The necessity of pretraining modern language models on large corpora were questioned in CamemBERT (Martin et al., 2020) and the effect of corpus size has been then thoroughly studied in Micheli et al. (2020), Zhang et al. (2021) as well as in Hoffmann et al. (2022). Samuel et al. (2023a) introduced the LTG-BERT – an improved language model optimized for pretraining on a low-resource corpus. They showed that a well-tuned language model can match the performance of BERT even when it is pretrained only on a small 100-million-word British National Corpus (BNC). We base our approach on this model due to the apparent similarity of the BabyLM training corpus to BNC.

6 Conclusion

In this paper, we presented a masked autoencoder language model trained with latent bootstrapping, an alternative self-supervised learning method. We showed that when pretrained on a low-resource corpus, the results of this method are varied – compared to a masked language modeling baseline, the performance is clearly better on (Super)GLUE, but worse on MSGS and mixed on BLiMP. We believe that it makes a promising alternative to traditional language modeling methods, but its reliable and effective utilization requires future work.

Acknowledgements

This paper would not be possible without the endless support and incredibly useful feedback from Andrey Kutuzov, Erik Velldal and Lilja Øvrelid from the Language Technology Group at the University of Oslo.

The efforts described in the current paper were funded by the HPLT project (High Performance Language Technologies; coordinated by Charles University). The computations were performed on resources provided through Sigma2 – the national research infrastructure provider for High-Performance Computing and large-scale data storage in Norway.

References

Ahmed Abdelali, Francisco Guzman, Hassan Sajjad, and Stephan Vogel. 2014. The AMARA corpus: Building parallel language resources for the educational domain. In *Proceedings of the Ninth International Conference on Language Resources and Evaluation (LREC'14)*, Reykjavik, Iceland. European Language Resources Association (ELRA).

Mahmoud Assran, Quentin Duval, Ishan Misra, Piotr Bojanowski, Pascal Vincent, Michael Rabbat, Yann LeCun, and Nicolas Ballas. 2023. Self-supervised learning from images with a joint-embedding predictive architecture. *arXiv preprint arXiv:2301.08243*.

Alexei Baevski, Wei-Ning Hsu, Qiantong Xu, Arun Babu, Jiatao Gu, and Michael Auli. 2022. data2vec: A general framework for self-supervised learning in speech, vision and language. In *Proceedings of the 39th International Conference on Machine Learning*, volume 162 of *Proceedings of Machine Learning Research*, pages 1298–1312. PMLR.

Roy Bar-Haim, Ido Dagan, Bill Dolan, Lisa Ferro, and Danilo Giampiccolo. 2006. The second pascal recognising textual entailment challenge. *Proceedings of the Second PASCAL Challenges Workshop on Recognising Textual Entailment*.

Adrien Bardes, Jean Ponce, and Yann LeCun. 2022. VICReg: Variance-invariance-covariance regularization for self-supervised learning. In *International Conference on Learning Representations*.

Yonatan Belinkov. 2022. Probing Classifiers: Promises, Shortcomings, and Advances. *Computational Linguistics*, 48(1):207–219.

Luisa Bentivogli, Ido Dagan, Hoa Trang Dang, Danilo Giampiccolo, and Bernardo Magnini. 2009. The fifth pascal recognizing textual entailment challenge. In *In Proc Text Analysis Conference (TAC'09*.

Ting Chen, Simon Kornblith, Mohammad Norouzi, and Geoffrey Hinton. 2020. A simple framework for contrastive learning of visual representations. In *Proceedings of the 37th International Conference on Machine Learning*, ICML'20. JMLR.org.

Xinlei Chen and Kaiming He. 2020. Exploring simple siamese representation learning. *arXiv preprint arXiv:2011.10566*.

Xinlei Chen and Kaiming He. 2021. Exploring simple siamese representation learning. In *Proceedings of the IEEE/CVF Conference on Computer Vision and Pattern Recognition (CVPR)*, pages 15750–15758.

Christopher Clark, Kenton Lee, Ming-Wei Chang, Tom Kwiatkowski, Michael Collins, and Kristina Toutanova. 2019. BoolQ: Exploring the surprising difficulty of natural yes/no questions. In *Proceedings of the 2019 Conference of the North American Chapter of the Association for Computational Linguistics: Human Language Technologies, Volume 1 (Long and Short Papers)*, pages 2924–2936, Minneapolis, Minnesota. Association for Computational Linguistics.

Ido Dagan, Oren Glickman, and Bernardo Magnini. 2006. The pascal recognising textual entailment challenge. In *Machine Learning Challenges. Evaluating Predictive Uncertainty, Visual Object Classification, and Recognising Tectual Entailment*, pages 177–190, Berlin, Heidelberg. Springer Berlin Heidelberg.

Jacob Devlin, Ming-Wei Chang, Kenton Lee, and Kristina Toutanova. 2019. BERT: Pre-training of deep bidirectional transformers for language understanding. In *Proceedings of the 2019 Conference of the North American Chapter of the Association for Computational Linguistics: Human Language Technologies, Volume 1 (Long and Short Papers)*, pages 4171–4186, Minneapolis, Minnesota. Association for Computational Linguistics.

William B. Dolan and Chris Brockett. 2005. Automatically constructing a corpus of sentential paraphrases. In *Proceedings of the Third International Workshop on Paraphrasing (IWP2005)*.

Allyson Ettinger. 2020. What BERT is not: Lessons from a new suite of psycholinguistic diagnostics for language models. *Transactions of the Association for Computational Linguistics*, 8:34–48.

Leo Gao, Jonathan Tow, Stella Biderman, Sid Black, Anthony DiPofi, Charles Foster, Laurence Golding, Jeffrey Hsu, Kyle McDonell, Niklas Muennighoff, Jason Phang, Laria Reynolds, Eric Tang, Anish Thite, Ben Wang, Kevin Wang, and Andy Zou. 2021. A framework for few-shot language model evaluation.

Martin Gerlach and Francesc Font-Clos. 2018. A standardized Project Gutenberg corpus for statistical analysis of natural language and quantitative linguistics. *Computing Research Repository*, arXiv:1812.08092.

Danilo Giampiccolo, Bernardo Magnini, Ido Dagan, and Bill Dolan. 2007. The third PASCAL recognizing textual entailment challenge. In *Proceedings of the ACL-PASCAL Workshop on Textual Entailment and Paraphrasing*, pages 1–9, Prague. Association for Computational Linguistics.

Ross Girshick. 2015. Fast r-cnn. In *Proceedings of the 2015 IEEE International Conference on Computer Vision (ICCV)*, ICCV '15, page 1440–1448, USA. IEEE Computer Society.

Thamme Gowda and Jonathan May. 2020. Finding the optimal vocabulary size for neural machine translation. In *Findings of the Association for Computational Linguistics: EMNLP 2020*, pages 3955–3964, Online. Association for Computational Linguistics.

Jean-Bastien Grill, Florian Strub, Florent Altché, Corentin Tallec, Pierre H. Richemond, Elena Buchatskaya, Carl Doersch, Bernardo Avila Pires, Zhaohan Daniel Guo, Mohammad Gheshlaghi Azar, Bilal Piot, Koray Kavukcuoglu, Rémi Munos, and Michal Valko. 2020. Bootstrap your own latent a new approach to self-supervised learning. In *Proceedings of the 34th International Conference on Neural Information Processing Systems*, NIPS'20, Red Hook, NY, USA. Curran Associates Inc.

Chuan Guo, Geoff Pleiss, Yu Sun, and Kilian Q. Weinberger. 2017a. On calibration of modern neural networks. In *Proceedings of the 34th International Conference on Machine Learning - Volume 70*, ICML'17, page 1321–1330. JMLR.org.

Chuan Guo, Geoff Pleiss, Yu Sun, and Kilian Q Weinberger. 2017b. On calibration of modern neural networks.

Kaiming He, Xinlei Chen, Saining Xie, Yanghao Li, Piotr Dollár, and Ross Girshick. 2022. Masked autoencoders are scalable vision learners. In *Proceedings of the IEEE/CVF Conference on Computer Vision and Pattern Recognition (CVPR)*, pages 16000–16009.

Kaiming He, Haoqi Fan, Yuxin Wu, Saining Xie, and Ross Girshick. 2020. Momentum contrast for unsupervised visual representation learning. In *2020 IEEE/CVF Conference on Computer Vision and Pattern Recognition (CVPR)*, pages 9726–9735.

Pengcheng He, Xiaodong Liu, Jianfeng Gao, and Weizhu Chen. 2021. Deberta: Decoding-enhanced bert with disentangled attention. In *International Conference on Learning Representations*.

Felix Hill, Antoine Bordes, Sumit Chopra, and Jason Weston. 2016. The Goldilocks principle: Reading children's books with explicit memory representations.

R Devon Hjelm, Alex Fedorov, Samuel Lavoie-Marchildon, Karan Grewal, Phil Bachman, Adam Trischler, and Yoshua Bengio. 2019. Learning deep representations by mutual information estimation and maximization. In *International Conference on Learning Representations*.

Jordan Hoffmann, Sebastian Borgeaud, Arthur Mensch, Elena Buchatskaya, Trevor Cai, Eliza Rutherford, Diego de Las Casas, Lisa Anne Hendricks, Johannes Welbl, Aidan Clark, Tom Hennigan, Eric Noland, Katie Millican, George van den Driessche, Bogdan Damoc, Aurelia Guy, Simon Osindero, Karen Simonyan, Erich Elsen, Jack W. Rae, Oriol Vinyals, and Laurent Sifre. 2022. Training compute-optimal large language models.

Mandar Joshi, Danqi Chen, Yinhan Liu, Daniel S. Weld, Luke Zettlemoyer, and Omer Levy. 2020. SpanBERT: Improving pre-training by representing and predicting spans. *Transactions of the Association for Computational Linguistics*, 8:64–77.

Daniel Khashabi, Snigdha Chaturvedi, Michael Roth, Shyam Upadhyay, and Dan Roth. 2018. Looking beyond the surface: A challenge set for reading comprehension over multiple sentences. In *Proceedings of the 2018 Conference of the North American Chapter of the Association for Computational Linguistics: Human Language Technologies, Volume 1 (Long Papers)*, pages 252–262, New Orleans, Louisiana. Association for Computational Linguistics.

Yann LeCun. 2022. A path towards autonomous machine intelligence version 0.9. 2, 2022-06-27. *Open Review*, 62.

Hector J. Levesque, Ernest Davis, and Leora Morgenstern. 2012. The winograd schema challenge. In *Proceedings of the Thirteenth International Conference on Principles of Knowledge Representation and Reasoning*, KR'12, page 552–561. AAAI Press.

Pierre Lison and Jörg Tiedemann. 2016. OpenSubtitles2016: Extracting large parallel corpora from movie and TV subtitles. In *Proceedings of the Tenth International Conference on Language Resources and Evaluation (LREC'16)*, pages 923–929, Portorož, Slovenia. European Language Resources Association (ELRA).

Yinhan Liu, Myle Ott, Naman Goyal, Jingfei Du, Mandar Joshi, Danqi Chen, Omer Levy, Mike Lewis, Luke Zettlemoyer, and Veselin Stoyanov. 2019. Roberta: A robustly optimized bert pretraining approach.

Brian MacWhinney. 2000. *The CHILDES project: The database*, volume 2. Psychology Press.

Louis Martin, Benjamin Muller, Pedro Javier Ortiz Suárez, Yoann Dupont, Laurent Romary, Éric de la Clergerie, Djamé Seddah, and Benoît Sagot. 2020. CamemBERT: a tasty French language model. In *Proceedings of the 58th Annual Meeting of the Association for Computational Linguistics*, pages 7203–7219, Online. Association for Computational Linguistics.

B.W. Matthews. 1975. Comparison of the predicted and observed secondary structure of t4 phage lysozyme. *Biochimica et Biophysica Acta (BBA) - Protein Structure*, 405(2):442–451.

Yu Meng, Jitin Krishnan, Sinong Wang, Qifan Wang, Yuning Mao, Han Fang, Marjan Ghazvininejad, Jiawei Han, and Luke Zettlemoyer. 2023. Representation deficiency in masked language modeling.

Vincent Micheli, Martin d'Hoffschmidt, and François Fleuret. 2020. On the importance of pre-training data volume for compact language models. In *Proceedings of the 2020 Conference on Empirical Methods in Natural Language Processing (EMNLP)*, pages 7853–7858, Online. Association for Computational Linguistics.

Alec Radford, Karthik Narasimhan, Tim Salimans, and Ilya Sutskever. 2018. Improving language understanding by generative pre-training.

Colin Raffel, Noam Shazeer, Adam Roberts, Katherine Lee, Sharan Narang, Michael Matena, Yanqi Zhou, Wei Li, and Peter J. Liu. 2020. Exploring the limits of transfer learning with a unified text-to-text transformer. *Journal of Machine Learning Research*, 21(140):1–67.

Pranav Rajpurkar, Jian Zhang, Konstantin Lopyrev, and Percy Liang. 2016. SQuAD: 100,000+ questions for machine comprehension of text. In *Proceedings of the 2016 Conference on Empirical Methods in Natural Language Processing*, pages 2383–2392, Austin, Texas. Association for Computational Linguistics.

Julian Salazar, Davis Liang, Toan Q. Nguyen, and Katrin Kirchhoff. 2020. Masked language model scoring. In *Proceedings of the 58th Annual Meeting of the Association for Computational Linguistics*, pages 2699–2712, Online. Association for Computational Linguistics.

David Samuel, Andrey Kutuzov, Lilja Øvrelid, and Erik Velldal. 2023a. Trained on 100 million words and still in shape: BERT meets British National Corpus. In *Findings of the Association for Computational Linguistics: EACL 2023*, pages 1954–1974, Dubrovnik, Croatia. Association for Computational Linguistics.

David Samuel, Andrey Kutuzov, Samia Touileb, Erik Velldal, Lilja Øvrelid, Egil Rønningstad, Elina Sigdel, and Anna Palatkina. 2023b. NorBench – a benchmark for Norwegian language models. In *Proceedings of the 24th Nordic Conference on Computational Linguistics (NoDaLiDa)*, pages 618–633, Tórshavn, Faroe Islands. University of Tartu Library.

Noam Shazeer. 2020. GLU variants improve transformer. *CoRR*, abs/2002.05202.

Sam Shleifer and Myle Ott. 2022. Normformer: Improved transformer pretraining with extra normalization.

Richard Socher, Alex Perelygin, Jean Wu, Jason Chuang, Christopher D. Manning, Andrew Ng, and Christopher Potts. 2013. Recursive deep models for semantic compositionality over a sentiment treebank. In *Proceedings of the 2013 Conference on Empirical Methods in Natural Language Processing*, pages 1631–1642, Seattle, Washington, USA. Association for Computational Linguistics.

Andreas Stolcke, Klaus Ries, Noah Coccaro, Elizabeth Shriberg, Rebecca Bates, Daniel Jurafsky, Paul Taylor, Rachel Martin, Marie Meteer, and Carol Van Ess-Dykema. 2000. Dialogue act modeling for automatic tagging and recognition of conversational speech. *Computational Linguistics*, 26(3):339–371.

Antti Tarvainen and Harri Valpola. 2017. Mean teachers are better role models: Weight-averaged consistency targets improve semi-supervised deep learning results. In *Proceedings of the 31st International Conference on Neural Information Processing Systems*, NIPS'17, page 1195–1204, Red Hook, NY, USA. Curran Associates Inc.

Ian Tenney, Patrick Xia, Berlin Chen, Alex Wang, Adam Poliak, R Thomas McCoy, Najoung Kim, Benjamin Van Durme, Sam Bowman, Dipanjan Das, and Ellie Pavlick. 2019. What do you learn from context? probing for sentence structure in contextualized word representations. In *International Conference on Learning Representations*.

Aaron van den Oord, Yazhe Li, and Oriol Vinyals. 2019. Representation learning with contrastive predictive coding.

Ashish Vaswani, Noam Shazeer, Niki Parmar, Jakob Uszkoreit, Llion Jones, Aidan N Gomez, Ł ukasz Kaiser, and Illia Polosukhin. 2017. Attention is all you need. In *Advances in Neural Information Processing Systems*, volume 30. Curran Associates, Inc.

Alex Wang and Kyunghyun Cho. 2019. BERT has a mouth, and it must speak: BERT as a Markov random field language model. In *Proceedings of the Workshop on Methods for Optimizing and Evaluating Neural Language Generation*, pages 30–36, Minneapolis, Minnesota. Association for Computational Linguistics.

Alex Wang, Yada Pruksachatkun, Nikita Nangia, Amanpreet Singh, Julian Michael, Felix Hill, Omer Levy, and Samuel Bowman. 2019. Superglue: A stickier benchmark for general-purpose language understanding systems. In *Advances in Neural Information Processing Systems*, volume 32. Curran Associates, Inc.

Alex Wang, Amanpreet Singh, Julian Michael, Felix Hill, Omer Levy, and Samuel Bowman. 2018. GLUE: A multi-task benchmark and analysis platform for natural language understanding. In *Proceedings of the 2018 EMNLP Workshop BlackboxNLP: Analyzing and Interpreting Neural Networks for NLP*, pages 353–355, Brussels, Belgium. Association for Computational Linguistics.

Alex Warstadt, Leshem Choshen, Aaron Mueller, Adina Williams, Ethan Wilcox, and Chengxu Zhuang. 2023a. Call for papers – the babylm challenge: Sample-efficient pretraining on a developmentally plausible corpus. *Computing Research Repository*, arXiv:2301.11796.

Alex Warstadt, Aaron Mueller, Leshem Choshen, Ethan Gotlieb Wilcox, Chengxu Zhuang, Juan Ciro, Rafael Mosquera, Adina Williams, Bhargavi Paranjabe, Tal Linzen, and Ryan Cotterell. 2023b. Findings of the 2023 BabyLM Challenge: Sample-efficient pretraining on developmentally plausible corpora. In *Proceedings of the 2023 BabyLM Challenge*. Association for Computational Linguistics (ACL).

Alex Warstadt, Alicia Parrish, Haokun Liu, Anhad Mohananey, Wei Peng, Sheng-Fu Wang, and Samuel R. Bowman. 2020a. BLiMP: The benchmark of linguistic minimal pairs for English. *Transactions of the Association for Computational Linguistics*, 8:377–392.

Alex Warstadt, Amanpreet Singh, and Samuel R. Bowman. 2019. Neural network acceptability judgments. *Transactions of the Association for Computational Linguistics*, 7:625–641.

Alex Warstadt, Yian Zhang, Xiaocheng Li, Haokun Liu, and Samuel R. Bowman. 2020b. Learning which features matter: RoBERTa acquires a preference for linguistic generalizations (eventually). In *Proceedings of the 2020 Conference on Empirical Methods in Natural Language Processing (EMNLP)*, pages 217–235, Online. Association for Computational Linguistics.

Adina Williams, Nikita Nangia, and Samuel Bowman. 2018. A broad-coverage challenge corpus for sentence understanding through inference. In *Proceedings of the 2018 Conference of the North American Chapter of the Association for Computational Linguistics: Human Language Technologies, Volume 1 (Long Papers)*, pages 1112–1122, New Orleans, Louisiana. Association for Computational Linguistics.

C. Wilson. 2006. Learning phonology with substantive bias: an experimental and computational study of velar palatalization. *Cogn Sci*, 30(5):945–982.

Yonghui Wu, Mike Schuster, Zhifeng Chen, Quoc V. Le, Mohammad Norouzi, Wolfgang Macherey, Maxim Krikun, Yuan Cao, Qin Gao, Klaus Macherey, Jeff Klingner, Apurva Shah, Melvin Johnson, Xiaobing Liu, Łukasz Kaiser, Stephan Gouws, Yoshikiyo Kato, Taku Kudo, Hideto Kazawa, Keith Stevens, George Kurian, Nishant Patil, Wei Wang, Cliff Young, Jason Smith, Jason Riesa, Alex Rudnick, Oriol Vinyals, Greg Corrado, Macduff Hughes, and Jeffrey Dean. 2016. Google's neural machine translation system: Bridging the gap between human and machine translation.

Jure Zbontar, Li Jing, Ishan Misra, Yann LeCun, and Stephane Deny. 2021. Barlow twins: Self-supervised learning via redundancy reduction. In *Proceedings of the 38th International Conference on Machine Learning*, volume 139 of *Proceedings of Machine Learning Research*, pages 12310–12320. PMLR.

Susan Zhang, Stephen Roller, Naman Goyal, Mikel Artetxe, Moya Chen, Shuohui Chen, Christopher Dewan, Mona Diab, Xian Li, Xi Victoria Lin, Todor Mihaylov, Myle Ott, Sam Shleifer, Kurt Shuster, Daniel Simig, Punit Singh Koura, Anjali Sridhar, Tianlu Wang, and Luke Zettlemoyer. 2022. Opt: Open pre-trained transformer language models.

Yian Zhang, Alex Warstadt, Xiaocheng Li, and Samuel R. Bowman. 2021. When do you need billions of words of pretraining data? In *Proceedings of the 59th Annual Meeting of the Association for Computational Linguistics and the 11th International Joint Conference on Natural Language Processing (Volume 1: Long Papers)*, pages 1112–1125, Online. Association for Computational Linguistics.

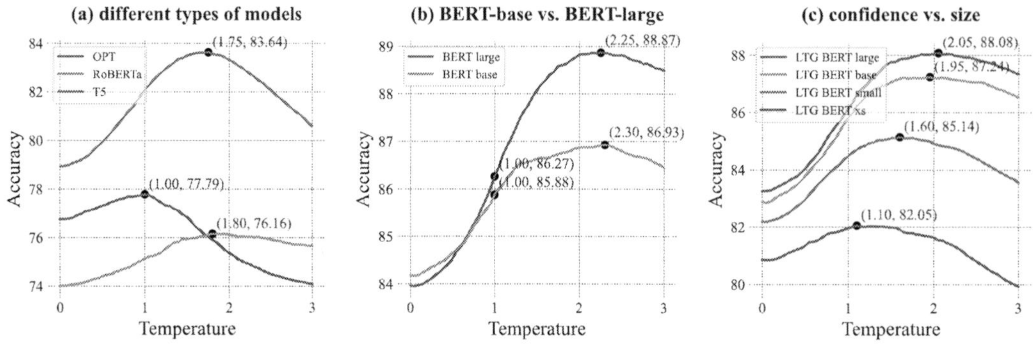

Figure 5: These plots show the BLiMP 'confidence profiles' of several language models – the influence of temperature scaling on the average BLiMP accuracy. **(a)** Models trained by different training objectives show different confidence profiles, judging their linguistic knowledge from BLiMP accuracy can be misleading. Here, we compare the three baseline from the BabyLM challenge trained on the STRICT track. **(b)** The linguistic knowledge of $\text{BERT}_{\text{base}}$ and $\text{BERT}_{\text{large}}$ appears comparable when judging from performance at temperature 1, but the potential of the larger model is much greater. **(c)** We train four sizes of LTG-BERT on the STRICT track and plot their confidence profiles. Larger models tend to be more confident and, therefore, measuring them at temperature 1 is more misleading.

A The Effect of temperature scaling on BLiMP

Our preliminary experiments with calibrating language models via temperature scaling (Guo et al., 2017b) revealed that the BLiMP scores are hugely dependent on the scalar temperature parameter – when these are calculated with the standard method by (Salazar et al., 2020). This single temperature value can increase the accuracy on some BLiMP subtasks by more than 10% (Figure 6), which challenges the usage of BLiMP as an appropriate evaluation tool. It is especially problematic when comparing different types of language models (Figure 5a) and different sizes of language models (Figure 5b,c).

Background. To better understand this problem, this section describes how are the BLiMP scores traditionally computed for masked language models. These models can estimate $P(s_t|s_{\setminus t})$ – the likelihood of a token s_t given its bidirectional context $s_{\setminus t} = (s_i|i \neq t)$. This probability distribution P is given by a softmax transformation of the output logits z, where τ is temperature:

$$P_i = \frac{\exp(z_i/\tau)}{\sum_k \exp(z_k/\tau)}.$$

Large temperature yields more even distribution and low temperature gives more 'peaky' distribution.

Salazar et al. (2020) proposed to use these probability estimates (with $\tau = 1$) to infer a *score* for each BLiMP sentence, with a higher *score* corresponding to a more likely sentence. Then, the BLiMP accuracy measures how many times is the score of a grammatically correct sentence greater than the score of an incorrect sentence. Specifically, we use the *pseudo-log-likelihood score* (PPL) by Wang and Cho (2019). The PPL score of a sentence s is defined as:

$$\text{PLL}(s) = \sum_{t=1}^{N} \log P(s_t|s_{\setminus t}).$$

Proposed solution. BLiMP should measure the linguistic knowledge of language models and we believe that this metric should be independent of the prediction confidence of these models. Formally speaking, the BLiMP score should be invariant to temperature scaling. Therefore, we propose to use the maximal average accuracy across all possible temperature values – instead of simply using the average accuracy at temperature equal to 1. As apparent from Figure 5b, such formulation can better reflect the difference of linguistic knowledge found in $\text{BERT}_{\text{base}}$ and $\text{BERT}_{\text{large}}$. There, the accuracy measured at temperature 1

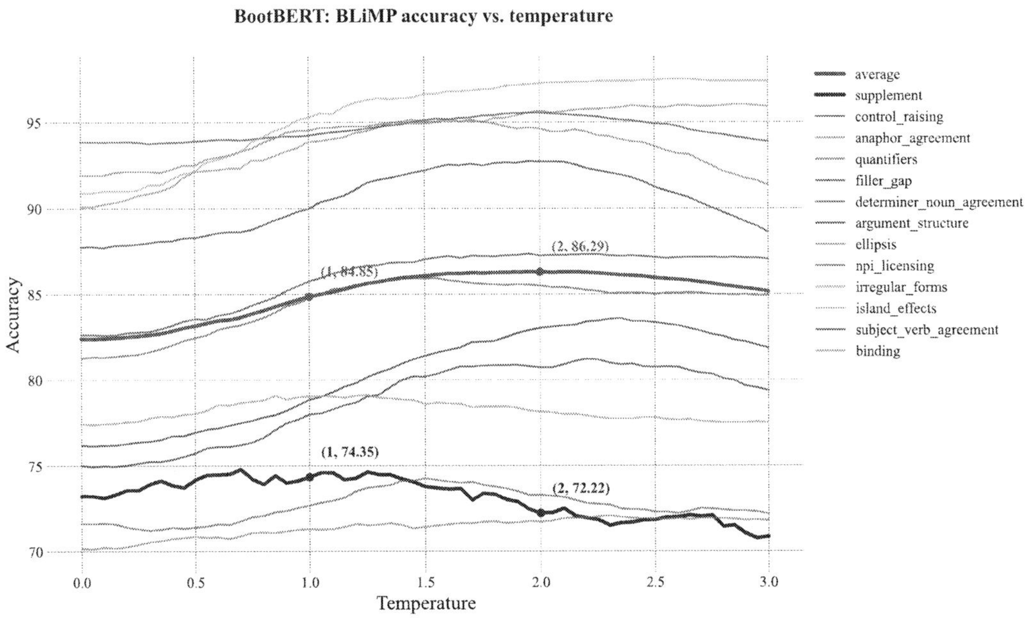

Figure 6: The confidence profile of our proposed $\text{BootBERT}_{\text{base}}$ model pretrained on the STRICT track. Apart from the average BLiMP accuracy (in red) and the average BLiMP supplement accuracy (in blue), this plot shows fine-grained BLiMP accuracies on all subtasks.

is at odds with other measures that show substantially better linguistic knowledge of $\text{BERT}_{\text{large}}$ (Devlin et al., 2019; Tenney et al., 2019; Ettinger, 2020).

Note that our approach bears only a negligible compute cost because the temperature modification is done ex-post, i.e., it does not require any additional passes through the language model.

Using one temperature for all subtasks does not account for the severe difference between the accuracy scores on these tasks (Figure 6), but it is a simple solution that also allows us to evaluate models on a held-out set, such as the BLiMP supplement. We believe that a scoring function that is (i) unified, (ii) invariant to temperature and (iii) fair to all subtasks, is an interesting future work.

B Data preprocessing

The pretraining datasets for the STRICT and STRICT-SMALL tracks are a mix 10 different corpora, as shown in Table 3. We applied light preprocessing and normalization to these corpora in order to cast them into a unified format. In particularly, we applied these modifications:

- **CHILDES**: We capitalize the first letter of each line, normalize punctuation with whitespaces (essentially detokenization) and put every line between double quotes (as directed speech).
- **British National Corpus**: Capitalization, normalization and double quotes.
- **Children's Book Test**: This corpus contains some remnants of the Penn Tree format where, for example, `-LRB-` and `-RRB-` tokens are used instead of '(' and ')'. We normalize all unnatural symbols and whitespaces.
- **Children's Stories Text Corpus**: We try to conserve the formatting with a special `[TAB]` symbol and apply whitespace normalization.
- **Standardized Project Gutenberg Corpus**: The text file is aligned into blocks by inserting a newline symbol after at most 70 characters, which ruins the sentence structure. We restore the original paragraphs by removing these additional newline symbols and apply whitespace normalization.

- **OpenSubtitles**: Some lines arbitrarily start with a dash symbol, which we remove. Then whitespace normalization is applied and every line is cast a directed speech with double quotes.
- **QED**: This corpus contains some incorrectly parsed HTML symbols, which we tried to clean up with some simple heuristics. The whitespace normalization is applied and every line is cast as directed speech with double quotes.
- **Wikipedia**: This dataset also needed to be cleaned of incorrectly parsed Wikipedia tags and hyperlinks. Whitespace normalization is applied.
- **Simple Wikipedia**: Heuristic HTML clean-up and whitespace normalization.
- **Switchboard**: The same as OpenSubtitles: removed leading dashes, whitespaces normalization and added double quotes.

Note that the preprocessed corpora and the preprocessing scripts are released alongside the training scripts.

Dataset	Domain	# Words		Proportion
		STRICT-SMALL	STRICT	
CHILDES (MacWhinney, 2000)	Child-directed speech	0.44M	4.21M	5%
British National Corpus (BNC),[1] dialogue portion	Dialogue	0.86M	8.16M	8%
Children's Book Test (Hill et al., 2016)	Children's books	0.57M	5.55M	6%
Children's Stories Text Corpus[2]	Children's books	0.34M	3.22M	3%
Standardized Project Gutenberg Corpus (Gerlach and Font-Clos, 2018)	Written English	0.99M	9.46M	10%
OpenSubtitles (Lison and Tiedemann, 2016)	Movie subtitles	3.09M	31.28M	31%
QCRI Educational Domain Corpus (QED; Abdelali et al., 2014)	Educational video subtitles	1.04M	10.24M	11%
Wikipedia[3]	Wikipedia (English)	0.99M	10.08M	10%
Simple Wikipedia[4]	Wikipedia (Simple English)	1.52M	14.66M	15%
Switchboard Dialog Act Corpus (Stolcke et al., 2000)	Dialogue	0.12M	1.18M	1%
Total	–	9.96M	98.04M	100%

Table 3: The contents of datasets for the the STRICT and STRICT-SMALL tracks; the table is taken from Warstadt et al. (2023b). [1]http://www.natcorp.ox.ac.uk [2]https://www.kaggle.com/datasets/edenbd/children-stories-text-corpus [3]https://dumps.wikimedia.org/enwiki/20221220/ [4]https://dumps.wikimedia.org/simplewiki/20221201/

C Implementation details

In order to reduce training time, pre-training is parallelized over multiple GPUs with the global batch size of 4 096. The number of GPUs used depends on the size of pre-trained language models, ranging from 32 to 128 AMD Instinct MI250X GPUs, each with 64GB memory. The amount of training steps is 62 500, reducing the training budget of the original BERT model by 50%. Unlike the BERT and LTG-BERT training recipe, we use the same sequence length, 256, throughout the whole training. This decision is necessary for keeping a reasonable exponential moving average of the parameters (it could be corrupted when switching to a longer sequence length in the middle of training).

The implementation of latent bootstrapping mainly follows I-JEPA (Assran et al., 2023). We also adopt their usage of a linearly increasing schedule of the EMA decay hyperparameter τ and a cosine schedule of weight decay.

The hyperparameters for pretraining are given in Table 5. Table 6 shows the finetuning hyperparameters.

D Finegrained MSGS scores

This section shows the full score distribution over all MSGS subtasks, including the control subtasks. This gives a better view on the behavior of different language models than the aggragated scores in Figure 4 and Table 1.

STRICT track (100M words)

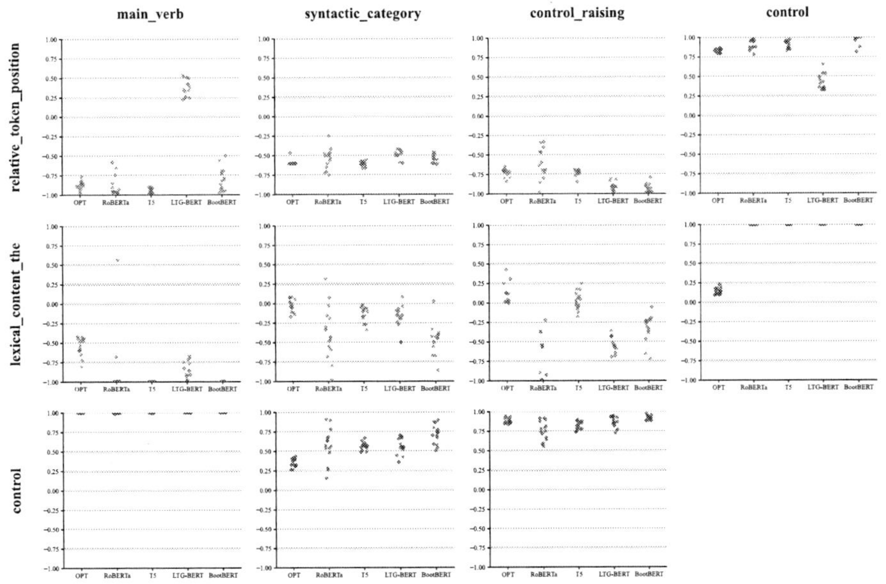

STRICT-SMALL track (10M words)

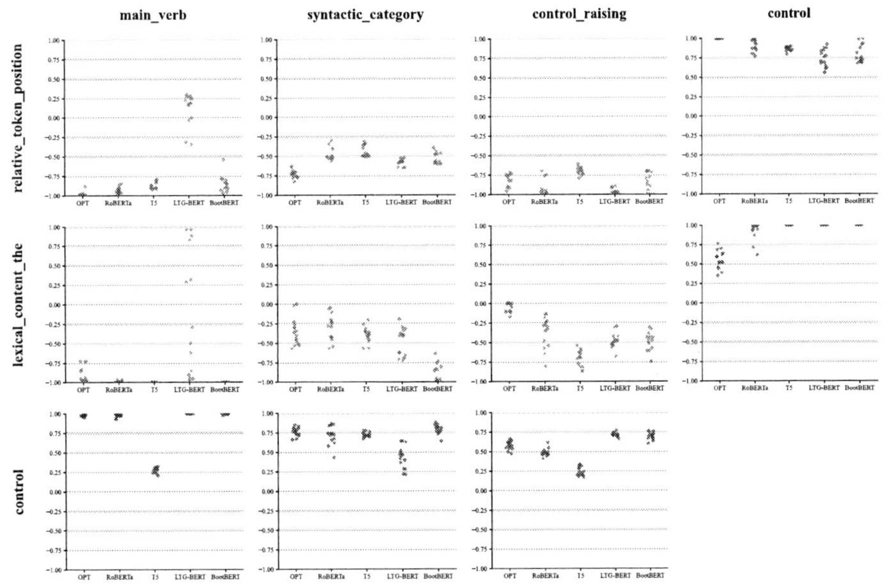

Figure 7: The MSGS linguistic bias scores of the control tasks (in blue) and non-control disambiguated tasks (in red). Values close to 1 indicate preference of linguistic explanations (columns) while values close to -1 indicate preference of surface explanations.

E The official BabyLM results from DynaBench

This section shows the official results for the BabyLM challenge as published on the DynaBench website.[5] We show the top 9 submissions (the official ones delivered on time) for the STRICT and STRICT-SMALL tracks with the aggregated scores in Table 4.

STRICT track (100M words)

Model	BLiMP	GLUE	MSGS	Average
BootBERT	[#2] 82.2	[#1] **78.5**	[#3] 27.7	[#3] 70.2
ELC-BERT	**82.8**	78.3	47.2	**74.3**
Contextualizer	79.0	72.9	**58.0**	73.0
MSLM	76.2	73.5	21.4	64.4
Bad babies	77.0	67.2	23.4	63.4
CogMemLM	72.8	72.2	-0.1	58.0
Pre-training LLMs	71.6	69.8	-3.8	56.0
BabyStories	73.9	59.1	0.2	54.7
AB-RoBERTa	68.3	64.1	-11.8	51.0

STRICT-SMALL track (10M words)

Model	BLiMP	GLUE	MSGS	Average
BootBERT	[#1] **75.9**	[#2] 71.7	[#9] -9.7	[#7] 57.5
ELC-BERT	75.8	**73.7**	**29.4**	**65.9**
MLSM	72.4	70.6	17.2	60.8
Contextualizer	74.3	69.6	12.7	60.5
Baby Llama	69.8	67.6	24.7	60.1
Too Much Information	75.7	70.9	3.9	59.9
McGill	72.4	69.3	5.2	58.0
CLIMB	71.8	65.6	9.7	57.5
William's college GPT2	70.9	64.8	9.9	56.9

Table 4: The DynaBench scores of the BabyLM challenge (Warstadt et al., 2023a), the table shows the top 9 submissions in the STRICT and STRICT-SMALL tracks. Higher scores are better, the best results in each evaluation suite are boldfaced.

F BabyLM subset of (Super)GLUE tasks

The BabyLM challenge involves slightly modified GLUE and SuperGLUE benchmarks. It uses only a subset of the subtasks, the datasets are filtered so that they do not contain out-of-vocabulary words, and it sometimes use non-standard metrics. We list all subtasks and their metrics below:

- **Boolean Questions** (BoolQ; Clark et al., 2019), a yes/no Q/A dataset evaluated with accuracy.
- **Corpus of Linguistic Acceptability** (CoLA; Warstadt et al., 2019) evaluated with accuracy (originally evaluated with the Matthews correlation coefficient (MCC; Matthews, 1975)).
- **The Multi-Genre Natural Language Inference Corpus** (MNLI; Williams et al., 2018). Its development set consists of two parts: *matched*, sampled from the same data source as the training set, and *mismatched*, which is sampled from a different domain. Both parts are evaluated with accuracy.
- **The Microsoft Research Paraphrase Corpus** (MRPC; Dolan and Brockett, 2005), evaluated with both F_1-score (originally also evaluated with accuracy).
- **Multi-Sentence Reading Comprehension** (MultiRC; Khashabi et al., 2018), a multiple choice question answering dataset, evaluated with accuracy (originally evaluated with the exact match accuracy (EM) and F_1-score (over all answer options)).
- **Question-answering Natural Language Inference** (QNLI) constructed from the Stanford Question Answering Dataset (SQuAD; Rajpurkar et al., 2016), evaluated with accuracy.
- **The Quora Question Pairs** (QQP),[6] evaluated with F_1-score (originally evaluated with accuracy).
- **The Stanford Sentiment Treebank** (SST-2; Socher et al., 2013), evaluated with accuracy.
- **The Recognizing Textual Entailment datasets** (RTE; Dagan et al., 2006; Bar-Haim et al., 2006; Giampiccolo et al., 2007; Bentivogli et al., 2009), evaluated with accuracy.
- **Winograd Schema Challenge** (WSC; Levesque et al., 2012) evaluated with accuracy.

[5] `https://dynabench.org/babylm` (22 October, 2023)

[6] `https://quoradata.quora.com/First-Quora-Dataset-Release-Question-Pairs`

Hyperparameter	**BootBERT$_{small}$**	**BootBERT$_{base}$**
Number of parameters	30 395 776	127 744 768
Number of layers	12	12
Hidden size	384	768
FF intermediate size	1 024	2 048
Vocabulary size	4 096	16 384
Attention heads	6	12
β parameter	0.1	0.1
Encoder hidden dropout	0.1	0.1
Encoder attention dropout	0.1	0.1
Decoder hidden dropout	0.0	0.0
Decoder attention dropout	0.0	0.0
Training steps	62 500	62 500
Batch size	4 096	4 096
Sequence length	256	256
Warmup steps	1 000	1 000
Initial learning rate	0.007	0.005
Final learning rate	0.0007	0.0005
Learning rate scheduler	cosine	cosine
Initial weight decay	0.04	0.02
Final weight decay	0.4	0.2
Weight decay scheduler	cosine	cosine
Initial EMA decay τ	0.996	0.996
Final EMA decay τ	1.0	1.0
EMA decay scheduler	linear	linear
Layer norm ϵ	1e-7	1e-7
Optimizer	LAMB	LAMB
LAMB ϵ	1e-6	1e-6
LAMB β_1	0.9	0.9
LAMB β_2	0.98	0.98
Gradient clipping	2.0	2.0

Table 5: Pre-training hyperparameters for the small-sized BootBERT (trained on STRICT-SMALL and for the base-sized BootBERT (trained on the STRICT track).

Hyperparameter	**BoolQ, MNLI MRPC, MultiRC, QNLI QQP, SST-2**	**CoLA, RTE, WSC**	**MSGS**
Batch size	32	16	16
Number of epochs	10	10	5
Dropout	0.1	0.1	0.1
Warmup steps	10%	10%	10%
Peak learning rate	3e-5	3e-5	{1e-5, 2e-5, 3e-5}
Learning rate decay	linear	linear	linear
Weight decay	0.01	0.01	0.01
Optimizer	AdamW	AdamW	AdamW
Adam ϵ	1e-6	1e-6	1e-6
Adam β_1	0.9	0.9	0.9
Adam β_2	0.999	0.999	0.999

Table 6: Hyperparameters for fine-tuning the GLUE, SuperGLUE task and MSGS tasks. We use the same hyperparameters for all models, not performing any per-model hyperparameter search. These values are adopted from LTG-BERT (Samuel et al., 2023a) and MSGS (Warstadt et al., 2020b). For all models, we measure the statistics over 5 random seeds: 1234, 2345, 3456, 4567 an 5678.

Not all layers are equally as important: Every Layer Counts BERT

Lucas Georges Gabriel Charpentier and **David Samuel**
University of Oslo, Language Technology Group

Abstract

This paper introduces a novel modification of the transformer architecture, tailored for the data-efficient pretraining of language models. This aspect is evaluated by participating in the BabyLM challenge, where our solution won both the STRICT and STRICT-SMALL tracks. Our approach allows each transformer layer to select which outputs of previous layers to process. The empirical results verify the potential of this simple modification and show that not all layers are equally as important.

1 Introduction

Modern language models (LLMs), with their deep architectures and large parameter counts, have displayed outstanding performance on a wide range of tasks. Their ability to understand, generate, and manipulate human language has been groundbreaking (Devlin et al., 2019; Raffel et al., 2020; Brown et al., 2020). However, this success largely relies on *vast amounts of unsupervised data* that these models need for pretraining, requiring extensive computational power and time. While this is feasible for high-resource languages like English, it becomes a bottleneck for languages with limited data resources (Joshi et al., 2020). Moreover, the environmental and economic costs of such massive training regimens are growing concerns (Strubell et al., 2019; Thompson et al., 2020).

The BabyLM challenge tries to address these concerns by providing a shared experimental ground for efficient language modelling (Warstadt et al., 2023). All models submitted to this shared task have to be trained on a restricted text corpus of 10M and 100M words – in the STRICT-SMALL and STRICT tracks, respectively. The challenge pushes the boundaries of what is possible with data-efficient language model pretraining.

In response to this challenge, we present a novel modification to the well-established transformer architecture (Vaswani et al., 2017). Instead of traditional residual connections, our model allows each layer to *selectively* process outputs from the preceding layers. This flexibility leads to intriguing findings: not every layer is of equal significance to the following layers. Thus, we call it the 'Every Layer Counts' BERT (ELC-BERT).

The BabyLM challenge provided us with a robust benchmark to evaluate the efficacy of ELC-BERT. Our approach emerged as the winning submission in both the STRICT and STRICT-SMALL tracks (Table 1), which highlights the potential of layer weighting for future low-resource language modelling.

Transparent and open-source language modelling is necessary for safe future development of this field. We release the full source code, together with the pre-trained ELC-BERT models, online.[1]

STRICT-SMALL track (10M words)

Model	BLiMP	GLUE	MSGS	Average
ELC-BERT *(ours)*	**75.8**	**73.7**	**29.4**	**65.9**
MLSM	72.4	70.6	17.2	60.8
Contextualizer	74.3	69.6	12.7	60.5
Baby Llama	69.8	67.6	24.7	60.1
Too Much Information	75.7	70.9	3.9	59.9

STRICT track (100M words)

Model	BLiMP	GLUE	MSGS	Average
ELC-BERT *(ours)*	**82.8**	78.3	47.2	**74.3**
Contextualizer	79.0	72.9	**58.0**	73.0
BootBERT	82.2	**78.5**	27.7	70.2
MSLM	76.2	73.5	21.4	64.4
Bad babies	77.0	67.2	23.4	63.4

Table 1: The DynaBench scores of the BabyLM challenge (Warstadt et al., 2023), the table shows the top 5 submissions in the STRICT-SMALL and STRICT tracks. Higher scores are better, the best results in each evaluation suite are boldfaced.

[1] `https://github.com/ltgoslo/elc-bert`

Proceedings of the 27th Conference on Computational Natural Language Learning: Volume 2: The BabyLM Challenge, pages 238–252
December 6-7, 2023 ©2023 Association for Computational Linguistics

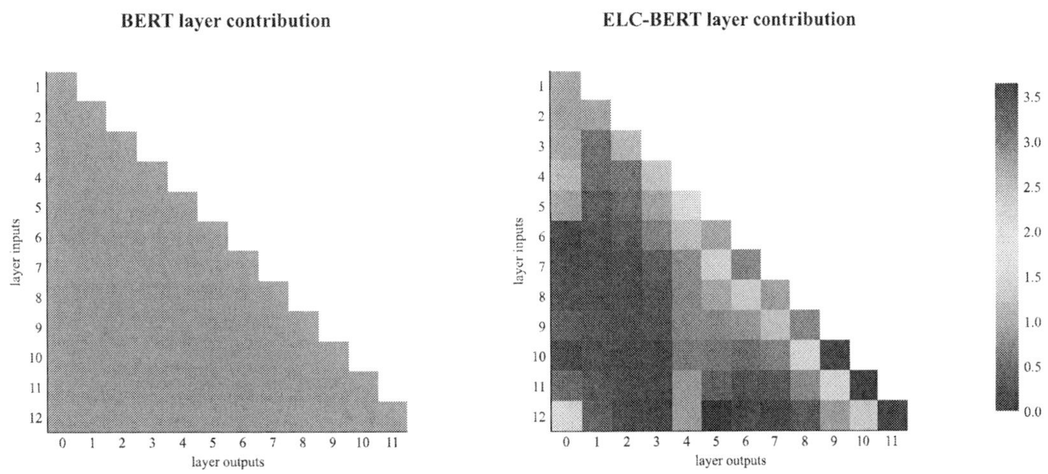

Figure 1: Every layer can select which outputs from previous layers it wants as its input, these heatmaps show the weights given to each previous layer output. The unit weights of the BERT model (and of any standard transformer-based model) are inferred from Equation (4). The right heatmap shows the α weights of the normalized ELC-BERT variant; for clear visual comparison between two the models, we rescale the α weights so that the kth row sums to k. Note that the layer 0 is the embedding layer, as in Equation (1).

2 Related work

Residual and highway networks. While the predecessor of residual models, highway networks, used a conditional gating mechanism to weigh layers (Srivastava et al., 2015), modern residual networks (including transformers) simply weigh all layers equally (He et al., 2016; Vaswani et al., 2017). Our work reintroduces layer weights into residual models – but without the computational cost of a gating mechanism.

Layer importance. The difference between various layers inside pre-trained language models has been extensively studied (Jawahar et al., 2019; Tenney et al., 2019; Niu et al., 2022). Different layers process different linguistic phenomena, thus their *importance* for downstream tasks varies – this has been successfully utilized by learning layer weights during finetuning, for example in ULMFiT (Howard and Ruder, 2018) or UDify (Kondratyuk and Straka, 2019). Following this direction, our system uses layer weights in the finetuning as well as in the pretraining phase.

ReZero transformer. A related approach to ours was proposed by Bachlechner et al. (2021). In that paper, the authors experimented with scaling the output of each layer. They showed that by initializing the scaling parameter to zero, their 'ReZero transformer' model tends towards setting the scale to $1/N$ (where N is the number of layers). Our approach can be considered as a generalization of this method – in ELC-BERT, every layer weights the outputs of previous layers *individually*.

3 ELC-BERT layer weighting

We modify the residual connections inside the transformer architecture, so that every layer can select which outputs from previous layers it wants to process – instead of always taking a simple sum of all preceding layers, as done in the Transformer (Vaswani et al., 2017) and in most works that use a variant of this architecture. This modification allows the model to form a complex inter-layer structure, as visible from Figure 1.

Transformer definition. To be more specific, we first formally define a *transformer encoder* as a function that maps subword indices $\boldsymbol{x}$ onto subword probabilities $\boldsymbol{y}$. First, $\boldsymbol{x}$ is embedded into a vector representation $\boldsymbol{h}^0_{\text{out}}$, which is then processed by N layers consisting of attention and multi-layer-perceptron (MLP) modules. Finally, $\boldsymbol{y}$ is produced by processing the final hidden representation with a language-modelling head. Formally for $n \in \{1, \dots N\}$:

$$\boldsymbol{h}^0_{\text{out}} \leftarrow \text{embedding}(\boldsymbol{x}), \tag{1}$$

$$\boldsymbol{h}^n_{\text{out}} \leftarrow \text{att}(\boldsymbol{h}^n_{\text{in}}) + \text{mlp}(\boldsymbol{h}^n_{\text{in}} + \text{att}(\boldsymbol{h}^n_{\text{in}})), \tag{2}$$

$$\boldsymbol{y} \leftarrow \text{LM\_head}(\boldsymbol{h}^N_{\text{out}}). \tag{3}$$

The original residual connection. The original transformer definition by Vaswani et al. (2017) can be recovered by simply assigning

$$\boldsymbol{h}_{\text{in}}^{n} \leftarrow \boldsymbol{h}_{\text{out}}^{n-1} + \boldsymbol{h}_{\text{in}}^{n-1}. \tag{4}$$

This recurrent assignment can also be rewritten as $\boldsymbol{h}_{\text{in}}^{n} \leftarrow \sum_{i=0}^{n-1} \boldsymbol{h}_{\text{out}}^{i}$, which highlights the implicit assumption of residual models that the output from every previous layer is equally important.

Layer weighting. In our formulation, we make two changes to the original definition: (i) the residual connections in all MLP modules are removed, (ii) the input to every layer is a convex combination of outputs from previous layers. Specifically, we replace Equation (2) and Equation (4) by:

$$\boldsymbol{h}_{\text{out}}^{n} \leftarrow \text{att}(\boldsymbol{h}_{\text{in}}^{n}) + \text{mlp}(\text{att}(\boldsymbol{h}_{\text{in}}^{n})), \tag{5}$$

$$\boldsymbol{h}_{\text{in}}^{n} \leftarrow \sum_{i=0}^{n-1} \alpha_{i,n} \boldsymbol{h}_{\text{out}}^{i}, \tag{6}$$

where $\sum_{i=0}^{n-1} \alpha_{i,n} = 1$. This constraint is satisfied by a softmax transformation of the raw learnable layer weights $\hat{\alpha}_{*,n} \in \mathbb{R}^{n}$ into $\alpha_{*,n}$. $\hat{\alpha}_{*,n}$ is initialized as a zero vector except for the value of $\hat{\alpha}_{n-1,n}$ set to one, in order to bias the weight towards the input from the previous layer.

4 Training

LTG-BERT backbone. We base our models around LTG-BERT (Samuel et al., 2023). This model has been specifically optimized for pretraining on small text corpora, similar to the one provided by BabyLM. We adopt all of their architectural modifications, their language modelling objective as well as all other pretraining settings. We also use the raw LTG-BERT (without our layer weighting) as a strong baseline in the following evaluation. Details on the pretraining hyperparameters can be found in Table 4.

BabyLM pretraining corpus. We pretrain all language models on a corpus from the BabyLM challenge (Warstadt et al., 2023). The goal of this challenge is to shed more light on data-efficient language modelling and on the question of human language acquisition. Thus, the organizers have constructed a small-scale text corpus of the same type and quantity that children learn from.

Specifically, the shared task consists of three tracks: STRICT, STRICT-SMALL and LOOSE. We participate in the first two tracks, where the submissions have to be pre-trained only on the BabyLM corpus, which corpus contains about 100M words in the STRICT track and about 10M words in the STRICT-SMALL track. We adopt the preprocessing pipeline from Samuel (2023) for unifying the format of texts from this corpus.

STRICT-SMALL track (10M words)

Model	**BLiMP**	**Supp.**	**MSGS**	**GLUE**
$\text{OPT}_{125\text{m}}$	62.6	54.7	$-0.64^{\pm 0.1}$	$68.3^{\pm 3.3}$
$\text{RoBERTa}_{\text{base}}$	69.5	47.5	$-0.67^{\pm 0.1}$	$72.2^{\pm 1.9}$
T5_{base}	58.8	43.9	$-0.68^{\pm 0.1}$	$64.7^{\pm 1.3}$
$\text{LTG-BERT}_{\text{small}}$	—	—	$\mathbf{-0.43}^{\pm 0.4}$	$74.5^{\pm 1.5}$
$\text{ELC-BERT}_{\text{small}}$	**80.5**	**67.9**	$-0.45^{\pm 0.2}$	$\mathbf{75.3}^{\pm 2.1}$

STRICT track (100M words)

Model	**BLiMP**	**Supp.**	**MSGS**	**GLUE**
$\text{OPT}_{125\text{m}}$	75.3	67.8	$-0.44^{\pm 0.1}$	$73.0^{\pm 3.9}$
$\text{RoBERTa}_{\text{base}}$	75.1	42.4	$-0.66^{\pm 0.3}$	$74.3^{\pm 0.6}$
T5_{base}	56.0	48.0	$-0.57^{\pm 0.1}$	$75.3^{\pm 1.1}$
$\text{LTG-BERT}_{\text{base}}$	**85.8**	**76.8**	$-0.42^{\pm 0.2}$	$77.9^{\pm 1.1}$
$\text{ELC-BERT}_{\text{base}}$	85.3	76.6	$\mathbf{-0.26}^{\pm 0.5}$	$\mathbf{78.3}^{\pm 3.2}$

Table 2: Results for the BabyLM challenge suite of evaluation datasets – BLiMP, supplemental dataset to BLiMP, MSGS and (Super)GLUE. We compare the results of our submitted model ($\text{ELC-BERT}_{\text{biased}}$) to the backbone model ($\text{LTG-BERT}_{\text{base}}$) and the baselines given by the organizers of the challenge on the STRICT dataset. On the STRICT-SMALL dataset, we compare a variation ($\text{ELC-BERT}_{\text{zero}}$) of small size to the backbone model and baselines.

5 Results

This section provides the results of the empirical evaluation of ELC-BERT. First, we compare our method to baselines, then we perform an ablation study of different ELC-BERT variations, and finally, we take a deeper look into the learnt layer weights.

5.1 BabyLM challenge evaluation

We adopt the BabyLM evaluation pipeline for all comparisons.[2] The pipeline itself is an adaptation of Gao et al. (2021) and it aims to provide a robust evaluation of syntactic and general language understanding.

[2] https://github.com/babylm/evaluation-pipeline

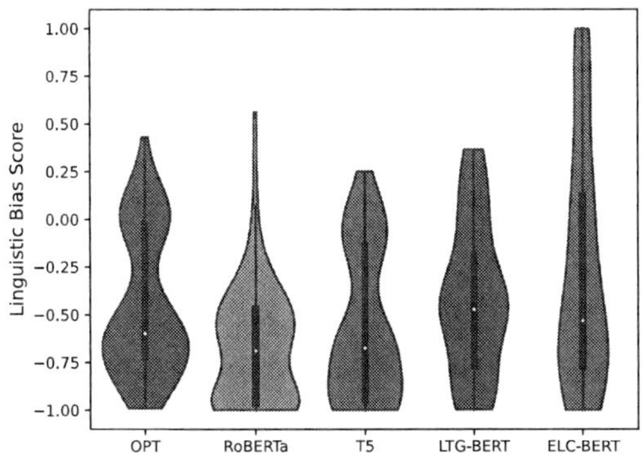

Figure 2: Violin plots of each model's Linguistic Bias Scores (LBS) and the base model. The white dot shows the median LBS and the edge of the boxes are the 1st and 3rd quartiles. The width of the violins shows the density of results at that score.

The syntactic understanding is measured by the Benchmark of Linguistic Minimal Pairs (BLiMP & BLiMP supplemental; Warstadt et al., 2020a) and the Mixed Signals Generalization Set (MSGS; Warstadt et al., 2020b). The general natural language understanding is measured by GLUE and SuperGLUE (Wang et al., 2018, 2019). All of these benchmarks use filtered subsets of the original datasets (provided by the organizers), which means that they are not directly comparable to previous literature. If applicable, we divide the training set into a train-development split and report the mean/std statistics over multiple runs on the former validation split.

BLiMP. This benchmark tests zero-shot preference of grammatical sentences. From the STRICT results in Table 2, we see that ELC-BERT outperforms the baseline models by a fair margin on this task. However, if we look at the LTG-BERT baseline, we see that our model slightly underperforms it (by 0.5 percentage points). Table 7 provides a more in-depth comparison of the models.

If we now look at the supplemental scores in, we see a very similar trend to the BLiMP results: our model outperforms the baseline RoBERTa model by 24.4 p.p. while slightly underperforming against the LTG-BERT model by 0.2 p.p. Table 8 shows a breakdown of the aggregated scores.

GLUE. A standard LM benchmark that tests the ability to be finetuned for general language understanding tasks. Focusing on the results in Table 2, we see that our model outperforms both the encoder baseline and the LTG-BERT model in the STRICT and STRIC-SMALL tracks. The improvement against LTG-BERT is rather modest and could be caused by random variation. If we look at Table 9 we see that the variation is greatly affected by the WSC task – ignoring it, we get a score of $80.49^{\pm1.44}$ for our model and $79.52^{\pm1.13}$ for LTG-BERT.

MSGS. Finally, this benchmark evaluates the preference towards linguistic explanations over spurious surface explanations. For the aggregated STRICT MSGS results of Table 2, the comparison appears unclear due to the large standard deviation. However, a closer inspection reveals that ELC-BERT *significantly* outperforms LTG-BERT by 0.16 LBS points.[3] Figure 2 and Table 10 shows a detailed view on the score distribution.

Shared task results. The official Dynabench results for the top-5 models for the STRICT and STRICT-SMALL track can be found in Table 1. Looking first at the STRICT track results, we see that our model achieves the highest total score and BLiMP score, while we are second for GLUE and MSGS. On the STRICT-SMALL track our model performs best on all benchmarks and by a substantial margin for all benchmarks.

5.2 Model variations

We compare the following modifications of the ELC-BERT architecture from Section 3:

1. **Zero initialization**: The layer weights are all initialized as zeros, without any bias towards the previous layer. This model also uses the residual MLP input from Equation (2). This variation is used in the STRICT-SMALL track.

2. **Strict normalization**: This follows the previous variant with every $\boldsymbol{h}^i_{\text{out}}$ normalized to a unit vector.

3. **Weighted output**: Follows the first variant and the input to the LM head is a weighted sum of all layers. To be more concrete, we replace Equation (3) by $\boldsymbol{y} \leftarrow \text{LM\_head}\left(\sum_{i=0}^{N} \alpha_{i,N+1}\boldsymbol{h}^i_{\text{out}}\right)$.

[3]Using the Almost Stochastic Order (ASO) significance test from Dror et al. (2019) and Del Barrio et al. (2018) (calculated using Ulmer et al. (2022)), we get a $\varepsilon_{\min}$ of 0.2 at a confidence level of 0.95 which implies that there is a high likelihood that ELC-BERT is better than LTG-BERT.

Model	BLiMP	Supp.	MSGS	GLUE
ELC-BERT	85.3	76.6	-0.26$^{\pm0.5}$	78.3$^{\pm3.2}$
+ zero initialization	84.9	**78.5**	-0.38$^{\pm0.3}$	**79.4**$^{\pm1.0}$
+ normalization	85.1	76.0	**-0.13**$^{\pm0.4}$	78.2$^{\pm3.3}$
+ weighted output	**86.1**	76.0	-0.28$^{\pm0.2}$	78.2$^{\pm0.6}$

Table 3: Results for the BabyLM challenge suite of evaluation datasets. We compare the performance of different variants of our model to the one submitted to the BabyLM challenge as well as the backbone model LTG-BERT on the STRICT dataset.

Evaluation. Based on Table 3, we see that different variations have varying effects on the evaluation scores.

When changing the $\hat{\alpha}$ initialization to zero, we see a significant increase in performance on both the BLiMP Supplemental and the GLUE benchmarks.[4] However, the model suffers in performance on both the BLiMP and MSGS.[5] Overall, we see that this variation leads to better zero-shot and fine-tuning results while biasing the model more towards spurious surface features rather than linguistic features, as can be seen in Figure 3.

If we then focus on the normalization variation, we see that it underperforms in all benchmarks but one, MSGS, where it significantly performs better by 0.13 LBS points,[6] as can be seen in more detail in Figure 3.

Finally, when looking at our weighted output variation, we see a substantial gain in performance on the BLiMP benchmark while the results on MSGS and GLUE are similar, and the results on Supplemental BLiMP slightly decrease. More detailed results on all these benchmarks can be found in Appendix D.

5.3 Layer importance

The empirical evaluation suggests that learnable layer weights are a simple but effective architectural change – but how do these learnt weights look like? In this section, we investigate the α values of the normalized ELC-BERT variant.[7]

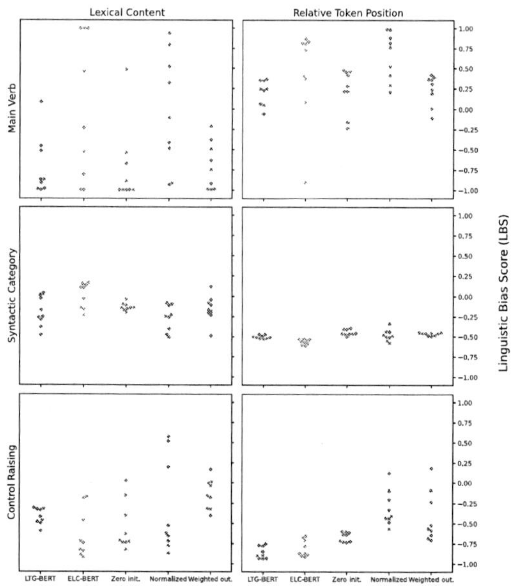

Figure 3: Detailed LBS for each model and each combination of surface and linguistic features. The Y-axis (Main Verb, Syntactic Category, and Control Raising) show the linguistic features, while the X-axis (Lexical Content, Relative Token Position) represent the surface features. Each dot represents a different fine-tuned model.

Looking at the importance matrix of ELC-BERT in Figure 1, we posit that the first 5 layers focus on surface-level information found in the embedding layer explaining its enhanced importance for the embedding layer. The next 5 layers (6-10) focus on more linguistic features by virtually ignoring the first 4 layers (0-3) and focusing primarily on the previous three layers as well as layers 4 and 5 to get some transformed information from the embedding layer. Layer 11 does much the same but focuses more on Layer 4, potentially trying to obtain some surface knowledge found in it. Finally, Layer 12 behaves similarly to Layer 11 but also puts high importance (3rd most) on the embedding layer. This is most likely to recuperate some surface information lost in previous layers to pass to the language modelling head.

6 Conclusion

In this paper, we proposed a novel and simple modification of the transformer architecture for language modelling. We empirically tested the efficacy of our approach by participating in the BabyLM challenge – a shared task for data-efficient language modelling. Our submission ranked first on both

[4]The increase in performance on the GLUE benchmark is significant when using the ASO significance test both against the original ELC-BERT and the backbone model LTG-BERT. Against both models, we get a $\varepsilon_{\min}$ of 0, indicating a very strong likelihood that the zero variation is better than ELC-BERT and LTG-BERT on GLUE

[5]This is a significant decrease with an $\varepsilon_{\min}$ of 0.28 that ELC-BERT is better.

[6]Significant with an $\varepsilon_{\min}$ of 0.31.

[7]The interpretation of α weights in a non-normalized variant is difficult due to different magnitudes of layer outputs.

tracks that we participated in. A more detailed evaluation shows that, when compared to a strong baseline, our approach reliably performs better on (Super)GLUE tasks. The evaluation on MSGS suggests that our approach is more likely to prefer linguistic features over spurious surface features, and the BLiMP benchmarks show comparable performance to the baseline. Finally, our proposed modification shows that the assumption that all layers are equally important is incorrect, and a more complex layer structure helps the model.

Acknowledgements

The efforts described in the current paper were funded by the HPLT project (High-Performance Language Technologies; coordinated by Charles University). The computations were performed on resources provided through Sigma2 – the national research infrastructure provider for High-Performance Computing and large-scale data storage in Norway.

References

Ahmed Abdelali, Francisco Guzman, Hassan Sajjad, and Stephan Vogel. 2014. The AMARA corpus: Building parallel language resources for the educational domain. In *Proceedings of the Ninth International Conference on Language Resources and Evaluation (LREC'14)*, Reykjavik, Iceland. European Language Resources Association (ELRA).

Thomas Bachlechner, Bodhisattwa Prasad Majumder, Henry Mao, Gary Cottrell, and Julian McAuley. 2021. Rezero is all you need: Fast convergence at large depth. In *Uncertainty in Artificial Intelligence*, pages 1352–1361. PMLR.

Roy Bar-Haim, Ido Dagan, Bill Dolan, Lisa Ferro, and Danilo Giampiccolo. 2006. The second pascal recognising textual entailment challenge. *Proceedings of the Second PASCAL Challenges Workshop on Recognising Textual Entailment.*

Luisa Bentivogli, Ido Dagan, Hoa Trang Dang, Danilo Giampiccolo, and Bernardo Magnini. 2009. The fifth pascal recognizing textual entailment challenge. In *In Proc Text Analysis Conference (TAC'09.*

Tom Brown, Benjamin Mann, Nick Ryder, Melanie Subbiah, Jared D Kaplan, Prafulla Dhariwal, Arvind Neelakantan, Pranav Shyam, Girish Sastry, Amanda Askell, Sandhini Agarwal, Ariel Herbert-Voss, Gretchen Krueger, Tom Henighan, Rewon Child, Aditya Ramesh, Daniel Ziegler, Jeffrey Wu, Clemens Winter, Chris Hesse, Mark Chen, Eric Sigler, Mateusz Litwin, Scott Gray, Benjamin Chess, Jack Clark, Christopher Berner, Sam McCandlish, Alec Radford, Ilya Sutskever, and Dario Amodei. 2020. Language models are few-shot learners. In *Advances in Neural Information Processing Systems*, volume 33, pages 1877–1901. Curran Associates, Inc.

Christopher Clark, Kenton Lee, Ming-Wei Chang, Tom Kwiatkowski, Michael Collins, and Kristina Toutanova. 2019. BoolQ: Exploring the surprising difficulty of natural yes/no questions. In *Proceedings of the 2019 Conference of the North American Chapter of the Association for Computational Linguistics: Human Language Technologies, Volume 1 (Long and Short Papers)*, pages 2924–2936, Minneapolis, Minnesota. Association for Computational Linguistics.

Ido Dagan, Oren Glickman, and Bernardo Magnini. 2006. The pascal recognising textual entailment challenge. In *Machine Learning Challenges. Evaluating Predictive Uncertainty, Visual Object Classification, and Recognising Tectual Entailment*, pages 177–190, Berlin, Heidelberg. Springer Berlin Heidelberg.

Eustasio Del Barrio, Juan A Cuesta-Albertos, and Carlos Matrán. 2018. An optimal transportation approach for assessing almost stochastic order. In *The Mathematics of the Uncertain*, pages 33–44. Springer.

Jacob Devlin, Ming-Wei Chang, Kenton Lee, and Kristina Toutanova. 2019. BERT: Pre-training of deep bidirectional transformers for language understanding. In *Proceedings of the 2019 Conference of the North American Chapter of the Association for Computational Linguistics: Human Language Technologies, Volume 1 (Long and Short Papers)*, pages 4171–4186, Minneapolis, Minnesota. Association for Computational Linguistics.

William B. Dolan and Chris Brockett. 2005. Automatically constructing a corpus of sentential paraphrases. In *Proceedings of the Third International Workshop on Paraphrasing (IWP2005)*.

Rotem Dror, Segev Shlomov, and Roi Reichart. 2019. Deep dominance - how to properly compare deep neural models. In *Proceedings of the 57th Annual Meeting of the Association for Computational Linguistics*, pages 2773–2785, Florence, Italy. Association for Computational Linguistics.

Leo Gao, Jonathan Tow, Stella Biderman, Sid Black, Anthony DiPofi, Charles Foster, Laurence Golding, Jeffrey Hsu, Kyle McDonell, Niklas Muennighoff, Jason Phang, Laria Reynolds, Eric Tang, Anish Thite, Ben Wang, Kevin Wang, and Andy Zou. 2021. A framework for few-shot language model evaluation.

Martin Gerlach and Francesc Font-Clos. 2018. A standardized Project Gutenberg corpus for statistical analysis of natural language and quantitative linguistics. *Computing Research Repository*, arXiv:1812.08092.

Danilo Giampiccolo, Bernardo Magnini, Ido Dagan, and Bill Dolan. 2007. The third PASCAL recognizing textual entailment challenge. In *Proceedings of the ACL-PASCAL Workshop on Textual Entailment and Paraphrasing*, pages 1–9, Prague. Association for Computational Linguistics.

Kaiming He, Xiangyu Zhang, Shaoqing Ren, and Jian Sun. 2016. Deep Residual Learning for Image Recognition. In *Proceedings of 2016 IEEE Conference on Computer Vision and Pattern Recognition*, CVPR '16, pages 770–778. IEEE.

Felix Hill, Antoine Bordes, Sumit Chopra, and Jason Weston. 2016. The Goldilocks principle: Reading children's books with explicit memory representations.

Jeremy Howard and Sebastian Ruder. 2018. Universal language model fine-tuning for text classification. In *Proceedings of the 56th Annual Meeting of the Association for Computational Linguistics (Volume 1: Long Papers)*, pages 328–339, Melbourne, Australia. Association for Computational Linguistics.

Ganesh Jawahar, Benoît Sagot, and Djamé Seddah. 2019. What does BERT learn about the structure of language? In *Proceedings of the 57th Annual Meeting of the Association for Computational Linguistics*, pages 3651–3657, Florence, Italy. Association for Computational Linguistics.

Pratik Joshi, Sebastin Santy, Amar Budhiraja, Kalika Bali, and Monojit Choudhury. 2020. The state and fate of linguistic diversity and inclusion in the NLP world. In *Proceedings of the 58th Annual Meeting of the Association for Computational Linguistics*, pages 6282–6293, Online. Association for Computational Linguistics.

Daniel Khashabi, Snigdha Chaturvedi, Michael Roth, Shyam Upadhyay, and Dan Roth. 2018. Looking beyond the surface: A challenge set for reading comprehension over multiple sentences. In *Proceedings of the 2018 Conference of the North American Chapter of the Association for Computational Linguistics: Human Language Technologies, Volume 1 (Long Papers)*, pages 252–262, New Orleans, Louisiana. Association for Computational Linguistics.

Dan Kondratyuk and Milan Straka. 2019. 75 languages, 1 model: Parsing Universal Dependencies universally. In *Proceedings of the 2019 Conference on Empirical Methods in Natural Language Processing and the 9th International Joint Conference on Natural Language Processing (EMNLP-IJCNLP)*, pages 2779–2795, Hong Kong, China. Association for Computational Linguistics.

Hector J. Levesque, Ernest Davis, and Leora Morgenstern. 2012. The winograd schema challenge. In *Proceedings of the Thirteenth International Conference on Principles of Knowledge Representation and Reasoning*, KR'12, page 552–561. AAAI Press.

Pierre Lison and Jörg Tiedemann. 2016. OpenSubtitles2016: Extracting large parallel corpora from movie and TV subtitles. In *Proceedings of the Tenth International Conference on Language Resources and Evaluation (LREC'16)*, pages 923–929, Portorož, Slovenia. European Language Resources Association (ELRA).

Brian MacWhinney. 2000. *The CHILDES project: The database*, volume 2. Psychology Press.

B.W. Matthews. 1975. Comparison of the predicted and observed secondary structure of t4 phage lysozyme. *Biochimica et Biophysica Acta (BBA) - Protein Structure*, 405(2):442–451.

Jingcheng Niu, Wenjie Lu, and Gerald Penn. 2022. Does BERT rediscover a classical NLP pipeline? In *Proceedings of the 29th International Conference on Computational Linguistics*, pages 3143–3153, Gyeongju, Republic of Korea. International Committee on Computational Linguistics.

Colin Raffel, Noam Shazeer, Adam Roberts, Katherine Lee, Sharan Narang, Michael Matena, Yanqi Zhou, Wei Li, and Peter J. Liu. 2020. Exploring the limits of transfer learning with a unified text-to-text transformer. *Journal of Machine Learning Research*, 21(140):1–67.

Pranav Rajpurkar, Jian Zhang, Konstantin Lopyrev, and Percy Liang. 2016. SQuAD: 100,000+ questions for machine comprehension of text. In *Proceedings of the 2016 Conference on Empirical Methods in Natural Language Processing*, pages 2383–2392, Austin, Texas. Association for Computational Linguistics.

David Samuel. 2023. Mean berts make erratic language teachers: the effectiveness of latent bootstrapping in low-resource settings.

David Samuel, Andrey Kutuzov, Lilja Øvrelid, and Erik Velldal. 2023. Trained on 100 million words and still in shape: BERT meets British National Corpus. In *Findings of the Association for Computational Linguistics: EACL 2023*, pages 1954–1974, Dubrovnik, Croatia. Association for Computational Linguistics.

Richard Socher, Alex Perelygin, Jean Wu, Jason Chuang, Christopher D. Manning, Andrew Ng, and Christopher Potts. 2013. Recursive deep models for semantic compositionality over a sentiment treebank. In *Proceedings of the 2013 Conference on Empirical Methods in Natural Language Processing*, pages 1631–1642, Seattle, Washington, USA. Association for Computational Linguistics.

Rupesh K Srivastava, Klaus Greff, and Jürgen Schmidhuber. 2015. Training very deep networks. In *Advances in Neural Information Processing Systems*, volume 28. Curran Associates, Inc.

Andreas Stolcke, Klaus Ries, Noah Coccaro, Elizabeth Shriberg, Rebecca Bates, Daniel Jurafsky, Paul Taylor, Rachel Martin, Marie Meteer, and Carol Van Ess-Dykema. 2000. Dialogue act modeling for automatic tagging and recognition of conversational speech. *Computational Linguistics*, 26(3):339–371.

Emma Strubell, Ananya Ganesh, and Andrew McCallum. 2019. Energy and policy considerations for deep learning in NLP. In *Proceedings of the 57th Annual Meeting of the Association for Computational Linguistics*, pages 3645–3650, Florence, Italy. Association for Computational Linguistics.

Ian Tenney, Dipanjan Das, and Ellie Pavlick. 2019. BERT rediscovers the classical NLP pipeline. In *Proceedings of the 57th Annual Meeting of the Association for Computational Linguistics*, pages 4593–4601, Florence, Italy. Association for Computational Linguistics.

Neil C. Thompson, Kristjan Greenewald, Keeheon Lee, and Gabriel F. Manso. 2020. The computational limits of deep learning.

Dennis Ulmer, Christian Hardmeier, and Jes Frellsen. 2022. deep-significance: Easy and meaningful signifcance testing in the age of neural networks. In *ML Evaluation Standards Workshop at the Tenth International Conference on Learning Representations*.

Ashish Vaswani, Noam Shazeer, Niki Parmar, Jakob Uszkoreit, Llion Jones, Aidan N Gomez, Łukasz Kaiser, and Illia Polosukhin. 2017. Attention is all you need. *Advances in neural information processing systems*, 30.

Alex Wang, Yada Pruksachatkun, Nikita Nangia, Amanpreet Singh, Julian Michael, Felix Hill, Omer Levy, and Samuel Bowman. 2019. Superglue: A stickier benchmark for general-purpose language understanding systems. In *Advances in Neural Information Processing Systems*, volume 32. Curran Associates, Inc.

Alex Wang, Amanpreet Singh, Julian Michael, Felix Hill, Omer Levy, and Samuel Bowman. 2018. GLUE: A multi-task benchmark and analysis platform for natural language understanding. In *Proceedings of the 2018 EMNLP Workshop BlackboxNLP: Analyzing and Interpreting Neural Networks for NLP*, pages 353–355, Brussels, Belgium. Association for Computational Linguistics.

Alex Warstadt, Aaron Mueller, Leshem Choshen, Ethan Gotlieb Wilcox, Chengxu Zhuang, Juan Ciro, Rafael Mosquera, Adina Williams, Bhargavi Paranjabe, Tal Linzen, and Ryan Cotterell. 2023. Findings of the 2023 BabyLM Challenge: Sample-efficient pretraining on developmentally plausible corpora. In *Proceedings of the 2023 BabyLM Challenge*. Association for Computational Linguistics (ACL).

Alex Warstadt, Alicia Parrish, Haokun Liu, Anhad Mohananey, Wei Peng, Sheng-Fu Wang, and Samuel R Bowman. 2020a. Blimp: The benchmark of linguistic minimal pairs for english. *Transactions of the Association for Computational Linguistics*, 8:377–392.

Alex Warstadt, Amanpreet Singh, and Samuel R. Bowman. 2019. Neural network acceptability judgments. *Transactions of the Association for Computational Linguistics*, 7:625–641.

Alex Warstadt, Yian Zhang, Haau-Sing Li, Haokun Liu, and Samuel R Bowman. 2020b. Learning which features matter: Roberta acquires a preference for linguistic generalizations (eventually). *arXiv preprint arXiv:2010.05358*.

Adina Williams, Nikita Nangia, and Samuel Bowman. 2018. A broad-coverage challenge corpus for sentence understanding through inference. In *Proceedings of the 2018 Conference of the North American Chapter of the Association for Computational Linguistics: Human Language Technologies, Volume 1 (Long Papers)*, pages 1112–1122, New Orleans, Louisiana. Association for Computational Linguistics.

A Pre-training details

Hyperparameter	Base	Small	Small (Submitted Model)
Number of parameters	98M	24M	24M
Number of layers	12	12	12
Hidden size	768	384	384
FF intermediate size	2 048	1 024	1 024
Vocabulary size	16 384	6 144	6 144
Attention heads	12	6	6
Hidden dropout	0.1	0.1	0.1
Attention dropout	0.1	0.1	0.1
Training steps	15 625	15 625	31 250
Batch size	32 768	32 768	8 096
Initial Sequence length	128	128	128
Initial Sequence length	512	512	512
Warmup ratio	1.6%	1.6%	1.6%
Initial learning rate	0.01	0.0141	0.005
Final learning rate	0.001	0.00141	0.005
Learning rate scheduler	cosine	cosine	cosine
Weight decay	0.1	0.4	0.4
Layer norm ϵ	1e-7	1e-7	1e-7
Optimizer	LAMB	LAMB	LAMB
LAMB ϵ	1e-6	1e-6	1e-6
LAMB β_1	0.9	0.9	0.9
LAMB β_2	0.98	0.98	0.98
Gradient clipping	2.0	2.0	2.0

Table 4: Pre-training hyperparameters for the small-sized models (trained on STRICT-SMALL) and for the base-sized models (trained on the STRICT track).

B Fine-tuning details

For the fine-tuning experiments, we will run multiple seeds and (for MSGS) multiple learning rates, to be able to get a more robust comparison of model performance. The detailed hyperparameters for fine-tuning can be found in Table 5.

B.0.1 GLUE

To finetune, we will use 5 different seeds: 12, 642, 369, 1267, and 2395. We will use a validation set to find our best model with early-stopping, and then test our model on a test set (here the validation set is 10% of the training sets from `https://github.com/babylm/evaluation-pipeline` and the test set is their validation set).

B.0.2 MSGS

To finetune, we use three different random seeds: 12, 369, and 2395, as well as three different learning rates: 1e-5, 2e-5, and 3e-5. In addition, we train for 5 epochs, with a batch size of 16 with no early stopping.

Hyperparameter	**QQP, MNLI QNLI, SST-2**	**CoLA, RTE, WSC MRPC, MultiRC**	**MSGS**
Batch size	32	16	16
Number of epochs	10	10	5
Dropout	0.1	0.1	0.1
Warmup steps	10%	1%	6%
Peak learning rate	5e-5	7e-5	{1e-5, 2e-5, 3e-5}
Learning rate decay	cosine	cosine	linear
Weight decay	0.1	0.1	0.1
Optimizer	AdamW	AdamW	AdamW
Adam ϵ	1e-8	1e-8	1e-8
Adam β_1	0.9	0.9	0.9
Adam β_2	0.999	0.999	0.999

Table 5: Hyperparameters for fine-tuning the GLUE, SuperGLUE task and MSGS tasks. We use the same hyperparameters for all ELC-BERT models, not performing any per-model hyperparameter search. The values for MSGS are adopted from (Warstadt et al., 2020b). For all models, we measure the statistics over 5 random seeds for GLUE tasks: 12, 642, 369, 1267, and 2395; and 3 seeds for MSGS tasks: 12, 369, and 2395

C BabyLM dataset

Table 6 is a detailed overview of the BabyLM dataset:

Dataset	Domain	# Words STRICT-SMALL	# Words STRICT	Proportion
CHILDES (MacWhinney, 2000)	Child-directed speech	0.44M	4.21M	5%
British National Corpus (BNC),[1] dialogue portion	Dialogue	0.86M	8.16M	8%
Children's Book Test (Hill et al., 2016)	Children's books	0.57M	5.55M	6%
Children's Stories Text Corpus[2]	Children's books	0.34M	3.22M	3%
Standardized Project Gutenberg Corpus (Gerlach and Font-Clos, 2018)	Written English	0.99M	9.46M	10%
OpenSubtitles (Lison and Tiedemann, 2016)	Movie subtitles	3.09M	31.28M	31%
QCRI Educational Domain Corpus (QED; Abdelali et al., 2014)	Educational video subtitles	1.04M	10.24M	11%
Wikipedia[3]	Wikipedia (English)	0.99M	10.08M	10%
Simple Wikipedia[4]	Wikipedia (Simple English)	1.52M	14.66M	15%
Switchboard Dialog Act Corpus (Stolcke et al., 2000)	Dialogue	0.12M	1.18M	1%
Total	–	9.96M	98.04M	100%

Table 6: The contents of datasets for the the STRICT and STRICT-SMALL tracks; the table is taken from Warstadt et al. (2023). [1]`http://www.natcorp.ox.ac.uk` [2]`https://www.kaggle.com/datasets/edenbd/children-stories-text-corpus` [3]`https://dumps.wikimedia.org/enwiki/20221220/` [4]`https://dumps.wikimedia.org/simplewiki/20221201/`

D Detailed Results

This section breaks down the aggregate scores of the benchmarks into their composing tasks. It also describes or name each task

D.1 BLiMP

The BabyLM challenge uses the BLiMP benchmark (Warstadt et al., 2020a) to evaluate the syntactic understanding of the models. Our detailed results can be found in Table 7. Its composing tasks are as follows (with descriptions taken from Warstadt et al. (2020a)):

- ANAPHOR AGREEMENT (AA): the requirement that reflexive pronouns like *herself* (also known as anaphora) agree with their antecedents in person, number, gender, and animacy.
- ARGUMENT STRUCTURE (AS): the ability of different verbs to appear with different types of arguments. For instance, different verbs can appear with a direct object, participate in the causative alternation, or take an inanimate argument.
- BINDING (B): the structural relationship between a pronoun and its antecedent.
- CONTROL/RAISING (CR): syntactic and semantic differences between various types of predicates that embed an infinitival VP. This includes control, raising, and *tough*-movement predicates.
- DETERMINER-NOUN AGREEMENT (DNA): number agreement between demonstrative determiners (e.g., *this/these*) and the associated noun.
- ELLIPSIS (E): the possibility of omitting expressions from a sentence. Because this is difficult to illustrate with sentences of equal length, our paradigms cover only special cases of noun phrase ellipsis that meet this constraint.
- FILLER-GAP (FG): dependencies arising from phrasal movement in, for example, *wh*-questions.
- IRREGULAR FORMS (IF): irregular morphology on English past participles (e.g., *awoken*).
- ISLAND EFFECTS (IE): restrictions on syntactic environments where the gap in a filler-gap dependency may occur.

- NPI LICENSING (NL): restrictions on the distribution of *negative polarity items* like *any* and *ever* limited to, for example, the scope of negation and *only*.
- QUANTIFIERS (Q): restrictions on the distribution of quantifiers. Two such restrictions are covered: superlative quantifiers (e.g., *at least*) cannot be embedded under negation, and definite quantifiers and determiners cannot be subjects in existential-*there* constructions.
- SUBJECT-VERB AGREEMENT (SVA): subjects and present tense verbs must agree in number.

Model	AA	AS	B	CR	DNA	E	FG	IF	IE	NL	Q	SVA	Average
STRICT (100M words)													
OPT_{125M}	94.9	73.8	73.8	72.2	93.1	80.5	73.6	80.8	57.8	51.6	74.5	77.3	75.3
$RoBERTa_{base}$	89.5	71.3	71.0	67.1	93.1	83.8	68.0	89.6	54.5	66.3	70.3	76.2	75.1
$T5_{base}$	66.7	61.2	59.4	59.8	53.8	49.1	70.0	75.5	43.6	45.6	34.2	53.2	56.0
$LTG\text{-}BERT_{base}$	**96.1**	79.5	**77.1**	80.3	95.4	**91.7**	87.8	94.5	79.8	84.4	72.2	**91.2**	85.8
$ELC\text{-}BERT_{base}$	92.8	**81.2**	74.0	79.2	**96.0**	**91.7**	87.1	93.6	**83.9**	83.5	70.2	90.8	85.3
+ zero initialization	93.8	79.1	73.6	79.8	95.5	91.0	87.1	93.3	78.8	84.8	**73.5**	88.7	84.9
+ normalization	93.0	79.1	74.6	79.8	95.6	**91.7**	87.4	93.9	82.0	83.7	71.3	89.1	85.1
+ weighted output	94.7	80.7	75.7	**81.3**	95.7	91.6	**88.9**	**95.9**	83.2	**85.7**	69.2	91.1	**86.1**
STRICT-SMALL (10M words)													
OPT_{125M}	63.8	70.6	67.1	66.5	78.5	62.0	63.8	67.5	48.6	46.7	59.6	56.9	62.6
$RoBERTa_{base}$	81.5	67.1	67.3	67.9	90.8	76.4	63.5	87.4	39.9	55.9	70.5	65.4	69.5
$T5_{base}$	68.9	63.8	60.4	60.9	72.2	34.4	48.2	77.6	45.6	47.8	61.2	65.0	58.8
$ELC\text{-}BERT_{small}$	89.5	**72.5**	**68.1**	**72.6**	93.4	87.4	**80.6**	**91.0**	**67.9**	79.4	**75.2**	**88.7**	**80.5**

Table 7: BLiMP results for models trained both on the 100M (above the mid-horizontal line) and the 10M (below the mid-horizontal line) Baby LM dataset. The **bold** results represent the best model for the task. The metric used to measure is accuracy. The results are in percentage.

D.2 BLiMP Supplemental

Model	Hypernym	QA Congruence Easy	QA Congruence Tricky	Subject Aux Inversion	Turn Talking	Average
STRICT (100M words)						
OPT_{125M}	46.3	76.5	47.9	85.3	82.9	67.8
$RoBERTa_{base}$	50.8	34.4	34.5	45.6	46.8	42.4
$T5_{base}$	**51.1**	45.3	25.5	69.2	48.9	48.0
$LTG\text{-}BERT_{base}$	47.0	90.6	60.6	90.7	92.1	76.8
$ELC\text{-}BERT_{base}$	47.3	85.9	63.0	94.5	92.1	76.6
+ zero initialization	47.1	**92.2**	**64.2**	95.9	**93.2**	**78.5**
+ normalization	46.1	85.9	59.4	**96.5**	92.1	76.0
+ weighted output	48.6	87.5	57.6	96.2	90.4	76.0
STRICT-SMALL (10M words)						
OPT_{125M}	**50.0**	54.7	31.5	80.3	57.1	54.7
$RoBERTa_{base}$	49.4	31.3	32.1	71.7	53.2	47.5
$T5_{base}$	48.0	40.6	21.2	64.9	45.0	43.9
$ELC\text{-}BERT_{small}$	48.0	**73.4**	**43.6**	**90.0**	**84.3**	**67.9**

Table 8: BLiMP supplemental results for models trained both on the 100M (above the mid-horizontal line) and the 10M (below the mid-horizontal line) Baby LM dataset. The **bold** results represent the best model for the task. The metric used to measure is accuracy. The results are in percentage.

D.3 GLUE

The BabyLM challenge involves slightly modified GLUE and SuperGLUE benchmarks. It uses only a subset of the subtasks, the datasets are filtered so that they do not contain out-of-vocabulary words, and it sometimes uses non-standard metrics. Our detailed results can be found in Table 9. We list all subtasks and their metrics below:

- **Boolean Questions** (BoolQ; Clark et al., 2019), a yes/no Q/A dataset evaluated with accuracy.
- **Corpus of Linguistic Acceptability** (CoLA; Warstadt et al., 2019) evaluated with accuracy (originally evaluated with the Matthews correlation coefficient (MCC; Matthews, 1975)).
- **The Multi-Genre Natural Language Inference Corpus** (MNLI; Williams et al., 2018). Its development set consists of two parts: *matched*, sampled from the same data source as the training set, and *mismatched*, which is sampled from a different domain. Both parts are evaluated with accuracy.
- **The Microsoft Research Paraphrase Corpus** (MRPC; Dolan and Brockett, 2005), evaluated with both F_1-score (originally also evaluated with accuracy).
- **Multi-Sentence Reading Comprehension** (MultiRC; Khashabi et al., 2018), a multiple choice question answering dataset, evaluated with accuracy (originally evaluated with the exact match accuracy (EM) and F_1-score (over all answer options)).
- **Question-answering Natural Language Inference** (QNLI) constructed from the Stanford Question Answering Dataset (SQuAD; Rajpurkar et al., 2016), evaluated with accuracy.
- **The Quora Question Pairs** (QQP),[8] evaluated with F_1-score (originally evaluated with accuracy).
- **The Stanford Sentiment Treebank** (SST-2; Socher et al., 2013), evaluated with accuracy.
- **The Recognizing Textual Entailment datasets** (RTE; Dagan et al., 2006; Bar-Haim et al., 2006; Giampiccolo et al., 2007; Bentivogli et al., 2009), evaluated with accuracy.
- **Winograd Schema Challenge** (WSC; Levesque et al., 2012) evaluated with accuracy.

Model	CoLA	SST-2	MRPC	QQP	$MNLI_m$	$MNLI_{mm}$	QNLI	RTE	BoolQ	MultiRC	WSC	Average
STRICT (100M words)												
OPT_{125m}	$74.9^{\pm0.6}$	$87.7^{\pm0.7}$	$81.9^{\pm0.7}$	$84.3^{\pm0.1}$	$75.7^{\pm0.3}$	$77.0^{\pm0.3}$	$82.8^{\pm0.8}$	$58.6^{\pm2.9}$	$66.4^{\pm0.7}$	$61.5^{\pm0.8}$	$52.3^{\pm12.5}$	$73.0^{\pm3.9}$
$RoBERTa_{base}$	$75.6^{\pm0.3}$	$88.3^{\pm0.6}$	$84.0^{\pm0.5}$	$85.5^{\pm0.2}$	$77.4^{\pm0.4}$	$78.3^{\pm0.3}$	$83.6^{\pm0.2}$	$50.7^{\pm1.5}$	$67.7^{\pm0.7}$	$64.3^{\pm0.5}$	$61.4^{\pm0.0}$	$74.3^{\pm0.6}$
$T5_{base}$	$76.7^{\pm0.9}$	$89.0^{\pm0.8}$	$85.2^{\pm1.1}$	$86.2^{\pm0.1}$	$77.9^{\pm0.3}$	$78.7^{\pm0.3}$	$84.7^{\pm0.9}$	$55.4^{\pm2.2}$	$67.7^{\pm1.5}$	$65.7^{\pm0.8}$	$61.0^{\pm1.1}$	$75.3^{\pm1.1}$
$LTG\text{-}BERT_{base}$	$82.7^{\pm0.8}$	$92.0^{\pm0.4}$	$87.4^{\pm0.7}$	$87.9^{\pm0.1}$	$83.0^{\pm0.4}$	$83.4^{\pm0.5}$	$89.1^{\pm0.5}$	$54.7^{\pm2.4}$	$68.4^{\pm0.5}$	$66.0^{\pm1.4}$	$61.4^{\pm0.0}$	$77.9^{\pm1.1}$
$ELC\text{-}BERT_{base}$	$82.6^{\pm0.5}$	$91.9^{\pm1.1}$	$\mathbf{89.3}^{\pm0.6}$	$88.0^{\pm0.1}$	$83.6^{\pm0.1}$	$83.3^{\pm0.2}$	$89.4^{\pm0.4}$	$60.0^{\pm2.8}$	$70.5^{\pm1.5}$	$\mathbf{66.2}^{\pm2.2}$	$56.4^{\pm9.4}$	$78.3^{\pm3.2}$
+ zero initialization	$82.0^{\pm0.7}$	$\mathbf{92.4}^{\pm0.4}$	$88.8^{\pm1.5}$	$\mathbf{88.2}^{\pm0.1}$	$\mathbf{84.4}^{\pm0.3}$	$\mathbf{84.5}^{\pm0.3}$	$\mathbf{90.5}^{\pm0.5}$	$\mathbf{63.0}^{\pm1.5}$	$\mathbf{72.6}^{\pm1.0}$	$65.8^{\pm1.1}$	$61.4^{\pm0.0}$	$\mathbf{79.4}^{\pm1.0}$
+ normalization	$\mathbf{83.1}^{\pm0.4}$	$91.9^{\pm0.4}$	$88.6^{\pm1.3}$	$88.0^{\pm0.1}$	$84.1^{\pm0.2}$	$84.3^{\pm0.2}$	$\mathbf{90.5}^{\pm0.4}$	$56.2^{\pm2.4}$	$72.0^{\pm1.5}$	$64.9^{\pm0.6}$	$56.9^{\pm10.2}$	$78.2^{\pm3.3}$
+ weighted output	$82.6^{\pm0.6}$	$91.7^{\pm1.2}$	$87.8^{\pm1.2}$	$87.9^{\pm0.1}$	$84.0^{\pm0.4}$	$84.0^{\pm0.3}$	$89.4^{\pm0.3}$	$55.2^{\pm5.5}$	$71.0^{\pm0.8}$	$64.4^{\pm0.8}$	$\mathbf{61.7}^{\pm0.5}$	$78.2^{\pm0.6}$
STRICT-SMALL (10M words)												
OPT_{125m}	$69.0^{\pm0.5}$	$85.4^{\pm0.9}$	$80.0^{\pm1.8}$	$80.3^{\pm0.3}$	$69.5^{\pm0.2}$	$71.0^{\pm0.5}$	$71.5^{\pm0.7}$	$51.3^{\pm2.1}$	$66.2^{\pm1.5}$	$56.5^{\pm2.0}$	$50.8^{\pm10.3}$	$68.3^{\pm3.3}$
$RoBERTa_{base}$	$70.4^{\pm0.4}$	$85.6^{\pm0.3}$	$82.2^{\pm0.4}$	$83.5^{\pm0.2}$	$72.5^{\pm0.4}$	$74.4^{\pm0.3}$	$80.3^{\pm0.7}$	$\mathbf{56.8}^{\pm5.5}$	$65.8^{\pm2.9}$	$61.2^{\pm1.5}$	$\mathbf{61.7}^{\pm0.5}$	$72.2^{\pm1.9}$
$T5_{base}$	$76.7^{\pm0.9}$	$69.4^{\pm0.1}$	$81.4^{\pm0.6}$	$76.8^{\pm0.3}$	$57.3^{\pm0.8}$	$58.6^{\pm1.1}$	$64.3^{\pm0.9}$	$52.7^{\pm2.4}$	$63.4^{\pm1.6}$	$48.4^{\pm1.4}$	$60.0^{\pm2.2}$	$64.7^{\pm1.3}$
$LTG\text{-}BERT_{small}$	$\mathbf{77.6}^{\pm0.8}$	$88.8^{\pm0.8}$	$82.3^{\pm0.4}$	$85.8^{\pm0.2}$	$78.0^{\pm0.2}$	$78.8^{\pm0.4}$	$85.0^{\pm0.2}$	$53.7^{\pm4.1}$	$64.8^{\pm2.1}$	$\mathbf{64.1}^{\pm0.3}$	$60.5^{\pm1.0}$	$74.5^{\pm1.5}$
$ELC\text{-}BERT_{small}$	$76.1^{\pm1.0}$	$\mathbf{89.3}^{\pm0.5}$	$\mathbf{85.0}^{\pm1.8}$	$\mathbf{86.7}^{\pm0.3}$	$\mathbf{79.2}^{\pm0.3}$	$\mathbf{79.9}^{\pm0.2}$	$\mathbf{85.8}^{\pm0.4}$	$55.4^{\pm2.6}$	$\mathbf{69.3}^{\pm2.0}$	$62.2^{\pm1.0}$	$59.0^{\pm5.4}$	$\mathbf{75.3}^{\pm2.1}$

Table 9: A subset of GLUE results (defined by the Baby LM challenge) for both the models trained on 100M and 10M words. All the results indicate the model accuracy for the task except for MRPC and QQP where the results are based on the F1-score of the positive class. To obtain the standard deviation, each model is trained with 5 seeds, and the average accuracy/F1-score is reported. The results are reported in percentage. The **bold** result indicates the best model for each dataset.

D.4 MSGS

The BabyLM challenge uses a reduced set of the MSGS benchmark (Warstadt et al., 2020b) to evaluate whether the model biases linguistic features or surface features. A score of 1 means only using the linguistic features, while a score of -1 is surface features only. Table 10 shows the detailed results of the reduced MSGS benchmark. The first 5 results (MVC to RTPC) are controls, checking whether the

[8] https://quoradata.quora.com/First-Quora-Dataset-Release-Question-Pairs

model can recognize the feature, while the next six evaluate whether the model biases linguistic or surface features. To evaluate the performance we use the Mathews Correlation Coefficient (MCC), also called Linguistic Bias Score (LBS) for the last six tasks. The surface features in this dataset are (definitions taken from Warstadt et al. (2020b)):

- LEXICAL CONTENT (LC): This feature is 1 *iff* the sentence contains *the*.
- RELATIVE TOKEN POSITION (RTP): This feature is 1 when *the* precedes *a*, and 0 when *a* precedes *the*.

The linguistic features are (definitions taken from Warstadt et al. (2020b)):

- MAIN VERB (MV): This feature is 1 *iff* the sentence's main verb is in the *-ing* form.
- CONTROL/RAISING (CR): This feature has value 1 *iff* the sentence contains the control construction.
- SYNTACTIC CATEGORY (SC): This feature is 1 *iff* the sentence contains an adjective.

Model	MVC	CRC	SCC	LCC	RTPC	MVLC	MVRTP	CRLC	CRRTP	SCLC	SCRTP
STRICT (10M words)											
OPT_{125M}	**1.00**$^{\pm0.00}$	0.88$^{\pm0.04}$	0.36$^{\pm0.06}$	0.14$^{\pm0.04}$	0.83$^{\pm0.03}$	-0.55$^{\pm0.12}$	-0.88$^{\pm0.06}$	**-0.02**$^{\pm0.08}$	-0.73$^{\pm0.05}$	**0.11**$^{\pm0.13}$	-0.59$^{\pm0.04}$
RoBERTa_{base}	**1.00**$^{\pm0.00}$	0.75$^{\pm0.12}$	0.57$^{\pm0.22}$	**1.00**$^{\pm0.00}$	0.92$^{\pm0.07}$	-0.87$^{\pm0.41}$	-0.89$^{\pm0.13}$	-0.37$^{\pm0.34}$	-0.54$^{\pm0.13}$	-0.70$^{\pm0.27}$	-0.61$^{\pm0.19}$
T5_{base}	**1.00**$^{\pm0.00}$	0.82$^{\pm0.05}$	0.56$^{\pm0.05}$	**1.00**$^{\pm0.00}$	0.90$^{\pm0.05}$	-1.00$^{\pm0.00}$	-0.95$^{\pm0.03}$	-0.13$^{\pm0.10}$	-0.61$^{\pm0.03}$	0.03$^{\pm0.12}$	-0.73$^{\pm0.04}$
LTG-BERT_{base}	**1.00**$^{\pm0.00}$	0.83$^{\pm0.07}$	0.65$^{\pm0.08}$	**1.00**$^{\pm0.00}$	0.50$^{\pm0.06}$	-0.72$^{\pm0.36}$	0.20$^{\pm0.15}$	-0.42$^{\pm0.10}$	-0.86$^{\pm0.08}$	-0.20$^{\pm0.18}$	-0.50$^{\pm0.02}$
ELC-BERT_{base}	**1.00**$^{\pm0.00}$	0.89$^{\pm0.10}$	**0.76**$^{\pm0.07}$	**1.00**$^{\pm0.00}$	0.77$^{\pm0.11}$	**-0.01**$^{\pm0.88}$	0.44$^{\pm0.57}$	-0.64$^{\pm0.29}$	-0.81$^{\pm0.10}$	0.01$^{\pm0.15}$	-0.57$^{\pm0.03}$
+ zero initialization	0.94$^{\pm0.17}$	**0.94**$^{\pm0.02}$	0.52$^{\pm0.14}$	**1.00**$^{\pm0.00}$	0.97$^{\pm0.03}$	-0.74$^{\pm0.49}$	0.23$^{\pm0.27}$	-0.54$^{\pm0.30}$	-0.67$^{\pm0.06}$	-0.13$^{\pm0.05}$	**-0.45**$^{\pm0.04}$
+ normalization	**1.00**$^{\pm0.00}$	**0.94**$^{\pm0.01}$	0.55$^{\pm0.09}$	**1.00**$^{\pm0.00}$	**0.99**$^{\pm0.01}$	-0.03$^{\pm0.71}$	**0.65**$^{\pm0.30}$	-0.32$^{\pm0.58}$	**-0.32**$^{\pm0.22}$	-0.27$^{\pm0.16}$	-0.48$^{\pm0.07}$
+ weighted output	**1.00**$^{\pm0.00}$	0.91$^{\pm0.02}$	0.40$^{\pm0.12}$	**1.00**$^{\pm0.00}$	0.84$^{\pm0.10}$	-0.71$^{\pm0.29}$	0.24$^{\pm0.18}$	-0.14$^{\pm0.19}$	-0.43$^{\pm0.31}$	-0.15$^{\pm0.16}$	-0.47$^{\pm0.02}$
STRICT-SMALL (100M words)											
OPT_{125M}	0.97$^{\pm0.01}$	0.58$^{\pm0.06}$	**0.76**$^{\pm0.06}$	0.55$^{\pm0.12}$	**1.00**$^{\pm0.00}$	-0.91$^{\pm0.10}$	-0.98$^{\pm0.03}$	-0.35$^{\pm0.17}$	-0.73$^{\pm0.05}$	**-0.05**$^{\pm0.06}$	-0.81$^{\pm0.08}$
RoBERTa_{base}	0.97$^{\pm0.02}$	0.49$^{\pm0.05}$	0.72$^{\pm0.12}$	0.93$^{\pm0.11}$	0.91$^{\pm0.08}$	-0.99$^{\pm0.01}$	-0.94$^{\pm0.04}$	-0.30$^{\pm0.17}$	-0.48$^{\pm0.08}$	-0.37$^{\pm0.20}$	-0.93$^{\pm0.10}$
T5_{base}	0.28$^{\pm0.04}$	0.25$^{\pm0.06}$	0.72$^{\pm0.03}$	**1.00**$^{\pm0.00}$	0.87$^{\pm0.03}$	-1.00$^{\pm0.00}$	-0.87$^{\pm0.05}$	-0.39$^{\pm0.10}$	**-0.44**$^{\pm0.07}$	-0.70$^{\pm0.10}$	**-0.70**$^{\pm0.05}$
LTG-BERT_{small}	**1.00**$^{\pm0.00}$	0.71$^{\pm0.02}$	0.43$^{\pm0.14}$	**1.00**$^{\pm0.00}$	0.75$^{\pm0.11}$	**-0.18**$^{\pm0.80}$	**0.12**$^{\pm0.21}$	-0.48$^{\pm0.10}$	-0.58$^{\pm0.04}$	-0.48$^{\pm0.10}$	-0.96$^{\pm0.04}$
ELC-BERT_{small}	**1.00**$^{\pm0.00}$	**0.79**$^{\pm0.04}$	0.68$^{\pm0.08}$	0.98$^{\pm0.04}$	0.77$^{\pm0.01}$	-0.86$^{\pm0.10}$	0.00$^{\pm0.24}$	**-0.14**$^{\pm0.21}$	-0.57$^{\pm0.02}$	-0.29$^{\pm0.17}$	-0.82$^{\pm0.16}$

Table 10: A subset of MSGS results (defined by the Baby LM challenge) for both the models trained on 100M and 10M words. All the results indicate the model MCC or LBS for the non-control tasks. To obtain the standard deviation, each model is trained with 3 seeds and 3 learning rates for the STRICT dataset and for ELC-BERT_{small}, the other STRICT-SMALL datasets are trained on 5 seeds with 3 learning rates, and the average MCC/LBS is reported. The results are reported in percentage. The **bold** result indicates the best model for each dataset.

E Almost Stochastic Order Significance Tests

In this section, we put all the ASO significance tests between the backbone model LTG-BERT, ELC-BERT, and all its variations trained on the STRICT dataset for both the MSGS and GLUE benchmarks.

E.1 GLUE - STRICT dataset

Model	LTG-BERT$_{base}$	ELC-BERT$_{base}$	zero initialization	normalized	weighted output
LTG-BERT$_{base}$	–	1.00	1.00	1.00	1.00
ELC-BERT$_{base}$	0.69	–	1.00	1.00	1.00
+ zero initialization	**0.00**	**0.05**	–	**0.00**	**0.00**
+ normalization	0.90	1.00	1.00	–	1.00
+ weighted output	0.55	1.00	0.95	1.00	–

Table 11: The $\varepsilon_{\min}$ from the ASO significance test between each model on the GLUE dataset. Each row compares whether the model in the row is better than the one in the column. Results in **bold** indicate that the row model is significantly better than the one in the column.

E.2 MSGS - STRICT dataset

Model	LTG-BERT$_{base}$	ELC-BERT$_{base}$	zero initialization	normalized	weighted output
LTG-BERT$_{base}$	–	1.00	1.00	1.00	1.00
ELC-BERT$_{base}$	**0.20**	–	**0.28**	1.00	0.83
+ zero initialization	0.62	1.00	–	1.00	1.00
+ normalization	**0.01**	**0.31**	**0.02**	–	**0.15**
+ weighted output	**0.06**	1.00	**0.25**	1.00	–

Table 12: The $\varepsilon_{\min}$ from the ASO significance test between each model on the MSGS dataset. Each row compares whether the model in the row is better than the one in the column. Results in **bold** indicate that the row model is significantly better than the one in the column.

WhisBERT: Multimodal Text-Audio Language Modeling on 100M Words

Lukas Wolf[ʕ] **Klemen Kotar**[ʃ] **Greta Tuckute**[ɱ] **Eghbal Hosseini**[ɱ]
Tamar I. Regev[ɱ] **Ethan Gotlieb Wilcox**[ʕ] **Alex Warstadt**[ʕ]
[ʕ]ETH Zürich [ɱ]MIT [ʃ]Stanford University
{wolflu, warstadt, ethan.wilcox}@ethz.ch
klemen@allenai.org {ehoseini, tamarr}@mit.edu

Abstract

Training on multiple modalities of input can augment the capabilities of a language model. Here, we ask whether such a training regime can improve the *quality* and *efficiency* of these systems as well. We focus on text–audio and introduce WhisBERT, which is inspired by the text–image approach of FLAVA (Singh et al., 2022). In accordance with BabyLM (Warstadt et al., 2023) guidelines, we pretrain WhisBERT on a dataset comprising only 100 million words plus their corresponding speech from the word-aligned version of the People's Speech dataset (Galvez et al., 2021). To assess the impact of multimodality, we compare versions of the model that are trained on text only and on both audio and text simultaneously. We find that while WhisBERT is able to perform well on multimodal masked modeling and surpasses the BabyLM baselines in most benchmark tasks, it struggles to optimize its complex objective and outperform its text-only WhisBERT baseline.

https://github.com/lu-wo/whisbert

1 Introduction

Recent advances in language modeling and their downstream applications have been driven, in large part, by bigger models, both in terms of model size and in terms of training data. Larger and larger pretraining datasets highlight the gap in terms of learning efficiency between humans and deep learning models—while state-of-the-art language models need billions of examples to approach human-level language performance, people learn their language from experience with about 100 million words or less (Warstadt and Bowman, 2022; Frank, 2023).

We hypothesize that one major reason for this data efficiency gap is the difference in input between humans and current deep learning systems. Human language learning involves multiple modalities, including both visual and auditory input. In contrast, typical language models are trained on representations of text alone. For this BabyLM submission, we ask whether training on inputs of multiple modalities can increase language models' training efficiency, with a focus on text-audio multimodal input. We conjecture that multimodal data sources have the potential to enrich the language learning process, enabling models to leverage complementary information from different modalities and thus augment their learning capacity (Baltrušaitis et al., 2017).

Multimodal language modeling has experienced a noteworthy surge in research productivity lately, in applications such as image retrieval, semantic embeddings, and image generation (Driess et al., 2023; Koh et al., 2023; Yasunaga et al., 2023) However, text-audio multimodal language modeling (e.g. (Chuang et al., 2019; Lakhotia et al., 2021)) remains largely unexplored, especially in low-resource settings such as the 100 million training regime we employ here. As a first step towards a text-audio language model, we introduce WhisBERT, a novel masked language model (MLM) architecture inspired by vision-text models such as FLAVA (Singh et al., 2022). The core idea is that WhisBERT is trained in a multitask setting on both unimodal (i.e. text- or audio-only) and multimodal objectives. In multimodal objectives, the model receives matched text-audio segments, and it can use information from one modality to learn representations for the other.

To accommodate the specific requirements of the BabyLM challenge (Warstadt et al., 2023), we pretrain WhisBert on a dataset of matched audio and text transcripts comprising 100 million words sampled from the People's Speech dataset (Galvez et al., 2021). We use an improved version of the audio-text-aligned training data, a subset of an upcoming speech production dataset release (see Section 3). This commitment to using high-quality pretraining data is in line with the data efficiency objectives of the BabyLM challenge.

Proceedings of the 27th Conference on Computational Natural Language Learning: Volume 2: The BabyLM Challenge, pages 253–258
December 6-7, 2023

We carry out a rigorous evaluation of the performance of the audio, text, and multimodal encoders within this new framework. We find that even though the optimization problem in the multimodal setting is much harder compared to a unimodal setting, the multimodal WhisBERT model outperforms the text-only baseline in a majority of the BabyLM challenge tasks even when trained for only a single iteration over the dataset.

2 WhisBERT

WhisBERT is a multimodal audio and text model that is inspired by *OpenAI*'s Whisper model (Radford et al., 2022) for speech recognition and BERT (Devlin et al., 2019) for bidirectional language encoding. WhisBERT contains two separate input streams, one of audio and of its corresponding text (i.e., a transcription). The model is trained using a combination of two unimodal and three multimodal masked training objectives. In the unimodal setting, the model must predict either a masked word or a masked patch of audio. In the multimodal training setting, the model must predict pairs of matched word/audio patches. This multi-objective training setup is inspired by the visual-audio model FLAVA (Singh et al., 2022).

2.1 Architecture details

Audio encoder In order to create audio patches that we can process with Whisper's bidirectional transformer encoder (Vaswani et al., 2017), the audio stream is first passed through the Whisper Feature Extractor available on Hugging Face[1].

All audio data is re-sampled to a rate of 16,000 Hz, and an 80-channel log-magnitude Mel spectrogram representation is computed using 25-millisecond windows with a 10-millisecond stride. We then pass the audio spectrogram through a patch embedding layer: a convolutional encoder processes the extracted frequency features using a stem of two 1-dimensional convolution layers (along the time dimension, filters cover all input frequencies), both with a filter width of 16 and incorporating the GELU activation function. The second convolution layer employs a stride of 10. This patch embedding layer creates overlapping 1-dimensional audio patches covering 100ms of the audio signal as input to the transformer.

After preprocessing and patch embedding, sinusoidal position embeddings are added to the stem's output, which is then processed by Whisper's transformer encoder blocks. A notable difference to the standard Whisper encoder is that we prepend a learnable classification (henceforth, CLS) token at the beginning of the audio patch sequence. Therefore, the audio encoder produces a list of audio hidden states $\{h_A\}$ each corresponding to a contextualized audio patch, as well as an additional audio classification state $h_{CLS,A}$.

Text encoder In order to encode the text input, we choose a standard bidirectional transformer architecture following the BERT (Devlin et al., 2019) model. We train a WordPiece (Wu et al., 2016) tokenizer on the 100M words in our People's speech (Galvez et al., 2021) subset (see Section 3). The WordPiece tokenizer automatically prepends a CLS token to the token sequence which is contextualized with the rest of the sequence. The text encoder produces a list of text hidden states $\{h_T\}$ corresponding to a text token, as well as an additional text CLS token $h_{CLS,T}$.

Multimodal encoder The multimodal encoder is a standard transformer encoder that gets as input the concatenated contextualized audio and text sequences. Additionally, we prepend a learnable multimodal CLS token and employ sinusoidal positional embeddings. The multimodal encoder contextualizes the multimodal sequence and outputs a list of multimodal hidden states $\{h_M\}$ each corresponding to an unimodal vector from $\{h_A\}$ or $\{h_T\}$, as well as an additional multimodal CLS token $h_{CLS,M}$.

Adapting to downstream tasks The WhisBert model can be readily applied to both unimodal and multimodal tasks. For audio recognition tasks (e.g., speaker identification or speech recognition), we apply a classifier head (e.g., a linear layer or a multi-layer perceptron) on top of the unimodal classification token, $h_{CLS,A}$, from the audio encoder. Similarly, for language understanding and multimodal reasoning tasks, we can apply a classifier head on top of the classification token, $h_{CLS,T}$, from the text encoder or $h_{CLS,M}$ from the multimodal encoder, respectively.

2.2 Pretraining objectives

Our goal is to pretrain models to have robust contextual representations for both text and audio on their own as well as for aligned text-audio pairs. We use the approach from FLAVA (Singh et al.,

[1]Documentation for Whisper is available here.

2022) of multitask training over a selection of unimodal and multimodal training objectives that have been demonstrated to facilitate joint learning on images and text. We adapt the five objectives used by FLAVA for the audio domain.

2.2.1 Unimodal pretraining objectives

Masked Language Modeling Masked Language Modeling (MLM) is a pretraining objective that encourages the model to learn a deep understanding of the language. In MLM, a portion of the input tokens is masked and the model is trained to predict the original identity of the masked tokens based on their context.

Given an input sequence of tokens $x = [x_1, x_2, ..., x_T]$, for MLM, a subset M of these tokens is selected to be masked. The objective is to minimize the negative log-likelihood of the masked tokens:

$$L_{\text{MLM}}(x) = -\frac{1}{|M|}\sum_{t\in M}\log p_{\text{model}}(x_t|x_{\neg t}) \quad (1)$$

Here, x_t is a masked token, $x_{\neg t}$ represents the sequence with the token x_t masked, and p_{model} is the model's probability distribution over possible tokens. $|M|$ is the size of the subset of masked tokens, and the sum is taken over all masked positions t. The goal is to adjust the model's parameters to minimize this loss. We obtain a probability distribution over the vocabulary by applying a linear prediction head on the text hidden states $\{h_T\}$.

Masked Audio Modeling We introduce the Masked Audio Modeling (MAM) objective L_{MAM} which follows the principles of Contrastive Predictive Coding (van den Oord et al., 2019). In MAM, we randomly mask audio patches in the input sequence to the audio encoder. The encoder is expected to generate outputs that are most similar to the unmasked input at a particular masked position t. The self-supervised loss function, which aims to encourage the model to align masked tokens with their unmasked identities given the context, is defined for a masked token localized at t as:

$$L_{\text{MAM}} = -\log\frac{\exp(sim(c_t, b_t)/\kappa)}{\sum_{b_i\in B_D}\exp(sim(c_t, b_i)/\kappa)} \quad (2)$$

Here, c_t is the output of the transformer at position t, and b_i is the audio representation vector of the (unmasked) patch at some offset i. B_D is a set of 20 uniformly selected negative samples from the same sequence, plus b_t, and $sim()$ is a similarity function. For our implementation, we use the cosine similarity function, adjusted by a temperature function, κ, which is set to 0.1. The loss function operates by adjusting the output of the transformer at position t to be most similar to the encoded representation at t, despite the fact that this input to the transformer is masked. In this way, the model is encouraged to predict the content of the masked spans based on the unmasked context.

2.2.2 Multimodal Pretraining Objectives

Multimodal Contrastive Loss Contrastive loss (Gutmann and Hyvärinen, 2010) has been successfully applied to image-text representation learning in approaches such as CLIP (Radford et al., 2021). Our audio-text contrastive loss L_{MMC} aims to maximize the cosine similarities between matched audio and text pairs and minimize those for the unmatched pairs across a given batch of audio clips and corresponding text. This is achieved by linearly projecting the classification token of each audio sequence $h_{CLS,A}$ and text sequence $h_{CLS,T}$ into a common embedding space, followed by L2-normalization, dot-product, and a softmax loss scaled by temperature.

The goal of this process is to ensure that the audio and text representations for the same data point are brought closer together in the embedding space, while representations for different data points are pushed apart. This encourages the model to learn meaningful representations that capture the shared information between the audio and text modalities.

Masked Multimodal Modeling (MMM) We introduce a Masked Multimodal Modeling (MMM) pretraining objective L_{MMM}, that uses the output of the multimodal encoder $\{h_M\}$ to attempt to reconstruct the masked tokens from both the audio and text sequences. For the multimodal contextualized audio tokens, we employ the Contrastive Predictive Coding strategy introduced in Section 2.2.1. For the multimodal text tokens, we add a multimodal masked language modeling head we compute the MLM loss as introduced in Section 2.2.1.

The MMM pretraining objective is designed to encourage the model to understand the interdependencies between audio and text modalities, which in addition to the MMC loss has been found to improve performance on multimodal downstream tasks (Singh et al., 2022). It is computed separately from the contrastive loss, which is applied on audio and text tokens without any masking.

Audio-Text Matching (ATM) Finally, we incorporate an Audio-Text Matching loss, L_{ATM}, in which we feed a batch of samples that include both matched and unmatched audio-text pairs. We apply a classifier on top of the output from the multimodal encode to decide if the input audio and text match each other.

2.3 Pretraining WhisBERT

We pretrain WhisBERT on both text and audio samples from the dataset introduced in Section 3 for five epochs with stochastic gradient descent. Although WhisBERT is able to learn both from paired and unpaired examples, in our pretraining dataset we only encounter text-audio pairs. This allows us to always apply all unimodal and multimodal objective functions. For further details and hyperparameters we refer to this GitHub repository.

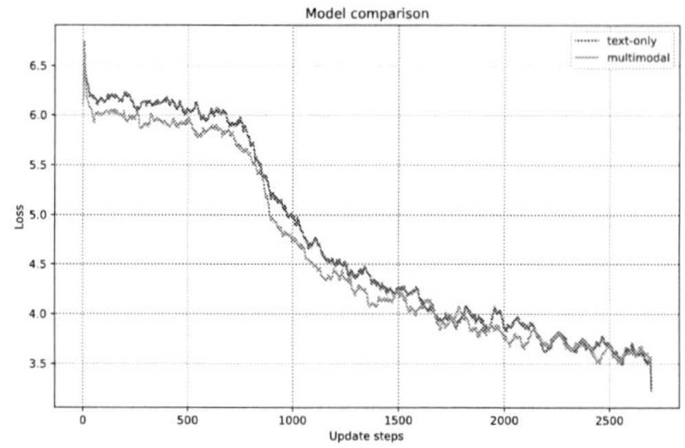

Figure 1: Text-only baseline vs WhisBERT on masked language modeling task during the first epoch. Interestingly, during the first epoch WhisBERT seems to perform better (outperforming the text-only baseline in 11 out of 17 tasks), but after five epochs does not outperform the text-only baseline across all benchmark tasks

3 People's Speech Dataset

The People's Speech dataset (Galvez et al., 2021) is a free-to-download, 30k hour English speech recognition dataset. The dataset is collected from appropriately licensed internet audio data with existing transcriptions, consisting of a clean and a dirty subset. We re-transcribed and re-aligned the People's Speech dataset using recently-released automatic speech recognition toolkits (Radford et al., 2022; Bain et al., 2023), which may provide better alignment than the baseline, publically available alignments. For this step we transcribe speech the Whisper large-v2 model from OpenAI (Radford et al., 2022). Numerals and non-standard characters were suppressed in the transcriptions, such that numbers were represented as words and non-standard characters were omitted. Otherwise, default parameters were used. The transcriptions were force-aligned to match the audio files using the WhisperX pipeline (Bain et al., 2023; Bredin et al., 2019; Baevski et al., 2020). We excluded very short transcripts (fewer than 100 words) or transcripts that contained more than 0.1% of words that could not be transcribed. The remaining files were sorted according to mean word-level transcription confidence (Whisper estimates a value between 0 and 1 that denotes the transcription confidence per word). We selected the files containing the first 100M words in this ordering. The average confidence of these final 100M words was 0.78 with 47M words from the clean audio subset and 53M words from the dirty audio subset. The transcribed, word-aligned dataset will be released as part of an upcoming speech production dataset.

4 Experimental Results

The main question we are interested in is whether pretraining on audio–text data can improve model performance. We assess this by comparing the text-encoder only version of WhisBERT compared to the exact same architecture trained with the multimodal objectives introduced in Section 2.2. (This is the MLM (text) vs. MM (multi-modal) comparison in Table 1.) Our results suggest that the answer is mixed. The MLM (text-only) version of the model achieves higher scores on 12 out of the 17 test suites, with the multi-modal model performing higher for Ellipsis, Island Effects, Quantifiers, Hypernym, and Question/Answer Congruence (tricky) tests. Interestingly, the three of these that were in the original BLiMP paper (Ellipsis, Island Effects and Quantifiers), were three of the four lowest-scoring tests for human accuracy, suggesting that where multi-modality *does* help, it is in processing particularly syntactically difficult material. Both of our trained models outperform the OPT-125M, RoBERTa and T5 baselines, averaging across tasks.

5 Discussion

Limitations We begin our discussion by noting the limitations of the current work. First, the People's Voice dataset presents a unique set of challenges, which likely resulted in limitations of the WhisBERT model. The most significant of these is

Task	MLM	MM	OPT-125m	RoBERTa-base	T5-base
anaphor_agreement	83.74%	81.29%	63.8%	81.5%	68.9%
argument_structure	68.60%	64.88%	70.6%	67.1%	63.8%
binding	66.95%	65.38%	67.1%	67.3%	60.4%
control_raising	65.25%	64.76%	66.5%	67.9%	60.9%
determiner_noun_agreement	92.24%	87.93%	78.5%	90.8%	72.2%
ellipsis	83.14%	88.68%	62%	76.4%	34.4%
filler_gap	73.12%	72.02%	63.8%	63.5%	48.2%
irregular_forms	89.62%	85.90%	67.5%	87.4%	77.6%
island_effects	53.51%	55.87%	48.6%	39.9%	45.6%
npi_licensing	64.77%	55.12%	46.7%	55.9%	47.8%
quantifiers	69.58%	71.69%	59.6%	70.5%	61.2%
subject_verb_agreement	75.05%	70.73%	56.9%	65.4%	65.0%
hypernym	50.12%	51.98%	50.0%	49.4%	48.0%
qa_congruence_easy	71.88%	67.19%	54.7%	31.3%	40.6%
qa_congruence_tricky	52.12%	53.94%	31.5%	32.1%	21.2%
subject_aux_inversion	77.90%	74.85%	80.3%	71.7%	64.9%
turn_taking	61.79%	58.21%	57.1%	53.2%	45.0%

Table 1: Evaluation scores of text-only (MLM), multimodal WhisBERT (MM), and the BabyLM baselines on *BLiMP* tasks. The BabyLM baselines were trained on the 100M words BabyLM dataset.

that it is primarily comprised of audio from movies, and thus includes things like background noise, music and audio effects that accompanied the dialog. This could have resulted in lower text–audio alignment accuracy, and likely made the audio-modeling challenge more difficult than for an in-studio recorded dataset.

Second, the requirements of the BabyLM challenge presented us with additional restrictions. Most notably, we were not allowed to use pre-trained audio encoders, and thus had to train these from scratch. Likely, this contributed to sub-optimal performance and requires further exploration. Furthermore, due to time limitations, we did not fully explore the space of the model's hyperparameters; it is well known that changes in hyperparameter settings can have large impacts on a model's performance.

Our mixed results when comparing WhisBERT against a text-only model suggest that small data settings are insufficient for effectively training a text-only masked language model. Given that the architectural basis for WhisBERT, Flava, was designed and built as a large-data foundation model, we suggest that such larger-data settings serve as the basis for future development and testing of the WhisBERT model.

Future Work We plan to train versions of WhisBERT on more than 100M words and their corresponding audio. This would enable investigations of the full capacity of the WhisBERT model and make it more comparable to similar vision-text models such as FLAVA (Singh et al., 2022). On the architecture level, one could replace the bidirectional transformer in the WhisBERT architecture with an autoregressive language model, allowing the use of the standard Whisper pretraining objectives in addition to the multi-modal ones.

Contribution Statement

LW, EH, TIR, EGW, and AW conceived of the ideas presented in this work. KK and GT provided the dataset used in pretraining WhisBERT. LW implemented the model and carried out the experiments. LW, KK, GT, EGW, AW, and TIR wrote the first draft of the manuscript. All authors edited the manuscript and reviewed the work.

References

Alexei Baevski, Henry Zhou, Abdel rahman Mohamed, and Michael Auli. 2020. wav2vec 2.0: A framework for self-supervised learning of speech representations. *ArXiv*, abs/2006.11477.

Max Bain, Jaesung Huh, Tengda Han, and Andrew Zisserman. 2023. Whisperx: Time-accurate speech transcription of long-form audio.

Tadas Baltrušaitis, Chaitanya Ahuja, and Louis-Philippe Morency. 2017. Multimodal machine learning: A survey and taxonomy.

Hervé Bredin, Ruiqing Yin, Juan Manuel Coria, Gregory Gelly, Pavel Korshunov, Marvin Lavechin, Diego Fustes, Hadrien Titeux, Wassim Bouaziz, and Marie-Philippe Gill. 2019. Pyannote.audio: Neural building blocks for speaker diarization. *ICASSP 2020 - 2020 IEEE International Conference on Acoustics,*

Speech and Signal Processing (ICASSP), pages 7124–7128.

Yung-Sung Chuang, Chi-Liang Liu, Hung-Yi Lee, and Lin-shan Lee. 2019. Speechbert: An audio-and-text jointly learned language model for end-to-end spoken question answering. *arXiv preprint arXiv:1910.11559*.

Jacob Devlin, Ming-Wei Chang, Kenton Lee, and Kristina Toutanova. 2019. Bert: Pre-training of deep bidirectional transformers for language understanding.

Danny Driess, Fei Xia, Mehdi SM Sajjadi, Corey Lynch, Aakanksha Chowdhery, Brian Ichter, Ayzaan Wahid, Jonathan Tompson, Quan Vuong, Tianhe Yu, et al. 2023. Palm-e: An embodied multimodal language model. *arXiv preprint arXiv:2303.03378*.

Michael C Frank. 2023. Bridging the data gap between children and large language models.

Daniel Galvez, Greg Diamos, Juan Ciro, Juan Felipe Cerón, Keith Achorn, Anjali Gopi, David Kanter, Maximilian Lam, Mark Mazumder, and Vijay Janapa Reddi. 2021. The People's Speech: A Large-Scale Diverse English Speech Recognition Dataset for Commercial Usage. ArXiv:2111.09344 [cs, stat].

Michael Gutmann and Aapo Hyvärinen. 2010. Noise-contrastive estimation: A new estimation principle for unnormalized statistical models. In *Proceedings of the Thirteenth International Conference on Artificial Intelligence and Statistics*, volume 9 of *Proceedings of Machine Learning Research*, pages 297–304, Chia Laguna Resort, Sardinia, Italy. PMLR.

Jing Yu Koh, Daniel Fried, and Ruslan Salakhutdinov. 2023. Generating images with multimodal language models.

Kushal Lakhotia, Eugene Kharitonov, Wei-Ning Hsu, Yossi Adi, Adam Polyak, Benjamin Bolte, Tu-Anh Nguyen, Jade Copet, Alexei Baevski, Abdelrahman Mohamed, et al. 2021. On generative spoken language modeling from raw audio. *Transactions of the Association for Computational Linguistics*, 9:1336–1354.

Alec Radford, Jong Wook Kim, Chris Hallacy, Aditya Ramesh, Gabriel Goh, Sandhini Agarwal, Girish Sastry, Amanda Askell, Pamela Mishkin, Jack Clark, Gretchen Krueger, and Ilya Sutskever. 2021. Learning transferable visual models from natural language supervision. In *Proceedings of the 38th International Conference on Machine Learning*, volume 139 of *Proceedings of Machine Learning Research*, pages 8748–8763. PMLR.

Alec Radford, Jong Wook Kim, Tao Xu, Greg Brockman, Christine McLeavey, and Ilya Sutskever. 2022. Robust speech recognition via large-scale weak supervision.

Amanpreet Singh, Ronghang Hu, Vedanuj Goswami, Guillaume Couairon, Wojciech Galuba, Marcus Rohrbach, and Douwe Kiela. 2022. FLAVA: A Foundational Language And Vision Alignment Model. ArXiv:2112.04482 [cs].

Aaron van den Oord, Yazhe Li, and Oriol Vinyals. 2019. Representation learning with contrastive predictive coding.

Ashish Vaswani, Noam Shazeer, Niki Parmar, Jakob Uszkoreit, Llion Jones, Aidan N. Gomez, Lukasz Kaiser, and Illia Polosukhin. 2017. Attention is all you need.

Alex Warstadt and Samuel R Bowman. 2022. What artificial neural networks can tell us about human language acquisition. In Shalom Lappin and Jean-Philippe Bernardy, editors, *Algebraic Structures in Natural Language*, pages 17–60. CRC Press. Publisher: CRC Press.

Alex Warstadt, Leshem Choshen, Aaron Mueller, Adina Williams, Ethan Wilcox, and Chengxu Zhuang. 2023. Call for papers – the babylm challenge: Sample-efficient pretraining on a developmentally plausible corpus.

Yonghui Wu, Mike Schuster, Zhifeng Chen, Quoc V. Le, Mohammad Norouzi, Wolfgang Macherey, Maxim Krikun, Yuan Cao, Qin Gao, Klaus Macherey, Jeff Klingner, Apurva Shah, Melvin Johnson, Xiaobing Liu, Łukasz Kaiser, Stephan Gouws, Yoshikiyo Kato, Taku Kudo, Hideto Kazawa, Keith Stevens, George Kurian, Nishant Patil, Wei Wang, Cliff Young, Jason Smith, Jason Riesa, Alex Rudnick, Oriol Vinyals, Greg Corrado, Macduff Hughes, and Jeffrey Dean. 2016. Google's neural machine translation system: Bridging the gap between human and machine translation.

Michihiro Yasunaga, Armen Aghajanyan, Weijia Shi, Richard James, Jure Leskovec, Percy Liang, Mike Lewis, Luke Zettlemoyer, and Wen-tau Yih. 2023. Retrieval-augmented multimodal language modeling.

A surprisal oracle for active curriculum language modeling

Xudong Hong[‡], **Sharid Loáiciga**[†] **and Asad Sayeed**[†]
[‡]Dept. of Language Science and Technology and Dept. of Computer Science, Saarland University
[†]Dept. of Philosophy, Linguistics, and Theory of Science, University of Gothenburg
{xhong}@lst.uni-saarland.de, {sharid.loaiciga, asad.sayeed}@gu.se

Abstract

We investigate the viability of surprisal in an active curriculum learning framework to train transformer-based language models in the context of the BabyLM Challenge. In our approach, the model itself selects the data to label (active learning) and schedules data samples based on a surprisal oracle (curriculum learning). We show that the models learn across all the tasks and datasets evaluated, making the technique a promising alternative approach to reducing the data requirements of language models. Our code is available at https://github.com/asayeed/ActiveBaby.

1 Introduction

We describe our submission to the BabyLM Challenge (Warstadt et al., 2023), a shared-task about language models trained from scratch on a developmentally plausible corpus. Inspired by expectation-based theories of sentence processing (Hale, 2001; Levy, 2008) and active curriculum learning (ACL) (Jafarpour et al., 2021), our approach relies on surprisal to select informative samples and streamline them into the model during training. We henceforth refer to our strategy as active curriculum learning modeling (ACLM).

There is a large volume of published studies describing how the processing difficulty of a sentence is correlated with its incremental probability in context (Linzen and Jaeger, 2016; Futrell and Levy, 2017; Hahn et al., 2019, among others). In other words, as people process sentences, they generate predictions about what is coming next and this can be measured using surprisal (Demberg et al., 2012). Here, we test to what extent this principle of syntactic predictability can also be used to guide the learning of a language model.

ACL, on the other hand, combines the strengths from Active Learning (AL) and Curriculum Learning (CL). AL is a classic paradigm for small data supervised scenarios, whereby an oracle labels informative examples selected by the model itself based (most often) on a uncertainty heuristic. The uncertainty metrics, however, tend to bias the model towards eccentric examples (Zhang et al., 2022b). To counteract this, Jafarpour et al. (2021) use CL, a technique that mimics how humans learn by regulating the training according to some schedule criterion, e.g., easy to difficult or short to long examples (Bengio et al., 2009).

In our approach, we use surprisal as sampling heuristic. A sample is formed from the sentence with the highest surprisal value s from an initial pool, along with the n most similar sentences to s from the rest of the training data. At each iteration, a new sample is added to the pool until convergence.

Our results show that the technique successfully learns steadily and incrementally in all the tasks, although its performance remains modest in comparison with equivalent systems with full access to the training data.

2 Background

AL specifically aims at reducing the amount of examples required for training. In AL, it is the algorithm itself that selects the most informative examples to annotate based on a probabilistic query heuristic. Each example is used to make the model better at selecting the next example. Nevertheless, AL is difficult to implement with neural networks frameworks due to their large number of parameters leading to poor uncertainty estimation and model instability (Lowell et al., 2019; Schröder et al., 2022). An excellent survey about the latest work on AL specifically for NLP is presented by Zhang et al. (2022b).

There is remarkably little research on surprisal and AL, or surprisal and CL. In the context of sentence classification, Yuan et al. (2020) exploit a pre-trained BERT model (Devlin et al., 2019) to generate surprisal embeddings as input to the

Proceedings of the 27th Conference on Computational Natural Language Learning: Volume 2: The BabyLM Challenge, pages 259–268
December 6-7, 2023

sentence labeling part of their model. In our case, sentence surprisal is used to select the sentence seeding the samples and the model is trained with a language modeling objective. Similar ideas are found in the context of machine translation.

Zhang et al. (2021) have experimented with adding training samples from a pool based on a difficulty criterion operationalized as sentence length (short sentences are easy, long ones are difficult) and word rarity (common sentences are easy, rare ones are difficult). In the second case, rare words are estimated based on the logarithms of word probabilities averaged over the sentence, which is effectively the same as surprisal. Likewise, Zhou et al. (2021) also report sampling based on sentence length and word rarity. In addition, they experiment with the probability of the sentence from an independent language model, source sentence word embeddings from another independent model, and the sentence score of the model under training itself. Last, Mohiuddin et al. (2022) rank their training sentences from easy to hard using the prediction scores of the model under training. They experiment with different window ranges over the distribution of these scores.

In keeping with the goals of the shared task, we train a language model from scratch. Elsewhere, a considerable amount of literature has been published on *compressing* state-of-the-art large language models (LLMs) into much smaller models without losing too much in accuracy and performance (Sanh et al., 2020; Zhang et al., 2022a, among others).

Cognitive studies, on their part, use LLMs to predict estimates about different effects attested in human language processing (Linzen et al., 2016; Futrell and Levy, 2019; Wei et al., 2021). This type of work also sheds light on the biases and mechanisms of learning of the LLMs themselves. Sinha et al. (2021), for instance, find the LLMs can account for word order due to their capacity for higher-order word co-occurrence statistics, while Arehalli et al. (2022) and Oh and Schuler (2023) have raised questions about the reliability of LLMs predictions due to their conflation of lexical and syntactic biases and their large capacity to memorize linguistic structures.

Humans acquire language in the context of interaction with a social and physical environment, which may explain at least part of the inductive bias humans display that allows them to learn from quantities of data far less than LLMs typically require to produce some of the spectacular-seeming recent results. The `strict` and `strict-small` settings of the BabyLM challenge effectively probe how small we can make the training data in an ungrounded setting. In this context, we still hypothesize that an interactive, environment-aware approach will be important in making learning efficient. We conceive of the learner as seeking out stimuli that represent domains of syntax and semantics on which the learner is furthest away from convergence, and we represent that distance by surprisal. We then hypothesize that the learner is motivated to seek out or pay attention to items that have a similar pattern of overall uncertainty, even if the specific syntactic or semantic conditions may be different in terms of, e.g., parts of speech or lexical semantics.

3 The model

Training a model with active learning (Cohn et al., 1996) involves (1) selecting an initial training set of sentences from a pool of sentences available for future training iterations and (2) iteratively adding sentences from the pool to the training set based on a criterion of uncertainty about the data. For classification tasks in scenarios with limited labelled data, this involves a human in the loop who labels a selection of "least certain" data from the pool, where the certainty is calculated based on model confidence. This form of active learning is intended to reduce the difficulty of labelling training data when, for example, annotators are difficult to find—only label what the model finds most "interesting" for the learning algorithm. This concept can be extended from classification to, for example, machine translation in low-resource contexts (Gupta et al., 2021), where a small group of proficient translators would be prompted for translations of items in the pool that the model is, e.g., most perplexed about.

Pre-training a language model is, however, not primarily a classification task. For a generative language model, the learning goal is for the model to be able to produce the next token or set of tokens given a prefix and to do so until a complete utterance is produced. Uncertainty for a generative LM over an utterance requires the aggregate of uncertainty over a number of decisions, each with low prior probability. Insofar as the model is intended to represent an approximation of human acquisition, it is implausible that the pool (representing

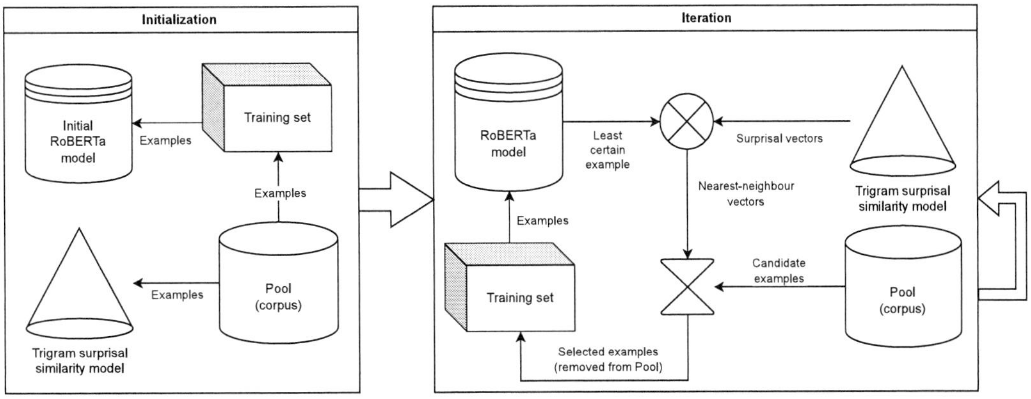

Figure 1: The architecture of our ACLM method.

the full environment over time of the learner) be fully evaluated in advance for uncertainty in the service of training data selection. This requires the introduction of an additional criterion for selecting new examples that are likely to represent utterances that are currently uncertain to the model.

To solve this, we adapt the concept of Active Curriculum Learning (ACL) from Jafarpour et al. (2021), who envision a joint scoring criterion for the selection of additional examples, composed of the scoring criterion for an active learning algorithm and the scoring criterion for a curriculum learning algorithm. Our approach is two-step, rather than a linear combination of two criteria. In the first step, we use a trained model to select the least certain example from the *existing* training set, rather than the pool. Then we apply a heuristic to select sentences that are structurally similar to the current least certain training example and add them to the next iteration's training set (see Figure 1).

Our heuristic is similarity based on a profile of the token-by-token incremental trigram surprisal of each sentence. Profiles of all the training and pool sentences are represented as seven-dimensional surprisal vectors by rescaling the sequence of surprisal values, which varies by the sentence length. This enables us to take the least certain training example's surprisal vector and request the nearest-neighbours, which are then added to the training set.

3.1 Base model

The base model is RoBERTa (Liu et al., 2019; Zhuang et al., 2021) trained from initialization on a 100K randomly selected subset—the initial training set—of the `strict-small` dataset of the BabyLM challenge.

The data for all our model variants was preprocessed in the same way. The documents where split at the sentence level and then BPE tokenized with a truncated maximum length of 512 tokens.

3.2 Surprisal space

The surprisal space for the corpus as a whole is generated by training a simple language model via Maximum Likelihood Estimation on n-grams up to trigrams via the nltk.lm module. Trigram surprisal can be used to explain part of human linguistic behaviour at a syntactic and semantic level in human dialogue (Sayeed et al., 2015).

Every sentence in the pool and training set is then labelled with a sequence of surprial values, one for each token. We use scikit-image's resizing function to stretch or shrink the surprisal sequences to vectors of dimension seven.[1]

All the vectors are placed in an instance of scikit-learn's KDTree (Sproull, 1991) implementation, which allows for an efficient search for the k nearest neighbours (kNN) of a given query vector and returns sentence identifiers for the vectors in the pool that are nearest to the surprisal vector of the least certain example. These are added to the training set.

For efficiency reasons, we do not re-evaluate the surprisal space at every iteration of active learning. This part of the model represents an oracle selecting items from the pool that bear a model uncertainty pattern that is similar to the least certain item in the training set.

[1]This is a random choice to get a small number such that the surprisal space can fit into the main memory.

3.3 Active curriculum language modeling

RoBERTa is allowed to train with the current training set for multiple epochs until the least certain training set example is found and the active learning loop initiated. This process thus combines active learning, in terms of the model being used to identify sets of data that need to be labelled, and curriculum learning, where a heuristic—a vector-based surprisal oracle—is used to schedule the newly delivered examples. We stop the model training after a set number of iterations.

The least certain example is the one with the highest cross-entropy loss or surprisal according to the model; that is, while the surprisal vectors do not change between iterations based on the RoBERTa model, the model under training changes to produce a different ranking of sentences in its training set, thereby allowing for variation in curriculum presented by the surprisal oracle.

4 Results

4.1 Shared task evaluation

We use the official evaluation tools (Gao et al., 2021) from the BabyLM Challenge to report our results. Our submissions mostly targeted the `strict-small` track, but we also report results for one system trained for the `strict` track. Tables 1, 2 and 3 in Appendix A contain the details of the obtained scores.

Strict-100M is trained with the data from the `strict` track, all other models rely on the `strict-small` data. 10ep10it and 10ep20it served as our internal baselines. They are RoBERTa models without ACLM that only differ in the number of iterations, 10 for the first and 20 for the second, both have a batch size of 64 sentences. The ACLM models are s50Kep1 and s50Kep5. Both have a batch size of 64 and use a sample size of 50K sentences; they differ in that the first runs one epoch per sample and the second 5 epochs per sample.

In summary, the results for the Strict-100M model tend to be overall higher, as it is trained on a larger amount of data. When considering the ACLM models, we observe that they performed the best when evaluated on the (Super)GLUE datasets and the worst on the MSGS one. There is also a clear gain in performance when training the model with more epochs per sample.

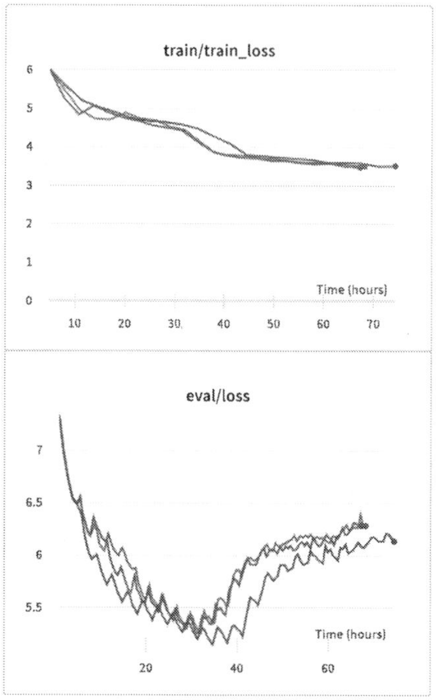

Figure 2: Comparison of the learning curves of systems with random sampling (green line), sampling with maximal surprisal (orange line), and sampling with minimal surprisal criterion (red line).

4.2 Hyper-parameter search

We experimented with batch sizes of 32 and 64 data points and observed that it produced minimum differences. As for the number of epochs, we tested different values between 1 and 5 for the ACLM systems, with 5 yielding the best performance. We expected to see some variation if changing the size of the sample size, but we also did not observe any important changes.

5 Analysis

5.1 Sampling Methods

Our method set out to determine the extent to which the principle of predictability as represented by surprisal can be used to guide language model training. In order to test this hypothesis, we compared the best performing ACLM system (s50Kep5) using three different values of surprisal for the query: minimum, maximum, and random (Figure 2). What we found is that the model with the maximal surprisal performed closely to the random one and learned faster, while the one with minimal surprisal did clearly well on evaluation. While this

Figure 3: Accuracy of the systems 10ep10it (blue line, without ACLM), 50Kep5min (red line, with ACLM and minimal surprisal sampling) and s50K_ep5 (orange line, with ACLM) in the zero-shot tasks over 20 checkpoints during training.

seemed counter-intuitive at first, we believe that the model with the minimal surprisal is actually selecting sentences that are overall more informative than those with the maximal surprisal which might be too divergent. Furthermore, this also accords with Mohiuddin et al.'s (2022) analysis that if a sample is too easy, the model might not gain any useful information from it, whereas if the sample is too hard, it might degrade the model's performance at that point. Taken together, this strongly suggests that surprisal does have an effect as a sampling query, but more work will need to be done to determine the optimal curriculum for its efficiency.

5.2 Zero-shot tasks

As a means to understand the way in which the ACLM models learn, we evaluated the 20 training checkpoints of the models 10ep10it, 50Kep5 and 50Kep5min (50Kep5 which samples data points with minimal surprisal) on the official zero-shot tasks. As mentioned, while all systems are trained on the `strict-small` data, the 10ep10it system uses all the data at once, in the standard way, while 50Kep5 and 50Kep5min are trained through ACLM with different sampling methods. These systems have a sample size of 50k sentences and runs 5 epochs per sample. Both have a batch size of 64. Results are depicted in Figure 3.

The plots from this figure indicate that the ACLM model learns in a steadier fashion than its non-ACLM counterpart, in particular for the "agreement" categories: determiner-noun, subject-verb and (somewhat less) anaphor agreement. This might indicate a frequency effect better caught on by the ACLM model, as basically every sentence contains a positive example of correct agreement, but it is unknown how many total examples there are of the other tested phenomena. For most of the other categories, the learning curves are similar overall, and the ACLM model shows consistent learning increments. The exception seems to be the island effects category, where the accuracy tends to drop over time. Surprisingly, the ACLM model with minimal surprisal sampling (50Kep5min) underperforms the ACLM model with maximal surprisal (50Kep5) across many tasks except congruence-tricky and island, effects even though 50Kep5min has a lower evaluation loss than 50Kep5. The results indicate that maximal surprisal sampling is an effective method to improve model performance on zero-shot grammatical tasks. Moreover, lower perplexity does not always imply better performance on linguistic tasks.

6 Conclusions and future work

To our knowledge, this is the first contribution to the literature in reducing the pre-training requirement of a transformer-based language model via active curriculum learning modeling. What we have shown is that learning does take place under these conditions and produces promising results. It is not the case, however, that we explored the full potential of this technique; there is a huge scope for plausible variants that may be even more effective than what we have proposed.

For example, we designed the surprisal oracle around a vector space defined by trigram surprisal over tokens which is never re-evaluated. A more realistic learner would re-evaluate the surprisal space based on what it knows now, i.e., compute per-token surprisal based on the current training state of the transformer model. We did not implement this for computational resource reasons.

Another likely possibility for improvement of our model lies in the fact that the surprisal space is created by resizing all the vectors to the same dimensionality, which is equivalent to representing all sentences as having the same length. It is implausible that longer sentences produce model uncertainty in the same way as shorter sentences. A future version of our work could attempt to bin the sentences by length, creating separate surprisal spaces.

Limitations

The models trained in this study are designed to test ACLM as a viable method to train language models and as such, they are not overly optimized. Furthermore, any claims are specific to English, in keeping with the shared-task constraints.

Acknowledgements

This research was funded in part by the Swedish Research Council (VR) grant (2014-39) for the Centre for Linguistic Theory and Studies in Probability (CLASP). Xudong Hong was funded by the Konrad Zuse School of Excellence in Learning and Intelligent Systems (ELIZA). We thank our student assistant Mattes Alexander Warning for searching hyperparameters for our models. We also thank the anonymous reviewers for their insightful comments.

References

Suhas Arehalli, Brian Dillon, and Tal Linzen. 2022. Syntactic surprisal from neural models predicts, but underestimates, human processing difficulty from syntactic ambiguities. In *Proceedings of the 26th*

Conference on Computational Natural Language Learning (CoNLL), pages 301–313, Abu Dhabi, United Arab Emirates (Hybrid). Association for Computational Linguistics.

Yoshua Bengio, Jérôme Louradour, Ronan Collobert, and Jason Weston. 2009. Curriculum learning. In *Proceedings of the 26th Annual International Conference on Machine Learning*, ICML '09, page 41–48, New York, NY, USA. Association for Computing Machinery.

David A Cohn, Zoubin Ghahramani, and Michael I Jordan. 1996. Active learning with statistical models. *Journal of artificial intelligence research*, 4:129–145.

Vera Demberg, Asad Sayeed, Philip Gorinski, and Nikolaos Engonopoulos. 2012. Syntactic surprisal affects spoken word duration in conversational contexts. In *Proceedings of the 2012 Joint Conference on Empirical Methods in Natural Language Processing and Computational Natural Language Learning*, pages 356–367, Jeju Island, Korea. Association for Computational Linguistics.

Jacob Devlin, Ming-Wei Chang, Kenton Lee, and Kristina Toutanova. 2019. BERT: Pre-training of deep bidirectional transformers for language understanding. In *Proceedings of the 2019 Conference of the North American Chapter of the Association for Computational Linguistics: Human Language Technologies, Volume 1 (Long and Short Papers)*, pages 4171–4186, Minneapolis, Minnesota. Association for Computational Linguistics.

Richard Futrell and Roger Levy. 2017. Noisy-context surprisal as a human sentence processing cost model. In *Proceedings of the 15th Conference of the European Chapter of the Association for Computational Linguistics: Volume 1, Long Papers*, pages 688–698, Valencia, Spain. Association for Computational Linguistics.

Richard Futrell and Roger P. Levy. 2019. Do RNNs learn human-like abstract word order preferences? In *Proceedings of the Society for Computation in Linguistics (SCiL) 2019*, pages 50–59.

Leo Gao, Jonathan Tow, Stella Biderman, Sid Black, Anthony DiPofi, Charles Foster, Laurence Golding, Jeffrey Hsu, Kyle McDonell, Niklas Muennighoff, Jason Phang, Laria Reynolds, Eric Tang, Anish Thite, Ben Wang, Kevin Wang, and Andy Zou. 2021. A framework for few-shot language model evaluation.

Kamal Gupta, Dhanvanth Boppana, Rejwanul Haque, Asif Ekbal, and Pushpak Bhattacharyya. 2021. Investigating active learning in interactive neural machine translation. In *Proceedings of Machine Translation Summit XVIII: Research Track*, pages 10–22, Virtual. Association for Machine Translation in the Americas.

Michael Hahn, Frank Keller, Yonatan Bisk, and Yonatan Belinkov. 2019. Character-based surprisal as a model of reading difficulty in the presence of errors. In *Proceedings of the 41th Annual Meeting of the Cognitive Science Society, CogSci 2019: Creativity + Cognition + Computation, Montreal, Canada, July 24-27, 2019*, pages 401–407. cognitivesciencesociety.org.

John Hale. 2001. A probabilistic Earley parser as a psycholinguistic model. In *Second Meeting of the North American Chapter of the Association for Computational Linguistics*.

Borna Jafarpour, Dawn Sepehr, and Nick Pogrebnyakov. 2021. Active curriculum learning. In *Proceedings of the First Workshop on Interactive Learning for Natural Language Processing*, pages 40–45, Online. Association for Computational Linguistics.

Roger Levy. 2008. Expectation-based syntactic comprehension. *Cognition*, 106(3):1126–1177.

Tal Linzen, Emmanuel Dupoux, and Yoav Goldberg. 2016. Assessing the ability of LSTMs to learn syntax-sensitive dependencies. *Transactions of the Association for Computational Linguistics*, 4:521–535.

Tal Linzen and Florian T. Jaeger. 2016. Uncertainty and Expectation in Sentence Processing: Evidence From Subcategorization Distributions. *Cognitive science*, 40(6):1382–1411.

Yinhan Liu, Myle Ott, Naman Goyal, Jingfei Du, Mandar Joshi, Danqi Chen, Omer Levy, Mike Lewis, Luke Zettlemoyer, and Veselin Stoyanov. 2019. Roberta: A robustly optimized bert pretraining approach.

David Lowell, Zachary C. Lipton, and Byron C. Wallace. 2019. Practical obstacles to deploying active learning. In *Proceedings of the 2019 Conference on Empirical Methods in Natural Language Processing and the 9th International Joint Conference on Natural Language Processing (EMNLP-IJCNLP)*, pages 21–30, Hong Kong, China. Association for Computational Linguistics.

Tasnim Mohiuddin, Philipp Koehn, Vishrav Chaudhary, James Cross, Shruti Bhosale, and Shafiq Joty. 2022. Data selection curriculum for neural machine translation. In *Findings of the Association for Computational Linguistics: EMNLP 2022*, pages 1569–1582, Abu Dhabi, United Arab Emirates. Association for Computational Linguistics.

Byung-Doh Oh and William Schuler. 2023. Why Does Surprisal From Larger Transformer-Based Language Models Provide a Poorer Fit to Human Reading Times? *Transactions of the Association for Computational Linguistics*, 11:336–350.

Victor Sanh, Lysandre Debut, Julien Chaumond, and Thomas Wolf. 2020. Distilbert, a distilled version of bert: smaller, faster, cheaper and lighter.

Asad Sayeed, Stefan Fischer, and Vera Demberg. 2015. Vector-space calculation of semantic surprisal for predicting word pronunciation duration. In *Proceedings of the 53rd Annual Meeting of the Association for Computational Linguistics and the 7th International*

Joint Conference on Natural Language Processing (Volume 1: Long Papers), pages 763–773, Beijing, China. Association for Computational Linguistics.

Christopher Schröder, Andreas Niekler, and Martin Potthast. 2022. Revisiting uncertainty-based query strategies for active learning with transformers. In *Findings of the Association for Computational Linguistics: ACL 2022*, pages 2194–2203, Dublin, Ireland. Association for Computational Linguistics.

Koustuv Sinha, Robin Jia, Dieuwke Hupkes, Joelle Pineau, Adina Williams, and Douwe Kiela. 2021. Masked language modeling and the distributional hypothesis: Order word matters pre-training for little. In *Proceedings of the 2021 Conference on Empirical Methods in Natural Language Processing*, pages 2888–2913, Online and Punta Cana, Dominican Republic. Association for Computational Linguistics.

Robert F Sproull. 1991. Refinements to nearest-neighbor searching in k-dimensional trees. *Algorithmica*, 6:579–589.

Alex Warstadt, Aaron Mueller, Leshem Choshen, Ethan Gotlieb Wilcox, Chengxu Zhuang, Juan Ciro, Rafael Mosquera, Adina Williams, Bhargavi Paranjabe, Tal Linzen, and Ryan Cotterell. 2023. Findings of the 2023 BabyLM Challenge: Sample-efficient pretraining on developmentally plausible corpora. In *Proceedings of the 2023 BabyLM Challenge*. Association for Computational Linguistics (ACL).

Jason Wei, Clara Meister, and Ryan Cotterell. 2021. A cognitive regularizer for language modeling. In *Proceedings of the 59th Annual Meeting of the Association for Computational Linguistics and the 11th International Joint Conference on Natural Language Processing (Volume 1: Long Papers)*, pages 5191–5202, Online. Association for Computational Linguistics.

Michelle Yuan, Hsuan-Tien Lin, and Jordan Boyd-Graber. 2020. Cold-start active learning through self-supervised language modeling. In *Proceedings of the 2020 Conference on Empirical Methods in Natural Language Processing (EMNLP)*, pages 7935–7948, Online. Association for Computational Linguistics.

Mingliang Zhang, Fandong Meng, Yunhai Tong, and Jie Zhou. 2021. Competence-based curriculum learning for multilingual machine translation. In *Findings of the Association for Computational Linguistics: EMNLP 2021*, pages 2481–2493, Punta Cana, Dominican Republic. Association for Computational Linguistics.

Minjia Zhang, Niranjan Uma Naresh, and Yuxiong He. 2022a. Scala: Accelerating adaptation of pre-trained transformer-based language models via efficient large-batch adversarial noise.

Zhisong Zhang, Emma Strubell, and Eduard Hovy. 2022b. A survey of active learning for natural language processing. In *Proceedings of the 2022 Conference on Empirical Methods in Natural Language Processing*, pages 6166–6190, Abu Dhabi, United Arab Emirates. Association for Computational Linguistics.

Lei Zhou, Liang Ding, Kevin Duh, Shinji Watanabe, Ryohei Sasano, and Koichi Takeda. 2021. Self-guided curriculum learning for neural machine translation. In *Proceedings of the 18th International Conference on Spoken Language Translation (IWSLT 2021)*, pages 206–214, Bangkok, Thailand (online). Association for Computational Linguistics.

Liu Zhuang, Lin Wayne, Shi Ya, and Zhao Jun. 2021. A robustly optimized BERT pre-training approach with post-training. In *Proceedings of the 20th Chinese National Conference on Computational Linguistics*, pages 1218–1227, Huhhot, China. Chinese Information Processing Society of China.

A Appendix

	Submitted RoBERTa models					Official baselines		
		Strict small 10M						
				ACL				
	Strict-100M	10ep10it	10ep20it	s50Kep1	s50Kep5	OPT-125m	RoBERTa-base	T5-base
Anaphor Agr.	82.31	77.76	74.34	42.02	75.30	63.8	**81.5**	68.9
Agr. Structure	74.03	**72.91**	68.83	61.52	60.36	70.6	67.1	63.8
Binding	68.63	69.09	67.62	64.02	**85.95**	67.1	67.3	60.4
Control/Raising	70.35	**68.96**	64.98	61.36	50.03	66.5	67.9	60.9
Det-N Agr.	94.84	**95.66**	91.94	55.49	55.79	78.5	90.8	72.2
Ellipsis	65.42	65.82	56.41	32.79	55.41	62	**76.4**	34.4
Filler-Gap	78.32	**75.61**	69.89	63.68	50.12	63.80	63.50	48.20
Irregular Forms	92.01	**89.41**	89.87	75.01	43.98	67.5	87.4	77.6
Island Effects	48.62	46.30	40.58	47.20	**50.00**	48.6	39.9	45.6
NPI Licensing	61.52	54.16	**56.77**	51.90	35.15	46.7	55.9	47.8
Quantifiers	66.82	66.87	63.96	45.96	**78.02**	59.6	70.5	61.2
S-V Agr.	80.85	**79.33**	70.66	50.44	60.39	56.9	65.4	65
				Supplement				
Hypernym	49.07	49.30	49.07	50.23	**62.15**	50	49.4	48
QA Cong. (easy)	57.81	56.25	53.13	50.00	**66.51**	54.7	31.3	40.6
QA Cong. (tricky)	33.33	35.76	35.76	30.30	**69.17**	31.5	32.1	21.2
Subj.-Aux. Inv.	78.92	75.38	**82.73**	75.82	62.03	80.3	71.7	64.9
Turn Taking	57.50	61.79	**66.79**	56.43	42.96	57.1	53.2	45

Table 1: Accuracy scores of the zero-shot evaluation on the BLiMP dataset. Comparisons per row highlighted with bold do not include the Strict-100M column. QA Cong. means QA Congruence. Inv. means inversion.

	Submitted RoBERTa models					Official baselines			
		Strict small 10M							
				ACL					
	Strict-100M	10ep10it	10ep20it	s50Kep1	s50Kep5	Majority	OPT-125m	RoBERTa-base	T5-base
CoLA	73.11	**72.62**	70.76	69.48	61.17	69.5	64.6	70.8	61.2
SST-2	86.42	**84.84**	83.27	81.3	75.97	50.2	81.9	87	78.1
MRPC	63.28	64.41	64.41	64.41	90.2	82	72.5	79.2	80.5
QQP	79.93	81.65	**79.88**	77.65	65.98	53.1	60.4	73.7	66.2
MNLI	69.02	70.34	68.62	65.27	**100**	35.7	57.6	73.2	48
MNLI-mm	71.94	**71.26**	69.51	67.06	66.6	35.7	60	74	50.3
QNLI	64.96	66.4	66.49	58.36	**68.44**	35.4	61.5	77	62
RTE	47.47	51.52	49.49	49.49	**98.93**	53.1	60	61.6	49.4
BoolQ	65.98	63.35	66.11	66.11	**74.9**	50.5	63.3	66.3	66
MultiRC	57.28	58.6	56.19	50.82	58.6	**59.9**	55.2	61.4	47.1
WSC	61.45	61.45	61.45	61.45	**81.89**	53.2	60.2	61.4	61.4

Table 2: Accuracy scores of the fine-tuning evaluation on the (Super)GLUE datasets. Comparisons per row highlighted with bold do not include the Strict-100M column.

	Submitted RoBERTa models					Official baselines		
		Strict small 10M						
				ACL				
	Strict-100M	10ep10it	10ep20it	s50Kep1	s50Kep5	OPT-125m	RoBERTa-base	T5-base
CR (Control)	91.55	86.68	86.89	75.51	**94.5**	86.4	84.1	78.4
LC (Control)	**100**	**100**	**100**	**100**	66.45	86.1	**100**	**100**
MV (Control)	99.72	99.77	99.63	97.57	84.33	**99.8**	99.4	72.7
RP (Control)	98.85	**100**	**100**	97.87	0	**100**	93.5	95.5
SC (Control)	81.27	89.54	90.54	88.17	66.78	94.3	**96.4**	94.4
CR_LC	66.76	66.74	66.69	66.32	**83.46**	66.5	67.7	66.7
CR_RTP	66.78	67.25	66.73	66.61	66.71	67	68.6	**69.7**
MV_LC	66.51	66.61	66.61	66.61	55.1	66.5	**66.7**	66.6
MV_RTP	67.18	69.08	67.04	66.71	**100**	67.6	68.6	66.9
SC_LC	63.83	66.28	67.49	67.44	66.73	80.2	**84.2**	73.6
SC_RP	62.32	65.05	64.86	64.07	66.19	67.5	65.7	**67.8**

Table 3: Accuracy scores of the fine-tuning evaluation on the MSGS datasets. Comparisons per row highlighted with bold do not include the Strict-100M column.

Mmi01 at The BabyLM Challenge: Linguistically Motivated Curriculum Learning for Pretraining in Low-Resource Settings

Maggie Mi
Department of Computer Science
The University of Sheffield
zmi1@sheffield.ac.uk

Abstract

This paper presents our findings for the BabyLM Challenge (Warstadt et al., 2023). Our exploration is inspired by vanilla curriculum learning (Bengio et al., 2009) and we explored the effect of linguistic complexity in forming the best curriculum for pre-training. In particular, we explore curriculum formations based on dependency-based measures (dependents per token, average dependency distance) and lexical-based measures (rarity, density, dispersion and diversity). We found that, overall, models pretrained using curriculum learning were able to beat the performance of a non-curriculum learning pre-trained model. Furthermore, we notice using different linguistic metric for measuring complexity lead to advantageous performance for some tasks, but not all. We share our results and analysis in the hope that it can provide beneficial insights for future work.

1 Introduction

Currently, pretraining language models (LMs) involve training models on large, diverse datasets before fine-tuning them on specific downstream tasks. As a byproduct of this procedure, datasets have grown substantially beyond developmentally plausible amounts. For instance, the recently released large variant of LLAMA-2 has 70 billion parameters and it was pre-trained with 2 trillion tokens (Touvron et al., 2023). This amount of data is well over the amount of exposure a child would have. Gilkerson et al. (2017) find that on average, a child aged 48-mo would be exposed to 12,128 tokens, from solely their parents. Calculations show LLAMA2's pretraining data is 165,000 times more than this developmental-plausible quantity.

Therefore, the goal of this task is to use human-development plausible methods for pretraining smaller-sized language models. In particular, we combine intuitions from linguistics and curriculum learning to explore whether different curricula designs affect models' performance. To do this, we investigate two strands of complexity measures, namely, structural complexity and lexical complexity.

Our research questions (RQs) are as follows:

1. Do pre-training LMs using CL produce better performance? If so:

2. Are linguistic complexity measures helpful in designing curricula for CL?

3. Which linguistic metric is advantageous and which is less? Is one strand of complexity measure inherently better than the other?

To answer RQ1, we aim to compare a baseline non-CL model to the results of CL-pretrained models. For RQ2, we make a similar comparison but this time using the results of a model that is trained on a random curriculum. For the last RQ, we make inter-model comparisons.

We provide an analysis of curriculum designs and the novel aspects of our work (§ 2). Following this, we explain the linguistic metrics in detail and provide details of our approach (§ 3). In § 4, we present our findings and discussions, before finally summarising the paper in § 5.

2 Related Works

Curriculum learning (CL) was first proposed by Bengio et al. (2009). The idea behind curriculum learning comes from the pedagogical observation that animals and humans learn better when knowledge is presented in a meaningfully organised way. For instance, starting with simple examples and gradually advancing to more complex ones (Skinner, 1958; Sweller, 1994; Krueger and Dayan, 2009). In the language modelling experiment carried out by Bengio et al. (2009), a corpus replacement method was used to make the data

Proceedings of the 27th Conference on Computational Natural Language Learning: Volume 2: The BabyLM Challenge, pages 269–278
December 6-7, 2023 ©2023 Association for Computational Linguistics

increasingly difficult. This way of pertaining was found to be more effective, producing improved results.

There have been then numerous works have explored using CL as the pretraining approach for language models. Whilst some works reported CL as beneficial to pretraining, others have reported the opposite results. Nagatsuka et al. (2021) investigated a CL-based pretraining scheme that utilises the length of the input text as the measure of "difficulty" in curriculum design. It was found that using length-based curriculum training alongside using the maximum available batch size, models achieved drastically faster convergence speed, and higher scores on downstream tasks (Nagatsuka et al., 2021, 2022).

Curriculum design greatly varies in each work. Linguistic features that have been used in curriculum formation include Parts-of-Speech (POS) information, n-gram frequency (Platanios et al., 2019), average number of dependents per word in the sentence parse tree (Jafarpour et al., 2021), edit distance (Kadotani et al., 2021; Chang et al., 2021). However, arguably, the most common curriculum formations are based on measures of frequency (Liu et al., 2018) and text length (Tay et al., 2019; Cirik et al., 2016).

Comparing curriculum learning studies becomes challenging due to the inherent variability in curriculum choices across different tasks. However, it is undeniable that the arrangement of data holds significance. As a result, in distinction from prior research, our work is oriented towards investigating diverse linguistic features in curriculum formation. Notably, we investigate 5 different measures of linguistic complexity. They are:

- Average dependency distance (ADD)
- Dependents per word (DPW)
- Lexical rarity (RARITY)
- Lexical density (DENSITY)
- Lexical Evenness (DISPERSION)
- Lexical diversity (TTR)

We choose these measures of linguistic complexity to address the multi-dimensionality of measuring language complexity. In particular, we consider not only lexical (vocabulary-based) information, but also syntactical (structural-based) complexity measures. To the best of our knowledge, this study is the first to consider curriculum formation using such a comprehensive set of measures. Moreover, we focus our experimentation specifically on low-resource, data-constrained scenarios. As a result, we adopt a simple CL approach to reflect these settings.

3 Methodology

Our submission considers GPT-2 models (Radford et al., 2019) pretrained using curricula formed by various linguistic measures detailed in § 2. The pretraining approach involves sequentially training the model using ten different curriculum levels of the dataset, with each level building upon the previous one in terms of difficulty. Each model is pretrained three times, with a random seed used each time.

3.1 Curricula Formations

We used the 10M words dataset provided by the task authors for the STRICT-SMALL track of the Challenge. As detailed in the task description, the dataset consists of 10 excerpts, sourced from 10 different corpora of mixed domains (Warstadt et al., 2023). We consider all of the models to qualify for the LOOSE track, and only the evenness and lexical diversity models are legible for the STRICT-SMALL track. This is due to the fact that we use existing scripts from `textcomplexity`[1], which makes use of external tools, such as POS taggers trained on much more data than the given amount for linguistic complexity calculations.

For each part of the overall dataset, a score for each linguistic metric was calculated. As an example, Table 1 provides the TTR scores of each subset of the data. Curriculum formation is based on this ranking, with the "easiest", or in this case, the least lexically diverse data being Open Subtitles and the "hardest" being the Wikipedia data. Using the same idea, other curricula were formed using each linguistic measure.

3.1.1 Syntactic Diversity (DPW)

DPW quantifies the average number of syntactic dependents (i.e., words that depend on another word for their grammatical function) in a given text per word. A DPW score indicates that, on average, each word in a sentence has a large number of syntactic dependents. This means that the sentence has a complex and intricate syntactic structure, with many words relying on each other to convey meaning and grammatical relationships. Sentences with

[1] https://github.com/tsproisl/textcomplexity

high DPW scores tend to be more challenging for humans to process and understand (Hawkins, 1994; Grodner and Gibson, 2005; Gibson, 1998).

3.1.2 Syntactic Proximity (ADD)

ADD is mathematically defined as (Liu et al., 2009):

$$\text{ADD} = \frac{1}{n-s}\sum_{i=1}^{n-s}|DD_i|$$

where:

- n is the total number of tokens in the sentence
- s is the total number of sentences in the document
- DD_i is the dependency length of the i-th syntactic link

Conceptually, this is calculating a ratio of calculating the total lengths of dependency links in a sentence to the total number of dependencies links in the same sentence. It gives an indication of how closely related the words are in a sentence syntactically. A lower average dependency distance suggests that the words in a sentence tend to be more closely connected, indicating a more compact sentence structure. Conversely, a higher average dependency distance suggests more complex and possibly longer distances between heads and their dependents in a sentence (Oya, 2011).

3.1.3 Lexical Rarity (RARITY)

As detailed in `textcomplexity`, rarity was calculated with the help of the COW frequency list (Schäfer, 2016). More frequent lexical items were given a smaller score.

3.1.4 Lexical Density (DENSITY)

Lexical density is calculated as the proportion of content words to function words. We consider a higher score on this metric as data that is harder to learn since it is more likely to be information-heavy.

3.1.5 Lexical Evenness (DISPERSION)

Dispersion is measured using Gini-based dispersion (Gini, 1912). It measures how evenly tokens of the same type are distributed in the text (Blombach et al., 2022). The Gini-based dispersion for a single type is computed as

$$1 - \frac{Gini}{Gini_{max}}$$

where $Gini$ is the Gini coefficient of the distances between tokens of the same type, and $Gini_{max}$ is the maximum value for a type with frequency f in a text of length N.

The formula for $Gini_{max}$ is:

$$\text{Gini\_max} = \frac{(N-f)\cdot(f-1)}{f\cdot N}$$

where

- N is the length of the entire text (total number of tokens in the text)
- f is the frequency of the type (number of times a particular token appears in the text)

In this work, evenness serves to illustrate the arrangement or spread of token types within a text.

3.1.6 Lexical Diversity (TTR)

Type-token ratio (TTR) is used to measure lexical diversity. It is calculated by dividing the number of unique words (types) to the total number of words (tokens) present in the text (Templin, 1957). This can be thought of as measuring the richness of the vocabulary of the corpus. A higher TTR indicates a more diverse vocabulary with a greater range of unique words in the text. Conversely, a lower TTR suggests a more repetitive or limited use of vocabulary.

TTR is given by :

$$\text{TTR} = \frac{\textit{Number of different word types}}{\textit{Total number of tokens}}$$

Table 1: TTR scores of each subset of the 10M words dataset, shown in increasing order.

Subset	TTR Score
open subtitles	1.623
bnc spoken	2.034
aochildes	2.068
qed	2.966
cbt	3.450
children_stories	3.570
switchboard	3.997
gutenberg	4.149
simple wikipedia	4.491
wikipedia	5.678

3.2 Model Description

We use the provided data to train a Unigram-16000 tokeniser, and our experiments all use this tokeniser.

In this Challenge, we focus specifically on smaller settings of the models. All models featured in this work are trained on architectures with 12 layers and 12 attention heads [2]. Our focus is directed towards this smaller setting since smaller models typically require less computational power and memory, making them more accessible and cost-effective for researchers with limited resources.

3.3 Model Evaluation

All models undergo evaluation on The Benchmark of Linguistic Minimal Pairs (BLiMP) benchmark as well as SuperGLUE and MSGS tasks. We run each evaluation suite three times for every model. Each run uses a different random seed.

BLiMP is an evaluation suite that tests LMs' abilities on a range of grammatical phenomena in the English language (Warstadt et al., 2020a). For BLiMP tasks, a zero-shot evaluation approach is used, allowing the models to be assessed without any additional fine-tuning. On the other hand, to gauge the models' performance on SuperGLUE tasks, they are subjected to fine-tuning using the respective datasets.

SuperGLUE is a benchmark that comprises challenging language understanding tasks. Inspired by GLUE, SuperGLUE aims to address the limitations of the original GLUE benchmark (Wang et al., 2018), which had gradually lost its challenge due to the improving capabilities of LMs.

Mixed Signals Generalization Set (MSGS) assess whether language models exhibit preferences for certain aspects of language, such as linguistic features (e.g., specific sentence structures) or surface features (e.g., word positioning). The MSGS dataset evaluates whether language models can identify and detect these linguistic and surface features and whether they prioritize linguistic features over surface features, which is a crucial aspect of human language understanding abilities (Warstadt et al., 2020b).

Taken together, these evaluation suites provide insights into the models' general language understanding capabilities as well as their adaptability and performance on specific downstream tasks. The code for this task's evaluation originates from *eval-harness* by Gao et al. (2021). Furthermore, as a fascinating aspect of cognitive modelling, we assess our models' capability to predict the **age of word acquisition (AoA)**. Based on the work of Portelance et al. (2023), computing this metric involves an estimation of the average surprisal of words in child-directed utterances sourced from CHILDES. Models are then evaluated using leave-one-out cross-validation. The metric used to measure prediction is mean absolute deviation (MAD). A lower MAD score indicates that the model's predictions are closer to the actual age of acquisition, signifying better performance on the task. Conversely, a higher MAD score suggests that the model's predictions are less accurate.

Baselines: The two baseline models we use are a model trained without CL (NONCL) and a model trained on a randomly formed curriculum (RANDOM). The non-CL model represents a conventional approach, where the model is trained on all available data simultaneously for a fixed number of steps (50000 in this case). On the other hand, the CL model trained on a randomly formed curriculum serves as a comparison to understand how much improvement linguistically justified curricula can provide.

4 Results

The results of models can be seen in Tables 2, 3, 4. We provide the performance results for the supplement BLiMP tasks and MSGS tasks (see Table 6 and 7). The analysis of the main BLiMP, SuperGLUE and AoA prediction tasks serves as a representative basis, and the conclusions drawn from these tasks can be extended to the results presented in the Appendices. The analysis presented takes into consideration the results of all evaluation metrics, however, we mainly focus on the BLiMP, SuperGLUE and AoA benchmarks; MSGS and the supplement BLiMP tasks will be referred to on a needs basis.

4.1 Non-CL vs. CL

By comparing the non-curriculum learning pre-trained baseline model (NONCL) with models pre-trained using curriculum learning, we observe that the latter exhibit slightly better performance. For most of the tasks, CL models (RANDOM, ADD, DPW, DISPERSION, DENSITY, RARITY, TTR) outperform NONCL. Higher scores are observed in these systems on BLiMP tasks such as ANA. AGR, ARG. STR, QUANTIFIERS and SuperGLUE tasks such as QQP, BoolQ, and MultiRC indicating that curriculum learning leads to better performance. Although the improvements are not substantial in some cases and there exist also situations where

[2] The code for curriculum formation and training can be found on Github: https://github.com/mi-m1/BabyLM-Entry.

Model	ANA. AGR	ARG. STR	BINDING	CTRL. RAIS	D-N AGR	ELLIPSIS	FILLER. GAP	IRREGULAR	ISLAND	NPI	QUANTIFIERS	S-V AGR
NONCL baseline	50.19	58.53	46.26	55.57	50.31	38.41	28.94	47.96	45.71	45.74	30.52	48.35
RANDOM baseline	61.28	59.53	48.74	56.87	49.24	40.36	28.99	56.49	52.14	23.70	38.01	46.91
ADD	**64.37**	59.53	47.03	55.04	49.58	37.30	29.05	48.50	48.13	31.49	55.15	**48.93**
DISPERSION	63.19	59.78	46.82	57.39	49.58	39.32	28.94	52.60	51.08	45.27	**46.68**	**48.93**
DPW	63.80	**59.86**	**49.80**	56.79	49.38	37.88	28.99	**59.29**	51.97	30.11	43.39	47.77
DENSITY	65.56	59.66	45.83	**57.56**	49.25	40.07	29.76	49.86	50.31	41.48	42.25	**48.93**
RARITY	59.01	59.78	49.01	57.11	49.47	38.51	29.03	56.28	50.75	18.91	41.60	48.43
TTR	59.00	59.13	44.99	56.99	**49.78**	36.76	**30.58**	47.75	49.00	**49.52**	33.08	48.55

Table 2: Table showing BLiMP results of models. All results are average performance accuracy over three runs. **Bold** values are results that are the best performance achieved average for the given task. These values are also statistically significantly better than the baseline CL model tested with Welch's t-test ($p < 0.05$).

the NONCL model has exceeded CL models, for instance, in CoLA and MRPC. Comparisons between the random CL baseline model (RANDOM) and models trained on structured curriculum suggest that training data on increasing lexical complexity can contribute to improved performance, albeit to a limited extent.

Since the models are trained on small amounts of data, they are likely to overfit. Future investigations can explore more computationally complex methods, such as competency-based scheduling functions to make more robust decisions on when to expose a new level of curriculum to the model (Platanios et al., 2019).

4.2 Best and Worst Curriculum Design

Considering the similarity of the results and the diverse nature of the evaluation tasks, we determine the best model as the one that outperforms the baseline CL model statistically significantly in the highest number of tasks. We find that the best curriculum depends on the evaluation suite. On BLiMP tasks, the best curriculum is found to be DENSITY; ADD on SuperGLUE tasks; TTR on MSGS tasks. Interestingly, the curriculum that demonstrated the fewest instances of outperforming the baseline across all evaluation suites is DISPERSION. From these observations, organising pretraining data according to syntactic complexity is perhaps more advantageous on the SuperGLUE and MSGS tasks, whereas lexical information is more effective for gaining the knowledge required to perform well on BLiMP tasks. The best aggregate model is found to be pretrained by ADD curriculum. This could indicate that exposing data incrementally to the model based on sentence structure is a modest choice for curriculum design.

4.3 Curriculum Design Variation

The variation in performance between each model is observed to be diverse across all evaluation schemes. On average, the gap in performance between the best and worst CL model on SuperGLUE tasks (3.072) and MSGS tasks (4.670) is smaller than on BLiMP (7.440) and supplement BLiMP tasks (5.763). This difference in spread shows that models perform more consistently on finetuning tasks than BLiMP ones. We attribute this to the nature of the evaluation tasks. SuperGLUE comprises a variety of natural language understanding tasks, but they may share certain linguistic or semantic characteristics that make them more predictable for models to generalize across tasks. On the other hand, BLiMP tasks are designed to test specific linguistic phenomena, making them more challenging and potentially leading to greater variation in model performance. Furthermore, given that a portion of the dataset comprises transcribed spoken speech, the exposure to intricate linguistic structures may be restricted, as spoken language tends to be less complex than written language. For instance, Chang and Bergen (2022) find that the average mean sentence length in the CHILDES corpus is 4.5 tokens. This adds plausibility to the fact that spoken language contains simpler syntactic structures.

4.4 Age-of-Acquisition Prediction Results

We find that some of the results for AoA predictions are statistically insignificant. In particular, we see that the models are unable to predict AoA for Overall and Nouns categories. Out of the results that are statistically significant, ADD is able to predict predicates more accurately than the NONCL model and functions words more accurately than the RANDOM model. DISPERSION and DENSITY models have higher accuracy on function words predictions than ADD model.

4.5 Difficulties

Overall, there are fewer instances where the models are able to exceed the CL baseline on SuperGLUE tasks. However, the hardest tasks, whereby models achieved the lowest scores are mostly BLiMP tasks.

Model	CoLA (MCC)	SST-2	MRPC (F1)	QQP (F1)	MNLI	MNLI-mm	QNLI	RTE	BoolQ	MultiRC	WSC
NONCL baseline	69.48	83.27	65.35	69.65	58.07	57.89	56.74	55.22	60.40	48.63	58.63
RANDOM baseline	68.92	83.14	63.65	71.30	57.76	58.84	58.30	50.84	64.08	52.39	61.45
ADD	68.56	83.07	62.90	70.56	58.56	58.94	57.58	**55.89**	62.52	50.38	**61.45**
DISPERSION	68.53	82.94	63.09	70.28	58.33	**59.44**	57.98	52.86	62.84	49.65	61.45
DPW	68.92	82.15	**63.65**	69.66	58.36	59.30	58.18	53.87	62.38	50.16	61.45
DENSITY	**69.12**	82.94	57.63	70.27	**58.94**	57.69	57.60	51.18	62.89	50.93	57.83
RARITY	67.71	82.87	59.32	**73.79**	58.31	57.89	56.39	51.18	62.24	51.92	61.45
TTR	69.09	82.35	60.83	73.53	58.61	59.20	55.89	53.20	57.81	48.67	60.24

Table 3: Table showing SuperGLUE results of models. All results are average performance accuracy over three runs. Matthews correlation is reported for CoLA; F1 scores are reported for MRPC and QQP; the rest are accuracy scores. **Bold** values are results that are the best-performing model for the given task. These values are also statistically significant, tested using Welch's t-test ($p < 0.05$).

Model	Overall (591 words)	Nouns (322 words)	Predicates (167 words)	Function words (102 words)
NONCL baseline	2.053	1.970	1.867	2.619
RANDOM baseline	2.050	1.968	1.850	2.640
ADD	2.051	1.970	1.851*	2.637*
DISPERSION	2.053	1.973	1.854	2.632*
DPW	2.051	1.971	1.847	2.640
DENSITY	2.051	1.970	1.852	2.632*
RARITY	2.049	1.969	1.845	2.637
TTR	2.052	1.969	1.862	2.626

Table 4: Table showing Age-of-Acquisition prediction results of models. The scores are mean absolute deviation in months across Leave-One-Out (LOO) cross-validation folds. Lower MAD scores denotes higher accuracy. Values* are results that are significant, tested using Welch's t-test ($p < 0.005$).

Namely, NPI (lowest = 18.91), FILLER GAP, and QUANTIFIERS (lowest = 33.08), as can be seen in Table 2).

As noted by Warstadt et al. (2020a), tasks such as NPI licensing and Quantifiers require in-depth semantic knowledge. LMs seem to lack such knowledge, as they tend to make errors that produce contradictory language and show a lack of understanding of assumptions and ideas (Marvin and Linzen, 2018). Interestingly, upon inspecting the predictions made by the models, it appears that there is a strong preference for constructions that contain the adverb "*ever*". In fact, all the predictions made by the models incorporated this adverb. The predictions for the Quantifier task also exhibit consistent patterns of ungrammatically. For instance, they do not seem to know superlative quantifiers cannot be embedded under negation.

Table 5 provides examples that illustrate these judgements. Taken together, this effectively shows the models have not been able to generalise conditions for NPI licensing, which is, that NPIs prefer not to occur in positive sentences and are restricted to specific contexts, primarily negative environments. In addition, the models seem to have also not learned that NPI licensing environments exist and can take the form of negation and negative quantifiers. Similarly, the model has not learned the required knowledge for resolving the right quantifier constructions.

In this light, solely relying on CL with varying kinds of lexical complexity for forming curricula may not be sufficient. Additional efforts are required to explicitly introduce language models with the knowledge necessary for completing both semantic and syntax tasks successfully. This draws questions to LMs' abilities to generalise syntactical patterns in language. Whilst this 10M-word corpus might be sufficient for humans acquiring language, LMs perhaps require more targeted training and additional data.

5 Conclusion

In this work, we investigated different CL curricula. We find that linguistically-motivated curriculum formation produces better results than (1) a non-CL pretrained model, and (2) a CL model trained on a randomly formed curriculum. In addition, we provide an analysis of the impact of linguistic curriculum on evaluation tasks. The findings underscore the potential of leveraging linguistic principles to address the challenges posed by sequential learn-

ID	Prediction
npi_licensing_9	"Should Mitchell ever know Eva?"
npi_licensing_43	"Sharon has ever climbed down a hill."
quantifiers_62	"There weren't most gates looking like most photographs."

Table 5: Example BLiMP predictions made by the models

ing tasks and pave the way for further research in this promising direction. One possible direction to explore is the adaptive CL approach, which dynamically adjusts the curriculum based on the model's learning progress and task complexities. This could involve incorporating feedback mechanisms to fine-tune the curriculum during training for optimal task mastery. With this work as a foundation, we hope it can provide insights to linguistically-oriented pertaining works.

6 Limitations

We would like to point out that more advanced features, such as discourse features and additional semantic features provided by Lee et al. (2021) form promising areas of exploration. Arguably, including these features will paint a more representative of linguistic complexity. However, as a starting point, we frame our work to first isolate each "dimensionality" of linguistic complexity, and explore each one's effect in pretraining independently.

Acknowledgements

This work is supported by the Centre for Doctoral Training in Speech and Language Technologies (SLT) and their Applications are funded by the UK Research and Innovation grant EP/S023062/1. We are grateful to the reviewers for their contributions and feedback. Special thanks to Aline Villavicencio for the insights and directions. Additional thanks to Ed Gow-Smith, Dylan Phelps, Bohua Peng and members of the CDT for making this work happen.

References

Yoshua Bengio, Jérôme Louradour, Ronan Collobert, and Jason Weston. 2009. Curriculum learning. In *Proceedings of the 26th Annual International Conference on Machine Learning*, ICML '09, page 41–48, New York, NY, USA. Association for Computing Machinery.

Andreas Blombach, Stephanie Evert, Fotis Jannidis, Steffen Pielström, Leonard Konle, and Thomas Proisl. 2022. *Digital Humanities 2022*, 2022 edition, page 130–134. University of Tokyo.

Ernie Chang, Hui-Syuan Yeh, and Vera Demberg. 2021. Does the order of training samples matter? improving neural data-to-text generation with curriculum learning. In *Proceedings of the 16th Conference of the European Chapter of the Association for Computational Linguistics: Main Volume*, pages 727–733, Online. Association for Computational Linguistics.

Tyler A. Chang and Benjamin K. Bergen. 2022. Word Acquisition in Neural Language Models. *Transactions of the Association for Computational Linguistics*, 10:1–16.

Volkan Cirik, Eduard H. Hovy, and Louis-Philippe Morency. 2016. Visualizing and understanding curriculum learning for long short-term memory networks. *ArXiv*, abs/1611.06204.

Leo Gao, Jonathan Tow, Stella Biderman, Sid Black, Anthony DiPofi, Charles Foster, Laurence Golding, Jeffrey Hsu, Kyle McDonell, Niklas Muennighoff, Jason Phang, Laria Reynolds, Eric Tang, Anish Thite, Ben Wang, Kevin Wang, and Andy Zou. 2021. A framework for few-shot language model evaluation.

Edward Gibson. 1998. Linguistic complexity: locality of syntactic dependencies. *Cognition*, 68(1):1–76.

Jill Gilkerson, Jeffrey A. Richards, Steven F. Warren, Judith K. Montgomery, Charles R. Greenwood, D. Kimbrough Oller, John H. L. Hansen, and Terrance D. Paul. 2017. Mapping the early language environment using all-day recordings and automated analysis. *American Journal of Speech-Language Pathology*, 26(2):248–265.

C. Gini. 1912. *Variabilità e mutabilità: contributo allo studio delle distribuzioni e delle relazioni statistiche. [Fasc. I.]*. Studi economico-giuridici pubblicati per cura della facoltà di Giurisprudenza della R. Università di Cagliari. Tipogr. di P. Cuppini.

Daniel Grodner and Edward Gibson. 2005. Consequences of the serial nature of linguistic input for sentenial complexity. *Cognitive Science*, 29(2):261–290.

John A Hawkins. 1994. *A performance theory of order and constituency*. 73. Cambridge University Press.

Borna Jafarpour, Dawn Sepehr, and Nick Pogrebnyakov. 2021. Active curriculum learning. In *Proceedings of the First Workshop on Interactive Learning for Natural Language Processing*, pages 40–45, Online. Association for Computational Linguistics.

Sora Kadotani, Tomoyuki Kajiwara, Yuki Arase, and Makoto Onizuka. 2021. Edit distance based curriculum learning for paraphrase generation. In *Proceedings of the 59th Annual Meeting of the Association for Computational Linguistics and the 11th International Joint Conference on Natural Language Processing: Student Research Workshop*, pages 229–234, Online. Association for Computational Linguistics.

Kai A Krueger and Peter Dayan. 2009. Flexible shaping: How learning in small steps helps. *Cognition*, 110(3):380–394.

Bruce W. Lee, Yoo Sung Jang, and Jason Lee. 2021. Pushing on text readability assessment: A transformer meets handcrafted linguistic features. In *Proceedings of the 2021 Conference on Empirical Methods in Natural Language Processing*, pages 10669–10686, Online and Punta Cana, Dominican Republic. Association for Computational Linguistics.

Cao Liu, Shizhu He, Kang Liu, and Jun Zhao. 2018. Curriculum learning for natural answer generation. In *Proceedings of the Twenty-Seventh International Joint Conference on Artificial Intelligence, IJCAI-18*, pages 4223–4229. International Joint Conferences on Artificial Intelligence Organization.

Haitao Liu, Richard Hudson, and Zhiwei Feng. 2009. Using a chinese treebank to measure dependency distance. 5(2):161–174.

Rebecca Marvin and Tal Linzen. 2018. Targeted syntactic evaluation of language models. In *Proceedings of the 2018 Conference on Empirical Methods in Natural Language Processing*, pages 1192–1202, Brussels, Belgium. Association for Computational Linguistics.

Koichi Nagatsuka, Clifford Broni-Bediako, and Masayasu Atsumi. 2021. Pre-training a BERT with curriculum learning by increasing block-size of input text. In *Proceedings of the International Conference on Recent Advances in Natural Language Processing (RANLP 2021)*, pages 989–996, Held Online. INCOMA Ltd.

Koichi Nagatsuka, Clifford Broni-Bediako, and Masayasu Atsumi. 2022. Length-based curriculum learning for efficient pre-training of language models. *New Gen. Comput.*, 41(1):109–134.

Masanori Oya. 2011. Syntactic dependency distance as sentence complexity measure. *Proceedings of the 16th International Conference of Pan-Pacific Association of Applied Linguistics*.

Emmanouil Antonios Platanios, Otilia Stretcu, Graham Neubig, Barnabas Poczos, and Tom Mitchell. 2019. Competence-based curriculum learning for neural machine translation. In *Proceedings of the 2019 Conference of the North American Chapter of the Association for Computational Linguistics: Human Language Technologies, Volume 1 (Long and Short Papers)*, pages 1162–1172, Minneapolis, Minnesota. Association for Computational Linguistics.

Eva Portelance, Yuguang Duan, Michael C. Frank, and Gary Lupyan. 2023. Predicting age of acquisition for children's early vocabulary in five languages using language model surprisal. *Cognitive science*, 47 9:e13334.

Alec Radford, Jeff Wu, Rewon Child, David Luan, Dario Amodei, and Ilya Sutskever. 2019. Language models are unsupervised multitask learners.

Roland Schäfer. 2016. CommonCOW: Massively huge web corpora from CommonCrawl data and a method to distribute them freely under restrictive EU copyright laws. In *Proceedings of the Tenth International Conference on Language Resources and Evaluation (LREC'16)*, pages 4500–4504, Portorož, Slovenia. European Language Resources Association (ELRA).

Burrhus F Skinner. 1958. Reinforcement today. *American Psychologist*, 13(3):94.

John Sweller. 1994. Cognitive load theory, learning difficulty, and instructional design. *Learning and Instruction*, 4:295–312.

Yi Tay, Shuohang Wang, Anh Tuan Luu, Jie Fu, Minh C. Phan, Xingdi Yuan, Jinfeng Rao, Siu Cheung Hui, and Aston Zhang. 2019. Simple and effective curriculum pointer-generator networks for reading comprehension over long narratives. In *Proceedings of the 57th Annual Meeting of the Association for Computational Linguistics*, pages 4922–4931, Florence, Italy. Association for Computational Linguistics.

Mildred C. Templin. 1957. *Certain Language Skills in Children: Their Development and Interrelationships*, new edition edition, volume 26. University of Minnesota Press.

Hugo Touvron, Louis Martin, Kevin Stone, Peter Albert, Amjad Almahairi, Yasmine Babaei, Nikolay Bashlykov, Soumya Batra, Prajjwal Bhargava, Shruti Bhosale, Dan Bikel, Lukas Blecher, Cristian Canton Ferrer, Moya Chen, Guillem Cucurull, David Esiobu, Jude Fernandes, Jeremy Fu, Wenyin Fu, Brian Fuller, Cynthia Gao, Vedanuj Goswami, Naman Goyal, Anthony Hartshorn, Saghar Hosseini, Rui Hou, Hakan Inan, Marcin Kardas, Viktor Kerkez, Madian Khabsa, Isabel Kloumann, Artem Korenev, Punit Singh Koura, Marie-Anne Lachaux, Thibaut Lavril, Jenya Lee, Diana Liskovich, Yinghai Lu, Yuning Mao, Xavier Martinet, Todor Mihaylov, Pushkar Mishra, Igor Molybog, Yixin Nie, Andrew Poulton, Jeremy Reizenstein, Rashi Rungta, Kalyan Saladi, Alan Schelten, Ruan Silva, Eric Michael Smith, Ranjan Subramanian, Xiaoqing Ellen Tan, Binh Tang, Ross Taylor, Adina Williams, Jian Xiang Kuan, Puxin Xu, Zheng Yan, Iliyan Zarov, Yuchen Zhang, Angela Fan, Melanie Kambadur, Sharan Narang, Aurelien Rodriguez, Robert Stojnic, Sergey Edunov, and Thomas

Scialom. 2023. Llama 2: Open foundation and fine-tuned chat models.

Alex Wang, Amanpreet Singh, Julian Michael, Felix Hill, Omer Levy, and Samuel Bowman. 2018. GLUE: A multi-task benchmark and analysis platform for natural language understanding. In *Proceedings of the 2018 EMNLP Workshop BlackboxNLP: Analyzing and Interpreting Neural Networks for NLP*, pages 353–355, Brussels, Belgium. Association for Computational Linguistics.

Alex Warstadt, Leshem Choshen, Ryan Cotterell, Tal Linzen, Aaron Mueller, Ethan Wilcox, Williams Adina, and Chengxu Zhuang. 2023. Findings of the BabyLM Challenge: Sample-efficient pretraining on developmentally plausible corpora. In *Proceedings of the BabyLM Challenge*. Association for Computational Linguistics (ACL).

Alex Warstadt, Alicia Parrish, Haokun Liu, Anhad Mohananey, Wei Peng, Sheng-Fu Wang, and Samuel R. Bowman. 2020a. BLiMP: The benchmark of linguistic minimal pairs for English. *Transactions of the Association for Computational Linguistics*, 8:377–392.

Alex Warstadt, Yian Zhang, Xiaocheng Li, Haokun Liu, and Samuel R. Bowman. 2020b. Learning which features matter: RoBERTa acquires a preference for linguistic generalizations (eventually). In *Proceedings of the 2020 Conference on Empirical Methods in Natural Language Processing (EMNLP)*, pages 217–235, Online. Association for Computational Linguistics.

A Additional Results

Results on the supplement BLiMP tasks and MSGS tasks are shown in Table 6 and Table 7, respectively.

	HYPERNYM	QA CONGRUENCE EASY	QA CONGRUENCE TRICKY	SUBJECT AUX INVERSION	TURN TAKING
NONCL baseline	50.85	27.60	32.73	62.63	51.31
RANDOM baseline	50.85	34.90	28.69	59.32	50.00
ADD	49.42	**37.50**	29.09	**67.16**	46.43
DISPERSION	50.81	28.65	30.30	64.16	50.95
DPW	50.58	30.73	28.69	57.37	48.10
DENSITY	49.92	32.81	30.71	65.37	47.98
RARITY	**50.54**	34.38	28.08	61.77	49.40
TTR	50.50	31.25	**32.32**	61.06	**50.83**

Table 6: Table showing results of supplement BLiMP tasks. All results are average performance accuracy over three runs. **Bold** values are results that are the best performance achieved average for the given task. These values are also statistically significantly better than the baseline CL model tested with Welch's t-test ($p < 0.05$).

	CR_CTRL	LC_CTRL	MV_CTRL	RP_CTRL	SC_CTRL	CR_LC	CR_RTP	MV_LC	MV_RTP	SC_LC	SC_RP
NONCL	59.64	79.23	82.98	98.85	60.58	54.61	23.22	29.39	23.92	40.82	35.40
RANDOM	59.78	93.15	82.34	99.75	60.21	51.90	24.95	23.59	26.22	40.82	34.69
ADD	**61.19**	**98.30**	76.38	99.75	60.18	48.78	23.43	22.81	22.81	40.84	30.09
DISPERSION	58.34	93.07	79.17	99.72	59.35	50.91	24.69	22.67	23.48	40.84	31.64
DPW	59.12	87.27	79.97	99.64	59.25	42.76	23.68	23.41	25.26	40.82	37.18
DENSITY	59.39	88.63	75.69	99.75	**61.39**	50.98	26.02	22.66	24.53	40.80	33.75
RARITY	58.70	92.71	76.71	**99.82**	59.96	49.84	24.49	27.18	25.62	40.82	35.10
TTR	59.17	85.87	81.26	99.09	59.20	46.57	**27.83**	**28.82**	**26.92**	**40.84**	**39.42**

Table 7: Results of MSGS evaluation. All results are Matthews correlation coefficients (MCCs). All results are average performance accuracy over three runs. **Bold** values are results that are average MCC for the given task. These values are also statistically significantly better than the baseline CL model tested with Welch's t-test ($p < 0.05$).

Baby Llama: knowledge distillation from an ensemble of teachers trained on a small dataset with no performance penalty

Inar Timiryasov*
Niels Bohr Institute,
University of Copenhagen,
Blegdamsvej 17, DK-2010,
Copenhagen, Denmark
inar.timiryasov@nbi.ku.dk

Jean-Loup Tastet*
Departamento de Física Teórica and
Instituto de Física Teórica UAM/CSIC,
Universidad Autónoma de Madrid,
Cantoblanco, 28049, Madrid, Spain
jean-loup.tastet@uam.es

Abstract

We present our submission[1] to the BabyLM challenge, whose goal was to improve the sample efficiency of language models. We trained an ensemble consisting of a GPT-2 and small LLaMA models on the developmentally-plausible, 10M-word BabyLM dataset, then distilled it into a small, 58M-parameter LLaMA model, which exceeds in performance both of its teachers as well as a similar model trained without distillation. This suggests that distillation can not only retain the full performance of the teacher model when the latter is trained on a sufficiently small dataset; it can exceed it, and lead to significantly better performance than direct training.

1 Introduction

Today's state-of-the-art language models are typically trained on the order of a trillion tokens. Hoffmann et al. (2022) have observed that in order to train a model in a compute-optimal way, the number of parameters and dataset size should follow a linear relation: the so-called Chinchilla scaling law, with an optimal ratio of about 20 tokens per model parameter. For models larger than $\sim 10^{11}$ parameters, this implies that the currently-available amount of training data ($\sim 10^{12}$ tokens) already constitutes a bottleneck, that prevents scaling up those models in a compute-optimal way.

A trillion tokens is already at least 4 orders of magnitude larger than the estimated number of words[2] ($\lesssim 10^8$) to which a typical 13-year-old child has been exposed. This suggests that current language models are significantly less *sample-efficient* than human beings.

Furthermore, the trend of scaling up models to improve their performance may limit their usage in embedded systems, personal devices, and other end-user technologies, as well as in specialized applications where domain-specific training material is scarce. Taylor et al. (2022) have shown that training models on higher-quality data can improve performance; however, the quantity of such high-quality data is limited, and often represents only a small fraction of the corpus.

This makes a strong case for trying to increase the sample efficiency of current models and training algorithms. In this context, the BabyLM challenge (Warstadt et al., 2023) has invited researchers to investigate ways of improving the sample efficiency of small-scale language models, by restricting the training set to a *developmentally plausible* corpus, consisting mostly of transcribed speech of either 10M (`strict-small` track) or 100M words (`strict` and `loose` tracks).

The present paper describes our submission to the `strict-small` track of the BabyLM challenge. As such, it focuses on the 10M-word dataset. Our proposed solution consists in distilling an ensemble of two larger "teacher" models, of different architectures (GPT-2 and LLaMA), into a smaller "student" LLaMA model. We show that this approach produces a model whose performance largely matches, and often exceeds, that of both teachers.

We introduce Baby Llama in section 2, describe the dataset in section 3, discuss the model performance in section 4, and finally conclude in section 5. The full numerical results of the evals are listed in appendix A, and in appendix B we briefly discuss a number of experiments (including some negative results) that we eventually chose not to include into the final model.

2 Pretraining using distillation

Knowledge distillation (Bucila et al., 2006; Hinton et al., 2015) is a technique that consists in training a (usually smaller) student model to reproduce the

*Equal contributions

[1]`https://huggingface.co/timinar/baby-llama-58m` for the checkpoint; the training code is available at `https://github.com/timinar/BabyLlama`.

[2]Extrapolating from Gilkerson et al. (2017).

Proceedings of the 27th Conference on Computational Natural Language Learning: Volume 2: The BabyLM Challenge, pages 279–289
December 6-7, 2023

behaviour of one or more teacher models. This method has been successfully applied to large language models, e.g. in Sanh et al. (2019).

In our submission to the `strict-small` track of the BabyLM challenge, we address the sample efficiency problem by distilling an ensemble of larger pre-trained teacher models into a smaller student model. Specifically, we train an ensemble consisting of GPT-2 (Radford et al., 2019) and a small LLaMA model (Touvron et al., 2023) on the 10M-word BabyLM dataset, and then distill this ensemble into a smaller, 58M-parameter LLaMA model. Despite its reduced size, our distilled LLaMA model not only retains the performance of the larger models, but also exceeds it. This shows that distillation can be a powerful tool to enhance sample efficiency when training on smaller datasets.

The distillation process involves guiding the training of the student model using the output of the teacher models. This output, also known as soft targets, is obtained by applying a temperature scaling factor to the teacher's output logits. The student model is then trained to approximate these soft targets (with the same temperature) in addition to the original hard targets, resulting in a model that generalizes better and therefore performs better on unseen data.

The loss function consists of a weighted sum of the original hard target loss (cross-entropy with the true labels) and the distillation loss (Kullback-Leibler divergence with the teacher's soft targets). Formally, it can be expressed as:

$$L = \alpha L_{CE} + (1 - \alpha) L_{KL} \quad (1)$$

where α is the weight factor, L_{CE} is the original cross-entropy loss, and L_{KL} is the Kullback-Leibler divergence.

The teacher models used for the distillation are newly-trained instances of GPT-2 and LLaMA. The GPT-2 model has 24 layers, 16 attention heads, an embedding dimension of 1536, intermediate size of 6144, and maximum sequence length of 128, resulting in 705M parameters. It was trained for 6 epochs with a batch size of 256 and maximum learning rate[3] of $2.5 \cdot 10^{-4}$. The LLaMA model has 24 layers, 8 attention heads, a hidden size of 1024, intermediate size of 3072, and maximum sequence length of 256, resulting in 360M parameters. It was trained for 4 epochs with a batch size of 128 and maximum learning rate of $3 \cdot 10^{-4}$. Both teacher models are pretrained exclusively on the 10M-word BabyLM dataset. We use the same tokenizer for both the teacher and student models, with a vocabulary size of 16000; the tokenizer is trained exclusively on the *training* split.

For the student model, we chose a smaller version of the LLaMA model with only 16 layers, 8 attention heads, a hidden size of 512 and an intermediate size of 1024, resulting in 58M parameters. This choice was mainly motivated by the requirement of being able to fine-tune the model with our limited computational resources[4] for the various benchmark tasks that require fine-tuning. The distillation process is carried out using a batch size of 32 and a maximum learning rate of $3 \cdot 10^{-4}$. The loss function (1) is used throughout the entire training, i.e. the student model is *not* trained conventionally before the distillation. The training lasts for 6 epochs. The temperature was set to 2 and $\alpha = 0.5$. We have tried various combinations of 2, 4, and 6 teacher models, with the best results being achieved using two teachers.

We observed that the eval loss did not correlate sufficiently well with the benchmarks to be able to use it as a proxy for the final model performance. Therefore, given the limited time and resources, we were not able to perform a systematic hyperparameter search.

The trained model can be downloaded from the HuggingFace repository `https://huggingface.co/timinar/baby-llama-58m`. When implementing the distillation loss, we largely followed repository `https://github.com/philschmid/knowledge-distillation-transformers-pytorch-sagemaker` to modify the original `Trainer` class from the HuggingFace Transformers library. Pretraining a 58M-parameter model with two teachers for 6 epochs takes less than 3 hours on a single NVIDIA RTX 3090. Training GPT-705M for 6 epochs takes around 12 hours, while training Llama-360M for 4 epochs takes around 2 hours.

3 Dataset

The "train" dataset used in the `strict-small` track consists of approximately 10M words (as counted by the UNIX `wc` tool) that form a *developmentally*

[3] We trained all three models using a cosine learning rate schedule with a warm-up of 200 steps.

[4] It would be interesting to see if a bigger model — possibly larger than the teachers — can be successfully pretrained in the same way.

plausible corpus, i.e. the sort of "input" that a typical child has access to: mostly transcribed speech and children's books. A separate, similar "dev" dataset of approximately 9.4M words is used for validation and testing. The entire dataset is in English, with some occasional foreign words such as e.g. proper nouns in Wikipedia articles.

Some simple, regex-based cleaning is performed on both datasets, e.g. to remove HTML tags from Wikipedia articles, non-verbal cues from subtitles, or even to correct I's that were incorrectly recognized as l's in OCR'ed uppercase text. The Python script responsible for the cleaning, `mrclean.py`, is included along with the model; it contains one function for each data source.

The cleaned dataset is then tokenized using Byte-Pair Encoding (BPE) with a vocabulary size of 16000. To avoid leakage, the tokenizer was trained *exclusively* on the training split. All the tokens are finally concatenated into a single one-dimensional vector.

Each split is divided into contiguous chunks of 128 tokens. During each epoch of pretraining, the model is presented with a new random permutation of the chunks from the training split.[5] The validation loss is computed at the end of each epoch, by iterating in order over a fixed (but randomly sampled at the beginning) subset of the "dev" split.

4 Performance

Baby Llama is evaluated using a suite of linguistic benchmarks consisting of the BLiMP (Warstadt et al., 2020a) zero-shot benchmark (plus some yet-unpublished supplementary evals) as well as two fine-tuning benchmarks: SuperGLUE (Wang et al., 2020) and MSGS (Warstadt et al., 2020b). In appendix A, we also discuss the model performance when used as part of an age-of-acquisition prediction task (Portelance et al., To Appear). These benchmarks are all run using the `lm-evaluation-harness` package (Gao et al., 2021), version `v0.2.0`.

We compare Baby Llama with three baseline models that are similar or larger in size and inference/fine-tuning computational cost: OPT (125M-parameter version, Zhang et al., 2022), RoBERTa (base, 125M parameters, Liu et al., 2019) and T5 (base, 222M parameters, Raffel et al., 2020). The baseline models have been re-trained on the same 10M-word dataset by the organizers of the BabyLM challenge.[6] For the BLiMP zero-shot benchmark, we add to the comparison the larger GPT-2 (705M) and LLaMA (360M) models that were used as teachers in the distillation procedure, a LLaMA (58M) model trained without distillation, as well as the ensemble model formed by averaging the output logits of both teachers. However, we do not evaluate the fine-tuning performance of these models due to the computational cost that it would incur.

The accuracy[7] of Baby Llama on the zero-shot benchmarks is presented in fig. 1 along with the accuracy of the baselines, and in fig. 2 with that of the non-distilled and teacher models. Its fine-tuning accuracy[8] is reported in fig. 3 for (Super)GLUE, and its Matthews correlation coefficient (MCC) in fig. 4 for MSGS. The performance is reported in the form of parallel-coordinates plots, with the lines serving as visual guides. The full numerical results of the evals are listed in tables 1 and 2 in appendix A.

Baby Llama's performance is generally superior to all three baselines, for both zero-shot and fine-tuning benchmarks. It only falls significantly behind *any* of the baselines on a handful of evals, thus showing a well-balanced and consistent overall performance.

Interestingly, Baby Llama not only performs better that both of the individual teacher models (as well as the non-distilled model) on most zero-shot tasks; it also performs better than the corresponding ensemble model. This clearly shows that the distillation procedure, by itself, leads to an improvement in the zero-shot accuracy.

When evaluating Baby Llama on the benchmarks that require fine-tuning, we noticed that the default fine-tuning hyperparameters suggested by the organizers lead to severe overfitting in a number of benchmarks (as evidenced by an increasing eval loss and no improvement — or a decrease — in the accuracy, while the training loss kept decreas-

[5] We noticed that adding a random offset between 0 and 127 to each chunk lead to marginally better performance; however, due to lack of time, the final teacher and student models were trained without such an offset.

[6] The checkpoints for those baseline models can be found at `https://huggingface.co/babylm`.

[7] We note that, despite seeding all the random number generators, we were not able to reproduce the numerical results across different machines (possibly due to different software versions) despite following as closely as possible the official procedure to install the evaluation pipeline. For consistency, all the reported results have been produced on the same machine.

[8] Or MCC or F_1 score when explicitly mentioned.

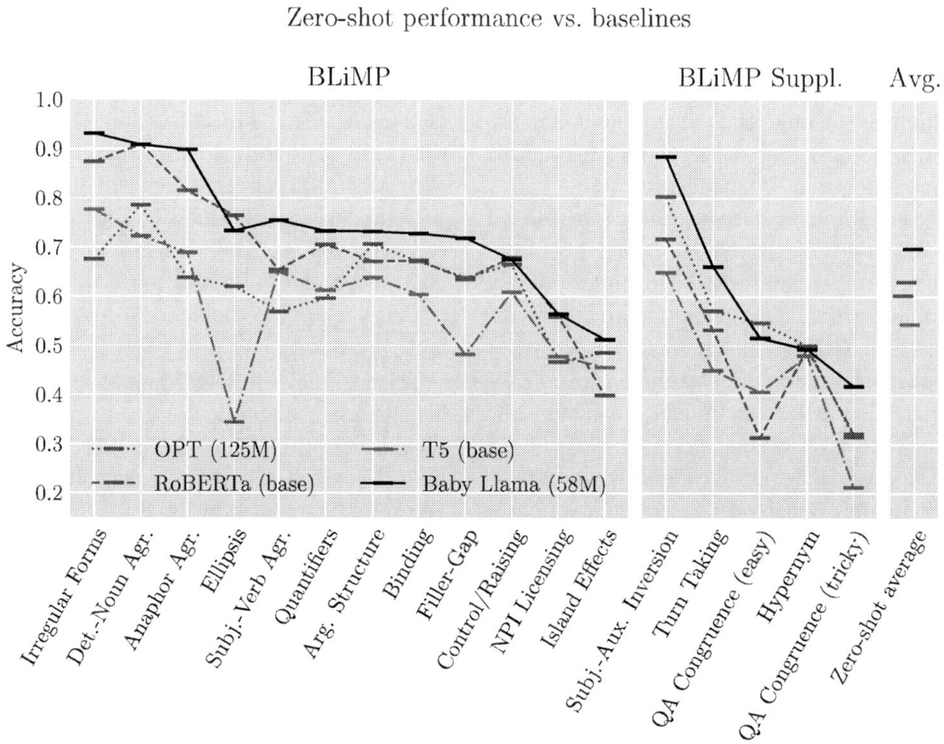

Figure 1: Parallel-coordinates plot summarizing the zero-shot performance of Baby Llama on the BLiMP and BLiMP Supplement benchmarks, compared with a number of baseline models.

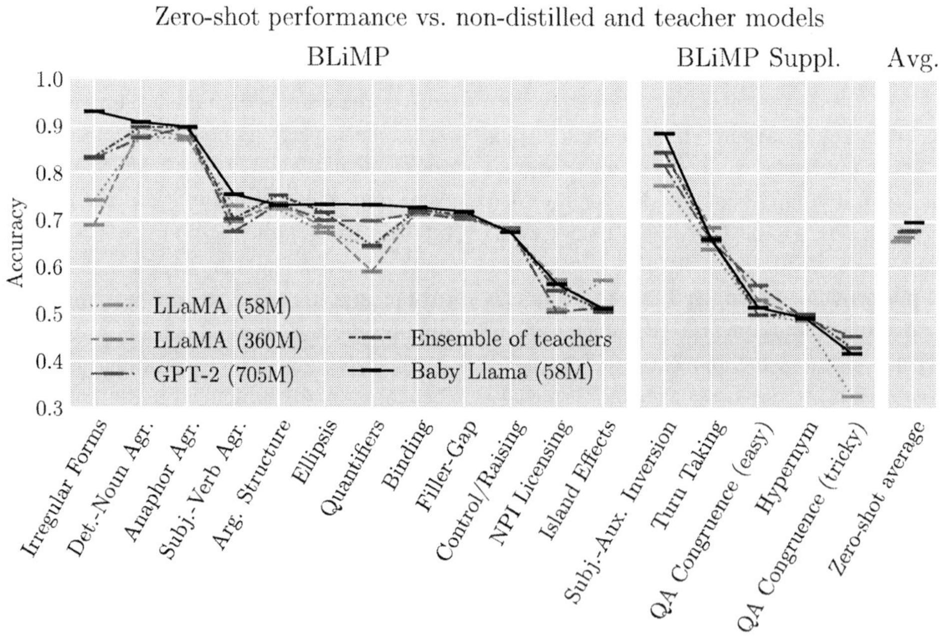

Figure 2: Parallel-coordinates plot summarizing the zero-shot performance of Baby Llama on the BLiMP and BLiMP Supplement benchmarks, compared with the same, non-distilled model, and both teacher models.

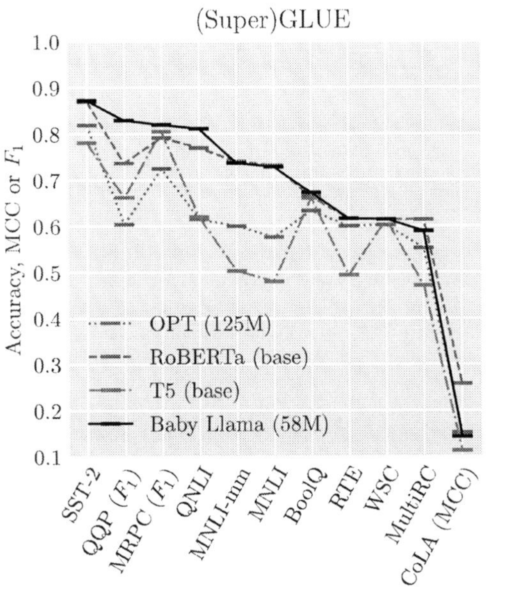

Figure 3: Parallel-coordinates plot summarizing the fine-tuning performance of Baby Llama on a subset of the GLUE and SuperGLUE benchmarks, compared with a number of baseline models. Unless specified otherwise, the metric used is the classification accuracy. The fine-tuning hyperparameters are listed in table 3.

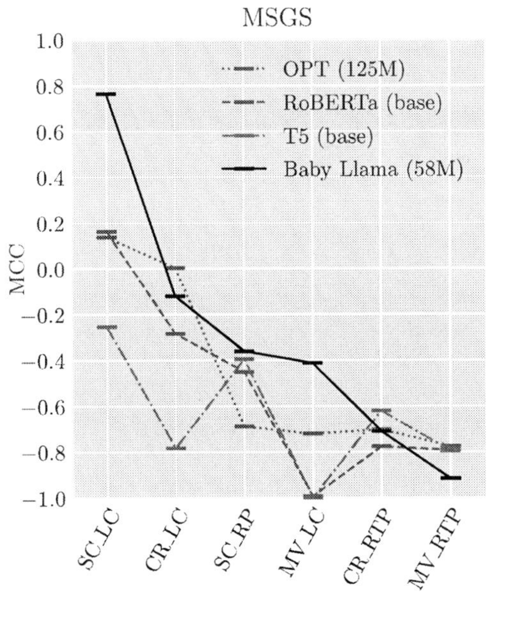

Figure 4: Parallel-coordinates plot summarizing the fine-tuning performance of Baby Llama on the MSGS benchmark, compared with a number of baseline models. The fine-tuning hyperparameters are listed in table 3.

ing). To avoid this issue, we have re-tuned the fine-tuning hyperparameters as needed. The selected sets of hyperparameters are listed in table 3. For a small number of benchmarks, the performance didn't evolve smoothly as a function of the hyperparameters. Since this is symptomatic of overfitting on the eval dataset (making any comparison potentially inaccurate), we explicitly identify those benchmarks with the † symbol in table 2.

5 Conclusion

In this work, we trained Baby Llama — a 58M-parameter model based on the LLaMA architecture — on the 10M-word BabyLM dataset using knowledge distillation. It was distilled from an ensemble of two, inhomogeneous teachers: a 360M-parameter LLaMA model and a 705M-parameter GPT-2 model, both trained on the same dataset. We observed that the model pretrained with the distillation loss (1) performs better that the similar 58M-parameter model trained in the usual way. Moreover, the smaller, distilled model outperforms both of its teachers individually, as well as the ensemble model formed by the two teachers.

If those findings continue to hold at scale (see Limitations), they could help improve the sample efficiency of large language models, while reducing the amount of memory and compute necessary to deploy them. The increased sample efficiency could allow training larger, higher-performing models on the already-available training corpora (but at a higher training cost). Alternatively, it could limit the data collection necessary to train today's state-of-the-art models. This would e.g. allow focusing on higher-quality data, and it could be particularly useful in a hypothetical scenario where data collection gets restricted by online platforms, regulations, or due to copyright. Finally, the reduced size and computing requirements of the distilled model would reduce its energy footprint and facilitate on-device/local processing, leading to potentially-improved user privacy.

Limitations

The results presented in this article have been obtained for models which are 10^3 to 10^4 times smaller that current state-of-the-art language models. Many important properties of these models have been shown to emerge as the model size increases (Radford et al., 2019; Brown et al., 2020). Therefore, the results obtained at small scales may not necessarily generalize to larger scales.

Furthermore, our results have been obtained in the regime where the number of parameters significantly exceeds the number of training tokens. This differs from today's state-of-the-art language models, which are usually trained on many more tokens than their number of parameters, e.g. ~ 20 times more for models trained in a compute-optimal way following Hoffmann et al. (2022). Such models may not have the luxury to dedicate as many parameters to a given piece of information or feature as ours. Therefore, there is no guarantee that the nearly lossless distillation that we have observed will generalize to such models.

Due to these differences in scale and tokens-to-parameters ratio, it is not clear if our proposed distillation procedure could be scaled up in order to increase the sample efficiency of today's largest language models. Although this hypothesis can in principle be tested experimentally, the authors lack the computational resources required to perform such a test.

Finally, our results have been obtained for a textual training corpus, in the context of language modeling. Further experimentation will be required in order to investigate whether our findings generalize to different data modalities and to other domains where transformer-based models are also being used.

Acknowledgements

We thank Oleg Ruchayskiy and Troels C. Petersen for their support. JLT acknowledges partial financial support by the Spanish Research Agency (Agencia Estatal de Investigación) through the grant IFT Centro de Excelencia Severo Ochoa No CEX2020-001007-S, by the grant PID2019-108892RB-I00 funded by MCIN/AEI/ 10.13039/501100011033, by the European Union's Horizon 2020 research and innovation programme under the Marie Skłodowska-Curie grant agreements No 860881-HIDDeN and Staff Exchange grant agreement No 101086085 - ASYMMETRY, and by the grant Juan de la Cierva FJC2021-047666-I funded by MCIN/AEI/10.13039/501100011033 and by the European Union "NextGenerationEU"/PRTR. The work of IT was partially supported by the Carlsberg foundation, and by the European Union's Horizon 2020 research and innovation program under the Marie Sklodowska-Curie grant agreement No. 847523 'INTERACTIONS'.

References

Dara Bahri, Hossein Mobahi, and Yi Tay. 2021. Sharpness-Aware Minimization Improves Language Model Generalization. *arXiv e-prints*, page arXiv:2110.08529.

Yoshua Bengio, Jérôme Louradour, Ronan Collobert, and Jason Weston. 2009. Curriculum learning. ICML '09, page 41–48, New York, NY, USA. Association for Computing Machinery.

Tom Brown, Benjamin Mann, Nick Ryder, Melanie Subbiah, Jared D Kaplan, Prafulla Dhariwal, Arvind Neelakantan, Pranav Shyam, Girish Sastry, Amanda Askell, Sandhini Agarwal, Ariel Herbert-Voss, Gretchen Krueger, Tom Henighan, Rewon Child, Aditya Ramesh, Daniel Ziegler, Jeffrey Wu, Clemens Winter, Chris Hesse, Mark Chen, Eric Sigler, Mateusz Litwin, Scott Gray, Benjamin Chess, Jack Clark, Christopher Berner, Sam McCandlish, Alec Radford, Ilya Sutskever, and Dario Amodei. 2020. Language models are few-shot learners. In *Advances in Neural Information Processing Systems*, volume 33, pages 1877–1901. Curran Associates, Inc.

Cristian Bucila, Rich Caruana, and Alexandru Niculescu-Mizil. 2006. Model compression. In *Knowledge Discovery and Data Mining*.

William Fedus, Barret Zoph, and Noam Shazeer. 2022. Switch transformers: Scaling to trillion parameter models with simple and efficient sparsity. *Journal of Machine Learning Research*, 23(120):1–39.

Pierre Foret, Ariel Kleiner, Hossein Mobahi, and Behnam Neyshabur. 2020. Sharpness-Aware Minimization for Efficiently Improving Generalization. *arXiv e-prints*, page arXiv:2010.01412.

Leo Gao, Jonathan Tow, Stella Biderman, Sid Black, Anthony DiPofi, Charles Foster, Laurence Golding, Jeffrey Hsu, Kyle McDonell, Niklas Muennighoff, Jason Phang, Laria Reynolds, Eric Tang, Anish Thite, Ben Wang, Kevin Wang, and Andy Zou. 2021. A framework for few-shot language model evaluation.

Jill Gilkerson, Jeffrey A. Richards, Steven F. Warren, Judith K. Montgomery, Charles R. Greenwood, D. Kimbrough Oller, John H. L. Hansen, and Terrance D. Paul. 2017. Mapping the early language environment using all-day recordings and automated analysis. *American Journal of Speech-Language Pathology*, 26(2):248–265.

Geoffrey Hinton, Oriol Vinyals, and Jeff Dean. 2015. Distilling the Knowledge in a Neural Network. *arXiv e-prints*, page arXiv:1503.02531.

Jordan Hoffmann, Sebastian Borgeaud, Arthur Mensch, Elena Buchatskaya, Trevor Cai, Eliza Rutherford,

Diego de Las Casas, Lisa Anne Hendricks, Johannes Welbl, Aidan Clark, Tom Hennigan, Eric Noland, Katie Millican, George van den Driessche, Bogdan Damoc, Aurelia Guy, Simon Osindero, Karen Simonyan, Erich Elsen, Jack W. Rae, Oriol Vinyals, and Laurent Sifre. 2022. Training compute-optimal large language models.

Yinhan Liu, Myle Ott, Naman Goyal, Jingfei Du, Mandar Joshi, Danqi Chen, Omer Levy, Mike Lewis, Luke Zettlemoyer, and Veselin Stoyanov. 2019. RoBERTa: A robustly optimized BERT pretraining approach.

Eva Portelance, Yuguang Duan, Michael C. Frank, and Gary Lupyan. To Appear. Predicting age of acquisition for children's early vocabulary in five languages using language model surprisal. *Cognitive Science.*

Alec Radford, Jeff Wu, Rewon Child, David Luan, Dario Amodei, and Ilya Sutskever. 2019. Language models are unsupervised multitask learners.

Colin Raffel, Noam Shazeer, Adam Roberts, Katherine Lee, Sharan Narang, Michael Matena, Yanqi Zhou, Wei Li, and Peter J. Liu. 2020. Exploring the limits of transfer learning with a unified text-to-text transformer.

Victor Sanh, Lysandre Debut, Julien Chaumond, and Thomas Wolf. 2019. DistilBERT, a distilled version of BERT: smaller, faster, cheaper and lighter. *CoRR*, abs/1910.01108.

Maxim Surkov, Vladislav Mosin, and Ivan Yamshchikov. 2022. Do data-based curricula work? In *Proceedings of the Third Workshop on Insights from Negative Results in NLP*, pages 119–128, Dublin, Ireland. Association for Computational Linguistics.

Ross Taylor, Marcin Kardas, Guillem Cucurull, Thomas Scialom, Anthony Hartshorn, Elvis Saravia, Andrew Poulton, Viktor Kerkez, and Robert Stojnic. 2022. Galactica: A large language model for science.

Hugo Touvron, Thibaut Lavril, Gautier Izacard, Xavier Martinet, Marie-Anne Lachaux, Timothée Lacroix, Baptiste Rozière, Naman Goyal, Eric Hambro, Faisal Azhar, Aurelien Rodriguez, Armand Joulin, Edouard Grave, and Guillaume Lample. 2023. LLaMA: Open and efficient foundation language models.

Alex Wang, Yada Pruksachatkun, Nikita Nangia, Amanpreet Singh, Julian Michael, Felix Hill, Omer Levy, and Samuel R. Bowman. 2020. SuperGLUE: A stickier benchmark for general-purpose language understanding systems.

Alex Warstadt, Leshem Choshen, Ryan Cotterell, Tal Linzen, Aaron Mueller, Ethan Wilcox, Williams Adina, and Chengxu Zhuang. 2023. Findings of the BabyLM Challenge: Sample-efficient pretraining on developmentally plausible corpora. In *Proceedings of the BabyLM Challenge*. Association for Computational Linguistics (ACL).

Alex Warstadt, Alicia Parrish, Haokun Liu, Anhad Mohananey, Wei Peng, Sheng-Fu Wang, and Samuel R. Bowman. 2020a. BLiMP: The benchmark of linguistic minimal pairs for English. *Transactions of the Association for Computational Linguistics*, 8:377–392.

Alex Warstadt, Yian Zhang, Xiaocheng Li, Haokun Liu, and Samuel R. Bowman. 2020b. Learning which features matter: RoBERTa acquires a preference for linguistic generalizations (eventually). In *Proceedings of the 2020 Conference on Empirical Methods in Natural Language Processing (EMNLP)*, pages 217–235, Online. Association for Computational Linguistics.

Dongkeun Yoon, Joel Jang, Sungdong Kim, and Minjoon Seo. 2023. Gradient Ascent Post-training Enhances Language Model Generalization. *arXiv e-prints*, page arXiv:2306.07052.

Susan Zhang, Stephen Roller, Naman Goyal, Mikel Artetxe, Moya Chen, Shuohui Chen, Christopher Dewan, Mona Diab, Xian Li, Xi Victoria Lin, Todor Mihaylov, Myle Ott, Sam Shleifer, Kurt Shuster, Daniel Simig, Punit Singh Koura, Anjali Sridhar, Tianlu Wang, and Luke Zettlemoyer. 2022. OPT: Open pre-trained transformer language models.

A Evals

The numerical results for the zero-shot accuracy on the BLiMP suite of benchmarks (Warstadt et al., 2020a) can be found in table 1, while the results for the fine-tuning accuracy on the SuperGLUE (Wang et al., 2020) and MSGS (Warstadt et al., 2020b) benchmarks are listed in table 2. Finally, the hyperparameters selected for the various fine-tuning tasks are summarized in table 3.

Age-of-acquisition prediction In addition to the above-mentioned benchmarks, we have tested our model on an age-of-acquisition task proposed by Portelance et al. (To Appear). Its aim is to predict the median age at which a word is learned by children, as a function of a number of variables (such as the lexical category, concreteness, frequency, etc.), using a *linear model*. One of these variables is the average *surprisal*, i.e. the average negative log-probability of the word across all the contexts where it appears, as predicted by a causal language model. This is the only place where the language model enters. The use of this task as a benchmark for language models fundamentally relies on the assumption of a linear relationship between the surprisal and the age of acquisition. If this assumption is true, then a more accurate estimation of the tokens probabilities by the language model should indeed translate into a more accurate prediction of the age of acquisition. If, however, this assumption is not justified, then the linear model — but not the language model — might be the bottleneck, and a better language model won't necessarily lead to a better prediction.

The mean absolute deviations of the predicted ages of acquisition are reported for various language models and lexical categories in table 4. We can only observe minor differences between the four considered language models (likely due to random noise), suggesting that the linear regression — and not the language model — is indeed the bottleneck. Therefore, this task is unlikely to be indicative of the performance of Baby Llama relative to the baselines.

B Other attempts and null results

In this appendix, we briefly describe various approaches that we have investigated in order to improve the performance of our models. Unlike distillation from an ensemble of teachers, those attempts had mixed results and we haven't pursued them further, in part due to our limited computational resources.

Curriculum learning We implemented a simple version of curriculum learning, directly inspired by the original paper from Bengio et al. (2009). We split the 10 files composing the training set into 5 buckets, in order of roughly increasing complexity according to some readability metrics[9] computed using the `textstat` Python package. We start training for 3 epochs using the lowest bucket only, then, every 3 epochs, we add the next bucket to the training set without removing the previous ones, until we have trained for 3 epochs on the full training set. The full validation set is always used to compute the eval loss.

After training a 10M-parameter GPT-2 model using the schedule described above, the eval loss[10] plateaued at 3.75, comparable to the 3.74 obtained by training the same model for the same wall-clock duration but using the full training set from the beginning. Although the model trained with curriculum learning scored on average 1 percentage point above the non-curriculum model on the zero-shot benchmarks, the overall picture was mixed, due to significant regressions in two of the evals. The absence of a significant improvement from curriculum learning is in line with previously-reported negative results in Surkov et al. (2022), although we should remain cautious since our attempt wasn't comprehensive and modern sampling methods may lead to significantly better results.

Switch Transformer Using the HuggingFace Transformers library, we have implemented a decoder Switch Transformer (Fedus et al., 2022) for causal language modeling, based on the encoder-decoder version available in said library. This mixture-of-experts model was initially introduced to scale up the number of parameters at a constant computational cost.

We train both a GPT2-10M baseline[11], as well as a number of Switch Transformers with the same number of layers and embedding dimension but different numbers of experts and expert capacities (tuning separately the other hyperparameters of each model). We observe, as expected, that a Switch Transformer with a single expert of capacity 1 closely matches the performance of the baseline GPT-2 model. However, as we scale up the number of experts and expert capacity, we observe a performance degradation (both in the loss and zero-shot scores), even after allowing for longer training of the larger models. This suggests that mixture-of-experts models may not bring any advantages for the model and dataset sizes considered here.

Ensembling of homogeneous models We averaged the predicted logits of 4 GPT2-10M models trained from different random initializations, but otherwise identical, and compared the results of the ensemble with those of its constituent GPT2-10M models. All models had their hyperparameters tuned to minimize the eval loss. While the individual models had an average eval loss of 3.77, the averaged model reached 3.66, an improvement of 0.11. This translates into an improvement of 1 to 2 percentage points (depending on the specific seed) in the average zero-shot BLiMP score; more importantly, the averaged model always scored higher

[9] The metrics used are the Flesch reading ease, Flesch-Kincaid grade level, Gunning fog index, automated readability index, and SMOG grade. The buckets are 1. `aochildes`, 2. `open_subtitles`, 3. `switchboard`, `cbt`, `qed`, `children_stories`, `bnc_spoken`, 4. `simple_wikipedia`, `gutenberg` and 5. `wikipedia`.

[10] In this experiment and the others described in this appendix, the exact tokenizer and sequence length may differ from the ones used for the final Baby Llama, therefore the loss isn't directly comparable.

[11] 8 layers, embedding dimension 256, 16 heads, and vocabulary size 16000.

	Model	OPT (125M)	RoBERTa (base)	T5 (base)	LLaMA (58M)	LLaMA (360M)	GPT-2 (705M)	Ensemble of teachers	Baby Llama (58M, distilled)
BLiMP	Anaphor Agr.	63.8	81.5	68.9	87.0	87.6	89.6	89.6	**89.8**
	Arg. Structure	70.6	67.1	63.8	72.3	73.5	73.5	**75.3**	73.1
	Binding	67.1	67.3	60.4	71.2	72.1	71.5	72.2	**72.7**
	Control/Raising	66.5	67.9	60.9	67.5	67.4	**68.4**	67.7	67.5
	Det.-Noun Agr.	78.5	**90.8**	72.2	87.8	89.6	87.4	89.8	**90.8**
	Ellipsis	62.0	**76.4**	34.4	67.3	68.5	69.9	71.7	73.3
	Filler-Gap	63.8	63.5	48.2	70.9	70.6	70.2	71.1	**71.8**
	Irregular Forms	67.5	87.4	77.6	74.1	68.9	83.1	83.4	**93.1**
	Island Effects	48.6	39.9	45.6	**57.3**	50.4	51.6	50.7	51.2
	NPI Licensing	46.7	55.9	47.8	51.1	**57.3**	50.5	55.1	56.5
	Quantifiers	59.6	70.5	61.2	64.2	59.0	69.8	64.6	**73.3**
	Subj.-Verb Agr.	56.9	65.4	65.0	73.0	69.7	67.5	70.3	**75.4**
BLiMP suppl.	Hypernym	50.0	49.4	48.0	48.7	49.4	49.2	**50.1**	49.3
	QA Congruence (easy)	54.7	31.3	40.6	50.0	53.1	**56.2**	50.0	51.6
	QA Congruence (tricky)	31.5	32.1	21.2	32.7	41.8	**45.5**	43.0	41.8
	Subj.-Aux. Inversion	80.3	71.7	64.9	77.4	84.3	81.7	84.5	**88.5**
	Turn Taking	57.1	53.2	45.0	63.9	**68.6**	65.7	66.4	66.1

Table 1: Zero-shot accuracy (in percent), as evaluated by the BLiMP suite of benchmarks (top) and some supplementary benchmarks (bottom).

	Model	OPT (125M)	RoBERTa (base)	T5 (base)	Baby Llama (58M, distilled)
(Super)GLUE	CoLA (MCC)	15.2	**25.8**	11.3	14.3
	SST-2	81.9	87.0	78.1	**87.2**
	MRPC (F_1)	72.5	79.2	80.5	**82.0**
	QQP (F_1)	60.4	73.7	66.2	**83.0**
	MNLI	57.6	**73.2**	48.0	72.9
	MNLI-mm	60.0	**74.0**	50.3	73.7
	QNLI	61.5	77.0	62.0	**81.1**
	RTE	60.0	**61.6**	49.4	**61.6**†
	BoolQ	63.3	66.3	66.0	**67.2**†
	MultiRC	55.2	**61.4**	47.1	58.9†
	WSC	60.2	**61.4**	**61.4**	**61.4**†
MSGS (MCC)	CR_LC	**0.4**	-28.3	-78.3	-12.0
	CR_RTP	-70.3	-77.7	**-62.0**	-71.1
	MV_LC	-72.1	-99.3	-100.0	**-41.2**
	MV_RTP	**-77.6**	-79.4	-79.7	-91.7
	SC_LC	13.8	16.3	-25.3	**76.4**
	SC_RP	-68.9	-45.0	-39.4	**-36.0**

Table 2: Fine-tuning accuracy (if not specified), Matthews correlation coefficient (MCC) or F_1 score — in percent — as evaluated by the SuperGLUE (top) and MSGS (bottom) suites of benchmarks. The † symbol indicates benchmarks for which the best performance was reached only for a narrow range of hyperparameters, suggesting possible overfitting of the validation set.

	Task	Max. learning rate	Batch size	Max. epochs	Patience	Eval every	Seed
(Super)GLUE	CoLA	$4 \cdot 10^{-5}$	64	3	10	20	12
	SST-2	$5 \cdot 10^{-5}$	64	6	10	200	12
	MRPC	$3 \cdot 10^{-5}$	64	3	10	20	12
	QQP	$4 \cdot 10^{-5}$	64	10	10	1000	12
	MNLI	$5 \cdot 10^{-5}$	64	6	10	200	12
	MNLI-mm	$5 \cdot 10^{-5}$	64	6	10	200	12
	QNLI	$5 \cdot 10^{-5}$	64	6	10	200	12
	RTE	$5 \cdot 10^{-5}$	64	6	10	200	12
	BoolQ	$3 \cdot 10^{-4}$	16	10	10	10	12
	MultiRC	$1 \cdot 10^{-4}$	64	7	10	1000	42
	WSC	$5 \cdot 10^{-7}$	1	10	1000	2000	12
MSGS	CR_LC	$1 \cdot 10^{-3}$	64	2	10	10	12
	CR_RTP	$5 \cdot 10^{-5}$	64	6	10	200	12
	MV_LC	$5 \cdot 10^{-5}$	64	6	10	200	12
	MV_RTP	$5 \cdot 10^{-5}$	64	6	10	200	12
	SC_LC	$1 \cdot 10^{-3}$	64	2	10	10	12
	SC_RP	$1 \cdot 10^{-3}$	64	2	10	10	12

Table 3: List of the hyperparameters selected when fine-tuning Baby Llama on the various evals that require fine-tuning.

Model	OPT (125M)	RoBERTa (base)	T5 (base)	Baby Llama (58M, distilled)
AoA Overall (591 words)	**2.03**	2.06	2.04	2.06
AoA Nouns (322 words)	1.98	1.99	**1.97**	1.99
AoA Predicates (167 words)	**1.81**	1.85	1.82	1.84
AoA Function words (102 words)	**2.57**	2.65	2.64	2.63

Table 4: Performance of the model, when used as part of an age-of-acquisition (AoA) prediction task for various lexical categories, as quantified by the mean absolute deviation (lower is better).

than the average score of its constituents, and often scored higher than all of them. Despite the initial success of this method, adding more teachers to the ensemble from which Baby Llama was distilled yielded no further improvement to the performance of the distilled model, suggesting that the gains from using this method do not sum with those from knowledge distillation.

Sharpness-Aware Minimization Foret et al. (2020) have introduced a Sharpness-Aware Minimization (SAM) procedure for simultaneously minimizing the loss value and its sharpness. It has been shown in Bahri et al. (2021) that applying SAM when fine-tuning on multiple downstream tasks can result in substantial performance gains.

Here we tried a rather different approach: we pretrained GPT2-10M in the usual way for 15 epochs and then trained it using SAM for one more epoch. This approach in some sense resembles the gradient ascent discussed in the next paragraph. We implemented a custom training loop for HuggingFace Transformers models based on `https://github.com/karpathy/nanoGPT`. This allowed us to use the two-step SAM optimization from `https://github.com/davda54/sam`. Unfortunately, we have not observed any improvement in the model's zero-shot capabilities resulting from this type of SAM application.

Post-training Gradient Ascent Yoon et al. (2023) have empirically demonstrated that a few steps of Gradient Ascent Post-training (GAP) enhances the zero-shot generalization capabilities across diverse NLP tasks.

In order to test GAP, we first applied it to GPT2-10M. We took a fully trained model and performed 15 to 100 steps of gradient ascent (following the original paper, we used batch size 1 and learning rate $5 \cdot 10^{-5}$). We observed some improvements on BLiMP (although those were not consistent among the various tasks). However, we did not manage to further improve the zero-shot performance of the distilled Baby Llama, suggesting again that the gains from using this method do not sum with those from knowledge distillation.

BabyLM Challenge: Curriculum learning based on sentence complexity approximating language acquisition

Miyu Oba[1] **Akari Haga**[1] **Akiyo Fukatsu**[2] **Yohei Oseki**[2]
[1]Nara Institute of Science and Technology
[2]The University of Tokyo
{oba.miyu.ol2, haga.akari.ha0}@is.naist.jp
{akiyofukatsu, oseki}@g.ecc.u-tokyo.ac.jp

Abstract

This paper describes our proposed models in the BabyLM Challenge (Warstadt et al., 2023). The goal of this shared task is to pretrain models efficiently using a developmentally plausible corpus. To simulate the increasing complexity of Child-Directed Speech (CDS) sentences, we employed curriculum learning and trained models with data reordered based on three metrics for sentence complexity. Among all the models, the best performing one was trained with data ordered by the max-dependency, although the models trained with curriculum learning did not outperform the baseline model without curriculum learning.

1 Introduction

Successful recent large language models (LLMs) are trained on extensive datasets, leading to a gap between the training data of models and the inputs that children receive during language acquisition. English-speaking children hear less than 100M words until the age of 12, while Chinchilla, one of the recent LLMs, uses 1.4 trillion words for training (Wertz et al., 2022). Training models with human-like input data can improve LLM data efficiency and shed light on efficient language acquisition in children with limited data. Thus, the BabyLM Challenge (Warstadt et al., 2023) aims to pretrain models on a developmentally plausible corpus, including Age-Ordered CDS (Huebner and Willits, 2021). We used a dataset of ~10M words, approximating the input that children receive until 2–3 years [1].

In model training, reordering data in a meaningful way (e.g., from easy to difficult samples), known as curriculum learning (Bengio et al., 2009), is suggested to enhance performance. In human language acquisition, mothers adjust their speech when addressing their children, using shorter and simpler sentences (Snow, 1972; Newport et al., 1977; Fernald et al., 1989). Notably, Snow (1972) and Fernald et al. (1989) report that the mean length of utterance and the use of nominal compounds increase as children age, suggesting that language-acquiring children receive easy inputs initially and gradually encounter more complexity as they grow. Thus, reordering data by sentence difficulty may improve model performance.

In this paper, we train models on data reordered by sentence difficulty and evaluate them on three designated datasets. The difficulty metrics include the number of subword tokens, that of constituents and max-dependency. The max-dependency yielded the highest scores, but curriculum learning did not outperform the baseline model.

2 Corpora and preprocessing

We used the BabyLM strict-small train/dev dataset (Warstadt et al., 2023). First, we split the corpora into sentences using the sentencizer from spaCy[2]. Next, we deleted sentences that were non-English, titles, and longer than 300 characters. For identifying non-English sentences, we used FastText (Joulin et al., 2017). Some corpora in the datasets contain much upper-case-only or lower-case-only data. Therefore we trained Moses truecaser (Koehn et al., 2007) using other training corpora, then true-cased all data. After true-casing, we tokenized all data. We trained the tokenizer from scratch using RobertaTokenizer (Liu et al., 2019) with the preprocessed training dataset.

3 Models

3.1 Baseline model

Our models are based on the RoBERTa-base (Liu et al., 2019). We trained them on randomly shuf-

[1]According to Gilkerson et al. (2017), children are exposed to adult 12,300 words within a 12-hour day.

[2]https://spacy.io

Proceedings of the 27th Conference on Computational Natural Language Learning: Volume 2: The BabyLM Challenge, pages 290–297
December 6-7, 2023

fled data from scratch. Their hyperparameters are shown in Appendix A.2.

3.2 Curriculum learning model

We employed curriculum learning in our baseline models. Training data were sorted by a particular difficulty metric. We focused on sentence complexity and used three metrics, the number of subword tokens (Ntoken), that of constituency (Nconst.), and maximum depth of dependency tree (Max-dep.). We split the data into several blocks and trained models on them in order with particular steps. Note that we adjusted the number of steps in each block to be proportional to the number of subwords in each block.

4 Experiments

To find optimal settings for curriculum learning, we begin with investigating which difficulty metrics are better and how many blocks of data should be split into for this task. To explore the effect of curriculum learning, we then compare the baseline model, which is trained on randomly shuffled data, with the curriculum learning models. We use parsers from spaCy to calculate the number of constituents and max-dependency.

4.1 Evaluation

We evaluated our models with the shared evaluation datasets (Gao et al., 2021). These consist of BLiMP (Warstadt et al., 2020a), (Super)GLUE (Wang et al., 2018) and MSGS (Warstadt et al., 2020b). BLiMP is used for zero-shot evaluation, and it includes supplement tasks that are specifically made for BabyLM. We report its accuracy. GLUE and MSGS are used for fine-tuning evaluation. We report F1 score for GLUE and Matthews Correlation Coefficient (MCC) for MSGS.

4.2 Results

Difficulty metrics We compare the models trained on the sorted data with the three difficulty metrics (See section 3.2). The bottom of Table 1 shows the performance of curriculum learning models in the different difficulty metrics. The results suggest that the difficulty metrics affect the performance of the models. Notably, the model trained on the data sorted by Max-dep. achieved slightly higher performance than the other metrics.

Model	Curr.	BLiMP	GLUE	MSGS	Avg.
Baseline		69.23	65.74	−0.57	44.80
+cleaning		**70.46**	**66.40**	**6.86**	**47.91**
Ntoken	✓	**68.37**	64.96	−5.56	42.59
Nconst.	✓	65.90	64.71	−2.73	42.63
Max-dep.	✓	68.27	**65.90**	**3.26**	**45.81**

Table 1: Performance of models. The models at the top are baseline models with and without data preprocessing. Those at the bottom are curriculum learning models in different difficulty metrics. ✓in Curr. denotes whether curriculum learning is applied to the models.

Model	n	BLiMP	GLUE	MSGS	Avg.
Max-dep.	3	**68.70**	65.06	0.37	44.71
	4	68.27	**65.90**	3.26	45.81
	6	67.85	64.97	**9.56**	**47.46**
	8	67.93	65.05	0.33	44.44

Table 2: Performance of models with different split blocks. n indicates the number of blocks.

Number of blocks We compare the models trained on the data split into {3, 4, 6, 8} blocks. As difficulty metrics, we use Max-dep., which achieves the highest score among the three models at the bottom of Table 1. Table 2 indicates the performance of models with different split blocks. This result shows that there is no significant difference between the models with different split blocks, suggesting that scores will not be improved by the simple increase or decrease in the number of split blocks.

Baseline model vs. Curriculum learning model Finally, we compare the curriculum learning model [3], in which difficulty metrics are Max-dep. and the number of blocks is 4, with the baseline model. The top of Table 1 shows that the baseline model obtains higher scores than the curriculum learning model. This result implies that at least the curriculum learning settings attempted in this work are inadequate in facilitating higher model performance. Investigating other effective training settings would be interesting for future work; e.g., warmup, optimizers.

5 Conclusion

In summary, our participation in the BabyLM Challenge centered on curriculum learning based on the three metrics of sentence complexity. While

[3]The model is available at https://huggingface.co/akari000/roberta-dependency-max-4split

the max-dependency demonstrated slightly higher performance scores than the other metrics, it did not outperform the baseline model without curriculum learning on the BLiMP dataset. These findings suggest the complexity of language acquisition and the need to improve the experimental setting in future research to enhance the models' performance. To enhance the validity of our research as a future work, we need to use multiple random seeds to train the model to verify how much those affect the results.

Acknowledgements

We would like to express our gratitude for the anonymous reviewers who provided many insightful comments that have improved our paper. This work was supported by JSPS KAKENHI Grant Number JP21H05054 and JST PRESTO Grant Number JPMJPR21C2.

References

Yoshua Bengio, Jérôme Louradour, Ronan Collobert, and Jason Weston. 2009. Curriculum learning. In *Proceedings of the 26th Annual International Conference on Machine Learning*, ICML '09, page 41–48, New York, NY, USA. Association for Computing Machinery.

Anne Fernald, Traute Taeschner, Judy Dunn, Mechthild Papousek, Bénédicte de Boysson-Bardies, and Ikuko Fukui. 1989. A cross-language study of prosodic modifications in mothers' and fathers' speech to preverbal infants. *Journal of Child Language*.

Leo Gao, Jonathan Tow, Stella Biderman, Sid Black, Anthony DiPofi, Charles Foster, Laurence Golding, Jeffrey Hsu, Kyle McDonell, Niklas Muennighoff, Jason Phang, Laria Reynolds, Eric Tang, Anish Thite, Ben Wang, Kevin Wang, and Andy Zou. 2021. A framework for few-shot language model evaluation.

Jill Gilkerson, Jeffrey A. Richards, Steven F. Warren, Judith K. Montgomery, Charles R. Greenwood, D. Kimbrough Oller, John H. L. Hansen, and Terrance D. Paul. 2017. Mapping the early language environment using all-day recordings and automated analysis. *American Journal of Speech-Language Pathology*, 26(2):248–265.

Matthew Honnibal and Mark Johnson. 2015. An improved non-monotonic transition system for dependency parsing. In *Proceedings of EMNLP*, pages 1373–1378, Lisbon, Portugal. Association for Computational Linguistics.

Philip A. Huebner and Jon A. Willits. 2021. Chapter eight - using lexical context to discover the noun category: Younger children have it easier. In Kara D. Federmeier and Lili Sahakyan, editors, *The Context of Cognition: Emerging Perspectives*, volume 75 of *Psychology of Learning and Motivation*, pages 279–331. Academic Press.

Armand Joulin, Edouard Grave, Piotr Bojanowski, and Tomas Mikolov. 2017. Bag of tricks for efficient text classification. In *Proceedings of EACL: Volume 2, Short Papers*, pages 427–431, Valencia, Spain. Association for Computational Linguistics.

Nikita Kitaev and Dan Klein. 2018. Constituency parsing with a self-attentive encoder. In *Proceedings of ACL (Volume 1: Long Papers)*, pages 2676–2686, Melbourne, Australia. Association for Computational Linguistics.

Philipp Koehn, Hieu Hoang, Alexandra Birch, Chris Callison-Burch, Marcello Federico, Nicola Bertoldi, Brooke Cowan, Wade Shen, Christine Moran, Richard Zens, Chris Dyer, Ondřej Bojar, Alexandra Constantin, and Evan Herbst. 2007. Moses: Open source toolkit for statistical machine translation. In *Proceedings of ACL Companion Volume Proceedings of the Demo and Poster Sessions*, pages 177–180, Prague, Czech Republic. Association for Computational Linguistics.

Yinhan Liu, Myle Ott, Naman Goyal, Jingfei Du, Mandar Joshi, Danqi Chen, Omer Levy, Mike Lewis, Luke Zettlemoyer, and Veselin Stoyanov. 2019. Roberta: A robustly optimized bert pretraining approach.

Elissa. Newport, Henry Gleitman, and Lila Gleitman. 1977. Mother, id rather do it myself: Some effects and non-effects of maternal speech style. In Catherine E. Snow and Charles A. Ferguson, editors, *Talking to Children*, pages 109–149. Cambridge University Press.

Joakim Nivre and Jens Nilsson. 2005. Pseudo-projective dependency parsing. In *Proceedings of ACL*, pages 99–106, Ann Arbor, Michigan. Association for Computational Linguistics.

Catherine E. Snow. 1972. Mothers' speech to children learning language. *Child Development*, 43(2):549–565.

Alex Wang, Amanpreet Singh, Julian Michael, Felix Hill, Omer Levy, and Samuel Bowman. 2018. GLUE: A multi-task benchmark and analysis platform for natural language understanding. In *Proceedings of the 2018 EMNLP Workshop BlackboxNLP: Analyzing and Interpreting Neural Networks for NLP*, pages 353–355, Brussels, Belgium. Association for Computational Linguistics.

Alex Warstadt, Leshem Choshen, Ryan Cotterell, Tal Linzen, Aaron Mueller, Ethan Wilcox, Williams Adina, and Chengxu Zhuang. 2023. Findings of the BabyLM Challenge: Sample-efficient pretraining on developmentally plausible corpora. In *Proceedings of the BabyLM Challenge*. Association for Computational Linguistics (ACL).

Alex Warstadt, Alicia Parrish, Haokun Liu, Anhad Mohananey, Wei Peng, Sheng-Fu Wang, and Samuel R. Bowman. 2020a. Blimp: The benchmark of linguistic minimal pairs for english. *Transactions of the Association for Computational Linguistics*, 8:377–392.

Alex Warstadt, Yian Zhang, Xiaocheng Li, Haokun Liu, and Samuel R. Bowman. 2020b. Learning which features matter: RoBERTa acquires a preference for linguistic generalizations (eventually). In *Proceedings of the EMNLP*, pages 217–235, Online. Association for Computational Linguistics.

Lukas Wertz, Katsiaryna Mirylenka, Jonas Kuhn, and Jasmina Bogojeska. 2022. Investigating active learning sampling strategies for extreme multi label text classification. In *Proceedings of LREC*, pages 4597–4605, Marseille, France. European Language Resources Association.

A Appendix

A.1 Difficulty Metrics

Number of constituents The number of constituents was counted using the Berkley Neural Parser (Kitaev and Klein, 2018) in spaCy. This parser uses a self-attentive encoder in place of LSTM along with a chart decoder. This parser outputs POS tags and surface strings in brackets as in (1), and we count the number of phrasal nodes (e.g., NP) in the outputs. In this case, the number of constituents is counted as 4.

(1) (S (NP (DT That)) (VP (MD might) (VP (VB be) (ADJP (JJR better)))) (. .))

Max-dependency We count max-dependency using the dependency parser in spaCy, which is a transition-based system by Honnibal and Johnson (2015) along with Nivre and Nilsson (2005)'s pseudo-projective dependency transformation. We count the number of dependent nodes from the root and choose the maximum depth as the value of max-dependency. For example, the dependency tree in (2) is an example of parsing by the dependency parser. In this case, the longest dependency is either 'told → happened → had' or 'told → happened → what'. Given that the root is counted as 0, the max-dependency of this sentence is 2.

(2)

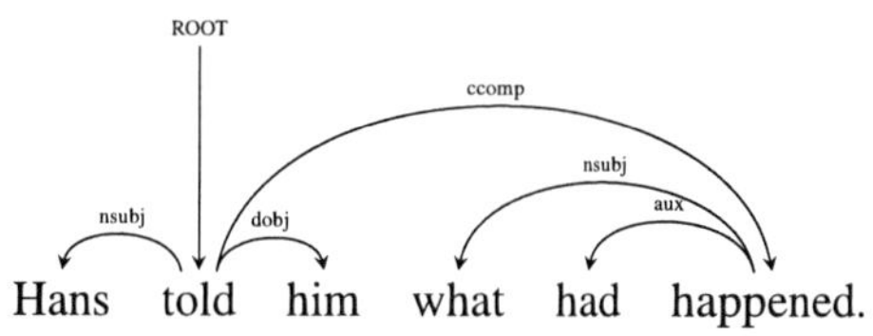

A.2 Hyperparameters

We arranged the number of instances that we input into our models for all steps to 28,800k instances. Other hyperparameters are shown in Table 3.

A.3 Detailed results

We show the details of the results for each task. Table 4 – 6 shows the accuracies for all measures in BLiMP and GLUE. Table 7 shows the F1 scors for all measures in GLUE, where we use macro-F1, and Table 8 shows the MCC scores for all measures in MSGS.

Model	architecture	roberta-base
	vocab size	50,265
	hidden size	768
	heads	12
	layers	12
	dropout	0.1
	layer norm eps	1e-12
Optimizer	algorithm	AdamW
	learning rates	3e-4
	betas	(0.9, 0.999)
	weight decay	0.1
	clip norm	0.0
Scheduler	type	cosine
	warmup updates	5000
Training	gradient accumulation	4
	line by line	true
	NGPU	4

Table 3: Hyperparameters of the models

Model	Curr.	n	Anaphor Agr.	Agr. Structure	Binding	Control/Raising	D-N Agr.	Ellipsis
Baseline model		-	86.09	73.68	67.84	68.03	95.57	73.44
+cleaning		-	91.82	74.32	74.16	73.75	96.29	77.19
Ntoken	✓	4	88.45	75.24	73.67	73.75	95.47	74.19
Nconst.	✓	4	83.44	72.50	73.75	71.74	91.45	75.17
Max-dep.	✓	3	90.85	73.82	73.76	72.45	95.62	79.68
	✓	4	91.21	74.98	73.49	71.06	95.48	78.58
	✓	6	87.68	71.59	73.79	68.43	93.86	76.21
	✓	8	91.26	72.25	73.43	67.21	94.55	74.54

Model	Curr.	n	Filler Gap	Irregular Forms	Island Effects	NPI Licensing	Quantifiers	S-V Agr.
Baseline model		-	75.26	90.69	37.56	52.73	74.86	78.14
+cleaning		-	76.39	90.99	44.96	56.71	73.98	82.48
Ntoken	✓	4	74.93	89.57	38.08	55.10	72.41	81.43
Nconst.	✓	4	77.65	74.66	39.57	61.75	65.10	76.50
Max-dep.	✓	3	71.49	87.48	35.24	57.91	72.05	81.70
	✓	4	71.88	88.80	33.15	53.72	71.95	83.04
	✓	6	71.94	89.87	26.76	60.04	69.91	81.43
	✓	8	72.08	91.40	28.70	58.56	75.94	78.34

Table 4: Accuracies for all measures in BLiMP

Model	Curr.	n	Hypernym	QA Congruence (easy)	QA Congruence (tricky)	Subj.-Aux. Inversion	Turn Taking
Baseline model		-	49.53	60.94	43.03	84.24	65.36
+cleaning		-	49.19	67.19	39.39	68.72	60.36
Ntoken	✓	4	48.72	59.38	40.00	64.85	57.14
Nconst.	✓	4	48.02	54.69	29.70	67.14	57.50
Max-dep.	✓	3	48.84	68.75	36.97	63.09	58.21
	✓	4	46.98	65.63	39.39	63.77	57.50
	✓	6	47.91	67.19	43.03	63.53	60.36
	✓	8	51.40	60.94	37.58	63.38	63.21

Table 5: Accuracies for all measures in BLiMP supplement task

Model	Curr.	n	CoLA	SST-2	MRPC	QQP	MNLI	MNLI-mm
Baseline model		-	72.91	87.01	64.97	80.61	70.04	71.13
+cleaning		-	76.84	88.39	69.49	82.32	72.19	74.06
Ntoken	✓	4	76.15	87.60	64.41	82.31	72.14	71.79
Nconst.	✓	4	73.01	87.01	66.67	82.74	70.41	72.14
Max-dep.	✓	3	75.17	87.40	70.62	83.46	72.90	73.01
	✓	4	75.17	87.20	67.23	82.75	72.37	73.50
	✓	6	75.47	87.60	70.06	82.13	72.04	73.98
	✓	8	75.47	88.39	66.67	83.14	71.96	73.22
Model	Curr.	n	QNLI	RTE	BoolQ	MultiRC	WSC	
Baseline model		-	69.25	51.52	65.15	60.35	61.45	
+cleaning		-	71.26	52.53	66.67	58.71	63.86	
Ntoken	✓	4	66.01	52.53	65.98	59.26	61.45	
Nconst.	✓	4	64.92	56.57	66.11	59.15	61.45	
Max-dep.	✓	3	71.00	48.48	66.11	60.46	61.45	
	✓	4	70.25	52.53	65.98	61.34	61.45	
	✓	6	70.73	46.46	64.04	59.04	61.45	
	✓	8	70.21	57.58	66.39	59.26	61.45	

Table 6: Accuracies for all measures in GLUE task

Model	Curr.	n	CoLA	SST-2	MRPC	QQP	MNLI	MNLI-mm
Baseline model		-	82.92	87.36	74.80	76.27	-	-
+cleaning		-	84.58	88.45	80.58	79.78	-	-
Ntoken	✓	4	83.77	87.52	76.92	79.10	-	-
Nconst.	✓	4	82.22	87.36	77.90	79.36	-	-
Max-dep.	✓	3	83.96	87.64	80.88	80.38	-	-
	✓	4	83.77	87.67	78.68	79.96	-	-
	✓	6	83.66	87.67	80.87	79.12	-	-
	✓	8	83.85	88.54	78.07	79.93	-	-
Model	Curr.	n	QNLI	RTE	BoolQ	MultiRC	WSC	
Baseline model		-	72.89	45.45	74.65	57.31	20.00	
+cleaning		-	74.47	47.19	76.11	54.63	11.76	
Ntoken	✓	4	71.36	52.53	73.72	59.74	00.00	
Nconst.	✓	4	71.44	59.05	75.57	49.53	00.00	
Max-dep.	✓	3	74.82	45.16	75.52	57.18	00.00	
	✓	4	74.46	53.47	74.11	60.99	00.00	
	✓	6	72.16	51.38	74.61	55.26	00.00	
	✓	8	72.51	55.32	75.92	51.31	00.00	

Table 7: F1 scores for all measures in GLUE task

Model	Curr.	n	CR (Control)	LC (Control)	MV (Control)	RP (Control)	SC (Control)
Baseline model		-	64.29	99.98	92.47	75.34	73.65
+cleaning		-	76.34	100.00	99.64	99.91	27.19
Ntoken	✓	4	66.43	100.00	96.66	90.15	53.17
Nconst.	✓	4	64.76	100.00	97.11	96.48	49.27
Max-dep.	✓	3	81.61	100.00	99.59	99.98	24.81
	✓	4	77.71	100.00	99.23	100.00	52.80
	✓	6	67.47	100.00	99.37	92.35	74.47
	✓	8	55.99	100.00	98.98	99.82	38.54

Model	Curr.	n	CR_LC	CR_TP	MV_LC	MV_RTP	SC_LC	SC_RP
Baseline model		-	-70.37	-69.93	-100.00	-81.71	-57.74	-32.27
+cleaning		-	33.37	-65.21	-99.54	-79.93	-59.83	-56.48
Ntoken	✓	4	-92.54	-44.48	-100.00	-89.32	-78.91	-62.35
Nconst.	✓	4	-47.57	-98.28	-98.55	-85.35	-52.81	-55.07
Max-dep.	✓	3	-39.21	-73.38	-100.00	-83.32	-48.79	-57.24
	✓	4	-32.06	-62.60	-100.00	-77.70	-59.96	-61.52
	✓	6	20.13	-65.46	-100.00	-86.16	-32.50	-64.47
	✓	8	-17.58	-63.82	-100.00	-99.03	-47.53	-61.69

Table 8: MCC scores for all measures in MSGS

Models	Curr.	n	Perplexity
Baseline model		–	14.58
+cleaning		–	19.80
Ntoken	✓	4	25.74
Nconst.	✓	4	32.20
Max-dep.	✓	3	24.42
	✓	4	27.35
	✓	6	38.61
	✓	8	40.16

Table 9: Perplexity for all measures

Better Together: Jointly Using Masked Latent Semantic Modeling and Masked Language Modeling for Sample Efficient Pre-training

Gábor Berend
University of Szeged
2 Árpád tér, Szeged, Hungary
berendg@inf.u-szeged.hu

Abstract

In this paper, we demonstrate the benefits of jointly using Masked Latent Semantic Modeling (MLSM) and traditional Masked Language Modeling (MLM) as the pre-training objective of masked language models. The core idea behind MLSM is to modify the pre-training objective in a way which ensures that the language models predict a (latent) semantic distribution for the masked tokens – instead of outputting their exact identity as in MLM. Language models pre-trained with MLSM behave more favorable in terms of fine-tuneability towards downstream tasks, however, their performance lags behind MLM pre-trained language models in evaluations that investigate the linguistic capabilities. In an attempt to combine the strengths of the two different pre-training paradigms, we propose their joint use in a multi-task learning setting. Our evaluations that we performed using the BabyLM evaluation framework (Warstadt et al., 2023) demonstrate the synergistic effects of the joint use of the two different kinds of pre-training objectives.

1 Introduction

Albeit being effective and easy to implement in practice, the highly stochastic batch-based masked language modeling (MLM) objective frequently used for pre-training language models, such as BERT (Devlin et al., 2019) and RoBERTa (Liu et al., 2019), is not sample efficient and works in a rather unnatural way from a human cognitive perspective. This is caused by the fact that traditional MLM expects the neural models to recover the exact identity of the masked (sub)words within an input sequence. In an attempt to overcome the unnaturalness of MLM, (Berend, 2023) has recently proposed masked latent semantic modeling (MLSM), a sample efficient alternative to traditional masked language modeling.

MLSM differs from MLM in that its objective is to recover the semantic distribution of masked (sub)tokens over an unsupervised inventory of latent semantic properties — as opposed to that of a one-hot distribution over the entire vocabulary of the language model. This kind of pre-training is arguably more plausible from a human cognitive perspective, i.e., traditional MLM acts as if there was a single proper substitute for a special [MASK] token (the one that got masked), whereas from a human perspective multiple viable tokens – tokens that share some common semantic properties – can substitute a masked token.

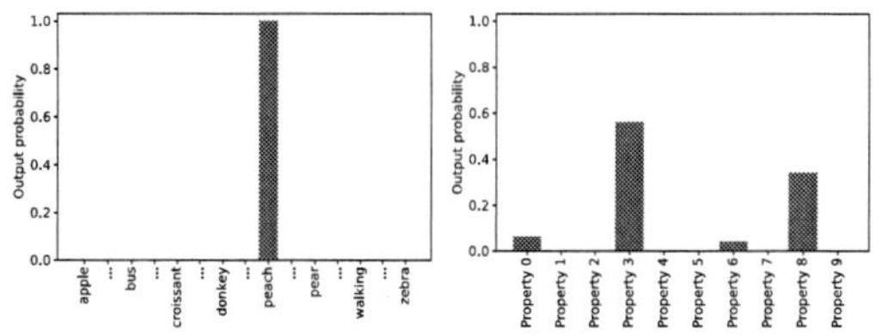

(a) MLM objective (b) MLSM objective

Figure 1: Comparisons of the probability distributions used in MLM (a) and MLSM (b) pre-training.

For instance, in the sentence *'She picked a delicious* [MASK].', human subjects would agree that any word referring to an edible concept is a viable substitute for the last word of the sentence. In Figure 1, we illustrate the different kinds of outputs that the MLM (Figure 1a) and the MLSM (Figure 1b) objectives could produce for some masked token such as the one in the above example.

Even though (Berend, 2023) has demonstrated the improved sample efficiency of MLSM, language models pre-trained with it perform poorly in evaluations that test the linguistic capabilities of language models. In this paper, we extend the results from (Berend, 2023) in several important aspects. On the one hand, – instead of using a medium-sized BERT model – we pre-train base-sized DeBERTa (He et al., 2021) models, illustrating that the MLSM pre-training objective gener-

Proceedings of the 27th Conference on Computational Natural Language Learning: Volume 2: The BabyLM Challenge, pages 298–307
December 6-7, 2023 ©2023 Association for Computational Linguistics

alizes across different model types and sizes. On the other hand, we investigate the added value of a multi-task learning setting during pre-training, in which the use of MLSM objective is coupled with traditional MLM. Our empirical results show vast improvements in the performance of the pre-trained language models using the joint objective. We release our source code[1] and pre-trained models that we created using the strict[2] and strict-small[3] datasets provided as part of the BabyLM shared task (Warstadt et al., 2023).

2 Methodology

In this section, we introduce the pre-training training objectives that we conducted experiments with.

2.1 Standard Masked Language Modeling

During MLM pre-training, we expect the masked language model to output a probability distribution over its entire vocabulary and the objective is to return one-hot distributions corresponding to the actually masked token, similar to what is illustrated in Figure 1a. The loss function for this kind of pre-training is the categorical cross entropy.

2.2 Knowledge distillation (KD)

During knowledge distillation (KD), we expect the language model to output such a probability distribution over its entire vocabulary that tries to mimic the output distribution of viable masked token substitutes, produced by another language model that is (partially) pre-trained using the standard MLM objective. This setting, hence, is basically a two phase pre-training, in which the first phase is a regular pre-training, followed by a knowledge distillation phase, during which we calculate the Kullback-Leibler divergence between the probability distribution outputted by the language model from the first phase and the model that is being trained.

In this two phase setting, we have the option to reinitalize the model weights, or to make a copy of the (partially) pre-trained model from the first phase, and start KD pre-training with the weights of the MLM pre-trained model in a transfer learning setting. As our preliminary experiments suggested that this latter form of continued pre-training is more beneficial, we opted for that variant of KD.

[1] https://github.com/SzegedAI/MLSM

[2] https://huggingface.co/SzegedAI/babylm-strict-mlsm

[3] https://huggingface.co/SzegedAI/babylm-strict-small-mlsm

2.3 Masked Latent Semantic Modeling

We also utilize Masked Latent Semantic Modeling (Berend, 2023). MLSM is based on an efficient *unsupervised* method for determining the context-sensitive latent semantic distribution of *any* token. We use this as the target distribution that the language model needs to recover during a pre-training as illustrated in Figure 1b.

MLSM is similar to knowledge distillation in that it also relies on a (partially) pre-trained model, however, the mechanism in which it gets utilized differs rather substantially. The partially pre-trained model was not only used for providing the training signal, but also for initializing the weights of MLSM pre-trained models.

The MLSM approach is based on the observation that (sub)tokens with overlapping semantic content tend to have an overlapping set of non-zero coordinates in their sparse contextualized representation, which can be obtained by performing sparse coding on the hidden representations of transformer architectures (Berend, 2020). We incorporate this property of sparse token representations into pre-training, i.e., we devise such distributions of latent semantic properties of masked tokens that are based on the sparsity structure of the sparse representations during the second phase of pre-training.

Suppose that the language model from the first phase of pre-training produces hidden vectors $\boldsymbol{h}^{(l)} \in \mathbb{R}^d$ by its lth layer for a particular token within its context. We then construct a collection of hidden representations as $\boldsymbol{H}^{(l)} \in \mathbb{R}^{d\times n}$, and, as a preparatory step for the second phase of pre-training, we jointly optimize for a dictionary matrix $\boldsymbol{D} \in \mathbb{R}^{d\times k}$ and $\boldsymbol{\alpha}_{\boldsymbol{H}^{(l)}} \in \mathbb{R}^{d\times n}$, such that

$$\min_{\boldsymbol{D},\boldsymbol{\alpha}_{\boldsymbol{H}^{(l)}}} \frac{1}{2}\|\boldsymbol{H}^{(l)} - \boldsymbol{D}\boldsymbol{\alpha}_{\boldsymbol{H}^{(l)}}\|_F^2 + \lambda\|\boldsymbol{\alpha}_{\boldsymbol{H}^{(l)}}\|_1,$$

where the norm of the columns vectors in $\boldsymbol{D}$ do not exceed 1, and the sparse linear coefficients in $\boldsymbol{\alpha}$ are non-negative, with the regularization coefficient λ controlling the sparsity level of $\boldsymbol{\alpha}$.

Once the dictionary matrix $\boldsymbol{D}$ is determined, we can obtain sparse contextualized representation for any token described by $\boldsymbol{h}^{(l)}$ via solving

$$\min_{\boldsymbol{\alpha}\in\mathbb{R}^k_{\geq 0}} \frac{1}{2}\|\boldsymbol{h}^{(l)} - \boldsymbol{D}\boldsymbol{\alpha}\|_2^2 + \lambda\|\boldsymbol{\alpha}\|_1. \quad (1)$$

As such, the determination of (1) can provide useful signal during the second phase of pre-training, i.e., by determining the sparse $\boldsymbol{\alpha}$ representation for the token which was assigned $h^{(l)}$ by the language model from the first phase of pre-training, we can obtain its latent semantic profile via investigating its non-zero coefficients. Due to the non-negativity of α, it can be conveniently transformed into a probability distribution of semantic profiles via ℓ_1-normalization, each coordinate corresponding to a (latent) semantic property as illustrated in Figure 1b.

Similar to KD pre-training, MLSM also employs the Kullback-Leibler divergence as its objective for comparing the expected semantic distribution and the model output. A major difference between KD and MLSM though is that for the former, the domain of the target distribution is the entire vocabulary, whereas for MLSM, there are k many latent semantic properties to consider.

2.4 Joint training objectives

We relied on standard MLM on its own as one of our baseline approaches, as well as in conjunction with other pre-training objectives, in order to assess its added value as a joint self-supervised pre-training task. In the case MLM was used as an additional pre-training task, the losses of the different pre-training paradigms were added together and backpropagation was performed over the joint loss. When using MLM as an additional loss, we add the `+MLM` suffix to the pre-training approach that we augment it with. For instance, `KD+MLM` refers to such a pre-trained model that we obtained by relying on the joint objective of knowledge distillation and MLM.

3 Experiments and results

We performed our experimental evaluation based on the BabyLM Challenge environment (Warstadt et al., 2023), the goal of which is to provide a unified framework for pre-training language models based on moderate amounts of texts, inspired by children language acquisition (Saffran et al., 2001; Gilkerson et al., 2017; Dupoux, 2018). The size and the contents of the pre-training dataset released as part of the BabyLM Challenge is guided by the amount and types of texts children are typically exposed to by reaching preadolescence.

That is, the size of the pre-training corpus is limited in either 100 million (strict) or 10 million (strict-small) tokens, and the released text is mostly composed of transcribed speech. The concrete subcorpora of the challenge are the CHILDES (Macwhinney, 2000), dialogue portion of the British National Corpus (BNC), Children's Book Test (cbt; Hill et al., 2016), Children's Stories Text Corpus, Standardized Project Gutenberg Corpus (Gerlach and Font-Clos, 2020), OpenSubtitles (Lison and Tiedemann, 2016), QCRI Educational Domain Corpus (qed; (Abdelali et al., 2014)), Wikipedia, Simple Wikipedia and the Switchboard Dialog Act Corpus (Stolcke et al., 2000).

The evaluation framework contains a collection of supervised fine-tuning and zero-shot evaluations for assessing the utility and the linguistic capabilities of the pre-trained language models.

3.1 Training a tokenizer

As the goal of the BabyLM Challenge is to create an environment in which language models are not exposed to colossal amounts of pre-training text, all components of the trained language models conformed to the standardized pre-training data. To this end, we first trained a unigram tokenizer (Kudo, 2018) over the corresponding BabyLM strict/strict-small dataset, that comprised of roughly 100/10 million (whitespace separated) tokens. The vocabulary size we employed is 25000.

As increased vocabulary size can potentially yield better downstream performance (e.g., one of the potential reasons why RoBERTa (Liu et al., 2019) often performs better than BERT (Devlin et al., 2019) is due to its increased vocabulary size), we also attempted to train a unigram tokenizer with 50000 subtokens as well. Our preliminary results, however, showed vastly degraded performance for the increased vocabulary size.

For this reason, we continued our experiments with the tokenizers with 25000 cased entries, which was likely more beneficial compared to the one with twice the number of subtokens, as the training corpus itself was intentionally limited in its size, and the increased vocabulary was too large for the relatively small number of unique tokens in the pre-training corpora.

3.2 Pre-training

We used almost identical hyperparameters to (Berend, 2023). That is, we employed a batch size of 128 and a gradient accumulation over 8 batches, yielding an effective batch size of 1024. The learning rate for pre-training was set to 1e-4 with linear scheduling.

We employed the kind of two-phase pre-training introduced earlier in Section 2, i.e., we first pre-

	KD	KD+MLM	MLM	MLSM	MLSM+MLM
anaphor agreement	0.801	0.893	0.801	0.476	0.718
argument structure	0.760	0.797	0.779	0.700	0.762
binding	0.655	0.645	0.660	0.680	0.654
control raising	0.763	0.771	0.766	0.706	0.770
determiner noun agreement	0.969	0.969	0.969	0.847	0.969
ellipsis	0.908	0.936	0.924	0.690	0.930
filler gap	0.826	0.850	0.850	0.714	0.850
hypernym	0.492	0.510	0.480	0.503	0.480
irregular forms	0.850	0.907	0.949	0.794	0.948
island effects	0.669	0.754	0.782	0.629	0.773
npi licensing	0.732	0.781	0.759	0.628	0.768
qa congruence easy	0.625	0.672	0.688	0.438	0.688
qa congruence tricky	0.358	0.394	0.467	0.442	0.424
quantifiers	0.733	0.752	0.768	0.484	0.754
subject aux inversion	0.929	0.949	0.951	0.808	0.951
subject verb agreement	0.893	0.904	0.893	0.764	0.903
turn taking	0.557	0.604	0.643	0.571	0.611
Average	0.736	0.770	0.772	0.640	0.762

(a) strict

	KD+MLM	MLM	MLSM+MLM
anaphor agreement	0.880	0.829	0.831
argument structure	0.765	0.739	0.737
binding	0.684	0.661	0.676
control raising	0.737	0.728	0.757
determiner noun agreement	0.948	0.933	0.939
ellipsis	0.830	0.819	0.827
filler gap	0.781	0.768	0.777
hypernym	0.477	0.495	0.479
irregular forms	0.910	0.896	0.902
island effects	0.630	0.650	0.685
npi licensing	0.719	0.712	0.743
qa congruence easy	0.734	0.688	0.703
qa congruence tricky	0.370	0.364	0.333
quantifiers	0.706	0.728	0.733
subject aux inversion	0.863	0.827	0.830
subject verb agreement	0.852	0.816	0.825
turn taking	0.525	0.521	0.521
Average	0.730	0.716	0.724

(b) strict-small

Table 1: BLiMP results for the models pre-trained on the strict (a) and the strict-small (b) corpora.

trained a model using standard MLM, then used this model for initializing the second-phase model, the pre-training objective of which can potentially differ from MLM. We performed 20,000 and 80,000 update steps during the first and second phases, respectively.

As such, we had a total of 100,000 update steps, which together with the fact that we had an effective batch size of 1024, means that we considered approximately 100,000,000 sequences during pre-training. This resulted in 17 and 166 epochs when using the strict and the strict-small pre-training corpora, respectively. We performed pre-training on NVIDIA A6000 or V100 GPUs (depending on their availability). One pre-training took approximately 5 days to finish.

For the strict scenario, we report results when using the different pre-training paradigms on their own and in conjunction with MLM. As our experiments revealed a superior performance for the joint pre-training with MLM, we only consider those models that jointly use one of the pre-training paradigms and MLM during the second phase of pre-training for the strict-small case.

When applying MLSM, we set the number of latent semantic properties to one tenth of the size of the vocabulary, i.e., we had $k = 2500$. For the joint objectives (KL+MLM and MLSM+MLM), we weighted the two loss terms equally by simply adding the two loss terms together. Investigating different weighting of the MLM term could have been an interesting, but computationally demanding ablation experiment to conduct.

3.3 Quantitative evaluation

We next report our experimental results towards zero-shot (§3.3.1) and fine-tuning (§3.3.2) evaluation, using the BabyLM evaluation framework.[4]

3.3.1 Zero-shot results on BLiMP

The BabyLM framework uses the BLiMP dataset (Warstadt et al., 2020a) for assessing the linguistic capabilities of language models. BLiMP contains English sentence pairs that differ in their linguistic acceptability regarding a variety of grammatical concepts and the task is to select the correct sentence based on the pre-trained model.

To decide which sentence is linguistically more acceptable, the pseudo-log-likelihood (PLL; Salazar et al., 2020) scores of the sentences are calculated, and the sentence with the higher PLL is considered grammatically acceptable. The BabyLM evaluation framework focuses on 17 grammatical phenomena, the results of which are included in Table 1.

Table 1a reveals that the MLSM pre-trained model performs poorly on BLiMP. This is not surprising, as PLL is based on the predictions over the vocabulary of the model, however, MLSM totally neglect the kind of objective that is related to the vocabulary of the model, making the PLL values

[4] `https://github.com/babylm/`

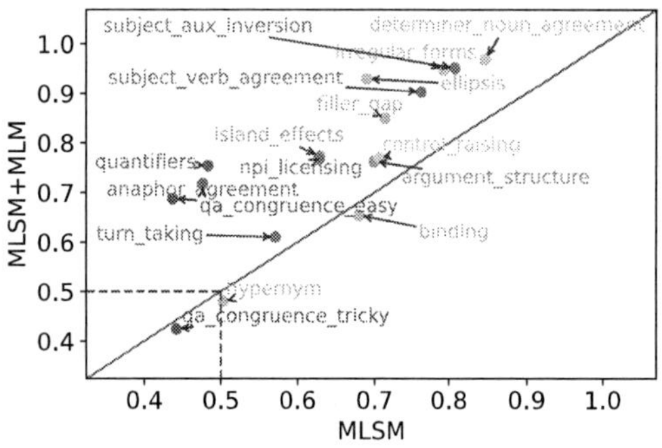

Figure 2: Pairwise comparison of BLiMP task performances between the MLSM (x-axis) and the MLSM+MLM (y-axis) pre-trained models.

calculated by MLSM-only models less useful for approximating linguistic acceptability.

The model pre-trained with the joint MLSM objective (MLSM+MLM), however, performs 0.122 points better on average (0.640→0.762), nearly as good as the model pre-trained with MLM alone (0.772). The additional use of MLM also improves the BLiMP performance of knowledge distillation by 0.034 points on average (0.736→0.770).

Table 1b reveals that when using the reduced amount of strict-small pre-training corpus, the MLSM+MLM pre-trained model in fact outperforms the purely MLM pre-trained model variant.

We depict the added value of using the joint MLSM+MLM objective over the MLSM only objective when conducting pre-training on the 100 million token strict corpus in Figure 2. Each of the 17 sub-task is visualized by a point in the figure, with its x and y coordinates displaying the performance of the pre-trained model that was based on the MLSM and MLSM+MLM objectives. The dashed line indicates chance performance, and the diagonal line helps in identifying the added value of joint pre-training, i.e., the further away a point above the diagonal line is, the bigger positive impact the joint pre-training had towards the evaluation on the subtask represented by the given point.

During the second phase of pre-training, we evaluated intermediate checkpoints. Figure 3a and Figure 3b illustrates the average BLiMP performance of the models pre-trained with varying strategies and at different readiness levels for using the strict and the strict-small pre-training corpora, respectively. The x-axis indicates the number of additional update steps performed during the second phase of the pre-training.

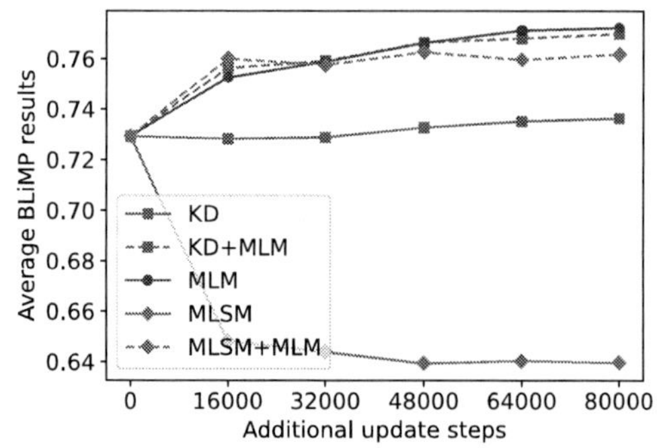

(a) Models pre-trained using the 100M token strict corpus

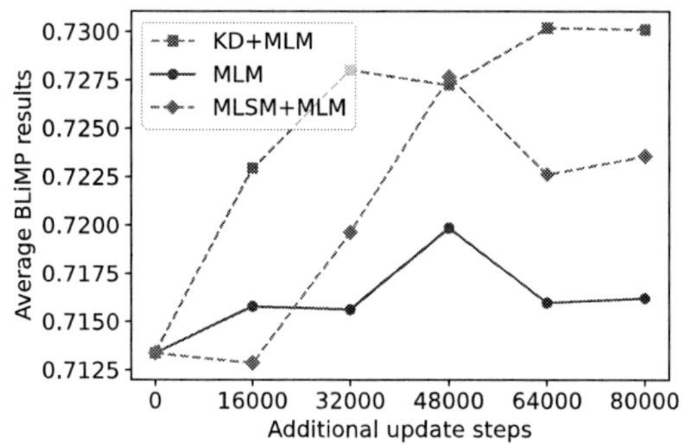

(b) Models pre-trained using the 10M token strict-small corpus

Figure 3: Average BLiMP performances as a function of the number of update steps performed in the second phase of pre-training.

The MLSM curve in Figure 3a shows that the masked language modeling capabilities of an MLSM-only pre-trained model fade out quickly, as the average BLiMP performance drops drastically already at the first investigated checkpoint, i.e., at 16,000 additional MLSM update steps performed on a model that had gone through 20,000 steps of first phase MLM pre-training.

Figure 3a further reveals that there is a large performance gap between the MLSM and MLSM+MLM pre-trained models at every checkpoint, with the performance of MLSM+MLM being nearly as good or better than that of the purely MLM pre-trained model. As the size of the pre-training corpus gets reduced from 100 million to 10 million tokens, the average BLiMP performance of the alternatively pre-trained models becomes favorable compared to the MLM-only models as it is illustrated in Figure 3b.

3.3.2 Fine-tuning results

The BabyLM evaluation framework also includes supervised learning tasks from the GLUE (Wang

	KD	KD+MLM	MLM	MLSM	MLSM+MLM
BoolQ	**0.6943**	0.6885	0.6936	0.6857	0.6826
CoLA	0.4551	0.4687	**0.4962**	0.4758	0.4854
MNLI	0.7620	0.7669	0.7695	0.7558	**0.7704**
MNLI-mm	0.7641	0.7761	0.7779	0.7687	**0.7808**
MRPC	0.8263	0.8406	**0.8496**	0.8325	0.8339
MultiRC	0.5578	0.6114	0.6238	**0.6309**	0.5983
QNLI	0.8350	0.8409	**0.8447**	0.8427	0.8438
QQP	0.8366	0.8451	**0.8492**	0.8421	0.8428
RTE	0.5985	**0.6010**	**0.6010**	**0.6010**	0.5808
SST2	0.8907	0.8922	0.8927	**0.8952**	0.8907
WSC	0.6024	0.5964	0.5843	0.6024	**0.6054**

(a) strict

	KD+MLM	MLM	MLSM+MLM
BoolQ	**0.6843**	0.6729	0.6670
CoLA	0.3889	0.3794	**0.4171**
MNLI	0.7503	0.7426	**0.7542**
MNLI-mm	0.7506	0.7527	**0.7535**
MRPC	0.7645	**0.7766**	0.7653
MultiRC	0.580	**0.6076**	0.5676
QNLI	0.8205	**0.8261**	0.8237
QQP	0.8343	0.8346	**0.8351**
RTE	0.5404	**0.5556**	0.5202
SST2	0.8903	**0.8937**	0.8917
WSC	0.5813	0.5964	**0.6084**

(b) strict-small

Table 2: (Super)GLUE results for the models pre-trained on the strict (a) and the strict-small (b) corpora. Metrics are reported as accuracy, except for CoLA (Matthew Correlation Coefficient), MRPC (F1) and QQP (F1).

et al., 2019b) and SuperGLUE (Wang et al., 2019a) benchmarks and selected subtasks of MSGS (Mixed Signals Generalization Set; Warstadt et al., 2020b). The original datasets are filtered to those cases that include words that are present at least twice in the 10 million token strict-small training corpus. Unless stated otherwise, we report performance metrics in the form of accuracy.

We made no modifications in the hyperparameters of the official evaluation framework, apart from reducing the batch size from 64 to 32, which was necessary for avoiding out-of-memory error on the NVIDIA 2080Ti GPUs that accommodated our fine-tuning experiments. In order to account for the high variability in fine-tuning results, we repeated all experiments involving fine-tuning four times with different random seeds and report the average of the scores that we obtained. Due to the computational need of fine-tuning, we only evaluated the intermediate checkpoints at the 20%, 60% and 100% readiness levels, i.e., after 16000, 48000 and 80000 additional second phase pre-training steps.

(Super)GLUE Vocabulary-filtered versions of 11 different subtasks from (Super)GLUE are included in the BabyLM evaluation environment. The individual results obtained by the differently pre-trained DeBERTa models are listed in Table 2. Fine-tuning MLSM+MLM models again yielded better results compared to the MLSM models, however, the performance gap is not that pronounced as it was for BLiMP. The average fine-tuning performance of MLSM+MLM pre-trained model is on par with the one that got pre-trained with traditional MLM considering the models pre-trained over the 100 million corpus.

Figure 4 displays the fine-tuning performance of the intermediate model checkpoints of second phase pre-training. Figure 4a reveals that when using the 100 million token training corpus, the intermediate checkpoints of the MLSM+MLM and MLM models have similar fine-tuning performances averaged over the (Super)GLUE tasks, with a slight advantage towards MLSM+MLM.

For the smaller training corpus in Figure 4b, the advantage of MLSM+MLM pre-trained model is more notable, confirming that jointly using MLSM with MLM offers better sample efficiency.

MSGS MSGS (Warstadt et al., 2020b) is a sentence classification challenge set that contains training instances towards different linguistic categories and surface form features of sentences. Control tasks are 'regular' training and evaluation splits in the sense that there is no purposefully encoded spurious correlation in the training dataset that is not present in the test set. The challenge tasks, however, are designed with the intention of conflating two properties with each other in the training set in a way that the given relation do not hold for the test instances. This way, one can measure to what extent the model was able to learn and rely on the actual target contept to be learned as opposed to the deliberately included surface level spruious correlation in the training data.

Table 3 contains the results for the control tasks as well as for the challenging cases with the purposefully malignant training data in which a surface form characteristic goes along with the linguistic properties to be tested. The different kinds of test

	KD	KD+MLM	MLM	MLSM	MLSM+MLM
CR (control)	0.7521	0.7609	0.7739	0.7842	0.7940
LC (control)	1.0	1.0	1.0	1.0	1.0
MV (control)	0.9999	0.9994	0.9997	0.9996	0.9995
RTP (control)	0.6905	0.8738	0.9117	0.9344	0.8785
SC (control)	0.7603	0.7786	0.7940	0.7130	0.7794
CR_LC	-0.4572	-0.6195	-0.6733	-0.6766	-0.5380
CR_RTP	-0.7686	-0.6571	-0.7805	-0.6051	-0.7613
MV_LC	-0.5329	-0.3928	-0.7954	-0.8370	-0.8558
MV_RTP	-0.0097	0.0729	-0.2217	-0.1047	-0.0385
SC_LC	-0.2849	-0.2673	-0.3011	-0.3087	-0.3223
SC_RP	-0.5758	-0.5601	-0.5039	-0.5346	-0.5173

(a) strict

	KD+MLM	MLM	MLSM+MLM
CR (control)	0.6311	0.6872	0.7351
LC (control)	1.0	1.0	1.0
MV (control)	0.9988	0.9956	0.9985
RTP (control)	0.8579	0.9857	0.8963
SC (control)	0.6657	0.6829	0.7845
CR_LC	-0.2261	-0.4080	-0.0729
CR_RTP	-0.6850	-0.8230	-0.6516
MV_LC	-0.9055	-0.9522	-0.9465
MV_RTP	-0.2882	-0.5484	-0.3947
SC_LC	-0.0300	-0.2715	-0.1664
SC_RP	-0.5290	-0.5681	-0.5275

(b) strict-small

Table 3: MSGS results for the models pre-trained on the strict (a) and the strict-small (b) corpora.

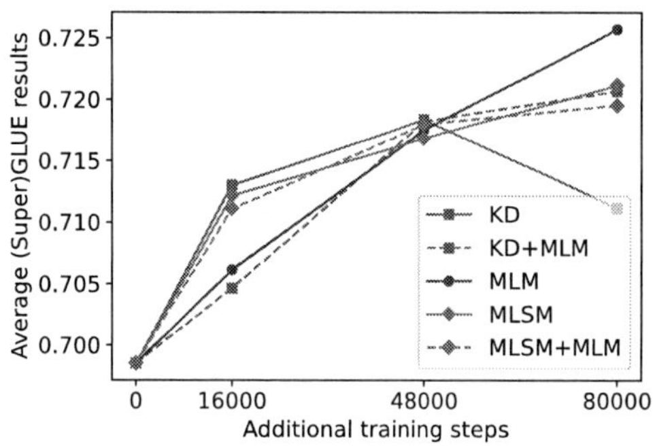

(a) Models pre-trained using the 100M token strict corpus

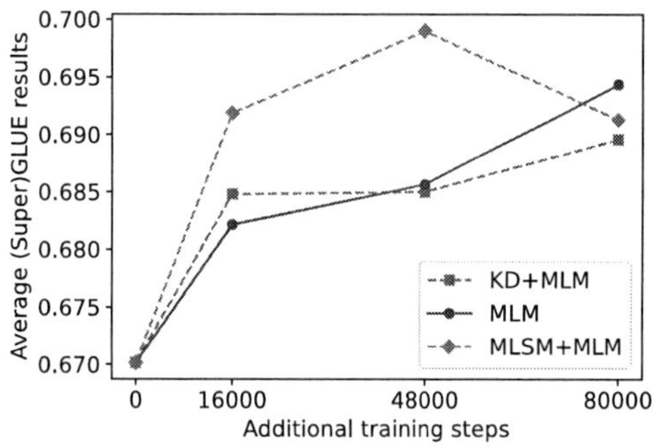

(b) Models pre-trained using the 10M token strict-small corpus

Figure 4: Average SuperGLUE performances as a function of the number of update steps performed in the second phase of pre-training.

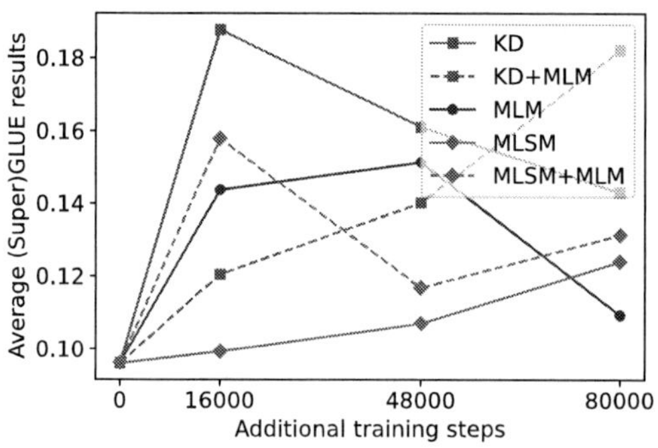

(a) Models pre-trained using the 100M token strict corpus

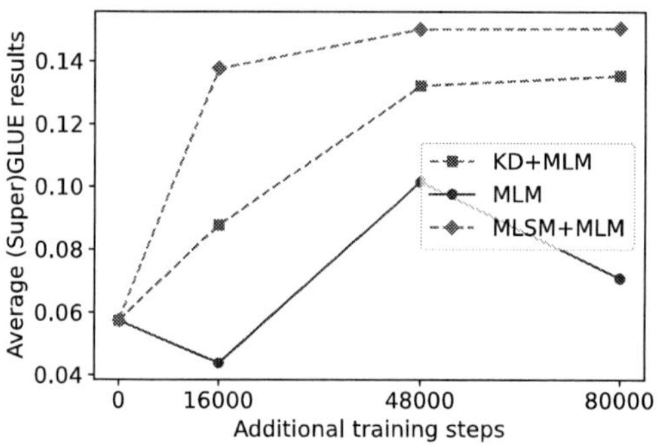

(b) Models pre-trained using the 10M token strict-small corpus

Figure 5: Average MSGS performances expressed in Matthew Correlation Coefficient as a function of the number of update steps performed in the second phase of pre-training.

cases are separated by an underscore. The five linguistic categories (and their combined challenge tasks) in the BabyLM evaluation framework are the control raising (CR), lexical content (LC), main verb (MV), relative token position (RTP) and SC (syntactic category) classes. The challenge sets are referenced as X_Y, where both X and Y corresponds to one of the above categories and they indicate the two categories that are purposefully conflated in the training, but not in the test set.

The performance of the differently pre-trained models on MSGS is similar to the previously re-

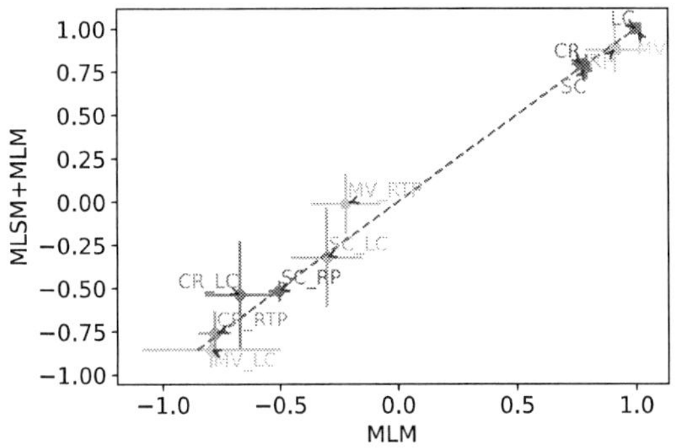

(a) Models pre-trained using the 100M token strict corpus

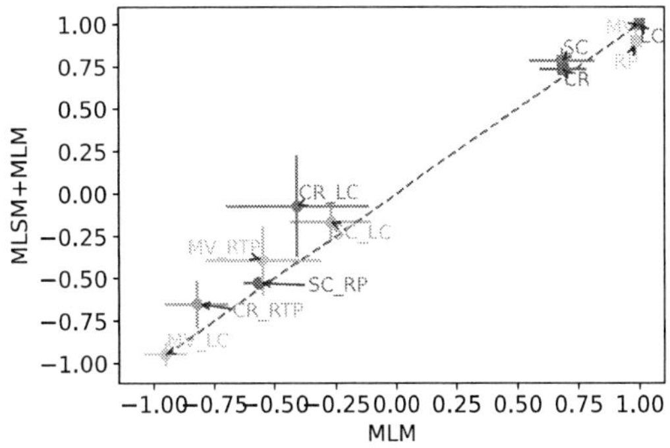

(b) Models pre-trained using the 10M token strict-small corpus

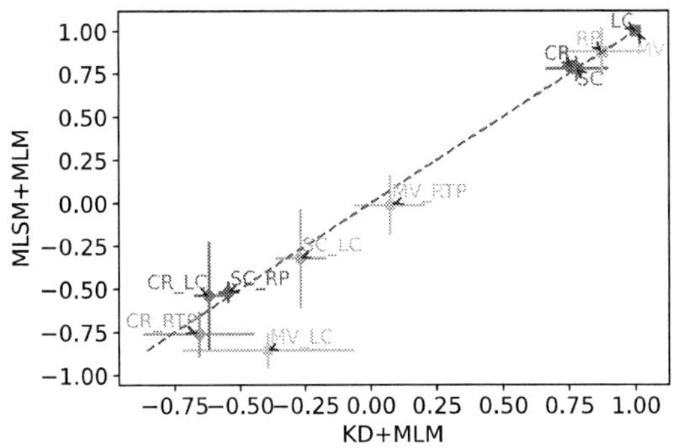

(c) Models pre-trained using the 100M token strict corpus

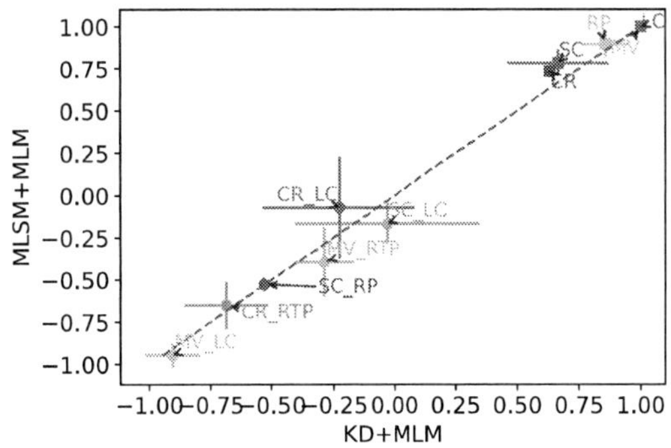

(d) Models pre-trained using the 10M token strict-small corpus

Figure 6: Pairwise performance comparison of best performing fully pre-trained models. MLSM+MLM performances are along the y-axis, the x-axis contains the performance of an alternatively pre-trained model. The fine-tuning performance on the unambiguous control tasks and the challenge tasks are denoted by squares and circles, respectively. For the task located above the main diagonal line, MLSM+MLM pre-trained models delivered better fine-tuning performance than the alternatively pre-trained model. The error bars correspond to the standard deviations of the Matthew Correlation Coefficient evaluation scores calculated over four experiments.

ported BLiMP and (Super)GLUE evaluations, i.e., MLSM+MLM pre-trained models perform well not only at the end of pre-training, but also across all the intermediate checkpoints as illustrated by Figure 5. The added value of MLSM+MLM pre-training is the most pronounced when the number of additional update steps is low. For the MSGS evaluation, we can see the largest average performance gain of MLSM+MLM when pre-training was conducted over the 10 million token strict-small training corpus (Figure 5b). The performance gains are already apparent (and actually the most pronounced) after performing only 16000 additional training steps.

Figure 6 contains scatter plots in which the MSGS fine-tuning performance of the best performing pre-trained models can be assessed on the individual tasks. The further a marker above the dashed diagonal line, the larger added value the use of the MLSM+MLM pre-trained model had over an alternatively pre-trained model for the given task. In case a point is located under the main diagonal, MLSM+MLM pre-trained model performed worse than a differently pre-trained model. The majority of the points are located above the diagonal line in each subplot, often by a large margin, confirming the additional benefits of jointly pre-training with masked latent semantic modeling and masked language modeling.

4 Conclusions

Even though MLSM is a cognitively more appealing pre-training objective than MLM, models exclusively pre-trained with MLSM fail at assigning reliable pseudo-log-likelihood scores to sequences (§3.3.1). To this end, we experimented with the coupled use of MLSM loss and the traditional MLM objective.

Our empirical results suggest that the joint use of masked latent semantic modeling and traditional masked language modeling can boost the performance of the pre-trained language models. This is especially the case for tasks that directly assess the linguistic capabilities of the pre-trained models that were obtained by relying on limited corpus size, i.e., the 10 million token strict-small dataset. Our ablation experiments also revealed that the advantages of MLSM pre-training are more pronounced during the earlier phase of pre-training.

Acknowledgments

The research received support from the European Union project RRF-2.3.1-21-2022-00004 within the framework of the Artificial Intelligence National Laboratory. Additionally, we are grateful for the possibility to use ELKH Cloud (see Héder et al., 2022; https://science-cloud.hu/) which helped us in achieving the results published in this paper.

References

Ahmed Abdelali, Francisco Guzman, Hassan Sajjad, and Stephan Vogel. 2014. The AMARA corpus: Building parallel language resources for the educational domain. In *Proceedings of the Ninth International Conference on Language Resources and Evaluation (LREC'14)*, pages 1856–1862, Reykjavik, Iceland. European Language Resources Association (ELRA).

Gábor Berend. 2020. Sparsity makes sense: Word sense disambiguation using sparse contextualized word representations. In *Proceedings of the 2020 Conference on Empirical Methods in Natural Language Processing (EMNLP)*, pages 8498–8508, Online. Association for Computational Linguistics.

Gábor Berend. 2023. Masked latent semantic modeling: an efficient pre-training alternative to masked language modeling. In *Findings of the Association for Computational Linguistics: ACL 2023*, pages 13949–13962, Toronto, Canada. Association for Computational Linguistics.

Jacob Devlin, Ming-Wei Chang, Kenton Lee, and Kristina Toutanova. 2019. BERT: Pre-training of deep bidirectional transformers for language understanding. In *Proceedings of the 2019 Conference of the North American Chapter of the Association for Computational Linguistics: Human Language Technologies, Volume 1 (Long and Short Papers)*, pages 4171–4186, Minneapolis, Minnesota. Association for Computational Linguistics.

Emmanuel Dupoux. 2018. Cognitive science in the era of artificial intelligence: A roadmap for reverse-engineering the infant language-learner. *Cognition*, 173:43–59.

Martin Gerlach and Francesc Font-Clos. 2020. A standardized project gutenberg corpus for statistical analysis of natural language and quantitative linguistics. *Entropy*, 22(1).

Jill Gilkerson, Jeffrey A. Richards, Steven F. Warren, Judith K. Montgomery, Charles R. Greenwood, D. Kimbrough Oller, John H. L. Hansen, and Terrance D. Paul. 2017. Mapping the early language environment using all-day recordings and automated analysis. *American Journal of Speech-Language Pathology*, 26(2):248–265.

Pengcheng He, Xiaodong Liu, Jianfeng Gao, and Weizhu Chen. 2021. DeBERTa: Decoding-enhanced BERT with disentangled attention. In *International Conference on Learning Representations*.

Mihály Héder, Ernő Rigó, Dorottya Medgyesi, Róbert Lovas, Szabolcs Tenczer, Ferenc Török, Attila Farkas, Márk Emődi, József Kadlecsik, György Mező, Ádám Pintér, and Péter Kacsuk. 2022. The past, present and future of the ELKH cloud. *Információs Társadalom*, 22(2):128.

Felix Hill, Antoine Bordes, Sumit Chopra, and Jason Weston. 2016. The goldilocks principle: Reading children's books with explicit memory representations. In *4th International Conference on Learning Representations, ICLR 2016, San Juan, Puerto Rico, May 2-4, 2016, Conference Track Proceedings*.

Taku Kudo. 2018. Subword regularization: Improving neural network translation models with multiple subword candidates. In *Proceedings of the 56th Annual Meeting of the Association for Computational Linguistics (Volume 1: Long Papers)*, pages 66–75, Melbourne, Australia. Association for Computational Linguistics.

Pierre Lison and Jörg Tiedemann. 2016. OpenSubtitles2016: Extracting large parallel corpora from movie and TV subtitles. In *Proceedings of the Tenth International Conference on Language Resources and Evaluation (LREC'16)*, pages 923–929, Portorož, Slovenia. European Language Resources Association (ELRA).

Yinhan Liu, Myle Ott, Naman Goyal, Jingfei Du, Mandar Joshi, Danqi Chen, Omer Levy, Mike Lewis, Luke Zettlemoyer, and Veselin Stoyanov. 2019. RoBERTa: A robustly optimized BERT pretraining approach.

Brian Macwhinney. 2000. The childes project: tools for analyzing talk. *Child Language Teaching and Therapy*, 8.

Jenny R. Saffran, Ann Senghas, and John C. Trueswell. 2001. The acquisition of language by children. *Proceedings of the National Academy of Sciences*, 98(23):12874–12875.

Julian Salazar, Davis Liang, Toan Q. Nguyen, and Katrin Kirchhoff. 2020. Masked language model scoring. In *Proceedings of the 58th Annual Meeting of the Association for Computational Linguistics*, pages 2699–2712, Online. Association for Computational Linguistics.

Andreas Stolcke, Klaus Ries, Noah Coccaro, Elizabeth Shriberg, Rebecca Bates, Daniel Jurafsky, Paul Taylor, Rachel Martin, Carol Van Ess-Dykema, and Marie Meteer. 2000. Dialogue act modeling for automatic tagging and recognition of conversational speech. *Computational Linguistics*, 26(3):339–374.

Alex Wang, Yada Pruksachatkun, Nikita Nangia, Amanpreet Singh, Julian Michael, Felix Hill, Omer Levy, and Samuel Bowman. 2019a. Superglue: A stickier benchmark for general-purpose language understanding systems. In *Advances in Neural Information Processing Systems*, volume 32. Curran Associates, Inc.

Alex Wang, Amanpreet Singh, Julian Michael, Felix Hill, Omer Levy, and Samuel R. Bowman. 2019b. GLUE: A multi-task benchmark and analysis platform for natural language understanding. In the Proceedings of ICLR.

Alex Warstadt, Aaron Mueller, Leshem Choshen, Ethan Gotlieb Wilcox, Chengxu Zhuang, Juan Ciro, Rafael Mosquera, Adina Williams, Bhargavi Paranjabe, Tal Linzen, and Ryan Cotterell. 2023. Findings of the 2023 BabyLM Challenge: Sample-efficient pretraining on developmentally plausible corpora. In *Proceedings of the 2023 BabyLM Challenge*. Association for Computational Linguistics (ACL).

Alex Warstadt, Alicia Parrish, Haokun Liu, Anhad Mohananey, Wei Peng, Sheng-Fu Wang, and Samuel R. Bowman. 2020a. BLiMP: The benchmark of linguistic minimal pairs for English. *Transactions of the Association for Computational Linguistics*, 8:377–392.

Alex Warstadt, Yian Zhang, Xiaocheng Li, Haokun Liu, and Samuel R. Bowman. 2020b. Learning which features matter: RoBERTa acquires a preference for linguistic generalizations (eventually). In *Proceedings of the 2020 Conference on Empirical Methods in Natural Language Processing (EMNLP)*, pages 217–235, Online. Association for Computational Linguistics.

Lil-Bevo: Explorations of Strategies for Training Language Models in More Humanlike Ways

Venkata S Govindarajan[♠] Juan Diego Rodriguez[♣] Kaj Bostrom[♣] Kyle Mahowald[♠]
[♠]Department of Linguistics [♣]Department of Computer Science
The University of Texas at Austin
{venkatasg,juand-r,kaj,kyle}@utexas.edu

Abstract

We present Lil-Bevo, our submission to the BabyLM Challenge. We pretrained our masked language models with three ingredients: an initial pretraining with music data, training on shorter sequences before training on longer ones, and masking specific tokens to target some of the BLiMP subtasks. Overall, our baseline models performed above chance, but far below the performance levels of larger LLMs trained on more data. We found that training on short sequences performed better than training on longer sequences. Pretraining on music may help performance marginally, but, if so, the effect seems small. Our targeted Masked Language Modeling augmentation did not seem to improve model performance in general, but did seem to help on some of the specific BLiMP tasks that we were targeting (e.g., Negative Polarity Items). Training performant LLMs on small amounts of data is a difficult but potentially informative task. While some of our techniques showed some promise, more work is needed to explore whether they can improve performance more than the modest gains here. Our code and models are available online.[1].

1 Introduction

Large Language Models (LLMs) generate complex and largely grammatical strings and display impressive performance with structures traditionally thought to require abstract and hierarchical syntax (Linzen et al., 2016; Linzen and Baroni, 2021; Wilcox et al., 2022; Futrell and Levy, 2019). They have achieved human-like performance at a wide range of natural language tasks (Bubeck et al., 2023; Frank, 2023), particularly those having to do with linguistic *form* (Mahowald et al., 2023). This state of affairs has led to claims that such models should be taken seriously as cognitive models of human language (Piantadosi, 2023; Baroni, 2022; Frank, 2023), in line with claims from the neuroscience literature to "take mechanistic abstraction seriously" (Cao and Yamins, 2021).

One reason that has been posited *not* to take LLMs seriously as cognitive models, though, is the immense amount of data they are trained on relative to what a human child is exposed to (Warstadt and Bowman, 2022; van Schijndel et al., 2019). Thus, it is possible that models memorize more than humans do and, relative to humans, over-rely on statistical heuristics and memorized chunks of language (Bender et al., 2021).

On the other hand, the quality of data that LLMs get during pretraining is, in many ways, much worse than what human learners get. Children get richly structured, interactive, multimodal input, tailored to their specific interests and needs. A baby might reach for a cup of water and be told "Water. You want some water?" Given that babies are known to conduct repeated experiments to learn about the world (Gopnik et al., 1999), the baby might try this again and again until mastering the concept of what water is. An LLM, meanwhile, might begin learning language by being asked to predict random tokens in the Wikipedia article on quantum mechanics.

In this paper, we describe our experiments with Lil-Bevo, a small language model trained on human-scale data for the BabyLM competition (Warstadt et al., 2023). The goal of the competition is to train a performant LM on a human-scale amount of data: 10M words for the small track, 100M for the larger track. We submitted to both strict tracks — however, we were notified through the meta-review that our models qualify only for the loose track due to the usage of additional non-linguistic data (music from the MAESTRO dataset (Hawthorne et al., 2019)). The evaluation is on a set of natural language tasks including grammatical acceptability judgments via minimal pairs in the BLiMP benchmark (Warstadt et al.,

[1]https://github.com/venkatasg/Lil-Bevo

Proceedings of the 27th Conference on Computational Natural Language Learning: Volume 2: The BabyLM Challenge, pages 308–316
December 6-7, 2023 ©2023 Association for Computational Linguistics

2020a), language understanding tasks in SuperGLUE (Wang et al., 2019), and MSGS (the Mixed Signals Generalization Set) (Warstadt et al., 2020b)

We started with a baseline DeBERTa model, trained from scratch on BabyLM data using a custom unigram SentencePiece tokenizer (Kudo and Richardson, 2018). Our strategy was not focused on the architecture, but on ways in which we could adjust the training regime to improve performance above the baseline.

Specifically, our strategy targets 3 ways in which typical LLM training regimes lead to lower-quality data than humans have access to. Here, we describe those strategies and their motivation. We give detailed methods in Section 2 and then present results, including a number of ablation studies that attempt to partition out what strategies were successful.

We treated these studies as proof-of-concept and did not exhaustively test these strategies. Thus, we think that there is still room for improvement.

Training on Short Sequences Unlike LLMs, babies do not start language by learning long complicated sequences all at once. Using databases of child and child-directed speech, it has been shown that there is some alignment of caretakers to the child's level in terms of linguistic complexity such that caregivers talk to younger children using shorter utterances and longer utterances as they develop (Schwab and Lew-Williams, 2016; Kunert et al., 2011). To that end, Mueller and Linzen (2023) showed that training on simpler data first could induce a better hierarchical bias for learning language. We specifically take inspiration from Press et al. (2021) who showed that LLMs learn better when trained on shorter sequences before being trained on longer sequences.

Training on Music Before Training on Language Unlike LLMs, babies are exposed to a wide range of input besides just text. Before and while learning language, they are also learning to map the visual world, to navigate the physical world, to process non-linguistic auditory stimuli, and to engage in a wide variety of cognitive operations. Thus, it is commonly observed that some of the machinery thought to be language-specific (e.g., hierarchical structure) might be induced in pre-linguistic infants through exposure to other kinds of stimuli. Papadimitriou and Jurafsky (2020) use this idea to show that training language models on structured data (e.g., music) can help models learn faster. We use a similar idea, with initial pretraining on a mix of music (piano performances) and text.

Targeted Masked Language Model The role of child-directed speech in human language learning is controversial (see Consortium and et. al., 2020, for discussion and a large-scale replication of infant-directed speech preferences). It is generally agreed that parents do not correct a child every time they make a grammatical error (Marcus, 1993), but there is also evidence that social feedback acts as a signal (Tomasello, 1992) and that parents structure input to be helpful (Weisleder and Fernald, 2013). When a child says something wrong, a parent might "recast" the utterance or highlight grammatical features that children are struggling with (Nicholas et al., 2001). Inspired by this idea, targeting the BLiMP (Warstadt et al., 2020a) syntactic evaluations as well as more general tasks, we trained with a targeted MLM objective.

We considered some variations of the idea of learning with some external feedback that distinguishes correct tokens against corrupted/noisy replacements. For example, ELECTRA (Clark et al., 2020) consists in learning to detect tokens which have been replaced by an auxiliary model. Unfortunately, replaced token detection approaches such as ELECTRA (Clark et al., 2020) suffer from an inability to learn probability distributions over the entire vocabulary, and so cannot be used for (pseudo)-likelihood scoring (Salazar et al., 2020). Another related approach is Corrective Language Modeling (CLM) (Bajaj et al., 2022), in which the model is trained to correctly replace corrupted tokens; however, it is not clear how to best use these models for scoring sentences in BLiMP.[2]

Given the problems outlined above, we decided to use masked language modeling (MLM) with targeted masks. The motivation is to make it easier for the model to learn syntactic phenomena that co-occur frequently with certain words. Other strategies for selecting masks were used in Sadeq et al. (2022); Gu et al. (2020); unlike these works, we mask specific words which are essential to the phenomena in BLiMP. For example, to target the filler-gap dependency subtask in BLiMP, we go through the original data set and mask every occurrence of "that" and "what" in the corpus. By

[2]Initial experiments with CLM performed worse than masked language modeling (MLM); we believe this is due to a mismatch between training and how the pseudo-likelihood scoring is done via masking.

focusing on these words, we anticipate that the model will more quickly learn to score "I know what you did last summer." more highly than "I know that you did last summer."

2 Experiments & Methods

We report all experiments and results for Lil-Bevo in this paper, as it enabled quick prototyping, and because we find similar trends with our larger model Lil-Bevo-X. Lil-Bevo-X differs from Lil-Bevo in the model used (`deberta-base` rather than `deberta-small`), training data (100M versus 10M), and vocabulary size. Final results for the Lil-Bevo-X are available on our online repository.

Tokenizer We trained a unigram SentencePiece tokenizer (Kudo and Richardson, 2018) from scratch on the BabyLM data combined with the MAESTRO (Hawthorne et al., 2019) dataset (described in detail below) using the `sentencepiece` library. Specifically, we trained a tokenizer with a vocabulary size of 16,640 and 33,280 for Lil-Bevo and Lil-Bevo-X respectively. `<mask>` and `<cls>` were included as control symbols in the vocabulary, along with an end-of-sequence token (`</s>`), a pad token (`<pad>`) and an unknown token (`<unk>`).

Model We chose to use an encoder-based language model, specifically DeBERTa since (a) encoder-based language models are known to capture many syntactic and semantic features in language when pretrained on relatively modest amounts of data (Zhang et al., 2021), (b) there were a wide variety of off-the-shelf DeBERTa architectures available on HuggingFace for easy prototyping and use.

We trained the model in three phrases: (1) pretraining on a combination of music and text for **5** epochs with a sequence length of 64 tokens, (2) continuing pretraining on text for **50** epochs with a sequence length of 128 tokens, and (3) finally pretraining on text using targeted MLM for **2** epochs with a sequence length of 512 tokens. Each of these is described in more detail below.

1. Music Pretraining Papadimitriou and Jurafsky (2020) find that pretraining on languages other than the target language — including music and code — lead to lower perplexities on target language as compared to random distributions of tokens, or even Zipfian token distributions. Inspired by this idea, we explored whether supplementing the 10M linguistic tokens with *non-linguistic* musical tokens from the MAESTRO dataset (Hawthorne et al., 2019) could lead to noticeable improvements in LM learning. The impetus behind pretraining on music is two-fold: (a) additional training data that nevertheless has structural biases that could help the model learn structural biases found in language (b) the model reaching a stable region in parameter space that enables it to learn desired linguistic properties much faster and/or better.

After several experiments, we found that pretraining on the combined *strict-small* and the entire MAESTRO dataset for 5 epochs provided the best results. We use V3.0.0 of the MAESTRO dataset, which contains 85M tokens using our custom trained tokenizer. The dataset consists of 200 hours of MIDI piano recordings, which we convert to text and tokenize with the shared unigram SentencePiece tokenizer. Our textual representation of MIDI consists of a chronological sequence of codes describing the channel and key of each note onset and release event (e.g. `c0n71` for 'note on, channel 0, key 71') delimited by spaces and optional codes for time between events (e.g. `t18` for 18 MIDI ticks). We chose a short sequence length of 64 tokens for pretraining inspired by the Shortformer, which we now explain in further detail.

2. Shortformer Press et al. (2021) introduce a few innovations to the training regime. In particular, we focused on their idea of training for shorter sequence lengths before moving onto longer ones. We used a similar training regime to (Press et al., 2021), where we started with a training sequence length of 128 for 50 epochs, before moving to a training sequence length of 512. We initially experimented with training on longer subsequence length for 150 epochs as in Press et al. (2021), but discovered lower evaluation results on most BLiMP categories (albeit with some improvements on some categories like Island Effects and Quantifiers). Results on BLiMP (Warstadt et al., 2020a) and SuperGLUE (Wang et al., 2019) saturated with as little as 2 epochs — we believe this is because of the much smaller size of the dataset as compared to that in (Press et al., 2021), leading to overfitting on the dataset.

3. Targeted MLM We specifically masked out words which were essential to some of the BLIMP subtasks. Some of these, such as quantifier and negation words, are also important to some of the

Category	Total	Avg
S-V agreement	124197	4.3
Animacy	100206	3.5
Quantifiers	89926	3.1
Modal verbs	58604	2.0
NPI licensing	47484	1.6
Filler gap	34988	1.2
D-N agreement	28675	1.0
Adverbs	19332	0.7
Anaphor agreement	3659	0.1

Table 1: Total number of masks and average number of masks per sample for each targeted category (*S-V agreement* stands for subject-verb agreement, and *D-N agreement* stands for determiner-noun agreement).

SuperGLUE tasks (e.g., textual entailment.) For anaphor agreement, we masked the words "himself", "herself", "itself", "themselves". For NPI licensing the masked words included "not", "often", and "probably"[3]. The list of words which were masked in each category are shown in Table 3 in Appendix A. We used a sequence length of 512 tokens, and additionally masked other random tokens in order to mask a total of 15% of tokens per sample.

The total number of words masked for each category across the 10M train set are given in Table 1.

The *Animacy* class consists of animate nouns, and was used to target the minimal pairs in the *Argument Structure* category with animate/inanimate subjects ("Amanda was respected by some *waitresses*." vs "Amanda was respected by some picture"). To obtain a list of animate nouns we used all the lemmas of (direct and indirect) hyponym synsets of *person.n.01* in WordNet.

In addition to targeting the BLiMP categories of S-V agreement, quantifiers, NPI licensing, filler gap, argument structure, DN- agreement and anaphor agreement, we also included some *modal verbs* (e.g., can, might, shall) and certain *adverbs* (e.g., never, maybe, always, perhaps), since these are important for textual entailment.

2.1 Ablations

We compare Lil-Bevo with ablations to explore how important our three strategies are for final performance. Specifically, we compare Lil-Bevo with the following:

Long-only Train DeBERTa with a sequence length of 512 tokens for 57 epochs.

Short-only Train DeBERTa with a sequence length of 128 tokens for 57 epochs.

Short+target Train DeBERTa with a sequence length of 128 tokens for 55 epochs. Then train with targeted MLM for 2 epochs.

Music+short Train DeBERTa on music and text for 5 epochs with a sequence length of 64 tokens. Then continue training on text with a sequence length of 128 tokens for 52 epochs.

Music+short+long Train DeBERTa on music and text for 5 epochs with a sequence length of 64 tokens. Then continue training on text with a sequence length of 128 tokens for 50 epochs, followed by training with a sequence length of 512 tokens for 2 epochs.

Lil-Bevo (music+short±target) This is the same as *Music+short+long* except that the final stage of pretraining for 2 epochs uses targeted MLM.

Implementation We train all our models using the `Trainer` API, part of the `huggingface` python package. Models are trained using 4 Nvidia A40 GPUs, with the maximum possible batch size that was permissible with each experiment. Apart from setting initial learning rate to 6e-4, weight decay to 0.1 and a warmup ratio to 0.0001, we use default training arguments in the API (except for the final targeted MLM/long stage, where we used all default parameters). Models are evaluated on the validation split of the BabyLM dataset. We did not use the test split of the BabyLM data. We release all of the above pretrained models online on the Huggingface Hub.

3 Results

Results for BLiMP, MSGS, SuperGLUE and the supplementary tasks are shown in Figure 1. The results are color-coded to represent each model's differences from the Short-only ablation. We highlight some results below.

Does pretraining on music help? Comparing *short-only* with *music+short*, we see that pretraining on music helps slightly on 8 of the 12 BLiMP subtasks, and on two of the 5 supplement tasks. However, it suffers from a large gap of 9.1 points

[3]Note that the masked words are not necessarily NPI items themselves, but rather that they are targets of single word substitutions in NPI items.

Group	Task	RoBERTa-baseline	Short - target	Short only	Long only	Music - short	Music-short-long	Lil Bevo
BLiMP	S-V Agr.	65.4	83.9	82.2	78.2	83.8	83.9	84.8
BLiMP	Quantifiers	70.5	66.7	72.7	69.4	71.3	73.1	68.7
BLiMP	NPI Licensing	55.9	77.2	61.0	54.9	65.1	63.7	78.5
BLiMP	Island Effects	39.9	44.1	50.8	44.5	58.3	55.5	55.8
BLiMP	Irregular Forms	87.4	88.5	87.0	84.2	87.0	85.3	85.3
BLiMP	Filler-Gap	63.5	76.1	76.3	72.1	77.1	76.0	77.5
BLiMP	Ellipsis	76.4	87.5	84.7	82.5	85.1	82.5	82.0
BLiMP	D-N Agr.	90.8	90.5	89.8	88.9	90.9	90.8	91.7
BLiMP	Control/Raising	67.9	69.8	69.8	68.9	72.1	71.9	70.0
BLiMP	Binding	67.3	64.1	72.4	69.5	72.9	72.6	63.3
BLiMP	Arg. Structure	67.1	73.7	71.7	69.8	71.1	69.9	72.5
BLiMP	Anaphor agreement	81.5	91.2	92.3	91.7	90.0	89.6	90.9
MSGS	syntactic-category-relative-position	-45.0	31.3	33.2	30.1	29.3	29.4	31.6
MSGS	syntactic-category-lexical-content-the	16.3	31.0	37.4	38.3	37.0	36.3	37.5
MSGS	main-verb-relative-token-position	-79.4	47.5	58.0	47.7	49.6	54.8	40.7
MSGS	main-verb-lexical-content-the	-99.3	67.2	40.6	42.1	42.2	54.8	36.7
MSGS	lexical-content-the-position	100.0	72.4	79.9	77.4	99.5	97.8	88.2
MSGS	control-raising-relative-token-position	-77.7	35.1	33.8	33.6	35.3	34.6	34.0
MSGS	control-raising-lexical-content-the	-28.3	44.2	40.1	43.8	44.0	44.1	44.0
SuperGLUE	WSC	61.4	61.4	60.2	59.0	60.2	61.4	61.5
SuperGLUE	SST-2	87.0	87.4	87.2	89.0	88.4	87.2	88.4
SuperGLUE	RTE	61.6	55.6	50.5	48.5	44.4	48.5	46.5
SuperGLUE	QQP (F1)	73.7	85.0	85.2	85.0	85.2	85.5	85.5
SuperGLUE	QNLI	77.0	82.1	81.9	82.2	80.9	81.6	81.6
SuperGLUE	MultiRC	61.4	63.1	64.2	63.6	65.5	64.8	66.0
SuperGLUE	MRPC (F1)	79.2	80.0	80.8	81.9	81.1	80.9	82.2
SuperGLUE	MNLI-mm	74.0	75.2	75.6	76.0	76.3	76.0	76.3
SuperGLUE	MNLI	73.2	75.0	74.9	75.4	75.9	75.0	75.4
SuperGLUE	COLA	25.8	71.6	72.3	71.7	74.1	73.9	73.7
SuperGLUE	BoolQ	66.3	65.6	66.4	66.0	64.2	65.3	65.4
supplement	Turn taking	53.2	65.7	68.9	68.2	68.2	67.9	68.2
supplement	Subj Aux Inversion	71.7	74.7	77.3	79.4	79.2	79.0	76.5
supplement	QA Congruence tricky	32.1	51.5	52.1	43.0	43.0	46.7	57.0
supplement	QA Congruence easy	31.3	79.7	76.6	65.6	73.4	73.4	82.8
supplement	Hypernym	49.4	47.1	48.1	47.1	49.4	48.7	48.1

Figure 1: Results for each model, for each task. The color reflects the difference in score between the given model and the RoBERTa baseline results released by the organizers of BabyLM.

on *QA Congruence tricky*. On SuperGLUE, *music+short* outperforms *short-only* on 6 of the 11 subtasks, and only slightly. Thus, we do not think there is strong evidence that pretraining on music improves over the short-only condition, in isolation.

Comparing *Lil-Bevo* (music+short+target) with *short+target*, we see that *Lil-Bevo* outperforms *short+target* on 69% of all tasks. Predicting score for each task in a mixed-effect linear regression with a fixed effect predictor for whether the model was *Lil-Bevo* or *short+target*, we found that *Lil-Bevo* was slightly better ($\beta = 1.3$, $\chi^2(1) = 4.11, p < .05$ by a likelihood ratio test). So, while music pretraining may help, the effect is small and inconsistent in our observed data.

What is the effect of targeted MLM? We compare *music+short+long* with Lil-Bevo (music+short+target) and *short-only* with *short+target* to ascertain whether targeted MLM helps over random masking. Targeted MLM does not systematically improve performance, except for two BLiMP tasks: NPI Licensing and Argument Structure. For NPI Licensing, Lil-Bevo outperforms *music+short+long* by 14.8 points, and *short+target* outperforms *short-only* by 16.2 points. We suspect that this difference could be meaningful since our Targeted MLM strategy specifically targets NPI terms that are substituted in BLiMP.

The effect of increasing sequence length When comparing *music+short* with *music-short-long*, and *short-only* with *long-only*, we find that pretraining with 512-token sequence lengths generally underperforms pretraining with 128-token sequence lengths. The difference between *short-only* and *long-only* conditions is quite large in fact. A linear mixed effect regression comparing the two using the same method as above found that performance was 1.8 points worse on average for the *long-only* method ($\beta = 1.8$, $\chi^2(1) = 14.2, p < .001$ by a likelihood ratio test). Thus, we believe pretraining with shorter sequences helps significantly compared to using longer sequences.

4 Discussion

Overall, we found that, for BabyLM's, sequence length matters, music pretraining may help a little (but may be spurious), and targeted MLM training may help on specific tasks.

These results are far from exhaustive, and we see a number of areas for future improvement using these methods. To fully understand the role of initial pretraining on music, one could construct a series of synthetically-generated music datasets, with varying degrees of complexity. Would pretraining on music that is more "language-like" (Lerdahl, 1996) in some sense improve performance on downstream tasks? Perhaps there is a principled way to interpolate between music and language, using the same kind of data format (MIDI). At one end of the spectrum one would have MAESTRO, and at the other end, text that has been encoded as into MIDI events.

Model	Dynabench score
Lil-Bevo	0.64
Music-short-long	0.64
Music-short	0.69
Short-only	0.63
Short-target	0.62
Long-only	0.61
Lil-Bevo-X	0.69

Table 2: Scores on Dynabench for different models.

Related to the use of varying sequence lengths, future work could consider improvements in data preprocessing and batching; in particular, knowing the beginning and ending of coherent chunks of text (e.g., dialogues or documents) could help improve the model. Beyond this, Mueller and Linzen (2023) provide some evidence that curriculum learning approaches may be fruitful to improving low-resource language models.

Finally, a more thorough analysis is needed on when (and by how much) targeted MLM is able to boost model performance. Other strategies are also possible, such as combining targeted MLM with information-theoretic strategies for picking random masks (Sadeq et al., 2022). Beyond MLM, contrastive objectives could be used to encourage the model to score grammatical sentences more highly than ungrammatical sentences.

5 Conclusion

A big motivating question for training models on human-scale data is whether it is possible for models to attain linguistic competence without the massive amounts of data used to train the massive LLMs that dominate NLP leaderboards. If so, that would make it more plausible that we should take LLMs seriously as cognitive models. So can BabyLMs learn like grown-up ones? While we find some hints of directions to pursue for making small language models learn more from less, we did not come close to matching LLM performance from larger amounts of data. Of course, that does not mean it is not possible to do so, and other teams might have different experiences. We did not fully explore optimizing all of our methods, and we treated our manipulations largely as proof-of-concept. Aggregating methods and results from a wider variety of teams will make it possible to more fully explore these questions.

References

Payal Bajaj, Chenyan Xiong, Guolin Ke, Xiaodong Liu, Di He, Saurabh Tiwary, Tie-Yan Liu, Paul Bennett, Xia Song, and Jianfeng Gao. 2022. METRO: efficient denoising pretraining of large scale autoencoding language models with model generated signals. *CoRR*, abs/2204.06644.

Marco Baroni. 2022. On the proper role of linguistically-oriented deep net analysis in linguistic theorizing. In Shalom Lappin, editor, *Algebraic systems and the representation of linguistic knowledge*, chapter 1, pages 5–22. Taylor and Francis, Abingdon-on-Thames.

Emily M. Bender, Timnit Gebru, Angelina McMillan-Major, and Shmargaret Shmitchell. 2021. On the dangers of stochastic parrots: Can language models be too big? In *Proceedings of the 2021 ACM Conference on Fairness, Accountability, and Transparency*, New York. Association for Computer Machinery – ACM.

Sébastien Bubeck, Varun Chandrasekaran, Ronen Eldan, Johannes Gehrke, Eric Horvitz, Ece Kamar, Peter Lee, Yin Tat Lee, Yuanzhi Li, Scott Lundberg, Harsha Nori, Hamid Palangi, Marco Tulio Ribeiro, and Yi Zhang. 2023. Sparks of artificial general intelligence: Early experiments with gpt-4.

Rosa Cao and Daniel Yamins. 2021. Explanatory models in neuroscience: Part 1–taking mechanistic abstraction seriously. *arXiv preprint arXiv:2104.01490*.

Kevin Clark, Minh-Thang Luong, Quoc V. Le, and Christopher D. Manning. 2020. Electra: Pre-training text encoders as discriminators rather than generators. In *International Conference on Learning Representations*.

The ManyBabies Consortium and Michael C. Frank et. al. 2020. Quantifying sources of variability in infancy research using the infant-directed-speech preference. *Advances in Methods and Practices in Psychological Science*, 3(1):24–52.

Michael C Frank. 2023. Large language models as models of human cognition.

Richard Futrell and Roger P Levy. 2019. Do RNNs learn human-like abstract word order preferences? *Proceedings of the Society for Computation in Linguistics*, 2(1):50–59.

Alison Gopnik, Andrew N Meltzoff, and Patricia K Kuhl. 1999. *The scientist in the crib: Minds, brains, and how children learn.* William Morrow & Co.

Yuxian Gu, Zhengyan Zhang, Xiaozhi Wang, Zhiyuan Liu, and Maosong Sun. 2020. Train no evil: Selective masking for task-guided pre-training. In *Proceedings of the 2020 Conference on Empirical Methods in Natural Language Processing (EMNLP)*, pages 6966–6974, Online. Association for Computational Linguistics.

Curtis Hawthorne, Andriy Stasyuk, Adam Roberts, Ian Simon, Cheng-Zhi Anna Huang, Sander Dieleman, Erich Elsen, Jesse Engel, and Douglas Eck. 2019. Enabling factorized piano music modeling and generation with the MAESTRO dataset. In *International Conference on Learning Representations*.

Taku Kudo and John Richardson. 2018. SentencePiece: A simple and language independent subword tokenizer and detokenizer for neural text processing. In *Proceedings of the 2018 Conference on Empirical Methods in Natural Language Processing: System Demonstrations*, pages 66–71, Brussels, Belgium. Association for Computational Linguistics.

Richard Kunert, Raquel Fernández, and Willem Zuidema. 2011. Adaptation in child directed speech: Evidence from corpora. In *Proceedings of the 15th SemDial Workshop on the Semantics and Pragmatics of Dialogue (Los Angelogue)*, pages 112–119, Los Angeles, California, USA.

Fred Lerdahl. 1996. Calculating tonal tension. *Music Perception: An Interdisciplinary Journal*, 13(3):319–363.

Tal Linzen and Marco Baroni. 2021. Syntactic Structure from Deep Learning. *Annual Review of Linguistics*, 7(1):195–212.

Tal Linzen, Emmanuel Dupoux, and Yoav Goldberg. 2016. Assessing the ability of LSTMs to learn syntax-sensitive dependencies. *Transactions of the Association for Computational Linguistics*, 4:521–535.

Kyle Mahowald, Anna A. Ivanova, Idan A. Blank, Nancy Kanwisher, Joshua B. Tenenbaum, and Evelina Fedorenko. 2023. Dissociating language and thought in large language models: a cognitive perspective.

Gary F. Marcus. 1993. Negative evidence in language acquisition. *Cognition*, 46:53–85.

Aaron Mueller and Tal Linzen. 2023. How to plant trees in language models: Data and architectural effects on the emergence of syntactic inductive biases. In *Proceedings of the 61st Annual Meeting of the Association for Computational Linguistics (Volume 1: Long Papers)*, pages 11237–11252, Toronto, Canada. Association for Computational Linguistics.

Howard Nicholas, Patsy M Lightbown, and Nina Spada. 2001. Recasts as feedback to language learners. *Language learning*, 51(4):719–758.

Isabel Papadimitriou and Dan Jurafsky. 2020. Learning Music Helps You Read: Using transfer to study linguistic structure in language models. In *Proceedings of the 2020 Conference on Empirical Methods in Natural Language Processing (EMNLP)*, pages 6829–6839, Online. Association for Computational Linguistics.

Steven T Piantadosi. 2023. Modern language models refute chomsky's approach to language. *Lingbuzz Preprint, lingbuzz/007180*.

Ofir Press, Noah A. Smith, and Mike Lewis. 2021. Shortformer: Better language modeling using shorter inputs. In *Proceedings of the 59th Annual Meeting of the Association for Computational Linguistics and the 11th International Joint Conference on Natural Language Processing (Volume 1: Long Papers)*, pages 5493–5505, Online. Association for Computational Linguistics.

Nafis Sadeq, Canwen Xu, and Julian McAuley. 2022. InforMask: Unsupervised informative masking for language model pretraining. In *Proceedings of the 2022 Conference on Empirical Methods in Natural Language Processing*, pages 5866–5878, Abu Dhabi, United Arab Emirates. Association for Computational Linguistics.

Julian Salazar, Davis Liang, Toan Q. Nguyen, and Katrin Kirchhoff. 2020. Masked language model scoring. In *Proceedings of the 58th Annual Meeting of the Association for Computational Linguistics*, pages 2699–2712, Online. Association for Computational Linguistics.

Jessica F Schwab and Casey Lew-Williams. 2016. Language learning, socioeconomic status, and child-directed speech. *Wiley Interdisciplinary Reviews: Cognitive Science*, 7(4):264–275.

Michael Tomasello. 1992. The social bases of language acquisition. *Social Development*, 1:67–87.

Marten van Schijndel, Aaron Mueller, and Tal Linzen. 2019. Quantity doesn't buy quality syntax with neural language models. In *Proceedings of the 2019 Conference on Empirical Methods in Natural Language Processing and the 9th International Joint Conference on Natural Language Processing (EMNLP-IJCNLP)*, pages 5831–5837, Hong Kong, China. Association for Computational Linguistics.

Alex Wang, Yada Pruksachatkun, Nikita Nangia, Amanpreet Singh, Julian Michael, Felix Hill, Omer Levy, and Samuel R. Bowman. 2019. SuperGLUE: A Stickier Benchmark for General-Purpose Language Understanding Systems. In *Proceedings of the 33rd International Conference on Neural Information Processing Systems*. Curran Associates Inc., Red Hook, NY, USA.

Alex Warstadt and Samuel R. Bowman. 2022. What artificial neural networks can tell us about human language acquisition.

Alex Warstadt, Aaron Mueller, Leshem Choshen, Ethan Gotlieb Wilcox, Chengxu Zhuang, Juan Ciro, Rafael Mosquera, Adina Williams, Bhargavi Paranjabe, Tal Linzen, and Ryan Cotterell. 2023. Findings of the 2023 BabyLM Challenge: Sample-efficient pretraining on developmentally plausible corpora. In *Proceedings of the 2023 BabyLM Challenge*. Association for Computational Linguistics (ACL).

Alex Warstadt, Alicia Parrish, Haokun Liu, Anhad Mohananey, Wei Peng, Sheng-Fu Wang, and Samuel R. Bowman. 2020a. BLiMP: The benchmark of linguistic minimal pairs for English. *Transactions of the Association for Computational Linguistics*, 8:377–392.

Alex Warstadt, Yian Zhang, Xiaocheng Li, Haokun Liu, and Samuel R. Bowman. 2020b. Learning which features matter: RoBERTa acquires a preference for linguistic generalizations (eventually). In *Proceedings of the 2020 Conference on Empirical Methods in Natural Language Processing (EMNLP)*, pages 217–235, Online. Association for Computational Linguistics.

Adriana Weisleder and Anne Fernald. 2013. Talking to children matters: Early language experience strengthens processing and builds vocabulary. *Psychological science*, 24(11):2143–2152.

Ethan Gotlieb Wilcox, Richard Futrell, and Roger Levy. 2022. Using computational models to test syntactic learnability. *Linguistic Inquiry*, pages 1–88.

Yian Zhang, Alex Warstadt, Xiaocheng Li, and Samuel R. Bowman. 2021. When do you need billions of words of pretraining data? In *Proceedings of the 59th Annual Meeting of the Association for Computational Linguistics and the 11th International Joint Conference on Natural Language Processing (Volume 1: Long Papers)*, pages 1112–1125, Online. Association for Computational Linguistics.

A Appendix

Table 3 shows the list of words selected for targeted MLM for each linguistic category, while age of acquisition results are presented in Table 4

Category	Words
S-V agreement	is, was, have, do, are, don't, were, has, does, isn't, doesn't, wasn't, haven't, aren't, weren't, hasn't
Quantifiers	all, some, more, any, little, many, much, most, every, both, each, few, enough, several,half, less,either, none,. lots, neither, plenty
Filler gap	that
Modal verbs	can, would, will, could, should, may, must, might, shall
NPI licensing	not, only, also, really, probably, often, certainly, clearly
D-N agreement	this, these
Adverbs	never, always, maybe, probably, perhaps, certainly, absolutely, likely, possibly, definitely, surely, truly, constantly, forever, potentially, positively, undoubtedly, consistently, invariably, eternally, perpetually, dubiously, uncertainly
Anaphor agreement	himself, themselves, itself, herself
Animacy	people, man, men, family, person, father, mother, girl, woman, son, children, guy, friend, wife, boy, guys, human, member, friends, women, members, daughter, child, brother, boys, husband, girls, lady, parents, kids, king, sister, dad, mommy, daddy, player, students, doctor, president, captain, kid, mom, leader, officer, director, players, soldiers, teacher, god, student, sir, officers, judge, patient, brothers, families, mark, actor, ladies, singer, uncle, author, manager, gentleman, humans, lad, writer, sweetie, prince, lawyer, artist, mum, host, owner, guest, teachers, princess, scientists, guard, professor, artists, leaders, agent, assistant, patients, mama, workers, minister, boss, sons, criminal, partner, babies, citizens, adult, politician, gods, mayor, actress, principal, cousin, witness, driver, hero, governor, lord, doctors, authorities, maiden, suspect, victims, aunt, candidate, individuals, producer, champion, gentlemen, founder, enemies, sisters, winner, passenger, client, bride, priest, prisoners, pilot, inhabitants, ghost, chairman, nurse, guests, user, pirate, graduate, merchant, cats, victim, passengers, pirates, noble, agents, expert, parent, editor, grandma, officials, subjects, cops, maid, commander, policeman, writers, servants, academic, peasant, eldest, engineer, musician, devil, critics, users, creatures, twin, composer, personality, lads, followers, poet, adults, boyfriend, fellows, actors, ruler, judges, witch, daughters, lieutenant, musicians, servant, secretary, slave, priests, scholars, prisoner, visitors, residents, lover, cop, companion, knight, deputy, customers, tourist, guards, grandfather, journalist, architect, rival, kings, colleagues, farmers, owners, farmer,...

Table 3: Words which were masked in targeted MLM in the 10M train set. For *Animacy* only words appearing over 100 times are shown in the table.

Model	Overall	Nouns	Predicates	Function words
RoBERTa-baseline	2.06	1.99	1.85	2.65
Lil-Bevo	2.06	2.0	1.84	2.65
Lil-Bevo-X	2.05	1.99	1.85	2.59

Table 4: Age of Acquisiton results

Towards more Human-like Language Models based on Contextualizer Pretraining Strategy

Chenghao Xiao G Thomas Hudson Noura Al Moubayed
Department of Computer Science
Durham University

Abstract

Taking inspiration from human children learning, we pose a question: can a "baby language model" gradually internalize a concept by exposing itself to the concept in unlimited, oftentimes irrelevant contexts, and what this means to limited pretraining resource (both data-wise and GPU-wise).

Throughout the study, we restrict our experiments to two data-limited settings, 10M and 100M tokens, which are respectively 1/3000 and 1/300 to what were available to the training of RoBERTa. Our best performing training recipe performs within 1.2% of RoBERTa, and on-par with BERT, on the BLiMP zero-shot linguistic knowledge benchmark, using 1/300 RoBERTa's pretraining data and can be trained on only 1 GPU in 4 days, trained for only 1 epoch.

1 Introduction

In recent years, the success of pretrained language models has relied on scaling up both parameter counts and the size of the datasets that models are exposed to, in order to improve performance. According to (Warstadt et al., 2023), the number of words that the modestly-sized language model, Chinchilla (Hoffmann et al., 2022) goes through (1.4 trillion words), is equivalent to over 10000 words for every one word a 13-year-old child has heard in their entire life.

In this work, we take a contextualization perspective to rethink, why can a human child build up their understanding of the world with an exposure to merely 2M-7M words per year (Gilkerson et al., 2017), and without largely changing the current pretraining techniques, how can we facilitate the learning of a language model to imitate such behaviors to the greatest extent.

With many nuanced experimental findings, our main findings can be summarized analogically as one trick:

"Learning to solve math problems in a history class".

Metaphorically, exposing a language model to datasets of different domains is like sending a kid to a kindergarden that teaches classes of diverse content. Taking the learning of math as an example, a child does not only do math in a math class, nor is their math capability only aroused when they see a math test paper. They do math in a math class, at home, and during playing time. If a child is good at math in a math class, they theoretically should be able to demonstrate their math abilities any time when presented with a real-life scenario that requires these skills.

We argue that such ability should also apply to language models, and find that, exposing a language model to knowledges of a domain surrounded by knowledges of that same domain, poses a **"contextualization trap"**. This induces overfitting to contexts, over-attendance to spuriously relevant tokens, and thus under-exploitation of semantics signals in the limited data available.

In fact, if a language model can recover masked Wikipedia texts surrounded by Wikipedia texts, it should be no worse at recovering them when it is "watching" cartoons.

We find that, designing training recipes solely based on this inspiration largely improves pretraining performance, enabling a baby language model to achieve similar performance to RoBERTa on zero-shot linguistic knowledge tasks, and competitive SuperGLUE performance, with less than 1/300 of its pretraining data.

2 Method: Contextualizer

To exploit the limited data available, we propose `Contextualizer`, a framework to create more (theoretically unlimited) contexts that a fixed input is surrounded by.

Proceedings of the 27th Conference on Computational Natural Language Learning: Volume 2: The BabyLM Challenge, pages 317–326
December 6-7, 2023 ©2023 Association for Computational Linguistics

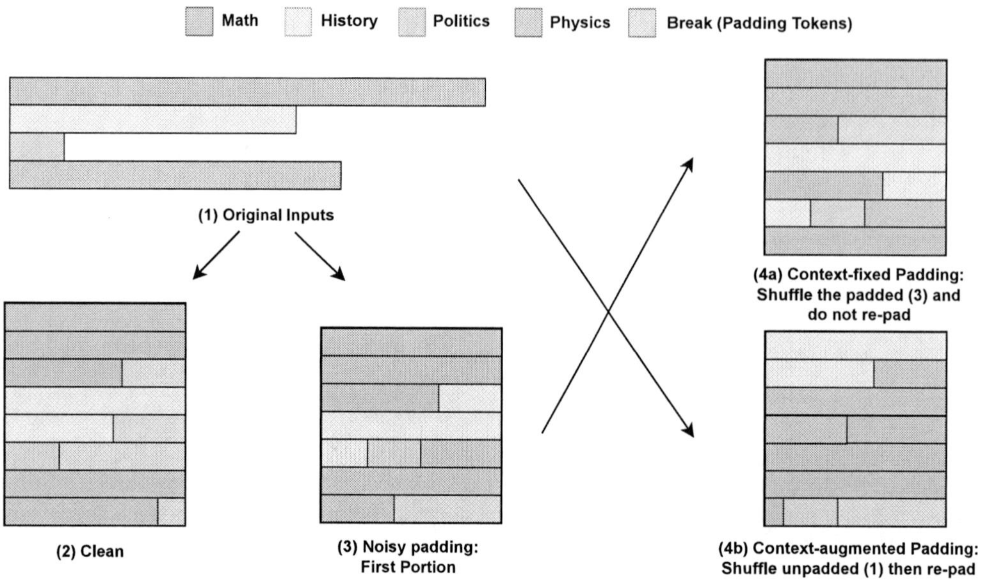

Figure 1: Concept of `Contextualizer`. Assume we build a training set with four datasets of different domains (say math, history, politics, and physics), each with one input. **Clean Padding** splits every input to different chunks, then pads the end of each input with padding tokens, and does not allow mixing components of different inputs to a same chunk. **Noisy Padding**, on the other hand, allows different inputs to be padded to the same chunk. **Context-fixed Padding** simply takes the chunks padded by Noisy Padding and does a round of shuffling. **Context-augmented Padding** shuffles the original inputs every time and re-pads them, allowing original inputs to be truncated at diverse positions and joint with different contexts. In our best training configuration, we do (4b) 40 times.

2.1 Recipes

We have designed two recipes to facilitate `Contextualizer`. 1) $\texttt{Context}^{\texttt{clean}}$. Aligning with the process of children learning, one would expect that teaching a concept to a baby for the first time requires exposing them to the concept in a "clean context", i.e., the context that the concept's supposed to be in. 2) $\texttt{Context}^{\texttt{noisy}}$. After a model/baby has attained certain level of knowledge, we consider augmenting this knowledge by practicing the knowledge in different contexts. As a further intuitive example, after a baby has remembered a quote from some cartoon character, they can repeat this sentence in a standalone manner in any context, and this does not require locating this sentence in a context with (max sequence length - quote length) of relevant cartoon dialogues any more.

Apart from intuitions from children learning, the spirit of the recipes has also seen its empirical ground in previous research. For one, research on shortcut learning (Geirhos et al., 2020) has attributed vulnerability of a model's prediction partly to its overfitting towards spurious correlation. Taking Tweet toxicity classification as an example, a model can easily learn its over-reliance on @ as an indicator for toxicity, because of the frequent appearance of @user in toxic tweets. Such vulnerability has hindered a real understanding towards the semantics of a large amount of tokens. Our contextualization method has largely removed learning shortcuts, by truncating complete inputs at diverse positions, making tokens in the input unseen from one another from time to time, while co-occurring with unlimited contexts from other inputs (be them relevant or irrelevant). This improves the model's robustness against irrelevant noise, while training its intra-input attentions to be activated by real relevant tokens.

2.2 Implementation Details

As discussed, we process data into $\texttt{Context}^{\texttt{clean}}$ and $\texttt{Context}^{\texttt{noisy}}$ on a high level. However, under the category of $\texttt{Context}^{\texttt{noisy}}$, we have designed three settings, namely, Noisy Padding, followed by either Context-fixed Padding and Context-augmented Padding (Figure 1). As we will show in later experiments, these techniques show large behavioral and performance gap.

Context^{clean} The concept of Context^{clean} is very straightforward and only facilitated by one setting: Clean Padding (Figure 1). Taking the original inputs, **Clean Padding** truncates and allocates each original input to different chunks, and extends each input with [pad] tokens, if the last portion of the input is shorter than the max chunk length by itself.

Context^{noisy} Context^{noisy}, on the other hand, is facilitated by three settings. As opposed to Clean Padding, techniques in Context^{noisy} allow text from different original inputs to appear in a same chunk. 1) **"Noisy Padding: First Portion"** is used to create the first portion of noisy training set, in a dataset curriculum order (will be discussed later). In this setting, datasets are first concatenated in a pre-defined easy-to-difficult order. At the end of each input, the next input will follow immediately, instead of starting a new chunk. 2) Later portions of the training set are created by two options: 2a) **Context-fixed Padding** directly takes the first portion created by noisy padding, and shuffles them on a chunk level. This will only enable different chunks to appear in different batches in later training, but will not re-pad different contexts in a same chunk. In other words, content in a chunk always stays the same, but is just shuffled to different indexes in the training set portion. 2b) **Context-augmented Padding** is the most noisy setting (and most beneficial, as will be shown). At each operation, it shuffles the original input order again, and conducts Noisy Padding. In other words, Context-augmented Padding is in essence Noisy Padding without the dataset curriculum scheme. Using Context-augmented Padding, we can theoretically create $n!$ training data examples by exhausting the order permutation of the original inputs, where n is the number of original inputs. As we will show, this technique leads to the most performance gain, by allowing the model/baby to revisit the same knowledge in many contexts, with different amounts of clean context available, and to develop different 'perspectives' to understand the same knowledge.

Datasets Our 10M and 100M datasets come from the two tracks of the BabyLM Challenge (Warstadt et al., 2023), including data sampled from CHILDES, Switchboard, OpenSubtitles, BNC, QED, CBT, Children Stories, Gutenberg, Simple Wikipedia, and Wikipedia, covering children speech, transcribed text, children stories, and Wikipedia data. In order to further imitate human learning, we apply a rough dataset-level curriculum for clean padding and the first portion of noisy padding, by manually arranging the order of importing the 10 datasets.

Notably, we did not apply any annotations or ordering to input-level data, but only arranged the training set at the dataset level following commonsense understanding (such as children speech datasets at the beginning, followed by children stories, and lastly Wikipedia datasets), further confirmed by manual inspection of linguistic statistics.

We leverage the TCT toolkit (Simig et al., 2022) to generate these statistics. For every dataset, we first compute the statistics on sentence level-inputs, and then average all outputs on the dataset level. As a further note, sentence-level statistics are just used to compute dataset-level statistics to roughly confirm our dataset order, and **none of these statistics provides signals to the training inputs in any form**. Also, there is no evidence that applying dataset-level curriculum in the first portion is useful to our method, but we would like to provide a starting point for future studies to combine our method with more human-like data orders.

Table 1 presents statistics of four of the representative properties: Age of Acquisition (Mean), Age of Acquisition (Max), Flesch Reading Ease, and Flesch-Kincaid Grade Level. We also ran computations on Word per Sentence, Average Word Length - syllables, Average Word Length - letters, type-token ratio computed over all words, lexical diversity, mean meaningfulness, etc. We find that, albeit we cannot find a dataset order that makes all linguistic statistics monotonically decrease or increase, statistics computed on all linguistic properties display a strong correlation. These statistics also align with one's common sense.

Following these inspections, the final data order is determined to be: CHILDES, Switchboard, OpenSubtitles, BNC, QED, CBT, Children Stories, Gutenberg, Simple Wikipedia, and Wikipedia. For Context^{clean} and the first portion of Context^{noisy}, all datasets are concatenated in this order before processing. They are then shuffled before creating later portions of Context^{noisy}.

2.3 Other technical Details

Tokenizer For 10M and 100M settings, we train separate BPE tokenizers (Sennrich et al., 2016)

	CHILDES	Switchboard	OpenSub.	BNC	QED	CBT	Child. Stories	Gutenberg	Sim. Wiki.	Wiki.
Age of Acquisition (Mean)	4.38	4.69	4.76	4.72	5.01	4.89	4.84	5.49	5.84	5.79
Age of Acquisition (Max)	5.43	6.80	6.66	6.94	7.88	8.62	9.58	9.38	9.99	11.37
Flesch Reading Ease	105.41	101.19	94.83	96.88	85.61	84.51	83.00	79.07	58.51	62.68
Flesch-Kincaid Grade Level	-0.28	1.03	1.53	2.15	3.86	6.19	6.80	4.35	7.67	9.30

Table 1: Dataset-level statistics of selected linguistic features, computed with TCT toolkit (Simig et al., 2022). These statistics align well with common sense, and confirm our manual dataset order.

from scratch with a fixed vocabulary size of 50k, in line with the original RoBERTa. We find that a vocabulary size of 10k and 30k degrades the performance of most BLiMP tasks (except on Irregular Forms, noticeably) in inital experiments with 10M datasets.

Arch./Size/Init. We use the architecture and parameter size of RoBERTa-base (Liu et al., 2019), and initialize the models with random weights.

Training Cost We fix the computation cost for models under the same track to be roughly the same. For 10M track, every model takes around 6-8 hours on a single RTX 3090; and for 100M track, every model takes around 3-4 days. The only factor that brings this around 10% - 20% training time difference is whether we add a round or two of $\texttt{Context}^{\texttt{clean}}$ before or after the training with $\texttt{Context}^{\texttt{noisy}}$. We will explain how we decide the computation cost in experiment setting section.

Chunk Length For 10M track, we set the max sequence length of each padded input to be 64 (i.e., max length of input chunks), and for 100M track, we set it to 128. We find that a max chunk length of 128 degrades the performance of models trained on 10M corpus on BLiMP tasks. Notably, in initial tokenization before post-processing with `Contextualizer`, we do not impose any max sequence length, and keep every token available before context augmentation padding with `Contextualizer`, i.e., the "max sequence length" only applies to padding complete inputs to chunks.

We hypothesize that there exists a training stability-oriented scaling law between corpus size and max sequence length to be padded to, due to the difficulty of learning robust long-range dependencies with limited amount of training examples.

Training Objectives We stick to MLM objective with 15% masking rate, and use dynamic masking (Liu et al., 2019). For all stratigies we use, we conduct random masking on the tokenized inputs on the fly (in training loop instead of before).

Interestingly, in initial experiments, we find that using reconstruction loss instead of MLM loss improves performance of checkpoints in early phase of training, and the isotropy of the embeddings encoded (Xiao et al., 2023) (also better zero-shot performance on sts-b). However, the gap could be bridged in later training. We leave further exploration of this phenomenon for future work.

We have also tried combining mlm loss and unsupervised contrastive loss (Gao et al., 2021b), and find unstable improvements (better on tasks related to representation - such as QQP and NLI tasks, and opposite otherwise). We have also tried masking rate curriculum and contrastive loss weighting curriculum, and find unstable improvements as well.

Therefore, we decide to only use a MLM loss with a static masking rate to focus on the study of contextualization.

Other Dataset Pre-processing We include a few extra pre-processing steps for all experiments. For $\texttt{Context}^{\texttt{clean}}$, we filter all original tokenized inputs that have only 2 tokens ([cls] and [sep] tokens) to make sure that the processed chunks later are not empty strings with only [cls], [sep] and the rest being all [pad] tokens. For $\texttt{Context}^{\texttt{noisy}}$, we only keep original tokenized inputs with at least 5 tokens before conducting noisy padding. This is because inputs with too few tokens are not self-contained. For instance, predicting "[cls] Hello! [sep]" with "hello" masked would only provide signals for the model's prediction to converge to token frequency-based probability distribution of the corpus (Chang and Bergen, 2022), and it is not useful for our noisy-context strategy. In terms of the datasets, we find that the Gutenberg dataset provided officially by BabyLM contains nextline splits in every paragraph once each line reaches certain length, and it is not ideal - because after tokenization, this would give unwanted [sep] tokens within a complete sentence that is not supposed to be split. Thus, we remove all nextline splits within same paragraphs. We find performance gains in initial experiments for all pre-

Task→ Model ↓	Anaph. Agr.	Agr. Struct.	Bndg.	Ctrl./ Raise.	D-N Agr.	Ell.	F-G.	Irreg. Forms	Island Effects	NPI Lic.	Qnts.	S-V Agr.	Main Avg.
Baseline	89.50	71.30	71.00	67.10	93.10	83.80	68.00	89.60	54.50	66.30	70.30	76.20	75.06
1-40 n (ours)	96.01	78.84	76.68	74.52	96.45	91.97	76.13	90.48	70.67	71.99	65.20	83.41	81.03
40-1 n (ours)	97.49*	79.58	**79.98***	78.26	**96.80**	**92.73****	83.94*	**94.50***	78.18	81.22	73.31**	**90.35**	85.53
40-1 cnc (ours)	**97.55***	**80.15***	77.06	**80.11**	96.57	92.26**	**84.97***	90.53	**80.12****	**83.71***	**73.80****	89.63	**85.54**
BERT	97.03	79.62	81.23	81.02	96.83	89.03	81.85	94.30	79.56	84.97	69.91	91.80	85.60
RoBERTa	97.70	83.04	79.21	81.90	97.28	92.15	89.39	95.67	79.67	82.58	70.40	91.47	86.70

Table 2: BLiMP Results of 100M recipes. **Bold Numbers** represent the best performance among our training recipes. Underlined Numbers represent second best. * denotes that the performance outperforms either BERT or RoBERTa. ** denotes that the performance outperforms both BERT and RoBERTa. Notably, our performances on Ellipsis, Island Effects, and Quantifiers outperform both BERT and RoBERTa, using respectively under 1/40 and 1/300 of their training data.

processing steps stated above.

Experiment Settings We conduct experiments with combinations of the above described `Contextualizer` data processing settings.

As stated, we fix the computation cost of experiments in the same track to be roughly the same. The exact cost is decided to align with the epoch number used in RoBERTa. We calculated that RoBERTa was roughly trained for 40 epochs on their training set. Therefore, for the noisy training set created by Context-fixed Padding, we train the model for 40 epochs (in result tables, we call this setting "1-40"). Then to align with this computation cost for context-augmented experiments, we perform Context-augmented Padding for 39 times on top of Noisy Padding first portion, creating a noisy training set 40 times larger than the context-fixed training set, and train it for only 1 epoch (we refer to this as "40-1" in result tables). Furthermore, we consider adding a round or two of Clean Padding data before or after the noisy data. This typically brings around 10% to 20% computation cost difference, since clean padding data has more examples (For instance, if we have 10 original inputs, each with 10 tokens, they could fit in one single chunk using Noisy Padding under a max chunk length of 128, but would create 10 chunks, using Clean Padding).

Concretely, "1-40 n" in result tables means: we train the model only on 1 portion of noisy data for 40 epochs. This is achieved by doing Noisy Padding to create one portion of data, and just shuffle this portion in the rest of the 39 epochs (essentially 39 times of "context-fixed padding"). On the other hand, "40-1 n" means that we create the first portion of data, and create 39 more portions with context-augmented padding, training on this 40-times larger training set for 1 epoch. "c" in the result tables denotes the number of clean data concatenated before and after noisy data. For instance, "1-40 ccn" denotes first training on clean data twice, then 1 portion of noisy data for 40 epochs.

3 Results

We evaluate our models on BLiMP, SuperGLUE and MSGS tasks (Warstadt et al., 2020a; Wang et al., 2019; Warstadt et al., 2020b; Gao et al., 2021a). Notably, we use the versions processed by BabyLM, where each word has appeared in the 10M training set at least twice.

3.1 BLiMP Results

100M Track For the 100M track (Table 2), we can clearly see the benefits brought by Context-augmented Padding (40-1 n), outperforming its Context-fixed Padding counterpart (1-40 n) by a large margin on the zero-shot BLiMP benchmark, and outperforming BabyLM official baseline for over 10 absolute percentage points. The model trained with Context-augmented Padding outperforms Context-fixed Padding on all BLiMP tasks, showing no trade-offs in introducing more noise from mixing contexts in the same inputs in the 100M setting.

Adding a round of clean data before and after noisy data (40-1 cnc) improves tasks like Agreement Structure, Control/Raising, Island Effects, and NPI Licensing, but degrades the model's performance largely on Irregular Forms, leading to only a small gain on average performance of all tasks. We hypothesize that there might exist a better data shuffling strategy when combining noisy and clean data, such as doing another round of training set-level shuffling after concatenating clean and noisy data. We leave this for future work.

Notably, our best performing models are on-

Model	CoLA	SST-2	MRPC	QQP	MNLI	MNLI-mm	QNLI	RTE	BoolQ	MuiltiRC	WSC	Main Avg.
Strict-Small (10M Track)												
Baseline	25.80	87.00	79.20	73.70	73.20	74.00	77.00	**61.60**	66.30	**61.40**	61.40	67.33
1-40 cnc (Ours)	**38.70**	**89.76**	**79.55**	**84.19**	**73.61**	**74.89**	**83.01**	52.53	**66.39**	61.23	**61.45**	**69.58**
Strict (100M Track)												
Baseline	45.30	88.60	80.50	78.50	68.70	78.00	82.30	51.50	59.90	61.30	**61.40**	68.73
40-1 cnc (Ours)	**56.09**	**90.55**	**83.74**	**85.63**	**77.92**	**78.36**	**83.60**	**53.54**	**68.46**	**64.40**	59.04	**72.85**

Model	CR	LC	MV	RP	SC	CR-LC	CR-RTP	MV-LC	MV-RTP	SC-LC	SC-RP	Main Avg.
Strict-Small (10M Track)												
Baseline	43.10	100.0	97.70	76.70	**86.20**	**-28.30**	**-77.70**	**-99.30**	-79.40	**16.30**	-45.00	8.21
1-40 cnc (Ours)	**75.68**	**100.00**	**99.93**	**99.96**	85.67	-46.28	-89.12	-100.00	**-62.37**	13.40	**-37.24**	**12.69**
Strict (100M Track)												
Baseline	74.7	100.0	99.9	100.0	59.2	-89.0	-91.2	-99.8	-15.3	-57.7	-39.2	3.78
40-1 cnc (Ours)	**96.48**	**100.00**	**100.00**	**100.00**	**96.68**	**88.03**	**71.76**	**-32.02**	**30.91**	**21.97**	**-35.93**	**57.99**

Table 3: SuperGLUE and MSGS results for 10M track and 100M track, comparing our selected models and baselines. Except CoLA (MCC), MRPC (F1) and QQP (F1), all other scores are Accuracy.

par with BERT, and is within a 1.2% gap with RoBERTa, using $1/40$ and $1/300$ of their training data respectively. This validates that, using Context-augmented Padding, we can create more pseudo-data that behaves closely like the real data. In our case, by running Context-augmented Padding 39 times, we actually create a 4B-token dataset using the 100M-token dataset. This is on-par with the training set with BERT, and actually gives us a model that behaves on-par with BERT on BLiMP. Given enough compute resource, we would expect running the augmentation 299 times would give us a model that performs more on-par with RoBERTa.

10M Track We find that, the best strategy for 10M deviates from the best strategy for 100M. We suggest this is because Context-Augmented padding dilutes the impact of informative datasets such as Wikipedia with noise (children mumbling, onomatopoeia data) from datasets such as CHILDES. Therefore, the decision for the optimal 10M strategy has been more difficult and nuanced. We leave the full 10M BLiMP results of 7 strategies that we have explored in Appendix A, and only present the SuperGLUE and MSGS results for one representative strategy (1-40 cnc, created by Context-fixed Padding) in the next section.

3.2 SuperGLUE and MSGS Results

Table 3 presents the results of SuperGLUE and MSGS tasks. Due to compute constraints, we only compare one of our models in each track with the BabyLM baselines. Our hyperparameter search space only concerns learning rate and batch size, with the rest of hyperparameters following BabyLM's offical repo. With limited compute resource (evaluating all fine-tuning tasks once takes around 13-15 hours on 2 RTX 3090s), we have only explored the combinations of $\{5e-5, 64\}$, $\{3e-5, 32\}$ and $\{2e-5, 16\}$, instead of exhaustive permutations of them. This follows the empirical intuition that, smaller batch sizes lead to more unstable optimization, and should be paired with small learning rates. We find that smaller learning rates and batch sizes generally work better for small datasets like CoLA, MultiRC and RTE.

For 100M track, our model outperforms baseline models on all SuperGLUE and MSGS tasks. On average, our model outperforms baselines by 4.1 and 54.2 absolute percentage points on SuperGLUE and MSGS respectively.

For 10M track, our methods also provide competitive results, outperforming baselines by 2.3 and 4.5 absolute percentage points on SuperGLUE and MSGS respectively.

This again confirms the universal effectiveness of our recipe pool, and also provides support for our hypothesis when evaluating BLiMP that, 10M datasets seem to work less well with our method compared to 100M dataset, because of the less self-contained original inputs provided by informative datasets like Wikipedia.

3.3 BabyLM challenge

The resultant models are submitted as part of the BabyLM challenge. Considering all results, we submitted the 1-40 cnc model for 10M track, and 40-1 cnc model for 100M track, and named

Tasks → Models ↓	BLiMP	BLiMP-sup	SuperGLUE	MSGS	Weighted Avg.
Contextualizer-RoBERTa-base-10M-v1	79.24	62.30	69.58	12.69	60.54
Contextualizer-RoBERTa-base-100	85.54	63.35	72.85	57.99	72.96

Table 4: Results on Dynabench Leaderboard. Notably, the BabyLM official evaluation has further included 5 BLiMP supplementary tasks, denoted as BLiMP-sup here.

them Contextualizer-RoBERTa-base-10M-v1[1] and Contextualizer-RoBERTa-base-100M[2].

Table 4 presents the official BabyLM Challenge results of our two models on the Dynabench Leaderboard.

4 Inner-workings Analysis

As simple as learning the same things repeatedly in different, oftentimes irrelevant contexts is, our method achieves surprising results without changing other technical details. It is a natural question to wonder how the method has facilitated better learning.

As partly discussed in the Recipe section, we hypothesize that the inner-working of this method is largely relevant to mitigating shortcut learning, and spurious correlation. For instance, if the same data keeps being displayed to the models throughout all epochs, the model might tend to overfit to the co-occurrence of words in certain inputs, or even simply remember the sequence.

For instance, without our method, if a padded input *"[cls] Figure 1 is an example figure for the concept. [cls] This is a completely irrelevant sentence."* is seen by the model 40 times, the model might incorrectly learn a rule that "example" is two tokens before "for", or even depends on "irrelevant" in the irrelevant chunk padded to the same input, due to stochasticity in optimization, instead of relying "example" on the information in "Figure 1" and "for the concept".

By contrast, our method makes sure 1) an input is padded with a different input in every portion, so it will not be padded with the same "This is a completely random sentence." and seen by the model multiple times. This way, the model learns to focus attention within one document, instead of "peeking" tokens in other text chunks that happen to be padded into the same input with them. 2) an input is cropped at different positions in different portions of the data, making sure the model utilize information in a flexible way, instead of building over-reliance on certain shortcuts. As an example, in one portion, it might be "an example figure for the concept. [cls] sentences from dataset 1"; and in a different portion, it might be "sentences from dataset 5 [cls] Figure 1 is an example".

We have conducted a proof-of-concept experiment to support this hypothesis. We take the 100M 1-40 n and 40-1 n models respectively. Note that the 1-40n model sees the same padded inputs 40 times, and is theoretically prone to shortcut learning; while the 40-1 n model is expected to learn more actual dependencies among tokens, as it keeps seeing the different combinations of inputs. Note that they are both trained with 15% masking probability. We take the padded training set that is exposed to the 1-40 model, and mask $\{50\%, 85\%, 95\%\}$ tokens in every input respectively, we then compare the mlm loss produced by both models. Masking more than 50% of tokens should have already made most documents lose its semantics. If the mlm loss produced by 1-40 n model is much lower than 40-1 n model, we can conclude that, it presents certain levels of overfitting and shortcut learning, shown by its ability to recover more tokens, with very broken evidence.

Mask Prob.→ Model ↓	50%	85%	95%
1-40 n	2.20	4.53	**6.23**
40-1 n	**2.67**	**4.69**	5.81

Table 5: Memory Analysis. Both models are trained with 15% mask probability. We get the mlm losses with different mask probabilities on data exposed to 1-40 n model in training.

As Table 5 shows, this pattern clearly holds. For 50% and 85%, 1-40n model produces much lower mlm losses, showing its imposed memory on the corpus.

However, when the masking rate is increased to 95%, the 40-1 n model produces a lower loss. We speculate that this is because with 95% tokens

[1]Dynabench ID: 1450

[2]Dynabench ID: 1343

masked (leaving around 6 tokens in every 128-token input), the documents are extremely broken, and knowledge about basic grammar depending on these $\sim$ 6 tokens are beneficial to recover parts of the tokens. Therefore, 40-1 n shows its robust grammar understanding towards more ubiquitous grammar phenomena.

5 Discussions

Due to limited time and compute resources, we position this work as a humble first step in studying contextualization as a data augmentation method for more human-like learning. We have proved the effectiveness of this context augmentation framework with its strong zero-shot linguistic knowledge performance gain, and leave design of other details such as the optimal way to tokenize, process and train the [cls] token for better performance on downstream fine-tuning tasks, as future work.

Moreover, while this work is largely restricted to studying pretraining of encoder models because of limited compute resources, we envision that the general findings are transferable to, or at least worth attention in several settings, including:

1) **Multilingual Models.** In the training of multilingual models, does practicing multiple languages in the same input chunk improve performance not only in code-switching scenarios, but also reflect in all languages individually? Does this performance manifest differently in low-resource languages, than in high-resource languages?

2) **Generative LLMs.** Does doing multiple instructions at the same time not only improve a LLM's multi-tasking abilities, but also improve abilities of individual tasks? How will this affect hallucinations?

Limitations

As discussed, our work is restricted to the study of encoder models. However, we envision certain transferability of our conclusions to encoder-decoder models and decoder-only models, and leave these for future work.

Moreover, again due to compute constraints, we have not been able to study the scaling law between model size and the number of times to augment the data with our Context-augmented Padding operation. We envision this to be very interesting, and SOTA-result-promising, as discussed in § 3.1.

References

Tyler A Chang and Benjamin K Bergen. 2022. Word acquisition in neural language models. *Transactions of the Association for Computational Linguistics*, 10:1–16.

Leo Gao, Jonathan Tow, Stella Biderman, Sid Black, Anthony DiPofi, Charles Foster, Laurence Golding, Jeffrey Hsu, Kyle McDonell, Niklas Muennighoff, Jason Phang, Laria Reynolds, Eric Tang, Anish Thite, Ben Wang, Kevin Wang, and Andy Zou. 2021a. A framework for few-shot language model evaluation.

Tianyu Gao, Xingcheng Yao, and Danqi Chen. 2021b. Simcse: Simple contrastive learning of sentence embeddings. In *2021 Conference on Empirical Methods in Natural Language Processing, EMNLP 2021*, pages 6894–6910. Association for Computational Linguistics (ACL).

Robert Geirhos, Jörn-Henrik Jacobsen, Claudio Michaelis, Richard Zemel, Wieland Brendel, Matthias Bethge, and Felix A Wichmann. 2020. Shortcut learning in deep neural networks. *Nature Machine Intelligence*, 2(11):665–673.

Jill Gilkerson, Jeffrey A Richards, Steven F Warren, Judith K Montgomery, Charles R Greenwood, D Kimbrough Oller, John HL Hansen, and Terrance D Paul. 2017. Mapping the early language environment using all-day recordings and automated analysis. *American journal of speech-language pathology*, 26(2):248–265.

Jordan Hoffmann, Sebastian Borgeaud, Arthur Mensch, Elena Buchatskaya, Trevor Cai, Eliza Rutherford, Diego de Las Casas, Lisa Anne Hendricks, Johannes Welbl, Aidan Clark, et al. 2022. Training compute-optimal large language models. *arXiv preprint arXiv:2203.15556*.

Yinhan Liu, Myle Ott, Naman Goyal, Jingfei Du, Mandar Joshi, Danqi Chen, Omer Levy, Mike Lewis, Luke Zettlemoyer, and Veselin Stoyanov. 2019. Roberta: A robustly optimized bert pretraining approach. *arXiv preprint arXiv:1907.11692*.

Rico Sennrich, Barry Haddow, and Alexandra Birch. 2016. Neural machine translation of rare words with subword units. In *Proceedings of the 54th Annual Meeting of the Association for Computational Linguistics (Volume 1: Long Papers)*, pages 1715–1725.

Daniel Simig, Tianlu Wang, Verna Dankers, Peter Henderson, Khuyagbaatar Batsuren, Dieuwke Hupkes, and Mona Diab. 2022. Text characterization toolkit (tct). In *Proceedings of the 2nd Conference of the Asia-Pacific Chapter of the Association for Computational Linguistics and the 12th International Joint Conference on Natural Language Processing: System Demonstrations*, pages 72–87.

Alex Wang, Yada Pruksachatkun, Nikita Nangia, Amanpreet Singh, Julian Michael, Felix Hill, Omer Levy, and Samuel Bowman. 2019. Superglue: A stickier benchmark for general-purpose language understanding systems. *Advances in neural information processing systems*, 32.

Alex Warstadt, Aaron Mueller, Leshem Choshen, Ethan Gotlieb Wilcox, Chengxu Zhuang, Juan Ciro, Rafael Mosquera, Adina Williams, Bhargavi Paranjabe, Tal Linzen, and Ryan Cotterell. 2023. Findings of the 2023 BabyLM Challenge: Sample-efficient pretraining on developmentally plausible corpora. In *Proceedings of the 2023 BabyLM Challenge*. Association for Computational Linguistics (ACL).

Alex Warstadt, Alicia Parrish, Haokun Liu, Anhad Mohananey, Wei Peng, Sheng-Fu Wang, and Samuel R Bowman. 2020a. Blimp: The benchmark of linguistic minimal pairs for english. *Transactions of the Association for Computational Linguistics*, 8:377–392.

Alex Warstadt, Yian Zhang, Haau Sing Li, Haokun Liu, and Samuel R Bowman. 2020b. Learning which features matter: Roberta acquires a preference for linguistic generalizations (eventually). In *2020 Conference on Empirical Methods in Natural Language Processing, EMNLP 2020*, pages 217–235. Association for Computational Linguistics (ACL).

Chenghao Xiao, Yang Long, and Noura Al Moubayed. 2023. On isotropy, contextualization and learning dynamics of contrastive-based sentence representation learning. In *Findings of the Association for Computational Linguistics: ACL 2023*, pages 12266–12283.

A 10M BLiMP results

The decision for which strategy to use for 10M track has been more nuanced and difficult. As shown in Table 6, we could see that Context-augmented Padding models (40-1) still outperform their Context-fixed Padding counterparts (1-40). However, this gap is not as large as the results in 100M, which as we discussed in main sections, is probably because of that, there exists much less self-contained data to resist against the noise brought by less semantic data (like children mumbling).

As shown in Table 2, using pure noisy data (entries with only "n" but no "c"), Context-augmented Padding (40-1 n) still outperforms Context-fixed Padding (1-40 n). However, when combining Clean Padding data, it seems to be detrimental to Context-augmented Padding data, while is consistently contributing to Context-fixed Padding data. We hypothesize that, mixing Clean data and Noisy data in essence is a context-augmenting operation itself. And as we discussed, for 10M track, a moderate amount of noisy context, instead of too much, is better.

We have also run some experiments on fine-tuning tasks on all model entries, and decided to use "1-40 cnc" for our final submission. Even though "40-1 n" provides the best BLiMP scores, it seems to rely on tasks with unstable behaviours such as irregular forms and quantifiers.

Task→ Model ↓	Anaph. Agr.	Agr. Struct.	Bndg.	Ctrl./ Raise.	D-N Agr.	Ell.	F-G.	Irreg. Forms	Island Effects	NPI Lic.	Qnts.	S-V Agr.	Main Avg.
Baseline	81.50	67.10	67.30	67.90	90.80	76.40	63.50	87.40	39.90	55.90	70.50	65.40	69.47
1-40 n	90.18	74.73	69.07	71.90	94.59	86.49	72.74	88.40	59.60	67.70	69.45	84.17	77.42
1-40 cn	91.62	76.13	69.83	71.23	94.51	89.03	77.30	82.29	58.67	67.04	72.21	83.96	77.82
40-1 n	92.02	76.02	70.66	73.07	95.66	82.39	77.48	93.13	61.47	66.75	81.43	85.56	79.64
40-1 cn	93.15	76.33	70.73	73.93	96.96	82.91	77.90	87.74	63.23	66.50	77.77	87.35	79.54
40-1 ccn	92.38	77.30	70.97	74.61	95.48	82.56	78.20	86.77	62.03	62.92	71.90	87.05	78.51
1-40 cnc	92.79	76.33	71.64	72.56	95.65	89.15	75 4.99	87.63	61.47	69.78	72.46	86.43	79.24
40-1 cnc	94.12	74.48	67.60	71.45	95.12	82.79	76.38	91.55	58.67	74.05	82.17	83.34	79.31

Table 6: BLiMP Results of 10M recipes. Clearly, while all of our strategies outperform the baseline by a large margin, results are more nuanced and it is not that straightforward to see which strategy is the best.

Increasing The Performance of Cognitively Inspired Data-Efficient Language Models via Implicit Structure Building

Omar Momen, **David Arps** and **Laura Kallmeyer**
Heinrich Heine University
Düsseldorf, Germany
{omar.hassan,david.arps,laura.kallmeyer}@hhu.de

Abstract

In this paper, we describe our submission to the BabyLM Challenge 2023 shared task on data-efficient language model (LM) pretraining (Warstadt et al., 2023). We train transformer-based masked language models that incorporate unsupervised predictions about hierarchical sentence structure into the model architecture. Concretely, we use the Structformer architecture (Shen et al., 2021) and variants thereof. StructFormer models have been shown to perform well on unsupervised syntactic induction based on limited pretraining data and to yield performance improvements over a vanilla transformer architecture (Shen et al., 2021). Evaluation of our models on 39 tasks provided by the BabyLM challenge shows promising improvements of models that integrate a hierarchical bias into the architecture at some particular tasks, even though they fail to consistently outperform the baseline model on all tasks.[1]

1 Introduction

Transformer-based Language Model (LM) performance is heavily influenced by three scaling factors: the number of model parameters, the pretraining dataset size, and the amount of computing. For optimal performance, all three factors must be simultaneously scaled up (Kaplan et al., 2020). This scaling law has introduced several challenges in advancing research on neural language modeling. One major obstacle lies in the unequal distribution of resources across languages. Consequently, the current approach of transformer-based models falls short of achieving equally high-performance levels for models dedicated to different languages (Choudhury and Deshpande, 2021).

Moreover, we see a considerable difference when comparing the way LMs learn how humans acquire language. One difference concerns the data that is input to learning: LMs such as BERT (Devlin et al., 2019), RoBERTa (Liu et al., 2019b) or GPT-3 (Brown et al., 2020) are exposed to billions of tokens during training, far surpassing what an individual human is exposed to when learning a language (Warstadt and Bowman, 2022). This fundamental discrepancy raises important considerations when drawing parallels between language learning in machines and humans.

To improve the data-efficiency of LMs, one direction is to adapt the model architecture. An effective approach in this endeavor involves incorporating an inductive bias into the models' architectures, which could potentially facilitate acquiring more knowledge from the same amount of data compared to standard models. However, the specific type of inductive bias to be added is still under exploration. Recently, there have been efforts to investigate the use of syntactic hierarchical inductive biases as a potential improvement (Mulligan et al., 2021; Papadimitriou and Jurafsky, 2023).[2]

One of these potential solutions is the StructFormer architecture (Shen et al., 2021), a transformer that is trained on the masked language modeling task. An additional convolutional neural network (CNN) component produces unlabeled dependency and constituency trees as a byproduct and influences the self-attention mechanism of the transformer layers. The model has obtained demonstrated competitive results in structure induction evaluations and a decrease in perplexity over a vanilla transformer baseline (Vaswani et al., 2017). However, it is an open question whether the inductive bias learned in this architecture enhances performance on downstream NLP tasks.

We pretrain the StructFormer architecture on a dataset from a different domain that had not been tested on that model before. Moreover, we use a

[1] Implementation and models checkpoints can be found here: https://github.com/omarTronto/structformer-babylm

[2] Note that we don't want to claim that humans integrate such an inductive bias and therefore can learn language with less data, compared to large LMs.

Proceedings of the 27th Conference on Computational Natural Language Learning: Volume 2: The BabyLM Challenge, pages 327–338
December 6-7, 2023

more sophisticated tokenizer in comparison to the most frequent words dictionary used to train the models in the original experiment. Additionally, we modify the model architecture to investigate whether injecting a hierarchical bias in the middle layers of the transformer architecture (rather than after the embedding layer) leads to improved downstream performance. Eventually, we evaluate seven model variants through the evaluation pipeline of the shared task and submit our best-performing model to the shared task challenge.

1.1 The BabyLM Challenge

The BabyLM Challenge is a shared task with the aim of data-efficient language modeling for English. Participants pretrain a LM from scratch on data that corresponds to the amount of linguistic data available to a child. The task is a great setting for conducting our experiments. It provides us with a pretraining dataset, a thorough evaluation pipeline, and, furthermore, an environment where we can compare our models' performance to other interesting architectures from the systems participating in the shared task.

Dataset The shared task is conducted in two tracks with different dataset sizes: a 100M words corpus, and a 10M words corpus as a sample of the larger corpus. The size is inspired by the assumption that children are exposed to 2M-7M words per year (Gilkerson et al., 2017). To account for the fact that children mostly interact with spoken rather than written language data, the datasets include a high proportion of transcribed data from different domains. For more details regarding the source domains, please refer to Warstadt et al. (2023).

Evaluation A thorough evaluation pipeline that comprises 39 different tasks is used to evaluate every model participating in the shared task. These tasks are supposed to represent a model's performance with respect to efficiency and applied NLP, as well as cognitive science, and linguistics. A group of 17 tasks, named *BLiMP* (Warstadt et al., 2020a) are performed via zero-shot predictions, while the other two groups of tasks; *SuperGLUE* (11 tasks, Wang et al., 2019) and *MSGS* (11 tasks, Warstadt et al., 2020b) need finetuning of the submitted models for classification. Refer to Appendix A for the complete list of tasks.

2 Language Modeling and Hierarchical Information

Transformer LMs use syntactic information in their predictions. This has been shown by work on interpreting their internal representations as well as by investigating the grammatical correctness of their predictions (Mahowald et al., 2023; Kulmizev and Nivre, 2022). However, the vanilla transformer architecture that underlies both encoder and decoder-based LMs does not encode hierarchical information explicitly. Rather, objectives such as masked language modeling and next-token prediction are based on linear relationships between tokens. This has inspired two lines of work that incorporate hierarchical knowledge into LMs. The first group of papers introduces models in which the training objective involves syntactic labels explicitly (e.g. Dyer et al., 2016; Sartran et al., 2022), The second group introduces models in which hierarchical information is encoded implicitly as a byproduct of a language modeling task (Shen et al., 2018, 2021; Li et al., 2019; Kim et al., 2019; Choi et al., 2018; Williams et al., 2018). We consider the second group of models more relevant for this shared task since it allows us to train models with a hierarchical architecture bias on raw text data. In particular, we use the StructFormer model (Shen et al., 2021), a transformer in which one architecture component, the parser network, predicts the position of each token in the hierarchical structure of the sentence. The prediction of the parser network puts soft constraints on the attention mask of the transformer layers. The model is pretrained on the masked language modeling task, and we view two experimental contributions of Shen et al. (2021) as most relevant for using this model: First, they show that a StructFormer achieves lower perplexity on limited training data than a transformer that replaces the parser network with standard self-attention. Second, the induced hierarchical structure corresponds to unlabeled dependency trees. Concretely, evaluation on the Penn Treebank (PTB) shows that 61.6% of the undirected dependency edges are recovered. We further implement a variant of the model in which the parser network predicts hierarchical information based on hidden states that are contextualized with classical transformer layers, rather than using uncontextualized token embeddings as direct input to the parser network (Sec. 3.2.4).

3 Experiment

This section introduces the objectives of our experiment, a description of the model architectures, and the technical aspects of the pretraining and evaluation process.

3.1 Objectives

In this work, we aim to validate the claim that the performance of LMs, in particular on syntax-sensitive tasks, can be improved through the implicit integration of an inductive bias into the model's architecture that yields a hierarchical structure of the tokens. Concretely, we conduct experiments towards pursuing the following three primary objectives:

1. Assess the robustness of the finding that LM performance is enhanced through the utilization of a linguistically informed model architecture (Shen et al., 2021).
2. Investigate whether the claim that transformer architectures better represent syntactic information in their middle attention layers is supported in a practical use case (Vig and Belinkov, 2019; Arps et al., 2022; Müller-Eberstein et al., 2022).
3. Develop models that surpass the performance of the baseline models offered by the organizers of the shared task.

3.2 Methodology

In order to address the questions posed by the experiment's objectives, we train a tokenizer, develop several model variants, and perform iterations of model pretraining, finetuning, and evaluation. Due to limited resources, we only conducted our experiments on the 10M words dataset. Furthermore, from the model architectures provided by the shared task, we chose the encoder-type models due to their adaptability for integrating a hierarchical bias in the model architecture.

3.2.1 Tokenizer

We use the same tokenizer across all variations of our models. Specifically, we train a Byte Pair Encoding (BPE) tokenizer (Sennrich et al., 2016; Gage, 1994) from scratch on the 10M BabyLM corpus. Since BPE tokenizers require specifying the vocabulary size as a hyperparameter before training on the corpus, we carefully determined an appropriate size. Our goal was to obtain a tokenizer that

Vocabulary Size	Least Frequent Tokens	Frequency
8K	sought, arts, stolen, ATOR	230
10k	accounts, seated, lemn, feathers	165
12k	sailors, goss, reun, irlines	126
16k	sophisticated, olleyball, AMES, poorly	80
32k	jets, estus, iesselin, UCLA, mannik	26

Table 1: Tokenizer Vocabulary Size Experiments

accurately represents tokens in our relatively small dataset while adhering to best practices for LMs. To achieve this, we train the tokenizer on the same corpus with different vocabulary sizes. We then observed the resulting vocabularies and identified the least frequent tokens within each (Table 1).

Based on our analysis, a vocabulary size of 32K tokens provides a fair representation relative to the corpus size for the least frequent tokens. Additionally, Geiping and Goldstein (2022) found that a BPE tokenizer with 32K tokens yielded the best results.

3.2.2 Baseline model

To achieve objective 1, we pretrained a standard transformer architecture that we call *transformer-base*, using our custom-trained tokenizer and following the same model and training hyperparameters to minimize any effects due to uncontrolled variables.

3.2.3 Hyperparameters

Due to resource limitations, and to assure fair comparisons between models, we use one set of pretraining and finetuning hyperparameters: We chose the default hyperparameters settings that were used to pretrain the shared task baseline models (Warstadt et al., 2023). In order to speed up the evaluation of finetuning tasks, we made modifications to the finetuning hyperparameters that were used to evaluate the baseline models. Our main hyperparameters are reported in Appendix B. We pretrain all models with the same batch size and the same number of steps. We use the training pipeline that Warstadt et al. (2023) introduced to train their baseline modes to minimize any effects due to uncontrolled variables.

However, one variable that could not be fixed during the experiment is the number of trainable parameters in each model. When adding a convolution parser network to a particular model, the increase in the number of parameters in that model is inevitable (parameter counts are listed in Appendix B). We are aware that this can have misleading effects on the results and conclusions, however, we still think that the experiment in its current setting can show interesting behaviors that may encourage further investigation in a fully controlled experiment.

3.2.4 Model Architectures

We develop two primary variants of model architectures for our experiment.

StructFormer This variant (Figure 1) closely follows the architecture in Shen et al. (2021). In brief, it incorporates a parser network that consists of 4 convolution layers. The input to the parser network is token embeddings, and the output is probability distributions for dependencies between tokens. These distributions are then integrated into the multi-head self-attention mechanism of a standard transformer model. For a complete description of the architecture, we refer readers to Shen et al. (2021). We name models of this variant by the prefix *structformer*.

StructRoBERTa The second variant (Figure 1) is similar to the StructFormer, but instead of employing a standard transformer, it utilizes a base RoBERTa encoder (Liu et al., 2019b). We modify the HuggingFace (Wolf et al., 2020) implementation, which has a few differences from the vanilla transformer implementation, mainly adding normalization and dropout layers after the embeddings layer, and also adding an additional intermediate block within each layer. The models following this architecture will be identified with the prefix *structroberta*.

Vanilla transformer For transformers without parser networks, we reuse the implementation by Shen et al. (2021) which follows the standard transformer introduced by Vaswani et al. (2017), except that a layer normalization is added in front of each layer.

Variants Subsequently, for each of the main variants, *structformer* and *structroberta*, we create two sub-variants to explore a different placement of the parser network within the architecture (Figure 2). This decision is based on insights from previous experiments, which indicate that syntactic information tends to be better represented in the middle layers of the transformer (Liu et al., 2019a; Vig and Belinkov, 2019; Arps et al., 2022).

In our approach, we divide the initial $n_{context}$ layers of either the transformer or RoBERTa component in *structformer* or *structroberta* respectively.

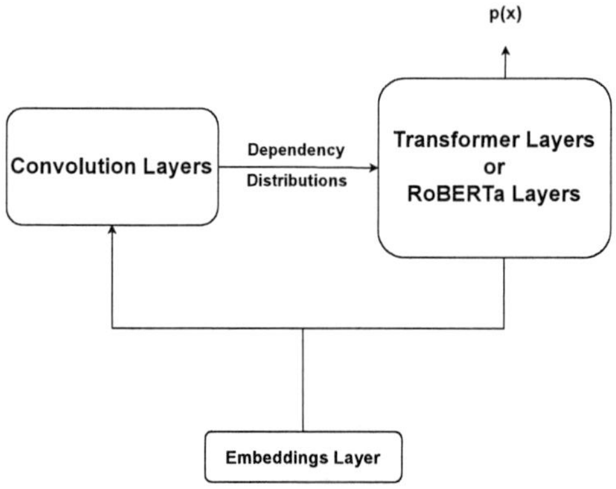

Figure 1: StructFormer and StructRoBERTa Architectures (s_1)

We label these $n_{context}$ layers as the Front Attention Layers, while the remaining attention layers are labeled as Rear Attention Layers. The input embeddings pass through the Front component, generating embeddings that are subsequently fed into the parser network. The parser network, in turn, outputs dependency distributions that are integrated into the Rear component of the architecture.

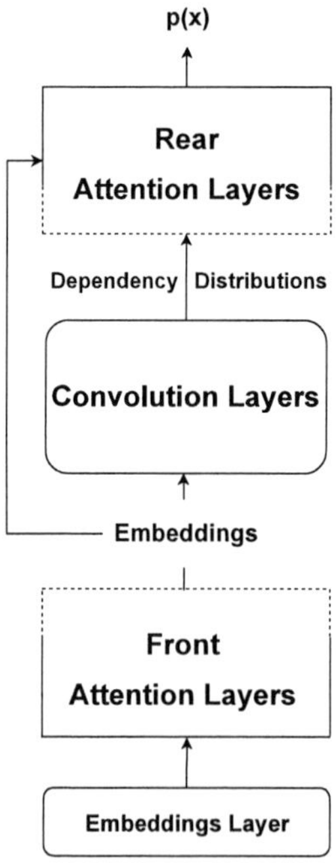

Figure 2: In-between Parser Architectures (s_2), dotted lines indicate intervening the encoder layers at two positions, where the parser network connects the two split parts of the encoder

To distinguish between the two sub-variants, we append the suffix s_1 to models with the parser network before the attention layers (Figure 1), and the suffix s_2 to models with the parser network in-between the middle attention layers (Figure 2).

To achieve objective 3, we introduce two additional models, *structroberta*$_{s1'}$ and *structroberta*$_{s2'}$, to enhance the evaluation scores so we could submit the best attainable results to the shared task. These two models are basically an upgrade in the number of convolution layers (from 4 to 6) of the parser network in *structroberta*$_{s1}$ and *structroberta*$_{s2}$ respectively.

4 Results

After completing the pretraining process of the 7 investigated models, a comprehensive linguistic evaluation is conducted for the seven models under study. The shared task evaluation pipeline is used for this purpose. Detailed evaluation results are presented in Tables 2 3, 4, and 5. We compare the scores of the following models: *transformer-base* (TF$_{base}$), *structformer*$_{s1}$ (SF$_{s1}$), *structformer*$_{s2}$ (SF$_{s2}$), *structroberta*$_{s1}$ (SR$_{s1}$), *structroberta*$_{s2}$ (SR$_{s2}$), *structroberta*$_{s1'}$ (SR$_{s1'}$) and *structroberta*$_{s2'}$ (SR$_{s2'}$). We are particularly interested in assessing to which extent the introduction of a hierarchical bias improves a model's performance on a specific task. Therefore, in addition to the scores of the individual models, we also report the differences in scores as follows:

- $\Delta_{SF_{s1}} = Score(SF_{s1}) - Score(TF_{base})$
- $\Delta_{SF_{s2}} = Score(SF_{s2}) - Score(TF_{base})$
- $\Delta_{SR_{s12}} = Score(SR_{s1}) - Score(SR_{s2})$
- $\Delta_{SR_{s1'}} = Score(SR_{s1'}) - Score(SR_{s1})$
- $\Delta_{SR_{s2'}} = Score(SR_{s2'}) - Score(SR_{s2})$

All numerical values in the result tables are measures of accuracy unless explicitly stated otherwise.

4.1 Pseudo-perplexity

We report the corpus-level pseudo-perplexity ($PPPL$, Salazar et al., 2020) on the test split of the BabyLM shared task dataset[3] (Table 2). $PPPL$ is computed by masking out each token in turn and collecting the log-likelihoods. This evaluation contributes to objective 1 in our experiment. Shen et al. (2021) found that *structformer* models incorporating hierarchical inductive bias achieve lower $PPPL$ than their baseline *transformer* model. We want to assess this finding on the BabyLM dataset and using our custom-trained tokenizer. SF$_{s1}$ shows lower $PPPL$ compared to TF$_{base}$, which follows the previous findings. However, the model with a parser network within the middle layers shows a higher $PPPL$ than the baseline TF$_{base}$. The addition of more convolution layers at the parser network shows an improvement at SR$_{s2'}$ but surprisingly shows a deterioration at SR$_{s1'}$.

4.2 BLiMP

BLiMP is a challenging benchmark comprising a set of tests designed to evaluate the linguistic knowledge of LMs with a specific focus on linguistic phenomena encompassing syntax, morphology, and semantics (Warstadt et al., 2020a). Originally, the benchmark consisted of 12 tasks (see Appendix A). Additionally, in the shared task (Warstadt et al., 2023), 5 more tasks were added to BLiMP as held-out tasks, aiming to assess the generalization capabilities of the submitted models. The random chance accuracy for all original BLiMP tasks is 50, while chance was not reported for the additional 5 supplement tasks.

According to the BLiMP scores in Table 3, within the *Set A* models, the models incorporating hierarchical inductive bias (SF$_{s1}$ and SF$_{s2}$) do not show consistent outperformance or underperformance in comparison to the baseline model TF$_{base}$.

However, on average, the SF$_{s1}$ model is on par with and occasionally outperforms the TF$_{base}$ model. In particular, SF$_{s1}$ excels in the following tests: Argument Structure, Determiner Noun Agreement, Filler Gap, Irregular Forms, Quantifiers, and Subj. Verb Agreement. Conversely, SF$_{s1}$ underperforms the TF$_{base}$ in the tasks of QA Congruence Easy, Subject Aux Inversion and Turn Taking. We hypothesize that this is because syntactic knowledge is helpful for the former list of tasks, but to a lesser degree for the latter, for example, Turn Taking, which focuses on knowledge of discourse and dialogue structure, in particular of referential properties of NPs, which is not reflected in the syntactic structure. A sample pair from this data set is *"Should you quit?" – "No, I shouldn't."* (good) versus *"Should she quit?" – "No, I shouldn't."* (bad). The negative and the positive data points have the same syntactic structure and the dependents are

[3]We use Kauf and Ivanova (2023)'s implementation for computing $PPPL$ scores and remove the 100 longest sentences from the dataset to reduce the computation time.

	Set A			Set B			
	TF$_{base}$	**SF**$_{s1}$	**SF**$_{s2}$	**SR**$_{s1}$	**SR**$_{s2}$	**SR**$_{s1'}$	**SR**$_{s2'}$
Perplexity	32.84	26.48	38.26	**21.15**	23.15	37.11	22.48

Table 2: Perplexity Results

	Set A					Set B						
	TF$_{base}$	**SF**$_{s1}$	**SF**$_{s2}$	$\Delta_{SF_{s1}}$	$\Delta_{SF_{s2}}$	**SR**$_{s1}$	**SR**$_{s2}$	**SR**$_{s1'}$	**SR**$_{s2'}$	$\Delta_{SR_{s12}}$	$\Delta_{SR_{s1'}}$	$\Delta_{SR_{s2'}}$
Anaphor Agreement	88	88	74	0	-14	89	87	90	87	-2	1	0
Argument Structure	68	69	68	1	0	69	72	73	68	3	4	-4
Binding	68	68	66	0	-2	72	70	70	67	-2	-2	-3
Control Raising	66	66	64	0	-2	69	70	68	63	1	-1	-7
Det. Noun Agreement	87	90	86	3	-1	92	93	93	88	1	1	-5
Ellipsis	79	79	72	0	-7	70	71	77	70	1	7	-1
Filler Gap	63	70	63	7	0	69	67	74	64	-2	5	-3
Irregular Forms	76	90	86	14	10	83	92	85	84	9	2	-8
Island Effects	44	44	37	0	-7	49	45	52	43	-4	3	-2
NPI Licensing	58	58	55	0	-3	55	59	68	53	4	13	-6
Quantifiers	73	78	73	5	0	71	68	68	71	-3	-3	3
Subj. Verb Agreement	64	70	60	6	-4	75	75	76	66	0	1	-9
Hypernym	50	50	50	0	0	48	48	50	49	0	2	1
QA Congruence Easy	59	56	56	-3	-3	64	69	66	64	5	2	-5
QA Congruence Tricky	38	35	35	-3	-3	28	34	28	28	6	0	-6
Subject Aux Inversion	82	78	81	-4	-1	70	71	76	70	1	6	-1
Turn Taking	67	65	55	-2	-12	61	59	60	61	-2	-1	2
Average	66.5	67.9	63.6	1.4	-2.9	66.7	67.7	**69.1**	64.5	0.9	2.4	-3.2

Table 3: BLiMP Results

perfectly fine as argument fillers.

While the model with a parser network in-between the middle layers SF$_{s2}$, underperforms TF$_{base}$ on average, but interestingly it demonstrates a noteworthy improvement in the specific task of Irregular Forms. Remarkably, similar to SF$_{s1}$, SF$_{s2}$ significantly outperform TF$_{base}$ in this particular task. The task of Irregular Forms involves aspects of lexical decisions but the syntax of course also plays a role.

Within the RoBERTa model variations in Set B, again the model with a parser network in-between the middle layers SR$_{s2}$ fails to improve over the one with a parser network ahead of the encoder layers SR$_{s1}$ in most of the tasks. It even gets worse with the upgrade in the number of convolution layers within the parser network at SR$_{s2'}$. On the other hand, the upgrade in the number of convolution layers at SR$_{s1'}$ shows also an upgrade in accuracies over SR$_{s1}$. Generally, SR$_{s1'}$ achieves the best results among all the investigated models on average.

Moreover, the Set B models exhibit improvements over Set A models in the tests of Binding, Det. Noun Agreement, Subject Verb Agreement, and QA Congruence Easy.

It is not so clear how to interpret the results of the two Question Answering (QA) Congruence tasks, where the baselines achieve only very low scores. For the QA Congruence Easy task, which tests for detecting selectional preference violations on object fillers in answers (e.g., *"What did you sell? - A chair."* (good) versus *"What did you sell? - Sarah."* (bad)), knowing about the syntactic structure of the first sentence probably helps to apply selectional restrictions and thereby assessing the quality of the second as a possible reply. This might be the reason why we see an improvement in model performance in the SR models when adding implicit hierarchical information that reflects syntactic dependencies. The QA Congruence Tricky task is similar, except that the selectional preference that is violated in the negative data points does not refer to the direct object. Furthermore, the object is dropped in most examples and sometimes the (incorrect) argument filler would be a plausible direct object (e.g., *"Who ate? - Sarah ate."* (good) versus *"Who ate? - Pasta ate."* (bad)). This is why the task is tricky. In this context, it is important to keep in mind that our StructFormer models learn only unlabeled dependencies and therefore cannot distinguish between object and subject. This means that for *Pasta ate*, a structure would be implicitly predicted where *pasta* is a dependent of *ate*, which is perfectly fine semantically (as a direct object). This might be a reason why the structformer models struggle with this test and partly lead to a decrease in the performance, compared to our baseline, since the unlabeled dependency tree actually licenses the negative data points.

4.3 SuperGLUE

SuperGLUE consists of eleven diverse tasks (see Appendix A) which evaluate various performance aspects. These tasks include sentiment analysis, linguistic acceptability judgments, entailment detection, and semantic similarity evaluations of words within contexts, among others (Wang et al., 2019).

The scores (see Table 4) in most of the tasks fall in a narrow range across all the investigated models. The incorporation of hierarchical inductive bias does not show clear improvements in most of the tasks. A noticeable result that is observed for the models with a parser network within the middle layers *(s2)* is the result of the MRPC task, where *s2* models consistently outperform the *s1* models in both sets for this particular task. The upgrade in the number of convolution layers also does not show a clear improvement in most of the tasks for both $SR_{s1'}$ and $SR_{s2'}$ models.

Notably, in the case of the WSC task, we observe that all models' predictions heavily favored one specific class. This raises concerns about the success of the finetuning process for this particular task.

4.4 MSGS

The MSGS tasks, listed in Appendix A, were introduced by the shared task as held-out tests specifically designed to evaluate generalization capabilities. Detailed information and further insights about these tasks are expected to be disclosed in an upcoming publication. MSGS tasks are measured using the Matthews correlation coefficient (MCC). MCC is used in machine learning as a measure of the quality of binary (two-class) classifications, introduced by Matthews (1975)

The MSGS results (Table 5), resemble to the SuperGLUE results. The models incorporating hierarchical inductive bias show contradicting behavior across the different tasks. While for some tasks e.g Control Raising (Control), Relative Position (Control), and Syntactic Category (Relative Position), SF_{s1} and SF_{s2} are strengthening the correlation in comparison to the baseline model, but with other tasks e.g Lexical Content (Control), Main Verb (Lexical Content) and Syntactic Category (Lexical Content), SF_{s1} and SF_{s2} are shown weakening the correlation.

4.5 Aggregation

Indeed, analyzing the performance changes across 39 tasks for 7 different models is a complex process. To simplify the assessment and present a concise summary of each model's overall performance, we report an aggregate score of all the 39 scores for each model (Table 6). This aggregation approach was internally computed by the shared task submission platform to represent each model with a single score, providing a more straightforward evaluation of the overall performance. Subsequently, we select the model with the best aggregate score $SR_{s1'}$ to represent our submission in the shared task.

5 Discussion

Although the evaluation pipeline of the shared task was meticulously designed to encompass a comprehensive analysis of pretrained LMs, covering aspects of efficiency, applied NLP standards, cognitive science, linguistics, and language acquisition (Warstadt et al., 2023), it was discussed in Warstadt et al. (2020a) that some tasks that involve semantic phenomena such as Island Effects and NPI Licensing are very difficult for LMs in general. Consequently, the consistently low performance observed across all models on these tests can be attributed to this matter. As a result, we refrain from considering the aggregate score as a single definitive metric for representing how a model's performance compares to another. Instead, we advocate for a thorough investigation of individual tests while considering the test's objectives, dataset, and evaluation strategy.

Overall, the models incorporating hierarchical inductive bias did not show significant improvement in the scores of the BabyLM evaluation tasks, however, some exceptions of the evaluation tasks that show improvements in terms of scores when using the *structformer* and *structroberta* models, encourage a deeper investigation for patterns in the outputs predictions that might lead to a different conclusion. Namely, the tasks that we think are worth more investigation are: *Argument Structure, Determiner Noun Agreement, Filler Gap, Irregular Forms, Quantifiers, Subj. Verb Agreement, Control Raising (Control), Relative Position (Control) and Syntactic Category (Relative Position).*

Contrary to our expectations, the modification of placing the parser in-between the middle attention layers has not demonstrated notable improvements but rather a decline in performance compared to the models with the parser placed right after the input

	Set A					Set B						
	$\mathbf{TF}_{base}$	$\mathbf{SF}_{s1}$	$\mathbf{SF}_{s2}$	$\Delta_{SF_{s1}}$	$\Delta_{SF_{s2}}$	$\mathbf{SR}_{s1}$	$\mathbf{SR}_{s2}$	$\mathbf{SR}_{s1'}$	$\mathbf{SR}_{s2'}$	$\Delta_{SR_{s12}}$	$\Delta_{SR_{s1'}}$	$\Delta_{SR_{s2'}}$
BoolQ	63	61	62	-2	-1	66	66	64	65	0	-2	-1
COLA (MCC)	0.16	0.19	0.14	—	—	0.23	0.23	0.19	0.26	—	—	—
MNLI	71	71	70	0	-1	72	72	69	72	0	-3	0
MNLI-MM	72	73	72	1	0	73	73	70	73	0	-3	0
MRPC (F1)	75	75	79	0	4	76	81	77	75	5	1	-6
MultiRC	61	58	62	-3	1	62	59	59	54	-3	-3	-5
QNLI	81	77	78	-4	-3	71	72	66	74	1	-5	2
QQP (F1)	81	82	81	1	0	82	82	80	81	0	-2	-1
RTE	48	42	47	-6	-1	46	57	53	56	11	7	-1
SST2	87	85	82	-2	-5	87	82	86	83	-5	-1	1
WSC	61	61	61	0	0	61	59	61	61	-2	0	2

Table 4: (Super)GLUE Results. Values are not aggregated across each model due to the presence of different metrics (Accuracy, F1 score, and MCC)

	Set A			Set B			
	$\mathbf{TF}_{base}$	$\mathbf{SF}_{s1}$	$\mathbf{SF}_{s2}$	$\mathbf{SR}_{s1}$	$\mathbf{SR}_{s2}$	$\mathbf{SR}_{s1'}$	$\mathbf{SR}_{s2'}$
Control Raising (Control)	0.54	0.56	0.69	0.57	0.56	0.69	0.56
Control Raising (Lexical Content)	-0.45	-0.04	-0.02	-0.03	-0.07	-0.36	-0.14
Control Raising (Relative Position)	-0.94	-0.89	-0.92	-1.00	-0.98	-0.77	-0.98
Lexical Content (Control)	1.00	0.88	0.6	1.00	0.98	1.00	0.78
Main Verb (Control)	0.93	0.96	0.84	0.85	0.98	0.96	0.98
Main Verb (Lexical Content)	-1.00	-0.79	-0.84	-1.00	-1.00	-0.99	-1.00
Main Verb (Relative Position)	-0.87	-0.78	-0.89	-0.98	-0.93	-0.83	-0.95
Relative Position (Control)	0.67	0.81	0.78	0.86	0.95	0.97	1.00
Syntactic Category (Control)	0.62	0.23	0.47	0.80	0.73	0.66	0.87
Syntactic Category (Lexical Content)	-0.61	-0.17	-0.17	-0.42	-0.59	-0.26	-0.76
Syntactic Category (Relative Position)	-0.32	-0.57	-0.44	-0.47	-0.47	-0.63	-0.52

Table 5: MSGS Results

	Set A			Set B			
	$\mathbf{TF}_{base}$	$\mathbf{SF}_{s1}$	$\mathbf{SF}_{s2}$	$\mathbf{SR}_{s1}$	$\mathbf{SR}_{s2}$	$\mathbf{SR}_{s1'}$	$\mathbf{SR}_{s2'}$
Aggregate Score	0.52	0.53	0.52	0.53	0.54	**0.55**	0.52

Table 6: Shared Task Leaderboard Results

embedding layer. We can only speculate about why this is so. It might be that it is an advantage to push the model very early towards identifying structural relations between words. More precisely to do so at a stage where the contributions of the single tokens are still separated from each other. The parsing network placed between the middle layers acts at a moment where single token contributions are already blurred.

To understand the effect of placing the parser network within the middle layers, we propose probing the layers of the Front and Rear modules and comparing them to the corresponding layers in the model where the parser network is placed ahead of the attention layers. Such a comparative analysis can provide valuable insights and either support or contradict our hypothesis regarding the learning of syntactic features in the middle layers of transformer models.

Regarding the aim of achieving competitive scores on the shared task challenge, the best score we could get was from the model $structroberta_{s1'}$, this model is an upscaling of the $structroberta_{s1}$.

6 Conclusion

In this paper, we extend the work of Shen et al. (2021) to explore the capabilities of the StructFormer architecture as an example of employing hierarchical bias in addressing the challenges posed by relatively small LLM pretraining datasets. Furthermore, we modify the StructFormer architecture to examine whether integrating the hierarchical bias within the middle attention layers leads to performance improvements. To accomplish these objectives, we pretrain seven model variants using the same dataset and configuration settings. We evaluate these models on 39 different tasks. The evaluation outcomes reveal varying behavior across the models, exhibiting inconsistencies in performance. We could not show strong evidence that models incorporating hierarchical bias are performing better in the context of this shared task, nor could we show practical evidence for the claim that syntactic information is better represented in the middle attention layers within the scope of our experiment. We have noted substantial enhancements in certain tasks when models incorporate hierarchical bias in their architectural designs. Nonetheless, to ensure the reliability of our findings and to eliminate potential confounding factors related to the varying number of parameters in each model, as well as the distinct objectives and complexities of individual tasks, we intend to carry out an in-depth analysis of each model's performance on a task-by-task basis.

Acknowledgements

We thank the authors of the StuctFormer model (Shen et al., 2021) for providing their implementation, which played an important role in the completion of this work. Additionally, we acknowledge the invaluable support received from the BabyLM shared task organizers, who provided the datasets, evaluation pipeline, and codes for pretraining and finetuning LMs. Their contributions enabled us to conduct a comprehensive and successful study. Furthermore, we are grateful for the comments of our reviewers that helped improve the paper. Lastly, we thank Hassan Sajjad and Younes Samih for fruitful discussions on hierarchical information in language models.

References

David Arps, Younes Samih, Laura Kallmeyer, and Hassan Sajjad. 2022. Probing for constituency structure in neural language models. In *Findings of the Association for Computational Linguistics: EMNLP 2022*, pages 6738–6757, Abu Dhabi, United Arab Emirates. Association for Computational Linguistics.

Tom B. Brown, Benjamin Mann, Nick Ryder, Melanie Subbiah, Jared Kaplan, Prafulla Dhariwal, Arvind Neelakantan, Pranav Shyam, Girish Sastry, Amanda Askell, Sandhini Agarwal, Ariel Herbert-Voss, Gretchen Krueger, Tom Henighan, Rewon Child, Aditya Ramesh, Daniel M. Ziegler, Jeffrey Wu, Clemens Winter, Christopher Hesse, Mark Chen, Eric Sigler, Mateusz Litwin, Scott Gray, Benjamin Chess, Jack Clark, Christopher Berner, Sam McCandlish, Alec Radford, Ilya Sutskever, and Dario Amodei. 2020. Language models are few-shot learners.

Jihun Choi, Kang Min Yoo, and Sang-goo Lee. 2018. Learning to compose task-specific tree structures. In *Proceedings of the Thirty-Second AAAI Conference on Artificial Intelligence and Thirtieth Innovative Applications of Artificial Intelligence Conference and Eighth AAAI Symposium on Educational Advances in Artificial Intelligence*, AAAI'18/IAAI'18/EAAI'18. AAAI Press.

Monojit Choudhury and Amit Deshpande. 2021. How linguistically fair are multilingual pre-trained language models? *Proceedings of the AAAI Conference on Artificial Intelligence*, 35(14):12710–12718.

Jacob Devlin, Ming-Wei Chang, Kenton Lee, and Kristina Toutanova. 2019. BERT: Pre-training of deep bidirectional transformers for language understanding. In *Proceedings of the 2019 Conference of the North American Chapter of the Association for Computational Linguistics: Human Language Technologies, Volume 1 (Long and Short Papers)*, pages 4171–4186, Minneapolis, Minnesota. Association for Computational Linguistics.

Chris Dyer, Adhiguna Kuncoro, Miguel Ballesteros, and Noah A. Smith. 2016. Recurrent neural network grammars. In *Proceedings of the 2016 Conference of the North American Chapter of the Association for Computational Linguistics: Human Language Technologies*, pages 199–209, San Diego, California. Association for Computational Linguistics.

Philip Gage. 1994. A new algorithm for data compression. *C Users J.*, 12(2):23–38.

Jonas Geiping and Tom Goldstein. 2022. Cramming: Training a language model on a single gpu in one day.

Jill Gilkerson, Jeffrey A. Richards, Steven F. Warren, Judith K. Montgomery, Charles R. Greenwood, D. Kimbrough Oller, John H. L. Hansen, and Terrance D. Paul. 2017. Mapping the early language environment using all-day recordings and automated analysis. *American Journal of Speech-Language Pathology*, 26(2):248–265.

Jared Kaplan, Sam McCandlish, Tom Henighan, Tom B. Brown, Benjamin Chess, Rewon Child, Scott Gray, Alec Radford, Jeffrey Wu, and Dario Amodei. 2020. Scaling laws for neural language models.

Carina Kauf and Anna Ivanova. 2023. A better way to do masked language model scoring. In *Proceedings of the 61st Annual Meeting of the Association for Computational Linguistics (Volume 2: Short Papers)*, pages 925–935, Toronto, Canada. Association for Computational Linguistics.

Yoon Kim, Alexander Rush, Lei Yu, Adhiguna Kuncoro, Chris Dyer, and Gábor Melis. 2019. Unsupervised recurrent neural network grammars. In *Proceedings of the 2019 Conference of the North American Chapter of the Association for Computational Linguistics: Human Language Technologies, Volume 1 (Long and Short Papers)*, pages 1105–1117, Minneapolis, Minnesota. Association for Computational Linguistics.

Artur Kulmizev and Joakim Nivre. 2022. Schrödinger's tree—on syntax and neural language models. *Frontiers in Artificial Intelligence*, 5.

Bowen Li, Lili Mou, and Frank Keller. 2019. An imitation learning approach to unsupervised parsing. In *Proceedings of the 57th Annual Meeting of the Association for Computational Linguistics*, pages 3485–3492, Florence, Italy. Association for Computational Linguistics.

Nelson F. Liu, Matt Gardner, Yonatan Belinkov, Matthew E. Peters, and Noah A. Smith. 2019a. Linguistic knowledge and transferability of contextual representations. In *Proceedings of the 2019 Conference of the North American Chapter of the Association for Computational Linguistics: Human Language Technologies, Volume 1 (Long and Short Papers)*, pages 1073–1094, Minneapolis, Minnesota. Association for Computational Linguistics.

Yinhan Liu, Myle Ott, Naman Goyal, Jingfei Du, Mandar Joshi, Danqi Chen, Omer Levy, Mike Lewis, Luke Zettlemoyer, and Veselin Stoyanov. 2019b. Roberta: A robustly optimized bert pretraining approach.

Kyle Mahowald, Anna A. Ivanova, Idan A. Blank, Nancy Kanwisher, Joshua B. Tenenbaum, and Evelina Fedorenko. 2023. Dissociating language and thought in large language models: a cognitive perspective.

B.W. Matthews. 1975. Comparison of the predicted and observed secondary structure of t4 phage lysozyme. *Biochimica et Biophysica Acta (BBA) - Protein Structure*, 405(2):442–451.

Max Müller-Eberstein, Rob van der Goot, and Barbara Plank. 2022. Probing for labeled dependency trees. In *Proceedings of the 60th Annual Meeting of the Association for Computational Linguistics (Volume 1: Long Papers)*, pages 7711–7726, Dublin, Ireland. Association for Computational Linguistics.

Karl Mulligan, Robert Frank, and Tal Linzen. 2021. Structure here, bias there: Hierarchical generalization by jointly learning syntactic transformations. In *Proceedings of the Society for Computation in Linguistics 2021*, pages 125–135, Online. Association for Computational Linguistics.

Isabel Papadimitriou and Dan Jurafsky. 2023. Pretrain on just structure: Understanding linguistic inductive biases using transfer learning.

Julian Salazar, Davis Liang, Toan Q. Nguyen, and Katrin Kirchhoff. 2020. Masked language model scoring. In *Proceedings of the 58th Annual Meeting of the Association for Computational Linguistics*, pages 2699–2712, Online. Association for Computational Linguistics.

Laurent Sartran, Samuel Barrett, Adhiguna Kuncoro, Miloš Stanojević, Phil Blunsom, and Chris Dyer. 2022. Transformer grammars: Augmenting transformer language models with syntactic inductive biases at scale. *Transactions of the Association for Computational Linguistics*, 10:1423–1439.

Rico Sennrich, Barry Haddow, and Alexandra Birch. 2016. Neural machine translation of rare words with subword units. In *Proceedings of the 54th Annual Meeting of the Association for Computational Linguistics (Volume 1: Long Papers)*, pages 1715–1725, Berlin, Germany. Association for Computational Linguistics.

Yikang Shen, Zhouhan Lin, Chin wei Huang, and Aaron Courville. 2018. Neural language modeling by jointly learning syntax and lexicon. In *International Conference on Learning Representations*.

Yikang Shen, Yi Tay, Che Zheng, Dara Bahri, Donald Metzler, and Aaron Courville. 2021. StructFormer: Joint unsupervised induction of dependency and constituency structure from masked language modeling. In *Proceedings of the 59th Annual Meeting of the Association for Computational Linguistics and the 11th International Joint Conference on Natural Language Processing (Volume 1: Long Papers)*, pages 7196–7209, Online. Association for Computational Linguistics.

Ashish Vaswani, Noam Shazeer, Niki Parmar, Jakob Uszkoreit, Llion Jones, Aidan N. Gomez, Lukasz Kaiser, and Illia Polosukhin. 2017. Attention is all you need.

Jesse Vig and Yonatan Belinkov. 2019. Analyzing the structure of attention in a transformer language model. In *Proceedings of the 2019 ACL Workshop BlackboxNLP: Analyzing and Interpreting Neural Networks for NLP*, pages 63–76, Florence, Italy. Association for Computational Linguistics.

Alex Wang, Yada Pruksachatkun, Nikita Nangia, Amanpreet Singh, Julian Michael, Felix Hill, Omer Levy, and Samuel R. Bowman. 2019. *SuperGLUE: A Stickier Benchmark for General-Purpose Language Understanding Systems*. Curran Associates Inc., Red Hook, NY, USA.

Alex Warstadt and Samuel R. Bowman. 2022. What artificial neural networks can tell us about human language acquisition.

Alex Warstadt, Aaron Mueller, Leshem Choshen, Ethan Gotlieb Wilcox, Chengxu Zhuang, Juan Ciro, Rafael Mosquera, Adina Williams, Bhargavi Paranjabe, Tal Linzen, and Ryan Cotterell. 2023. Findings of the 2023 BabyLM Challenge: Sample-efficient pretraining on developmentally plausible corpora. In *Proceedings of the 2023 BabyLM Challenge*. Association for Computational Linguistics (ACL).

Alex Warstadt, Alicia Parrish, Haokun Liu, Anhad Mohananey, Wei Peng, Sheng-Fu Wang, and Samuel R. Bowman. 2020a. BLiMP: The benchmark of linguistic minimal pairs for English. *Transactions of the Association for Computational Linguistics*, 8:377–392.

Alex Warstadt, Yian Zhang, Xiaocheng Li, Haokun Liu, and Samuel R. Bowman. 2020b. Learning which features matter: RoBERTa acquires a preference for linguistic generalizations (eventually). In *Proceedings of the 2020 Conference on Empirical Methods in Natural Language Processing (EMNLP)*, pages 217–235, Online. Association for Computational Linguistics.

Adina Williams, Andrew Drozdov, and Samuel R. Bowman. 2018. Do latent tree learning models identify meaningful structure in sentences? *Transactions of the Association for Computational Linguistics*, 6:253–267.

Thomas Wolf, Lysandre Debut, Victor Sanh, Julien Chaumond, Clement Delangue, Anthony Moi, Pierric Cistac, Tim Rault, Rémi Louf, Morgan Funtowicz, Joe Davison, Sam Shleifer, Patrick von Platen, Clara Ma, Yacine Jernite, Julien Plu, Canwen Xu, Teven Le Scao, Sylvain Gugger, Mariama Drame, Quentin Lhoest, and Alexander M. Rush. 2020. Huggingface's transformers: State-of-the-art natural language processing.

Appendix

A Evaluation Tasks

BLiMP

1. Anaphor Agreement
2. Argument Structure
3. Binding
4. Control Raising
5. Determiner Noun Agreement
6. Ellipsis
7. Filler Gap
8. Irregular Forms
9. Island Effects
10. Negative Polarity Items NPI Licensing
11. Quantifiers
12. Subject Verb Agreement
13. Hypernym
14. QA Congruence Easy
15. QA Congruence Tricky
16. Subject Aux Inversion
17. Turn Taking

SuperGLUE

18. Corpus of Linguistic Acceptability CoLA (MMC)
19. Stanford Sentiment Treebank SST-2

20. Microsoft Research Paraphrase Corpus MRPC (F1)

21. Quora Question Pairs QQP (F1)

22. MultiNLI Matched MNLI

23. MultiNLI Mismatched MNLI-mm

24. Question NLI QNLI

25. Recognizing Textual Entailment RTE

26. Boolean Questions BoolQ

27. Multi-Sentence Reading Comprehension MultiRC

28. Winograd Schema Challenge WSC

MSGS

29. Main Verb (Control)

30. Control Raising (Control)

31. Syntactic Category (Control)

32. Relative Position (Control)

33. Lexical Content The (Control)

34. Main Verb Lexical Content The

35. Main Verb Relative Token Position

36. Control Raising Lexical Content The

37. Control Raising Relative Token Position

38. Syntactic Category Lexical Content The

39. Syntactic Category Relative Position

B Hyperparameters and Models Configurations

In Table 7, we report the number of trainable parameters per model. In Table 8, we report all the important hyperparameters values for all our pretraining and finetuning experiments. Also, we report the main configuration settings for all our models. Unless specified otherwise, these values were used across all models.

Model	# of trainable parameters
transformer-base	110M
structformer$_{s1}$	133M
structformer$_{s2}$	133M
structroberta$_{s1}$	133M
structroberta$_{s2}$	133M
structroberta$_{s1'}$	144M
structroberta$_{s2'}$	144M

Table 7: Number of trainable parameters per model

Training Hyperparameters	
Batch size	96
Sequence Length	128
Optimizer	AdamW
Weight Decay	0.1
Learning Rate (Linear)	1e-4
Max Steps	62K
Masking Probability	0.15
Finetuning Hyperparameters	
Initial learning rate	5e-5
Batch size	120
Maximum epochs	10
Evaluate every (steps)	400
Patience	5
Random seed	12
Models configurations	
Number of Attention Heads	12
Number of Attention Layers	12
Embeddings (Hidden) Size	768
FFN inner hidden size	3072
Attention Dropout	0.1
Front Attention Layers (where applicable)	4
Rear Attention Layers (where applicable)	8
Parser Convolution Layers (where applicable)	4
Convolution Kernel Size	9

Table 8: Pretraining and Finetuning Hyperparameters, and Models Configurations Settings

Pre-training LLMs using human-like development data corpus

Khushi Bhardwaj, Raj Sanjay Shah, Sashank Varma
Georgia Institute of Technology
{khushi.bhardwaj, rajsanjayshah, varma}@gatech.edu

Abstract

Pre-trained Large Language Models (LLMs) have shown success in a diverse set of language inference and understanding tasks. The pre-training stage of LLMs looks at a large corpus of raw textual data. This shared task compares LLM pre-training to human language acquisition, where the number of tokens seen by 13-year-old kids is magnitudes smaller than the number of tokens seen by LLMs. In this work, we pre-train and evaluate LLMs on their ability to learn contextual word representations using roughly the same number of tokens as seen by children. We provide a strong set of baselines; with different architectures, evaluation of changes in performance across epochs, and reported pre-training metrics for the strict small and strict tracks of the task. We also try to loosely replicate the RoBERTa baseline given by the task organizers to observe the training robustness to hyperparameter selection and replicability. We provide the submission details to the strict and strict-small tracks in this report.

1 Introduction

Transformer-based LLMs (Vaswani et al., 2017) show state-of-the-art performance on a variety of language processing tasks. In the last few years, pre-training methods for LLMs have evolved rapidly to meet task-driven demands. This evolution has focused on model expansion (Brown et al., 2020), more pre-training data (Hoffmann et al., 2022), use of higher quality data (Raffel et al., 2019), model alignment (von Werra et al., 2020), quicker run-time inference (Sanh et al., 2020), quicker pre-training (Clark et al., 2020), faster fine-tuning (Sanh et al., 2020), domain adaptation (Alsentzer et al., 2019; Caselli et al., 2021; Beltagy et al., 2019; Shah et al., 2022), and the addition of multi-modal capabilities (OpenAI, 2023; Gatti et al., 2022). The task-driven nature of this development optimizes performance at scale but fails to account for human-like learning.

Humans typically encounter fewer than 100 million tokens through language exposure by the time they are 13 years old (Warstadt et al., 2023). LLMs, on the other hand, parse tens of billions to trillions of tokens in their pre-training stage, typically from sources like Wikipedia (Wikipedia contributors, 2004), and Open Book Corpus (Zhu et al., 2015), which consist of different tokens than the ones seen by children. In this paper, we evaluate the capabilities of popular architectures on various tasks when trained on a number of tokens comparable to that seen by 13-year-old children. Such scaled-down pre-training has several potential benefits:

- A better sandbox for the development of new LLM training techniques inspired by the cognitive science literature (Yiu et al., 2023).
- Robust evaluation of models on human behavioral signatures (Shah et al., 2023).
- Building plausible human cognition models using LLMs aligned to actual human actions (Park et al., 2022).

Track	Data size	Datasets	Our work
Strict-small	10M words	Child-directed speech, transcribed speech from multiple sources, children's books, and Wikipedia, etc.	✓
Strict	100M words		✓
Loose	100M words	Strict track data + unlimited non-linguistic data	×

Table 1: Task Summary

1.1 Task Descriptions

The shared task has three tracks: Strict, Strict small, and Loose. The details of each track are summarized in Table 1. The Strict and Strict-small tracks

Proceedings of the 27th Conference on Computational Natural Language Learning: Volume 2: The BabyLM Challenge, pages 339–345
December 6-7, 2023

use pre-released datasets containing Child-directed speech, transcribed speech from multiple sources, children's books, and Wikipedia. These tracks are meant to encourage explorations of architectural variation and self-supervised approaches.

1.2 Key Contributions

Given the benefits of using scaled-down human-like pre-training data, our work focuses on the following aspects of the shared task:

1. Replication details: Can we replicate the results of the baselines given by the task organizers?
2. Can we understand the impact of more training epochs on the same architecture?
3. Providing each training checkpoint for the different model architectures to facilitate future modeling of development. All checkpoints can be found **here.**

We provide details of training and evaluation for the strict and strict-small tracks of this task.

2 Related Work

2.1 Cognitive science driven LLM architecture development

With the efforts put into LM pre-training, learning frameworks informed by cognitive science have received increasing attention. For instance, unsupervised and adversarial pre-training methods have been employed to enhance the logical reasoning capabilities of language models (Pi et al., 2022b). Using pre-training to inject numerical (Pi et al., 2022a) and commonsense reasoning (Zhong et al., 2019) has also been recently explored. Huebner et.al have constructed pre-training paradigms using curriculum learning (Huebner et al., 2021) to show the advantages of incremental learning.

2.2 Pre-training with limited data

Previous experiments show that pre-training data size is positively correlated with the syntactic capabilities of RoBERTa in terms of generalization and robustness (Pérez-Mayos et al., 2021). However, it has been discovered that model performance gains bring a high financial and environmental cost (Tay et al., 2021). This justifies the appeal of small-scale pretraining with data limitations. There have also been explorations of how human-like data scales could improve our understanding of language acquisition and solidify current cognitive models (Dupoux, 2018).

Track	Model	Competition Scores (Dynabench)	Perplexity
Strict Small	Distilbert Epoch 20	0.62	86.283
	Distilbert Epoch 60	**0.65**	17.278
	RoBERTa Epoch 20	0.58	49.586
	GPT2 Epoch 20	0.64	79.318
	Competition Max	0.73	
Strict	Distilbert Epoch 20	0.66	39.427
	Distilbert Epoch 60	**0.71**	10.332
	RoBERTa Epoch 20	0.63	27.566
	GPT2 Epoch 20	0.67	34.950
	Competition Max	0.81	

Table 2: Model scores on dynabench

3 Methodology

3.1 Models

We use the simple-transformers library (Rajapakse, 2019) to pre-train the models below from scratch. The library uses the Huggingface trainer for pre-training. Note: We build new vocabularies for all models and limit the number of training epochs due to computational constraints in certain models.

- RoBERTa: We train the RoBERTa-base model (Liu et al., 2019) for comparison to the baseline given by the task organizers. This model is trained for 20 epochs on both datasets (strict and strict-small). The size of this model is roughly 125M parameters.
- DistilBert (uncased): Because this model (Sanh et al., 2020) is smaller (roughly 66M parameters) and quicker to pre-train, we additionally train it for 60 epochs. This allows us to explore the impact of more training epochs on performance.
- GPT2: We include a decoder-based architecture (Radford et al., 2019) in our pre-training to explore the impact of architecture type on the evaluation tasks. This model has a similar size to RoBERTa (117M parameters). We train it for 20 epochs due to computational constraints.

All of the checkpoints for the three architectures and the two tracks are uploaded on Huggingface (Wolf et al., 2020). **Hyperparameters:** We perform a grid search over the hyperparameters for all three architecture types. We use a subset of 0.5 GB of the training data for the search. The learning

Tasks		Super GLUE										
	Model	CoLA	SST-2	MRPC (F1)	QQP (F1)	MNLI	MNLI-mm	QNLI	RTE	BoolQ	MultiRC	WSC
Strict Small	Majority label	69.50	50.20	**82.00**	53.10	35.70	35.70	35.40	53.10	50.50	59.90	53.20
	OPT-125m	64.60	81.90	72.50	60.40	57.60	60.00	61.50	60.00	63.30	55.20	60.20
	RoBERTa-base	**70.80**	**87.00**	79.20	73.70	73.20	**74.00**	**77.00**	**61.60**	66.30	**61.40**	61.40
	T5-base	61.20	78.10	80.50	66.20	48.00	50.30	62.00	49.40	66.00	47.10	61.40
	Distilbert Epoch 20	69.38	83.46	79.69	80.21	69.80	71.56	60.15	54.55	65.42	53.67	51.81
	Distilbert Epoch 60	69.68	85.63	78.81	**82.28**	**71.62**	73.11	76.73	60.61	**67.77**	56.74	61.45
	RoBERTa Epoch 20	65.55	81.30	79.71	76.37	65.16	65.82	62.73	56.57	62.38	44.91	**61.45**
	GPT2 Epoch 20	69.58	83.07	75.47	73.13	63.88	65.95	59.84	56.57	64.45	58.38	46.99
Strict	OPT-125m	73.70	86.60	82.10	77.80	70.10	71.90	80.10	**67.70**	66.00	61.10	59.00
	RoBERTa-base	75.90	**88.60**	80.50	78.50	68.70	**78.00**	82.30	51.50	59.90	61.30	61.40
	T5-base	**76.30**	88.00	**85.90**	79.70	71.50	74.00	**83.10**	60.60	69.00	62.40	60.20
	Distilbert Epoch 20	69.48	86.22	62.98	83.81	73.44	74.97	79.00	60.61	67.91	62.98	44.58
	Distilbert Epoch 60	74.78	87.01	81.40	**84.37**	74.95	75.27	80.97	55.56	65.56	**65.83**	**61.45**
	RoBERTa Epoch 20	67.81	84.06	82.00	82.12	72.22	73.19	77.17	53.54	60.30	51.48	38.55
	GPT2 Epoch 20	69.58	87.20	79.29	82.23	**74.00**	74.98	81.01	52.53	**69.58**	57.83	48.19

Table 3: Results for the Super GLUE tasks

Tasks		Blimp											
	Model	Anaphor Agr.	Agr. Structure	Binding Binding	Control/ Raising	D-N Agr.	Ellipsis	Filler-Gap	Irregular Forms	Island Effects	NPI Licensing	Quantifiers	S-V Agr.
Strict Small	OPT-125m	63.8	**70.6**	67.1	66.5	78.5	62	63.8	67.5	48.6	46.7	59.6	56.9
	RoBERTa-base	81.5	67.1	67.3	**67.9**	**90.8**	76.4	63.5	87.4	39.9	**55.9**	**70.5**	65.4
	T5-base	68.9	63.8	60.4	60.9	72.2	34.4	48.2	77.6	45.6	47.8	61.2	65
	Distilbert Epoch 20	83.49	64.12	63.98	62.22	77.72	62.76	62.36	85.24	42.94	41.38	67.47	55.81
	Distilbert Epoch 60	**89.62**	68.44	64.08	65.20	89.70	**81.64**	63.57	**89.92**	39.69	44.58	66.20	**78.09**
	RoBERTa Epoch 20	84.76	60.54	**67.97**	60.69	56.47	52.25	**65.48**	64.53	**54.22**	52.51	52.42	66.63
	GPT2 Epoch 20	81.24	72.56	67.81	67.43	86.98	59.82	67.72	84.38	52.62	51.76	58.14	64.12
Strict	OPT-125m	**94.9**	73.8	**73.8**	**72.2**	93.1	80.5	**73.6**	80.8	**57.8**	51.6	**74.5**	**77.3**
	RoBERTa-base	89.5	71.3	71	67.1	93.1	83.8	68	89.6	54.5	**66.3**	70.3	76.2
	T5-base	66.7	61.2	59.4	59.8	53.8	49.1	70	75.5	43.6	45.6	34.2	53.2
	Distilbert Epoch 20	92.43	67.06	67.66	65.27	94.38	87.24	65.42	85.04	42.86	50.43	67.41	66.25
	Distilbert Epoch 60	94.68	70.39	68.39	68.25	**96.39**	**89.03**	68.69	**90.08**	45.59	64.67	70.20	72.32
	RoBERTa Epoch 20	85.94	67.68	65.27	63.74	91.04	75.52	62.98	87.23	46.41	44.47	61.46	60.51
	GPT2 Epoch 20	91.56	**74.88**	73.21	69.22	91.89	75.52	71.91	75.32	55.04	51.20	66.13	67.19

Table 4: Results for the Blimp tasks

Tasks		Blimp Supplement Tasks				
	Model	Hypernym	QA Congruence (easy)	QA Congruence (tricky)	Subj.-Aux. Inversion	Turn Taking
Strict Small	OPT-125m	50.00	54.7	31.5	80.3	57.1
	RoBERTa-base	49.4	31.3	32.1	71.7	53.2
	T5-base	48	40.6	21.2	64.9	45
	Distilbert Epoch 20	50.00	65.63	**42.42**	**77.31**	61.79
	Distilbert Epoch 60	48.95	**70.31**	41.21	60.87	62.86
	RoBERTa Epoch 20	**51.28**	48.44	31.52	53.86	**66.07**
	GPT2 Epoch 20	47.44	48.44	45.45	72.41	62.86
Strict	OPT-125m	46.3	**76.50**	**47.9**	**85.3**	**82.9**
	RoBERTa-base	50.8	34.4	34.5	45.6	46.8
	T5-base	51.1	45.3	25.5	69.2	48.9
	Distilbert Epoch 20	48.26	64.06	40.61	81.53	65.36
	Distilbert Epoch 60	48.95	73.44	47.88	83.43	65.36
	RoBERTa Epoch 20	**51.16**	46.88	37.58	76.85	64.29
	GPT2 Epoch 20	49.53	57.81	45.45	81.85	65.00

Table 5: Results for the Blimp supplemental tasks

rate ranges from 5e-5 to 4e-4 across the searches, with weight decay in place but no early stopping mechanisms.

4 Results

Table 2 shows the results obtained from the dynabench submission portal. The individual results for each of the tasks in different benchmarks are available in Tables 3, 4, 5, 6, 7. Looking at these tables, we observe the following patterns:

1. We see that training for more epochs leads to better overall performance (compare 20 and 60 epochs of DistilBert in Table 2).

2. Variation among architecture types exists when limiting the training to the same number of epochs, but it is difficult to identify a definitively better architecture.

Tasks		MSGS Tasks										
	Model	CR (Control)	LC (Control)	MV (Control)	RP (Control)	SC (Control)	CR_LC	CR_RTP	MV_LC	MV_RTP	SC_LC	SC_RP
Strict-Small	OPT-125m	86.40	86.10	**99.80**	**100.00**	94.30	66.50	67.00	66.50	**67.60**	80.20	67.50
	RoBERTa-base	84.10	**100.00**	99.40	93.50	96.40	**67.70**	68.60	**66.70**	68.60	**84.20**	65.70
	T5-base	78.40	**100.00**	72.70	95.50	94.40	66.70	**69.70**	66.60	66.90	73.60	67.80
	Distilbert Epoch 20	79.22	**100.00**	97.17	98.57	96.36	66.53	66.71	66.61	67.47	67.89	67.58
	Distilbert Epoch 60	81.68	**100.00**	98.61	99.14	95.66	67.24	66.72	66.61	67.03	67.76	**68.27**
	RoBERTa Epoch 20	73.02	**100.00**	73.91	99.59	86.47	66.70	67.19	66.61	66.84	67.44	71.93
	GPT2 Epoch 20	**89.78**	96.30	99.23	**100.00**	**97.13**	66.46	66.72	66.58	66.83	78.78	64.87
Strict	OPT-125m	**97.20**	82.60	**100.00**	99.80	88.10	75.30	67.10	66.30	66.80	84.80	62.00
	RoBERTa-base	93.00	**100.00**	**100.00**	**100.00**	89.00	68.30	66.80	66.60	**80.20**	67.40	67.40
	T5-base	95.10	**100.00**	**100.00**	99.80	88.70	**76.70**	**69.40**	**67.00**	67.70	72.70	68.00
	Distilbert Epoch 20	81.44	**100.00**	97.36	97.35	94.77	67.26	66.72	66.61	66.97	67.67	68.63
	Distilbert Epoch 60	93.23	**100.00**	99.33	99.17	95.64	68.91	66.77	66.61	67.45	67.89	66.59
	RoBERTa Epoch 20	84.63	97.38	92.12	98.15	95.54	66.47	66.59	66.41	66.05	68.17	**72.78**
	GPT2 Epoch 20	95.35	76.53	99.55	99.83	**96.76**	67.21	68.46	66.78	66.70	**91.90**	65.90

Table 6: Results for the MSGS tasks

Tasks		Age of Acquisition tasks (mean absolute deviation)			
	Model	Overall (591 words)	Nouns (322)	Predicates (167)	Function words (102)
Strict Small	OPT-125m	2.03	1.98	1.81	2.57
	RoBERTa-base	2.06	1.99	**1.85**	2.65
	T5-base	2.04	1.97	1.82	2.64
	Distilbert Epoch 20	2.06	2.00	1.84	2.65
	Distilbert Epoch 60	**2.09**	**2.00**	1.84	**2.76**
	RoBERTa Epoch 20	2.06	2.00	1.84	2.63
	GPT2 Epoch 20	2.06	2.00	1.85	2.64
Strict	OPT-125m	2.04	1.97	1.83	2.61
	RoBERTa-base	2.06	1.99	1.82	2.66
	T5-base	2.06	2.00	1.83	2.65
	Distilbert Epoch 20	2.06	2.00	1.83	2.65
	Distilbert Epoch 60	**2.08**	**2.00**	1.81	**2.79**
	RoBERTa Epoch 20	2.06	2.00	**1.84**	2.62
	GPT2 Epoch 20	2.04	1.98	1.81	2.60

Table 7: Results for the Age of Acquisition tasks

3. Tables 3, 4, 5, 6, and 7 show that pre-training (RoBERTa) is not robust to initialization, and the competition scores would greatly benefit from a warm-up or a grid search over different hyper-parameters.

4. In most cases, the pre-training improves performance over the majority label in the Super GLUE tasks.

5. Tables 8, 9 shows that the performance on the BLIMP tasks becomes better with more training epochs. While this is orthogonal to wisdom performance saturates at one epoch(Biderman et al., 2023). Our results hint that training saturation or stability may be a function of model size divided by the number of tokens seen.

5 Conclusions

We pre-train popular LLM architectures on the kind of textual data seen by children when they are around 13 years old. We show that pre-training paradigms like Masked Language Modeling or Causal Language Modeling lead to only minor variations. Our results show that models are not robust to the initialization of weights. Our work provides each and every checkpoint of the model architectures on Huggingface to facilitate future research. All checkpoints can be found **here.**

6 Limitations

Our work trains some of the popular Language Model architectures on human-like scaled-down training data, it does not introduce new training methodologies or architectures which may be better suited for such tasks. Furthermore, our work does not exhaustively cover different model types in the literature. Our results are preliminary as they do not account for all possible confounds.

	Epochs																			
BLIMP Tasks	1	2	3	4	5	6	7	8	9	10	11	12	13	14	15	16	17	18	19	20
Anaphor Agr.	50.77	70.81	82.21	79.75	84.46	84.00	86.71	88.14	87.27	87.88	87.42	87.32	83.54	86.91	86.30	84.76	85.22	85.99	85.22	85.94
Agr. Str.	58.69	59.81	60.46	60.83	59.80	60.39	60.43	60.84	61.02	60.60	59.69	62.08	63.70	65.22	65.39	66.56	67.54	67.34	67.92	67.68
Binding	64.43	68.06	64.84	65.32	64.31	67.17	64.31	66.00	63.92	64.10	64.00	59.45	61.52	62.60	62.72	63.67	64.54	65.21	65.18	65.27
Control Rais.	59.17	59.19	58.17	58.24	59.06	59.01	59.79	59.70	59.70	60.01	58.51	62.22	60.25	59.41	60.87	62.88	62.79	63.57	63.85	63.74
Det-N Agr.	51.47	56.72	58.87	59.57	58.63	58.62	58.18	60.09	60.16	59.06	59.63	63.47	71.69	80.95	85.20	87.18	88.49	90.51	90.98	91.04
Ellipsis	37.93	44.05	46.54	50.87	50.98	54.27	56.12	58.43	59.70	61.61	55.02	51.96	54.62	65.47	68.30	73.85	72.92	75.64	75.23	75.52
Filler Gap	69.39	64.53	66.48	63.66	65.38	61.95	61.31	61.95	61.84	65.39	60.58	61.86	60.21	62.14	61.47	61.80	62.40	63.35	63.38	62.98
Hypernym	53.84	49.77	52.09	51.74	48.02	48.49	48.72	50.12	49.88	51.28	50.35	50.70	48.84	50.35	51.28	49.77	51.51	50.47	51.86	51.16
Irr. Forms	45.90	59.75	60.87	61.32	63.66	59.54	65.24	63.36	64.83	64.99	69.97	78.07	76.39	81.53	86.92	86.87	88.96	88.85	87.74	87.23
Island Effects	53.66	42.68	56.20	55.53	54.67	44.66	48.28	51.91	49.93	52.88	47.31	45.22	51.76	50.67	47.83	48.92	46.82	46.38	45.40	46.41
NPI Lic.	34.89	43.58	35.71	46.96	40.81	43.41	43.29	42.97	39.60	44.02	37.25	38.23	39.20	40.80	40.10	43.77	44.05	44.46	43.65	44.47
QA_cong. Easy	34.38	35.94	39.06	42.19	39.06	35.94	40.63	40.63	37.50	37.50	37.50	46.88	56.25	57.81	56.25	50.00	45.31	45.31	48.44	46.88
QA_cong. Tricky	38.18	34.55	32.73	31.52	31.52	30.91	30.30	29.70	28.48	28.48	27.27	24.85	23.64	30.30	33.94	32.73	35.76	35.15	38.18	37.58
Quantifiers	37.92	38.15	36.22	40.96	43.07	41.96	49.00	50.05	43.07	51.91	51.52	66.95	65.35	67.85	60.72	64.30	61.98	64.09	61.39	61.46
S-Aux Inv.	74.68	75.04	69.85	68.87	63.19	52.74	55.40	50.65	47.89	48.65	52.28	62.94	66.85	72.82	70.36	77.92	73.82	76.38	75.43	76.85
S-V Agr.	49.67	50.89	52.10	51.91	52.34	53.68	53.80	54.47	55.54	55.83	54.87	52.72	54.27	57.58	58.10	58.70	60.09	60.31	60.23	60.51
Turn-Taking	59.64	59.64	60.00	59.29	61.43	60.36	58.57	59.64	58.93	58.57	61.07	63.57	64.64	67.14	63.57	63.57	64.29	63.93	64.64	64.29

Table 8: Results for the BLIMP tasks across different epochs of the RoBERTa-base model architecture for the strict (100M token) track.

	Epochs												
Behavior/ Model +Epoch	1	5	10	15	20	25	30	35	40	45	50	55	60
Anaphor Agr.	46.57	82.87	89.88	91.21	92.43	93.10	94.07	94.17	95.19	94.94	94.58	94.43	94.68
Agr. Str.	58.06	59.71	61.78	65.69	67.06	68.02	70.05	69.07	69.67	70.55	70.49	70.27	70.39
Binding	59.65	65.24	63.15	67.14	67.66	66.93	68.48	66.55	69.07	68.76	68.95	68.27	68.39
Control Rais.	58.33	58.93	60.01	64.14	65.27	66.00	65.91	67.12	67.30	67.41	68.10	67.87	68.25
Det-N Agr.	50.76	60.30	70.41	92.16	94.38	95.24	95.94	95.97	96.34	96.14	96.27	96.37	96.39
Ellipsis	37.53	54.16	55.08	81.99	87.24	86.49	86.20	89.32	89.32	89.38	88.57	88.86	89.03
Filler Gap	70.23	64.89	58.56	62.06	65.42	64.74	66.64	67.49	67.54	67.24	69.00	68.88	68.69
Hypernym	51.40	50.23	50.70	48.84	48.26	50.00	48.60	51.40	50.23	50.00	49.77	48.49	48.95
Irr. Forms	56.39	65.24	87.38	85.55	85.04	86.92	88.50	89.16	88.85	88.85	89.72	89.72	90.08
Island Effects	46.52	44.62	48.09	45.52	42.86	45.07	43.20	46.49	44.81	43.80	44.39	45.44	45.59
NPI Lic.	53.23	46.90	41.06	46.67	50.43	55.25	58.56	57.39	61.69	64.36	64.09	64.15	64.67
QA_cong. Easy	31.25	43.75	59.38	67.19	64.06	68.75	70.31	73.44	75.00	70.31	70.31	73.44	73.44
QA_cong. Tricky	333.33	22.42	23.03	35.15	40.61	42.42	46.06	43.03	44.24	41.82	46.06	46.06	47.88
Quantifiers	54.87	69.55	62.31	65.43	67.41	70.40	70.50	72.82	70.74	70.63	70.25	70.81	70.20
S-Aux Inv.	58.45	65.77	73.65	79.21	81.53	81.19	81.85	81.75	83.17	82.80	83.63	82.53	83.43
S-V Agr.	48.93	54.60	55.56	62.06	66.25	68.24	70.82	70.05	71.64	72.50	71.73	72.41	72.32
Turn-Taking	59.29	60.71	65.36	64.29	65.36	63.93	64.64	65.36	65.36	65.00	66.07	65.00	65.36

Table 9: Results for the BLIMP tasks across different epochs of the DistilBERT-base model architecture for the strict (100M token) track.

7 Ethical Considerations

All researchers in this study have active responsible code of conduct in research certifications. The models shared on Huggingface have the same risks associated with any other Large Language Model. Researchers in this study have tried to be mindful of the environment while doing the pre-training runs and hope that publically available checkpoints will help other researchers avoid computation and environmental costs associated with repeat pre-training.

8 Computational Resources

The models are trained on Nvidia-RTX 2080 GPUs with 12 GB RAM. The models are trained for nearly 975 GPU hours.

References

Emily Alsentzer, John Murphy, William Boag, Wei-Hung Weng, Di Jin, Tristan Naumann, and Matthew McDermott. 2019. Publicly available clinical BERT embeddings. In *Proceedings of the 2nd Clinical Natural Language Processing Workshop*, pages 72–78, Minneapolis, Minnesota, USA. Association for Computational Linguistics.

Iz Beltagy, Kyle Lo, and Arman Cohan. 2019. Scibert: Pretrained language model for scientific text. In *EMNLP*.

Stella Biderman, Hailey Schoelkopf, Quentin Anthony, Herbie Bradley, Kyle O'Brien, Eric Hallahan, Mohammad Aflah Khan, Shivanshu Purohit, USVSN Sai Prashanth, Edward Raff, Aviya Skowron, Lintang Sutawika, and Oskar van der Wal. 2023. Pythia: A suite for analyzing large language models across training and scaling.

Tom B. Brown, Benjamin Mann, Nick Ryder, Melanie Subbiah, Jared Kaplan, Prafulla Dhariwal, Arvind Neelakantan, Pranav Shyam, Girish Sastry, Amanda

Askell, Sandhini Agarwal, Ariel Herbert-Voss, Gretchen Krueger, Tom Henighan, Rewon Child, Aditya Ramesh, Daniel M. Ziegler, Jeffrey Wu, Clemens Winter, Christopher Hesse, Mark Chen, Eric Sigler, Mateusz Litwin, Scott Gray, Benjamin Chess, Jack Clark, Christopher Berner, Sam McCandlish, Alec Radford, Ilya Sutskever, and Dario Amodei. 2020. Language models are few-shot learners.

Tommaso Caselli, Valerio Basile, Jelena Mitrović, and Michael Granitzer. 2021. Hatebert: Retraining bert for abusive language detection in english.

Kevin Clark, Minh-Thang Luong, Quoc V. Le, and Christopher D. Manning. 2020. Electra: Pre-training text encoders as discriminators rather than generators. *ArXiv*, abs/2003.10555.

Emmanuel Dupoux. 2018. Cognitive science in the era of artificial intelligence: A roadmap for reverse-engineering the infant language-learner. *Cognition*, 173:43–59.

Prajwal Gatti, Anand Mishra, Manish Gupta, and Mithun Das Gupta. 2022. VisToT: Vision-augmented table-to-text generation. In *Proceedings of the 2022 Conference on Empirical Methods in Natural Language Processing*, pages 9936–9949, Abu Dhabi, United Arab Emirates. Association for Computational Linguistics.

Jordan Hoffmann, Sebastian Borgeaud, Arthur Mensch, Elena Buchatskaya, Trevor Cai, Eliza Rutherford, Diego de Las Casas, Lisa Anne Hendricks, Johannes Welbl, Aidan Clark, Tom Hennigan, Eric Noland, Katie Millican, George van den Driessche, Bogdan Damoc, Aurelia Guy, Simon Osindero, Karen Simonyan, Erich Elsen, Jack W. Rae, Oriol Vinyals, and Laurent Sifre. 2022. Training compute-optimal large language models.

Philip A. Huebner, Elior Sulem, Fisher Cynthia, and Dan Roth. 2021. BabyBERTa: Learning more grammar with small-scale child-directed language. In *Proceedings of the 25th Conference on Computational Natural Language Learning*, pages 624–646, Online. Association for Computational Linguistics.

Yinhan Liu, Myle Ott, Naman Goyal, Jingfei Du, Mandar Joshi, Danqi Chen, Omer Levy, M. Lewis, Luke Zettlemoyer, and Veselin Stoyanov. 2019. Roberta: A robustly optimized bert pretraining approach. *ArXiv*, abs/1907.11692.

OpenAI. 2023. Gpt-4 technical report.

Joon Sung Park, Lindsay Popowski, Carrie J. Cai, Meredith Ringel Morris, Percy Liang, and Michael S. Bernstein. 2022. Social simulacra: Creating populated prototypes for social computing systems.

Laura Pérez-Mayos, Miguel Ballesteros, and Leo Wanner. 2021. How much pretraining data do language models need to learn syntax? *arXiv preprint arXiv:2109.03160*.

Xinyu Pi, Qian Liu, Bei Chen, Morteza Ziyadi, Zeqi Lin, Qiang Fu, Yan Gao, Jian-Guang Lou, and Weizhu Chen. 2022a. Reasoning like program executors.

Xinyu Pi, Wanjun Zhong, Yan Gao, Nan Duan, and Jian-Guang Lou. 2022b. Logigan: Learning logical reasoning via adversarial pre-training. *Advances in Neural Information Processing Systems*, 35:16290–16304.

Alec Radford, Jeff Wu, R. Child, David Luan, Dario Amodei, and Ilya Sutskever. 2019. Language models are unsupervised multitask learners.

Colin Raffel, Noam Shazeer, Adam Roberts, Katherine Lee, Sharan Narang, Michael Matena, Yanqi Zhou, Wei Li, and Peter J. Liu. 2019. Exploring the limits of transfer learning with a unified text-to-text transformer.

T. C. Rajapakse. 2019. Simple transformers. `https://github.com/ThilinaRajapakse/simpletransformers`.

Victor Sanh, Lysandre Debut, Julien Chaumond, and Thomas Wolf. 2020. Distilbert, a distilled version of bert: smaller, faster, cheaper and lighter.

Raj Sanjay Shah, Kunal Chawla, Dheeraj Eidnani, Agam Shah, Wendi Du, Sudheer Chava, Natraj Raman, Charese Smiley, Jiaao Chen, and Diyi Yang. 2022. When flue meets flang: Benchmarks and large pretrained language model for financial domain. In *Proceedings of the 2022 Conference on Empirical Methods in Natural Language Processing (EMNLP)*. Association for Computational Linguistics.

Raj Sanjay Shah, Vijay Marupudi, Reba Koenen, Khushi Bhardwaj, and Sashank Varma. 2023. Numeric magnitude comparison effects in large language models.

Yi Tay, Mostafa Dehghani, Jinfeng Rao, William Fedus, Samira Abnar, Hyung Won Chung, Sharan Narang, Dani Yogatama, Ashish Vaswani, and Donald Metzler. 2021. Scale efficiently: Insights from pre-training and fine-tuning transformers. *arXiv preprint arXiv:2109.10686*.

Ashish Vaswani, Noam M. Shazeer, Niki Parmar, Jakob Uszkoreit, Llion Jones, Aidan N. Gomez, Lukasz Kaiser, and Illia Polosukhin. 2017. Attention is all you need. *ArXiv*, abs/1706.03762.

Leandro von Werra, Younes Belkada, Lewis Tunstall, Edward Beeching, Tristan Thrush, and Nathan Lambert. 2020. Trl: Transformer reinforcement learning. `https://github.com/lvwerra/trl`.

Alex Warstadt, Aaron Mueller, Leshem Choshen, Ethan Gotlieb Wilcox, Chengxu Zhuang, Juan Ciro, Rafael Mosquera, Adina Williams, Bhargavi Paranjabe, Tal Linzen, and Ryan Cotterell. 2023. Findings of the 2023 BabyLM Challenge: Sample-efficient pretraining on developmentally plausible corpora. In *Proceedings of the 2023 BabyLM Challenge*. Association for Computational Linguistics (ACL).

Wikipedia contributors. 2004. Wikipedia, the free encyclopedia.

Thomas Wolf, Lysandre Debut, Victor Sanh, Julien Chaumond, Clement Delangue, Anthony Moi, Pierric Cistac, Tim Rault, Rémi Louf, Morgan Funtowicz, Joe Davison, Sam Shleifer, Patrick von Platen, Clara Ma, Yacine Jernite, Julien Plu, Canwen Xu, Teven Le Scao, Sylvain Gugger, Mariama Drame, Quentin Lhoest, and Alexander M. Rush. 2020. Transformers: State-of-the-art natural language processing. In *Proceedings of the 2020 Conference on Empirical Methods in Natural Language Processing: System Demonstrations*, pages 38–45, Online. Association for Computational Linguistics.

Eunice Yiu, Eliza Kosoy, and Alison Gopnik. 2023. Imitation versus innovation: What children can do that large language and language-and-vision models cannot (yet)?

Wanjun Zhong, Duyu Tang, Nan Duan, Ming Zhou, Jiahai Wang, and Jian Yin. 2019. Improving question answering by commonsense-based pre-training. In *Natural Language Processing and Chinese Computing: 8th CCF International Conference, NLPCC 2019, Dunhuang, China, October 9–14, 2019, Proceedings, Part I 8*, pages 16–28. Springer.

Yukun Zhu, Ryan Kiros, Rich Zemel, Ruslan Salakhutdinov, Raquel Urtasun, Antonio Torralba, and Sanja Fidler. 2015. Aligning books and movies: Towards story-like visual explanations by watching movies and reading books. In *The IEEE International Conference on Computer Vision (ICCV)*.

On the effect of curriculum learning with developmental data for grammar acquisition

Mattia Opper[a] and **J. Morrison**[a,b] and **N. Siddharth**[a,c]
[a] University of Edinburgh; [b] University of St Andrews; [c] The Alan Turing Institute
{m.opper,j.morrison,n.siddharth}@ed.ac.uk

Abstract

This work explores the degree to which grammar acquisition is driven by language 'simplicity' and the source modality (speech vs. text) of data. Using BabyBERTa (Huebner et al., 2021) as a probe, we find that grammar acquisition is largely driven by exposure to speech data, and in particular through exposure to two of the BabyLM (Warstadt et al., 2023) training corpora: AO-Childes and Open Subtitles. We arrive at this finding by examining various ways of presenting input data to our model. First, we assess the impact of various sequence-level complexity based curricula. We then examine the impact of learning over 'blocks'—covering spans of text that are balanced for the number of tokens in each of the source corpora (rather than number of lines). Finally, we explore curricula that vary the degree to which the model is exposed to different corpora. In all cases, we find that over-exposure to AO-Childes and Open Subtitles significantly drives performance. We verify these findings through a comparable control dataset in which exposure to these corpora, and speech more generally, is limited by design. Our findings indicate that it is not the proportion of tokens occupied by high-utility data that aids acquisition, but rather the proportion of training steps assigned to such data. We hope this encourages future research into the use of more developmentally plausible linguistic data (which tends to be more scarce) to augment general purpose pre-training regimes.

1 Introduction

Pre-training modern LLMs has become an increasingly resource intensive process, often requiring hundreds of GPU hours, and enough electricity to power a small village. These requirements have led to model creation increasingly becoming restricted to the few actors that are able to muster the resources necessary, excluding many from being able to participate in researching the field.

On the other hand, recent work (Huebner et al., 2021; Mueller and Linzen, 2023) has shown that Transformer LLMs can acquire knowledge of grammar and syntax with less data scale than was previously thought necessary, provided that they are exposed to simpler forms of language. These findings provide a hope that research on pre-training can once again become accessible to the community as a whole.

However, even if scale may not be such a strict requirement for the acquisition of linguistic knowledge, there are two tendencies exhibited by transformer models that may still be barriers to accessibility. Firstly, simply increasing the number of training steps generally yields better results. In fact, recent work by Murty et al. (2023) has shown that continuing training long past *train loss saturation* can lead to acquisition of a bias towards tree-likeness. While a fascinating finding in its own right (as hierarchical structure is considered a central feature of natural language) many groups simply won't have the GPU hours necessary to reach this point, so resources may remain a barrier. Secondly, it is often the case that simply increasing the complexity of a model can be beneficial (e.g. greater depth can aid syntactic generalisation (Mueller and Linzen, 2023)), but increasing complexity also increases cost.

This work investigates whether we can use the starting small approach to curriculum learning (Elman, 1993) combined with a small scale developmentally plausible pre-training set to aid model grammar acquisition without necessitating an increased budget of training steps. Our findings are mixed. We were unable to significantly outperform a random sampling baseline over all the pre-training corpora contained in the strict-small track. However, we are able to attribute this to the prevalence of high-utility simple speech data. We demonstrate through the use of a control corpus that in a setting where this high-utility data is more scarce, the benefits of developmentally ordered learning start to show themselves.

Proceedings of the 27th Conference on Computational Natural Language Learning: Volume 2: The BabyLM Challenge, pages 346–355

2 Related Work

Elman (1993)'s seminal early work presented the idea of starting small, whereby a model is first exposed to simpler data before moving on to more complex types of input. The idea is that complex data might get the model to learn 'false friend' heuristics that are actually harmful in the long run, but simple data might get it to learn in a way that generalises well. However, this hypothesis is not without controversy. Rohde and Plaut (1999) found that networks trained on complex sentences from the start performed better than those trained on simpler sentences initially, contradicting the starting-small hypothesis. They argue that previous studies supporting the starting small hypothesis may have terminated the training of complex networks too early. Bengio et al. (2009) train a language model using a curriculum learning strategy where only spans of text containing the first 5k most frequent words are included, then expanding to the first 10k and so on. They find that while a random sampling baseline initially achieves a superior loss, with sufficient updates the curriculum strategy comes to a better minimum and converges more stably.

These approaches have in common that they gradually reveal more and more of the dataset. An alternative approach is a single-phase curriculum where the input data is sorted by some criterion and then presented to the model in a fixed ordering. The model goes through the curriculum once, and does not revisit simpler data once it transitions to more complex data. The success of the single phase approach depends heavily on how complexity is defined, and has shown dubious results when applied to NLP (Campos, 2021; Surkov et al., 2022). Even under a developmentally plausible setting, the efficacy of the single phase approach has been shown to be mixed (Huebner et al., 2021).

3 BabyBERTa

3.1 Model and Training Details

The baseline model architecture we use in this work is an adaptation of BabyBERTa (Huebner et al., 2021). BabyBERTa is a variant of RoBERTa (Liu et al., 2019), with a few key differences:

No Unmasking: RoBERTa had used unmasking to minimise the disparity between pre-training and fine-tuning (where no mask tokens are used). Instead, BabyBERTa prioritises the finding that removing unmasking substantially improves model grammar acquisition.

No length truncation: Sequences which exceed the max length set in BabyBERTa are excluded instead of truncated. This ensures the model is only provided with whole utterances that correspond to a coherent linguistic unit.

Smaller Size: BabyBERTa is both shallower (fewer layers) and narrower (lower hidden and feed-forward size) than the original RoBERTa.

Training Data and Vocab Size: BabyBERTa is pre-trained on child directed speech and uses a substantially smaller vocabulary size in order to mimic that of a 6-year-old (theorised to be roughly 6k words).

We adopt this architecture for use in our paper with some alterations:

Increased Vocabulary: The BabyLM training corpora consist of more diverse data than AO-Childes, and encompass a wider range of developmental complexity. Consequently, a greater vocabulary size may be beneficial. We performed a grid search over vocabulary sizes 10k, 20k, 30k, 40k and 50k and found 30k to be optimal.

Increased Width: We double the hidden size and feed-forward network dimension of the original BabyBERTa from 256 to 512 and 1024 to 2048 respectively. These changes yielded slight improvements in BLiMP performance, but without them the model performed substantially worse on NLI tasks than the RoBERTa baseline provided for the challenge. However, increased width yields only minimal improvements in terms of grammar acquisition. We tested increasing the depth of the model (more layers), but found this yielded no improvements within the pre-training step budget we had available, neither did increasing the number of attention heads.

Our remaining model parameters are the defaults for RoBERTa from the transformer's library (Wolf et al., 2019). We use relative key query positional embeddings and set our max sequence length during training to 128 for efficiency reasons, and follow the no-truncation strategy. We set the learning rate to 1e-5 and the max number of steps to 120k using batch size 128. Unless stated otherwise, all our experiments utilise these same hyperparameters. We utilise dynamic masking as with the original RoBERTa, and no unmasking following BabyBERTa in all cases without exception. While the latter choice may impact downstream performance in the fine-tuning tasks, the focus of this paper is largely on grammar acquisition as measured by the zero-shot evaluation suite and here removing unmasking proved beneficial.

4 Sequence Complexity Curricula

Our first point of investigation was to examine whether we could use sequence complexity based curricula to improve grammar acquisition. In the original BabyBERTa paper, the authors found that training on AO-Childes in its original ordering (which corresponds to age ordering, hence AO) led to better grammar acquisition than the reverse, but failed to outperform a random sampling baseline. They attribute this failure to a lack of vocabulary diversity in each batch when using age ordering. By contrast, the BabyLM pre-training corpora exhibit varying complexities (AO-Childes or Open Subtitles are on average much simpler than Wikipedia, see Figure 2), as well as variance in complexity within the corpora. Consequently, we hypothesised that we may be able to scaffold learning by presenting sequences to the model in order of complexity, while mitigating the potential issue of vocabulary and domain diversity by drawing these sequences from across all the source corpora.

4.1 Curriculum Types

We tested three kinds of curricula using different measures for complexity. As we were submitting to the strict small track, we only used sequence complexity metrics that could be easily inferred from the raw data. We call lines of the corpora 'sequences' for lack of a better term. Each corresponds to a linguistically coherent unit, but they can vary from short transcribed utterances to full articles. It is likely that better curricula can be created by using more complex and linguistically motivated metrics, but without the use of external resources this is difficult to achieve. The three types we tried are:

Entropy: Entropy favours highly likely sequences, but penalises based on length. This should order data such that the most likely shortest sequences appear first, allowing the model to learn simple local dependencies before moving to more complex data.

Unigram Probability: Orders sequences by the average unigram probability of their tokens. This is similar to entropy, except without penalising length directly. The idea here is that the model can learn good representations for highly likely tokens first and use that to inform its decision around more complicated/rarer tokens later down the line. The approach is similar to that of Bengio et al. (2009).

Block: Introduced by Nagatsuka et al. (2021) in the block curriculum, block size is increased during the course of training. This allows the model to first learn to optimise local dependencies before moving to longer range ones. The block curriculum differs from the other two in that each stage of learning does not present a subset of sequences, but rather is over the entirety of data in all the corpora, with each stage providing a greater context window for the model to consider. Secondly, by utilising blocks, each input consists of a span of tokens rather than a linguistically coherent unit like a transcribed utterance or article, and can include segments that represent partial units both at the start or end of a block. This means that the model must learn to identify the boundaries between coherent units during training, which may be a burden.

4.2 Creation

We first tokenised all sequences using the model's tokeniser, then calculated probabilities for each token using MLE, and scored each sequence, and subsequently re-ranked the data. The re-ranked sequence were then divided into different stages, by chunking according to rank. We used 4 stages for all curricula, with each stage containing a roughly equal number of sequences. Increasing this number did not yield significant improvements.

In the original block curriculum Nagatsuka et al. (2021) use block sizes 64, 128, 256 and 512, with the maximum batch size that could fit on their GPU at each step. We adopt this approach, but following initial findings that significantly smaller block sizes proved more beneficial than larger ones (potentially as a result of us limiting the max number of steps to 120k to enforce consistency across experiments), we instead switched to block sizes 16, 32, 64, 128.

In some preliminary training runs, we tested both the single phase and starting small approaches to curriculum learning. The single phase approach proved significantly inferior and exhibited a tendency towards catastrophic forgetting. Instead, we

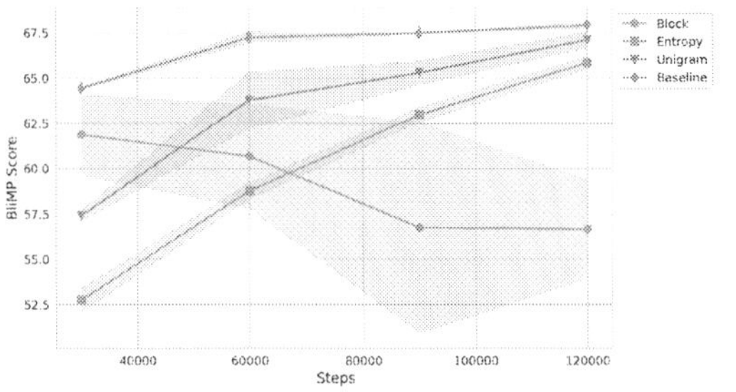

Figure 1: Zero-shot performance for curricula vs. random-sampling baseline with training (over 3 seeds).

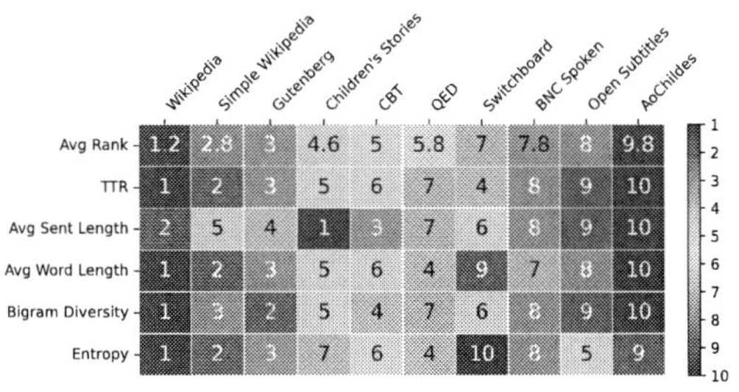

Figure 2: Heatmap ranking of the BabyLM Strict Small training corpora according to complexity measures.

used the following strategy: Each stage introduces new data for training, and the model is trained on the data in the current stage concatenated with that of all stages seen prior. This approach worked best for us. Each stage was trained on for 30k steps, totalling a combined 120k. As a baseline, we trained using random sampling over the whole data, also for 120k steps.

4.3 Summary

Figure 1 shows results. None of the curricula were able to outperform a baseline measure of simply sampling random sequences from the concatenation of all the datasets. Though the sequence complexity based curricula showed improvement throughout training, the block curriculum got worse with each stage. This raised two follow-up questions for us. First, what causes the random sampling baseline to do so well? Second, is using blocks as inputs rather than sequences causing the block curriculum to fail, or some other factor [1]?

5 Investigating Random Sampling

Why might random sampling be successful? Let us begin by examining how we present our data.

[1]The large variance exhibited by the block curriculum suggests significantly more steps would be needed to perform well.

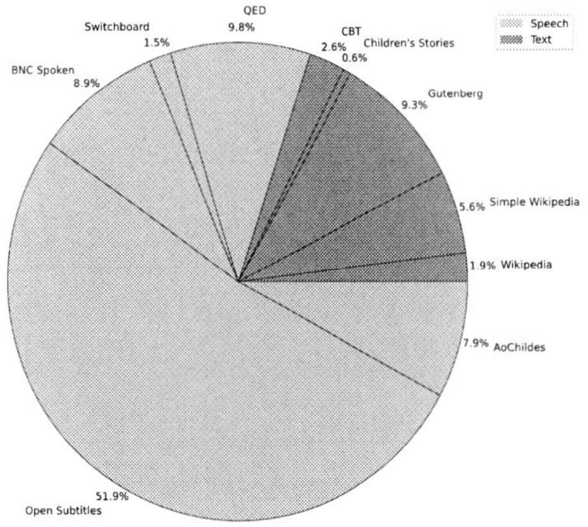

Figure 3: Distribution of line counts across the ten language corpora, with each line treated as a unique sequence. The percentages represent the proportion of total lines that each individual corpus contributes to the overall dataset.

In terms of number of tokens, the BabyLM pretraining corpora are roughly equally divided between the source modalities: text and (transcribed) speech. Though there is a slight weighting in favour of speech, which comprises 56% of total tokens. Now let us contrast this with the relative complexity of each corpus (see Figure 2). We can see that the speech corpora on average, across all metrics, contain far simpler language than the text corpora. Secondly, as we were submitting to the strict small track we do not perform any augmentation on the data, including sentence tokenisation. This means that the random sampling baseline takes as input lines from each corpus. If we examine the distribution of number of lines between corpora, we find a very different division compared with the number of tokens. Figure 3 shows the breakdown. Looking at the number of lines, the balance between transcribed speech and text data becomes highly unequal, with transcribed speech now comprising a total of 80% of all examples. Secondly, the two corpora which contain on average the simplest language (AO-Childes and Open-Subtitles) represent 59.8% of all lines, and these may be responsible for driving the majority of grammar acquisition. If this is the case, then it may explain the performance of the random sampling baseline, as it is more likely to see sequences from these two corpora than any others, while still being provided a degree of diverse examples in each batch. By contrast, when the input is treated as blocks rather

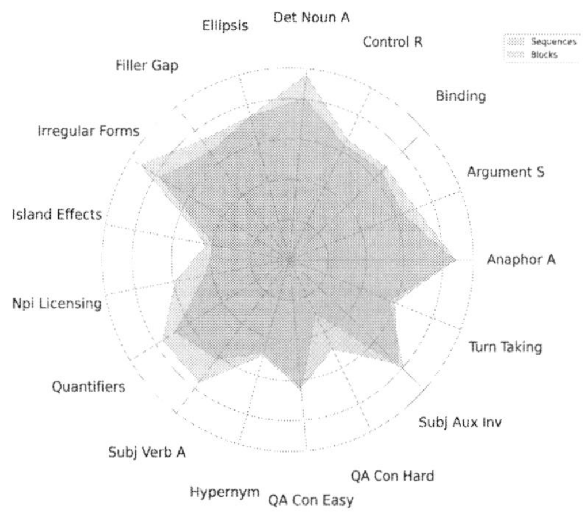

Figure 4: By-task breakdown of zero-shot performance when input data is either a linguistically coherent sequence or a block. Results averaged over 3 seeds.

than lines, the balance between speech and text inputs corresponds to the proportion of number of tokens. Alternatively, it may simply be that training on blocks requires more steps so that the model can identify linguistically coherent units.

To test this hypothesis, we train on both models, taking either blocks or lines from the corpora (henceforth referred to as sequences) as input. We train for an equal number of steps (120k). We report results for block size 32, as when trained for the full number of steps, this worked best out of all the variations tested in the block curriculum.

5.1 Summary

Even when trained for a greater number of steps we find that sequences as input still quite substantially outperform blocks. Results are shown in Figure 4 and Table 1. The only exception is on the held out tasks, however, this is due to the block variant of the model essentially having random accuracy on the QA congruence tasks (close to 50%) while the sequences variants appear to have learned to solve the easy tasks, but fail at the hard ones (see Table 7 for full results by for each task).

We can conclude from this that providing linguistically coherent units as input is beneficial for overall efficient grammar acquisition, despite the fact that the model is disproportionately being exposed to speech data, and therefore only a subset of the overall tokens throughout pre-training. However, we still need to disentangle whether it is speech that is driving this effect or the fact that the model is being presented linguistically coherent units.

Table 1: By-task breakdown of zero-shot performance between models utilising random sampling strategies where inputs are either linguistically coherent sequences or blocks. Results averaged over 3 seeds.

Tasks	Blocks	Sequences
Original	65.98 ± 1.02	$\mathbf{73.11 \pm 0.89}$
Held Out	$\mathbf{59.59 \pm 0.6}$	56.45 ± 0.88
Overall	64.1 ± 0.2	$\mathbf{68.21 \pm 0.23}$

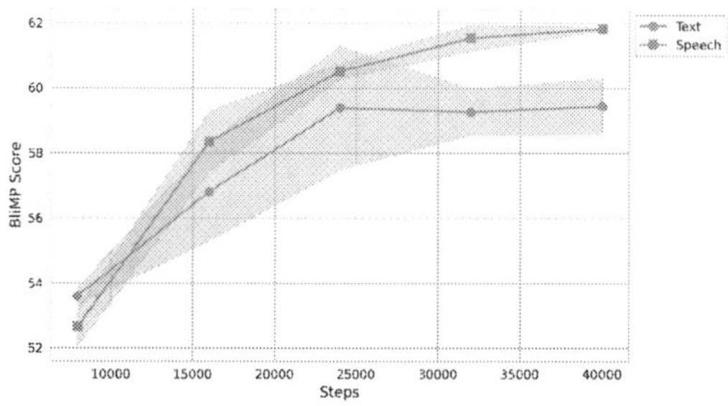

Figure 5: Zero-shot performance by step when the model is trained on either the transcribed speech or text portions of the pre-training corpora (over 3 seeds).

6 Speech vs Text

6.1 Efficient Acquisition by Modality

Prior work examining the impact of pre-training on AO-Childes (Huebner et al., 2021; Mueller and Linzen, 2023) has shown that utilising this simpler form of language enables more efficient acquisition of grammatical knowledge and encourages a bias towards hierarchical generalisation in transformer language models. As such, it is not improbable that simply over exposing the model to simpler data such as speech may be driving performance. To test this, we perform two ablations. First, we assess the impact of training on only one source modality for an equal, but reduced, number of steps to assess whether one provides a better starting point for acquisition. This instance actually in some respects favours the textual data, which contains longer sequences and therefore should provide more signal per step, as each input will contain more masks and contexts while still representing a linguistically coherent unit. Figure 5 shows results on the first comparing the two modalities when trained for 40k steps each. Training on transcribed speech consistently outperforms training on text alone, and leads to more stable improvements than just text. Indicating that it is a better starting point.

Table 2: Comparison of Ordering Effects Given Source Modality. Results averaged across 3 seeds.

Training Data	Original	Held Out	Overall
Speech → Speech+Text	**72.99 ± 0.53**	**56.26 ± 1.3**	**67.74 ± 0.77**
Text → Speech+Text	71.69 ± 0.6	**53.77 ± 2.78**	66.42 ± 1.2
Speech+Text	**73.11 ± 0.89**	**56.45 ± 0.88**	**68.21 ± 0.52**

6.2 Speech Data as a Foundation

As a second follow-up investigation, we once again trained on two different settings. In the first we train on speech first and then the concatenation of text and speech for 60k steps respectively. This is to check whether we can build a foundation from speech data alone, and then transition to including both modalities. However, here text data only occupies 10% of the overall proportion of inputs, and is only observed in the later stages of training. As a control, we also try the inverse, starting with text first and then transitioning to the concatenation of all the corpora, this means that the text data now provides 60% of all the total inputs and speech is only introduced once the model later in training, no longer acting as a foundation. Results are in Table 2. Further, weighting things towards speech improves over the text control on the original BLiMP tasks, and secondly makes performance indistinguishable from random sampling if we account for standard deviation overlap. The only area where this does not hold is in the held out tasks.

6.3 Summary

We find that transcribed speech leads to improved BLiMP performance and lower variance compared with text only data. Based on this finding, we investigated whether we could design a simple two stage curriculum where we first train the model on speech only and then transfer to the full dataset. Under this setting, performance is roughly equal to random sampling, and shows some very slight improvements compared to the reverse curriculum. This is despite the fact that the model is only exposed to the $\approx$ 50% of total tokens contained in the text portion in the latter half of training.

7 Corpora Complexity Curricula

Having found that speech data can provide a better foundation than text, and that over exposure may be behind the random sampling baselines performance, we conduct a follow-up investigation. How much exposure to more complex data is necessary in order to achieve grammar acquisition? To probe this question, we use the same strategy

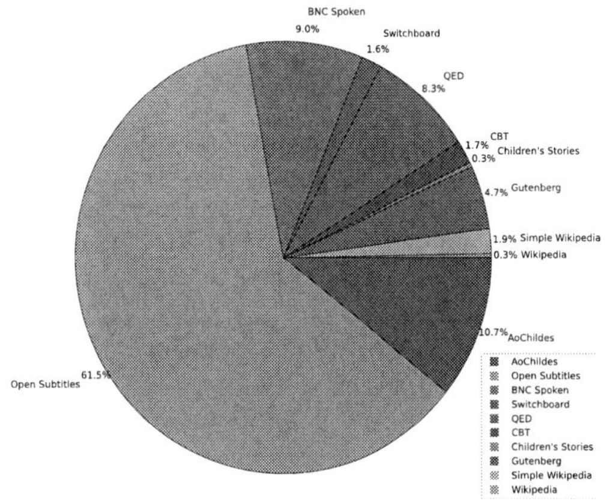

Figure 6: Proportion of total inputs comprised by each of the corpora using the corpus complexity curriculum.

for our curriculum by training on a stage and the concatenation of all previous stages. This time we define our ordering using the average rank across our various corpus complexity measures as shown in Figure 2. So our ordering starts with AO-Childes and ends with Wikipedia. The curriculum is simply the corpus complexity ordering, with two caveats. We treat BNC spoken and switchboard as one corpus, as switchboard is too small to warrant a new stage. We also do the same for CBT and children's stories, as they are very similar in terms of complexity. Using this form of curriculum further increases the model's exposure to simple data, with AO-Childes and Open Subtitles now representing 72.2% of all total training examples, compared with 59.8% before, and Wikipedia representing only 0.3% (see Figure 6). We again implement the reverse curriculum as a control measure, starting with Wikipedia and finishing with AO-Childes, and compare results to the random sampling baseline (see Table 3). The simple to complex curriculum yields marginally better results overall compared to the random sampling baseline, and the gap with the reverse curriculum is wider here than for the previous speech versus text curriculum.

However, the marginality of the increase compared to the random sampling baseline makes it

Table 3: Comparison of performance by corpora complexity ordering. Results averaged across 3 seeds.

Training Data	Original	Held Out	Overall
Simple → Complex	**74.14 ± 0.39**	**55.9 ± 0.74**	**68.77 ± 0.04**
Complex → Simple	71.89 ± 0.9	**54.29 ± 2.74**	66.72 ± 0.42
Random Sampling	**73.11 ± 0.89**	**56.45 ± 0.88**	**68.21 ± 0.52**

Table 4: Control Dataset Statistics

Name	Tokens %	Input %	Curriculum Input %
AO-Childes	4%	15.8%	26%
CBT	50%	51.8%	56%
Wikipedia	46%	32.4%	18%

difficult to make any strong claims regarding the effect of ordering. We wondered if this was because the BabyLM training data is already favourable for grammar acquisition and weighted towards speech, and whether we would observe greater benefits over random sampling in a setting where the data did not have these properties.

7.1 Summary

We wanted to test whether we could design a curriculum based on the complexity of the various pre-training corpora (see Figure 2). We find that following this approach led to improvements over the reverse, especially on the original set of BLiMP tasks, but failed to show a significant difference over random sampling. We hypothesise that this due to AO-Childes and Open Subtitles, two of the most high utility corpora for grammar acquisition, already making up a large percentage of inputs in the random-sampling setting. Thus, the introduction of a curriculum may have little impact.

8 Control Dataset

To test whether complexity ordering helped more when the training data was less optimal, we created a new dataset. It consists of the AO-Childes portion of BabyLM 10M, and the CBT and Wikipedia portions of BabyLM 100M, representing the simplest, middle, and most complex corpora respectively. We set max sequence length to 512 to allow training on as much of the data as possible. Combined, these three corpora have approximately 10 million tokens (similar to the 'strict-small' track), but with the vast majority of these coming from text data. It also means that the number of inputs that come from simpler, more beneficial data is reduced. Descriptive statistics can be found in Table 4.

We train a new tokeniser on the data, and then compare results between a random sampling base-

Table 5: Control Dataset Results on Zero-shot Tasks. Results averaged across 3 seeds.

Training Data	Original	Held Out	Overall
Simple → Complex	**72.18 ± 0.88**	**55.52 ± 1.08**	**67.28 ± 0.52**
Random Sampling	70.77 ± 0.37	**55.88 ± 1.11**	66.38 ± 0.1

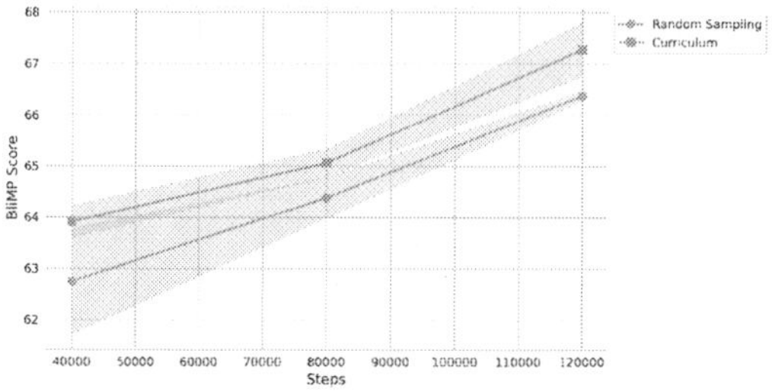

Figure 7: Zero-shot performance by step when the model is trained using the curriculum or random sampling on our control dataset (over 3 seeds).

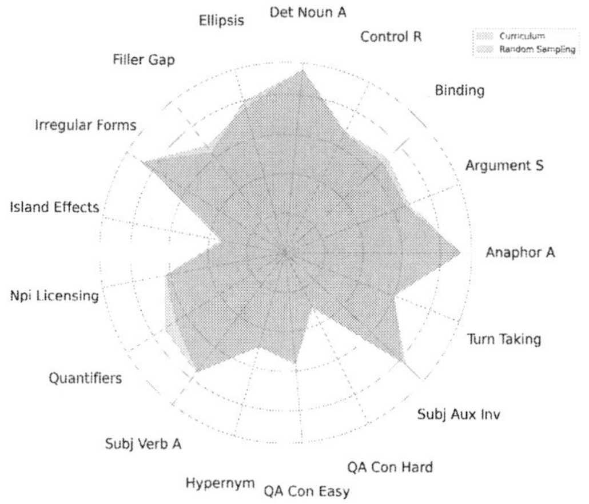

Figure 8: By-task breakdown of zero-shot performance on the control dataset curriculum vs random sampling. Results averaged across 3 seeds.

line and corpus complexity curriculum approach described in the previous section. Both versions are trained for 120k steps, but we had to lower the batch size to 64 due to GPU memory constraints with longer sequences. Results are in Table 5, and a plot of the by task scores can be found in Figure 8. Under this setting, the curriculum approach begins to demonstrate modest, but visible improvements over random sampling, though this does not extend to the held out tasks. Figure 7 shows the performances patterns as the number of steps increases. The curriculum consistently offers slight improvements over random sampling.

9 Summary

We wanted to test whether curriculum learning can be beneficial in a scenario where the majority of data is not high utility, i.e., simple transcribed speech. To do so, we created a control corpus where the majority of data comes from long form text. Under this setting, we find a slight, but discernable improvement from using the curriculum.

10 Conclusion

We began our exploration by attempting to design a learning curriculum to further grammar acquisition for the BabyLM strict-small track. We found that when the majority of the data is high-utility, as is the case here, curriculum learning shows no substantial benefits. However, such training data is not always available or may be dwarfed by the number of tokens of low utility data available. In these settings—common for pre-training NLP models—our results indicate some promise in starting small after all. However, extensive further experimentation, most likely requiring larger scale corpora, is necessary to properly test and verify this claim.

11 Limitations

The work presented in this paper represents an initial foray into starting-small-style learning. There are a number of extensions and further questions one could ask, building upon the work presented here, that could help shine further light on the nuances of this style of learning.

- Although the control-dataset experiments in Section 8 show better performance when starting small compared to random sampling, we don't yet definitively discount that starting large *in the same setting* does not achieve the same results. This could be remedied by constructing a careful 'complementary' large-to-small-complexity curriculum.
- Given our training regime, for both random sampling and corpus curricula, on both the original data and the control, we don't know if the eventual trends over training will resemble that reported by Rohde and Plaut (1999) or that of Bengio et al. (2009). We could explore this by attempting to train over longer horizons to see if a comparable trend emerges.
- In our submission for the competition, we used an additional technique: layer stacking (Gong et al., 2019), which involved progressively growing the model as we advanced through the curriculum (following Elman (1993)). The hypothesis was that we would be starting small in two ways: from simple data and/or a simple model. This yielded some slight improvements over only using the corpora curriculum over the entirety of the strict-small training data, which had been our previous best scoring model. We do not yet have a complete picture of how layer-stacking affects all the various training regimes discussed in this manuscript, and hence only describe the basic algorithm in the appendix A.
- Follow on work could probe how much of a token disparity can be tolerated before loseing the benefits of starting small from transcribed speech. This could be, for example, replacing CBT with a larger proportion of Wikipedia; e.g. Wiki-103 (Merity et al., 2016).

12 Full Results

While our focus here has been grammar acquisition, we present results on all tasks in Table 6. We perform favourably compared to the official RoBERTa baseline for the challenge, but one area shows a notable disparity—MSGS tasks (Warstadt et al., 2020) measuring syntactic category. This may be because our model is too shallow (RoBERTa base has 12 layers vs. our 8).

Table 6: Full results from Dynabench for our submission vs. the official RoBERTa baseline for the challenge.

Task	Ours	RoBERTa Base
Anaphor Agreement	**84**	82
Argument Struct	**70**	67
Binding	**69**	67
Control R	**70**	68
DN Agreement	**92**	91
Ellipsis	**77**	76
Filler Gap	**76**	64
Irregular Forms	87	87
Island Effects	**42**	40
NPI Licensing	**65**	56
Quantifiers	**78**	71
SV Agreement	**77**	66
Hypernym	45	**49**
QA Cong Easy	**69**	31
QA Cong Hard	**33**	32
SA Inversion	**77**	72
Turn Taking	**57**	53
CoLA	**32**	26
SST-2	87	87
MRPC	79	79
QQP	**82**	74
MNLI	73	73
MNLI-MM	74	74
QNLI	**78**	77
RTE	49	**62**
BoolQ	62	**66**
MultiRC	60	**61**
WSC	61	61
CR	**0.73**	0.43
LC	1.0	1.0
MV	**1.0**	0.98
RP	0.84	**0.94**
SC	0.16	**0.86**
CR_LC	-0.58	**-0.28**
CR_RTP	-0.92	**-0.77**
MV_LC	-1.0	**-0.99**
MV_RTP	**-0.26**	-0.79
SC_LC	-0.43	**0.16**
SC_RP	-0.59	-0.45

Acknowledgements

MO was funded by a PhD studentship through Huawei-Edinburgh Research Lab Project 10410153. We also wish to thank Victor Prokhorov for his suggestions and tireless willingness to answer questions.

References

Yoshua Bengio, Jérôme Louradour, Ronan Collobert, and Jason Weston. 2009. Curriculum learning. In *Proceedings of the 26th Annual International Conference on Machine Learning*, ICML '09, page 41–48, New York, NY, USA. Association for Computing Machinery.

Daniel Campos. 2021. Curriculum learning for language modeling. *CoRR*, abs/2108.02170.

Jeffrey L. Elman. 1993. Learning and development in neural networks: the importance of starting small. *Cognition*, 48:71–99.

Linyuan Gong, Di He, Zhuohan Li, Tao Qin, Liwei Wang, and Tieyan Liu. 2019. Efficient training of BERT by progressively stacking. In *Proceedings of the 36th International Conference on Machine Learning*, volume 97 of *Proceedings of Machine Learning Research*, pages 2337–2346. PMLR.

Philip A. Huebner, Elior Sulem, Fisher Cynthia, and Dan Roth. 2021. BabyBERTa: Learning more grammar with small-scale child-directed language. In *Proceedings of the 25th Conference on Computational Natural Language Learning*, pages 624–646, Online. Association for Computational Linguistics.

Yinhan Liu, Myle Ott, Naman Goyal, Jingfei Du, Mandar Joshi, Danqi Chen, Omer Levy, Mike Lewis, Luke Zettlemoyer, and Veselin Stoyanov. 2019. Roberta: A robustly optimized BERT pretraining approach. *CoRR*, abs/1907.11692.

Stephen Merity, Caiming Xiong, James Bradbury, and Richard Socher. 2016. Pointer sentinel mixture models. *CoRR*, abs/1609.07843.

Aaron Mueller and Tal Linzen. 2023. How to plant trees in language models: Data and architectural effects on the emergence of syntactic inductive biases. *ArXiv*, abs/2305.19905.

Shikhar Murty, Pratyusha Sharma, Jacob Andreas, and Christopher D. Manning. 2023. Grokking of hierarchical structure in vanilla transformers. *ArXiv*, abs/2305.18741.

Koichi Nagatsuka, Clifford Broni-Bediako, and Masayasu Atsumi. 2021. Pre-training a BERT with curriculum learning by increasing block-size of input text. In *Proceedings of the International Conference on Recent Advances in Natural Language Processing (RANLP 2021)*, pages 989–996, Held Online. INCOMA Ltd.

Douglas L. T. Rohde and David C. Plaut. 1999. Language acquisition in the absence of explicit negative evidence: how important is starting small? *Cognition*, 72:67–109.

Maxim Surkov, Vladislav Mosin, and Ivan Yamshchikov. 2022. Do data-based curricula work? In *Proceedings of the Third Workshop on Insights from Negative Results in NLP*, pages 119–128, Dublin, Ireland. Association for Computational Linguistics.

Alex Warstadt, Leshem Choshen, Ryan Cotterell, Tal Linzen, Aaron Mueller, Ethan Wilcox, Williams Adina, and Chengxu Zhuang. 2023. Findings of the BabyLM Challenge: Sample-efficient pretraining on developmentally plausible corpora. In *Proceedings of the BabyLM Challenge*. Association for Computational Linguistics (ACL).

Alex Warstadt, Yian Zhang, Xiaocheng Li, Haokun Liu, and Samuel R. Bowman. 2020. Learning which features matter: RoBERTa acquires a preference for linguistic generalizations (eventually). In *Proceedings of the 2020 Conference on Empirical Methods in Natural Language Processing (EMNLP)*, pages 217–235, Online. Association for Computational Linguistics.

Thomas Wolf, Lysandre Debut, Victor Sanh, Julien Chaumond, Clement Delangue, Anthony Moi, Pierric Cistac, Tim Rault, Rémi Louf, Morgan Funtowicz, and Jamie Brew. 2019. Huggingface's transformers: State-of-the-art natural language processing. *CoRR*, abs/1910.03771.

Appendices

A Layer Stacking

We grew our model during training by adding a layer when we reached each new stage of our curriculum. We cloned the existing uppermost layer at the beginning of each new stage of our curriculum, then stacked that layer on top of the existing layers of our model. Our model then proceeds to learn from our new mix of datasets for the new stage of the curriculum, with the uppermost layer most responsive to the newly revealed datasets in our curriculum. In this way we progressed from 1 to 8 layers over the course of our training regime.

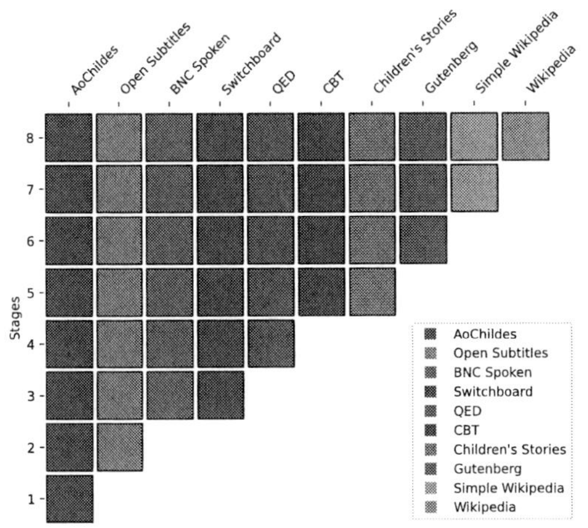

Figure 9: Our learning curriculum exposes our model to additional datasets stage-by-stage as it progresses through our training regime.

B Full Results Table

Table 7: Sequence vs block input performance on zero-shot tasks. Results are averaged across three random seeds. 4

Model	Anaphor A	Argument S	Binding	Control R	Det Noun A	Ellipsis	Filler Gap	Irregular Forms	Island Effects
Sequences	**86.78**	**70.84**	**68.58**	**66.60**	**92.31**	**74.12**	**74.20**	**89.47**	**42.91**
Blocks	86.39	63.59	65.36	63.66	80.91	73.81	67.19	77.89	39.08

Model	Npi Licensing	Quantifiers	Subj Verb A	Hypernym	QA Con Easy	QA Con hard	Subj Aux Inv	Turn Taking	Score
Sequences	**58.97**	**76.06**	**76.52**	**49.19**	**65.63**	29.90	**81.21**	56.31	**68.21**
Blocks	43.85	68.20	61.81	48.22	64.06	**49.50**	76.99	**59.17**	64.01

Optimizing GPT-2 Pretraining on BabyLM Corpus with Difficulty-based Sentence Reordering

Nasim Borazjanizadeh
Williams College
nb11@williams.edu

Abstract

This paper focuses on enhancing the performance of GPT-2, pre-trained on the BabyLM Strict-Small challenge datasets, for the BLiMP zero-shot tasks. We explored various curriculum learning optimizations to supervise the order of training samples presented to the model. We discovered that training GPT-2 on a corpus consisting of one dataset sorted based on difficulty leads to improved BLiMP scores. Additionally, we measured the loss of contextual information by comparing the semantic similarity of neighboring sentences before and after reordering inputs of each dataset. A positive correlation is found between the measured contextual similarity of sentences in the difficulty-sorted dataset and the BLiMP performance of the model trained on the rearranged dataset. We conclude that reordering sentences based on difficulty while minimizing the loss of contextual and semantic similarity between sentences that follow each other in a context length can enhance the model's performance. Using this approach we trained a model with an average of 75.77% across all BLiMP's tasks. Additionally, data cleaning using ASR further enhanced the model performance on BLiMP to 75.84%, an improvement of over 6% compared to the baselines released for the BabyLM Strict-Small challenge.

1 Introduction

Language models have shown significant progress in natural language processing tasks, but their performance heavily relies on the diversity and quality of large-scale training data. This paper aims to enhance the performance of language models trained exclusively on the datasets from the BabyLM Strict-Small challenge (Warstadt et al., 2023). We evaluate the models using the average across all BLiMP's zero-shot tasks, which assess language models' knowledge of major English grammatical phenomena (Warstadt et al., 2020). The reason we exclusively relied on BLiMP results to optimize the performance of our models is that other evaluation tasks within the BabyLM evaluation pipeline, like (Super)GLUE and held-out MSGS tasks, require fine-tuning the model and demand more computational resources than we had available.

In this paper, we attempt to optimize the performance of language models on the BLiMP evaluation by using heuristics inspired by difficulty metrics proposed in Competence-based Curriculum Learning (Platanios et al., 2019) to reorder sentences in the datasets and remove semantically meaningless inputs. As a result, we achieved an improvement of over 6 percent on BLiMP compared to the baseline results released for the BabyLM Strict-Small track (Table 1).

We first manually analyzed the training data to gain a better understanding of the training data. The analysis revealed the sentences in the `gutenberg` dataset were fragmented across lines. This fragmentation could disrupt the intrinsic structure and the contextual information provided by each sentence during training, as irrelevant fragments would follow each other in a single context length due to the shuffling of training samples at each training epoch. To rectify this, we preprocessed the `gutenberg` dataset by merging subsegments of each sentence into a coherent sentence printed in one line (Table 1).

We then attempted to optimize the use of limited training samples by supervising the order of samples presented to the model using Curriculum Learning (CL) and Competence-based Curriculum Learning. These methods involve starting the training of the model with simpler examples and gradually introducing harder ones. In Competence-based CL, the training corpus is constructed using the competence function which samples from the difficulty-sorted training inputs based on the competence of the model at time `t` compared to

Proceedings of the 27th Conference on Computational Natural Language Learning: Volume 2: The BabyLM Challenge, pages 356–365
December 6-7, 2023

Baselines	BLiMP
OPT-125 - BabyLM baseline	62.63%
RoBERTa-base - BabyLM baseline	69.47%
T5-base - BabyLM baseline	58.83%
GPT-2 - gutenberg not merged	73.40%
GPT-2 - gutenberg merged	75.05%

Table 1: The BLiMP evaluation results comparing the baselines released for the BabyLM Strict-Small challenge and our baseline GPT-2 models. GPT-2 gutenberg not merged is trained on all raw datasets in the Strict-Small track, and GPT-2 - gutenberg merged model is trained on 9 unchanged datasets and the preprocessed gutenberg dataset, where sentences are merged into a single line.

Excluded	BLiMP	Excluded	BLiMP
aochildes	74.40%	open_subtitles	72.81%
bnc_spoken	73.91%	qed	74.12%
cbt	74.21%	simple_wikipedia	73.64%
children_stories	73.36%	switchboard	73.93%
gutenberg	73.48%	wikipedia	72.70%

Table 2: BLiMP evaluation results for GPT-2 model trained on all datasets in Strict-Small track beside the dataset listed under the 'Excluded' column. The sentences in the gutenberg dataset are merged into one line, and thus the baseline model for this experiment is GPT-2 - gutenberg merged with a BLiMP score of 75.05%.

the competence of the model at convergence time. Using this method leads to an overrepresentation of shorter sentences (which are sorted as easier using length-dependent difficulty metrics such as sentence length (SL) or sentence rarity (SR) suggested in Platanios et al. (2019)) in the training corpus. Shorter sentences tend to contain more grammatical errors in the BabyLM datasets, as these datasets consist largely of spoken language sentences. We hypothesize this could result in suboptimal results on BLiMP when implementing Competence-based CL optimizations. To address this, we proposed a novel length-independent difficulty metric, *average sentence rarity* (ASR), calculated by taking the average frequency of words in a sentence to determine the singular score for the difficulty of the sentence.

We hypothesize that when using CL optimizations, the performance of the model is also negatively impacted because the contextual information provided by neighboring sentences is disrupted when reordering sentences based on difficulty. To tackle the loss of contextual information, we narrow our focus to a smaller optimization problem, supervising the order of sentences within a context length rather than the order of all sentences in the training corpus, as determined by the competence function. To measure contextual information provided by nearby sentences, we propose a new heuristic, *local coherence*, calculated by quantifying the similarity between a central sentence and its adjacent ones using sup-simcse-roberta-large model (Gao et al., 2021) within a specific window of seven inputs. The size of this window is determined by the average number of samples combined into a context length after tokenization.

To enhance the model's performance and investigate our hypothesis about the correlation between the local coherence of sentences in the datasets sorted based on difficulty and the resulting improvement in the language model's performance on BLiMP, we conducted a series of 20 experiments. In these experiments, we exclusively reordered sentences from one dataset based on SR or ASR, while leaving the other 9 datasets unchanged. Upon analyzing the results, we found a positive correlation between the expected local coherence of the sorted datasets and the BLiMP performance of the models trained on the corpus compromising of one sorted dataset. The positive correlations indicate that reordering sentences based on difficulty while minimizing the loss of contextual and semantic similarity between sentences that follow each other in a context length can enhance the model's performance.

We were also able to improve the model's performance with data cleaning. ASR sorts inputs with high counts of frequent words and low counts of other words, as easy inputs. Through manual evaluation of datasets, we discovered that these characteristics often correspond to meaningless or grammatically incoherent inputs in the 3 following datasets: cbt, gutenberg, and bnc_spoken. Removing these redundant inputs from the gutenberg dataset, led to improved BLiMP performances for the model trained on the sorted and cleaned dataset (Table 6).

While we did achieve improvements in the BLiMP evaluation by training models only on the Strict-Small datasets using the described methods, the most significant intellectual contribution of this paper is highlighting the importance of considering contextual and knowledge-based similarity when reordering training inputs with any performance-enhancing metrics for language models. This concept reflects how humans learn effectively. In schools, subjects like math and English are not mixed in the same class period, regardless of the difficulty of the subjects, unless students are already proficient in both.

If we compare a context length-sized input to a human's attention span of 5 minutes, teaching math to a model or human is more effective if we present 10 similar examples of arithmetic operations that follow the same logical pattern within that 5-minute span, rather than presenting examples of different mathematical operations (like basic combinatorics mixed with calculus and geometry) without any logical pattern connecting the examples, even if these examples share the same level of difficulty. Therefore, in curriculum learning for language models, we argue that sentences that are presented together within a context length should be semantically and contextually similar beyond having the same level of difficulty.

2 Model Architecture & Training Loop

To identify the optimal base model architecture for our experiments, we trained BERT(Devlin et al., 2018), RoBERTa(Liu et al., 2019), and GPT-2(Radford et al., 2019) on the given datasets, adhering to the conventional guidelines for language model training, and utilizing identical hyperparameters, without any extra optimizations. Our results revealed that GPT-2 not only converged at a faster rate but also marginally outperformed the other models in the BLiMP evaluation. Consequently, we selected GPT-2 as the base model architecture for all our following experiments.

The GPT2 models were trained for six epochs, with convergence typically occurring around the fifth epoch. Throughout the training process, we assessed the models on the evaluation dataset every 500 steps, with the gradient accumulation set to 1. We then selected the best checkpoint based on the evaluation loss to assess with BLiMP evaluation. For all experiments, we utilized the DataLoader function to load data in batches of size 64. We set the shuffle boolean to True, which rearranges the indices of all samples at each epoch for the baseline experiments and the ablation experiments (results in Table 2) that did not involve reordering the data.

The data preparation process involved reading each line of the dataset files as a separate sample. We then joined all the tokenized samples in a batch with an `eos_token_id` token in between and then divided the concatenated samples into sequences of size context-length. During experiments that involved sorting the sentences based on difficulty, we eliminated any duplicated inputs from the dataset. We used the preprocessed `gutenberg` dataset, with sentence fragments merged into one line, as our baseline `gutenberg` dataset for all the experiments besides GPT-2 `gutenberg` not merged (Table 1).

In our experimental setup, we tested our baseline model using different context length sizes. We observed that a context length of 64 resulted in a decline in the model's performance on BLiMP. On the other hand, context lengths of 512 and 256 did not yield any performance improvements over a context length of 128. However, they significantly increased the GPU memory usage and extended the training time. Consequently, we chose a context length of 128, the smallest size that did not adversely affect the model's performance, for all subsequent experiments.

We repeated a subset of baseline experiments multiple times to understand the effect of randomness on the outcome of experiments. The limited volume of data used to train our models introduces an inherent instability in the training process, resulting in some variation in the BLiMP evaluation results. We observed a variance of up to 0.6% in the experiments with the same setup when altering the seed before instantiating the model. To neutralize the randomness effect and ensure a valid comparison of different optimizations, we standardized the seed value to 1 for all the experiments discussed in this paper.

3 Dataset Analysis

In order to gain a better understanding of the training data, we conducted a manual analysis of the datasets. This examination revealed that the sentences in the Gutenberg dataset were fragmented across multiple lines. Given that each line is read as a separate sample in our baseline training loop, shuffling the sample indices results in unrelated sentence segments following one another in a context length. This disrupts the inherent structure of the sentences and interrupts the contextual information provided by the surrounding words when learning word embeddings during training.

To address this issue, we preprocessed the Gutenberg dataset by consolidating subsegments of each sentence into a single, coherent sentence printed in one line. This modification led to an improvement of over 1.6% percent in the model's BLiMP evaluation results compared to the baseline (Table 1). This notable enhancement over the baseline, achieved through a straightforward preprocessing step, highlights the importance of maintaining the contextual information provided by the surrounding sentences when feeding the training data to the model.

To evaluate the influence of each dataset on the model's performance during the BLiMP assessment, we conducted an ablation study consisting of 10 experiments. In each of these experiments, the model was trained on nine datasets, with one dataset being excluded in each iteration (Table 2). The results show that removing the `aochildes` dataset has the least influence on the model's performance. However, excluding the `wikipedia` dataset significantly reduced the model's BLiMP score. A comparison between sentences in the `aochildes` and `wikipedia` datasets highlights their distinct grammatical characteristics. Sentences in the `aochildes` dataset, which are compiled from child-directed speech (Huebner et al., 2021), are short, informal, and often contain grammatical errors, including missing or misplaced pronouns and verbs. On the other hand, the `wikipedia` dataset contains longer sentences that strictly adhere to grammatical rules while avoiding unnecessary repetition.

As BLiMP is specifically designed to assess the sensitivity of language models to acceptability contrasts using grammar templates (Warstadt et al., 2020), it follows that the impact of excluding spoken language sentences in `aochildes`, which are incomplete and error-prone, on improving the model's performance in BLiMP evaluation is less significant. Additionally, we can observe that shorter sentences in the BabyLM datasets are less effective in training the model for BLiMP evaluation.

4 Curriculum Learning

To optimize the use of the limited training samples available and improve the model's performance, we chose to supervise the order in which samples are presented to the model. To this end, we implemented Curriculum Learning (CL) (Bengio et al., 2009) and Competence-based Curriculum Learning (Platanios et al., 2019). The fundamental idea behind CL is to initiate learning with simpler examples and gradually incorporate harder ones by sorting the samples based on their difficulty. In Competence-based CL, the training data is filtered based on the estimated difficulty of the sample and model competence.

Difficulty Metric	BLiMP
Sentence Length	69.93%
Sentence Rarity	71.49%
Average Sentence Rarity	74.51%

Table 3: BLiMP results for competence-based CL using different difficulty metrics. The `gutenberg` dataset is preprocessed to have complete sentences in each line before reordering the samples based on difficulty. Shuffle is set to false, and the number of training epochs is 1, as the competence function samples from the difficulty-sorted datasets multiple times when constructing the training corpus.

To implement Competence-based CL, we sorted the training samples based on the difficulty metrics outlined in the Platanios et al. (2019): Sentence Length (SL), which ranks samples based on length, considering shorter samples as easier, and Sentence Rarity (SR), which is the overall likelihood of a sentence, incorporating both word frequency and sentence length, with less likely or more rare sentences being considered more difficult. To build the training corpus with a supervised order of samples, we employed the square root competence function which determines which examples should be incorporated into the training corpus, based on the competence of the model at time `t` of training, and the pace at which new examples are introduced during the training process, where the rate of new examples added decreases over time, allowing the learner more time to assimilate the information (Table 3).

However, BLiMP results for models trained using SL or SR difficulty metrics were worse than the performance achieved when training the model on the base datasets (with `gutenberg` sentences merged) without any CL optimizations. We hypothesize that the sub-optimal performance is linked to the competence function's design and the unique attributes of the BabyLM datasets. The competence function samples more from easier sentences when constructing the training corpus, and both SR and SL heuristics employ sentence length as a criterion, either implicitly or explicitly, to determine the difficulty of sentences. Consequently, this leads to an overrepresentation of shorter sentences in the training data created using this competence function. Furthermore, a higher portion of the BabyLM datasets includes transcribed speech, and shorter spoken language sentences are often fragmented and contain more grammatical errors due to the spontaneous flow of the speech. Our prior observations also show a negative correlation between sentence length and the importance of the sentence in training the model for BLiMP evaluation. Thus, we can deduce that the overrepresentation of short sentences in the Competence-based CL training dataset adversely affects the model's performance on BLiMP.

5 Proposed Methods

5.1 Average Sentence Rarity

Using word frequencies as a difficulty heuristic can be helpful when training language models with limited data. Training examples with rare words need repeated exposure for effective learning, making them difficult to learn (Platanios et al., 2019). Moreover, limited data can lead to high variance in gradients for rare word embedding due to insufficient contextual information. This suggests that word frequencies can be an effective difficulty heuristic.

Given a corpus of M sentences, $\{s_i\}_{i=1}^{M}$, where each sentence is a sequence of words, $s_i = \{w_1^i, ..., w_{N_i}^i\}$, word frequencies are defined as:

$$\hat{f}(w_j) \triangleq \sum_{i=1}^{M} \sum_{k=1}^{N_i} \mathbb{1}_{w_k^i = w_j}$$

where $j = 1, ...,, \#\{\text{unique words in corpus}\}$ and $\mathbb{1}_{condition}$ is the indicator function which is equal to 1 if its condition is satisfied and 0 otherwise. Here, we argue that using the product of the unigram probabilities of word frequency counts, which is employed to compute SR, is not an appropriate strategy for aggregating word frequencies into a singular difficulty score for sentences in the BabyLM Corpus. This approach implicitly incorporates sentence length into the difficulty score, resulting in shorter sentences being classified as easy and subsequently overrepresented in the training dataset when sampling from the difficulty-sorted datasets with the competence function. Instead, we propose using the average of the word frequencies as the singular score for sentence difficulty. This ensures that the difficulty metric is independent of sentence length. We thus propose the *average sentence rarity* difficulty heuristic:

$$d_{avg\_rarity}(s_i) \triangleq \frac{-1}{N_i} \sum_{k=1}^{N_i} \hat{f}(w_j)$$

For the easier sentences to receive a higher score using this metric, we incorporate the -1 factor in our difficulty metric. Implementing this difficulty metric along with the competence function to construct the training corpus led to a performance increase of over 3% on BLiMP, reaching 74.51% (Table 3).

5.2 Local Coherence

There is semantic similarity between consecutive sentences that convey information about the same concept. For instance, sentences from a Wikipedia article on engines are more similar compared to sentences from a conversation between parents and children about lunch. Therefore, adjacent sentences encoding the same concept tend to be more semantically similar. This semantic coherence between adjacent sentences is preserved when sentences from a dataset are in their original order. However, reordering sentences based on difficulty metrics can disrupt the semantic distribution of nearby sentences.

Learning contextualized word embeddings heavily relies on the sequence of words presented together within a context length. We hypothesize that the inferior performance of models developed using Competence-based CL optimizations, in comparison to baselines achieved with simple preprocessing steps, is likely due to the language model's inability to capture important context encoded by nearby sentences. This is because as a consequence of reordering sentences based on difficulty metrics, sentences are followed by others that are grammatically and semantically different, potentially sampled from other datasets, and encoding a completely different concept.

The objective here is to reorder sentences based on difficulty in a manner that minimizes the loss of contextual information encoded by nearby semantically similar sentences, to enhance model performance. To achieve this, we diverge from the competence algorithm proposed, which controls the order of all sentences that the model sees during training. Instead, we focus on a smaller-scale optimization problem by supervising the sequence of sentences that follow each other within a given context length. The order of sentences grouped at the context length level has a significant impact on the

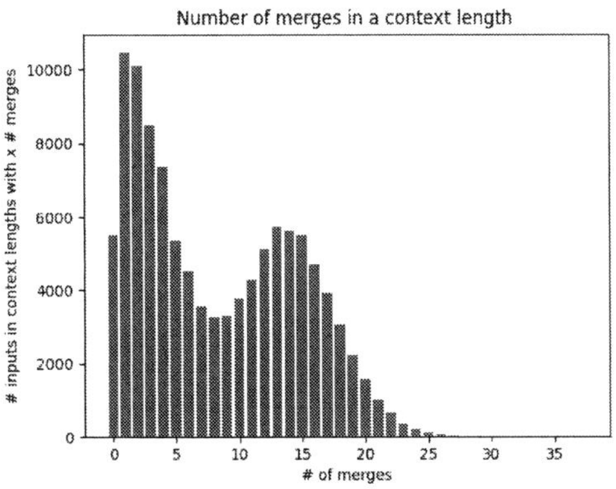

Figure 1: Frequency of context length size samples that are a merge of x number of tokenized inputs in the BabyLM datasets. The average number of merged inputs in a context length is 8.512. However, for the 80% longer portion of inputs, the average is 6.55.

model's performance, because, due to the shorter length of sentences in the BabyLM datasets, an average of 8 sentences are grouped within a context length of 128 tokens when using the concatenation algorithm to merge tokenized inputs (Figure 1).

To assess the extent of contextual information that is lost during sentence reordering, we use *local coherence* as a heuristic. This metric quantifies the pair-wise contextual similarity between a central sentence and its adjacent sentences within a window of seven sentences, as measured by `sup-simcse-roberta-large`, a model specifically designed to produce contextualized sentence embeddings (Gao et al., 2021). It's important to note that this measurement, produced by a pretrained Roberta model, is completely independent of the training process of our models. We define local coherence for sentence s_i as:

$$c(s_i) \triangleq \frac{1}{6} \sum_{\substack{k=-3 \\ k \neq 0}}^{3} sim(s_i, s_{i+k})$$

Where $sim(s_i, s_j)$ is the cosine similarity between the sentence embeddings encoded for s_i and s_j using `sup-simcse-roberta-large`. To determine the size of the local similarity window, we consider the average number of inputs concatenated in a context length of 128, which is 8.512 for all sentences in the BabyLM datasets. However, for the subset of sentences that make up the 80% of longer inputs, which are more influential in optimizing the model's performance for BLiMP, the average number of inputs merged in a context length of 128 reduces to 6.55. Thus, we opt for a window size of seven for this particular metric.

To unify the local coherence of individual sentences into a single metric for a given corpus, we use an average pooling function. However, due to limited computational resources and to enhance time efficiency, we opt for calculating the expected local coherence of a corpus. To compute this, instead of calculating the local coherence of all sentences in the corpus, we take the average of the local coherence values of 1000 randomly selected unique sentences from each dataset in the BabyLM Strict-Small track.

5.3 Data Cleaning With ASR

ASR sorts sentences based on the relative frequency of the words, classifying sentences with a high concentration of common words as the easiest and those with a high concentration of rare words as the hardest. Manual evaluation of datasets sorted using this metric indicates that sentences classified as easy tend to lack semantic meaning and appear fragmented in some datasets. This is expected, as this metric ignores sentence length, and thus, sentences classified as easy have few words besides the most frequent words, which include numbers, articles, and pronouns. This leaves limited room for meaningful development of concepts in those sentences. The datasets that display this pattern most prominently are `gutenberg`, `bnc`, and `cbt`. `gutenberg` contains thousands of lines consisting of a few words and a long series of numbers, likely corresponding to Project Gutenberg catalog numbers. These lines are isolated when the dataset is sorted by ASR and ranked as the easiest sentences.

We found that cleaning the datasets by removing redundant or semantically meaningless lines with a high count of common words can improve the model's performance. ASR also effectively identifies meaningless inputs containing a high count of rare words, as hard samples; however, we found that removing such samples did not provide an improvement in the model's performance. This might be because removing the limited contextual information available for the rare words either entirely erases them from the model's vocabulary or increases the variance in gradients of their embeddings, given the small size of our dataset. Alternatively, removing meaningless contextual information for high-frequency tokens from the datasets can be advantageous, because when learning embeddings for the common words, the noise introduced by meaningless samples can be amplified due to the small size of our training datasets.

When employing SR to sort inputs in the datasets, the isolation of semantically meaningless lines does not occur, because this metric is dependent on sentence length. This difficulty metric fails to identify inputs with a high count of frequent tokens and a low count of all other tokens, which is a marker for meaningless inputs in the target datasets. Examples classified as hard tend to be very long, and at least segments of those sentences are coherent. On the other hand, the frequency of common words is lower compared to the frequency of other words in the inputs classified as easy, primarily due to the imposed short length limit for these inputs. As a result, sentence rarity cannot be used as an effective metric to clean these datasets.

6 Experiments

6.1 Reordering One Dataset

The primary objective of these experiments is to enhance the performance of the language model on BLiMP by grouping training samples with a similar difficulty, as quantified by either SR or ASR, in the same context length, and to measure the loss of contextual information when sentences are rearranged to this new order.

The BabyLM datasets are derived from various sources, each encoding distinct conceptual information. As a result, sentences from the same database exhibit a higher level of grammatical and semantic similarity. Thus, to preserve the maximum contextual information when rearranging sentences, we reorder sentences only within each dataset in this series of experiments.

To quantify the extent of contextual information loss following sentence reordering, we calculate the expected local coherence of each dataset in the Strict-Small track separately with the sentences of the dataset in their original order and with the sentences sorted based on either of the difficulty metrics (Table 4). As expected, rearranging sentences using either difficulty metric significantly reduced the expected local coherence across all datasets. When it comes to arranging sentences with a similar context close to each other, both metrics demonstrated comparable performance.

To assess the potential improvement of GPT-2's performance on the BLiMP evaluation through organizing sentences of a single dataset based on a difficulty metric, we conducted a series of 20 experiments. In each experiment, GPT-2 is trained on a training corpus consisting of 9 unchanged datasets concatenated with one dataset sorted based on difficulty. The model's performance is then evaluated on the BLiMP evaluation (Table 5). We also measure the correlation between the expected local coherence of the difficulty-sorted dataset and model performance to test our hypothesis that even though sorting inputs based on difficulty can improve performance, interrupting the semantic distribution of nearby contextual sentences can reduce the model performance.

We observed a positive correlation between the expected local coherence of datasets sorted by either difficulty metric and the evaluation results of the model on BLiMP (Figure 2). To assess the relationship between these two variables, we used Spearman's Rank correlation coefficient. The correlation coefficient between the coherence score of datasets sorted with SR and the BLiMP score of the models is 0.693, indicating a strong correlation. For datasets sorted with average sentence rarity, the coefficient is 0.559, indicating a moderate correlation.

The larger correlation coefficient achieved for datasets sorted with SR may be caused by the implicit similarity in length among neighboring sentences within the window of local coherence when sentences are sorted by SA. And this similarity in turn increases the local coherence score and BLiMP performance of the model. This suggests that considering sentence length when sorting sentences by difficulty is beneficial, however, it is the high sampling frequency from shorter sentences in our datasets, ranked as easier using SA, that reduces the model's performance when using the competence function.

Out of the 20 experiments conducted, 8 resulted in an improvement in the BLiMP evaluation relative to our baseline of 75.05% achieved by preprocessing `gutenberg`, and all results were above the 73.40% BLiMP score achieved with no optimizations. Notably, the model trained on `aochildes` sorted with SA achieved a 0.72% increase in BLiMP and reached a score of 75.77%.

The lower performance of certain models in this experiment on BLiMP is most likely attributed to the loss of significant contextual information in the dataset during the reordering of sentences based

	Datasets									
Order of Sentences	aochildes	bnc_spoken	cbt	children_stories	gutenberg	open_subtitles	qed	simple_wikipedia	switchboard	wikipedia
Original Order	0.303	0.228	0.227	0.326	0.307	0.204	0.240	0.348	0.249	0.400
SA	0.149	0.114	0.127	0.180	0.121	0.104	0.090	0.108	0.147	0.124
ASR	0.152	0.108	0.124	0.172	0.120	0.110	0.086	0.115	0.120	0.127

Table 4: Comparing the expected local coherence of each dataset when its sentences are in their original order to when the sentences are sorted based on sentence rarity (SA) or average sentence rarity (ASR).

	Rearranged Dataset In The Training Data									
Order of Sentences	aochildes	bnc_spoken	cbt	children_stories	gutenberg	open_subtitles	qed	simple_wikipedia	switchboard	wikipedia
SA	75.77%	75.19%	74.64%	75.42%	75.42%	74.58%	74.54%	74.29%	74.81%	75.48%
ASR	74.85%	75.37%	75.59%	75.40%	74.71%	74.69%	74.11%	74.32%	74.88%	74.74%

Table 5: BLiMP results for models trained on the BabyLM Strict Small Corpus with one dataset sorted based on SA or ASR.

on difficulty. This is evident from the positive correlation between the local coherence score of the dataset and the model's performance on BLiMP, which suggests that models that achieved lower performance on BLiMP were trained on datasets with higher contextual information loss.

The loss of contextual information may also be attributed to higher subject variance in certain datasets. In that case, to improve the preservation of local contextual information, it may be beneficial to sort sentences at a sub-dataset level. For instance, rearranging sentences from only a single story in the children_stories dataset instead of rearranging all sentences in the dataset could potentially lead to better results. Furthermore, to enhance the model's performance on these datasets, it may be essential to implement a larger-scale supervision of the sentence order. This can be achieved through the development of a difficulty metric that considers the semantic similarity of consecutive sentences when reordering sentences from different datasets, leading to a minimum loss of contextual information when sorting sentences with different meanings and grammar styles.

6.2 Data Cleaning

In this series of experiments, we applied the previously discussed data-cleaning method to 3 datasets: bnc, cbt, and gutenberg. To set up these experiments, we initially sorted the datasets using ASR. Next, we determined the number of lines to eliminate from the easiest sentences in the dataset through manual evaluation. For every 200 lines, we assessed 10 lines and removed the preceding 200 lines if more than 1 out of the 10 lines contained grammatically incoherent or semantically meaningless sentences. Subsequently, the sorted and cleaned dataset was concatenated with the 9

	Data Cleaning with ASR		ASR
Dataset	BLiMP	# Lines Cut	BLiMP
bnc_spoken	75.53%	4600	75.37%
cbt	75.69%	800	75.59%
gutenberg	75.84%	3200	74.71%

Table 6: A comparison between the results of training GPT-2 on the training corpus consisting of one dataset cleaned and sorted with ASR and the earlier experiment results obtained by simply reordering the dataset with ASR. The number of lines eliminated from the sorted dataset (after duplicates were removed) is also stated.

base datasets to create the training corpus. We trained a model on each corpus and evaluated their performance using BLiMP. Table 6 compares the results of training GPT-2 on the training corpus composed of one dataset cleaned and sorted with ASR with the experiment results achieved earlier by only reordering the dataset with ASR.

By employing this method, we achieved a considerable improvement in the performance of the model trained on the cleaned gutenberg dataset. However, the improvement achieved in the performance of the two other models was negligible. We believe the substantial enhancement on gutenberg is because a higher portion of the excluded inputs was meaningless relative to the inputs cut from the other two datasets. The model trained on ASR sorted and cleaned gutenberg performed the best on BLiMP among the other models we trained and is the model submitted for the challenge. This model's perplexity on the BabyLM test datasets is 54.8.

7 Conclusion and Future Work

In conclusion, the primary objective of this paper was to enhance GPT-2's performance on BLiMP zero-shot tasks by pre-training the model on the

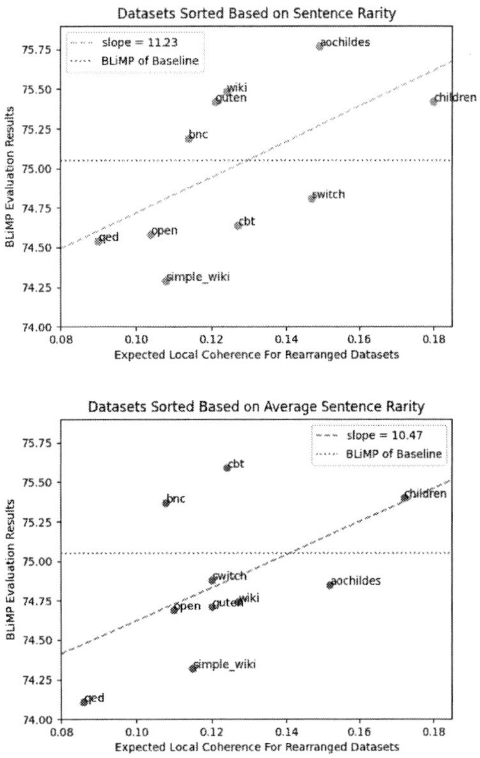

Figure 2: The graph illustrates a positive correlation between the expected local coherence of the sorted dataset and the BLiMP score of the model trained on it. The Spearman's Rank correlation coefficient is 0.693 for datasets sorted with SA (represented in orange) and 0.559 for those sorted with ASR. The green line indicates the best BLiMP score obtained without any CL optimizations, achieved by preprocessing the `gutenberg` dataset.

datasets provided in the BabyLM Strict Small track. Various difficulty metrics were explored to supervise the order of sentences presented to the model. It was observed there's a positive correlation between the BLiMP result of models trained on a corpus comprised of one dataset sorted based on difficulty and the contextual coherence of nearby sentences in the rearranged dataset. Thus, Training models on a dataset sorted by difficulty with preserved contextual coherence could lead to better performance on BLiMP. By employing difficulty-based sentence reordering, we trained a model that achieved an average accuracy of 75.77% on BLiMP's zero-shot tasks. Additionally, we used *average sentence rarity*, a length-independent sentence rarity metric, to clean and sort the `gutenberg` dataset, which further improved the performance to 75.84%.

Hence, to improve curriculum learning optimizations for language models, we argue that sentences presented together within a context length should exhibit not only the same level of difficulty but also semantic and contextual similarity. In our study, we employed similarity measures to assess the contextual coherence of rearranged datasets after the sentences were ordered based on word frequencies; the semantic similarity of sentences had no impact on the actual order of the sentences. A critical future advancement arising from this research lies in the development of more sophisticated difficulty metrics that consider both the similarity among sentences and their individual difficulty levels.

8 Limitations

No measure of grammatical similarity of sentences: When assessing the correlation between the expected local coherence of a dataset and the performance of the model trained on the rearranged dataset, we are considering the semantic similarity of sentences within a context length, but using a grammar-based evaluation to assess the model's performance. While we hypothesize that training the model on difficulty-sorted datasets that have more semantically similar sentences sequenced after each other improves the model's overall performance, leading to better BLiMP results, it might be more effective to optimize for higher BLiMP scores by evaluating the grammatical similarity of sentences that follow each other. Nevertheless, there is currently no reliable method to solely measure the grammatical similarity of two sentences to the best of our knowledge. Alternatively, using an evaluation pipeline that assesses the model's semantic understanding of sentences would be a good way to compare against the received local coherence scores. However, our available resources did not allow us to optimize our models using such pipelines.

Lack of scalability: Our current approaches to enhance model performance are not scalable as reordering two or more datasets did not yield any improvement in BLiMP scores in our experiments. This lack of scalability is the motivation behind the investigation of the semantic similarity of sentences that follow each other in a context length. We hypothesize that although sorting a higher number of datasets increases the number of context-length samples where the concatenated sentences have the same difficulty, sequencing sentences from different sources with distinct grammar styles and semantic meanings within a context length results in a decrease in the model's performance. The resolution to this scalability issue lies in the development of more advanced difficulty metrics that take into account both the similarity between sentences and their individual difficulty levels when reordering the training samples.

References

Yoshua Bengio, Jérôme Louradour, Ronan Collobert, and Jason Weston. 2009. Curriculum learning. In *Proceedings of the 26th annual international conference on machine learning*, pages 41–48.

Jacob Devlin, Ming-Wei Chang, Kenton Lee, and Kristina Toutanova. 2018. Bert: Pre-training of deep bidirectional transformers for language understanding. *arXiv preprint arXiv:1810.04805*.

Tianyu Gao, Xingcheng Yao, and Danqi Chen. 2021. Simcse: Simple contrastive learning of sentence embeddings. *arXiv preprint arXiv:2104.08821*.

Philip A. Huebner, Elior Sulem, Fisher Cynthia, and Dan Roth. 2021. BabyBERTa: Learning more grammar with small-scale child-directed language. In *Proceedings of the 25th Conference on Computational Natural Language Learning*, pages 624–646, Online. Association for Computational Linguistics.

Yinhan Liu, Myle Ott, Naman Goyal, Jingfei Du, Mandar Joshi, Danqi Chen, Omer Levy, Mike Lewis, Luke Zettlemoyer, and Veselin Stoyanov. 2019. Roberta: A robustly optimized bert pretraining approach. *arXiv preprint arXiv:1907.11692*.

Emmanouil Antonios Platanios, Otilia Stretcu, Graham Neubig, Barnabas Poczos, and Tom M Mitchell. 2019. Competence-based curriculum learning for neural machine translation. *arXiv preprint arXiv:1903.09848*.

Alec Radford, Jeffrey Wu, Rewon Child, David Luan, Dario Amodei, Ilya Sutskever, et al. 2019. Language models are unsupervised multitask learners. *OpenAI blog*, 1(8):9.

Alex Warstadt, Aaron Mueller, Leshem Choshen, Ethan Gotlieb Wilcox, Chengxu Zhuang, Juan Ciro, Rafael Mosquera, Adina Williams, Bhargavi Paranjabe, Tal Linzen, and Ryan Cotterell. 2023. Findings of the 2023 BabyLM Challenge: Sample-efficient pretraining on developmentally plausible corpora. In *Proceedings of the 2023 BabyLM Challenge*. Association for Computational Linguistics (ACL).

Alex Warstadt, Alicia Parrish, Haokun Liu, Anhad Mohananey, Wei Peng, Sheng-Fu Wang, and Samuel R. Bowman. 2020. BLiMP: The benchmark of linguistic minimal pairs for English. *Transactions of the Association for Computational Linguistics*, 8:377–392.

Author Index

Association for Computational Linguistics
209 N. Eighth Street
Stroudsburg, Pennsylvania 18360

ISBN 978-1-7138-8586-3

9 781713 885863

CURRAN ASSOCIATES INC.
proceedings.com